GLOBAL COMPETITIVENESS: BUSINESS TRANSFORMATION
IN THE DIGITAL ERA

T0384172

PROCEEDINGS OF THE FIRST ECONOMICS AND BUSINESS
COMPETITIVENESS INTERNATIONAL CONFERENCE (EBCICON 2018),
BALI, INDONESIA, 21-22 SEPTEMBER 2018

Global Competitiveness: Business Transformation in the Digital Era

Editors

Ade Gafar Abdullah, Isma Widiaty & Cep Ubad Abdullah
Universitas Pendidikan Indonesia

Routledge
Taylor & Francis Group

LONDON AND NEW YORK

Published by: CRC Press/Balkema
P.O. Box 447, 2300 AK Leiden, The Netherlands
e-mail: Pub.NL@taylorandfrancis.com
www.crcpress.com – www.taylorandfrancis.com

First issued in paperback 2021

Routledge is an imprint of the Taylor & Francis Group, an informa business

© 2019 Taylor & Francis Group, London, UK

Typeset by Integra Software Services Pvt. Ltd., Pondicherry, India

DOI: https://doi.org/10.1201/9780429202629
ISBN 13: 978-0-367-77943-6 (pbk)
ISBN 13: 978-0-367-19442-0 (hbk)

Global Competitiveness: Business Transformation in the
Digital Era – Abdullah, Widiaty & Abdullah (eds)
© 2019 Taylor & Francis Group, London, ISBN 978-0-367-19442-0

Table of contents

Information System and Technology

International Issues

Operation and Supply Chain

Other Related Issues

Global Competitiveness: Business Transformation in the
Digital Era – Abdullah, Widiaty & Abdullah (eds)
© 2019 Taylor & Francis Group, London, ISBN 978-0-367-19442-0

Preface

The 2018 Economics and Business Competitiveness International Conference (EBCICON) is a seminar conducted by the Economics Faculty of Parahyangan Catholic University, Indonesia, in collaboration with Politeknik APP Jakarta (Ministry of Industry), Indonesia. The conference has been proven to receive enthusiastic response from scholars and practitioners in the fields of business and economy. Participants from several countries such as Australia, Vietnam, Malaysia, United Kingdom, Singapore, Japan, and many cities in Indonesia attended this year's conference.

Discussing its theme "Global Competitiveness: Business Transformation in the Digital Era", the conference welcomed Ir. Airlangga Hartarto, MBA, MT, the Minister of Industry, Republic of Indonesia, as the keynote speaker. In addition, the conference also invited several invited speakers such as Dr. Arief Gusnanto from the University of Leeds; UK, Prof. Lorne Cummings, Associate Dean – Higher Degree Research – Faculty of Business and Economics; Dr. Ir. Ngakan Timur Antara, Head of Industry R&D Agency Ministry of Industry, Republic of Indonesia; and Michiko Miyamoto, Deputy Director ILO Indonesia & Timor Leste. To have more practical insights, the conference held a workshop entitled "theoretical and methodological suggestions for publishing in leading scholarly journals" delivered by Prof. Chris Patel, Dr. Pei Pei Pan, and Dr. Ranjith Appuhami, all from the Department of Accounting and Corporate Governance Macquire University.

There were approximately 200 submissions from authors from various countries to the conference. The committee went through rigorous selection and decided to have 54 papers accepted in the proceedings of EBCICON 2018, published by CRC Press/ Balkema by Taylor & Francis.

Ade Gafar Abdullah
Universitas Pendidikan Indonesia

Isma Widiaty
Universitas Pendidikan Indonesia

Cep Ubad Abdullah
Universitas Pendidikan Indonesia

Acknowledgements

Ahmad Cahyo Nugroho, S. Pt., M.M. (Politeknik APP Jakarta, Ministry of Industry – Indonesia)

Aji Kresno Murti, S.T., MM. (Politeknik APP Jakarta, Ministry of Industry – Indonesia)

Annisaa Novieningtyas, SE., MSM. (Parahyangan Catholic University – Indonesia)

Aria Bayu Pangestu, B.Mgt., M.HRM. (Bandung Institute of Technology – Indonesia)

Assoc. Prof. Dr. Corina Joseph (Universiti Teknologi MARA Cawangan Sarawak – Malaysia)

Atty Yuniawati SE., MBA. (Parahyangan Catholic University – Indonesia)

Bayu Prabowo Sutjiatmo, S. T., M.M. (Politeknik APP Jakarta, Ministry of Industry – Indonesia)

Bayu Prabowo Sutjiatmo, ST., MM. (Politeknik APP Jakarta, Ministry of Industry – Indonesia)

Christian Wibisono SE., MSM. (Parahyangan Catholic University – Indonesia)

Dhany Surya Ratana, S.T., M.M. (Politeknik APP Jakarta, Ministry of Industry – Indonesia)

Disma Prasaja, S.Si., M.I.L. (Politeknik APP Jakarta, Ministry of Industry – Indonesia)

Dr. Budiana Gomulia (Parahyangan Catholic University – Indonesia)

Dr. Indrani Dharmayanti, SP., M.Si. (Politeknik APP Jakarta, Ministry of Industry – Indonesia)

DR. Ir. Darmawan Napitupulu (Budi Luhur University – Indonesia)

Dr. Ir. Yandra Arkeman, M. Eng. (Bogor Agricultural University – Indonesia)

Dr. Istiharini (Parahyangan Catholic University – Indonesia)

Dr. Miryam B. Lilian Wijaya (Parahyangan Catholic University – Indonesia)

Dr. Nacanieli Rika (University of South Pacific – Fiji)

DR. Parulian Silaen (University of Wolongong – Australia)

Dr. Pei Pei Pan (Macquarie University – Australia)

Dr. Ranjith Apuhami (Macquarie University – Australia)

Dr. Toni Irawan, SE., M.Ec. App (Bogor Agricultural University – Indonesia)

Erika Fatma, S.Pi., MT., MBA. (Politeknik APP Jakarta, Ministry of Industry – Indonesia)

Fajria Fatmasari, S.Pd., M.A. (Politeknik APP Jakarta, Ministry of Industry – Indonesia)

Fernando Mulia, SE., M.Kom. (Parahyangan Catholic University – Indonesia)

Gandhi Pawitan, Ph.D. (Parahyangan Catholic University – Indonesia)

Inge Barlian, Dra., M.Si. (Parahyangan Catholic University – Indonesia)

Irfa Ampri, Ph.D. (Ministry of Finance – Indonesia)

Ivan Prasetya SE., M.S.M, M.Eng. (Parahyangan Catholic University – Indonesia)

Januarita Hendrani, Ph.D. (Parahyangan Catholic University – Indonesia)

Juniati Gunawan, Ph.D. (Trisakti University – Indonesia)

Lilian Danil, SE., MM. (Parahyangan Catholic University – Indonesia)

Meiliani, S.E., M.Com., Ph.D. (Bengkulu University – Indonesia)

Meylianti Sulungbudi SE., MSi. (Parahyangan Catholic University – Indonesia)

Michelle Kurniawan SE., M.Ak. (Parahyangan Catholic University – Indonesia)

Nalal Muna, S.I.Kom., MBA. (Politeknik APP Jakarta, Ministry of Industry – Indonesia)

Natalia Christi, S.T., MBA. (Parahyangan Catholic University – Indonesia)

Nina Septina, SP., MM. (Parahyangan Catholic University – Indonesia)

Global Competitiveness: Business Transformation in the
Digital Era – Abdullah, Widiaty & Abdullah (eds)
© 2019 Taylor & Francis Group, London, ISBN 978-0-367-19442-0

Committees

SCIENTIFIC COMMITTEE

1. Ahmad Cahyo Nugroho, S. Pt., M.M. (Politeknik APP Jakarta, Ministry of Industry – Indonesia)
2. Aria Bayu Pangestu, B.Mgt., M.HRM. (Bandung Institute of Technology – Indonesia)
3. Assoc. Prof. Dr. Corina Joseph (Universiti Teknologi MARA Cawangan Sarawak – Malaysia)
4. Bayu Prabowo Sutjiatmo, S. T., M.M. (Politeknik APP Jakarta, Ministry of Industry – Indonesia)
5. DR. Ir. Darmawan Napitupulu (Budi Luhur University – Indonesia)
6. Dr. Ir. Yandra Arkeman, M. Eng. (Bogor Agricultural University – Indonesia)
7. Dr. Miryam B. Lilian Wijaya (Parahyangan Catholic University – Indonesia)
8. Dr. Nacanieli Rika (University of South Pacific – Fiji)
9. DR. Parulian Silaen (University of Wolongong – Australia)
10. Dr. Pei Pei Pan (Macquarie University – Australia)
11. Dr. Ranjith Apuhami (Macquarie University – Australia)
12. Dr. Toni Irawan, SE., M.Ec. App (Bogor Agricultural University – Indonesia)
13. Gandhi Pawitan, Ph.D. (Parahyangan Catholic University – Indonesia)
14. Irfa Ampri, Ph.D. (Ministry of Finance – Indonesia)
15. Januarita Hendrani, Ph.D. (Parahyangan Catholic University – Indonesia)
16. Juniati Gunawan, Ph.D. (Trisakti University – Indonesia)
17. Meiliani, S.E., M.Com., Ph.D. (Bengkulu University – Indonesia)
18. Prof. Charles H. Cho, Ph.D, CPA (York University -Toronto, Ontario, Canada)
19. Prof. Chris Patel (Macquarie University – Australia)
20. Prof. Dr. Muhammad Firdaus, Sp, M.Si. (Bogor Agricultural University – Indonesia)
21. Prof. Fahlino F. Sjuib, Ph.D. (Boston College – USA)
22. Prof. Hasan Fauzi, Ph.D., CA, CSRS (Sebelas Maret University – Indonesia)
23. Prof. Ir. Roy Sembel, Ph.D. (IPMI International Business School – Indonesia)
24. Prof. Lorne Cummings (Macquarie University – Australia)
25. Prof. Ujang Sumarwan (Bogor Agricultural University – Indonesia)
26. Prof. Umesh Sharma (Waikato University – New Zealand)

ORGANIZING COMMITTEE

Chairman

1. Dr. Istiharini
2. Rinandita Wikansari, S.Psi., M.Psi., Psikolog

Secretariat

1. Annisaa Novieningtyas, SE., MSM.
2. Erika Fatma, S.Pi., MT., MBA.
3. Natalia Christi, S.T., MBA.

Treasury

1. Dr. Budiana Gomulia
2. Fajria Fatmasari, S.Pd., M.A.

Event

1. Meylianti Sulungbudi SE., MSi.
2. Bayu Prabowo Sutjiatmo, ST., MM.
3. Probowo Erawan SE., MSc.
4. Aji Kresno Murti, S.T., MM.

Publication and Documentation

1. Fernando Mulia, SE., MKom.
2. Disma Prasaja, S.Si., M.I.L.
3. Ronny T. Surbakti, SIP., MM.
4. Dhany Surya Ratana, S.T., M.M.

Sponsorship

1. Inge Barlian, Dra., MSi.
2. Nalal Muna, S.I.Kom., MBA.
3. Ivan Prasetya SE., M.S.M, M.Eng.
4. Christian Wibisono SE., MSM.

Call for Paper

1. Atty Yuniawati SE., MBA.
2. Dr. Indrani Dharmayanti, SP., M.Si.
3. Michelle Kurniawan SE., M.Ak.
4. Oei Venny Febrianti, SE., Ak., MM., CA., CSRS.

Seminar

1. Nina Septina, SP., MM.
2. Lilian Danil, SE., MM.

Accounting and Governance

Global Competitiveness: Business Transformation in the
Digital Era – Abdullah, Widiaty & Abdullah (eds)
© 2019 Taylor & Francis Group, London, ISBN 978-0-367-19442-0

The application of management accounting in micro and small enterprises

V. Suryaputra
Parahyangan Catholic University, Bandung, Indonesia

ABSTRACT: The purpose of this research is to investigate how management accounting is applied in micro and small enterprises in Bandung and its surrounding areas in Indonesia. To this end, a descriptive study was conducted. The findings indicated that the application of management accounting in micro and small enterprises was rather limited to simple accounting techniques. Data were collected through questionnaires and interviews. Since the respondents of this research were mostly micro and small enterprises in the culinary industry, generalization to a wider context could not be made.

1 INTRODUCTION

1.1 Background

The growth of micro and small enterprises (MSEs) in Indonesia has been mushrooming. They create a strong competition both between themselves and with medium and large enterprises. In order to win the competition and keep the business going, the MSEs must be highly productive. However, Mourougane's (2012) work indicates that micro, small and medium enterprises play in Indonesia are still struggling with productivity problems.

Studies have shown that management accounting can affect MSE performance (e.g., Ahmad 2017; Shields & Shelleman 2016). The more often the management accounting system is used to calculate the profitability of products or services and to assess the profitability of customers, the more positive and significant the impacts on return on investment are. This seems to imply that the application of management accounting can improve MSE performance.

The present research attempts to investigate how management accounting is applied in MSEs in Indonesia. It is expected that the findings can help improve their performance and productivity. This research is also particularly useful for other researchers whose interests and concerns are related in one way or another to the field of the same kind as that of this research.

2 RESEARCH METHOD

This research employed a descriptive study design. The aim was to describe the application of management accounting in micro and small enterprises in Indonesia. The samples were 30 micro and small enterprises in Bandung selected out of 300 thousand (data from www.jabarprov.go.id) randomly. Data were collected through questionnaires and interviews in January - June 2018.

3 SMALL AND MEDIUM ENTERPRISES (SMES)

In Indonesia, small and medium enterprises (SMEs) are defined in many different ways and from many different perspectives.

1) Ministry of Cooperatives and Small and Medium Enterprises (Menegkop and UKM) classifies MSMEs based on their net worth as follows:
   - A small enterprise (UK), including Micro Enterprises (UMI), is a business entity having a net worth of IDR 200,000,000, excluding land and building of business premises, and has annual sales of up to IDR 1,000,000,000.
   - A medium enterprises (UM) is a business entity owned by an Indonesian citizen with a net worth between IDR 200,000,000 and IDR 10,000,000,000, excluding land and buildings.

2) Law of the Republic of Indonesia Number 20 of 2008 defines SMEs based on the amount of assets and turnover per year as follows:
   - A micro enterprise is a productive business owned by individual and/or individual business entity fulfilling micro business criteria as regulated in this law.
   - A small-scale business is a stand-alone productive economic enterprise conducted by an individual or a business entity that is not a subsidiary or not a company owned, controlled, or a part, directly or indirectly, of a medium-sized or large-scale business that meets the criteria small business as referred to in this law.
   - A medium-sized enterprise is a stand-alone productive economic enterprise, carried out by an individual or a business entity that is not a subsidiary or not a company owned, controlled, or a part, directly or indirectly, of a small business or large business with net worth or annual sales proceeds as provided in this law.

Table 1. Classification of enterprise Based on Net Worth and Annual Sales.

Type of enterprise	Net Worth (excluding land and business building)	Annual sales
Micro Enterprise	Max. IDR 50millions	Max. IDR 300 million
Small Enterprise	> IDR 50 million - IDR500 millions	> IDR 300 million – IDR 2.5 billion
Medium Enterprise	> IDR 500 million – IDR 10 billion	> IDR 2.5 billion – IDR 50 billion

Source: Law Number 20 Year 2008.

3) Bank Indonesia through Bank Indonesia Circular Letter no. 3/9/Bkr of 2001 defines a small business by referring to Law No. 9 of 1995, which is small scale business criteria based on fixed asset value (excluding lands and buildings) of IDR 200 million with maximum turnover per year of IDR 1 billion. Based on Presidential Decree No.10 of 1999 on medium enterprises, the maximum fixed asset criterion (excluding land and buildings) of a medium business ranges between IDR 200 million and IDR 10 billion.
4) According to the Ministry of Industry and Trade, businesses with asset value (excluding land and buildings) of less than IDR 200 million are called small industries, whereas a business with asset between IDR 200 million and IDR 5 billion is classified as a small and medium enterprise.
5) Ministry of Finance, through Ministerial Decree number 316/KMK.016/1994 dated June 27, 1994, defines a small business as an individual or business entity that has engaged in business/sales turnover per year as high as IDR 600,000,000 or assets of up to IDR 600,000,000 (excluding land and buildings occupied). They could be:
   a. Field of business (Fa, CV, PT, and cooperative), and
   b. Individuals (craftsmen/home industry, farmers, fishermen, forest encroachers, miners, traders of goods and services).
6) Statistics Indonesia (BPS) classifies a business based on the number of workers as follows:
   • Micro-enterprises (households) are businesses with 1-5 people.
   • Small businesses are businesses with 6-19 employees.
   • Medium enterprises have 20-99 employees.
   • Large businesses have workers at least 100 people.

In this study, small and medium micro enterprises are defined based on their annual turnover in accordance with Law No.20 of 2008 and based on the number of employees according to Statistics Indonesia.

4 MANAGEMENT ACCOUNTING

Management accounting helps managers with their financial statement creation (Horngren et al. 2015). According to Management Accounting Practices Committee (MAPC) management accounting is the process of identification, measurement, analysis, preparation and communication of financial information used by management for planning, evaluation, control in an organization and to ensure the ac-curacy of the use of resources and accountability.

The purpose of management accounting is to help managers plan and control the company's current operations and hence helps make specific decisions and long-term plans (Horngren 1962). Management accounting is broader than cost accounting and is used for planning and control (Williams 1986).

The role of accounting is to help managers and professionals with the planning and controls within an organization and does not merely perform a bookkeeping function (Birnberg 2011). Management accounting is different from cost accounting. Cost accounting is concerned with the cost measurement of the product whereas management accounting is rather a managerial-related activity (2003).

According to Keong (1997), the primary purpose of management accounting is to ensure that we un-derstand how internal information in the form of fi-nancial data can be used to help businesses generate more profit. Kaplan and Johnson in a book entitled Relevance Lost advised the Chief Financial Officer established a simplified accounting management sys-tem to help them make important decisions (Pearl-stein 1988). With the use of management account-ing, companies or managers can create their own management accounting system suitable with their needs and can support decision making processes.

Management accounting is an abstract construct; therefore, the application of management accounting is usually seen from the use of methods (techniques) such as cost calculations, planning in the form of budget, control in the form of variance (compare actual results with budget).

4.1 The use of management accounting outside Indonesia

Laureano et al (2016) conducted a study of management accounting practices in SMEs in Portugal, to find out which SMEs in Portugal belong to which category of Kaplan's four stage model. The Kaplan model groups companies based on the level of development of their management accounting practices. Stage 1 uses insufficient methods for financial reporting needs, stage 2 implements methods for financial reporting, stage 3 produces innovation and is relevant for management, stage 4 integration. The re-search results show that all studied SMEs have implemented management accounting methods for product valuation, but the method used is considered inadequate for decision making, 24.14% of them do valuation of products using direct cost, the rest using the basis of allocations relating to the amount of production, usually using machine hours. None is using activity-based costing.

Studies on management accounting practices in SMEs were also conducted in Romania. The results of Cuzdriorean's (2017) study; for example, indicate that most respondents use some (slightly) traditional management accounting methods, while modern accounting method uses are rather limited. The most commonly used traditional management accounting methods are budgeting systems for cost control and cash flow planning. The commonly used modern management accounting methods are benchmarking and reporting performance based on financial and non-financial size.

The results of a survey of 226 SMEs in Italy show that there is a positive correlation between firm size and diffusion of management accounting tools. The most widely used accounting management tools are cost analysis, budget and cash flow budget. And the use of business plan, gross margin contribution and analysis of variance is limited (Broccardo 2014).

Ahmad and Zabri (2015) conducted research on the application of management accounting in medium-sized businesses in Malaysia. The results indicate that the use of costing system, budgeting system, and performance evaluation system is significantly higher than decision support and strategic management accounting. Traditional management accounting practice (MAP) is more commonly used than sophisticated MAP.

Shields and Shelleman's (2016) research on the application of management accounting in micro enterprises in the US suggests that management accounting systems are implemented to facilitate decision making, including calculating the profitability of products/services, taking action based on actual and budget performance comparisons, and assessment of customer profitability.

McChlery et al. (2005) conducted research on small business in Scotland. The results showed that only 54.8% of respondents made estimates of profits, and 53.6% made estimates of cash. Only 48.1% compared the budget with the actual results. 36.8% of respondents did not have a product cost calculation system.

It can be concluded that some SMEs in the above-mentioned countries demonstrate a limited technique use of management accounting, usually in the form of simple product cost and budget calculations.

4.2 The use of management accounting in Indonesia

There were several studies related to the use of management accounting in small and medium enterprises in Indonesia. For example, Alliyah and Hidayat's (2014) study indicate that 186 small and medium enterprises in Rembang Regency have implemented management accounting system. The study on 82 SMEs in Surabaya shows that, on a scale of 1-5, the measurement of management accounting resulted in the average score of 2.1265 (low) (Surenggono & Djamilah 2016). 19 small and medium businesses in Yogyakarta are reported to use management accounting for planning, control, and decision making, (Wirjono & Raharjono 2012). Research on 8 businesses of *enting-enting gepuk* in Salatiga indicates that the information used for business decision making is sales/income information, purchase information, cost information, profit and loss information, cash inflow information, and inventory amount information (Christian & Rita 2016). Purwati et al (2014) found that small and medium enterprises in Banyumas used management accounting make financial statements as requirements for proposing bank loans (Purwati et al. 2014).

The abovementioned studies may lead to a conclusion that management accounting helps SMEs with decision making processes.

4.3 Management accounting indicators

Scholars used different indicators for management accounting. Shield and Shelleman (2016) use the ability to calculate products/services, take remedial action if actual performance is not profitable relative to budgeted performance, assess customer profitability, compare actual and budgeted performance, calculate differences between actual and budgeted amounts, evaluate performance relative to the target, calculate breakeven point, prepare operating budget, use operating budget to set performance targets, assess customer costs. Ahmad (2017) uses Costing System, Budgeting system, Performance Measurement System, Decision Support System, Strategic Management Accounting. Wijewardena et al (2004) uses the use of budget and variance. Chand and Ambardar use (2013) Costing System, Budgeting System, Performance evaluation, information and decision making, strategic analysis. Chiarini uses (2012) activity-based costing.

The following are indicators this study considered appropriate is considered able to describe the use of management accounting in micro, small, and medium enterprises.

1) Calculation of product cost
2) Calculation of product profits
3) The calculation of customer profit
4) Preparing a sales plan
5) Production cost plan
6) Making operational cost plan
7) Creating a profit plan
8) Making cash usage plans
9) Making cash usage plans
10) Evaluate expenses
11) Compare sales results with sales plans
12) Compare production costs with production cost plans
13) Compare profit with profit plan
14) Calculate breakeven point
15) Compare the selling price with competitors
16) Compare product costs with competitors

5 DATA AND ANALYSIS

The number of returned questionnaires was 30. The results reveal that the maximum annual sales of the respondents were three hundred million rupiah, and hence they can be categorized into micro enterprises. As for the number of employees, 22 respondents who had 1-5 employees, seven respondents 6-19 employees, and one respondent had 20 employees. Therefore, based on the classification according to the number of employees, there were 22 micro enterprises, seven small enterprises, and one medium enterprise. Based on the type of business, there were 16 respondents doing the manufacturing businesses, six respondents doing trading businesses, and eight respondents doing service businesses.

All of these respondents used management accounting. Respondents with the manufacturing business use more management accounting techniques than respondents with the trading and service businesses. Respondents with the of manufacturing business used 10 management accounting techniques on average (65% of the total 16 management accounting techniques), respondents with the service businesses used 9 management accounting techniques (63% of the total 14 management accounting techniques), and respondents with trading businesses used 7 management accounting techniques (49% of the 14 management accounting techniques). These findings seem to confirm previous studies on small and medium enterprises in Indonesia.

Table 2. The use of management accounting based on kind of business.

Kind of business	Number of respondents	Averang score	%
Trading	6	6.83	48.81%
Manufacturing	16	10.38	64.84%
Service	8	8.75	62.50%

The most commonly used management accounting technique were calculation of product costs (80%), comparing the selling price with competitors (77%) and profit calculation (73%). And the most rarely used management accounting technique is comparing actual and target profit (40%), comparing actual production costs and production cost plans (44%) and making operational costing plans (50%). Most respondents seem to use the cost accounting technique (calculating product cost, calculating profit) and not to maximize the use of management accounting. This is in agreement with findings of studies on SMEs conducted outside Indonesia that SMEs usually use simple management accounting methods.

Table 3. Management Accounting Techniques used by respondent.

Question no.	Description	Number of respondents	%
1	Calculation of product cost	24	80.00%
2	Calculation of product profits	22	73.33%
3	The calculation of customer profit	18	60.00%
4	Preparing a sales plan	20	66.67%
5	Production cost plan	11	68.75%
6	Making operational cost plan	15	50.00%
7	Creating a profit plan	18	60.00%
8	Making cash usage plans	18	60.00%
9	Making cash usage plans	18	60.00%
10	Evaluate expenses	18	60.00%
11	Compare sales results with sales plans	18	60.00%
12	Compare production costs with production cost plans	7	43.75%
13	Compare profit with profit plan	12	40.00%
14	Calculate breakeven point	17	56.67%
15	Compare the selling price with competitors	23	76.67%
16	Compare product costs with competitors	18	60.00%

6 VALIDITY AND RELIABILITY TEST

The item validity test was performed using Pearson Product Moment, with a significance level of 5%. The results revealed that all the questionnaire items were valid

Table 4. Result of validity test.

Question no.	Rxy	t calculation	t table (95%,28)	Description
1	0.48594659	2.942129821	1.701130934	valid
2	0.418446644	2.437910849	1.701130934	valid
3	0.457298535	2.720971949	1.701130934	valid
4	0.687232258	5.005922704	1.701130934	valid
5	0.568310418	3.654793432	1.701130934	valid
6	0.420055527	2.449287964	1.701130934	valid
7	0.356423858	2.018589941	1.701130934	valid
8	0.675860335	4.85233721	1.701130934	valid
9	0.52454832	3.260173595	1.701130934	valid
10	0.541360766	3.407046348	1.701130934	valid
11	0.659047889	4.636815714	1.701130934	valid
12	0.540995154	3.40379283	1.701130934	valid
13	0.467386003	2.797539606	1.701130934	valid
14	0.625510108	4.24227151	1.701130934	valid
15	0.448540473	2.655574641	1.701130934	valid
16	0.60861055	4.058714271	1.701130934	valid

Reliability test is done using the split half method. The results showed that the questionnaire was highly reliable.

7 CONCLUSION

Micro and small enterprises in Bandung and its surrounding areas were found to have implemented management accounting. The most commonly used management accounting techniques were calculating product cost, calculating profit, and comparing selling price with competitors. The most rarely used techniques were comparing actual profit with profit plans, comparing actual production costs and production cost plans. Most respondents used simple management accounting techniques such as cost accounting, as stated by Horngren, cannot help organizations with the decision-making and long-term budgeting processes. The results of this study cannot be generalized to describe the condition of management accounting application in small and medium micro enterprise in Indonesia or in Bandung and surrounding areas. more in-depth research is needed with larger numbers of respondents.

REFERENCES

Ahmad, K. 2017. The Implementation of Management Accounting Practices and its Relationship with Performance in Small and Medium Enterprises. *International Review of Management and Marketing*: 342-353.

Ahmad, K., & Zabri, S. M. 2015. Factors explaining the use of management accounting practices in Malaysian medium-sized firms. *Journal of Small Business and Enterprise Development* 22(4): 762-781.

Alliyah, S., & Hidayat, R. 2014. Peningkatan Kinerja UKM dengan Mengimplementasikan Informasi Akuntansi Manajemen yang Didukung oleh Informasi antar Unit. *Fokus Ekonomi* 9(1): 100-111.

Anthony, R. N. 2003. Management Accounting: A Personal History. *Journal of Management Accounting Research* 15(1): 249-253.

Birnberg, J. G. 2011. Memorial Robert N.Anthony: A Pioneering Thinker in Management Accounting. *Accounting Horizons* 25(3): 593-602.

Broccardo, L. 2014. Management Accounting System in Italian SMEs: Some Evidence and Implications. *Advances in Management & Applied Economics* 4(4): 1-16.

Chand, M., & Ambardar, A. 2013. Management Accounting Practices in Hospitality and Service Enterprises: A Comparative Research. *Journal of Commerce & Accounting Research* 2(3): 1-9.

Chiarini, A. 2012. Lean Production: mistakes and limitations of accounting systems inside the SME sector. *Journal of Manufacturing Technology Management* 23(5): 681-700.

Christian, A. B., & Rita, M. R. 2016. Peran Penggunaan Informasi Akuntansi dalam Pengambilan Keputusan untuk Menunjang Keberhasilan Usaha. *EBBank* 7(2): 77-92.

Cuzdriorean, D. D. 2017. The Use of Management Accounting Practices by Romanian Small and Medium-Sized Enterprises: A Filed Study. *Accounting and Management Information Systems* 16(2): 291-312.

Horngren, C. T. 1962. Choosing Accounting Practices for Reporting to Management. National Association of Accountants. *NAA Bulletin (pre-1986)* 44 (1):44.

Horngren, C. T., Datar, S. M., & Rajan, M. V. 2015. *Cost Accounting: A Managerial Emphasis*. Pearson.

Keong, C. K. 1997. Management and accounting management practice: An essential perspective. *Management Services*: 41.

Laureano, R. M., Machado, M. J., & Laureano, L. M. 2016. Maturity in Management Accounting: Exploratory Study in Portuguese SME. *Society and Economy* 38(2): 139-156.

McChlery, S., Godfrey, P. A., & Meechan, L. 2005. Barriers and catalysts to sound financial management systems in small sized enterprises. *The Journal of Applied Accounting Research* 7(3): 1-26.

Mourougane, A. 2012. Promoting SME Development in Indonesia. *OECD Economics Department Working Papers*.

Pearlstein, S. 1988, April. Accounting Critic Robert Kaplan. *Inc* 10(4): 54.

Purwati, A. S., Suparlinah, I., & Putri, N. K. 2014. The Use of Accounting Information in the Business Decision Making Process on Small and Medium Enterprises in Banyumas Region, Indonesia. *Economy Transdisciplinarity Cognition* 17(2),63-75.

Shields, J., & Shelleman, J. M. 2016. Management Accounting Systems in Micro-SMEs. *The Journal of Applied Management and Entrepreneurship* 21(1): 19-32.

Surenggono, & Djamilah, S. 2016. Variabel Mediasi Pengaruh Persepsi dan Pengetahuan Pelaku Usaha Kecil dan Menengah (UKM) terhadap Kinerja UKM. *Dinamika Global: Rebranding Keunggulan Kompetituf Berbasis Kearifan Lokal*: 787-799.

Wijewardena, H., Zoysa, A., Fonseka, T., & Perera, B. 2004. The Impact of Planing and COntrol Sophistication on Performance of Small and Medium-Sized Enterprises: Evidence from Sri Lanka. *Journal of Small Business Management* 42(2),209-216.

Williams, K. 1986. Charles T. Horngren: Management Accounting's Renaissance Man. *Management Accounting*: 22.

Wirjono, E. R., & Raharjono, D. B. 2012. Survei Pemahaman dan Pemanfaatan Informasi Akuntansi dalam Usaha Kecil Menengah di Daerah Istimewa Yogyakarta. *AUDI Jurnal Akuntansi dan Bisnis*: 205-216.

*Global Competitiveness: Business Transformation in the
Digital Era – Abdullah, Widiaty & Abdullah (eds)*
© 2019 Taylor & Francis Group, London, ISBN 978-0-367-19442-0

The future of accountancy profession in the digital era

S. Fettry
Universitas Katolik Parahyangan, Bandung, Indonesia

T. Anindita & R. Wikansari
Politeknik APP Jakarta, Indonesia

K. Sunaryo
Universitas Pembangunan Jaya, Tangerang Selatan, Indonesia

ABSTRACT: The technology evolution is escalating rapidly. It has changed the business environment, including accountancy profession. Digitization makes various disruptive changes in accounting practices. Failure to keep pace with the digitization will be a disaster for the accountancy profession. The digital technology generates hard challenges for accountants. This study aims at examining the perception of accountants of the digital era and to identify some important impacts of digitization on accountancy profession. A strategy on how to exploit the digitization is required for the benefit of accountancy profession. The study is based on a perception survey. Data are collected by distributing questionnaires to Indonesian accountants. An inclusive literature review is conducted to get more comprehensive understanding. The finding of this study indicates that the digitization has changed the way of thinking and practicing in accounting field. It is revealed that most accountants recognize the digitization as both benefits and challenges. It is concluded that most of accountants have confronted the technological revolution. Furthermore, it is suggested that advanced research should explore the topic in a larger area for a comparative study. The main contribution of this study is some identified strategies for accountancy profession to cope with the future digital era.

1 INTRODUCTION

Nowadays, digital era has already evolved very fast in all aspects of life. The invention of computing and networking made everything become digitized. Digitizing has changed the business environment significantly, including the accounting field (Arnaboldi et al. 2017). It will affect the accounting profession permanently so that accountancy profession must respond to it in an effective way (Hunton 2015). The new modern technology of social, mobile and cloud platform (SoMoClo) has an effect on accountants' work and way of thinking (Al-Htaybat & von Alberti-Alhtaybat 2017, Stanciu & Gheorghe 2017). Radical innovation in digital technology such as cloud computing, mobile devices, internet of things, big data, analytics software, and artificial intelligence is altering all aspects of business (Bhimani & Willcocks 2014).

Technology advancement improves the efficiency and quality of accounting services and expands the scope of accounting services (Liu & Vasarhelyi 2014). The new IT solution and computing based solutions offer high level of accuracy, effectiveness, and efficiency in accounting services (Stanciu & Gheorghe 2017). However, it is perceived that the technology will replace some works in accounting (Accountancy Europe 2017, Guthrie & Parker 2016, Frey & Osborne 2013). This technology revolution will reduce the demand for accountants (Samkin & Stainbank 2016). Hood (2015) mentions that the technology forces will devalue the accountancy professional services. Therefore, the impact of digital era is questioned on whether it has a positive or negative effect on the accountancy profession.

This study explores the perception of the digital era and identifies some important impacts of digitization on accountancy profession by conducting survey on Indonesian accountants and literature review on various relevant readings. This paper is divided into five section. The first section introduces the background of the study. The second section provides a brief description of digitizing in accounting. The third section describes how survey and literature review were conducted. The fourth section presents and discusses the findings. The last section draws a conclusion based on the finding and offers some recommendations for future and further studies.

2 DIGITIZATION IN ACCOUNTING

The term digitization refers to the process of converting analogue data, e.g. images, video, and text, into a digital form (Oxford English Dictionary 2010). When used to improve business activities, this process is called digitalization (Brennen &

1983
- **Job duties:** Tax return preparation, financial statement auditing and preparation, business management consulting, establishment and evaluation of accounting system and controls
- **Tools/Technologies Used:** Spreadsheet programs VisiCalc and Lotus 1-2-3, electronic calculator, copiers, printers, and word processing software

1938
- **Job duties:** Tax return preparation, financial statement auditing and preparation, business management consulting, cost accounting, establishment and evaluation of accounting systems and controls
- **Tools/Technologies Used:** Large mechanical adding machines, comptometers, and typewriters

2012
- **Job duties:** Everything in 1983 plus outsourced CFO services, performance measurement attestation, business valuation, forensic accounting and fraud investigations, corporate governance and systems auditing, and business consulting
- **Tools/Technologies Used:** Desktop and laptop computers, tablets, and smartphones; cloud computing; Excel, Word, Powerpoint, QuickBooks; videoconferencing and virtual meeting

1887
- **Job duties:** Bookkeeping, financial statement preparation and attestation, cost accounting, fraud investigation, establishment of accounting systems and controls
- **Tools/Technologies Used:** No equipment other than a slide rule for percentages. Reports were handwritten on accounting ruled paper

Figure 1. Transformation Duties of Accountancy Profession and Related Technologies Used.
Source: Mendlowitz & Drew (2012).

Kreiss 2014). The digitization is about utilizing a new technology and integrating it with existing technology (Barashyan 2017).

Accounting has evolved from a simply book keeping to a sophisticated computerized information system to support decision making by both internal and external parties. The digitization in accounting has already started in the 90s, since the complex accounting information system was invented and evolved in more sophisticated ERP system, cloud computing, big data, mobile technology, social media, and internet of things (Rîndaşu 2017). This chronicle of technology advancement has effect on accounting profession as depicted in the Figure 1.

Today, the technology has brought the accountancy profession to the digital era to which accountancy professionals has responded by improving the accounting standards and procedures in accordance with the technology advancement. Accountants have been forced to change significantly in their services of compilation, assurance, tax and managerial consultation (Hunton 2015). There are some benefits and costs of digitization in accounting as listed in Table 1.

Table 1. Benefit and cost of digitizing in accounting.

Benefit	Cost
• Faster cycle times – these include credit approvals, payment and collections, posting of transactions, closing of the books, generation of reports and more time available for higher-level analysis • Broader geographic reach • Continuous service availability, 24/7 access, and more satisfied internal and external customers • Reduced error rates – that means fewer transactions with errors as well as fewer errors • Reduced accounting staff and improved productivity • Better cash management – efficient payments and effective collections • Cost saving in mail, paper and storage of paper • Improved audit trails and security	• Investment required in computer hardware and software • Initial need for expensive consultants • Cost involved in system, processes, processing of information and report generation changes • Continual training or retraining needs and/or requirements for personnel with specialized skills • User resistance • Careful attention needs to be paid to security, control and audit requirements for financial transactions during the initial configuration. If the initial configuration of the system is not correct or the integration with ERP software or legacy system is faulty, then there are recurring costs and fewer benefits from the implementation.

Source: Deshmukh (2006).

3 RESEARCH METHOD

This study was an on-line perception survey by distributing a questionnaire to Indonesian accountants, both practitioners and academicians. The items of the questionnaire were developed by adapting the concept of technology barometer introduced by the Accountancy Europe (2017). Only valid data were tabulated and analyzed using the perception descriptive technique. In addition, inclusive literature review from relevant accounting studies was conducted for the extensive analysis to get more comprehensive understanding on empirical evidence from the survey result. The questionnaire was distributed and collected in July 2018, by which 166 data were captured. The participants were selected using a snowball sampling technique. The first target participants were well-known accountants registered as member of accountancy profession association in Indonesia. The sampling method was purposive in nature based on certain criteria such as respondents' willingness to fill out the on-line short survey and at least one year working experience in accounting field. The respondents consisted of 102 academicians, 46 practitioners, and 19 mixed respondents from various area in Indonesia, i.e. Ambon, Bandung, Batam, Bekasi, Bogor, Cilegon, Citeureup, Depok, Garut, Jakarta, Jambi, Jayapura, Jember, Jombang, Makassar, Manado, Medan, Palembang, Pangkalpinang, Pekanbaru, Pontianak, Probolinggo, Serang, Sidoarjo, Sidrap, Solo, Surabaya, Surakarta, Tangerang Selatan, Tarakan, Tegal, and Yogyakarta. The survey captured their perception about the effect of digital era toward accountancy profession. This heterogeneous samples will give different perspectives into account.

4 RESULTS AND DISCUSSION

4.1 Survey results from Indonesian accountants

The internal consistency reliability of the survey questionnaire was measured by the Kuder–Richardson Formula 20. The KR-20 coefficient 0.725 shows that the test had a high reliability.

The survey results are depicted in Figures 2-10. Figure 2 shows that the technology

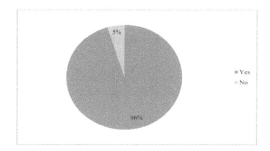

Figure 3. As accountant, I do some technology related activities.

development was perceived an opportunity to enhance the accountancy profession. Most agreed that the technology development had no impact on the accountancy profession. Therefore, as Figure 3 suggests, almost every accountant do some technology related activities.

Figure 4 gives an obvious picture that in order to confront the technology advancement, training in newest technology the most frequent activity in accountants' workplace. Special survey on technology advancement is very rarely conducted by accountants. Figure 5 depicts that mostly accountants' technology-related activities are aimed to simplify their day-to-day works. The standardized technology framework is not much of their concern.

Figure 6 shows that most accountants are supported by internal staff with specific technology expertise. IT consulting services are rarely used because of the high consultation fee. Figure 7

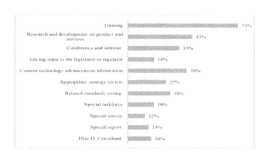

Figure 4. Activities have been initiated at my workplace to confront the technology advancement.

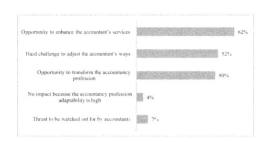

Figure 2. The impact of technology development on accountancy profession.

Figure 5. The focus of my technology-related activities.

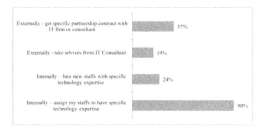

Figure 6. The way of my works is supported by the technology advancement

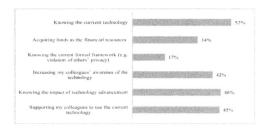

Figure 7. My challenges in the fast advancement of technology.

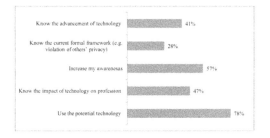

Figure 8. Support from the accountancy profession association for me.

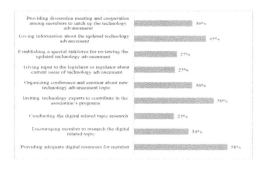

Figure 9. Kinds of technology advancement related activity must be conducted by the accountancy profession association.

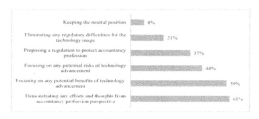

Figure 10. Issues to take into account by the accountancy profession association when meeting the legislators or regulators.

explains that the strongest challenge of technology advancement for accountants is knowing the current technology. The formal technology framework does not concern them much.

Figure 8 outlines some types of assistance provided by the accountancy profession association to its individual member. The most expected assistance is about how to use various potential technologies. Socialization on current formal technology framework is the least expected assistance. Based on Figure 9, the accountancy profession association is expected to organize some technology advancement related activities. The provision of adequate digital resource is highly expected by members of the accountancy profession association. Giving inputs to legislator or regulator and conducting digital related topic research do not concern them much.

Figure 10 lists the most important issues the accountancy profession association is expected to discuss with the legislators or the regulators.

4.2 The impact of digital era on accountancy profession

Digital era makes accountants engage new technologies. The new analytical tools, cloud computing, and social media are challenges for accountants. Accountants have to employ these kinds of new technology to address the many radical changes expected to happen. Mobile devices make it easy to connect with every one in any where and any time. Accountants have been touched by the technology advancement. Big data concept stems from the internet of things gives potential new area to be explored by accountants. Unstructured or semi-structured data will be counted. Artificial intelligence and modern robotic automation will replace any regular repetitive duties of accountants. Accountants will have more complex duties to create value for organization (Richins et al. 2016).

In the future, Association of Chartered Certified Accountants (ACCA) and Institute of Management Accountants (IMA) Report (2013) predict that accountancy profession, as shown in Figure 11, will become new professional hybrids

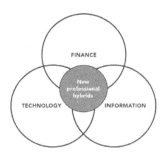

Figure 11. New professional hybrids.
Source: ACCA and IMA Report (2013).

responsible for interpreting every analytical data and transforming them into valuable insight so that the business can makes commercial value on it (CGMA Report 2014). Consequently, the new professional hybrids will work with IT professionals, data scientists and business managers to have more comprehensive analysis for a more meaningful insight. Data analytic will be very crucial for businesses, and accountants must have the high level of analytical skill in addition to technical skills.

Figure 12 illustrates a digital accounting value chain as general framework for understanding the impact of digital era on accountancy profession (Hunton 2015). The highest value is how to manage the business knowledge optimally. Available digital technology will be used to get this highest value by capturing any economic phenomena, redesigning the business processes, and disseminating knowledge to decision makers.

Some studies give list of potential impacts of digitalizing era on accountancy profession (Taylor et al. 2017) as follow:

a. The rapid pace on global financial accounting and reporting standards;
b. The importance of real-time dynamic reporting;
c. The new format of management control systems;
d. The audit risk assessment based on data analytic and population;

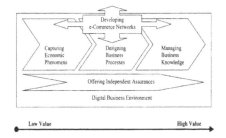

Figure 12. The Digital Accounting Value Chain.
Source: Hunton (2015).

e. The improved productivity by forecasts and sensitivity analysis based on external data;
f. The continuous assurance in timelier and more relevant audit reporting; and
g. The better understanding of restatements, fraud, and going-concern issues.

Furthermore, accountants will be required to protect sensitive information in the business system and application (Chorafas 2008). Cyber-crime is another challenge to be coped by accountants. Information security will be the area to be solved. The new IT-based environment causes other problems. Web-based applications are at risk of being hacked. The cloud computing makes data management related works tougher. Privacy protection development will be crucial. Digital exchange of information between organization and external parties causes a set of risk exposure such as questionable data integrity. Hence, the system architecture of organization needs to be developed well and secure.

In this digital era, the role of accountancy profession will be changed into more strategic ones. Accountants will take a position as important partners of organizational changes (Nga & Mun 2013). Accountants will have more tasks in planning and strategic area. Accountant will be the future middle man in every organization (King 2014).

4.3 Strategies to exploit the digital era

A strategy to exploit the digital era can be developed based on the accountancy academicians and practitioners' perspectives. Accountancy academicians concern that the beneficial digital era must be anticipated with highly prepared human resources; i.e., the accountants themselves. An appropriate accounting education becomes an absolute requirement. The accounting curriculum must be evaluated and revised to address the new needs and challenges in the digital era. In this regard, there are some topics specific suggested by Gamage (2016) to be included in courses of accounting education as illustrated in Figure 13.

The basic strategy is developing a comprehensive framework for competency-based curriculum in accounting education. Hard skills and soft skills of accountants must be sharpened. There are various must-have skills for an accountant including perception skills, communication skills, interpersonal skills, personal/self skills, and technical/analytical skills. These skills will be created by integrating development of all competencies, i.e. foundational competencies, broad-management competencies, and accounting competencies (Lawson et al. 2014). The proposed competency-based curriculum framework is as follows (Figure 14):

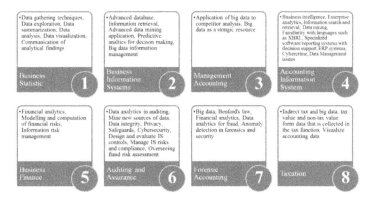

Figure 13. New topics in courses of accounting education.
Source: Gamage (2016).

Foundational Competencies	Accounting Competencies					
Communication	External Reporting & Analysis	Planning, Analysis & Control	Taxation: Compliance & Planning	Information Systems	Assurance & Internal Control	Professional Values, Ethics & Attitudes
Quantitative						
Analytical Thinking & Problem Solving	Broad Management Competencies					
Interpersonal	Leadership	Ethics & Social Responsibility	Process Management & Improvement	Governance, Risk & Compliance	Additional Core Business Competencies	
Technological						

Figure 14. Integrated competency of professional accountant.
Source: Lawson et al. (2014).

From the accountancy practitioners' perspectives, accountants must aware of the latest technology advancement. Accountants have to pay a closer attention to how the technology will impact their works. Accountants must be ready for any potential radical changes in accounting. The accountancy profession associations must familiarize their members with the new emerging technology knowledge. The fast technology evolution must be anticipated by the accountancy profession. The technology advancement will always give new opportunities for accountants. But at the same times, it is always followed by other consequences such as new kinds of threat to the accounting works. The accountancy profession must aware of the high impact of increasingly digital era on their works.

confronted the technological revolution. Accountancy executives must have relevant technology literacy. Accountancy academicians are responsible for preparing the next generation to get ready the digitalized world. It is suggested that further research explore the impact of a particular digitization on accountant profession for more detailed empirical study. Further research can be carried out in a longer time and larger area of survey and an in-depth interview with some accounting experts as informants for a comparative study. The main contribution of this research is some identified strategies which can be implemented by the accountancy profession both academicians and practitioners in order to gain extra advantages of the digital era.

5 CONCLUSION

Digital era with its emerging technologies has already changed the most accountants' works and the way of thinking. It is concluded that accountants have

REFERENCES

Association of Chartered Certified Accountants (ACCA) & Institute of Management Accountants (IMA). 2013. *Big Data: Its power and perils*. Retrieved from http://www.accaglobal.com/bigdata.

Accountancy Europe. 2017. *Technology Barometer: Survey Results.* Brussels: Accountancy Europe.

Al-Htaybat, K. & von Alberti-Alhtaybat, L. 2017. Big Data and corporate reporting: impacts and paradoxes. Accounting. *Auditing & Accountability Journal* 30(4): 850-873.

Arnaboldi, M, Busco, C. & Cuganesan, S. 2017. Accounting, accountability, social media and big data: revolution or hype? *Accounting, Auditing & Accountability Journal* 30(4): 762-776.

Barashyan, A. 2017. *Bibliometric Study on Digital Accounting Linked with Pedagogical View.* (Master's Thesis). Saimaa University of Applied Sciences.

Bhimani, A. & Willcocks, L. 2014 Digitisation, 'Big Data' and the transformation of accounting information. *Accounting and Business Research* 44(4): 469-490.

Brennen, S. & Kreiss, D. 2014. *Digitalization and Digitization. Culture Digitally.* Retrieved from http://culture digitally.org/2014/09/digitalization-and-digitization.

Chartered Global Management Accountants Report (CGMA). 2013. *From insight to impact: unlocking Opportunities in Big Data.* United Kingdom: CGMA.

Chorafas, D.N. 2008. *IT auditing and Sarbanes-Oxley compliance: key strategies for business improvement.* New York: CRC Press.

Deshmukh, A. 2006. *Digital accounting: The effects of the internet and ERP on accounting.* IGI Global.

Frey, C. & Osborne, M. 2013. The Future of Employment: How susceptible are Jobs to Computerisation. *Oxford University Programme on the Impacts of Future Technology.*

Gamage, P. 2016. Big Data: are accounting educators ready? *Accounting and Management Information Systems* 15(3): 588-604.

Guthrie, J. & Parker, L.D. 2016. Whither the accounting profession, accountants and accounting researchers? Commentary and projections. *Accounting, Auditing & Accountability Journal* 29(1): 2-10.

Hood, D. 2015. Losing sleep: Leaders of the profession on its biggest nightmares. *Accounting Today.* Retrieved from https://www.accountingtoday.com/news/losing-sleep.

Hunton, J.E. 2015. The impact of digital technology on accounting behavioral research. *Advances in Accounting Behavioral Research* 5: 3-17.

King, E. 2014. *London jobs: big drive for big data.* Retrieved from http://www.icaew.com/en/members/local-groups-and-societies/london.

Lawson, R.A., Blocher, E., Brewer, P.C., Cokins, G., Sorensen, J.E., Stout, D.E., Sundem, G.L., Wolcott, S. & Wouters, M. J.F. 2014. Focusing accounting curricula on students' long-run careers: Recommendation for an integrated competency-based framework for accounting education. *Issues in Accounting Education* 29(2): 295-317.

Liu, L. & Vasarhelyi, V. 2014. Big Questions in AIS Research: Measurement, Information Processing, Data Analysis and Reporting. *JIS.* Spring editorial. M68

Mendlowitz, E. & Drew, J. 2012. Carousel of Progress. *Journal of Accountancy* 213(6): 15-20.

Nga, J. & Mun, S.W. 2013. The perception of the undergraduate students towards accountants and the role of accountants in driving organizational change. A case of study of a Malaysian business school. *Education + Training* 55(6): 500-519

Oxford English Dictionary. 2010. *Oxford Advanced Learner's Dictionary.* New York: Oxford University Press.

Richins, G., Stapleton, A., Stratopoulos, T. C. & Wong, C. 2016. *Data Analytics and Big Data: Opportunity or Threat for the Accounting Profession?* Retrieved from https://papers.ssrn.com/sol3/papers.cfm?abstract_id=2813817.

Rîndaşu, S. 2017. Emerging information technologies in accounting and related security risks – what is the impact on the Romanian accounting profession. *Accounting and Management Information Systems* 16(4): 581-609.

Samkin, G. & Stainbank, L. 2016. Teaching and learning: Current and future challenges facing accounting academics, academicians, and the development of an agenda for future research. *Meditari Accountancy Research* 24(3): 294-317.

Stanciu, V. & Gheorghe, M. 2017. An exploration of the accounting profession – The stream of mobile devices. *Accounting and Management Information Systems* 16 (3): 369-385.

Taylor, A.M., Chen, Y., Estes, T.E., Hanks R.L. & Ramey, Z.M. 2017. Big Data Analytics: Megatrends to Business Success. *Internal Auditing.* July/August 2017: 26-32.

Effects of good corporate governance, ownership structure, political connections on tax aggressiveness of manufacturing companies listed in Indonesia Stock Exchange

M.S. Kurniawan, B.P. Sutjiatmo & R. Wikansari
Politeknik APP Jakarta, Jakarta, Indonesia

K. Haryono
Edinburgh Napier University, Edinburgh, Scotland, UK

ABSTRACT: This research aims to provide empirical evidence of the effects of good corporate governance, ownership structure, and political connection on tax aggressiveness. This research used linier regression as analysis tool. 64 sample manufacturing companies listed in Indonesia Stocks Exchange were selected purposively. The finding indicates that board of commissioners significantly and positively affected tax aggressiveness, that board of directors did not significantly affect tax aggressiveness, that audit committee did not significantly affect tax aggressiveness, that family ownership significantly and positively affected tax aggressiveness, and that political connection did not significantly affect tax aggressiveness.

1 INTRODUCTION

Companies' main purpose is to make profit. In doing so, good corporate governance is one of the most important aspects (Desai & Darmapala 2007).

National committee on governance policy (KNKG) is an organization that publishes guidelines for implementation of good corporate governance in Indonesia. KNKG states there are three important elements in the application of good corporate governance, there are board of committee, board of commissioners, board of directors, and audit committee (KNKG 2006).

In agency theory, one of the most frequently occurring agency conflicts was a conflict between company an owner and management. This conflict occurs because of differences in the interests; the company owner wants the addition of wealth from company profits, while management wants to gain benefit from the facilities provided by the company that sometimes can reduce company profit (Watt & Zimmerman 1986, Godfrey et al. 2010). This conflict can be reduced with good corporate governance that consists of board of commissioner helped by audit committee to oversee board of director in company's operations.

Another type of agency conflict is a conflict between controlling shareholders and non-controlling shareholders. This conflict occurs because of differences in interest between controlling and non-controlling parties. The controlling parties want to maximize their wealth using company assets which sometimes harms non-controlling parties. In companies with family ownership, commonly the family own the

control of company, despite the fact that family ownership is more effective organizational structure compared with other type of structure to overcome agency conflicts between company owners and management. This is because company owner is likely to place people on the board of directors or board of commissioners as representative of company owner, who are usually parts of the family (Randoy & Goel 2003, Gaaya et al. 2017).

Political connections are important resources for companies in developing countries. Political connections provide an option for companies to resolve issues related to law and taxes (Rajan & Zingales 1998, Leuz & Gee 2006). Commonly in Indonesia, retired soldiers, retired policemen, retired senate members, members of political parties become directors or commissioners in a company.

2 LITERATURE

2.1 *Agency theory*

In agency theory, there are two types of agency conflicts, conflict between company owners and the management and conflict between controlling shareholders and non-controlling shareholders. These conflicts can be resolved by the establishment of a board of commissioners and audit committee that can represent shareholders in overseeing operations of the company. Conflicts between controlling shareholder and non-controlling shareholder occurs because of the interest of controlling shareholders to transfer company assets into their assets, so it may harm the non-controlling shareholders (Watts & Zimmerman 1986, Godfrey et al. 2010).

2.2 *Good corporate governance*

Good corporate governance will help companies maintain sustainability, business efficiency, reduce the possibility of companies violating legislation, laws, and related regulations (IICG 2012).

Good corporate governance can be implemented properly if supported by the company's organs that perform their duties and functions as they must do. According to KNKG, there are 3 important organs in the company including:

a. General meeting of shareholders
   This meeting is one of the most important agendas for the company and the owners of the company because the ultimate decision making in the company is taken during this meeting (KNKG 2006).
b. Board of commissioners
   The board of commissioners is the organ of the company responsible for ensuring the proper implementation of corporate governance in the company, overseeing and advising management with the help of audit committee, and audit committee themselves help board of commissioners oversee and advise on management (KNKG 2006).
   The relations between board of commissioners and tax aggressiveness is the board of commissioners responsible for overseeing the operation of the company by management in accordance with rules and laws, including rules and laws in tax. Thus, the existence of board of commissioners can reduce agency conflicts between company owners and management. In Indonesia the board of commissioners of a company usually serves as the board of director or commissioners in other companies; that can cause difficulty in coordination between each member board of commissioners, so it can be assumed that the larger size of the board of commissioners will inhibit the function of the board of commissioners to conduct supervision. The larger size of the board of commissioners can lead to a greater tax aggressive action by company (Annisa & Kurniasih 2013).
c. Audit committee
   The audit committee is tasked with assisting the commissioners in overseeing the operations of the company whether it is in compliance with applicable laws and regulations. Financial Services Authority (OJK in Indonesia) rules state that minimum number of audit committee for companies listed on Indonesia Stock Exchange are at least 3 people. Relationship between audit committee and tax aggressiveness is audit committee in charge of ensuring the operational implementation of company in accordance with applicable tax regulation so that the lager audit committee made the chances of management

taking tax aggressive action can be reduced (Annisa & Kurniasih 2013).
d. Board of Directors (BoD)
   Board of Directors is the organ of the company responsible for company operations. Board of directors are appointed in general meeting of shareholder. Board of directors are responsible to shareholders. The bonus plan hypothesis stated that one of objectives of management with the bonus plan is to maximize the bonus she/he earns, one way to maximize management bonus with increased company profit and minimize amount of tax using tax aggressive policy (Watt & Zimmerman 1986, Godfrey et al. 2010).

2.3 *Family ownership*

Company with family ownership is one of the most effective types of corporate organizations because family firms have clear long-term goals, have almost absolute and clear policies, tend to maintain family name reputation, and with some of family members becoming directors or commissioners make firm management more likely effective (Chen et al. 2010). In Indonesia, majority of companies are owned by family or government (Dyanti et al. 2012).

There are two opinions concerning relationship between family ownership and tax aggressive action. The first opinion states that companies with family ownership will tend to reduce agency conflicts between controlling shareholders and non-controlling shareholders (Shleifer & Vishny 1986). Companies with family ownership will tend to have views for the future and minimize actions that will harm the company and damage family name such as tax avoidance action (Chen et al. 2010). The second opinion states that in a company with family ownership, agency conflicts will likely to happen between the family members serving as controlling shareholders and those of the non-controlling shareholders. The family members serving as controlling shareholders will tend to take advantage of the company, resulting in loss for non-controlling shareholding family members (Shleifer & Vishny 1986; Desai & Dharmapala 2007).

2.4 *Political connections*

Businesses in Asia are characterized with a connection system consisting of bankers, politicians, and members of government (Rajan & Zingales 1998). Company with political connections will generally find it easier to get credit from bank and leniency in law and taxation (Bliss & Gull 2012). In Indonesia, politics and business have been inseparable since the early Indonesian independence era. For example, many former military and police officers, former members of parliament, or politicians were appointed to the board of directors or commissioners (Leuz & Gee 2003).

Kim and Zhang (2015) state that there are 5 reasons why companies with political connections are more likely to engage in tax aggressive action than companies with no political connections: First, companies with political connections tend to have less control than companies with no political connections. This is due to the fact that companies with political connections tend to rely on assistance from their political connections. Second, companies with political connections tend to have wider access than those without political connections to changes in tax rules, so they can anticipate the rules earlier than others. Third, companies with political connections will tend not to be financially transparent as they have protections from their political connections. Fourth, companies with political connections will be more tax aggressive than those with non-political connections. Fifth, companies with political connections tend to be associated with the possibility of tax aggressive action due to consequences of their risk averse decision making.

3 RESEARCH DESIGN

3.1 Sample and data collection

The samples were chosen by using a purposive sampling technique based on the following criteria: being a manufacturing company listed on Indonesia Stock Exchange, publishing a complete annual report in the 2016 period, using rupiah (IDR) currency in reporting, and having a positive profit value. The number of samples was 64 companies.

3.2 Variable measured

3.2.1 Board of commissioners
This variable is measured using number of commissioners in a company.

3.2.2 Board of Directors
This variable is measured using number of directors in a company.

3.2.3 Audit committee
This variable is measured using number of audit committee in a company.

3.2.4 Family ownership
This variable is measured using the presence of the shareholding family members serving as board of commissioners or board of directors. If any family members become board of commissioner or board of directors, it is measured with value of 1, whereas if none it is measured with value of 0.

3.2.5 Political connection
This variable is measured by the presence of retired military officers, retired police officers, former members of the parliament, members of political parties in the board of commissioners and board of directors. Any presence of these figures in the board of

commissioners and board of directors is valued 1, and no presence is valued 0.

3.2.6 Tax aggressiveness
This variable is measured by using effective tax rate (ETR), which is obtained by the following formula:

$$ETR = \frac{\text{Tax Expenses}}{\text{Earning before tax}}$$

3.3 Model

$$TA = \alpha\,BOC + \alpha\,BOD - \alpha\,AC + \alpha\,FOWN + \alpha\,PCON + \varepsilon$$

BOC = Board of commissioner size
BOD = Board of director size
AC = Audit Committee size
FOWN = Family ownership
PCON = Political Connections
TA = Tax aggressiveness

4 RESULTS

Table 1 presents the result of sample selection. The number of samples reached 47.76% of the total population.

Table 2 summarizes the descriptive statistical computation results.

The board of commissioner variable has a minimum value of 2, maximum value of 10, mean of 4.2, standard deviation of 1.858. The board of

Table 1. Sample Selection.

NO	Sample Critera	Companies
1.	Manufacturing companies listed on IDX and publishes a complete annual report for the reporting period 2016	134
2.	Companies not using rupiah (IDR) currency in reporting	(29)
3.	Companias with negative profit value	(41)
	TOTAL SAMPLE	64

Table 2. Descriptive Statistics.

Variable	Data	Max. Value	Min. Value	Mean	Standard deviation
BOC	64	10	2	4.42	1.858
BOD	64	16	2	5.54	2.850
AC	64	6	3	3.4	0.812
FOWN	64	1	0	0.51	0.503
PCON	64	1	0	0.29	0.460
TA	64	4.96	0.02	0.30	0.614

Table 3. Regression test results.

Model	B	Sig.
Constant	0.323	0.409
BOC	0.128	0.013
BOD	0.020	0.505
AC	-0.161	0.170
FOWN	0.273	0.042
PCON	-0.165	0.407

director variable has a minimum value of 2, maksimum value of 16, mean of 5.54, and standard deviation of 2.85. The audit committee variable has a minimum value of 3, maximum value of 6, mean of 3.4, and standard deviation 0.812. In Indonesian Stock Exchange rules, each company must have an audit committee with a minimum of 3. Table 1 show that the audit comittee variable has a mean of 3.4 and hence indicates that manufacturing companies in Indonesia tend to appoint audit committees in minimal account, or just to meet requirements set by the regulator. The family ownership variable has a minimum value of 0, maximum value of 1, mean of 0.51, standard deviation of 0.503. This implies that the majority of manufacturing companies in Indonesia are owned by family. The political connection variable has a maximum value of 1, minimum value of 0, mean of 0.29, and standard deviation of 0.460, indicating that most of sample companies do not have BOD/BOC with political affiliation. The tax aggressiveness variable has a maximum value of 4.96, minimum value of 0.02, mean of 0.3, and standard deviation of 0.614.

Table 3 shows that the board of commissioners positively and significantly affected tax aggressiveness, indicating that larger size of the board of commisioners will inhibit the function of the board of commissioners to conduct supervision. The board of directors did not significantly affect tax aggressiveness. The audit committee did not significantly affect tax aggressiveness. This is due to the fact that most sample companies appoint an audit committee in minimum size as shown in Table 2, only to meet aplicable regulations. The family ownership positively and significantly affected tax aggressiveness. Political connections did not significantly affect tax aggressiveness because in the context of this study politicians who served as directors or commissioners in companies tend to conduct good business practices for the future of their political carreers.

5 CONCLUSIONS

This study investigates the effect of board of commissioners, board of directors, audit committee,

family ownership, and political connections on tax aggressiveness. This study used 64 sample of manufacturing companies listed in Indonesia Stock Exchange. Using linear regression, we found an evidence that board of commissioners positively and significantly affected tax aggressiveness, that board of directors did not significantly affect tax aggressiveness, that audit committee did not significantly affect tax aggressiveness, family ownership significantly and positively affected tax aggressiveness, and political connections did not significantly affect tax aggressiveness.

REFERENCES

Annisa, A., Ayu, N. & Kurniasih, L. 2012. *Pengaruh Corporate Governance Terhadap Tax Avoidance.* Surakarta: UNS.

Bliss, M.A, & Gull F.A. 2012. Political connection and cost of debt: Some Malaysian evidence. *Journal of Banking & Finance* 36(5): 1520-1527.

Chen, S, Chen, X, Chen, Q, & Shevlin, T. 2010. Are family firms more tax aggressive than non family firms. *Nan kai Business Review International.* 5(1): 25-42.

Desai, A., Mihir, M. & Dharmapala, D. 2007. *Taxation and corporate governce: an economic approach.* Harvard University, Working paper.

Komite Nasional Kebijakan Governance (KNKG). 2006. *Pedoman umum good corporate governance.* Jakarta. KNKG.

Dyanty, V., Utama, S., Rossieta, H. & Veronica, S. 2012. Pengaruh Kepemilikan pengendali akhir terhadap transaksi pihak berelasi. *SNA XV Banjarmasin.*

Gaaya, S., Lakhal, N. & Lakhal, F. 2017. Does family ownership reduce corporate tax avoidance? The moderating effect of audit quality. *Managerial Auditing Journal.* 32(7): 731-744.

Godfrey, J., Hodgson, A., Tarca, A., Hamilton, J. & Holmes, S. 2010. *Accounting Theory 7th edition.* New York: John Wiley & Sons.

Indonesian Institute Corporate Governance (IICG). 2012. Laporan Corporate Governance Perception Index: Good Corporate Governance dalam Perspektif Risiko. Jakarta. IICG.

Kim, C. & Zhang, L. 2015. Corporate political connections and tax aggressiveness. *Contemporary Accounting Research.* 3(1): 78-114.

Leuz, C & Gee O.F. 2006. Political Relationship, Global Financing, and corporate transparency: Evidence from Indonesia. *Journal of Financial Economics.* 81(2): 411-439.

Rajan, R, & Zingales, L. 1998. Which capitalism? Lesson from the East Asian Crisis. *Journal of applied corporate finance.* 11(3): 40-48.

Randoy, T, & Goel, S. 2003. Ownership structure, founder leadership, and performance in Norwegian SME's: implication for financing entrepreneurial opportunities. *Journal of bussiness Venturing.* 18: 619-637.

Shleifer, A. & Vishny, R. 1986. Large shareholders and corporate control. *Journal of Political Economy.* 94(3): 461-488.

Watts, R., & Zimmerman, J. 1986. *Positive accounting theory.*

Global Competitiveness: Business Transformation in the
Digital Era – Abdullah, Widiaty & Abdullah (eds)
© 2019 Taylor & Francis Group, London, ISBN 978-0-367-19442-0

The use of earnings and cash flows model in predicting corporate financial distress: Evidence from retail merchandizing enterprises listed in IDX

A. Selowidodo, R. Wikansari, B.P. Sutjiatmo & M.S. Kurniawan
Polytechnic APP Jakarta, Ministry of Industry, Indonesia

A.T. Rachmadi
Hokkaido University, Hokkaido, Japan

ABSTRACT: This research is aimed to examine and analyze the empirical effect of earnings and cash flows in predicting corporate financial distress of the retail merchandizing enterprises. This study used secondary data obtained from the company's financial statements in the period from 2014 to 2017 that are listed in IDX. Purposive sampling is used for collecting samples, and hence 15 firms were chosen for data research. The hypothesis testing was conducted using multiple discriminant analysis (MDA). The results of this study show that the earnings model is strong enough to predict corporate financial distress, while the cash flows model cannot be used as a predictive model of corporate financial distress. In other words, it is better to predict corporate financial distress based on earnings model than cash flows model.

1   INTRODUCTION

Corporate financial distress is the situation when a company cannot meet or face difficulty to pay off its financial obligation to the creditors. Recently, corporate financial distress has become a famous topic in finance. Thus, firm's financial health is a crucial indicator for interested users to know more about company's financial condition. That is why corporate financial distress has a big impact on management, shareholders, employees, creditors, customers, and other stakeholders.

The prediction of corporate financial distress and bankruptcy has been a great interest of research in the late 1960s. In addition, corporate financial distress prediction has become an integral part of corporate governance as it helps all the stakeholders analyze to which direction a company is taking. According to Warner (1977), companies that are in financial distress tend to exhibit decline in market value over time.

Some studies found that earnings may be more useful in predicting corporate financial distress. McCue (1991) investigated the hospitals' financial health in California. He showed that earnings model is more powerful than cash flows model. Similar research has been conducted by Djongkang & Rita (2014) on whether earnings or cash flows model can be used in predicting corporate financial distress of the company sector of textile mill product and apparel and other textile products listed in IDX. The result shows that earnings model can better predict corporate financial distress. In other words, it is harder to predict corporate financial distress by cash flows model than by earnings model. In contrast, Azis & Lawson (1989) found that cash flows-based model is more effective to predict corporate financial distress. However, according to Sharma (2001), studies using cash flows model for predicting company failure is not conclusive due to the limitations such as improperly measured cash flow operations.

In Indonesia, little empirical research has been done so far to assess the factors that are significant under corporate financial distress. Lack of research on the factors that contribute to corporate financial distress signifies that users do not have proper information about future prospects of a firm. Therefore, it is important to study the factors that are significant to financially distressed companies in Indonesia and thus provide a clearer picture in determining the significance of financial indicator while detecting financially distressed companies.

An interesting discussion issue in predicting corporate financial distress should be focus on both earnings and cash flows. Hence, the objective of this study is to empirically examine and analyze whether earnings model or cash flows model can better to predict corporate financial distress of the retail merchandizing enterprises listed in IDX for the period of 2014–2017.

2   LITERATURE REVIEW AND HYPOTHESIS

In modern concepts, financial distress is defined in many ways. Lau (1987) defined financial distress as a three-stage process: incubation, deficit funds-flow, and financial distress or recovery. Gilberst et al.

(1990) defined distress firms as firms that declared bankruptcy and firms that had negative cumulative earnings over three consecutive years. Ross (1996) stated, "Financial distress is a situation where a firm's operating cash flows are not sufficient to satisfy current obligations and the firm is forced to take corrective action". It is difficult to define precisely what distress or bankruptcy is, due to the variety of accounting procedures or rules in different countries or at different time spots as well as various events that put firms into financial distress.

2.1 *Earnings–financial distress relationships*

Corporate financial distress happens before bankruptcy. According to Wruck (1990), there are several pointers that can be used to detect corporate financial distress such as a reduction in the level of dividends issued out and retrenchment of employees and resignation of top management. In addition, Whitaker (1999) stated that the process of financial distress starts with a company's inability to pay short-term obligations at the due date. The main reasons behind financial distress can be attributed to inappropriate asset management, corporate governance, or financial structure (Gilberst et al. 1990). Adeyemi (2012) suggested that lack of adequate funds is one of the major factors leading to financial distress as capital has the capability to absorb losses. Nevertheless, most managers focus on and blame external factors when their businesses fail instead of evaluating the internal factors (Scherrer 2003).

There have been many models developed in order to predict corporate financial distress. Many of these models involve the use of ratio analysis to analyze failed companies. Beaver (1966) and Altman's (1968) studies consider five independent variables, and each of them represents the financial ratios. In their studies, earnings before taxes (EBT) is considered as a proxy for earnings. According to surveys, EBT-based ratio is by far the most popular type of valuation technique in debt contract. The popularity of EBT is confirmed by Lie & Lie (2002), according to which EBT-based ratio is one of the most of frequently used valuation indicators. Due to its popularity, managers of many companies use EBT as a primary metric to reflect company's performances (Isidro & Marques 2008). Thus, corporate financial distress is when the company is characterized by declining in financial conditions within a few years, negative net income, amount of cash flows less than long-term debt, and interest coverage ratio less than one. Based on the above arguments, the first hypothesis is proposed:

H1: Earnings can predict corporate financial distress.

2.2 *Cash flows–financial distress relationships*

The information contained on a cash flow statement shows the decrease or increase in cash flow balance over an accounting period. Significance of a cash flow analysis towards a corporate financial distress prediction has been augmented by Ward and Foster in 1997. They compared the trends in three components of a cash flow statement, i.e., operating cash flow, investing cash flow, and financing cash flow (Tam & Kiang 1992).

The observations of Ward and Foster (1997) concluded that healthy companies have a tendency towards comparatively stable association among the three components of cash flow, i.e., operating, investing, and financing activities. In addition, it is noted that unhealthy companies were characterized by decreasing cash flow from operating, investing, and financing cash flow about one or two years before they failed for financial distress. This study is vital as it portrays the significance of assessing cash flow information while examining corporate financial distress. Based on the above arguments, the second hypothesis is developed as follows:

H2: Cash flows can predict corporate financial distress.

3 METHOD

3.1 *Populations and samples*

The populations in this study related to all retail merchandizing enterprises listed in IDX. The samples were classified into two groups, namely analysis samples and holdout samples. The analysis samples were retail merchandizing enterprises listed in IDX for the period of 2014–2016. And the holdout samples were retail merchandizing enterprises listed in IDX for the period of 2017. The samples were selected by using purposive sampling method using the following criteria: (1) retail merchandizing enterprises that are listed in IDX for the period of 2014–2017, (2) having published audited financial statements for the fiscal period of 2014–2017, (3) companies are grouped into two groups for each model. Groups in the earning model are those with positive earnings and negative earnings. Groups in the cash flows model are positive cash flows and negative cash flows; and (4) the analysis samples consist of 45 firm-year from 15 different firms in earnings model and 45 firm-year from 15 different firms in cash flows model. The holdout samples consist of 15 firms.

3.2 *Dependent variables*

Dependent variables, corporate financial distress based on earnings model and cash flows model, are expressed as dummy variable (1) if the firm has positive earnings, and (0) if the firm has negative earnings; (1) if the firm has positive cash flows, and (0) if the firm has negative cash flows. In this study, EBT is used as a proxy for earnings, where extraordinary items and discontinued operations are not included in order to avoid the effect of different tax tariffs at different periods. In other words, the reason for excluding extraordinary items and discontinued operations is to eliminate elements that may show increased profit growth in one period but will not appear in any other periods. However, the data of cash flows are derived from the cash flow figures presented in the audited financial statements of the company.

3.3 Independent variables

The list for independent variables which may influence financial distress is as follows: Sales, Inventory turnover, Size, Employees, Current ratio, Acid ratio, Days in account receivables, Return on assets, Operating profit margin, Operating expenses, Total assets turnover, Net fixed assets turnover, Net fixed assets, Total debt to total assets, Long-term debt to total assets, and Equity to total assets (Atmini & Wuryana 2005).

The independent variables in this study are the variables used to measure the company's product market, institutional factors, operations, liquidity, income and expenses, profitability, activity and investment, and coverage (McCue 1991).

The institutional factor variable is the company size data. The operating variable is the number of employees. The liquidity variables are the current ratio, acid ratio, and days in account receivable. The income and expenses variables are sales and operating expenses. The Profitability variables are operating profit margins and return on assets. The activity and investment variables are inventory turnover, total asset turnover, net fixed assets turn over, and net fixed assets. The coverage variables are ratios of total debt to total assets, long-term debt to total assets, and equity to total assets.

3.4 Analysis method

In this study, data analysis is performed by using discriminant analysis. The following equation is used for judging corporate financial distress: equation (1) for the earnings model and equation (2) for the cash flows model.

$$
\begin{aligned}
EBT = \alpha &+ \beta 1 SALES + \beta 2 INVTO + \beta 3 SIZE \\
&+ \beta 4 EMPL + \beta 5 CR + \beta 6 AR + \beta 7 DAYSinAR \\
&+ \beta 8 ROA + \beta 9 OPM + \beta 10 OPREXP \\
&+ \beta 11 TATO + \beta 12 NFIXATO + \beta 13 NETFA \\
&+ \beta 14 TDTA + \beta 15 LTDTA + \beta 16 ETA \\
&+ \varepsilon \ldots (1).
\end{aligned}
$$

$$
\begin{aligned}
CF = \alpha &+ \beta 1 SALES + \beta 2 INVTO + \beta 3 SIZE \\
&+ \beta 4 EMPL + \beta 5 CR + \beta 6 AR + \beta 7 DAYSinAR \\
&+ \beta 8 ROA + \beta 9 OPM + \beta 10 OPREXP \\
&+ \beta 11 TATO + \beta 12 NFIXATO + \beta 13 NETFA \\
&+ \beta 14 TDTA + \beta 15 LTDTA + \beta 16 ETA \\
&+ \varepsilon \ldots (2).
\end{aligned}
$$

The effect of discriminant analysis on sample analysis is to determine whether the model can be used to predict corporate financial distress. If a model is statistically significant, the model is strong enough to predict corporate financial distress (Atmini & Wuryana 2005). The first step is done by carrying out the classical assumption test.

4 RESULTS AND DISCUSSION

4.1 Classical assumption test

The first test is testing the normality using Kolmogorov–Smirnov test. The result shows that both models are statistically significant at the level of 5 percent. The significance level of earnings model and cash flows model are 0.120 and 0.849, respectively. Thus, it is assumed that error of both models is normally distributed. Therefore, all the used data are normally distributed. The second test is heteroscedasticity testing using Glejser test. The result shows that the if significance values of the earnings model and cash value flows model are more than 5 percent, then there is no heteroscedasticity. The third one is testing Multicollinearity using the correlation coefficient among independent variables. The results found that the R values of any relation among independent variables in both earnings model and cash flows model are less than 0.8. This means that there is no multicollinearity or there is no linear relationship among independent variables. Finally, the fourth test is testing autocorrelation using Durbin Watson test. The output of the regression model for earnings model is 2.445, and for the cash flows model is 1.932. Durbin Watson test with significant level of 5 percent and samples total of 45 was dL = 0.6915, and dU = 2.5856 was used. The models' values are between dL and 4-dU. Therefore, there is no autocorrelation.

4.2 Earnings models

Table 1 presents the Wilks' Lambda of the earnings model. Table 1 shows that the value of discriminant analysis for this model is statistically significant (sig = 0.000) at the level of 1 percent. Thus, earnings model has significant ability to predict corporate financial distress. Besides, Table 2 shows that the earnings model is able to predict corporate financial distress, in terms of whether company reports

Table 1. Earnings model.

Wilks' Lambda				
Test of Function(s)	Wilks' Lambda	Chi-square	df	Sig.
1	0.29641	41.344	16	0.000

Table 2. Classification results.

| | | | Predicted Group Membership | | |
			Negative	Positive	Total
Original	Count	Negative	4	2	6
		Positive	0	38	38
	%	Negative	66.67	33.33	100
		Positive	–	100.00	100
Cross-validated data	Count	Negative	2	4	6
		Positive	1	37	38
	%	Negative	33.33	66.67	100
		Positive	2.63	97.37	100

a Cross-validation is done only for those cases in the analysis. In cross-validation, each case is classified by the functions derived from all cases other than that case.
b 95.5% of original grouped cases correctly classified.
c 88.6% of cross-validated grouped cases correctly classified.

Table 3. Holdout samples predicted earnings model.

No.	Code.	Score	Predicted earnings	Reported earnings
1	ACES	15.527	Positive earnings	Positive earnings
2	AMRT	22.171	Positive earnings	Positive earnings
3	CSAP	19.387	Positive earnings	Positive earnings
4	ERAA	19.127	Positive earnings	Positive earnings
5	HERO	19.526	Positive earnings	Negative earnings
6	KOIN	20.628	Positive earnings	Negative earnings
7	LPPF	18.698	Positive earnings	Positive earnings
8	MAPI	20.624	Positive earnings	Positive earnings
9	MIDI	21.156	Positive earnings	Positive earnings
10	MPPA	22.400	Positive earnings	Negative earnings
11	RALS	17.771	Positive earnings	Positive earnings
12	RANC	19.243	Positive earnings	Positive earnings
13	RIMO	12.712	Positive earnings	Positive earnings
14	SONA	18.738	Positive earnings	Positive earnings
15	TELE	19.066	Positive earnings	Positive earnings

Table 4. Cash flows model.

Wilks' Lambda

Test of Function(s)	Wilks' Lambda	Chi-square	df	Sig.
1	0.54659	20.5381	16	0.197

negative earnings or positive earnings, with a total of 95.50 percent for the original grouped cases, and of 88.60 percent for the cross-validated grouped cases accurately.

Further, to examine the power of earnings model in predicting corporate financial distress is to perform prediction on the holdout samples. The prediction of earnings model is as follows:

$$EBT = 0.000SALES + 0.909INVTO + 0.000SIZE \\ - 0.019EMPL + 0.122CR - 0.146AR \\ + 0.005DAYSinAR - 10.216ROA \\ + 8.495OPM + 0.000OPREXP \\ + 0.893TATO + 0.011NFIXATO \\ + 0.467NETFA + 2.977DAR - 2.989LDA \\ - 4.393ETA + \varepsilon$$

The model is used to determine the Z (EBT) scores of each firm in the holdout samples. Based on discriminant analysis, the centroids group A of firms with positive earnings is 3,788 and centroids group B of firms with negative earnings is 0.598. The optimal cutting score is calculated by basic formula as follows: ZCE = (ZA + ZB)/2, where ZCE = the critical cutting score between groups A and B, ZA = centroid for group A, and ZB = centroid for group B. The cutting score (Z) = (3.788 − 0.598)/2 = 1.595. This means that if a company has a score lower than 1.595, these companies are predicted to report negative earnings. Otherwise, companies would be predicted to report positive earnings when their score is higher than 1.595.

To determine the predictive accuracy of the earning model, we can see Table 3 which demonstrates that the earnings model is able to classify approximately 80 percent of holdout samples or 12 of 15 companies. Therefore, it can be seen that earnings model is powerful enough to predict corporate financial distress, since the number of holdout samples

test indicates more than 50 percent classification accuracy.

4.3 Cash flows model

Based on the Wilks' Lambda (see Table 4), we found that discriminant analysis for cash flows model is statistically insignificant (sig = 0.197 ≥ 1%) at α level of 0.01. Since the cash flows model is not significant, it cannot be used as a predictor model for corporate financial distress. Thus, there is no further testing of the holdout samples is needed.

5 CONCLUSIONS

The following results were obtained. The earnings model is strong enough to use as a model in predicting corporate financial distress. This model is able to predict correctly corporate financial distress of 95.5 percent for original grouped case by grouping companies into negative earnings and positive earnings. Further, holdout samples indicate that earnings model is able to classify 80 percent accurately, above 50 percent. Therefore, it can be concluded that the earnings model is a strong predictor model.

The cash flows model cannot be used as a predictive model of corporate financial distress, because of statistical insignificance. This model has a significance level of 0.197 which is more than 1 percent. Thus, there is no further testing of the holdout samples required.

Investors, creditors, fund managers, and stockholders can use earnings model to screen out undesirable investments, and reduce losses by withdrawing investments from unhealthy retail merchandizing enterprises listed in IDX. Government and the market authorities can use earnings model as guideline to increase the transparency of regulatory objectives.

REFERENCES

Adeyemi, B. 2012. Bank failure in Nigeria: A Consequence of Capital Inadequacy, Lack of Transparecy and Non-Performane Loans. *Bank and Bank System* 6(1): 99-109.

Altman, E.I. 1968. Financial Ratios, Discriminant Analysis and the Prediction of Corporate Bankruptcy. *The Journal of Finance* 23(9): 589-609.

Atmini, S. & Wuryana, 2005. The Benefit of Earnings and Cash Flows to Predict Financial Distress Condition: Textile Mill Products, Apparel and Other Textile Products Listed in The Jakarta Stock Exchange. *Call for Paper Accounting National Symposium VIII*: 460-474.

Azis, A. & Lawson. G.H. 1989. Cash Flow Reporting and Financial Distress Models: Testing Hypotheses. *Financial Management* 19(1): 55-63.

Beaver, W.H. 1966. Financial Ratios as Predictors of Failure. Empirical Research in Accounting: Selected Studies. *Journal of Accounting Research* 4: 71-111.

Djongkang, F. & Rita, M.R. 2014. The Benefit of Earnings and Cash Flows to Predict Financial Distress Condition. *Call for Paper Research Method and Organizational Studies.*

Gilberst, L.R. Menon, K. & Schwartz, K.B. 1990. Predicting Bankruptcy for Firms in Financial Distress. *Journal of Business Finance*:161-171.

Isidro, L. & Marques, A.L. 2008. An Investigation of Thai Listed Firms' Financial Distress Using Macro and Micro Variables. *Multinational Finance Journal* 3: 103-125.

Lau, A.H. 1987. A Five State Financial Distress Prediction Model. *Journal of Accounting Research* 25: 127-138.

Lie, E. & Lie, H.J. 2002. Multiples Used to Estimate Corporate Value. *Financial Analysts Journal* 58: 44-54

McCue, M.J. 1991. The Use of Cash Flow to Analyze Financial Distress in California Hospitals. *Hospital and Health Service Administration* 36: 223-241.

Ross, S.A. 1996. Corporate Finance. 4th edition, *McGraw-Hill Companies.*

Scherrer, P.S. 2003. Directors' responsibilities and participation in the strategic decision-making process. *Corporate Governance: International Journal of Business in Society* 3(1): 86–90.

Sharma, D.S., 2001. The role of cash flow information in predicting corporate failure: the state of the literature. *Managerial Finance* 27(4): 3-28.

Tam, K.Y. & Kiang, M.Y. 1992. Managerial Applications of the Neural Networks: The Case of Bank Failure Predictions. *Management Science*: 926-947.

Ward, T.J. & Foster, B.P. 1997. A Note on Selecting a Response Measure for Financial Distress. *Journal of Business Finance and Accounting* 24(6): 78-869.

Warner, J.B. 1977. Bankrupcy Costs: Some Evidence. *Journal of Finance* 32: 337-347.

Whitaker, R.B. 1999. The Early Stages of Financial Distress. *Journal of Economics and Finance* 23: 123-133.

Wruck, K. 1990. Financial Distress, Reorganization, and Organizational Efficiency. *Journal of Economics and Finance* 23(2): 123-133.

Global Competitiveness: Business Transformation in the
Digital Era – Abdullah, Widiaty & Abdullah (eds)
© 2019 Taylor & Francis Group, London, ISBN 978-0-367-19442-0

The effect of information privacy concern and security concern on online purchase decision among university students

S. Windiarti
Parahyangan Catholic University, Bandung, Indonesia

ABSTRACT: The aim of this research was to acknowledge the effect of privacy and security concern on the online purchase decision among university students. Data were gathered through the questionnaire from accountancy students at University of Achmad Yani regarding online purchase experience, before being analyzed by SPSS. The results show that both information privacy concern and security concern impact the online purchase decision. In order to reduce risk of insecurity among the online buyers, the privacy and security data problems should be handled carefully. E-commerce companies need to consider their company regulations related to the information privacy problems and develop their security apps in order to incline the online purchase decision.

1 INTRODUCTION

Technological developments in the world are increasing rapidly. The existence of the Internet is very supportive of all forms of activities, including commercial activities for a company or independent business (SWA 2017). Currently, no business can compete without digital marketing. The Internet has become a place where everyone on the earth interacts, learns, works, and exchanges information with each other.

Based on the APJII (Association of Indonesian Internet Service Providers) survey released in 2014, Internet users in Indonesia reached 88.1 million. When compared with the population of Indonesia reached 252.5 million people, it can be said that the penetration of Internet users in Indonesia reached 34.9% higher. The high level of Internet user penetration in Indonesia is also followed by the growth of e-Commerce in Indonesia. In years 2013–2015, the average growth of e-Commerce reached 33%, and as predicted, in 2016, the value of e-Commerce reached US$ 24.6 billion or Rp. 332 trillion (SWAOnline 2016a). Annual report issued by We Are Social shows that the percentage of Indonesian people who buy goods and services online in a month in 2017 reached 41% of the total population, an increase of 15% compared to the year 2016 which is only 26%. Recently, ShopBack conducted a survey of more than 1,000 respondents in Indonesia, to see the online purchasing pattern of Indonesian society. From the survey, 70.2% of respondents admitted that the existence of online stores affected their shopping behavior (Iskandar 2018). E-commerce provides convenience to consumers where they can shop anytime, anywhere indefinitely. Nevertheless, the issue of information privacy concern and security concern has become a troubling issue. Government and industry

organizations have stated that the problems of information privacy and security concern have become a major obstacle in the development of consumer-related e-commerce (Fernandez 2001). There are some surprising facts about e-commerce in Indonesia. From all that is summarized from the results of a survey conducted by MARS Indonesia, one is the issue of consumer trust in online shopping which is found to be still low (Prahadi 2017). Although consumers explore online shopping, there are concerns about trust regarding sharing personal information and bank information with third parties who may send unwanted emails to customers (SWAOnline 2016b). Lack of protection against fraud can reduce the trust in online purchases (Goldsmith & Wu 2006). Therefore, protecting consumer privacy is an important factor for e-commerce success (Liu et al. 2004). Furthermore, when viewed from the perspective of individual and consumer behavior, in turn, the issue of privacy concern encourages accounting information system (AIS) researchers to see the beliefs and attitudes of people about privacy, ways such as attitudes affecting intentions and consumer behavior as well as how individual behavior can be affected by the organization's privacy policies and practices (Kauffman 2011).

The issue of information privacy and security concern is treated as a single construct in most of the privacy literature (Liu et al. 2004, Xu et al. 2012). Belanger et al. (2002) mentioned that privacy and security issues should be conceptualized as two different things. As for other researchers who agree with Belanger et al. (2002) revealed, that the issue of information and security privacy are two different constructs (Chang et al. 2005, Vijayasarathy 2004). In response to two different views, this study attempts to provide a clear picture of the impact of privacy and security issues as two different constructs. Further information privacy and security concern issues will impact consumer decisions in purchase products on e-commerce.

2 RESEARCH METHOD

2.1 Privacy concern and risk

The issue of privacy or reluctance to disclose personal information is seen as a major threat to e-commerce and the digital economy (Culnan 2000, Malhotra et al. 2004). The perceived control over personal information is a key factor in influencing privacy concern (Xu et al. 2012). Consumers may have concern over the flow of personal information between online consumers and websites and concern about how personal information is managed by websites (Hong & Thong 2013). The effect of privacy concern on online trust may depend on consumer characteristics such as gender, age, and education (Riquelme & Roman 2014). Measures taken to protect consumer privacy include industrial policy and procedural fairness (Culnan 2000, Culnan & Armstrong 1999).

The problem of privacy refers to individual view about fairness in context of information privacy (Campbell 1997). Consumer have possibly a different opinion about what is fair and what is not when the company uses consumers' online personal information (Malhotra et al. 2004). Liu et al. (2004) proposed that the risks of this kind of information system depend on the consumer's trust that their privacies have been maintained. In the e-commerce context, positive relationship between privacy and risk is showed (Malhotra et al. 2004). The Internet user with high-level privacy concern tends to have high-level risk. Risk perception related to online purchasing can reduce consumer's control perception and, thus, possibly negatively influences to online purchasing (Jarvenpaa et al. 2000).

HI: Information privacy concern has positive impact on risk.

2.2 Security concern and risk

E-commerce has been associated with risky purchases, due to privacy issues and security issues (Miyazaki & Fernandez 2001). Case points out the importance of security payments and money-back guarantees. Other factors affecting consumer evaluations and decisions regarding online purchases involve consumer concern about the security and reliability of corporate processes in online settings (Miyazaki & Fernandez 2001, Wolfinbarger & Gilly 2003).

These security and reliability concern have also been suggested to influence consumer perceptions of risk (Olivero & Lunt 2004). Consumers have found distrust in online shopping because they worry about merchants who are unscrupulous and dubious and thereby susceptible to ineffective security from shopping using the Internet (Hoffman et al. 1999, Lee & Turban 2001).

Security practices are also seen in information privacy concern instruments developed by Smith et al. (1996). Bansal and Zahedi (2014) reported in their research about customers revealing that when security issues are high, customers prefer to transform sensitive information only to trusted websites, thus demonstrating a higher risk perception.

H2: Security concern will have a positive impact on Risk.

2.3 Risk and trust influence on each other and on online purchases decision

According to Bauer (1960), consumer behavior generally contains certain risks, because the actions performed produce consequences which can't be predicted accurately. In the e-commerce literature, two risk categories are identified: product risk and transaction risk (Chang et al. 2005). Product risk refers to the uncertainty that the purchase will match the level of acceptance in buying with a goal. The risk of a transaction is the uncertainty that something unfavorable and unpredictable may occur during the transactional process. Transaction risks include authentication, privacy, and transactional security.

In order to reduce the risk perception, creating the trust has been admitted as an important point (McKnight et al. 1998). The trust has yielded many researches in organizational study. The trust of e-commerce consumer and perceived risk have strong impact on the decision of online purchase (Kim et al. 2008). However, the trust is also considered subjective since it is formed by social factors which are strange in certain contexts. (Webster & Martocchio 1992).

Perceived Risk has a negative relationship with trust (Eastlick et al. 2006, Kimery & McCord 2002). Greater confidence is likely to reduce perceived Risk. Jarvenpaa et al. (1999) suggest that higher trust in online sellers reduces perceived risk so as to increase buyer desire to buy online.

H3: Perceived risk has a negative impact on trust.
H4: Information privacy concern, security concern, and risk have a positive impact on trust.
H5: Trust has a positive impact on online purchase decisions.
H6: Information privacy concern, security concern, risk, and trust have positive impact on online purchase decision.

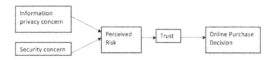

Figure 1. Research method.

3   RESULTS

3.1   *Profile of respondents*

Respondents are all accounting students of Achmad Yani University consisting of men and women. The data of respondents is presented in Table 1.

The data were analyzed using the path analysis method by SPSS 21. The population in this research came from the undergraduate student of Economy Faculty, enrolled in the period of 2014–2017. The population in this research can be categorized as the finite population, which implies that the amount of population can be quantified exactly. The sampling technique used in this research was probability sampling with the 100 respondents per class and gathered using the proportional random sampling technique.

- Information privacy concern, security concern, and perceived risk.

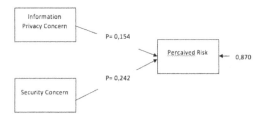

Figure 2.   Information privacy concern.

The R square number also shows that the information privacy concern and security concern affect the risk by 87 percent. The results of F calculation (7,219) are also way bigger than the F table (3,090), which implies that H0 must be rejected and accepting H1 and H2. The privacy issue refers to an individual's view of fairness in the context of information privacy (Campbell 1997). If a consumer is too concerned about privacy, it will affect how he or she will see the risks in buying from (Gurung 2016), and thereby a positive relationship between privacy and risk issues is demonstrated (Malhotra et al. 2004). Internet users with high levels of privacy concern tend to have high risk perceptions. Bansal and Zahedi (2014) reported in their research

Table 1.   Respondents.

Student	Number of students	Sample (10% × Number of student)
Freshmen year (2017–2018)	266	26.6
Sophomore year (2016–2017)	250	25
Junior year (2015–2016)	247	24.7
Senior year (2014–2015)	234	23.4
Total respondents	997	99.7 = 100

about customers that when security issues are high, customers prefer to transform sensitive information only to trusted websites, thus demonstrating a higher risk perception.

- Perceived risk and trust.

Figure 3.   Perceived risk and trust.

The magnitude of effect given by risk to the trust that stands on the R square column is 0.019 or 1.9 percent. Hence, it can be concluded that risk affecting the trust is 1.9%. Sitkin and Pablo (1992) suggest that perceived risk may mediate the influence of trust on purchase intentions. Several studies have investigated the effect of trust on perceived risk.

- Information privacy concern, security concern, perceived risk, and trust.

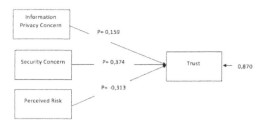

Figure 4.   Perceived risk and trust.

The magnitude of the effect given from information privacy concern, security concern, and perceived risk to trust in the R square column is 0.229 or 22.9%. Hence, it can be concluded that the influence of information privacy concern, security concern, and perceived trust on trust is 22.9%. The value of F arithmetic of 9.492 is greater than F table of 2.698. Therefore, H0 is rejected and H3 is accepted.

- Trust and online purchase decision.

Figure 5.   Trust and online purchase decision.

The result of R square value is 0.041 or 4.1%, so it can be concluded that trust influences online purchase decision by 4.1%. The results of F calculation (4.221) are also way bigger than the F table (3.938) which implies that H0 must be rejected and H5 accepted. In the online purchase environment, favorable relationships have been found between perceptions of consumer confidence and attitudes in purchases (Verhagen et al. 2006). Online companies can build trust if they convince consumers that online transactions will happen as expected by consumers (Culnan & Armstrong, 1999).

• Information privacy concern, security concern, risk, trust and online purchase decision.

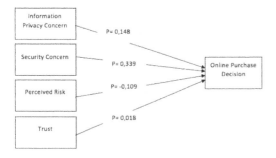

Figure 6. Information privacy concern, security concern, risk, trust and online purchase decision.

The magnitude of the effect of the privacy, security, risk, and trust of online purchasing decisions in the R square column is 0.185 or 18.5%. It can be concluded that the information privacy concern, security concern, risk, and trust affect the purchasing decision online by 18.5%. The F value of 5.398 is greater than F table of 2.467. Therefore, H0 is rejected and H6 is accepted. Van der Heijden et al. (2003) reported that reducing perceived risk can increase trust and attitudes toward online purchases, which in turn increases buyers' willingness to purchase online.

4 CONCLUSION

The study of e-commerce adoption is largely centered on the website usability features. The main obstacles that need to be addressed before the consumer reaches the adoption level are the concern of privacy and security. This study is one of the first attempts to develop an integrative framework of e-commerce adoption with the construction of privacy and security issues. The results of the study show information on privacy concerns and security concerns affecting online purchasing decisions through risk and trust of university students. The managerial implication of this research is that the usability features of the website can be improved not only aesthetically but also by adding security features. As consumers become more experienced with their online habits, issues about privacy and security features can be a problem for businesses. Further, deficiencies in securing personal information can even lead to serious consequences such as loss of consumers.

REFERENCES

Anil Gurung, M. R. 2016. Online privacy and security concerns of consumers. *Information & Computer Security.*

Bansal, G. and Zahedi, F.M. 2014. Trust-discount tradeoff in three contexts: frugality moderating privacy and security concerns. *Journal of Computer Information Systems* 55(1): 13-29.

Bauer, R.A. 1960. *Consumer behavior as risk taking, in Hancock, R.S. Ed., Dynamic Marketing for a Changing World,* American Marketing Association, Chicago, IL.

Belanger, F., Hiller, J.S. & Smith, W.J. 2002. Trustworthiness in electronic commerce: the role of privacy, security, and site attributes. *The Journal of Strategic Information Systems* 11 Nos ¾: 245-270.

Campbell, A.J. 1997. Relationship marketing in consumer markets: a comparison of managerial and consumer attitudes about information privacy. *Journal of Interactive Marketing* 11(3): 44-57.

Chang, M.K., Cheung, W. & Lai, V.S. 2005. Literature derived reference models for the adoption of online shopping. *Information & Management* 42(4): 543-559.

Culnan, M. 2000. Protecting privacy online: is self-regulation working? *Journal of Public Policy & Marketing* 19(1): 20-26.

Culnan, M. & Armstrong, P. 1999. Information privacy concerns, procedural fairness, and impersonal trust: an empirical investigation. *Organization Science* 10(1): 104-115.

Eastlick, M., Lotz, S. & Warrington, P. 2006. Understanding online B-to-C relationships: an integrated model of privacy concerns, trust, and commitment. *Journal of Business Research* 59(8): 877-86.

Fernandez, A. D. 2001. Consumer Perception of Privacy and security Risk for Online Shopping. *The Journal of consumer Affairs,* 35.

Goldsmith, J. & Wu, T. 2006. *Who Controls the Internet? Illusions of a Borderless World.* Oxford University Press: New York, NY.

Hoffman, D., Novak, T. & Peralta, M. 1999. Building consumer trust online. *Communications of the ACM* 42(4): 80-85.

Hong, W. & Thong, J.Y.L. 2013. Internet privacy concerns: an integrated conceptualization and four empirical studies. *MIS Quarterly* 37(1): 275-298.

Iskandar, E. D. 2018. Retrieved 05, 23, 2018, from SWA: https://swa.co.id/swa/listed-articles/prediksi-tren-e-commerce-indonesia-2018

Jarvenpaa, S.L., Tractinsky, N. and Vitale, M. 2000. Consumer trust in an internet store. *Information Technology and Management.* 1(2): 45-71.

Jarvenpaa, S.L., Tractinsky, N., Saarinen, L. & Vitale, M. 1999. Consumer trust in an internet store: a cross-cultural validation. *Journal of Computer-Mediated Communication.* 5(2): 1-35.

Kim, D., Ferrin, D. & Rao, H. 2008. A trust-based consumer decision-making model in electronic commerce: the role of trust, perceived risk, and their antecedents. *Decision Support System.* 44(2): 544-564.

Kimery, K.M. & McCord, M. 2002. Third-party assurances: mapping the road to trust in e-retailing. *Journal of Information Technology Theory and Application.* 4(2): 63-81.

Lee, M.K.O. & Turban, E. 2001. A trust model for consumer internet shopping. *International Journal of Electronic Commerce.* 6(1): 75-91.

Liu, C., Marchewka, J., Lu, J. & Yu, C. 2004. Beyond concern: a privacy-trust-behavioral intention model of electronic commerce. *Information & Management* 42(1): 127-142.

Malhotra, N.K., Kim, S.S. & Agarwal, J. 2004. Internet users' information privacy concerns IUIPC: the construct, the scale, and a causal model. *Information Systems Research* 15(4): 336-355.

McKnight, D., Cummings, L.L. & Chervany, N.L. 1998. Initial trust formation in new organizational relationships. *Academy of Management Review* 23(3): 473-490.

Miyazaki, A.D. & Fernandez, A. 2001. Consumer perceptions of privacy and security risks for online shopping. *Journal of Consumer Affairs* 35(1): 27-44.

Olivero, N. and Lunt, P. 2004. Privacy versus willingness to disclose in e-commerce exchanges: the effect of risk awareness on the relative role of trust and control. *Journal of Economic Psychology* 25: 243-62.

Prahadi, Y. Y. 2017. Retrieved 05, 23, 2018, from SWA: https://swa.co.id/swa/trends/business-research/ini-dia-fakta-mengejutkan-e-commerce-di-indonesia

Riquelme, U. & Roman, S. 2014. Is the in uence of privacy and security on online trust the same for all types of consumers?. *Electronic Markets* 24(2): 135-149.

Robert J. Kauffman, Y. J. 2011. A Survey of Consumer Information Privacy From the Accounting Information Systems Perspective. *Journal of Information System* 25.

Sitkin, S.B. & Pablo, A.L. 1992. Reconceptualizing the determinants of risk behavior. *Academy of Management Review* 17(1): 9-38.

Smith, H.J., Milberg, S.J. & Burke, S.J. 1996. Information privacy: measuring individuals' concerns about organizational practices. *MIS Quarterly* 20(2): 167-196.

SWA, M. 2017. *swa*. Retrieved 5, 23, 2018, from https://swa.co.id/swa/business-update/seberapa-penting-peran-website-dalam-peningkatan-sebuah-bisnis-mari-kenali-manfaatnya.

SWAOnline. 2016a. *SWA*. Retrieved 05, 23, 2018, from https://swa.co.id/swa/trends/business-research/tren-trans aksi-e-commerce-di-indonesia.

SWAOnline. 2016b. Retrieved 05, 23, 2018, from https://swa.co.id/swa/my-article/memahami-perilaku-belanja-online.

Van der Heijden, H., Verhagen, T. & Creemers, M. 2003. Understanding online purchase intentions: contributions from technology and trust perspectives. *European Journal of Information Systems*. 12(1) 41-48.

Verhagen, T., Meents, S. & Tan, Y.-H. 2006. Perceived risk and trust associated with purchasing at electronic marketplaces. *European Journal of Information Systems* 15(6): 542-556.

Vijayasarathy, L.R. 2004. Predicting consumer intentions to use on-line shopping: the case for an augmented technology acceptance model. *Information & Management* 41(6): 747-762.

Webster, J. & Martocchio, J.J. 1992. Microcomputer playfulness - development of a measure with workplace implications. *MIS Quarterly* 16(2): 201-226.

Wolfinbarger, M. and Gilly, M.C. 2003. eTailQ: dimensionalizing, measuring, and predicting etail quality. *Journal of Retailing* 79(3): 183-98.

Xu, H., Teo, H.-H., Tan, B.C.Y. & Agarwal, R. 2012. Effects of individual self-protection, industry self-regulation, and government regulation on privacy concerns: a study of location-based services. *Information Systems Research* 23(4): 1342-1363.

Global Competitiveness: Business Transformation in the
Digital Era – Abdullah, Widiaty & Abdullah (eds)
© 2019 Taylor & Francis Group, London, ISBN 978-0-367-19442-0

Maturity level of Good Corporate Governance (GCG) principles implementation – Case study from micro and small enterprises in Bandung

C.T.L. Soei, A. Setiawan, K. Fitriani & R. Satyarini
Parahyangan Catholic University, Bandung, Indonesia

ABSTRACT: This study investigates the maturity level of Good Corporate Governance implementation in micro and small enterprises in Bandung. We first identified five major good corporate governance indicators to implementation of good corporate governance principles. We then used maturity model to measure the success rate of good corporate governance implementation in micro and small enterprises. The first result of this study is maturity level as a map to assess the good corporate governance implementation. The next result indicates that micro and small enterprises in Bandung focus on fairness. The reason micro and small enterprises in Bandung focus on fairness is the unawareness of informal business of doing business with standard. These results indicate the need to improve micro and small enterprises' awareness of the importance of good corporate governance implementation to have sustainability of doing business.

1 INTRODUCTION

Good corporate governance becomes a hot topic since the 1998 economic crisis. One of the main causes is the implementation of bad corporate governance. Corporate governance is one of the best practices that ensures the company is properly directed, managed and monitored to achieve the company's objectives. The purpose of corporate governance is to create a balance among shareholders, directors, and management by increasing shareholder value and protecting the interest of stakeholders (Alnaser et al. 2014). For investors, one of the most important aspects when making investment decisions is the application of corporate governance principles and the company's profit to ensure the return on investment (Todorovic 2013).

Since the Asian crisis, Asian countries have sought to introduce corporate governance guidelines to direct companies to improve their best corporate governance practices. However, corporate governance has not been accepted by most companies in Asia. In Indonesia, during the economic crisis in 1997, the value of the currency depreciated by 80% and many companies in the banking sector went bankrupt. One of the main causes is the implementation of bad corporate governance (Susanty et al. 2013).

Good governance practices in corporate listed in the Indonesia capital market is necessitated in order to increase Indonesian position in the international rating regarding governance implementation as a reference for the practice of a good governance system, which the National Committee on Governance

Policy (KNKG) refers to the principles issued by the OECD. KNKP established a regulation for public companies to put the application of GCG in the annual reports. The application of GCG in public companies became a must. Corporate governance is a series of corporate control activities involving management, board members and stakeholders in order to encourage the creation of an efficient, transparent market and a high compliance with the laws and regulations (KNKG 2006).

Micro, Small and Medium Enterprises (MSMEs) have contributed more than 50% to Indonesia GDP. MSMEs are sole proprietorship business entities that strive for corporate governance in accordance with the principles of good corporate governance. At present, there have not been many studies that assess the application of good corporate governance to small and medium enterprises because since good corporate governance is commonly applied to large companies. Good corporate governance will be important to an MSME provided that the company expands into a larger scale business. The company needs good corporate governance to increase shareholder values and interests of stakeholders. (Alnaser et al. 2014). Therefore, it is important to know whether MSMEs apply the principle of GCG. The study was conducted on micro and small enterprises in Bandung. The research questions were:

RQ#1: How is the implementation of the maturity model in assessing the company's good corporate governance?
RQ#2: How is the maturity level of the implementation of good corporate governance in small and medium enterprises?

2 LITERATURE REVIEW

2.1 *Good corporate governance*

Corporate governance is a process and structure as a basis for all members of the company to take action to protect the interests of stakeholders (Ehikioya 2009). Corporate governance can be seen from two points of view, behavior and normative (Cosneanu et al. 2013). Corporate governance from behavioral perspective is related to company interactions with stakeholders, and corporate governance from normative perspectives is related to regulation regulating this relationship (Cosneanu et al. 2013). Behaviors related to corporate governance include structures and processes or mechanisms. The corporate governance structure relates to the company's ownership structure (Ehikioya 2009), including the composition, expertise, independence and size of the board of commissioners. In addition to the board of commissioners, the corporate governance structure also includes two basic ownership structures, namely concentrated or scattered (Ehikioya 2009). In developed countries, company ownership structure is scattered. However, in developing countries, where investor protection systems are weaker, company ownership structure is usually concentrated (Ehikioya 2009).

Corporate governance can consist of formal and informal mechanisms. Formal mechanisms are based on formally defined structures and processes, while informal mechanisms arise in relation to culture and values that are influenced by the organization's leaders. Organizational governance systems vary depending on the size and type of organization and the environmental, economic, political, cultural and social conditions in which the organization operates (ISO/TMB Working Group on Social Responsibility 2010).

The principles of good corporate governance in Indonesia are based on 5 principles of corporate governance, namely (1) transparency, (2) accountability, (3) responsibility, (4) independence, and (5) fairness (KNKG 2006). One of the implementations of this transparency principles is to carry out adequate company disclosures about corporate governance and other important information. The information disclosed must be in accordance with the needs of the stakeholders.

2.2 *Maturity model*

Maturity model is a model developed by Software Engineering Institute to assess the capability of information system applications in a company (Visconti & Cook 1998). In 2007, ISACA implemented this model maturity in COBIT 4.1 by conducting a benchmark maturity model and applied to the performance assessment and information technology processes in the company (IT Governance Institute 2007).

2.3 *Micro, small and medium enterprises*

Micro enterprises are productive business owned by private company or business entity that has net assets of no more than IDR 50,000,000 excluding lands and business premises. Usually micro enterprises have not even carried out simple financial administration. They do not separate family finances from business finance (Bank Indonesia, 2015).

Small enterprises are productive businesses owned by companies or individual business entities that have net assets more than Rp. 50,000,000.00 excluding lands and buildings of business premises. In addition, usually small businesses have better management and organization, with a clear division of tasks, among others, finance, marketing and production (Bank Indonesia 2015).

One characteristic of micro and small enterprises is insufficient knowledge related to business management due to numbers of employees and managerial experience (Oliveira et al. 2014). Oliveira et al. (2014) concluded the application of knowledge management to small and medium enterprises is often difficult due to insufficient of documentation. It can analogously be assumed the implementation of good corporate governance is also often difficult due to documentation problems.

3 METHODOLOGY

The population of this study is Micro and Small Businesses in the Bandung. We choose 4 micro and small enterprises using a purposive sampling technique that met the criteria for micro and small businesses and the willingness to involve in this study.

The questions for each GCG principle were formulated based on previous literature with some adjustment. Each question was answered using maturity scale to know maturity level. Semi-structured interviews were conducted with 4 owners of micro and small enterprises to determine the maturity level of each GCG principle. The data obtained from interviews and observation were processed qualitatively. After then, we did mapping using MS Excel to analyze the result.

4 RESULTS AND DISCUSSION

4.1 *The implementation of maturity model in assessing the company's good corporate governance*

The maturity model was implemented by mapping the five principles of good corporate governance in measurement in maturity models (non-existent, initial, repeatable but intuitive, defined, managed and measurable, and optimized). This mapping was done by making indicators for each of the principles of good corporate governance and making measurements to reflect each score in the maturity model.

Indicators for each principle were made to identify the measurement of the application of each principle of good corporate governance in the company. For small and medium enterprises, according to the objectives in this study, indicators were designed as follows:

1) Transparency (T): an assessment was made for the availability of information, including clarity, accessibility, accuracy, socialization and timeliness. However, an assessment was also carried out for the ability to maintain information confidentiality.
2) Accountability (A): an assessment was made for the company's accountability to employees, interested parties, the surrounding environment and the country.
3) Responsibility (R): an assessment was made for the clarity of tasks and responsibilities, the availability of business ethics standards, compliance with regulations and performance appraisal.
4) Independence (I): an assessment was made for freedom from the influence of outside parties in carrying out company operations.
5) Fairness (F): an assessment was made for the implementation of fairness for company stakeholders.

Based on indicators for each good corporate governance principle, the score is assigned to the application in the company. The scoring system applied in this study were: (1) inadequate application, meaning that the application of GCG principle is poorly applied, (2) basic application, meaning that the application of GCG principle is applied at a minimum effort, (3) adequate application, meaning that the application of GCG principle is applied well, (4) effective application, meaning that the application of GCG principle is effectively applied in daily life, and (5) the application of the lead, meaning that the application of GCG principle is applied so it can help company create a proactive solution. In each score for each indicator, the status of implementing good corporate governance principle was made. After the interviews, the results of GCG indicator were interpreted into maturity level. The result of the mapping can be seen in Table 1.

4.2 The maturity level of good corporate governance implementation in small and medium enterprises

Based on the characteristics of small and medium enterprises according to (Oliveira et al. 2014), there are limitations in the application of normal

Table 1. Comparison table of good corporate governance principles application.

Principles	MSME 1	MSME 2	MSME 3	MSME 4	Average
T	3.85	2.71	2.57	3	3.03
A	3.25	2.25	2.25	3.25	2.75
R	2.5	2.5	2.25	3	2.56
I	2.5	3	2.5	3	2.75
F	4	3	2.67	3.67	3.33

procedures, namely documentation and socialization, so this research was conducted to assess the implementation of good corporate governance in small and medium enterprises. However, based on previous research, the existence of good corporate governance in small and medium enterprises is still rarely studied because good corporate governance is commonly applied to large companies, especially companies that go public and must account for the management of the company to the company holders.

Table 1 shows the mean score of GCG principles (TARIF). The table also reveals the score for each MSME. Based on the data, fairness is the highest score among all principles.

Data from Table 1 is mapped into radar analysis using MS Excel. The result can be seen in Figure 1. It was found the principle with the greatest value was fairness, while the one with the smallest value was accountability. This is not surprising because MSMEs are managed and supervised directly by the owners.

Figure 2 shows the detailed mapping for each indicator of each GCG principle. In MSME 1, transparency obtained the highest point. Fairness obtained the highest score in MSMEs 2, 3, and 4. Figure 2 also shows that there were 20 indicators consisting

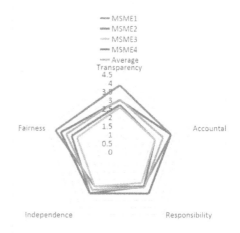

Figure 1. Maturity model – good corporate governance (by principles).

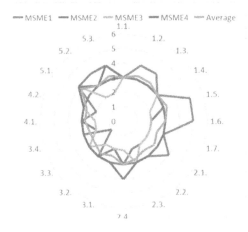

MSME1 — MSME2 — MSME3 — MSME4 — Average

Figure 2. Maturity model – good corporate governance in detail.

of 7 transparency indicators, 4 accountability indicators, 4 responsibility indicators, 2 independence indicators, and 3 fairness indicators.

5 CONCLUSION

To conclude, most micro and small enterprises have applied some of GCG principles well. The limitation of this study is that the results obtained cannot be generalized due to its case specific context. However, this is only a preliminary research. In further research, we want to expand the sample size and also want to know the factors that can affect application of GCG principles.

REFERENCES

Alnaser, N., Shaban, O. S. & Al-Zubi, Z. 2014. The Effect of Effective Corporate Governance Structure in Improving Investors' Confidence in the Public Financial Information. *International Journal of Academic Research in Business and Social Sciences* 4(1): 556-570.

Cosneanu, S., Russu, C., Chiritescu, V. & Badea, L. 2013. Foundations and Principles of Corporate Governance. *Valahian Journal of Ecionomic Studies*: 31-38.

Ehikioya, B. I. 2009. Corporate governance structure and firm performance in developing economies: evidence from Nigeria. *Corporate Governance*: 231-243.

ISO/TMB Working Group on Social Responsibility. 2010. *ISO/FDIS 26000 - Guidance on Social Responsibility*. Geneva: The International Organization for Standardization.

IT Governance Institute. 2007. *COBIT 4.1*. Illinois: ISACA.

Komite Nasional Kebijakan Governance (KNKG). 2006. *Pedoman Umum Corporate Governance Indonesia*. Jakarta: Komite Nasional Kebijakan Governance.

Oliveira, M., Pedron, C. D., Nodari, F. & Ribeiro, R. 2014. *Knowledge Management in Small and Micro Enterprises: Applying a Maturity Model*. Porto Alegre: Pontifícia Universidade Católica do Rio Grande do Sul.

Susanty, A., Suprayitno, G. & Jie, F. 2013. Preliminary Study The Relationship Between Organizational Culture and Implementation of Independence Principle: Indonesia Public Listed Company Case Study. *International Journal of Information, Business and Management* 5(1): 60-73.

Todorovic, I. 2013. Impact Of Corporate Governance On Performance Of Companies. *Montenegrin Journal of Economics*: 47-53.

Visconti, M. & Cook, C. R. 1998. Evolution of a maturity model - critical evaluation and lessons learned. *Software Quality Journal*: 223-237.

Customer Relations

Global Competitiveness: Business Transformation in the Digital Era – Abdullah, Widiaty & Abdullah (eds)
© 2019 Taylor & Francis Group, London, ISBN 978-0-367-19442-0

Preferences of domestic low-cost carrier airlines passenger in the Greater Jakarta area with conjoint analysis method

S. Novela
Bina Nusantara University, Tangerang, Indonesia

E.L. Ray, N.T.H. Ningsih & S. Fathin
Polytechnic APP, Jakarta, Indonesia

ABSTRACT: Since the air transportation is increasingly needed by society, the airline industry sees considerable market opportunities in Indonesia, resulting in many airlines attempting to establish low-cost carriers. Low-cost carrier domestic airlines are in great demand in many circles. Knowing the preference for low-cost carrier domestic airlines passengers is very important in order to determine the appropriate strategy in reaching the number of passengers. Preferences are calculated based on attributes using the conjoint analysis method. Respondents were asked to assign values to the level of each attribute. The results show that prices have the highest relative importance (NRP), followed by brand equity, facilities, time, and cabin staff. However, the most preferred combination of low-cost carrier domestic airlines is the price at the time of off-peak, has on-time brand equity, has a 5 kg baggage facility, 7–9 a.m. flight time, and organized cabin staffs. This result implies how low-cost carrier airlines should deliver excellent services by evaluating their marketing and operational strategies.

1 INTRODUCTION

Indonesia is an archipelagic nation, connected by various straits and beaches. Therefore, airlines industry has become the necessity of the Indonesian people to travel. In the law No. 1 of year 2009 verses 97 on aviation, airlines industry in Indonesia have three types of services: full service carrier, medium service, and minimum or low-cost airlines (no frills or low-cost carrier) (Azmarani 2016). According to the Statistics Indonesia (BPS 2016), domestic flights reached the level of high number of passengers in 2012 which was 19.24% compared to the previous year. In 2013, the number of passengers reached the highest level, with total number in the period of 2011–2015 being 73.59 million passengers.

Indonesia has five major airlines that implement low-cost carrier, such as Lion Air, Citilink, Wings Air, Tiger Mandala, and Indonesia Air Asia (International Civil Aviation Organization 2017). The growing number of passengers of low-cost carrier airlines in Indonesia from year to year has increased. In 2010, passengers of low-cost carriers reached 51.77 million passengers, while in 2014 the number increased to 76.49 million passengers. It can be seen that the increasing number of passengers of low-cost carriers was 24.72 million (Azmarani 2016).

The tight competition among airlines in Indonesia makes airlines need to improve their services. However, they have to pay attention to the effectiveness and efficiency of the service itself. The service has to meet the needs and wants of customers (Suhartanto & Noor 2012). Everyone has their own classification to decide what kind of airline they choose to travel. The classification can be regarded as an attribute. The purpose of customer preferences is to acknowledge customer behavior pattern to purchase or ignore a product or service (Isik & Yasar 2015). This research will elaborate customer preference of the attributes and its combination for domestic airline in Indonesia.

2 LITERATURE REVIEW

Service is a form of product consisting of activities, benefits, or satisfaction offered to consumer. In this case, service includes value which cannot be seen directly, and it does not result in any kind of ownership (Kotler & Armstrong 2014).

Customer preference is defined as the attitude to behave consistently either profitable or unprofitable to related object. These objects can be specific consumption/marketing or concept such as product, product use, cause or issue, price, and so on. Attitudes relevant to buying behavior are formed as a result of the direct experience of the product or service. Bogicevic et al. (2017) identified some service attributes such as value, seat comfort, staff/service, and catering as airline attributes that had significant effect on passengers' recommendations.

3 RESEARCH METHODOLOGY

This research used all selected attributes that have quality which is obtained based on literature review in previous studies.

Figure 1. Customer preference.

Conjoint analysis method is used to obtain a combination of attributes of product or service. Sample sizes for conjoint studies generally range from about 150 to 1200 respondents for infinite or very large populations (Orme 2010). Moreover, non-probability sample technique is used to collect 156 respondents. In this research, the customer will be asked to ensure the attribute that becomes the most preferred (Wingdes 2012). The preference is calculated using choice-based conjoint (CBC) because attributes used are for five items, which however do not exceed six items.

4 RESULTS AND DISCUSSION

Among respondents, there were 65% women and 35% men. As many of 93% of them were those who frequently used the airline service one to three times in the last 3 months; 4% had used 4–5 times, and 3% stated used more than 5 times. The most frequent airline used was Air Asia (34%), followed by Lion Air and Citilink (33%) respectively.

After forming the stimuli from the entire level, the costumer preference was calculated by the score from respondents using Microsoft Excel by ordering the stimuli. Names were assigned to the first to sixteenth preference. Each preference is designed by Microsoft Excel formula which then formed group of level, so it could be used automatically to calculate costumer preference for all respondents.

The ranks of Usage Level Value (ULV) were orderly: 0.1098, 0.6442, 0.0609, 0.3494, and 0.3694. In general, by using ULV and IRV (Important Relative Value), it can be stated that customers who run a domestic trip low-cost carrier should consider the off-peak airfare along with the aviation company branding in accordance with the punctual departure flight.

As summarized in Table 1, the results from this study are:

1) **Airfare has the highest Important Relative Value or the most crucial attribute.** Airfare is the most crucial attribute with IRV 36.76%. This finding is in line with Ayantoyinbo and Boye's (2015) finding stating that the airfare has contributed 3.30 from the total of utility;

2) **Passengers tend to pay the off-peak airfare.** With ULV value at 0.6442, passengers mostly love the ticket cost when it is off-peak with the utility value 1.650. This finding is in agreement with the previous research conducted by Ayantoyinbo and Boye (2015),

3) **Airline domestic *Low-Cost Carrier* passengers have awareness on company branding equity, particularly for *on-time* case.** The brand equity is the second crucial attribute for passengers with an important relative value of 30.77% with "on-time" at the highest level. This result is incompatible with Amegbe's (2016) finding stating that the brand equity, specifically on the premium class, does not create any burden over passengers to purchase.

4) **Facility as the third preferred attribute with IRV 17.74% and "additional luggage of 5 kg" as the highest level.** This fact is in contradiction with the finding of Sinaga et al. (2015) which stated that from the four attributes which are tested, facility had the lowest value of IRV. They found that the highest level was the entertainment such as magazine or newspaper, because both of them have important value.

5) **Departure flight is preffered at 7–9 a.m.** Most of passengers prefer morning departure flight, with an IRV of 10.65%. It shows that airline domestic low-cost carrier is unconsidered when purchased the airfare.

6) **Cabin crew service is unimportant attribute.** Kankaew (2013) found that the cabin crew is less significant attribute while having trip. This research supports that finding that the crew service turns to be the unimportant one when passengers booked the flight with an IRV of 4.07%.

Table 1. Usage Level Value (ULV) and Important Relative Values (IRV) entirely.

Attributes	Level	ULV	IRV (%)	Rank
Departure Flight	7 a.m.–9 a.m.	0.1098	10.65	IV
	9 a.m.–12 p.m.	0.0825		
	12 p.m.–4 p.m.	0.0713		
	4 p.m –7 p.m.	−0.2636		
Airfare	Peak	−0.6442	36.76	I
	Off-peak	0.6442		
Cabin Crew	Friendliness	0.0208	4.07	V
	Informative	−0.0817		
	Alertness	0.0609		
Facility	Baggage	0.3494	17.74	III
	Food/Beverage	−0.2724		
	Magazine/ Newspaper	−0.0769		
Equity	On time	0.3694	30.77	II
	Route	0.0601		
	Reputation	0.2796		
	Loyalty	−0.7091		

Based on Pearson or Kendall's tau test, the correlation between estimated preferences and the observed are closely related. The value has almost reached 1 or surpassed 0.5 which means the prediction is congruent with reality, so as to represent entire population.

5 CONCLUSIONS

The combined attributes which are strongly preferred include the departure of flight at 7–9 a.m., the off-peak airfare, the cabin crew services, additional 5 kg luggage, and the company branding equity in accordance with the punctual departure time. For domestic low-cost carrier industry, this research can be used as a reference to reevaluate marketing and operational strategies. The limitation of this research is that it was conducted in the Greater Jakarta area and may not represent the entire airline passengers. Therefore, further research with bigger samples on a wider area is necessary to better represent the population.

REFERENCES

Amegbe, H. 2016. The influence of customer based brand equity on consumer responses-the newly opened West Hills Mall in Ghana. *Trendy v podnikani-Business Trends-Scientific Journal of the Faculty of Economics*: 2016/1.

Ayantoyinbo, A. & Boye, B. 2015. Preferences for Nigerian domestic passenger airline industry: a Conjoint Analysis. *European Journal of Logistics Purchasing and Supply Chain Management* 3(2): 21-27.

Azmarani, A. W. 2016. Analisis kualitas pelayanan maskapai penerbangan *Low Cost Carrier* (Studi deskriptif di PT. Citilink Indonesia cabang Surabaya). *Kebijakan dan Manajemen Publik* 4(3).

Badan Pusat Statistik (BPS). 2016. Retrieved from http://www.bps.go.id.

Bogicevic, V., Yang W., Bujisic, M. & Bilgihan, A. 2017. Visual data mining: analysis of airline service quality attributes. *Journal of Quality Assurance in Hospitality & Tourism*.

International Civil Aviation Organization. 2017. *List of Low-Cost-Carriers (LCCs)*. Retrieved from https://www.icao.int/sustainability/Pages/GATO2030.aspx.

Isik, A. & Yasar, M. F. 2015. Effect of brand on consumer preferences: A study in Turkmenistan. *Eurasian Journal of Business and Economics 2015* 8(16): 139-150.

Kankaew, K. 2013. Importance-Performance Analysis in airlines service quality: a case study of legacy airlines in Thailand. *The International Conference on Tourism, Transport, Logistics 2013*. Paris: UP Organizer and Publication Co., Ltd.

Kotler, P. & Armstrong, G. 2014. *Principle of Marketing*, Pearson Education.

Orme, B. 2010. *Getting started with Conjoint Anaysis: strategies for product design and pricing research*. Second Edition, Madison, Wis.: Research Publisher LLC.

Sinaga, V. D. M., Safitri, D. & Rusgiyono, A. 2015. Analisis preferensi konsumen pengguna jasa maskapai penerbangan untuk rute Semarang-Jakarta dengan metode Choise-Based Conjoint (Full Profile). *Jurnal Gaussian* 4(4): 1055-1064.

Suhartanto, D. & Noor, A.A. 2012. Customer satisfaction in the airline industry: The role of service quality and price. *Paper presented at Asia Tourism Forum Conference at Indonesia*.

Wingdes, I. 2012. Conjoint analysis pada produk dengan media internet. *Jurnal Ilmiah SISFOTENIKA* 2(1).

Global Competitiveness: Business Transformation in the
Digital Era – Abdullah, Widiaty & Abdullah (eds)
© 2019 Taylor & Francis Group, London, ISBN 978-0-367-19442-0

The effect of endorser's perceived credibilities in brand image establishment

H. Liem
Sekolah Tinggi Ilmu Ekonomi Harapan Bangsa, Indonesia

ABSTRACT: Television has become the primary means of promotion. However, advertising expenditure in print media like newspapers, magazines, and tabloids actually showed a decrease. In creating effective advertising, there are various important factors, including the selection of celebrities as supporters. The attributes that can be used to say if the endorser is effective or not include attractiveness, trust, and expertise. The purpose of this research is to examine the effect of attractiveness, expertise, and trustworthiness using the celebrity endorser Maudy Ayunda either simultaneously or partially on the brand image of Teh Javana and to measure which of these three attributes has a dominant influence on the brand image. The samples of this research were 25 students of Sekolah Tinggi Ilmu Ekonomi Harapan Bangsa. This research was tested by using multiple linear regression analysis method. The results of the analysis show that attractiveness, trust, and expertise of the endorser simultaneously have a significant influence on the brand image. Partially, only trust and expertise affected the brand image significantly. Attractiveness partially has no significant effect on the brand image.

1 INTRODUCTION

Nielsen Advertising Services data show that television advertising spending in 2016 grew 22 percent to Rp 103.8 trillion. Meanwhile, newspaper ad spending in 2016 dropped by 4.6 to Rp 29.4 trillion from the previous year. Similarly, magazine and tabloid ad spending also fell 15.8 percent to Rp 1.6 trillion from a year earlier. Total spending on television, newspaper, magazine, and tabloid advertisements in 2016 grew 14 percent to Rp 134.8 trillion. About 77 percent of this is television advertising expenditure (The Nielsen Company 2017a). One factor in creating effective advertising is the selection of endorsers.

Teh Javana is a brand-new player in the packaged tea beverage industry. Teh Javana is in perfect competition market so that it has to face various brands of competitors such as Teh Pucuk Harum, Teh Gelas, Frestea, Ichi Ocha, Mytea, The Kotak, Teh Sosro, Nü Green Tea, Fiesta Black Tea, and others (The Nielsen Company 2017b).

According to Nielsen Advertising Information Services, Teh Pucuk Harum is the largest shopping and advertising manufacturer in print and television media in 2016. Its value reached IDR 381.7 billion, a 26 percent increase from the previous year (The Nielsen Company 2017b). Figure 1 shows that Teh Javana advertising spending is very big, reaching IDR 138.7 billion.

Teh Javana television advertisement using celebrity endorser Maudy Ayunda is expected to be one solution for brand image and positioning addressed by Wings Food that can be well received by consumers and can stick in the minds of consumers. However, there are attributes that become a reference that can state if the use of such endorser can effectively improve the company's brand image or not. Attributes that can be used to say an endorser is effective or not are attractiveness, trust, and expertise (Ohanian 1990). Therefore, it is necessary to research on how effective the influence of endorser used in the formation of Teh Javana brand image.

2 LITERATURE REVIEW

2.1 *Endorser in advertising*

In order for products offered by marketers through advertising media have an appeal to potential consumers, it requires the support of the figure (endorser) to deliver messages in advertising. Shimp (2000a) divides the role of endorsers in advertising into two types, namely typical person endorsers and celebrity endorsers.

1. Typical Person Endorser
   Very often the advertising use ordinary people instead of the celebrities to support the product. Some advertisers play with the common people often in large quantities rather than one individual because a lot of resources shall be more effective than a single source. Actions that describe more than one person will increase the likelihood of advertising and will lead to the involvement of the message and its relationship to a higher level.

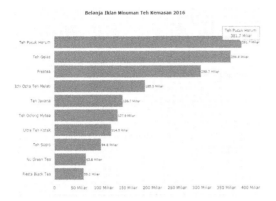

Belanja Iklan Minuman Teh Kemasan 2016

Figure 1. Advertising expenditures of tea beverage package year 2016. Source: The Nielsen Company (2017a).

2. Celebrity Endorser

Friedman and Friedman (1979) stated that celebrities can be interpreted as someone who is known by the public (actors, athletes, etc.) for their achievements in other fields. There are factors that companies pay attention to when making their celebrity selection decisions. McCracken (1989) defines celebrity endorser as everyone who is popular or known to the public and uses its popularity for a product with an appearance in an advertisement. Celebrity endorsers become one of the alternatives in marketing communication to build images that are appropriate to the brand and target audience (Byrne et al. 2003).

Shimp (2000b) states that today many consumers easily identify with these stars, often by looking upon them as heroes for their personal achievements, personalities, and attractiveness. Advertisers are proud to use celebrities in their ads because their popularity attributes, including beauty, courage, talent, athleticism, elegance, power and sexual attraction are often the desired enthusiasts for the brands they support. Repeated association of a brand with a celebrity ultimately leads consumers to think that the brand has interesting properties similar to those of a celebrity.

2.2 *Attribute of the endorser*

In choosing endorsers, companies need to pay attention to attributes that can affect the success of the campaign or in other words the endorser can represent what is desired by the company. Perceptions of endorsers will be measured using instruments developed by Ohanian (1990). In his research, Ohanian developed and validated the scale to measure the credibility of the endorser through perceived attractiveness, trustworthiness, and perceived expertise of the endorser. The following is Ohanian's developed scale, called the Source Credibility Scale.

Table 1. Source credibility scale.

A. Attractiveness	1. Attractive – Unattractive
	2. Classy – Not Classy
	3. Beautiful – Ugly
	4. Elegant – Plain
	5. Sexy – Not Sexy
B. Trustworthiness	1. Dependable – Undependable
	2. Honest – Dishonest
	3. Reliable – Unreliable
	4. Sincere – Unsincere
	5. Trustwothiness – Untrustworthiness
C. Expertise	1. Expert – Not an expert
	2. Experienced – Inexperienced
	3.Knowledgeable – Unknowledgeable
	4. Qualified – Unqualified
	5. Skilled – Unskilled

Source: Ohanian (1990).

2.3 *Brand image*

Identity consists of various ways that the company directs to identify itself or promote themselves or their products, while the image is a public perception of the company or its products (Kotler & Keller 2009). Identity is the introduction of the image. An effective image does three things: establishing product character and value proposals; conveying the character in different ways so as not to be confused by the competitor; and providing an emotional power that is just a mental image. In order to function, the image must be conveyed through available communication means and brand contacts. According to Kamins (1994), matching star ads with starred ads requires that celebrities have to be attractive because these conditions are more effective to support products that can ultimately improve consumer appeal to the item.

Brand image is a series of interrelated brand associations. The brand association is all the impression that comes to the mind of a person associated with his memory of a brand. Brand-related impressions will increase with the increasing number of consumer experiences in consuming a brand or with the more frequent appearance of the brand in its communications strategy, plus if it is supported by a network of other links. An established brand will have a prominent position in the competition when supported by a strong association. The more interconnected the associations, the stronger the brand image of the brand. Generally, brand associations (especially those that form the brand image) have become the basis of consumers in their purchasing decisions and loyalty to the brand (Durianto et al. 2003).

Goldsmith in Seno and Lukas (2007) states that the basic factors that influence brand image are

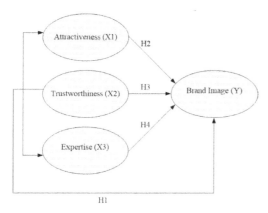

Figure 2. Proposed conceptual framework of the research.

celebrity credibility. Celebrity credibility is the perception of expertise related to messages communicated and can be trusted opinions or objective opinions of the message source. Perception, attractiveness, expertise, and trustworthiness regarding source credibility have a positive impact in persuading consumers and influencing consumers' attitudes to the products associated.

2.4 Conceptual framework and hypotheses development

A research conducted by Ramadhani (2014) suggests that celebrity credibility, attractiveness, and charisma simultaneously have significant influence on the brand image, and partially credibility had the most significant influence.

Using Principal Component Analysis, Multidimensional Scaling, and Importance Performance Analysis, Anggraesti (2010) conducted a study on the use of celebrity endorsers in shampoo ads. She concluded the the attractiveness, trustworthiness, and expertise of the endorsers will affect the creation of a positive brand image. The relationship between the four variables can be seen in Figure 2.

3 METHODOLOGY

3.1 Sampling and population

The sample of the study includes prospective buyers of Teh Javana product at Sekolah Tinggi Ilmu Ekonomi Harapan Bangsa, and selected purposively using the following criteria: respondents had seen on TV Maudy Ayunda's Teh Javana ad. In this study, the sample size was determined using Slovin formula with 90% confidence level so that the error value (e) was 10% (0.10). The total number of population members was 438 students. The minimum required sample (n) is:

$$\frac{438}{1 + (438 + 0.1^2)} = 81,41 = 125$$

4 DATA ANALYSIS

4.1 Demographic characteristics of respondents

The number of questionnaires collected was 125. The profile of the respondents involved in this study shows that:

- 54.4% respondents were male;
- 124 of the respondents were between 15 and 25 years old, while 1 respondent was between 26 and 35 years old.;
- 59 respondents had monthly expenses of less than 1 million rupiahs, 59 respondents had monthly expenses between 1 million to 3 million rupiahs, 3 respondents had monthly expenses between 3 to 5 million rupiahs, 2 respondents had monthly expenses between 5 to 10 million rupiahs, and 2 respondents had monthly expenses of more than 10 million rupiahs.

4.2 Validity and reliability of the instrument

Validity test is used to measure the validity of the questionnaire. A questionnaire is said to be valid if the question on the questionnaire is able to reveal something to be measured by the questionnaire. In this study, the validity measurement was done by doing bivariate correlation between each indicator score with the value of construct score. The result of validity test shows that all items were valid. The research instrument was reliable because it had a value of Cronbach's Alpha > 0.60. The result of reliability test is presented in Table 2.

Table 2. Reliability coefficients for attractiveness, trustworthiness, expertise, and brand image.

Variables	Dimension	Cronbach's α for Dimension	Cronbach's α for Variable
Attractiveness	a. Attractive – Unattractive	0,814	0,854
	b. Beautifull – Ugly	0,788	
	c. Elegant – Plain	0,828	
	d. Sexy – Not Sexy	0,827	
Trustworthiness	a. Dependable – Undependable	0,763	0,823
	b. Honest – Dishonest	0,754	
	c. Reliable – Unreliable	0,778	
	d. Trustwothiness – Untrustworthiness	0,811	
Expertise	a. Expert – Not an expert	0,801	0,844
	b. Experienced – Inexperienced	0,797	
	c. Knowledgeable – Unknowledgeable	0,826	
	d. Qualified – Unqualified	0,784	
Brand Image	a. Brand popularity	0,876	0,897
	b. Brand credibility	0,863	
	c. Brand image in the eyes of the public	0,870	
	d. Trust or warranty of the product.	0,895	
	e. Interest / attract people to the product.	0,865	

Table 3. Anova test results (F).

ANOVA[a]					
Model	Sum of Squares	df	Mean Square	F	Sig.
1 Regression	601,618	3	200,539	42,534	0.000[b]
Residual	570,494	121	4,715		
Total	1172,112	124			

a. Dependent Variable: BRANDIMAGE
b. Predictors: (Constant), ATTRACT, TRUST, EXPERTISE

4.3 Anova test (F)

The Anova test (F-test) was performed using IBM SPSS 24. The results show that at least one variable X had a significant effect on the variable Y. This result was obtained because the value of F arithmetic > F table using level 95% confidence, α = 5% by specifying degrees of freedom or df 1 (number of variables free − 1) i.e. 3−1 = 2 and df1 2 (the number of samples − the number of independent variables), i.e., 100 − 3 = 97. The F value = 42.534 > F table = 3.07 with probability value (0,000) < α = 5%. H0 was then rejected and H1 accepted. The result of Anova test results are presented in Table 3.

H2: The Influence of Attractiveness of Endorser Attention on Brand Image.

The result of T test (partial) indicates that attractiveness has no significant influence on the brand image. The result of this test indicates that the stage action, beauty, dressing, and sex appeal of Maudy Ayunda do not affect the psychological process where the recipient of the message can receive and understand the position of the endorser inside the ad. The results can be seen in Table 4.

H3: Effect of Endorser Trustworthiness Attribute on Brand image.

Table 4. T-Test results.

Coefficients[a]					
Model	Unstandardized Coefficients		Standardized Coefficients		
	B	Std. Error	Beta	t	Sig.
1 (Constant)	3,813	1,377		2.769	0.007
ATTRACT	0.159	0.094	0.137	1.688	0.094
TRUST	0.532	0.135	0.413	3.927	0.000
EXPERTISE	0.320	0.120	0.252	2.660	0.009

a. Dependent Variable: BRANDIMAGE

Trusthworthiness means how much the level of consumer trust in the endorser can affect the image of Teh Javana. Such trustworhincss can be seen on the basis of how to deliver advertising messages by endorsers.

This research resulted in the regression coefficient of trustworthiness of 0.532. This result means if trustworthiness is increased by one unit, then the brand image Teh Javana will increase by 0.532 assuming that other attributes have fixed value. This regression coefficient was the greatest compared with other attributes.

The result of T test (partial) indicates that trustworthiness had the most significant influence on the brand image. Thus, trust to Maudy Ayunda is very influential in Teh Javana brand image creation.

H4: Effect of Endorser Attribute Attitude on Brand image.

The regression coefficient of expertise was 0.320, meaning that if expertise is increased by one unit, then the brand image Teh Javana will experience an increase of 0.320 assuming that other attributes have fixed values. The indicators of expertise include knowledge, experience, and expertise in delivering advertising messages.

The result of T test (partial) indicates that expertise had significant influence on the brand image. Thus, the expertise of Maudy Ayunda has a significant effect on image the Teh Javana brand.

Each independent variable positively affected the brand image. This can be seen from the beta value which indicates a positive value. Based on the value of the coefficient, the regression equation can be stated as follows:

Brand image = 3.813 + 0.532 trustworthiness + 0.320 expertise.

• The constant of 3.813 means if the variable of trustwothiness and expertise is worth 0, then the brand image will be worth as much as 3.813
• The regression coefficient of trustworthiness variable of 0.532 means that if variable confidence increases by one unit, then the brand image Teh Javana will experience an increase of 0.532 units assuming the other variables have fixed values.
• The regression coefficient of expertise variable of 0.320 means that if the variable expertise increases by one unit, then the brand image Teh Javana will experience an increase of 0.2576 units with assuming the other variables have fixed values.

The determination analysis was performed to find out the contribution of variable X to variable Y. The result is presented in Table 5.

The adjusted R square number was 50.1%. This indicates that the independent variables had influence on the dependent variable as much as 50.1%; the rest is influenced by factors other than the studied variables.

41

Table 5. The result of determination analysis

Model Summary				
Model	R	R Square	Adjusted R Square	Std. Error of the Estimate
1	0.716[a]	0.513	0.501	2.17137

a. Predictors: (Constant), EXPERTISE, ATTRACT, TRUST

5 DISCUSSION

5.1 Managerial Implications

The management of Wings Food needs to make efforts to be able to maintain and enhance its positive image in the eyes of consumers. This can be done by hiring a celebrity to be a brand ambassador. People's admiration towards the celebrity will affect the product image.

5.2 Suggestion

Based on the results of the overall research, it is suggested that company promotion pays more attention to trust factor of the endorser because this variable is the highest variable to affect the brand image.

REFERENCES

Anggraesti H.P. 2010. *Analisis Efektivitas Penggunaan Celebrity Endorser Dalam Meningkatkan Brand Image Sampo Menurut Pandangan Mahasiswa Strata 1 IPB [skripsi]*. Bogor: Institut Pertanian Bogor.

Byrne, A., Whitehead, M. & Breen, S. 2003. The Naked Truth of Celebrity Endorsement. *British Food Journal* 4(5). 288.

Durianto, D., Sugiarto, S., Widjaja, A.W. & Hendrawan, S. 2003. *Invasi Pasar Dengan Iklan Yang Efektif*. Jakarta: PT. Gramedia Pustaka Utama.

Friedman, H.H. & Friedman, L. 1979. Endorser affectiveness by product type. *Journal of Advertising Research* 19(5): 63-71.

The Nielsen Company. 2017a. Perang Iklan Minuman Teh Kemasan. [Online]. Retrieved from: https://databoks.katadata.co.id/datapublish/2017/02/06/televisi-masih-menjadi-pilihan-utama-produsen-beriklan. Accessed on 1 December 2019.

The Nielsen Company. 2017b. Televisi Masih Menjadi Pilihan Utama Produsen Beriklan. [Online]. Retrieved from: https://databoks.katadata.co.id/datapublish/2017/02/04/perang-iklan-minuman-teh-kemasan. Accessed on 1 December 2019.

Kamins, M.A. & Gupta, A. 1994. Congruence between Spokesperson and Product Type: A Matchup Hypothesis Perspective. *Psychology and Marketing* 11(6): 569-586.

Kotler, P. & Keller, K.L. 2009. *Manajemen Pemasaran. Jilid 1. Ed ke-13*. Jakarta: Penerbit Erlangga.

McCracken, G. 1989. Who is the celebrity endorser? Cultural foundations of the endorsement process. *Journal of consumer research* 16(3): 310-321.

Ohanian, R. 1990. Construction and Validation of a Scale to Measure Celebrity Endorser's Perceived Expertise, Trustworthiness, and Attractiveness. *Journal of Advertising*, 19(3): 39-52.

Ramadhani, R. 2014. *Pengaruh Penggunaan Endorser Terhadap Brand Image Pada PT Nike Indonesia [skripsi]*. Bogor: Institut Pertanian Bogor.

Seno, D. & Lukas, B.A. 2007. The Equity Effect of Product Endorsement by celebrities. *European Journal of Marketing. Emerald Group Publishing*.

Shimp, S. & Terence, A. 2000a. *Periklanan Promosi: Komunikasi Pemasaran Terpadu. Jilid 1. cetakan V*. Jakarta: Penerbit Erlangga.

Shimp, S. & Terence, A. 2000b. *Periklanan Promosi: Komunikasi Pemasaran Terpadu. Jilid 2. cetakan V*. Jakarta: Penerbit Erlangga.

Global Competitiveness: Business Transformation in the
Digital Era – Abdullah, Widiaty & Abdullah (eds)
© 2019 Taylor & Francis Group, London, ISBN 978-0-367-19442-0

Entrepreneurship and small medium enterprises in ASEAN

L. Danil & N. Septina
Parahyangan Catholic University, Bandung, Indonesia

ABSTRACT: Entrepreneurship and small and medium-sized enterprises (SMEs) have grown positively all over the world, especially in ASEAN countries. This phenomenon has received attention from many scholars from various disciplines. In this research, we conducted in-depth in interviews with entrepreneurs from Indonesia, Cambodia, Brunei Darussalam, Lao Peoples Democratic Republic, Myanmar, Vietnam and Thailand. SMEs in ASEAN could be improved by the provision of marketing training and supports from the government. The results of this study are expected to be provide relevant information particularly useful for SMEs in ASEAN countries.

1 INTRODUCTION

Minister of Cooperatives and SMEs Anak Agung Gede Ngurah Puspayoga say the National Entrepreneurship Movement (GKN) makes the entrepreneurial ratio of Indonesia go up to 3.1 percent from 1.67 percent in 2013/2014. Based on data from Statistics Indonesia (BPS) in 2016, out of a population of 252 million, the number of non-agricultural full-time entrepreneurs has reached 7.8 million people or 3.1 percent. Thus, the level of entrepreneurship Indonesia has reached 2 percent of the population, meeting a minimum criterion of a welfare of society. The Entrepreneur ratio of 3.1 percent is still lower than those of other countries such as Malaysia 5%, China 10%, Singapore 7%, Japan 11% and the US 12%.

The development of entrepreneurship and SMEs in Indonesia itself is an integral part of the economic unification among ASEAN member countries. The Blueprint for SME Development in ASEAN, the ASEAN SME Blueprint for 2004-2014 and the ASEAN Strategic Action Plan for SME Development 2010-2015 constitute a framework of cooperation and action plans to develop competitive, dynamic and innovative ASEAN SMEs. This study was conducted in order to examine the competitiveness of Indonesian SMEs compared to other ASEAN countries and to develop strategies to improve the competitiveness of Indonesian SMEs anticipating the ASEAN Economic Community (MEA).

As an important contributor to economic growth, employment creation and gender empowerment in ASEAN, SMEs are increasingly becoming important forces in ASEAN economic integration. Their expansion and progress are important for ASEAN. SMEs play an important role in helping ASEAN achieve its fair economic development goals because of its wide range and diversity. ASEAN SMEs have been facing a number of challenges in terms of access to finance, technology and competitive markets. ASEAN countries are increasingly paying attention to these challenges and helping them to deal with these issues.

The ASEAN Strategic Action Plan for SME Development (SAPSMED) in 2016-2025 serves to strengthen the involvement of SMEs in an increasingly competitive economic environment and to support their growth and development through the vision of "Global and Innovative Partnership SME" and by 2025 ASEAN will have created more competitive and globally resilient SMEs. The overall achievement of SMEs will be traced through a series of 10 key policy indicators and other operational indicators to be developed. The plan was launched on the sidelines of the 27th ASEAN Summit on 21 November 2015. The plan was developed by the ASEAN SME Working Group. This study aims to examine the factors affecting entrepreneurship so as to increase the number of SMEs in ASEAN Countries.

Over the past few decades many scholars have conducted research on entrepreneurship and micro, small and medium-sized enterprises (MSMEs) in relation to poverty alleviation and state revenues. This study focuses on various aspects of entrepreneurship and SMEs.

Entrepreneurship is one aspect that can increase employment and economic growth in Indonesia. However, the number of entrepreneurs in Indonesia is unfortunately rather limited. The difference between business and entrepreneurship, according to Shane and Venkataraman in Campbell and Mitchell (2012), is that entrepreneurship is greater than starting new businesses or managing a small business: entrepreneurship does not require, but can include, the creation of new organizations.

Morrison et al. (1998) also argue the process of entrepreneurship initiation has its foundations in person and intuition, and society and culture. It is much more holistic than simply an economic

Table 1. Criteria for Indonesian MSMEs Source: Law of the Republic of Indonesia Number 20 of 2008 on Micro, Small and Medium Enterprises, 2018.

	Micro-sized Enterprise (in millions of IDR)	Small-sized Enterprise (in millions of IDR)	Medium-sized Enterprise (in millions of IDR)
Wealth (Investment Capital)	50	50 – 500	500 – 10,000
Turnover/ Sales	300	300 – 2,500	2,500 – 50,000

Figure 2. Indonesian Small Enterprises 2006 until 2013. Source: www.aseansme.org, 2018.

function, and represents a composite of material and immaterial, pragmatism and idealism.

It can be concluded that entrepreneurship is not just a matter of running a new business or managing a small business, but it can also create an organization. The difference between these can be observed in the Table 1.

The total number of micro enterprises in Indonesia from 2006 to 2013 is described in Figure 1.

The total number of small enterprises in Indonesia from 2006 to 2013 is described in Figure 2.

The total number of medium enterprises in Indonesia from 2006 to 2013 is described in Figure 3.

Storey (1994) states that SMEs has been the majority of businesses around the world. For studying entrepreneurship, the authors usually use start-up rates as a dependent variable (Van Stel et al. 2005). But there are some limitations in using this proxy:

1) The decision to become an entrepreneur could be affected more by social capital than by existing institutions. This assumption is confirmed by Engle et al. (2011) who empirically defined that parental experience and social norms have a significant positive effect on entrepreneurial intent.
2) Start-up rate does not cover the decision of entrepreneurs to act productively, i.e. it is impossible

Figure 3. Indonesian Medium Enterprises 2006 until 2013. Source: www.aseansme.org, 2018.

to make an assumption that all business will behave in a productive way (properly pays taxes to the state budget and so on).

The results of Nataliia's (2015) research also uphold the contradictive results of previous research that revealed the influence of national culture on business development/entrepreneurship. The outcome also shows that power distance has an impact on entrepreneurship development (Kreiser et al. 2010). The results of research conducted by Roland & Gorodnichenko (2010) show the causal effect of the personal income of individuals. The research done by Zhao et al. (2012) also shows that the modernistic culture creates high-growth and high-innovation entrepreneurship.

ASEAN SME sector is characterized by heterogeneity (Tambunan 2011). SMEs are keen to improve productivity and innovative capabilities to meet the increased competition in the global market. While the development gap between the ASEAN countries is often seen as a major defect. The gap could be turned into a source of dynamism, as indicated by classic models of the flying geese and product cycles. Some ASEAN countries have had experience with SME policies since the 1970s (Sato 2015).

This implies that it is necessary for Indonesia to increase the number of entrepreneurs to improve the performance of SMEs.

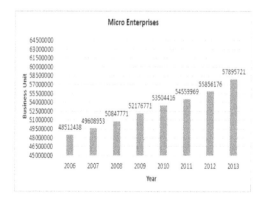

Figure 1. Indonesian Micro Enterprises 2006 until 2013. Source: www.aseansme.org, 2018.

Quantitative indicators refer to the economic, financial and operational results of the business. They are also called extrinsic indicators (Weber 2014) of business performance (Zolin et al. 2013, Robb & Watson 2012), or organisational variables (Baron & Henry 2011). Qualitative indicators refer to subjective aspects also known as intrinsic indicators (Weber 2014), such as effects on the entrepreneur (Baron & Henry 2011), success perception of positive consequences (Fisher et al. 2014) or development platform ascent (Dalborg 2012). With regard to qualitative indicators, Dej (2010) proposes a measurement in two dimensions: perception of the entrepreneur's financial success (and of the success of the business) and perception of the entrepreneur's personal success. The latter encompasses social recognition, establishment of loyalty relationships with customers also indicated by Lewis (2013), the accomplishment of personal goals and personal development. Dijkhuizen et al. (2014) establish an association between what they call *demand* factors: working hours, uncertainty and risk and responsibility, and factors that operate like *resources*: autonomy, variety of work, feedback, learning opportunities, organization and independence and perception of success as measured by Dej's (2010) proposed instrument.

However, some studies reveal that business results' indicators should be combined for a better explanation of business venturing success. In this regard, Fried and Tauer (2009) proposed an index combining total business resource cost, the entrepreneur's hours of dedication, total earnings and profit growth.

The literature on entrepreneurial tendencies focuses on recognizing individuals with the inclination to behave entrepreneurially by considering personal characteristics of entrepreneurs (e.g., Cromie 2000). Both academics and practitioners appear to believe that, relative to any other factor, the success of a venture is more dependent on the individual entrepreneur (Lee & Tsang 2001). Studies such as Collins et al. (2004), Rauch & Frese (2007a, 2007b), Stewart & Roth (2007), Zhao et al. (2012), Gurel et al. (2010) and Brandstätter (2011) have revealed various findings, arguments and meta-analytical evidence in support of the validity of personality traits as predictors of entrepreneurial behavior, as well as established differences between entrepreneurs and other occupational groups such as managers.

This study is focused on five key personality traits: need for achievement (nAch), need for autonomy, internal locus of control, calculated risk-taking and creative tendency (Dada et al, 2015).

It is believed that the "need to achieve" motivates individuals to prevail over obstacles and difficult situations and also motivates individuals to make every effort to attain their goals and excellence quickly (Tajeddini & Mueller 2009). Most studies have found achievement to be a robust characteristic of successful entrepreneurs (Sebora et al. 2009).

Particular emphasis has been on differentiating entrepreneurs and professional managers on their risk-taking propensity, and a notable premise is that entrepreneurs personally take the risk of profit and loss (Gürol & Atsan 2006).

Locus of control refers to the extent to which individuals believe that they are able to influence events encountered in their lives (Lee & Tsang 2001, Shane et al. 2003).

Need for autonomy is associated with entrepreneurs' avoidance of restrictive environments. They prefer to make decisions independent of supervisors to set their own goals and develop their own plans of actions, and to control goal achievement themselves (Rauch & Frese 2007b).

2 RESEARCH METHOD

Given the varied dimensions of entrepreneurship and small medium enterprises as gauged in some previous studies, it will be identified in advance what particular dimensions are most appropriate for the context of this research. The method of this research is In-depth interviews with entrepreneurs in Indonesia, Cambodia, Brunei Darussalam, Lao Peoples Democratic Republic, Myanmar, Vietnam and Thailand.

3 RESULTS

The main motivation of entrepreneurship is to earn money with the desired passion, in contrast to merely being an employee who goes through the motions of performing tasks that may not suit the heart. Other motivations may range from improving the economy and contributing to society to sustaining ourselves and taking care of those around us.

Indonesia has the opportunity to become a more powerful country of entrepreneurs with a population of 250 million people (but only about 3% of whom become entrepreneurs) and with its increasing middle market resulting in higher purchasing power.

Prices are becoming more and more efficient in terms of production cost, whether it is derived from raw materials or access to information, which creates the right time and conditions for becoming a businessman.

Products of Indonesian MSMEs are unique and cannot be found in other countries such as Jepara carving/furniture, Cirebon rattan, and batik. Unfortunately, these MSMEs still haven't got a firm grasp of sufficient network marketing. There must be awareness on the part of entrepreneurs of their own MSMEs to be able to improve their own marketing tools enabling them sell their products. One of these could be digital marketing, where the cost incurred is not too high while it can make a considerable impact.

But the obstacles frequently encountered by MSMEs, among others, include investment capital and the difficulty of finding other craftsmen. The position of Indonesian SMEs in ASEAN countries can be classified as a leading one because there is a strong domestic demand for products as many Indonesian people purchase domestic products. Another contributing factor is that the Indonesian middle market is expanding so the products are well absorbed by the consumers. Indonesia even shows the potential of becoming the third leading market in Southeast Asia and according to McKenzie, in 2030 Indonesia will be the seventh largest economy in the world due to its considerable market purchasing power, greater investment, enhanced by more flexible regulation and a more efficient infrastructure.

Table 2. ASEAN'S Export in January 2017.

Country	Value (US$)	Weight (kg)
BRUNEI DARUS-SALAM	4.678.950,31	6.366.347,02
CAMBODIA	39.837.006,74	244.085.497,94
INDONESIA	13.401.704.047,89	43.595.887.615,63
LAO PEO-PLES DEM-OCRATIC REPUBLIC	674.489,70	252.862,54
MALAYSIA	738.684.360,45	2.831.184.510,43
MYANMAR (FORM. BURMA)	51.572.817,59	59.811.490,97
PHILIPPINES	489.115.510,62	1.779.676.889,32
SINGAPORE	844.702.525,41	1.761.239.152,28
THAILAND	479.951.566,03	1.375.526.326,90
VIETNAM	234.363.132,31	451.897.951,22

Source: www.asean.org, 2017.

The distribution of SMEs by sector shows that the majority of Indonesian SMEs are involved in agriculture. The second largest sector is trade, hotel, and restaurant while the third largest is manufacturing as seen in Table 3.

Tambunan's (2011) research result show that SMEs are indeed very important not only as a source of employment, but, potentially, as a growth engine for the economy.

3.1 *The Indonesian Government's involvement in the process of raising the standard of MSMEs in ASEAN*

The Government of the Republic of Indonesia has been heavily involved in improving MSMEs in

Table 3. SMEs in ASEAN countries.

Member Country	Number	Year	As a percentage of all firms (for last year of data available)
Brunei Darussalam	30,000	2004	98
Cambodia[a]	369	mid-1950s	99
	1,000	1958	
	24,097	1998	
	25,406	2000	
	25,985	2003	
	28,747	2005	
Indonesia	377,652,000	1997	99,9
	378,563,000	1999	
	434,659,220	2003	
	488,229,005	2006	
Lao PDR	22,000	1998	99,4
	25,993	2004	
Malaysia	516,855	2003	99,2
	518,996	2005	
Myanmar	34,000	1998/1999	96
Philippines	68,000	2001	99,5
	72,696	2003	
Singapore	72,000	2002	97,8
Thailand	779,033	1997	99,8
	1,639,427	2001	
	1,995,929	2003	
	2,274,525	2006	
Vietnam	59,831	2002	96,8
	98,233	2005	

Note: [a]In manufacturing industry only
Source: Asia-Pacific Economic Cooperation (APEC) (2003a, 2003b, 2003c, 2003d), RAM Consultancy Services (2005), UNCTAD (2003), Myint (2000), Regnier (2000), Ministry of Industry, Mines and Energy of the Kingdom of Cambodia, Indonesian National Agency of Statistics, SMIDEC, Dhungana (2003), Rasiah (2001), Jajri & Ismail (2007), OSMEP; National SME Development Agenda 2000/2001, Kyophilavong et al. (2007a, 2007b), Sang (2007), Aldaba (2007), Cuong et al. (2007), and Bailey (2007), Tambunan (2011).

ASEAN as over the past two years there have been several meetings with ASEAN countries and those cooperating with ASEAN. In a session entitled 'Promoting an Innovative, Entrepreneurial ASEAN Economic Community', the President of Indonesia emphasized two priorities that deserved to receive the attention of ASEAN and the US. The two main priorities are MSME cooperation as well as technology and the digital economy.

President Joko Widodo (popularly known as "Jokowi") went on to suggest this particular cooperation should take precedence because MSMEs are the backbone of the economy of Indonesia and

ASEAN. Approximately 88.8 percent to 99.9 percent of business establishments in ASEAN are MSMEs, taking up 51.7 percent to 97.2 percent of the workforce in ASEAN.

"High-end SMEs are able to support the country's economy, even in times of global crisis", Jokowi explained. But MSMEs often face challenges, especially in terms of capacity building, access to capital and alternative funding, access to technology, global market access, and regional and global link integration.

Therefore, technology and the digital economy are absolute necessities in the era of digitalization. Every government, according to the President, must ensure that this era brings benefits to the people, especially MSMEs. As a consequence, these MSMEs must have access to technology and the digital economy.

In the ASEAN-Korea Free Trade Area (AKFTA) meeting, the Indonesian government stated that ASEAN and Korea should be able to maintain their ideals based on the notion of mutual economic openness. This statement was made by President Joko Widodo at the 19th ASEAN-South Korea Summit held at Philippine International Convention Center (PICC) in Manila, the Philippines on Monday, 13 November 2017.

SMEs play a very important role for the ASEAN economy. As a matter of fact, 96 percent of ASEAN consists of MSMEs. As stated by the President of the Republic of Indonesia "When we talk about ASEAN economic integration then it is our duty incorporate SMEs into our integration."

President Jokowi expressed his appreciation to the ASEAN Business Advisory Board for seeing the importance of ASEAN's partisanship towards MSMEs. In addition, attention should also be paid to empowering women in MSMEs. Indonesia will promote efforts to increase cooperation, both between ASEAN Members and between ASEAN and its partner countries. AKTFA will provide tangible benefits that can be felt by all Indonesian people as well as people in ASEAN and the Asia Pacific region.

Another meeting at the 28th ASEAN Summit was held at the National Convention Center (NCC), Vientienne, Laos, on September 6, 2016. The President asked ASEAN to ensure the involvement and progress of MSMEs through technological development and innovation as well as expansion of financial access and markets.

"If the people of ASEAN do not feel the benefits of ASEAN's existence, it will be difficult for ASEAN to grow in a sustainable manner," or so the President predicted.

Indonesia's ranking on the Global Competitive Index went up by five from 41st rank out of 138 countries in 2016/2017 to 36th rank from 137 countries in 2017/2018. Out of 10 ASEAN countries, only 9 countries made the top 138 countries in the 2016 and 2017 CGI.

Table 4. GCI Index.

Country of ASEAN	2011	2012	2013	2014	2015	2016	2017
Singapore	2	2	2	2	2	2	3
Malaysia	21	25	24	20	18	25	23
Thailand	39	38	37	31	32	34	32
Indonesia	46	50	38	34	37	41	36
Brunei Darussalam	28	28	26	-	-	58	46
Vietnam	65	75	70	68	56	60	55
Philippines	75	65	59	52	47	57	56
Cambodia	97	85	88	95	90	89	94
Laos	-	-	81	93	83	93	98

Source: presidenri.go.id, 2018.

The development of entrepreneurship has been very rapid under two periods of government when there was a strong focus on MSMEs and these enterprises took up 98% of the workforce. Many university and college students are under the impression that a businessman is not an employee. The Government of Indonesia has helped the development of MSMEs by providing working space in the shape of business centers.

Indonesia has the opportunity to become a more powerful entrepreneur with a population of 250 million people (only about 3% of whom become entrepreneurs) and aided by its increasing middle market resulting in higher purchasing power. Prices are becoming more and more efficient in terms of production costs, whether it is derived from raw materials or access to information, creating the right time and conditions for becoming a businessman.

There is something unique about products of Indonesian MSMEs not available in other countries, such as Jepara carving/furniture, Cirebon rattan, and batik. Unfortunately, these MSMEs still haven't got a firm grasp of sufficient network marketing. There must be awareness on the part of entrepreneurs of their own MSMEs to be able to improve their own marketing tools enabling them sell their products. One of these could be digital marketing, where the cost incurred is not too high while it can make a considerable impact.

SMESCO helps MSMEs by holding national and international exhibitions in various parts of the world, such as Europe and Middle East.

4 CONCLUSIONS

Based on the available data, it can be summarized as follows:

1) The main motivation of entrepreneurship is to earn money with the desired passion, in contrast to merely being an employee who goes through the motions of performing tasks that may not suit

the heart. Other motivations may range from improving the economy and contributing to society to sustaining ourselves and taking care of those around us.

2) But the obstacles encountered by MSMEs, among others, include investment capital and the difficulty of finding other craftsmen capable of making handmade products.

3) Although MSMEs include micro-sized businesses, 96% of all enterprises in ASEAN countries still show limited contribution to the formation of added value, even though MSMEs contribute 42% of the total GDP of ASEAN countries.

4) In general, the performance of Indonesian SMEs is still relatively low compared to ASEAN countries with relatively similar levels of development, especially in terms of productivity, export contribution, participation in global and regional production and contribution to added value.

5) The position of Indonesian SMEs in ASEAN countries can be classified as a leading one because there is a strong domestic demand for products as many Indonesian people purchase domestic products. Another contributing factor is that the Indonesian middle market is expanding so the products are well absorbed by the consumers. Indonesia even shows the potential of becoming the third leading market in Southeast Asia, and according to Mc Kenzie, in 2030 Indonesia will be the seventh largest economy in the world due to its considerable market purchasing power, greater investment, enhanced by more flexible regulation and a more efficient infrastructure.

6) Two ways of improving SMEs in ASEAN would be providing training for SMEs (especially in the field of marketing), and creating policies that support SMEs to run smoothly and make progress such as ease of business licensing as well as providing facilities such as work space for SMEs.

REFERENCES

Aldaba, R.M. 2007. *SMEs in the Philippines manufacturing industry and globalisation*. Paper presented at the Third Workshop, the ERIA Related Joint research of SME project, IDE-JETRO, Bangkok, 13-14 November.

APEC. 2003a. *APEC informatization survey for small and medium enterprises*. APEC Small and Medium Enterprises Working Group, APEC Secretariat, Singapore.

APEC. 2003b. *From income generation to patent creation – mapping out APEC best practices guidelines for industrial clustering*. Chung-Hua Institution for Economic Research and the APEC Secretariat, Singapore, December.

APEC. 2003c. *Profile of SMEs and SMEs issues in APEC 1990-2000*. APEC Small and Medium Enterprises Working Group, APEC Secretariat, Singapore.

APEC. 2003d. *Providing financial support for micro-enterprise development*. Paper presented at the SMEs Ministerial Meeting, Chiang Mai, Thailand, 7-8 August.

Bailey, P. 2007. Cambodian Small and Medium sized Enterprises Constraints, Policies and Proposals for their Development. In *third workshop for the ERIA Related Joint Research of SME Project, IDE-JETRO, Bangkok, November*.

Baron, R.A. & Henry, R.A., 2011. *Entrepreneurship: The genesis of organizations*. American Psychological Association.

Brandstätter, H. 2011. Personality aspects of entrepreneurship: a look at five meta-analyses. *Personality and Individual Differences* 51(3): 222-230.

Campbell, N. & Mitchell, D. T. 2012. A (partial) review of entrepreneurship literature across disciplines. *Journal of Entrepreneurship and Public Policy* 1(2): 183-199.

Collins, C.J., Hanges, P.J. & Locke, E.E. 2004. The relationship of achievementmotivation to entrepreneurial behavior: a meta-analysis. *Human Performance* 17(1): 95-117.

Cromie, S. 2000. Assessing entrepreneurial inclinations: some approaches and empirical evidence. *European Journal of Work and Organisational Psychology* 9(1): 7-30.

Cuong, T.T., Sang, L.X. & Anh, N.K. 2007. Small and medium enterprises development in Vietnam: the case of electronics and motorcycle. *Draft Report for the ERIA Related Joint Research of SME Project, IDE-JETRO, Central Institute for Economic Management, Vietnam, Hanoi*.

Dada, O., Watson, A., & Kirby, D. 2015. Entrepreneurial tendencies in franchising: evidence from the UK. *Journal of Small Business and Enterprise Development* 22(1): 82-98.

Dalborg, C.A. 2012. Beyond the numbers: qualitative growth in womens business. *International Journal of Gender and Entrepreneurship* 4(3): 289-331.

Dej, D. 2010. Defining and measuring entrepreneurial success", in Lagun, M.L. (Ed.), *Entrepreneurship: A Psychological Approach*, Oeconomica Publishers, Prague: 89-102.

Dhungana, B.P. 2003. Strengthening the competitiveness of small and medium enterprises in the globalization process: prospects and challenges. *Investment Promotion and Enterprises Development Bulletin for Asia and the Pacific, No.1, Economic and Social Commission for Asia and the Pacific, United Nations, New York, NY, ESCAP works towards reducing poverty and managing globalization*.

Dijkhuizen, J.G., Gorgievski, M., van Veldhoven, M. & Schalk, R. 2014. Feeling successful as an entrepreneur: a job demands – resources approach. *International Entrepreneurship and Management Journal* 12(2): 555-573.

Engle, R.L., Schlaegel, C. & Dimitriadi, N. 2011. Institutions and entrepreneurial intent: a cross-country study. *Journal of developmental entrepreneurship* 16(2): 227-250.

Fisher, R., Maritz, A. & Lobo, A. 2014. Evaluating entrepreneurs' perception of success: Development of a measurement scale. *International Journal of Entrepreneurial Behavior & Research* 20(5): 478-492.

Fried, H.O. & Tauer, L.W. 2009. Understanding the entrepreneur: an index of Entrepreneurial success. *Frontiers of Entrepreneurship Research* 29(5): 7.

Gurel, E., Altinay, L. & Daniele, R. 2010. Tourism students' entrepreneurial intentions. *Annals of Tourism Research* 37(3): 646-669.

Gürol, Y. & Atsan, N. 2006. Entrepreneurial characteristics amongst university students: some insights for entrepreneurship education and training in Turkey. *Education and Training* 48(1): 25-38.

Jajri, I. & Ismail, R. 2007. Source of output growth in small and medium scale enterprises in Malaysia. *MPRA Paper No 2779, January, University of Malaya, Kuala Lumpur.*

Kreiser, P., Marino, L., Dickson, P. & Mark, K. 2010. Cultural influences on entrepreneurial orientation: the impact of national culture on risk taking and proactiveness in SMEs. *Entrepreneurship Theory and Practice* 34(5): 959-983.

Kyophilavong, P., Sanesouphap, C., Suvannaphakdy, S. & Nakiengchan, A. 2007a. Determine the performance of SME in Vientiane and other provinces. *Lao journal of Economic and Business Management* 2: 31-61.

Kyophilavong, P., Wongpit, P. & Inthakesone, B. 2007b. SMEs development in Lao PDR. In *Third Workshop, the ERIA Related Joint Research of SME Project, IDE-JETRO, Bangkok, 13-14 November.*

Law of the Republic of Indonesia Number 20 of 2008 concerning Micro, Small and Medium Enterprises, 2017.

Lee, D.Y. & Tsang, E.W.K. 2001. The effects of entrepreneurial personality, background and network activities on venture growth. *Journal of Management Studies* 38(4): 583-602.

Lewis, P. 2013. The search of authentic entrepreneurial identity: difference and professionalism among women business owners. *Gender, Work and Organization* 20(3): 252-266.

Morrison, A., Rimmington, M. & Williamson, C. 1998. *Entrepreneurship in the Hospitality, Tourism and Leisure Industry.* Butterworth-Heinemann: Oxford.

Myint, S. 2000. The SMEs and skill development in Myanmar. In *the Leadership Forum 2000, Bangkok, 15-17 January.*

Nataliia, O. 2015. National culture, institutions and economic growth: The way of influence on productivity of entrepreneurship. *Journal of Entrepreneurship and Public Policy.* 4(3): 331-351

RAM Consultancy Services. 2005. SME access to financing: addressing the supply side of SME financing. *REPSF Project No. 04/003, Final Main Report, Ram Consultancy Services, Bangkok.*

Rasiah, R. 2001. Government-business coordination and small business performance in the machine tools sector in Malaysia. *Research Report, World Bank Institute/The World Bank, Washington, DC.*

Rauch, A. & Frese, M. 2007a. Born to be an entrepreneur? Revisiting the personality approach to entrepreneurship. In *Baum, R.J., Frese, M. and Baron, R. (Eds), The Psychology of Entrepreneurship, Lawrence Erlbaum Associates, Mahwah, NJ, pp.* 41-66.

Rauch, A. & Frese, M. 2007b. Let's put the person back into entrepreneurship research: a meta-analysis on the relationship between business owners personality traits, business creation, and success. *European Journal of Work and Organisational Psychology* 16(4): 353-385.

Regnier, P. 2000. Small and Medium Enterprises in Distress – Thailand. *The East Asian Crisis and Beyond, Gower, Aldershot.*

Robb, A.M. & Watson, J. 2012. Gender differences in firm performance: Evidence from new ventures in the United States. *Journal of Business Venturing* 27(5): 544-558.

Roland, G. & Gorodnichenko, Y. 2010. Culture, Institutions and the wealth of nations. *IZA Discussion Paper No. 5187, available at:* http://ftp.iza.org/dp5187.pdf *(accessed 20 October 2014).*

Sang, L.X. 2007. Vietnam's small and medium-sized enterprises development: the cases of motorcycle and electronic industries. In *the Third Workshop, the ERIA Related Joint Research of SME Project, IDE-JETRO, Bangkok, 13-14 November.*

Sato, Y. 2015. *Development of Small and Medium Enterprises in the ASEAN* Economies: 154-181.

Sebora, T.C., Lee, S.M. & Sukasame, N. 2009. Critical success factors for e-commerce entrepreneurship: an empirical study of Thailand. *Small Business Economics* 32(3): 303-316.

Shane, S., Locke, E.A. & Collins, C.J. 2003. Entrepreneurial motivation. *Human Resource Management Review* 13(2): 257-279.

Stewart Jr, W.H. & Roth, P.L., 2007. A meta-analysis of achievement motivation differences between entrepreneurs and managers. *Journal of Small Business Management* 45(4): 401-421.

Storey, D. 1994. *Understanding the Small Business Sector.* Routledge: London.

Tajeddini, K. & Mueller, S.L. 2009. Entrepreneurial characteristics in Switzerlandand the UK: a comparative study of techno-entrepreneurs. *Journal of International Entrepreneurship* 7: 1-25.

Tambunan, T. 2011. Development of small and medium enterprises in a developing country: The Indonesian case. *Journal of Enterprising Communities: People and Places in the Global Economy* 5(1): 68-82.

UNCTAD. 2003. *Improving the Competitiveness of SMEs through Enhancing Productive Capacity, TD/B/Com.3/51/Add. 1, United Nations, Geneva.*

Van Stel, A., Carree, M. & Thurik, R. 2005. The effect of entrepreneurial activity on national economic growth. *Discussion papers on Entrepreneurship, Growth and Public Policy, Max Planck Institute for Research into Economic Systems Group Entrepreneurship, Growth and Public Policy Kahlaische Str. 10 07745 Jena.*

Weber, P.G. 2014. Gender related perceptions of SME success. *International Journal of Gender and Entrepreneurship* 6(1): 15-27.

Zhao, X., Li, H. & Rauch, A. 2012. Cross-country differences in entrepreneurial activity: the role of cultural practice and national wealth. *Frontiers of Business Research in China* 6(4): 447-474.

Zolin, R., Stuetzer, M. & Watson, J. 2013. Challenging the female underperformance hypothesis. *International Journal of Gender and Entrepreneurship* 5(2): 116-129.

Global Competitiveness: Business Transformation in the Digital Era – Abdullah, Widiaty & Abdullah (eds)
© 2019 Taylor & Francis Group, London, ISBN 978-0-367-19442-0

Service-performance chain: A triangle conceptual model

N. Septina & M. Widyarini
Parahyangan Catholic University, Bandung, Indonesia

ABSTRACT: The service-profit chain demonstrates links between profitability, customer loyalty, and employee satisfaction, loyalty, and productivity. This chain involves employee, customer and company perspective as one framework. The conceptual model of this research was modified from the Heskett et al. service-profit chain framework as data for some variables in the service-profit chain were not accessible by adjusting profitability and revenue growth to daily business performance. Based on literature study combined with qualitative approach, this research aims to propose the service-performance chain model (Indonesian context).

1 INTRODUCTION

Globalization leads to the changing of business environment and increases the business competition as well. In this competitive world, every manager of every enterprise must learn how to handle changes. In modern market sector, preliminary research found that there was a significant customer shifting from supermarket and hypermarket to mini market as a priority channel on daily spending.

Service-profit chain suggested a framework connecting an enterprise's profitability not only to service operations, but also employee and customer assessments (Heskett et al. 1994). It is known as the service-profit chain, redefined by incorporating employee capability. This framework consists of four elements, namely internal elements (internal service quality, employee satisfaction, and employee loyalty), service elements (the value and delivery of the service), external elements (customer satisfaction and customer loyalty) and the financial elements (profitability and other financial performance measures).

The service-profit chain demonstrates links between profitability, customer loyalty, and employee satisfaction, loyalty, and productivity. The links along this chain are as follows: the first link explains that profit and growth are stimulated primarily by customer loyalty, the second link explains that loyalty is a direct result of customer satisfaction, the third link explains that customer satisfaction is largely influenced by the value of services provided, the fourth link explains that value is created by satisfied, loyal and productive employees, and the last link explains that employee satisfaction, in turn, results primarily from high-quality support services and policies that enable employees to deliver the result to customers. This framework provides an integrative approach for an enterprise to understand better how service and human resource input affect customer evaluations, customer behavior, and financial metrics (Kamakura et al. 2002).

The previous empirical research considers the service-profit chain scattered among various sector (Silvestro & Cross 2000, Xu & Goedegebuure 2005, Yee et al. 2011) explored different elements within the chain. The research mostly tries to answer some links within the framework; for example, research in Islamic banking in Indonesia conducted to explain all links within this framework (Lubis et al. 2015). However, little explanation has been provided about this framework, especially in the context of Indonesian small-scale enterprises (SMEs). This research aims to propose the service-performance chain model to be applied in Indonesian SMEs in the modern retailer sector.

2 LITERATURE REVIEW

There are two kinds of customers, internal and external customer (Hauser et al. 1996, Piercy 1995). Internal customers must have their needs met before they can provide service to external customer satisfaction (Berry 1981). A previous study suggested that employee job satisfaction is positively related to employee perception of internal service quality (Schlesinger & Zornitsky 1991). Other studies found that external customer satisfaction is the reflection of the internal customer satisfaction (Reynoso 1994), and there are positive associations among customer retention, employee satisfaction, and internal service quality (Conduit & Mavondo 2001). Meanwhile, it

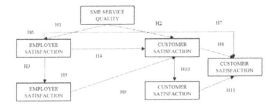

Figure 1. The Conceptual Proposed Model of Research.

was reported that the quality of internal processes, available resources, and recognition support the employee serving ability (Newman et al. 2001).

Previous studies suggested the link between employee loyalty and employee satisfaction (Griffeth et al. 2000, Wangenheim 2007). Some studies found a relationship between employee job satisfaction and customer satisfaction (Koys 2001, Brown & Lam 2008). Other studies found that a friendly service worker produces more customer satisfaction than an unfriendly service worker (Hennig-Thurau et al. 2006, Soderlund & Rosengren 2008).

While some studies established a strong relationship between customer satisfaction and customer loyalty (e.g., McDougall & Levesque 2000), others previous studies reported positive correlations between customer satisfaction and retention, loyalty, and word of mouth (Mittal & Kamakura 2001, Parasuraman et al. 1988). Other studies suggested that enterprises that stressed the weight of internal service quality tended to have better achievements such as growth rates and financial performance (Lau & May 1998, Lau 2000). Another study indicates it is necessary for an enterprise not only to integrate complementary paths in this framework, but also to maximize employee satisfaction and external service quality to optimize business performance (Hogreve 2017).

3 METHODOLOGY

The research process began with studying previous studies. Focus group discussions and in-depth interviews were conducted to confirm measurable indicators in Indonesian context. The focus group discussions involved customers and employees of the SME was held in different sessions. The in-depth interviews with managers who involved in associations of Indonesian SME were conducted in several sessions. All participants were related to the small sized modern retail sectors such as Alfamart, Indomaret and Yomart, in the Province of West Java, Indonesia.

4 PROPOSED MODEL

Based on those studies, a conceptual model of this research as seen on Figure 1 and proposition are proposed as follows. Theoretical propositions are derived to explain the links within the model proposed.

Data about profitability and growth were not accessible in most of Indonesian SMEs. This is not only in regards to the 'non-trust business society environment' and tight competition, but also most Indonesian SMEs have no accountable financial report yet. These are the reasons why in this research the profitability and revenue growth variables, as part of a service-profit chain, could not be measured by financial performance data as having been previously done in other study (Xu & van der Heijden 2005, Keiningham 2006).

In-depth interviews with several associations of Indonesian SMEs on preliminary research have discussed a possible measurement on SME performance, as a proxy of profitability and growth in the original chain.

The link in the proposed model explained by these propositions.

H1: SME Service Quality positively correlated with Employee Satisfaction.
H2: SME Service Quality positively correlated with Customer Satisfaction.
H3: Employee Satisfaction positively correlated with Employee Loyalty.
H4: Employee Satisfaction positively correlated with Customer Satisfaction.
H5: Employee Loyalty mediates the positive relationship between Employee Satisfaction with Customer Satisfaction.
H6: Employee Satisfaction positively correlated with SME Performance.
H7: Customer Satisfaction mediates the positive relationship between Employee Satisfaction with SME Performance.
H8: Customer Satisfaction positively correlated with SME Performance.
H9: Customer Loyalty mediates the positive relationship between Customer Satisfaction with SME Performance.
H10: Customer Satisfaction positively correlated with Customer Loyalty.
H11: Customer Loyalty positively correlated with SME Performance.

5 CONCLUSION

The research framework for investigating the chain from the service to business performance is required. This research adopted the service-profit chain as a research framework. It helped explain the role of service performance to business performance in the context of SMEs in Indonesia (Figure1). The propositions developed from an interpretation of preliminary findings and contextual theory were formulated into a two stages research framework using the case research method. The first stage will be applied to one sector which is small sized of modern retail sector which will be followed with multiple case study to grasp a comprehensive understanding.

REFERENCES

Berry, L.L. 1981. The Employee as Customer. *Journal of Retail Banking* 3(1): 33-40.
Brown, S.P. & Lam, S.K. 2008. A Meta Analysis of Relationships Linking Employee Satisfaction to Customer Responses. *Journal of Retailing* 84(3): 243-255.
Conduit, J. & Mavondo, F.T. 2001. How Critical is Internal Customer Orientation to Market Orientation?. *Journal of Business Research* 51(1): 11-24.

Griffeth, R., Hom, P. & Gaertner, S. 2000. A Meta Analysis of Antecedents and Correlates of Employee Turnover: Update, Moderator Tests, and Research Implications for the Next Millennium. *Journal of Management* 18(3): 463-488.

Hauser, J., Simester, D., & Wernerfelt, B. 1996. Internal Customer and Internal Suppliers. *Journal of Marketing Resourse* 33(3): 268-280.

Hennig-Thurau, T, Groth, M., Paul, M. & Gremler, D.D. 2006. Are All Smiles Created Equal? How Emotional Contagion and Emotional Labour Effect Service Relationships. *Journal of Marketing* 70: 58-73.

Heskett, J.L., Jones, T.O, Loveman, G.W., Sasser, W.E. Jr., Schlesinger, L.A. 1994. Putting the Service Profit Chain to Work. *Harvard Business Review* 72(2): 164-174.

Hogreve, J., Iseke, A., Derfuss, K., & Eller, T. 2017. The Service–Profit Chain: A Meta-Analytic Test of a Comprehensive Theoretical Framework. *Journal of Marketing* 81(3): 41-61.

Kamakura, W.A., Mittal, V., de Rosa, F., Mazzon, J.A. 2002. Assessing the Service-Profit Chain. *Marketing Science* 21(3): 294-317.

Keiningham, T.L., Aksoy, L., Cooil, B., Peterson, K., Vavra, T.G. 2006. A Longitudinal Examination of the Asymmetric Impact of Employee and Customer Satisfaction on Retail Sales. *Managing Service Quality* 16(5): 442-459.

Koys, D.J. 2001. The Effects of Employee Satisfaction, Organizational Citizenship Behavior, and Turnover on Organizational Effectivennes: A Unit-Level, Longitudinal Study. *Personnel Psychology* 54(1): 101-114.

Lau, R.S.M., May, B.E. 1998. A Win-Win Paradigm for Quality of Work Life and Business Performance. *Human Resource Development Quarterly* 9(3): 211-226.

Lau, R.S.M. 2000. Quality of Work Life and Performance – An Investigation of Two Key Elements in the Service Profit Chain Model. *International Journal of Service Industry Management* 11(5): 422–437.

Lubis, P.H., Sucherly, A.R., & Kaltum, U. 2015. Implementing Service Profit Chain at Islamic Banking, *International Journal of Economics, Commerce and Management* 3(6): 1271-1292.

McDougall, G.H. & Levesque, T. 2000. Customer satisfaction with Service: Putting Perceived Value Into the Equation. *Journal of Services Marketing* 14(5): 392-410.

Mittal, V. & Kamakura, A. 2001. Satisfaction, Repurchase Intent, and Repurchase Behavior: Investigating the Moderating Effect of Customer Characteristics. *Journal of Marketing Research* 38: 131-142.

Newman, K., Maylor, U. & Chansarkar, B. 2001. The Nurse Retention, Quality of Care and Patient Satisfaction Chain. *International Journal of Health Care Quality Assurance* 14(2): 57-68.

Parasuraman, A., Zeithaml, V.A. & Berry, L.L. 1988. SERVQUAL: A Multiple-item Scale for Measuring Consumer Perceptions of Service Quality. *Journal of Retailing* 64(1): 12-40.

Piercy, N.F. 1995. Customer Satisfaction and the Internal Market - Marketing Our Customers to Our Employees. *Journal of Marketing Practice: Applied Marketing Science* 1(1): 22-44.

Reynoso, J. 1994. Development of a Multiple-item Scale for Measuring Internal Service Quality in Hospitals. In *the 3rd International Seminar on Service Management & Marketing, Aix-en Provence, 24-27 May.*

Schlesinger, L.A. & Zornitsky, J. 1991. Job Satisfaction, Service Capability, and Customer Satisfaction: An Examination of Linkages and Management Implications. *Human Resource Planning* 14: 141-149.

Silvestro, R. & Cross, S. 2000. Applying the Service Profit Chain in a Retail Environment: Chalenging the Satisfaction Mirror. *International Journal of Service Industry Management* 11(3): 244-268.

Soderlund, M. & Rosengren, S. 2008. Revisiting the Smiling Service Worker and Customer Satisfaction. *International Journal of Service Industry Management* 19(5): 552-574.

Wangenheim, F.V., Evanschitzky, H. & Wunderlich, M. 2007. The Employee-customer Satisfaction Link: Does it Hold for All Employee Groups?. *Journal of Business Research* 60(7): 690-697.

Xu, Y. & van der Heijden, B. 2005. The Employee Factor in the Service-Profit Chain Framework. *Journal of International Consumer Marketing* 18(1): 137-155.

Xu, Y. & Goedegebuure, R. 2005. Employee Satisfaction and Customer Satisfaction: Testing the Service-Profit Chain in a Chinese Securities Firm. *Innovative Marketing* 1(2): 49-59.

Yee, R.W.Y., Yeung, A.C.L. & Cheng, T.C.E. 2011. The Service-profit Chain: An Empirical Analysis in High-contact Service Industries. *International Journal Production Economics* 130: 236-245.

Entepreneurship

Global Competitiveness: Business Transformation in the
Digital Era – Abdullah, Widiaty & Abdullah (eds)
© 2019 Taylor & Francis Group, London, ISBN 978-0-367-19442-0

Creativity in capital management by young entrepreneurs in West Java SMEs

I. Barlian & E.M. Manurung
Parahyangan Catholic University, Bandung, Indonesia

ABSTRACT: The resilience of small- and medium-scale businesses during the economic crisis is no longer doubted. While other companies with large capital collapsed due to the crisis, small and medium-scale businesses actually survived and were persistent to run. The research is a continuation of previous research which was conducted in 2014–2015 on several small- and medium enterprises in West Java. The previous research was conducted using mixed-method, while this research was conducted in 2016–2017 with qualitative method using case study. Several in-depth interviews and observations have been carried out on five young entrepreneurs in Bandung who are mostly students. Their major business sectors are fashion and culinary. Bourdieu's theory of capital was used to analyze the findings. The results showed that financial capital and good bookkeeping were necessary for business development. Each young entrepreneur shows a different way of managing their finance creatively. The same factors which are key to their success are not profit-money-oriented only, but they are more concerned with networking which is social capital. In addition, mastery of smartphone usage and social media to win the competition is an absolute requirement to sustain their businesses.

1 INTRODUCTION

Entrepreneurship is becoming an important issue in many countries to support economic development. The same phenomenon happened in Java, one of the regions with most dense population in Indonesia. Young entrepreneurs are classified as young people between age 17 and 39 years. Based on the statement given by Mayor of Bandung city, Mr. Ridwan Kamil, especially in Bandung city, they occupy 60% of the total population.

Some research was conducted to see how young entrepreneurs enhance the regional economic development. The first research was done by Dash & Kaur (2012) in Orissa, India. They found that entrepreneurship by young people in recent years has managed to boost competition and improve economic development in that area. Dash and Kaur findings showed some reasons behind entrepreneurship increase by young people, on the obstacles and challenges that hinder or motivate young people to start their business, as well as on assessment of their performance.

A similar study was also conducted by Baker (2008) in the article "Fostering a Global Youth Spirit of Enterprise". Baker describes the challenges faced by young unemployed people and how young people deal with these challenges. Baker examined the possibility of collaboration between public and private sectors to achieve social and economic changes. Entrepreneurship among young people is rarely explored; even policies and programs are often made

to be applied to all. The emergence of entrepreneurship by young people is caused by, for example, the high unemployment among young people and social gap between them. Bell et al. (2004) also found that traditional firm in the UK can be an internalization firm with knowledge-intensiveness as business strategy. This research looks at creativity of young entrepreneurs in Java in managing the capital, how financial capital matters, and what kind of capital needs for ongoing business.

Small- and medium-scale businesses play important role for economic development, absorb enough numbers of labors, contribute to GDP and development, and increase social welfare. It can be said that small- and medium-scale businesses are the labor organizers. They not only serve in monetary aspect, their contribution serves as innovation driving force in business. In an article entitled "*Small Business Administration and Small Business Innovation Research Program*", in 2006, it was stated that small- and medium-scale businesses could be seen in the development of national security, progress and maintenance of healthcare, data improvement, and information management.

Some other research regarding the role of financial capital in small- and medium-scale family business was explained in the following. Rogoff & Heck (2003) defined family as "oxygen" that ignited the "fire" of entrepreneurship in business. Without the time from the family members, talent, and common property, some family businesses will be possibly failed to reach their success.

On the other hand, Hanlon & Saunders (2007) found that the businessmen who joined family business would also rely on friendship as much as they depended on their family. The biggest support is provided by family and closest friends in the form of attentions, emotions, and actions that will encourage them. It is clear that resources owned by business owners are not limited to economic or financial capital, but also human capital, social capital, and cultural capital.

This research is a continuation from that previous research to seek how young and creative entrepreneurs manage their capital to sustain their businesses in the era of digitalization. The previous study in 2014–2016 by Barlian (2013) showed some results as follows: (i) Bandung as cosmopolitan city made by Dutch then developed into a city of students, city of tourism, and now city of creativity of young people, (ii) many communities developing in Bandung ranging from fashion lovers, movie lovers, food lovers, and so forth, (iii) those communities have triggered the creation of some businesses in Bandung initiated by young entrepreneurs, (iv) creative industries grew rapidly in Bandung and its surroundings which started from amateurs toward professionals, some young entrepreneurs are even capable of selling their products abroad, (v) many of those new businesses by young entrepreneurs need huge capital and funding.

This research is different from any other research on young entrepreneur's topic. The study is not focused on how the role of young entrepreneurs is enhancing regional economic, but it is more focused and emphasized on how they manage their creativity in capital management using Bourdieu's capital framework. This research aimed to seek the answers of two questions, namely, Will small- and medium-scale businesses in West Java continue to sustain in digital era? Does financial capital still play an important role in business sustainability?

2 THEORITICAL FRAMEWORK

2.1 Creativity

In a research article entitled "Perspectives in Business Anthropology: Cultural Production, Creativity and Constraints" in 2011, Brian Moeran argued that the words "creative" and "creativity" have other different meanings when they attached to the boundaries that work in the creativity. Being creative does not merely mean being innovative, talented, and occurring in an empty space without process. Moeran emphasized that creativity in cultural products is limited by a number of factors and the agreements and has to do with the social system in which the creative process (lasting cultural products) happens.

Creativity is unique, but the impact can be devastating not only to the way-habit-patterns of human life socially, culturally, and politically, but also on the economic growth of the nation. The term *creative* appeared around 2001 when John Howkins argued that new economy has emerged around creative industries controlled by the law of intellectual property such as patent, copyright, trademark, royalties, and design.

The creative era focuses on the creation and exploitation of intellectual property such as works of art, movie and TV programs, software, games, or fashion design. It also includes creative services such as advertising, publishing, and design companies. Creative era arrived in the third millennium wave which was characterized by increased prosperity and by emerging new needs to find meaning in experiencing and consuming goods/services. Design workers are now replacing the knowledge workers to produce goods and services with full meaning and uniqueness (Simatupang 2007).

Gartner (2001) and Low (2001) explained entrepreneurship process which includes all functions, activities, and actions related to the opportunity and creating organization to reach the opportunity. Zimmerer (1997) also defined entrepreneurship as one who creates a new business in the face of risk and uncertainty for the purpose of achieving profit and growth by identifying opportunities and assembling the necessary resources to capitalize on them.

2.2 Capital

Pierre Bourdieu, a French sociologist, offered ideas of capital which were not only limited to financial habitus, and so on. Capital, in Bourdieu's theory, was a broad definition. Capital in Bourdieu's theory was not limited to material objects, but also intangible ownership. Capital became a meaning of a field. Capital acted as social relation in exchange system. Capital also meant as domination basis for Bourdieu, even though it was not always known by the participants. Some types of capital could not be exchanged with other types of capital (inconvertible). Capitals with the highest level of conversion, or powerful, were types of capital that could be converted into symbolic capital. Symbolic capital provided legitimation (legitimate authority) to someone regarding their class and status.

There were four types of capital influencing the society in determining the power related to social relationships and social gaps; they were (i) *material capital*, (ii) *social capital*, (iii) *cultural capital*, and (iv) *symbolic capital*. The structure of this capital formed a structure of social environment based on differentiation and distribution. The actors and groups of people were defined by their position based on the size of owned capital and the composition weight of the whole capital.

Material capital showed the ownership of economic sources, while social capital was the network of social relation owned by someone that could be beneficial in determining the reproduction of its social stance (used in mobilizing his/her interest). Cultural capital had several dimensions; they were: objective knowledge, taste and preference, formal qualification (such as degree), cultural skills such as writing skills, language skills, politeness, communication skills, and practical skills (such as playing music).

Symbolic capital showed the owner's high status, authority, and prestige. For example, the inherited good reputation, luxurious car with its chauffer, ways of making guest to wait, and so on. Another example is the position in a career (Director, Minister, Lecturer) that referred and explained the activity and group name.

Out of the four types of capital, material capital and cultural capital were the determining types of capital in the most relevant differentiation criteria in advanced society. Material capital was the easiest type of capital to be converted into other types of capital. In every kind of struggle condition or social condition, the existence of material capital would be highly needed and impossible to deny. However, if it's compared to other capitals, the conversion of capital with the highest authoritative level was the symbolic capital. Among various kinds of capital forms, symbolic capital was perceived and recognized as the legitimate one that received recognition and was accepted by the public.

Someone's condition on that day, either in business or other conditions, was determined by habitus. Habitus was the formed disposition and they were continually formed through someone's background and experience from time to time. The center of attitude was the idea of habitus. Some experts defined habitus as:

"Habitus refers to a set of dispositions, created and reformulated through the conjuncture of objective structures and personal history. Dispositions are acquired in social positions within a field and imply a subjective adjustment to that position" (Harker et al. 2016).

"A system of durable, transposable disposition, structured structure predisposed to function as structuring structure which is the principle which generates and organizes practice and representation that can be objectively adapted to its outcomes without presupposing a conscious aim at the end or an express mastery of the necessary operation in order to attain it" (Swartz, 1994).

Habitus is a system that can last long, change dispositions, and act as structured structures that function as structuring structures (principles of generalization and practice of creation). For example, attitudes and patterns of one's mind and adjustments to these attitudes are sometimes included in views, thought patterns, and even reflected through his posture. This affects one's position and habitus which is formed through friendship, professional experience, love, and other personal relationships.

In the process of a person acquiring abilities in their life, skills are trained and structures are shifted into forming new structures. Artists, pianists, writers or thinkers, or other professionals can only create brilliant and creative works after experiencing the process of reflecting on the standard skills of their profession. A person can begin to develop his/her abilities and potential only after being processed in his professional experience.

3 RESEARCH METHOD: CASE STUDIES

The research was conducted in qualitative method, using case studies combined with some interviews with young entrepreneurs in West Java.

From previous research, it was found that the two largest sectors were engaged by young entrepreneurs, namely fashion and culinary. From a total of 388 respondents of previous research, 50 young entrepreneurs were invited to focus on group discussion in 2016–2017. The result of discussion shows that every entrepreneur has his uniqueness to manage his creativity.

During 2016–2017, five young student entrepreneurs came in to ask for help. They needed some training in financial recording. While providing training in finance, the research continued to observe how these young entrepreneurs manage their capital in line with the development and expansion of their businesses. Their business field varies, such as fashion accessories, design in event organizer, and culinary. During the training, some reports of financial transactions were summarized and explained in Tables 1–7.

3.1 *"B-Meatball": Culinary business in Jakarta*

B-Meatball was a family business established by a university student. Previously, the owner and his family had tried to engage in fashion field by producing bags, but the business failed. As the business only ran for nine months, the owner served as the owner and manager. By employing simple financial record, the business which had been recently established started to show its profit. Even though there was still no financial report such as cash flow, they knew the exact number of money they had and the cost they made for each month. On August 2015, the owner planned to buy a storehouse to open a new branch, as an expansion of the business they had. The owner did not need huge capital to run the business due to the workshop located in his own house. B-Meatball Loss and Profit Report during 2015–2016 is presented in Figure 1.

3.2 *"YY": Ricebox in Bandung*

YY was a boxed meal culinary business established by a student and her husband with their siblings. The business started from her hobby in cooking and having culinary travel to various regions in Indonesia and overseas. The owner wanted to serve complete meal for employees in office who did not have much time to have lunch. Her strategy was to pack

Table 1. Revenue and expense of —B-Meatball.

	2015		2016					
	Nov (Rp)	Dec (Rp)	Jan (Rp)	Feb (Rp)	Mar (Rp)	Apr (Rp)	May (Rp)	Jun (Rp)
Income	85,800,000	117,000,000	128,700,000	168,750,000	168,750,000	128,700,000	172,500,000.00	89,700,000.00
Raw Material Costs								
Bakso Urat	1,200,000	1,600,000	1,760,000	1,760,000	1,600,000	1,760,000	2,000,000	1,040,000
Bakso Daging	1,500,000	2,000,000	2,200,000	2,200,000	2,000,000	2,200,000	2,500,000	1,300,000
Bakso Urat Besar	300,000	420,000	350,000	450,000	480,000	540,000	750,000	264,000
Mie Telor	300,000	400,000	440,000	440,000	400,000	440,000	500,000	260,000
Mie Tepung	187,500	250,000	275,000	275,000	250,000	275,000	312,500	162,500
Bihun	112,500	150,000	165,000	165,000	150,000	165,000	187,500	97,500
Garam	150,000	200,000	220,000	220,000	200,000	220,000	250,000	130,000
Merica	277,500	370,000	407,000	407,000	370,000	407,000	462,000	240,500
Sawi	240,000	320,000	352,000	352,000	320,000	253,000	400,000	208,000
Seledri	150,000	200,000	220,000	220,000	200,000	220,000	250,000	130,000
Tulang Sapi	300,000	400,000	440,000	440,000	400,000	440,000	500,000	260,000
Bumbu Kuah	225,000	300,000	330,000	330,000	300,000	330,000	375,000	195,000
Cabai	330,000	440,000	484,000	484,000	440,000	484,000	550,000	286,000
Saos Sambal	15,000	20,000	22,000	22,000	20,000	22,000	25,000	13,000
Bawang Goreng	150,000	200,000	220,000	220,000	200,000	220,000	250,000	130,000
Ayam	1,140,000	1,520,000	1,672,000	1,672,000	1,520,000	1,672,000	1,900,000	988,000
Minyak	114,000	152,000	167,200	167,200	152,000	167,200	190,000	98,800
Profit	79,108,500	108,058,000	118,965,800	127,455,800	159,748,000	118,785,800	161,097,500	83,895,700
Biaya Gaji	9,500,000	9,500,000	9,500,000	10,400,000	10,400,000	10,400,000	10,400,000	10,400,000
Biaya Listrik	750,000	750,000	750,000	750,000	750,000	750,000	750,000	750,000
Biaya Gas	1,500,000	1,500,000	1,500,000	1,650,000	1,650,000	1,650,000	1,650,000	1,300,000
Biaya Marketing	255,000	1,250,000	1,000,000	2,500,000	1,000,000	875,000	1,500,000	450,000
Total Biaya	12,005,000	12,000,000	15,200,000	15,300,000	13,800,000	13,675,000	14,300,000	12,900,000
Net Profit	67,103,500	106,215,800	106,215,800	112,155,800	145,948,000	105,110,800	146,797,500	70,996,700

Source: B-Meatballl, 2016.

the lunch in a box. Table 2 shows the financial and sales record of YY in 2015–2016.

The product sale was carried out by two means, namely store (restaurant) and exhibition (event).

Table 2. Sales target and achievement of —YY (2015–2016).

No	Month & Year	Target	Achieved (✓), or, Not (✗)
1	October 2014	*Sales* target 5 *box* per day	✓
2	November 2014	*Sales* target 5 *box* per day	✓
		Event 50 box per day	✓
3	December 2014	*Sales* target 10 *box* per day;	✗
		Event 50 *box* per day; and	✓
		New Store	✓
4	January 2015	*Sales* target 15 *box* per day in *store* 1; 5 *box* per day in store 2	✗
		Event 75 *box per* day	✓
5	February 2015	*Sales* target 15 *box* per day in *store* 1 and 5 *box* per day store 2	✓ ✓
6	March 2015	*Sales* target 20 *box* per day in *store* 1 and 10 *box* per day in *store* 2	✗ ✗
7	April 2015	*Sales* target 30 *box* per day in *store* 1 and *Event* 100 *box/* day	✓ ✓
8	Mei 2015	*Sales* target 30 *box* per day in *store* 1 and *Event* 125 *box/* day	✗ ✓
9	June 2015	*Sales* target 30 *box* per day in *store* 1	✓
10	July 2015	*Sales* target 30 *box* per day in *store* 1 and *Event* 130 *box* per day	✗ ✓
11	August 2015	*Sales* target 35 *box* per day in *store* 1 and *Event* 140 *box/* day	✓ ✓
12	September 2015	*Sales* target 35 *box* per day in *store* 1 and *Event* 140 *box/* day	✓ ✓
13	October 2015	*Sales* target 35 *box* per day in *store* 1 and *New Work Shop*	✓ ✓
14	November 2015	*Sales* target 35 *box* per day and *Event* 150 *box per day*	✗ ✓
15	December 2015	*Sales* target 35 *box* per day and *Event* 150 *box per day*	✗ ✓
16	January 2016	*Sales* target 35 *box* per day	✗
17	February 2016	*Sales* target 35 *box* per day and *Event* 150 *box* per day	✗ ✓
18	March 2016	*Sales* target 40 *box* per day and *New Store*	✗ ✓

Source: YY, 2016.

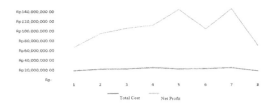

Figure 1. Loss/Profit obtained in 2015–2016. Source: B-Meatball, 2016.

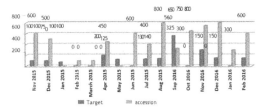

Figure 2. Graphic of —YY sales through store and events. (Source: —YY, 2016).

Sometimes, sales from event were more obtained than sales from store, as shown in Figure 2.

It could be seen that the sale achievement of YY was proven to be more maximum and exceeded its sales target if an event or exhibition was held than in-store (restaurant) sales. The owner admitted that her business required quite huge amount of capital and financing at the beginning, due to material and equipment purchases and employee training. However, she also believed that the business would not run without her brilliant idea of how to put rice, vegetables, and meat in a simple box to eat and good promotion through exhibition.

3.3 *"SP": Event organizer in Bandung*

SP was a creative service in organizing surprise events (birthday, wedding anniversary, etc.), which was established by some university students, S and friends. For approximately eight months organizing the business, the income of SP is as presented in Table 3.

The income for the end of 2015–2016 was still not significantly huge. The owner only did simple recording of his business. This business was considered as a quite interesting one because as the owner and manager, S almost did not need a starting capital since all of the incurred fees were covered by the customers who usually gave downpayment (approximately half of the price) prior to ordering the service.

3.4 *"CC accessories": Fashion business in Cirebon and Bandung*

CC Accessories was a business on manufactured handmade cellphone case, tablet phone case, and so on by D and his sister. The sale record for the last six months in 2015 is presented in Table 4.

Table 3. —SP Income.

No.	Date	Event	Total Cost
1	Nov 25, 2015	Birthday Dinner Couple	IDR 1.250.000
2	Dec 15,	Surprise Birthday	900.000
3	Jan 14, 2016	Wedding Anniversary	1.250.000
4	Jan 29,	Birthday	1.250.000
5	Feb 2,	Birthday	1.250.000
6	Feb 16,	Birthday	1.250.000
7	March 15,	Birthday	1.250.000
8	March 27,	Birthday	1.250.000
9	April 26,	Birthday Dinner Couple	1.500.000

Source: SP, 2016.

Table 4. CC evaluation of sales achievement (2015).

No.	Description	July	August	Sept	Oct	Nov	Dec
1	Production	✓	✗	✗	✓	✓	✓
2	Product Variation	✓	✗	✗	✓	✓	✓
3	Marketing				✓	✓	✓
4	Marketing Area						✓
5	Selling				✗	✗	✓
6	Article	✓			✓	✓	✓
7	Carftsmen	✓					
8	Supplier	✗					
9	Design	✓					

Source: CC, 2015.

The data of product sold in units could be seen in Table 5.

The table of inventory shows that there are still plenty of inventories to make the products. CC products seem to take time to increase awareness and need more branding strengthening. In the first three months, this business requires quite large financing for material inventory. Since the production was still conducted by the owner, it seemed that CC did not add more financial capital in the near future. If there are more orders in the future, the owner will ask for for 50% downpayment at the beginning of production process to prevent liquidity difficulties.

3.5 "PS Veil": Hijab store in Subang and Serang

PS Veil was a hijab store business established by P and S with their family.

In the early stages of production, the owner plans to produce a minimum of 15 products with the consideration that they still need to make some adjustments to market conditions, consumer preferences, models, and so on. Production continued in March 2015 until November 2016. Based on the inventory

Table 5. Merchandise inventory of product 2015

Month	Beginning balance	Sold	Ending balance
October, 2015	30	10	20
November, 2015	50	4	46
December, 2015	76	38	38

Source: CC, 2015.

Table 6. PS Veil Selling Achievement (2015–2016).

No	Description	Target	Mar	Apr	Nov	Dec	Jan–Mar
1	Production	15–50 pcs/ month	✓	✗	✓	✗	✗
2	Variation	Auare hijab, pashmina hijab, cover inner hijab.	✓	✗	✓	✗	✗
3	Marketing	Instagram, Line, Twitter, Event, Shop	✓	✗	✓	✓	✓
4	Selling	100% per month	✓	✗	✓	✗	✗
5	Employee	1–2 people	✓	✗	✓	✓	✓
6	Supplier	Textile shop	✓	✗	✓	✗	✗

Source: PS Veill, 2016.

Table 7. Inventory 2015

Month	Stock, beginning	Production	Selling	Stock, ending
March 2015	0	25	5	20
April–October	20	0	0	20
November	20	15	29	6

Source: —PS Veill, 2016.

tables, the sales have not reached the expected target so there will be more promotions to increase awareness and branding.

Because there are still some stocks left in November 2015, the remaining stock is sent to HD Cloth in Serang, Banten for sale.

There seems to be no sales during April–October 2015. PS Veil products have a simple model. The veil design is suitable for modern children. The choice of material does not feel hot when used and is comfortable to do many activities. The veil design with limited stocks make PS Veil products unique.

The weakness of the PS Veil business was the fact that the company had no network with other business partners. This was a lack of social capital because products were handled by only one person. The owner targetted products for Muslim women because basically Muslim women are advised to wear a veil. Furthermore, because the product offered was simple, the targeted segment was young people. In the future, market segments need to be expanded to get more customers. One business threat was the number of competitors who have released similar products and they also have creative marketing strategies. The new strategy through several promotional events was a threat because the sales of PS Veil were still done online.

4 CONCLUSION

Five young entrepreneurs in West Java as participants in this study were advised to explore their creativity in managing their capital, especially in this digital era. Most of them only use their smartphones to communicate with the work team but have not used it for marketing. Only "B-Meatball" and "YY Ricebox" have started using smartphones to promote their products via Line and Instagram. Three other businesses only use telephone and text messages to buy materials or production processes. Only "YY Ricebox" serves shipping orders.

Nowadays, young entrepreneurs are not only looking for profit as a result of their investment and financing at the beginning of the business. They want more than profit. They are now looking for more benefits to explore their creativity that will enhance the sustainability of their business and a good reputation for the future.

REFERENCES

Baker, K. 2008. *Fostering a Global Spirit of Youth Enterprise Preparatory Briefing of the Global Forum on Youth Entrepreneurship.*

Barlian, I. 2013. *The Role of Creative Young Entrepreneur for Entrepreneurship Expansion in Bandung.* LPPM Report: UNPAR.

Bell, J., Crick, D. & Young, S. 2004. Small firm internationalization and business strategy: an exploratory study of 'knowledge-intensive'and 'traditional'manufacturing firms in the UK. *International Small business journal* 22(1): 23-56.

Dash, M. & Kaur, K. 2012. Youth entrepreneurship as a way of boosting Indian economic competitiveness: A study of Orissa. *International Review of Management and Marketing* 2(1): 10-21.

Gartner, W.B. 2001. Is there an elephant in entrepreneurship? Blind assumptions in theory development. *Entrepreneurship Theory and practice* 25(4): 27-39.

Hanlon, D. & Saunders, C. 2007. Marshaling resources to form small new ventures: Toward a more holistic understanding of entrepreneurial support. *Entrepreneurship Theory and Practice* 31(4): 619-641.

Harker, R., Mahar, C. & Wilkes, C. (eds) 2016. *An introduction to the work of Pierre Bourdieu: The practice of theory.* Springer.

Low, M.B. 2001. The adolescence of entrepreneurship research: specification of purpose. *Entrepreneurship theory and practice* 25(4): 17-26.

Rogoff, R. & Heck, H. 2003. Evolving Research in Entrepreneurship and Family Business: Recognising Family as The Oxygen that Feeds the Fire of Entrepreneurship. *Journal of Business Venturing*, Elsevier.

Simatupang, T.M. 2007. *Industri Kreatif Jawa Barat. Bahan Masukan Kepada Dinas Perindustrian dan Perdagangan Provinsi Jawa Barat.*

Schwartz, H. 1994. Small states in big trouble: State reorganization in Australia, Denmark, New Zealand, and Sweden in the 1980s. *World Politics* 46(4): 527-555.

Zimmerer, K.S. 1997. *Changing fortunes: Biodiversity and peasant livelihood in the Peruvian Andes (Vol. 1).* Univ of California Press.

Global Competitiveness: Business Transformation in the
Digital Era – Abdullah, Widiaty & Abdullah (eds)
© 2019 Taylor & Francis Group, London, ISBN 978-0-367-19442-0

Critical study of business models of music education in the context of hyper-competition

S. Setiadi & S. Dwikardana
Magister Administrasi Bisnis, Universitas Katolik Parahyangan, Bandung, Indonesia

ABSTRACT: At present, competition in the music education business in Indonesia, especially Bandung, can be categorized as a hyper-competition condition characterized by competition that has gone crazy. The competitive advantages of each company are irrelevant because of the aggressive and innovative movements of competitors. The purpose of this study is to see the assumption that under hyper-competition conditions, businesses will be very difficult to compete if they do not have good competitive advantages, including in the music education business in Bandung. By examining 3 business models in Bandung, namely local school model, course model, and international certification model, this study found that despite the hyper-competition conditions, each of these music school businesses still survives because of the different adjustment factors of consumer needs. This is different from the hyper-competition theory assumption which states that the possibility of a business not surviving if it does not form a new strategy and top management cannot see the changes in market direction that occur, thereby reducing the flexibility of changes is needed in hyper-competition.

1 INTRODUCTION

In the music education business, there is a rapidly changing environment, so that to become a market leader in this fast-changing environment, business people must determine the right strategy, especially in hyper-competition conditions, because competition will usually not survive in this condition, thus demanding companies to think more. According to Murthy in his research, it is very difficult to survive in a hyper-competition situation where the worst companies can go bankrupt or experience a drastic decline in income. Therefore, to determine the strategy, Murthy points out that there is top management awareness about current competitive conditions and current markets that can determine competitive advantage with information seeking, information diagnosis, and behavioral choices (Murthy 2014). These are all aimed at answering strategic problems, where the success alone is a change from top manager cognition (Shang et al. 2010), where competitive strategies relate to questions about how to create competitive advantage in each business and the units in which companies compete (Salavou 2015). This strategy can also be enhanced by competitiveness potential that offers two basic strategies for survival by maintaining strength in a well-known business environment and progress secure all possibilities in the future.

On the other hand, three sets of strategy development ment tools are proposed for competitive market analysis. The principle underlying strategic action is

that companies must try to disrupt their own benefits and those of competitors. There are four analyzes that look at how competition accumulates in each of the fields below to identify patterns and predict future strategic actions. The areas of analysis are Cost and Quality, Timing and Know-how, Strong-holds, and deep pockets (D'Aveni 2010), and also use a 7-S framework (adapted from the McKinsey framework by D'Aveni) which proposes a series of hypercompetitive approaches to harmonizing strategy. The objective is to develop strategies in three categories, namely vision for disruption – creating temporary advantage, capabilities for disruption – sustaining competitive momentum, tactics for disruption – maintaining the equilibrium.

The hyper-competition concept and the above theory can help us mapping the existing market competition. Some studies that have used the hyper-competition concept found that competitive advantage has no effect if it is not adaptive to the existing changes. However, this study shows that despite the imbalance of power among education business, the models still survive and even grow in this hyper-competition situation.

The study of hyper-competition like Murphy, Salavou, and also D'Aveni has an assumption that if competing in hyper-competition market is very hard, it requires a lot of effort from top management and will not be able to survive if it does not have sufficient competitive advantage. On the other hand, this study found a different result that is even though under hyper-competition conditions, each of these music school businesses persisted. They have their own strengths and weaknesses and can be an initial reflection of the difference strategy in each model to compete.

The aim of this study is to answer the question: Does the company in the music education business residing in the hypercompetitive business environment have a particular model that enables them to survive and continue to innovate and create new competitive advantages? Or a hypercompetitive situation does not require companies to have a particular business model as such model can potentially make the company become less innovative and inflexible particularly in creating competitive advantage? Thus, from this research, we can learn what model or strategy has been taken by the companies is what that make them able to compete and continue to survive.

2 RESEARCH METHOD

This study evaluates three business models, namely Efata Cantata-Trinity College (open system model), Yamaha (closed system model), and Do to do Music Edutaiment (local model) to find out how they survive in business competition in the same market share and also in hyper-competition. The following is a hyper-competition framework used to identify strategic actions and patterns of competition among business models.

This framework explains that in the hyper-competition situation, it is required for a company to have awareness from Top Management that can produce the best survival strategy as well as necessary advancement. This strategy coupled with top management cognition will be split into four arenas of analysis. But in this case, the strategy will be more focused on the arena, which becomes a strategy to generate enterprise performance.

The research method is done qualitatively with data collection technique through in-depth iinterview and a six-month observation with Owner of Efata Cantata-Trinity College; Owner of Do to Do Music Edutaiment; and Owner of Yahama Music School Mekar Wangi. Data analysis for this research uses triangulation. The multiple perspective was also obtained from in-depth interview with customers (parents & students) as a user of music education business. Data triangulation involves using different sources of information to increase the validity of a study (Patton 2002).

Figure 1. Hyper-competition framework.

3 RESULTS

From this research, in terms of the map, there are three types of business models, namely: Open System; Half System; and Closed System. On the one hand, the business model of Local music education embraces Open system, which is characterized by the ability to maintain the flexibility side so that it can adjust to the willingness of consumers; on the other hand, other schools cannot provide it, they survive because the investment is not too large, and the cost of payroll is based on the number of students. In contrast, music schools like Trinity with embraced Half System can survive because of the name of the Centre of Trinity College, and as it offers the level of education of formal music up to S3 level, which cannot be given by other music schools, and do not spend much investment because it emphasizes on cooperation that benefits both parties.

The strengths of Yamaha's hyper-competition market winners can be categorized as Closed System models, mastering the flow of music business from upstream to downstream independently, providing all the needs with completeness ranging from musical instrument, internationally qualified teachers, curriculum, to its internationally standardized certification as well. This strength makes consumers feel ease and make Yamaha the winner in the market. Nevertheless, in this study, it is found out that the winner in the hypercompetitive market in the music education business in Indonesia does not necessarily have to "kill" their competitors, even though it is the fact that some competing schools show good development.

Mapping of each music school business with hyper-competition framework as well as the 7-Ss framework (adapted from the McKinsey framework by D'Aveni) is provided in Table 1. This map proposes a set of hypercompetitive approaches to realign strategy. From the tables, it can be concluded that Yamaha seems to be really well prepared with a long-term strategy, which shows that Yamaha has prepared all of the 7-Ss framework and mastered all elements of music from upstream to downstream, which make Yamaha being a leader in the market, but it can be seen that other music school models do not have a strategy like the one by Yamaha still can survive because they answer the needs of customers. This mapping is indeed very necessary to get what is potential and what should be prepared to formulate a strategy in dealing with existing markets.

4 CONCLUSION

In conclusion, the results of the study state that the theory of hyper-competition using the 4 arenas and 7s strategies can only map competition of the existing competition in the business of music education

Table 1. Four areas analysis of Yamaha, Trinity, and local model.

	Yamaha	Trinity	Local
Cost and quality (C–Q)	Offering excellent quality and the price is equivalent to the quality offered	When compared to its competitors, it is still cheaper for the same quality as competitors in the same model business	The quality offered is not as high as Yamaha and Trinity; however, comparing the price offered, it is cheaper
Timing and know-how (T–K)	Very masterful and deep-seated so that mastery is fully controlled from upstream to downstream	Not too concerned about this	Not too concerned about this
Strongholds (S)	Mastering upstream to downstream by maintaining its own brand	Nothing, because similar competitors have what Trinity has	For its uniqueness, mostly puts forward the uniqueness of teachers and curriculum but in reality, one teacher does not teach only in one place, so this cannot be a force that can be imitated by competitors
Deep pockets (D)	The source of funds used is very large and scattered everywhere, as the funds have many sources, especially coupled with the form of business model Yamaha	Has a university so that it will be a source from the university itself	More to the owner's investment directly to the source of funds used

Table 2. 7-Ss Framework of local model, Trinity, and Yamaha

		Local	Trinity	Yamaha
Vision for disruption	Stakeholder satisfaction	-	Raises the school's music brand that works or join it	Convenience for consumers ranges from learning to facilities provided to buying a musical instrument
	Strategic soothsaying	Increases the uniqueness of songs and local music, traditional musical instruments	In collaboration with high-quality local schools	Becomes the ruler of the music industry because it controls from upstream to downstream
Capabilities for disruption	Speed	Low, but flexible as needed	Low	Very highly prepared for the possibility of change
	Surprise	Low, nothing unique and can distribute competitor	Low	Many strategies that greatly disrupt competitors such as the emergence of new cooperation that can enhance the brand YAMAHA
Tactics for disruption	Shifting rules	-		Makes a number of musical instrument innovations that are then offered primarily to the music school students, so Yamaha will benefit from school music through the sales of musical instruments
	Signaling intent of selective strategies	-	-	Yes
	Simultaneous and sequential strategy thrust	-	-	Very attentive and always want to lead the market

in Bandung yet cannot predict companies to remain silent in market competition. The study found that in a highly competitive business environment, the music education business still survives and nothing collapses. Each has a model and excellence because each model can answer specific customer needs. This is in stark contrast to previous research which said that in very tight competition, it would be very difficult to survive and competitive advantage must be replaced.

REFERENCES

D'Aveni, R.A. 2010. *Hyper-competition*. New York: Simon & Schuster.

Murthy, V. 2014. Learning from praxis: How high-profile winners and losers inform business's extant theories on longevity, environment, and adaptation. *World Journal of Entrepreneurship, Management and Sustainable Development* 10(1): 33-47.

Patton, M.Q. 2002. *Qualitative Research & Evaluation Methods. 3rd edition.* Sage Publications, Inc.

Salavou, H.E. 2015. Competitive strategies and their shift to the future. *European Business Review* 27(1): 80-99.

Shang, H., Huang, P. & Guo, Y. 2010. Managerial cognition: the sources of sustainable competitive advantage in hyper-competition: A case study. *Nankai Business Review International* 1(4): 444-459.

Global Competitiveness: Business Transformation in the
Digital Era – Abdullah, Widiaty & Abdullah (eds)
© *2019 Taylor & Francis Group, London, ISBN 978-0-367-19442-0*

The impact of entrepreneurial orientation and business environment towards business performance: Small and medium fashion Moslem industry in Bandung

B.F. Putria & T. Gunawan
Parahyangan Catholic University, Bandung, Indonesia

ABSTRACT: This study aims to investigate the effect of entrepreneurial orientation (EO) and business environment (BE) on business performance (BP). This research will explore the important aspects that may improve the BP of Moslem fashion small and medium enterprises (SMEs) in Bandung. Differently from previous studies, EO and BP were studied separately. In this study, we try to comprehend the collaboration between EO and BP. This study is important to be conducted because it may provide insight for these businesses in dealing with intense competition in Moslem industry. Thus, firms need to understand their position and competitive environment. This is a quantitative study which involves 60 SMEs of Moslem fashion industry in Bandung. The data will be processed by using ordinary least square (OLS). The result of this paper shows that there is a positive relationship between EO and BE, and BP; thus, SMEs must begin to improve EO since, based on research, EO factor greatly influences BP.

1 INTRODUCTION

The fashion industry in the world has evolved and managed to changed people's perception of the prime function of clothing into a way of expressing identity, creating the welfare of creativity, and linking global society (Pratt et al. 2012). Besides, fashion is regarded as a unique reflection of social, cultural, and environmental characteristics and it also plays a crucial role in complementing one's self-image (Azuma & Fernie 2003). The Moslem fashion industry is a creative industry sub-sector that is interesting to be studied in Indonesia. Along with the emergence and development of creative industries in Indonesia, the Moslem fashion industry also emerges as important industry that has great potential to be developed in Indonesia. By the fact, Moslem fashion industry has a very tight competition, especially in Bandung which is known as fashion city in Indonesia.

A general tendency in today's business environment (BE) is the shortening of product and business model life cycles (Hamel 2000). Consequently, the future profit streams from existing operations are uncertain and businesses need to constantly seek out new opportunities. Based on previous studies, we found that one of the factors that may improve firms' performance is through applying entrepreneurial orientation (EO) (Gunawan et al. 2015). Therefore, they may benefit from adopting an "entrepreneurial strategic orientation". This involves a willingness to innovate and rejuvenate market offerings, take risks to try out new and uncertain products, services, and markets, and be more proactive than competitors

toward new marketplace opportunities (Covin & Slevin 1991). EO refers to a firm's strategic orientation, capturing specific entrepreneurial aspects of decision-making styles, methods, and practices. As such, it reflects how a firm operates rather than what it does (Lumpkin & Dess 1996). Miller (1983) summarizes the definition of an entrepreneurial firm as "firm that engages in product market innovation undertakes somewhat risky and proactive ventures". Based on this, several researchers have agreed that EO is a combination of the three dimensions: innovativeness, reactiveness, and risk-taking. Thus, EO involves a willingness to innovate and rejuvenate market offerings, take risks to try out new and uncertain products, services, and markets, and be more proactive than competitors toward new marketplace opportunities. The BE can also affect business performance (BP). In a research, Wispandono (2010) argued that the BE includes factors outside the company that may cause opportunities or threats to the company. Therefore, this study will show whether the EO and BE have a significant effect on BP. The findings of this research will give some contribution to entrepreneurship literature, as well as new views for small and medium business actors in designing business strategy for the future.

2 LITERATURE REVIEW

2.1 *Orientation of entrepreneurship*

Researchers have agreed that EO is a combination of three dimensions: innovation, proactive, and risk-taking. Thus, the entrepreneurial orientation involves a willingness to innovate and rejuvenate market supply, take risks to try uncertain, new, and more proactive products, services and new markets, rather than competitors against new market opportunities (e.g. Covin & Slevin 1991, Miller 1983, Wiklund 1999, Zahra and Covin 1995).

2.2 Business environment

Glueck and Jauch in Wispandono (2010) argued that the BE includes factors outside the company that may cause opportunities or threats to the company. Environmental analysis is defined as the process used by strategic planners to monitor the environmental sector in determining opportunities or threats to the company. Based on the results of research from Wispandono (2010), there are 4 indicators of BE: (1) Business Costs, (2) Availability of Labor, (3) Competitor Level, and (4) Market Dimensions.

2.3 Business performance

Performance is a multidimensional concept. According to Rivai (2004), BP is something that is produced by a company within a certain period with a certain standard. BP is an assessment of the indicators owned. According Hadjimanolis in Ratna Kusumawati (2010), the indicators are: (1) Total Sales, (2) Number of New Products, (3) Amount of Profit. Performance (BP) is at the performance level. The variables in this study were also developed by Lee & Tsang (2001).

2.4 Relationship of entrepreneurial orientation and business environment to business performance

Miller (1983) argues that entrepreneurial-type strategies tend to be more successful when handling customers who are premium on unique innovations and services. This is consistent with a dynamic environment. The dynamic environment is associated with uncertainty height of customers and competitors as well as high levels of market and trend changes industry innovation (Dess & Beard 1984, Miller 1983). In such a dynamic environment where demand continues to shift, opportunities result in abundant firms that should have higher entrepreunerial orientation to pursue new opportunities. Thus, entrepreunerial orientation and BE performance are aligned to be able to work together to change BP. In other words, we would expect the alignment of EO and dynamic environment to have a positive implication on firms performance. Study of Zahra (1993) suggests it is important firms to apply EO in a dynamic growth environment. Thus, we hypothesized:

Hypothesis 1: Orientation entrepreneurship has a significant influence on business performance.
Hypothesis 2: Business environment has a significant influence on business performance.

2.5 Hypothesized research model

Figure 1 shows the conceptual framework that explains the relationships proposed in our hypotheses, depicting how the interplay between EO and BE affects BP.

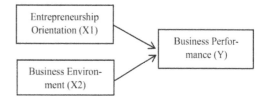

Figure 1. Research Model.

3 RESEARCH METHOD

3.1 Research design and data collection

We collected data in 2018 based on extensive surveys, using questionnaires and interviews with business owners. We selected owners as respondents to this research because they are the souls of small organizations and their "rational analysis" and "creative intuition" are directly reflected in the SME's decision and its performance (Van Gils 2005). We used convenience sampling, because we consider it fast and appropriate to test hypotheses in the initial stages, with 60 owners representing 60 Muslim fashion stores in Pasar Baru Trade Center Bandung taken as sample members. We combed each floor at Pasar Baru Trade Center Bandung and collected contact addresses. We then distributed questionnaires to all Muslim fashion store owners we found, and followed them with interviews.

3.2 Analytical approach

In processing our data, we used validation test of questioner entrepreneurial orientation variable (X1), BE (X2), and company performance (Y), and then we checked the test reliability. This test aims to show errors extending consistent measurement results and multiple regression analysis. Data analysis method used in this research is multiple regression analysis. In relation to this research, independent variables are entrepreneurship orientation (X1), BE (X2), and company performance variable (Y). Then, we also performed hypothesis testing by using F-test, to determine the effect of all independent variables simultaneously to the dependent variable.

4 RESULTS AND DISCUSSION

The results of research and data analysis are obtained by distributing questionnaires to 60 SMEs clothing businessmen in the city of Bandung. The method of data analysis used is descriptive analysis method.

4.1 Analysis descriptive

In this study with the number of respondents as many as 60 companies, the maximum score that may be obtained is $5 \times 60 = 300$ and the minimum score that may be obtained is $1 \times 60 = 60$. If divided into five categories, then the score range of each category is 48.

Interpretation interval amount of respondent response score can be seen in Table 1.

Based on Table 2, it can be seen that the average total score of respondents on statements on variables EO 232.5, BE 218.846, and BP 225, and when referring to the categorization guidelines contained in the interval interpretation table, the number of respondents' scores can be categorized as Agree.

4.2 Test validity and reliability

Validity test result using the correlation of the validity index of the question item is considered valid if the validity of the question index ≥ 0.2108. The reliability test used the Cronbach's alpha method and the result is considered reliable if the reability coefficient is greater than 0.70.

Based on Table 3, all items of question has a validity index greater than 0.2108. It means the questionnaires submitted are all valid and the data can be used for further analysis. Then, the value of reevaluation variable coefficient is greater than 0.70, and thus can be concluded that the questionnaire is reliable.

4.3 Multiple regression analysis

By using SPSS software, the results obtained from multiple linear regression analysis are as follows:

Table 1. Respondents answer recapitulation against variables.

No	Interval	Categories
1	60–108	Very Much Disagree
2	109–156	Disagree
3	157–204	Neutral
4	205–252	Aggre
5	253–300	Very Much Agree

Table 2. Score of respondents.

Means Variable	Total Score
Means Variable EO	232.5
Means Variable BE	218.846
Means Variable BP	225

Table 3. Validity and reliability test results.

Questions	Validity index	Info	Questions	Validity index	Info
1	0.6004	Valid	5	0.8100	Valid
2	0.6231	Valid	6	0.8022	Valid
3	0.6219	Valid	7	0.6814	Valid
4	0.7144	Valid	8	0.6729	Valid

Cronbach alpha > 0.70

Questions	Validity index	Info	Questions	Validity index	Info
9	0.2907	Valid	16	0.6635	Valid
10	0.3834	Valid	17	0.4332	Valid
11	0.3919	Valid	18	0.5253	Valid
12	0.3180	Valid	19	0.6869	Valid
13	0.2407	Valid	20	0.5636	Valid
14	0.2660	Valid	21	0.6447	Valid
15	0.5197	Valid			

Cronbach alpha > 0.70

Questions	Validity index	Info	Questions	Validity index	Info
22	0.7842	Valid	26	0.8134	Valid
23	0.8262	Valid	27	0.8032	Valid
24	0.7301	Valid	28	0.8315	Valid
25	0.6870	Valid	29	0.7458	Valid
			30	0.7511	Valid

Cronbach alpha > 0.70

Table 4. Coefficients

	Coefficients[a]				
Model	Unstandardized Coefficients		Standardized Coefficients	t	Sig.
	B	Std. Error	Beta		
(Constant)	9.316	6.374		1.462	0.149
EO	0.605	0.139	0.496	4.351	0.000
BE	0.120	0.114	0.119	1.048	0.299

a Dependent Variable: BP.

Table 5. Model summary.

Model	R	R Square	Adjusted R Square	Std. Error of the Estimates
1	0.529[a]	0.279	0.254	3.867

a Predictors: (Constant), BE, EO.

Based on Table 4, EO has a significant effect on BP but BE has no significant effect on BP. However from Table 5, the coefficient of determination or R square is obtained as 0.279 or 27.9%. This shows that EO (X1) and BE (X2) is simultaneously contributing to influence BP (Y) (27.9%). While the rest of 100% − 27.9% = 72.1% is the influence of other variables that are not researched. The finding of this study is quite interesting because the BE does not have a significant effect. Based on our observation, this may occur because entrepreneurs have a high EO, especially seen from their desire to achieve goals and belief that success is an effort from within themselves, and the attitude of the entrepreneurs who are always proactive and innovate that make them more confident in running their business. The entrepreneur characteristics have greatly affected the success of the BP (Idrus, 1999). These characteristics are: self-confidence, task result-oriented, risk-taker, originality, future-oriented. The success of a business is largely determined by how much of these traits are inherent in the spirit of the entrepreneur.

4.4 Simultaneous hypothesis testing (F-statistic test)

Table 6. Annova.

	Annova[a]				
Model	Sum of Squares	df	Mean Squares	F	Sig.
1 Regression	330.693	2	165.347	11.055	.00[b]
Residual	852.557	57	14.957		
Total	1183.250	59			

a Dependent Variable: BP.
b Predictors: (Constant), BE, EO.

Based on Table 6, the calculated F-value is 11.055 > F-table (3.16). In accordance with the result, H1 is accepted and H2 is rejected, thus both EO and BE significantly influence the company performance.

5 CONCLUSION

Based on the results of data analysis and discussion, it is true that there is a significant influence of entrepreneurship orientations on company performance. However, in this study, the BE has not significantly affected the BP, so that according to the hypothesis testing criteria, H1 is accepted and H2 is rejected, but EO and BE simultaneously have a significant effect on BP. Based on observations in the field, this might be caused by entrepreneurs who have a high EO, especially seen from their desire to achieve goals and the belief that success is an effort within themselves. In addition, entrepreneurial attitudes are always proactive and innovative to make them more confident in running their business. Therefore, improving the performance of Muslim fashion SMEs in the city of Bandung is inseparable from the entrepreneurial ability to understand EO. In this harsh environment, we recommend SMEs to maintain an entrepreneurial spirit to remain high to win the competition and perform well. In addition, entrepreneurs must be more active in finding new ideas, continue to innovate, and also focus on changing the BE in an effort to maintain the stability of their business.

REFERENCES

Azuma, N. & Fernie, J. 2003. Fashion in the globalized world and the role of virtual networks in intrinsic fashion design. *Journal of Fashion Marketing and Management: An International Journal* 7(4): 413-427.

Covin, J.G. & Slevin, D.P. 1991. *A conceptual model of entrepreurship as firm behaviour*: 7-25.

Covin, J. & Lumpkin, T. 2011. entrepreneurial orientation theory and research: reflections on a needed construct. *Entrepreneurship: theory and practice*: 855-872.

Covin, J. & Miles, M. 1999. Corporate entrepreneurship and the pursuit of competitive advantage. *Entrepreunership: theory and practice*: 47-63.

Dess, G.G. & Beard, D.W. 1984. Dimensions of organizational task environments. Administrative science quarterly: 52-73.

Gunawan, T., Jacob, J. & Duysters, G. 2015. *Network ties and entrepreunerial orientation: innovative performance of SMEs in a developing country.*

Hamel, G. 2000. *Leading the revolution.* Harvard Univ: Press, Cambridge, MA.

Idrus, M.S.I. 1999. *Strategi pengembangan kewirausahaan (Entrepreneurship) dan peranan perguruan tinggi dalam rangka membangun keunggulan bersaing (competitive advantage) bangsa Indonesia pada millenium ketiga.* Makalah tidak dipubilkasikan, Universitas Brawijaya.

Lee, D.Y. & Tsang, E.W. 2001. The effects of entrepreneurial personality, background and network activities on venture growth. *Journal of management studies* 38(4): 583-602.

Lumpkin, G., & Dess, G.G. 1996. Clarifying the entrepreneurial orientation construct and linking it to performance. *Acad manage. Rev.* 21: 135-172.

Miller, D. 1983. the correlates of entrepreneurship in three types of firms. *Management Science*: 770-791.

Pratt, A., Borrione, P., Lavanga, M. & D'Ovidio, M. 2012. *International change and technological evolution in the fashion industry.*

Kusumawati, R. 2010. Pengaruh Karakteristik Pimpinan Dan Inovasi Produk Baru Terhadap Kinerja Perusahaan Untuk Mencapai Keunggulan Bersaing Berkelanjutan. *AKSES: Jurnal Ekonomi dan Bisnis* 5(9).

Rivai, B. 2004. *Manfaat Penilaian Kinerja*. Jurnal http://jurnalsdm.blogspot.com/2004/04/penilaian-|kinerja-karyawan-definisi.htm.

Van Gils, A. 2005. Management and governance in Dutch SMEs. *European Management Journal* 23(5): 583-589.

Wiklund, J. 1999. The sustainability of the entrepreneurial orientation—performance relationship. *Entrepreneurship theory and practice* 24(1): 37-48.

Wispandono, W. & Moch, R. 2010. pengaruh lingkungan bisnis terhadap kinerja pengrajin industri batik di kabupaten Bankalan. *Jurnal Mitra Ekonomi dan Manajemen Bisnis* 1 (2) Oktober 2010.

Zahra, S.A., 1993. Environment, corporate entrepreneurship, and financial performance: A taxonomic approach. *Journal of business venturing* 8(4): 319-340.

Zahra, S.A. & Covin, J.G. 1995. Contextual influences on the corporate entrepreneurship-performance relationship: A longitudinal analysis. *Journal of business venturing* 10(1): 43-58.

Global Competitiveness: Business Transformation in the
Digital Era – Abdullah, Widiaty & Abdullah (eds)
© 2019 Taylor & Francis Group, London, ISBN 978-0-367-19442-0

The effect of strategic entrepreneurship to innovation with creativity as a moderating variable at culinary industry in Bandung city

A.L. Lahindah
Sekolah Tinggi Ilmu Ekonomi Harapan Bangsa, Bandung, Indonesia

ABSTRACT: Culinary industry in Bandung has become one of the national culinary tourism destinations. This condition arises due to the richness of Bandung culinary variations and innovations. Innovation is an instrument for realizing an entrepreneurial economy, which encourages the culinary industry to exploit the opportunity for profit. This research was conducted on 203 culinary actors in Bandung, to find the effect of the strategic entrepreneurship variables to innovation on culinary industry in Bandung through creativity variables as a moderation variable. By using partial least square technique, it is found that the strategic variables of entrepreneurship have effects on innovation variable, while creativity as a moderating variable has no impact on the relationship.

1 INTRODUCTION

Creative economy is the trigger of the birth of industry 4.0. This era was followed by the birth of new innovative and creative business models. The birth of industry 4.0 began with the emergence of generation Z who had a very high level of innovation and creativity. Bandung is designated as the city of national culinary destinations by the Ministry of Tourism along with other cities namely Bali, Solo, Semarang, and Yogyakarta (Budhiman 2017). The Mayor of Bandung stated that this condition occurred because of the many culinary varieties of Bandung and innovation.

According to data from the Bandung City Culture and Tourism Office, the culinary industry that has permits in August 2014 totaled 660 restaurants. This number consists of three classifications: 301 restaurants, 13 bars, and 346 canteens. From the classification, the culinary business in Bandung has a variety of business themes and specifications starting from the culinary business that serves certain types of food to culinary businesses that even offer a variety of the beauty of nature. This intense competition makes culinary players in Bandung to have a certain strategy for survival. Innovation is an instrument to realize entrepreneurial economy (Drucker 1985). Some researchers argue that the key to prosperity creation is how organizations can focus on creating new products, creating new processes, and creating new markets (Covin & Slevin 2002); (Kusumawardhani et al. 2012). If innovation is the key to creating prosperity, culinary practitioners who understand how to innovate will survive in this competition. However, Shane & Venkataraman (2000) revealed that the basis of prosperity creation was found by looking for and exploiting opportunities for profit.

This study attempts to analyze the factors of human capital and organizational social capital and relate them to innovation variables. Human resources are important variables for organizational success (Pfeffer 1994, Hitt et al. 2001a, b) where human resources include skills, abilities, knowledge, and experience.

Social capital is a series of organizational capital that includes relationships between individuals and between individuals and organizations. Variables of human capital and social capital of creative industry players then join the entrepreneurial variable which includes the entrepreneurial mindset and entrepreneurial culture. Entrepreneurship leadership which is rooted in the ability to know the opportunities and behaviors that produce superior organizational performance is called strategic entrepreneurship (Ireland et al. 2003).

Strategic entrepreneurship is expected to illustrate the condition of the culinary industry in Bandung, which is influenced by creativity and innovation that can make culinary actors in the city of Bandung survive. Creativity is sensitivity in dealing with problems (Cheng 2007) to form unusual patterns and then create ideas that ultimately create innovation (Tang 1998, Cook 1998).

Based on that situations, this research objective is to understand the effect of strategic entrepreneurship to innovation on culinary industry in Bandung City with creativity as a moderating variable.

1.1 Strategic entrepreneurship

Strategic entrepreneurship includes a combination of the ability to recognize the opportunities and behaviors that result in superior organizational performance (Ireland et al. 2003). Strategic entrepreneurship is a very unique and specific concept because of its ability to create organizational well-being.

Ireland et al. (2003) suggested that entrepreneurship and strategic management focus on growth and the creation of organizational welfare. The creation of welfare and growth of organizations are interconnected with each other even though growth is a predictable factor that can help organizations create prosperity and build economies of scale as much as market forces. Strategic entrepreneurship creates output that is an additional resource and contributes to achieving competitive advantage.

Strategic entrepreneurship consists of actions with a strategic perspective to create organizational skills and identify opportunities (Ireland et al. 2003). Without these skills, the organization will not innovate and will be disturbed.

1.2 *Creativity*

Creativity is an important part of research on creative behavior. How to assess creativity can be seen from how many new products, processes, and market systems are produced to deal with environmental dynamics and limited resources. Creativity is a response or level of sensitivity in dealing with problems (Cheng 2007), or forming unusual patterns to create ideas that ultimately create innovation (Tang 1998, Cook 1998).

1.3 *Innovation*

Innovation is an instrument to realize an entrepreneurial economy (Drucker 1985). Innovation comes from Latin "innovatio" or "innovo" which means updating or making something new (Abouzeedan 2011). Innovation can be seen in several characteristics such as introducing new products, introducing new methods, opening new markets, acquiring new sources of raw materials, and updating organizations (Schumpeter 1934). With the realization of innovation, delivery of products, processes, marketing techniques, and organizational updates can be carried out (Mazzarol & Rebound 2008) through new technology, intellectual property, and business and physical change (Abouzeedan 2011).

1.4 *The effect of strategic entrepreneurship to innovation with creativity as a moderation variable*

Strategic entrepreneurship consists of finding a balance between looking for potential opportunities (to identify areas of activity in the future) and how organizations experience learning, the absorption of new knowledge and technology, and several other strategies that bring organizations towards prosperity and achievement.

Ireland et al. (2003) argue that strategic entrepreneurship includes entrepreneurial action with a strategic perspective so that the organization is able to identify opportunities. Organizations that have the ability to exploit opportunities will

innovate and ultimately achieve their goals. Innovation is a real act of sensitivity when individuals face problems (Cheng 2007), and is a measure of the level of creativity that is formed as an unusual pattern (Tang 1998, Cook 1998). Thus, innovation as an action to achieve competitive advantage of an organization arises because of the existing strategic entrepreneurial spirit, which is supported by creativity.

From the above explanation, the hypothesis compiled in this study is:

H_1: Strategic Entrepreneurship influences innovation with creativity as a moderating variable.

2 RESEARCH METHODOLOGY

This study is a causal explanative research to understand the influence of strategic entrepreneurial causal relationships, creativity, and innovation. Data was taken from 203 culinary actors in the city of Bandung from 660 culinary actors registered in the city of Bandung. The questionnaire was distributed to culinary owners or managers by simple random sampling method. By using partial least square (PLS) method, the data is analyzed to find out the hypothesis. In-depth interviews were conducted to ascertain the results after the data was analyzed.

3 RESULTS AND DISCUSSION

In this research, WarpPLS 3.0 software was used to test the previously described hypothesis. The following research models were tested to answer the research questions that have been stated previously, as follows:

Figure 1 shows that strategic entrepreneurship influences innovation but the influence of creativity moderating on the relationship between strategic entrepreneurship and innovation is not significant with a P value of 0.28. These results indicate that creativity is not a moderating variable in the relationship between strategic entrepreneurship and innovation. Furthermore, several main outputs will be interpreted from the results of the testing of the moderation model above, as follows:

Table 1 shows that fit model indicators have been met, i.e., APC and ARS are significant with P value

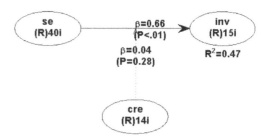

Figure 1. Research model.

Source: WarpPLS 3.0, 2016.

Table 1. Model fit indices and *P* values.

Average path coefficient (APC)=0.352, *P*<0.001
Average *R*-square (ARS)=0.470, *P*<0.001
Average block VIF=1.359

Source: WarpPLS 3.0, 2016.

Table 2. Path coefficients and *P* values.

Path coefficients

	se	Cre	inv	cre*se
Se				
Cre				
Inv	0.663			0.041
cre*se				
P value				
	se	Cre	inv	cre*se
Se				
Cre				
Inv	<0.001			0.276
cre*se				

Source: WarpPLS 3.0, 2016.

less than 0.001 and also AVIF indicator of 1.359 or below the limit of 3.3.

Table 2 shows that strategic entrepreneurship has a significant effect on innovation, but creativity does not give a moderating effect.

4 CONCLUSIONS

The model shows the strategic character of entrepreneurship owned by culinary actors in Bandung City. That factor has a huge impact on the innovation process. This condition is in line with the model developed by Ireland et al. (2003) beforehand, that strategic entrepreneurship is categorized into four main sections: entrepreneurial mindset, entrepreneurial culture, entrepreneurial networks, and entrepreneurial leadership are entrepreneurial actions with strategic perspective that generate innovation in organization. However, it was found that creativity variables did not moderate strategic entrepreneurship toward innovation.

The result of data processing shows the insignificant value of the relationship between strategic entrepreneurship to innovation and creativity as moderation. This condition illustrates that the strategic ability of culinary entrepreneurs in Bandung City will directly bring innovation. So this ability should be developed to create new innovations. The strategic ability of culinary entrepreneurship in Bandung City includes entrepreneurial thinking, entrepreneurship culture, and entrepreneurial leadership.

Based on the results of interviews, some culinary actors have the ability to process information received with different perceptions and views compared to public views. In the theory that has been described earlier that the process of identifying and exploring business opportunities is a driving factor to enter a market process, so an entrepreneur is responsible for collecting the data needed to identify alternative options even in ambiguous and fragmented conditions. The alternative options that are successfully developed are then processed so that alternative and logical alternatives can be created and implemented in concrete action to create a product innovation (Alvarez & Barney 2002). For example, the difficulty of looking for dinner at night is now mitigated because one of the culinary industries in Bandung has opened cafes functioning at night up to 9:00 pm. The ability of culinary actors lies in a mindset that other entrepreneurs may not have. Starting from dexterity or vigilance sees opportunities to bring up the ability to see opportunities from these different sides.

Next, culinary performers create new products, new designs, and new qualities in the culinary industry (innovation), matching the entrepreneurial awareness of culinary actors. Precautions make culinary actors aware of opportunities, so that entrepreneurial awareness raises product innovation. Entrepreneurship awareness also makes culinary performers capable of identifying consumer needs (in terms of product, design, and quality expected by consumers), and are able to make choices in accordance with the needs of consumers from a variety of alternative options available.

In addition to the strategic capabilities of culinary actors in Bandung city, innovation arises because of the culture of entrepreneurship that is built continuously. An effective entrepreneurial culture is an organization's effort to manage its resources strategically by using the organizational culture. With entrepreneurial culture, it is expected that various processes of organizational resource management can be facilitated. Developing an entrepreneurial culture in an organization will continuously create cultural patterns of member organizations that want to continuously develop and create innovation. The success of cultivators in developing their entrepreneurial culture is due to the form of culinary organization in Bandung city on average on the small and medium scales. On the scale of small and medium organizations, the formation of culture is usually easier and more focused.

Effective entrepreneurial leadership gains information disclosure with organizational members to describe innovations that may be disengaged as a potential advantage (for example, stimulating the development of new competitive advantages). By stimulating the development of new products, it will create a product innovation that is an advantage for the organization. Entrepreneurship leadership in the culinary sub-sector in Bandung influences Innovation. This condition can occur, because most culinary in Bandung are companies that are in the middle business category, and in this category, owners have full power to manage and develop the company (Mintzberg et al. 1998). In the culinary sub-sector in Bandung city, it is found that the members of the company are very much dependent on the owner or manager (in line with the concept of "design school" put forward by Mintzberg, Ahlstrand & Lampel 1998). Therefore, Product Innovation happens due to the spirit of Leadership Entrepreneurship.

REFERENCES

Abouzeedan, A. 2011. *SME Performance and Its Relationship to Innovation*. Linkoping, Sweden: Linkoping University.

Alvarez, S. & Barney, J. 2002. Resources-based theory and the entrepreneurial firm. In M. Hitt, R. Ireland, S. Camp, & D. Sexton, *Strategic Entrepreneurship: Creating a new mindset* (pp. 89-105). Oxford: Blackwell Publishers.

Budhiman, I. 2017, September 29. *Bisnis.com*. Retrieved from Bisnis.com: http://bandung.bisnis.com/read/20170929/13/574517/emil-bersyukur-bandung-ditetapkan-sebagai-destinasi-wisata-kuliner-nasional

Cheng, Y. 2007. *An Examination of the Relationship Between Creative Potential and Personality Types Among American and Taiwanese College Student of Teacher Education*. Michigan: Eastern Michigan University.

Cook, P. 1998. The Creative advantage- is your organization the leader of the pack? *Industrial and Commercial Training*, 179-184.

Covin, J. & Slevin, D. 2002. The Entrepreneurial imperatives of Strategic Leadership. In M. Hitt, R. Ireland, S.

Camp, & D. Sexton, *Strategic Entrepreneurship: Creating a new Mindset* (pp. 309-327). Oxford: Blackwell Published.

Drucker, P. 1985. *Innovation and Entrepreneurship*. London, UK: Heinemann.

Hitt, M., Bierman, L., Shimizu, K. & Kochhar, R. 2001a. Direct and moderating effect of human capital on strategy and performance in profesional service firm: A resource-based perspective. *Academy of Management Journal 44*, 13-28.

Hitt, M., Ireland, R. & Harrison, J. 2001b. Mergers and aquisitions. In M. Hitt, R. Freeman, & J. Harrison, *Handbook of Strategic Management* (pp. 384-408). Oxford: Blackwell Publishers.

Ireland, R., Hitt, M. A. & Sirmon, D. G. 2003. A Model of Strategic Entrepreneurship: The Construct and its Dimentions. *Journal of Management Vol. 29 No. 6*, 963-989.

Kusumawardhani, A., McCarthy, G. & Perera, N. 2012. Autonomy and innovativeness: understanding their relationship with the performance of Indonesian SMEs. *The Joint ACERE-DIANA International Entrepreneurship Conference* (pp. 1-16). Fremantle, Western Australia: ACERE-DIANA.

Mazzarol, T. & Rebound, S. 2008. The Role of Complementary Actors in The Development of Innovation in Small Firm. *International Journal of Innovation Management 12(2)*, 223-253.

Mintzberg, H., Ahlstrand, B. & Lampel, J. 1998. *Strategy Safary*. United States of America: The Free Press, a Division of Simon & Schuster, Inc.

Pfeffer, J. 1994. *Competitive advantage through people*. Boston: Harvard Business School Press.

Schumpeter, J. 1934. *The theory of economic development*. Cambridge, Massachusetts: Harvard University Press.

Tang, H. 1998. An Integrative model of innovation in organization. *Technovation, Vol.18*, 297-309.

Global Competitiveness: Business Transformation in the Digital Era – Abdullah, Widiaty & Abdullah (eds)
© 2019 Taylor & Francis Group, London, ISBN 978-0-367-19442-0

Evaluating entrepreneurship ecosystem at different phases of entrepreneurship activity

G. Pawitan & C.B. Nawangpalupi
Parahyangan Catholic University, Bandung, Indonesia

N.T. Tuan
University of Social Sciences and Humanities, Vietnam National University, Ho Chi Minh City, Vietnam

ABSTRACT: The entrepreneurship ecosystem plays a key role in achieving global competitiveness. This paper aims to analyze entrepreneurship ecosystem in different phases of entrepreneurial activities in achieving global competitiveness. The GEM model is used to analyze the entrepreneurship ecosystem for Indonesian entrepreneurs in 2015–2017. The entrepreneurs' activities were classified into three phases, namely nascent, new business, and established business. Meanwhile, the entrepreneurship ecosystem is defined into factors of entrepreneurial framework conditions. The result shows that there are different conditions faced by the entrepreneurs at different phases. All entrepreneurs need firm and definite regulations to support their business. Innovation or research and development (R&D) transfer is not very important for nascent entrepreneurs, but it is one of the most important factors for new and established businesses. The competitiveness and the strategies to win the competition are more important for those who have been operating the business for more than 3 months.

1 INTRODUCTION

1.1 *Important role of entrepreneurship*

Fritsch & Schmude (2007) noted that entrepreneurship has several important factors in regional dimension. Some factors are related to entrepreneurial attitude, aspiration, performance, and also local environment for entrepreneurship, as quoted below:

Differences in startup rates, in entrepreneurial attitudes, and the success of newly founded businesses between regions indicate a distinct importance of space and the local environment for entrepreneurship (Fritsch & Schmude 2007).

Literatures stated the importance of entrepreneurship as a key driver in achieving socio-economic development in the social, cultural, and political context, including new job creation, innovation, and social value creation (Fritsch & Wyrwich 2017, Mueller et al. 2008, Rocha 2012). Individuals, in relation to their environment, perform their activity to gain a better life, either economically or politically. The resulting entrepreneurship activity is motivated by the entrepreneurial spirit, which contains entrepreneurial attitude, aspiration, and activity (Acs et al. 2013, Stough & Nijkamp 2009). This activity requires attitude and aspiration, but then the entrepreneurship activities are supported by entrepreneurship ecosystem (Fuerlinger et al. 2015). Hence, understanding the entrepreneurship ecosystem becomes a necessity to develop a good entrepreneurship.

Isenberg (2014) defined entrepreneurship ecosystem as a dynamic community within a geographic region, composed of varied and inter-dependent actors, factors, and processes that evolve over time and whose actors and factors coexist and interact to promote new enterprise creation.

The literatures discussed the importance of entrepreneurship, and also the role of the entrepreneurship ecosystem in promoting the enterprises. However, still there is a lack of discussion on entrepreneurship ecosystem priority in each phase of their entrepreneurship activities. The knowing of priority for each phase will guide policy-maker to design a better intervention program that fits with the entrepreneurs' needs.

This paper aims to compare the entrepreneurship ecosystem in different phases of entrepreneurship activities. The research question "What is the priority of entrepreneurship ecosystem according to the entrepreneur's perception at different phases of their activities?"

1.2 *Entrepreneurship framework: GEM model*

Global Entrepreneurship Monitor (GEM) has developed a conceptual framework that identifies essential elements within the relationship between entrepreneurship and economic growth and how these elements interact with each other (Kelley et al. 2016, Nawangpalupi et al. 2014). The conceptual framework incorporates three main components (Levie & Autio 2008), namely capture aspects

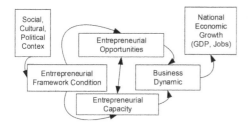

Figure 1. Entrepreneurship framework based on GEM model.

of entrepreneurial ecosystem, entrepreneurial opportunities and capacity, and entrepreneurial activity (see Figure 1).

The entrepreneurship ecosystem in the GEM model is defined by entrepreneurial framework conditions (Nawangpalupi et al. 2014). The entrepreneurship ecosystem measures supporting environmental factors for entrepreneurs in running and developing their ventures.

2 RESEARCH METHOD

2.1 Design of study and data

The GEM defines nine entrepreneurial framework conditions (EFC), namely (A) entrepreneurial finance, (B) government policy, (C) government entrepreneurship programs, (D) education and training, (E) research and development transfer, (F) commercial and professional infrastructure, (G) market openness, (H) physical infrastructure, and (I) cultural and social norms. The entrepreneurship activity's phase in the GEM model is defined by three phases (Figure 2) which initially involves in setting up a business – nascent, then grew a new business up to 3.5 years ventures, and finally blossoming into an established business. The surviving entrepreneurs (more than 3.5 years) are considered to own and manage an established business.

The data was sourced from the GEM – Adult Population Survey, conducted in 2015–2017, covering 23 major provinces in Indonesia, with 11,702

random selected adult of ages 18–64 years. The respondents were collected from 23 provinces in Indonesia covering 80% of the population.

Based on GEM conceptual framework, entrepreneurial ecosystem is called as entrepreneurial framework conditions (EFC). The EFC measures supporting factors for entrepreneurship activity. The entrepreneurs were asked to complete a closed questionnaire consisting of 55 indicators about factors relating to the conditions that make up the country's entrepreneurial environment (Nawangpalupi et al. 2015). Each response was measured on a 5-point scale, which is designed as 1=completely unsupported condition to 5=completely supported condition. The variables are defined as follows:

a. Variable: **EE** = Entrepreneurship Ecosystem, scale 1 = completely unsupported condition to 5 = completely supported condition, dimension: **EEa** = Entrepreneurial finance (8 indicators), **EEb** = government policy (7 indicators), **EEc** = government entrepreneurship programs (6 indicators), **EEd** = education and training (6 indicators), **EEe** = R&D transfer (6 indicators), **EEf** = commercial and professional infrastructures (6 indicators), **EEg** = market openness (6 indicators), **EEh** = physical infrastructures (5 indicators), **EEi** = cultural and social norms (5 indicators).

b. Variable: **PEA** = phase of entrepreneurship activities, scale 1 = nascent, 2 = new business, 3 = established business.

2.2 Method

The research question is answered by using Principal Component Analysis (PCA). PCA is a linear statistical approach for analyzing the covariance structure of multidimensional data X_{ij}, where $i=1,\ldots,m$, and $j=1,\ldots,n$. In this paper, X_{1j} is **EEa** for $j=1,\ldots,8$, X_{2j} is **EEb** for $j=1,\ldots,7$, and so on. Meanwhile, the **PEA** is a grouping variable.

It is assumed that indicators of entrepreneurship ecosystems were correlated each other, hence it is possible to extract most of the variability present in the $(m \times n)$ indicators into k principal components that are retained to capture the majority of variability in X_{ij}. The first principal component is considered as a basis to arrange priority of the entrepreneurship ecosystem to be developed, since it represents the largest X_{ij}'s variance explained (Johnson & Wichern 2014). The priority arrangement is defined by using its components loadings.

2.3 Entrepreneurs profile

There are 3375 entrepreneurs who consist of 17% nascent, 33% new business, and 50% established. Based on gender, 48.1% are male entrepreneurs and 51.9% are female. The entrepreneurs' ages were 12.6% of 18–24 years, 28.6% of 25–34 years, 27.6%

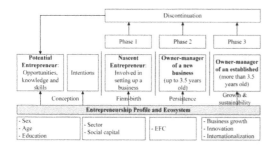

Figure 2. Phases of entrepreneurial activities.

of 35–44 years, 19.5% of 45–54 years, and 11.7% of 55–64 years. The entrepreneur profiles show that the number of female entrepreneurs was higher, but their ages are mostly within 25–34 years.

The types of their business for the early entrepreneurship activities were classified into 3.5% extractive, 11.7% transforming, 6.0% services, and 78.8% consumer-oriented. Meanwhile, the established business activities were classified into 4.6% extractive, 13.3% transforming, 5.3% services, and 76.8% consumer-oriented.

3 RESULTS AND DISCUSSION

3.1 *Principal component analysis for each phase*

Priority of the entrepreneurship ecosystem for each entrepreneurship phase was determined by applying PCA for each entrepreneurship phase. The results are presented in Tables 1–3.

Table 1 shows the priority arrangement of entrepreneurship ecosystem for the nascent entrepreneurship activities which are mostly dominated by education and training, government policy, bureaucracy, regulation, licensing, government entrepreneurship program, R&D transfer, and entrepreneurial finance. The first and second priorities of entrepreneurship ecosystem indicate a prominent role of education, training, and government in fostering individuals to become entrepreneurs. It is interesting business in terms of funding. R&D transfers are also considered as priority for the nascent entrepreneurs. It's the reason why majority of youth entrepreneurs are around 25–34 years old.

Table 1. Priorities of nascent's entrepreneurship ecosystem ordered by component loading.

D^*	Aspect/Indicators	L^*
EEd	Teaching in primary and secondary education provides adequate attention to entrepreneurship and new firm creation	0.99
EEd	Teaching in primary and secondary education provides adequate instruction in market economic principles	0.99
EEc	The people working for government agencies are competent and effective	0.99
EEb	Government bureaucracy, regulations, and licensing requirements are not excessively difficult for new and growing firms	0.99
EEb	Government policies consistently favor new firms	0.99
EEe	New tech, science, and other knowledge are efficiently transferred from universities and public research centers	0.99
EEa	Professional Business Angels funding available	0.99

Source: first principal component for nascent.
Note: D=dimension, L=component loading.

Table 2. Priorities of entrepreneurship ecosystem for new business ordered by component loading.

D^*	Aspect/Indicators	L^*
EEe	The science and technology base efficiently supports the creation of world-class new technology-based ventures	0.88
EEd	Colleges and universities provide good and adequate preparation for starting up and growing new firms	0.84
EEe	New and growing firms can afford the latest technology	0.82
EEd	The vocational, profession, and continuing education systems provide good and adequate preparation for starting up and growing new firms	0.77
EEg	New and growing firms can enter markets without being unfairly blocked by established firms	0.58

Source: first principal component for new business.
Note: D=dimension, L=component loading.

Table 3. Priorities of entrepreneurship ecosystem for established business ordered by component loading.

D^*	Aspect/Indicators	L^*
EEb	Government policies consistently favor new firms	0.935
EEh	It is not too expensive for a new or growing firm to get good access to communications	0.910
EEb	The amount of taxes is NOT a burden for new and growing firms	0.870
EEh	The physical infrastructures provide good support for new and growing firms	0.868
EEa	Debt funding available for new and growing firms	0.840

Source: first principal component for established business.
Note: D=Dimension, L= component loading.

For the new business (see Table 2), the first principal components consist of education and training, R&D transfer, and market openness. It is a typical ecosystem for the new business in encountering the market. They need education and training, technology transfers, and also market openness.

For the established business (see Table 3), the first principal factors are consistency of government policy, taxes, regulations, and financial support. They are followed by physical infrastructures/communication and entrepreneurial finance.

3.2 *Discussion*

These findings reveal that financial support is essential for starting up a business (for nascent entrepreneurs) and also to develop the business (for established businesses), while the new entrepreneurs require sustainable access to the market and a good physical infrastructure. All entrepreneurs need firm and definite regulations to support their business.

Innovation or research and development (R&D) transfer is a priority for nascent entrepreneurs, and new businesses. Innovation that represents the support for creating new products and new technologies, including the use of proprietary technology, is important when a business enters the world of real competition. The competitiveness and the strategies to win the competition are more important for those who have been operating the business for more than 3 months (where nascent ones are those just started their businesses and are under three months). This issue is an alarming message for Indonesia. Based on the Global Entrepreneurship Index of 2017, Indonesia has a very low absorption of technology, commenting to a value of 0.03 and this has been mentioned as the weakest area in Indonesian entrepreneurship. Hence, to improve the entrepreneurial climate and to strengthen the entrepreneurship ecosystem, it is important to prioritize the enforcement of policies and programs in the R&D transfer.

Based on these results, then the policy-makers may focus on suitable programs related with strengthening a particular entrepreneurship ecosystem. Such as, the nascent and new businesses need an innovation program in developing their enterprises. Meanwhile, the established business needs a supporting ecosystem by reforming policy, tax, and regulations, financial support, and physical infrastructures.

4 CONCLUSIONS

Each entrepreneurship activity has different characteristics and conditions, thus revealing that entrepreneurship ecosystem for each phase gives important information for policy-makers or entrepreneurs themselves.

Comparing entrepreneurship ecosystem among activities of their doing business, indicates a different priority between nascent, new business, and established business. The principal factors of entrepreneurship ecosystem for nascent entrepreneurs are mostly dominated by education and training, government policies, bureaucracy, regulation, and licensing.

The new business mostly considers market openness and R&D transfers, and the established business prioritizes physical infrastructures, consistency of government policy, taxes, regulations, and financial support.

ACKNOWLEDGMENTS

This paper was part of research project supported by a grant from the Indonesian government, the Ministry of Research, Technology, and Higher Education 2016-2018 (NES).

REFERENCES

Acs, Z. J., Audretsch, D. B. & Lehmann, E. E. 2013. The knowledge spillover theory of entrepreneurship. *Small Business Economics* 41(4): 757-774.
Fritsch, M. & Schmude, J. 2007. *Entrepreneurship in the Region*: Springer.
Fritsch, M. & Wyrwich, M. 2017. The effect of entrepreneurship on economic development—an empirical analysis using regional entrepreneurship culture. *Journal of Economic Geography* 17(1): 157-189.
Fuerlinger, G., Fandl, U. & Funke, T. 2015. The role of the state in the entrepreneurship ecosystem: insights from Germany. *Triple Helix* 2(1): 1-26.
Isenberg, D. 2014. What an Entrepreneurship Ecosystem Actually Is. *Harvard Business Review*.
Johnson, R. & Wichern, D. 2014. *Applied Multivariate Statistical Analysis* (Sixth Edition ed.): Pearson Education Limited.
Kelley, D., Singer, S. & Herrington, M. 2016. *Global Entrepreneurship Monitor 2015/16 Global Report*. Boston, USA: Global Entrepreneurship Research Association.
Levie, J. & Autio, E. 2008. A theoretical grounding and test of the GEM model. *Small Business Economics* 31 (3): 235-263.
Mueller, P., van Stel, A. & Storey, D. J. 2008. The effects of new firm formation on regional development over time: The case of Great Britain. *Small Business Economics* 30(1): 59-71.
Nawangpalupi, C. B., Pawitan, G., Gunawan, A., Widyarini, M., Bisowarno, B. H. & Iskandarsjah, T. 2015. *Global Entrepreneurship Monitor 2014 Indonesia Report*. Bandung, Indonesia: UNPAR PRESS.
Nawangpalupi, C. B., Pawitan, G., Gunawan, A., Widyarini, M. & Iskandarsjah, T. 2014. *Global Entrepreneurship Monitor 2013 Indonesian Report*: Universitas Katolik Parahyangan.
Rocha, E. A. G. 2012. The Impact of the Business Environment on the Size of the Micro, Small and Medium Enterprise Sector; Preliminary Findings from a Cross-Country Comparison. *Procedia Economics and Finance* 4: 335-349.
Stough, R. & Nijkamp, P. 2009. Knowledge spillovers, entrepreneurship and economic development. *The Annals of Regional Science* 43(4): 835.

Environmental Issues

Global Competitiveness: Business Transformation in the
Digital Era – Abdullah, Widiaty & Abdullah (eds)
© *2019 Taylor & Francis Group, London, ISBN 978-0-367-19442-0*

Competitiveness with (out) sacrificing environment: Estimating economic cost of groundwater pollution

E. Wardhani & S. Nugraheni
Parahyangan Catholic University, Bandung, Indonesia

ABSTRACT: Indonesia is one of the largest textile producers because of its high competitiveness. Most of the textile and apparel industries are located in West Java province. There are cases where the Indonesian textile industry causes pollution of ground water. This study aims to estimate the economic costs of groundwater pollution in two hamlets in Lagadar village, Bandung Regency, West Java province, which is caused by wastewater from the textile industry. Environmental assessment methods using replacement and prevention costs were carried out with primary data collected from the field with a survey of 84 households. The results show that the average expenditure of households to buy clean water (bottled water and/or tap water), build public wells, and operate public water treatment, is Rp 67,048 per month; or IDR 804,576 per year. Therefore, the total economic cost of pollution of groundwater for two hamlets (of 546 households), is IDR 36,608,208 per month; or IDR 439,298,496 per year.

1 INTRODUCTION

Indonesia is one of the largest textile producing countries in the world. In 2017, the value of Indonesia's exports from the textile industry reached $ 12.58 billion; it is the fourth largest export commodity after the food industry, chemical industry, and basic Meta industry (Ministry of Industry of the Republic of Indonesia, n.d.). Some reports state that Indonesian textiles and clothing have high competitiveness. Quoting the UN Commtrade report, the Coordinating Ministry for Economic Affairs of the Republic of Indonesia (2018) noted that Indonesian textile products' Revealed Comparative Advantage (RCA) was 55, the highest among other Indonesian export commodities.

Most of Indonesia's textile industries are located in West Java, especially in Bandung and its surrounding areas. In 2013, there were 1,658 factories (of 2,886), or 57 percent of all textile and apparel factories, located in West Java province (Badan Pusat Statistik Jawa Barat 2014).

In some cases, high competitiveness of Indonesia's textile products has to sacrifice environment. Greenpeace's report (2013) states that textile factories are the main cause of water pollution. Waste water from textile factories is disposed to rivers without being processed, and flows along the rivers, or seeps into the soil, and causes groundwater pollution around the factories' areas. Water is also an important input in textile production process, and the factories often use groundwater to fulfill their water needs. They drill deep wells that deplete groundwater quantity in the areas around the factories.

Lagadar Village, Bandung District, is one of the areas where several textile factories are located. Research by Suhari (2012) concluded that Lagadar Village is one of the areas in Bandung District that experienced shallow groundwater contamination. This is confirmed by Greenpeace's report (2013) and Lagadar's local people who stated that, before the textile industries built their factories in Lagadar's neighborhood, local people of the village used groundwater as their clean water resources. Once the textile factories established and operated in Lagadar village, the majority of the local people rely their clean water need from sources other than groundwater, such as: 'bottled' water (i.e. clean water in *gallons* that is sold based on refill system), tap water, and communal artesian wells that were built by the local community.

This study aims to estimate the economic costs borne by local people of Lagadar due to groundwater pollution in their areas. The study covered two hamlets (sub-villages), namely RW 04 and RW 17 of Lagadar village. Those two hamlets were chosen as the object of this research because the distance between the two hamlets and the textile factory complex is quite close, about 1.5 to 4 kilometers. Lagadar village is about 318.90 ha, with number of population is 22,567, and 5,548 households. There are 546 households living in RW 04 and RW 17 of the village.

2 EXTERNALITY AND ECONOMIC COST OF POLLUTION

Theoretically, pollution in the production process is the impact of externalities without compensation from one-child actions on third party welfare (Mankiw 2009). Externality is a type of market failure that can be negative or positive, depending on whether the impact by the stander is detrimental or profitable.

Research by Suhari (2012) and Greenpeace (2013) and statements by local residents of Lagadar state that the main cause of Lagadar groundwater pollution is textile industry wastewater. Suppose the statements are scientifically proven, cases of groundwater pollution in RW 04 and RW 17 Lagadar Village are negative externalities from textile factories located adjacent to the village. Externalities ignore Lagadar residents because they have to provide additional budgets to buy clean water. Lagadar villagers must bear the costs of groundwater pollution caused by the textile industry. As long as the costs are not included in the production costs of the textile industry, externalities occur.

Externalities will make the production costs of textile factories 'too low' because they do not take into account the costs of externalities (Tietenberg & Lewis 2012). Graphically, this is illustrated in Figure 1. Suppose marginal costs represent the costs of producing textile factories, the MPC curve is the cost of production without including negative externality costs. When we take into account the cost of pollution, this gives a factory 'real' production cost symbolized by the MSC curve. We can see that the externalities produce 'too much' out-put (Q1 compared to Q *), and the price is 'too low' (P1 compared to P *).

In Economics, externalities are overcome by internalization. One method of internalization is to provide compensation to the affected parties. The amount of payment must be more or less the same as the expenditure of the affected parties to avoid the risks caused by externalities. Industrial pollutants usually contain hazardous chemical substances that are very dangerous for humans, therefore, cause high economic, environmental and social costs (Fatma 2017). When there is groundwater pollution, the affected parties will do anything to avoid costs. In the case of local residents of Lagadar, they replaced ground water with other clean water sources. They also did water treatment and made artesian wells. All efforts have financial consequences. This is the economic cost of groundwater pollution.

Estimating economic costs from pollution not only for the purpose of providing compensation, but these costs can be used as information to develop a green growth strategy. Another use of the estimation results is to calculate the "net economic contribution" of the industrial sector.

3 RESEARCH METHOD

This paper aims to estimate economic cost of groundwater pollution in two hamlets (i.e. RW 04 and RW 17) of Lagadar village. The importance of this study is to raise villagers' awareness by proving that water pollution generates economic loss which showed in monetary values. The object of this study are RW 04 and RW 17 as they harmed the most compared to other sub district in that village (Suhari 2012).

There are studies on economic cost of water pollution and five of them are summarized in Table 1.

The estimation method used in this study is replacement and prevention costs. Data obtained from the survey at household level. Total number of household in RW 04 and RW 17 is 546 households. Using the following Slovin's formula, the sample size is 84 households.

$$n = \frac{N}{\left(1 + N(\mathbf{e})^2\right)}$$

n : number of sample
N : total population
E : limit of error tolerance

Each household is given a questionnaire to gather information about two types of costs associated with additional costs (referring to replacement and prevention costs) to provide clean water. Replacement costs refer to costs incurred by households to buy clean water (i.e. bottled water and tap water), instead of using ground water. Meanwhile, prevention costs consist of costs for using communal water treatment and artesian wells. Data on costs per household are collected and then the average cost per household is calculated using the following formula:

$$Average\ Economic\ Cost\ per\ Household = \frac{\sum_{i=1}^{n} (ReplCost + PrevCost)_i}{n}$$

ReplCost: Replacement Cost of Respondent (household) i (Rp.).
PrevCost: Prevention Cost of Respondent (household) i (Rp.).
n: Number of Respondents.
i: Respondent (household) to-i (1,2,3,... n).

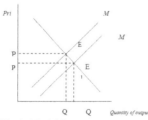

- MSC : Marginal Social Cost
- MPC : Marginal Private Cost
- D : Demand

Figure 1. Negative externalities and the cost of production.

Table 1. Previous studies on estimation of economic costs of water pollution.

No.	Researcher(s) & Year of Publication	Research Method & Object	Research Result
1.	Laughland et al. (1993)	Averting costs due to groundwater contamination in Milesburg, Pennsylvania, US.	$33.47 per month per household
2.	Lewandowski et al. (2008)	Well remediation cost, well maintenance cost, and cost for building new well because of groundwater pollution in Minnesota, US.	Remediation cost: US$800; Maintenance cost: $100; Cost to build new well: US$7.200; (costs per household/year)
3.	Ahyar & Perkasa (2011)	Prevention costs due to sea water intrusion into groundwater, in Kapuk Muara Village, Jakarta, Indonesia.	Rp. 9.9 million per year (total cost at village level)
4.	Rinita, Prabang & Kusno (2012)	Health costs due to mercury contamination from gold mining activities in Kalirejo vill., KulonProgo District, Indonesia	Replacement Cost: Rp 561.100/year. Remediation cost: Rp 16.706.400/year
5.	Greenpeace (2016)	Total economic value of waste water contamination in Rancaekek sub-district, Sumedang, Indonesia	Rp.11.4 trillion per year

Table 2. Household expenditure related to water consumption in Lagadar Village.

Type of Household Expenditure	Descriptive Statistic (in Rupiah)		
	Minimum	Maximum	Mean
Replacement Costs per Household per month			
- Cost to buy bottled water (gallon)	12.000	70.000	26.550
- Cost to buy tap water	0	50.000	22.500
Prevention Costs per Household per month			
- Cost to build public artesian well	0	50.000	22.500
- Cost for water treatment	0	50.000	39.451
Total expenditure related to clean water consumption per household per month	20,000	120.000	67.048

Source: authors' calculation based on survey.

calculation of economic costs in this study does not include health costs due to pollution. Thus, the real costs will be more than the costs estimated by this study. Indeed, textile factories have provided employment for the local community. Our survey shows that 55 percent of respondents (49 heads of households) work in factories. However, this should not reduce the company's obligation to preserve the environment around their industrial location, including groundwater. Workers are paid for their work, not to receive pollution.

5 CONCLUSION

This study aims to estimate the economic costs of groundwater pollution borne by residents of two hamlets (RW 04 and RW 17) in Lagadar village due to textile factory wastewater. Economic costs are estimated by calculating replacement and prevention costs from 84 sample households. The average cost of pollution of ground water per household is Rp. 67,048 per month or Rp. 804,576 per year. Because the total number of households in RW 04 and RW 17 from Lagadar is 546, the value of economic losses due to groundwater pollution borne by the population in the two hamlets is Rp. 36,608,208 per month or Rp. 439,298,496 per year. As long as residents bear the costs of pollution, externality exists.

Estimates of the economic costs of pollution can be used as information for compensation payments. However, there are ways to prevent contamination of ground water. Government regulation is one of them. Under these regulations, textile factories must treat their wastewater before disposal. Law enforcement

4 FINDINGS AND DISCUSSION

Based on the survey, the average cost of replacement and prevention per household is Rp. 67,048 per month or Rp. 804,576 per year. If there are 546 households in the study area (ie two hamlets: RW 04 and RW 17 in Lagadar village), the total economic costs due to groundwater pollution are Rp. 36,608,208 per month or Rp. 439,298,496 per year. The results of data collection are presented in Table 2.

The total economic cost of groundwater pollution is Rp. 36,608,208 per month or Rp. 439, 298,496 per year. This is not cheap for two reasons. First, this amount of money is only estimated for two hamlets. Water pollution caused by the textile industry affects communities along the river basin. Second, the is the main problem. Another way is to make spatial zoning into action. Industrial sites may not be in the same zone as residential areas.

Indonesian textile products that have high competitiveness make Indonesia the 11th largest textile and garment exporter in the world (Greenpeace 2013). However, high product competitiveness must not sacrifice the environment and people who live around textile factories.

REFERENCES

Ahyar, I. & Perkasa, B. 2011. Estimasi nilai kerugian ekonomi dan willingness to pay masyarakat akibat pencemaran air tanah (Studi kasus di kelurahan Kapuk Muara, Jakarta Utara). *Jurnal Ekonomi Lingkungan*, 15, 51-69.

Badan Pusat Statistik Jawa Barat. 2014. *Jumlah industri besar sedang menurut subsektor industri menurut golongan industri di Jawa Barat, 2010-2014*. Retrieved 27 Mei, 2018, from https://jabar.bps.go.id: https://jabar.bps.go.id/statictable/2016/11/11/148/jumlah-industri-besar-sedang-menurut-subsektor-industri-menurut-golongan-industri-di-jawa-barat-2010-2014.html

Fatma, D. 2017, Januari 2. *Pencemaran limbah pabrik*. Diakses melalui Ilmugeografi.com: https://ilmugeografi.com/bencana-alam/pencemaran-limbah-pabrik/pada tanggal 6 Mei 2018.

Freeman, A. M., Herriges, J. A. & Kling, C. L. 2014. *The measurement of environmental and resource values*. New York: RFF Press.

Greenpeace. 2013. *Kisah merek-merek ternama dan polusi air di Indonesia*. Jakarta: Green Peace Indonesia.

Greenpeace. 2013, April 26. *Toxic threads: meracuni surga*. Amsterdam: Green Peace International.

Greenpeace. 2016, April. *Konsekuensi tersembunyi: valuasi kerugian ekonomi akibat pencemaran industri*. Bandung: Greenpeace.

Ministry of Economic Coordinator of Republic Indonesia. 2018.

Kementerian Lingkungan Hidup Republik Indonesia. 2013. Program penilaian peringkat kinerja perusahaan Dalam Pengelolaan Lingkungan Hidup. *Peraturan Menteri Lingkungan Hidup Republik Indonesia Nomor 06 Tahun 2013*. Indonesia.

Kementerian Perindustrian Republik Indonesia. (n.d.). *Statistik Industri*. Retrieved Mei 27, 2018, from www.kemenprin.go.id: http://www.kemenprin.go.id/statistik/peran.php?ekspor=1

Kusumawardani, D. 2011, Desember 3. Valuasi ekonomi air bersih di Kota Surabaya. *Majalah Ekonomi*, hal. 216-229.

Laughland, A. S., Musser, M. L., Musser, N. W. & Shortle, S. J. 1993. The opportunity cost of time and averting expenditures for safe drinking water. *American Water Resources Association* 29(2): 291-299.

Lewandowski, A., Montgamery, C. & Moncrief, J. 2008. Groundwater nitrate contamination cost; a survei of private well owners. *Journal of Soil and Water Concervation* 63(3): 153-161.

Mankiw, N. G. 2009. *Principles of economics*. China-South Western: Cengage Learning.

Rinita, L., Prabang, S. & Kusno, A. 2012. Valuasi ekonomi eksternalitas penggunaan merkuri pada pertambangan emas rakyat dan peran pemerintah daerah mengatasi pencemaran merkuri (pertambangan emas rakyat di Kecamatan Kokap Kulon Progo). *Jurnal Ekonomi dan Sains* 4(8): 48-63.

Suhari. (2012). Prediksi tingkat pencemaran air tanah dangkal daerah Bandung, Jawa Barat. *Jurnal Lingkungan dan Bencana Geologi* 3(3): 169-179.

Tietenberg, T. & Lewis, L. 2012. *Environmental and natural resource economics*. New York: Pearson.

Global Competitiveness: Business Transformation in the Digital Era – Abdullah, Widiaty & Abdullah (eds)
© *2019 Taylor & Francis Group, London, ISBN 978-0-367-19442-0*

Synergy of green industry with industrial revolution 4.0 in Indonesia

D. Prasaja & M.W. Rini
Polytechnic APP Jakarta, Ministry of Industry, Indonesia

B.D. Yoga
Kumamoto University, Kumamoto, Japan

R. Wikansari
Polytechnic APP Jakarta, Ministry of Industry, Indonesia

ABSTRACT: This study aims to identify and analyze the synergy of the Green Industry with the Industrial Revolution 4.0 which is both programs from the Ministry of Industry and the Government of Indonesia. This study uses a comparative research method with a descriptive analysis approach. The method of data collection is done by studying the literature and reviewing regulations regarding related information, while the data is analyzed through the process of reduction, presentation, and conclusion. The results showed that the green industry synergy with the industrial revolution 4.0 was 77.1% and there were at least 27 characteristics that could be matched with each other out of a total of 35 characteristics.

1 INTRODUCTION

Industrial development is increasing rapidly, both globally and in Indonesia. In its journey, the current industrial revolution has reached the 4th generation, called Industry 4.0, which is characterized by various characteristics, especially increasingly high technology and increasingly unlimited information technology. Since the first industrial revolution recorded in history began in England in the mid-18th century, the other side of industrial development has the effect of decreasing the quality of the environment which is the habitat of humans and other living things.

The Green Industry Movement is increasing because of the growth of industrial technology that has an impact on the environment. The development of the green industry movement in the world cannot be separated from the development of a UN institution called UN-IDO (United Nations Industrial Development Organization) which was established on 17 November 1966. The Green Industry (According to UNIDO 2008) basically means the economy is struggling for the growth path more sustainable by making green public investments and implementing public policy initiatives that encourage private investment that is environmentally responsible. The Indonesian Ministry of Industry then adopted the UNIDO policy as a basis for setting green industry standards. As compensation for the adoption of green industry standards by industries in Indonesia, the Ministry of Industry launched the Green Industry Award program since 2010.

Based on above, this study is about the synergy of Green Industry and Industrial Revolution 4.0, which we will restrict to include its implementation by the Government of the Republic of Indonesia through the Ministry of Industry program.

2 INDUSTRIAL REVOLUTION 4.0

2.1 *A brief history of industrial revolution*

Industry 4.0 is continuing a series of industrial revolutions. European Parliament Research Services in Davies (2015) said that the industrial revolution had taken place four times. The first industrial revolution occurred at the end of the 18th century which was a mechanical production based on water and steam (Bahrin et al. 2016). It began to replace human power for industry. The second industrial revolution occurred at the beginning of the 20th century, starting with the introduction of conveyor belts and mass production. The machines are powered by electricity. The use of computer technology for manufacturing automation occurred in 1970 (Prasetyo & Sutopo 2018). This was marked as the beginning of the third industrial revolution. In the third industrial revolution, electronic systems and information technology (IT) were used by industry. At present, the rapid development of sensor, interconnection and data analysis technology has led to the idea of integrating this technology into various industrial fields. This idea is predicted to become the next industrial revolution. The fourth industrial revolution became public as Industry 4.0 was recognized in 2011 (Bahrin et al. 2016).

2.2 Characteristic of industry 4.0

The principles of cyber physical systems (CPS), internet and future technology, and intelligent systems with enhanced para-digma human-machine interaction are applied to industry 4.0 (Sanders et al. 2016). CPS is a technology for combining the real world and the virtual world. This combination can be realized through integration between physical and computational processes (embedded and networked computer technology) in a closed loop (Lee 2008). Industry 4.0 focuses on creating smart products, processes and procedures that can make activities more effective and efficient (Crnjac et al. 2017). Industry 4.0 is related to the Internet of Things, Internet of Services, and Internet of Data. This is the essence of industry 4.0. There are six industry principles 4.0 namely interoperability, virtualization, decentralization, real time, service oriented, and modular (Prasetyo & Sutopo 2018). Based on research using literature review as a method, there are several characteristic approaches to industry 4.0 such as horizontal integration, vertical integration, Internet of Things, Internet Service, Internet Computing Cloud Data, Cyber-Physical Systems, new business models, flexible production, and cluster concepts (Crnjac et al. 2017). Industrial 4.0 is estimated to have big advantages for industries such as rapid product development, product customization, flexible production, increased productivity, optimality in decision making, and revenue growth (Prasetyo & Sutopo 2018). In conclusion, industry 4.0 is an industrial era in which all entities within it can connect with each other in real time using internet technology and CPS to achieve optimization in every process in the industry.

3 GREEN INDUSTRY BASED ON MINISTRY OF INDUSTRY

Green industry is an industry that in its production process prioritizes efforts to efficiency and effectiveness of sustainable use of resources so that it can harmonize the development of industries with the sustainability of environmental functions and can provide benefits to the community. It means that green industry is an approach oriented to increasing efficiency through efficient measures in the use of materials, water and energy. It is also oriented to alternative energy use, the use of materials that are safe for humans and the environment, and the use of low-carbon technology with the aim of increasing productivity and minimizing waste which emphasizes a business approach to improve environmental health (Ministry of Industry 2018b). The Ministry of Industry has two main strategies related to the Green Industry. The first strategy is the greening of existing industries and the second strategy is the creation of new green industries.

Green industry means implementing 4R in its production process which consists of reduction, reuse, recycling, and recovery. Some of the characteristics of a green industry are the production process using fewer raw materials, supporting materials, energy and water, using alternative energy, using recycled packaging, etc. which produce less waste (Hutahaean 2017).

The implementation of the Green Industry in Indonesia has so far been in the form of government recommendations. The registration of the Green Industry Awards is voluntary by the industry itself. The Green Industry Award is an award given to industries that have made efforts to preserve the use of natural resources. this is done through various stages of selection and verification based on a scoring system to be evaluated regularly (Ministry of Industry 2018b). Green Industry Awards are given to every industry that has succeeded in implementing and running its industry in green industry standards.

4 MAKING INDONESIA 4.0 BASED ON MINISTRY OF INDUSTRY

Industry 4.0 can have a direct and indirect impact on Indonesia. The direct impact is to revive the production sector and regain the position of net exporters. Indirect impacts are increasing the country's financial strength, increasing government spending, increasing investment, and building a strong economy (Ministry of Industry 2018a).

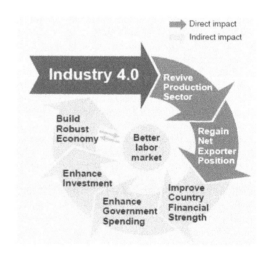

Figure 1. Direct and indirect impact of industry 4.0 (Ministry of Industry 2018a).

In making Indonesia 4.0, there are 5 top priority sectors of the industry such as food, textile and apparel, automotive, electronics and chemical beverages. Indonesia has set 10 National Priorities to Make Indonesia 4.0 such as material material reforms by redesigning industrial zones, embracing sustainability, empowering small micro-enterprises, building national digital infrastructure, attracting foreign investment, increasing human capital, building ecosystem innovations, investing incentive technology, and optimizing regulations and policies.

Indonesia 4.0 can create a large increase in overall GDP growth, job creation, and manufacturing GDP contributions. Making Indonesian policy 4.0 also needs to be well coordinated with several stakeholders and policies. Collaboration from government, industry and education is needed. Making Indonesia 4.0 will trigger immediate action with long-term aspirations based on the focus sector. For food and beverages, the sector's aspirations focus is establishing the ASEAN food and beverage center. In the field of textiles and apparel, becoming a leading functional clothing manufacturer is the aspiration of the focus sector. Automatically, this is the focus for building export leadership on ICE and EV. In addition, developing leading biochemical producers is the aspiration of the focus sector of the chemical industry. For the electronics industry, the sector aspirations focus on maintaining very capable domestic champions. Immediate actions must be taken by Indonesia such as technology incentives, investor roadshows, vocational schools, and support for small micro businesses.

5 DISCUSSION

The government has set 10 national priority steps in an effort to implement the Making Indonesia 4.0 roadmap. In the third priority, as stated by the Minister of Industry, Mr. Airlangga, that Industry 4.0 must accommodate sustainability standards. Indonesia views the challenges of sustainability as an opportunity to build national industrial capacity based on clean technology, electricity, biochemistry and renewable energy.

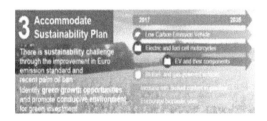

Figure 2. The third key national priority for making Indonesia 4.0 (Ministry of Industry 2018a).

Indonesia will strive to meet the sustainability requirements in the future by identifying the applications of technology and green growth opportunities and to promote a conducive environment.

When the government program Making Indonesia 4.0 runs well, either directly or indirectly, processes in the industry are increasingly leading to green industry. The demand for efficient use of raw materials and energy as well as every process become online and real-time, will have a positive impact on the reduction of waste and contamination by industry.

Table 1. Comparison characteristic between industry 4.0 and green industry (Ministry of Industry 2018b).

Code	Industry 4.0 characteristics	Code	Green Industry characteristic
A	Using cyber-physical system	1	Reduce the use of raw materials
B	Make activities more effective and efficient	2	Replace raw materials that are more environmentally friendly
C	Real-time data		
D	Improve productivity		
E	Related to internet of thing, internet of service, and internet of data	3	Reduce energy use
		4	Reduce water use
		5	Beneficial to the environment and society
F	Product customization		
G	Accommodate sustainability plan		

Table 2. Relationship and influence between industry 4.0 and green industry.

Matrix	1	2	3	4	5
A	V	X	X	V	V
B	V	V	V	V	V
C	V	V	X	X	V
D	V	V	V	V	V
E	X	X	X	X	V
F	V	V	V	V	V
G	V	V	V	V	V

Table 1 show the characteristics of the two programs which will then be compared to connect with each other. The relationship between them shows synergy and relationships for each characteristic seen in table 2 below.

Based on Table 2, there are 27 characteristics which can be matched each other from total 35 characteristics.

6 CONCLUSION

The synergy of the Green Industry with Industrial Revolution 4.0 was 77.1% with at least 27 characteristics that could be matched with each other from a total of 35 characteristic items. The Indonesia 4.0 program from the Ministry of Industry is in line with the Green Industry concept. Collaboration from government, industry and education is needed to maintain this synergy.

REFERENCES

Bahrin, M. A. K., Othman, M. F., Azli, N. H. N., & Talib, M. F. 2016. Industry 4.0: A Review on Industrial Automation and Robotic. *Jurnal Teknologi (Science and Engineering)* 78(6-13): 136-143.

Crnjac, M., Veza, I. & Banduka, N. 2017. From Concept to the Introduction of Industry 4.0. *International Journal of Industrial Engineering and Management* 8(1): 21-30.

Davies, R. 2015. *Industry 4.0 Digitalisation for productivity and growth.* Retrieved: http://www.europarl.europa.eu/RegData/etudes/BRIE/2015/568337/EPRS_BRI(2015)568337_EN.pdf., Online accessed on 26th June 2018.

Hutahaean, L.S. 2017. *Kebijakan Pengembangan Industri Hijau di Indonesia.* Bekasi: IHLH

Lee, E.A. 2008. Cyber physical systems: Design challenges. In Object Oriented Real-Time Distributed Computing (ISORC). *11th IEEE International Symposium*: 363-369.

Ministry of Industry. 2018a. *Presentation Material of Indonesia's Fourth Industrial Revolution: Making Indonesia 4.0.*

Ministry of Industry. 2018b. *Pedoman Penilaian Penghargaan Industri Hijau.* Jakarta: IHLH.

Prasetyo, H., & Sutopo, W. 2018. Industry 4.0: Telaah Klasifikasi Aspek dan Arah Perkembangan Riset. *Jurnal Teknik Industri* 13(1).

UNIDO. 2018. *Global Value Chains And Industrial Development.*

Sanders, A., Elangeswaran, C. & Wulfsberg, J. 2016. Industry 4.0 Implies Lean Manufacturing: Research Activities in Industry 4.0 Function as Enablers for Lean Manufacturing. *Journal of Industrial Engineering and Management*: 811-833.

Finance and Investment

Global Competitiveness: Business Transformation in the
Digital Era – Abdullah, Widiaty & Abdullah (eds)
© 2019 Taylor & Francis Group, London, ISBN 978-0-367-19442-0

Influence of intellectual capital on financial performance in real estate and property subsector companies

T. Jaya & S. Setiawan
Sekolah Tinggi Ilmu Ekonomi, Bandung, Indonesia

ABSTRACT: Science-based economic developments encourage companies to improve the management of their intangible assets such as intellectual capital. The purpose of this study was to determine the effect of intellectual capital consisting of three basic elements, namely Value Added Capital Employed (VACA), Value Added Human Capital (VAHU), and Structural Capital Value Added (STVA) on the performance of Return on Assets (ROA) on real estate & property companies listed on the Indonesia Stock Exchange (IDX) for the period of 2014–2016. This type of research is quantitative research with secondary data sourced from financial statements. Data analysis in this study used the method of multiple regression analysis. Data testing used the SPSS version 22 application. The results showed that VACA, VAHU, and STVA simultaneously affected 61.80% ROA, VACA affected 47.75% ROA, VAHU affected 50.41% ROA, and STVA did not affect ROA.

1 INTRODUCTION

In general, guidelines are used as a benchmark for investors to invest in terms of their financial performance. In terms of attracting investors, companies must have a consistent and good final performance. Financial performance is an illustration of the success of the company in various activities (Fahmi 2012). Economic progress, technological innovation, and competitive levels have an impact on companies to improve their financial performance. Competition makes companies change their business strategies based on workforce into knowledge-based business strategies (Oktavianti & Wahidahwati 2014). Science-based economic development encourages companies to improve the management of intangible assets.

The success of the company today is not only produced by tangible assets but the most important is how to manage intangible assets to provide added value and excellence to the company (Mashali 2018). One such intangible asset is intellectual capital. The phenomenon of intellectual capital in Indonesia began to develop after the emergence of PSAK No.19 concerning intangible assets (Yuniasih 2010). Pulic (1998) developed a model as a solution designed to provide information about the value creation of tangible assets and intangible assets owned by the company. This model is called "Value-Added Intellectual Coefficient (VAIC)". The main components of VAIC are Capital Employed, Human Capital, and Structural Capital owned by the company. Based on the Global Industry Classification Standards (GICS) in Woodcock & Whiting (2009), a real estate & property subsector company, belonging to one of the Intensive High-IC Industry classifications,

is an Intellectual Capital-intensive company. Therefore, effective management of intellectual capital is needed by real estate and property subsector companies to encourage growth in the company's financial performance.

Based on the above phenomenon, researchers are interested in knowing how the influence of intellectual capital is on the company's financial performance. The company's financial performance will be measured using one of the profitability ratios of Return on Assets (ROA). ROA is a profitability ratio that can show management effectiveness in using total assets (both tangible and intangible assets) owned by the company to generate profits (Devi et al. 2017). Like previous studies conducted by Ramadani et al. (2014) which examined the effect of Intellectual Capital on the financial performance of banking companies listed on the Indonesia Stock Exchange (IDX) in 2010–2012, this study will examine the effect of Intellectual Capital on the company's financial performance in real estate and property subsectors listed in IDX in the period 2014–2016. Based on the situation, the purpose of this study was to examine and analyze the influence of intellectual capital on financial performance in the real estate subsector and property listed on the IDX for the period 2014–2016.

1.1 Intellectual capital

Intellectual capital is a form of intangible assets that are very important for the company. Intangible assets are a combination of intellectual and human-centered markets that enable companies to function. Intellectual capital is the key to the success of the company

(Bontis 1998). Without intellectual capital, the company will not be able to run its business even with abundant assets because basically people use all these assets to achieve company goals (Baroroh 2013). According to Ulum (2008), intellectual capital is divided into three components. The first component that becomes a major part of intellectual capital is Human Resources. Human resources are a source of knowledge, skills, and competencies in an organization or company. Customer Capital or Relational Capital is the second component of intellectual capital which is the company's ability to interact with outside parties. The final component of intellectual capital is Structural Capital which is the ability of an organization or company to create routine processes and structures that support employee efforts to produce optimal performance.

1.2 *Value-Added Intellectual Coefficient (VAIC)*

The measurement model developed by Pulic (1998) is designed to provide information about the efficiency of the value creation of tangible assets and intangible assets owned by the company. The VAIC™ model measures the efficiency of Intellectual Capital in creating value based on the relationship of its three main components that use Value-Added Capital (VACA), which gives an idea of how much added value is created from management. Physical capital is in the form of financial capital and tangible assets such as buildings, land, equipment, and technology used for company operations. Value-Added Human Capital (VAHU) identifies the ability of the workforce to generate added value for the company from the funds spent on labor and Structural Capital Value Added (STVA) shows the value-added efficiency of Structural Capital which includes procedures, routines, and systems within the company in value creation.

1.3 *Financial performance*

According to Utomo (2014), financial performance is the achievement of something that is always measured by the company by using various measuring instruments in order to increase the effectiveness and efficiency of the company in generating income for the survival of the company. Ross et al. (2009) states that ratio is one of the financial analysis tools used for comparing and investigating the relationships that exist between various parts of financial information, such as are liquidity, solvency, profitability, activity, and market ratio. Financial performance is evaluated in three dimensions. The first is the productivity of the company or the process of processing inputs into output efficiently. The second is the dimension of profitability or the level of corporate income that exceeds costs. The third dimension is the market premium or the level of the company's market value that exceeds the book value (Iswati & Anshori 2007). According to Hery (2016), profitability is the

ratio used to measure a company's ability to generate profits from its business operations. The business operational goal for most companies is to maximize profits, both short and long term.

1.4 *Return on assets*

One type of profitability ratio is Return on Assets (ROA). ROA is the ratio between net income after tax and the number of assets that describes the rate of return of all assets owned by the company. According to Cashmere (2012), ROA is the result of the number of assets used in the company and can provide a good measure of company profitability because it shows management effectiveness in using assets to earn revenue.

1.5 *Research hypothesis*

In this research, there are four hypotheses, namely:

1) Value-Added Capital Employed (VACA), Value-Added Human Capital (VAHU), and Structural Capital Value Added (STVA) affect company's financial performance (ROA).
2) Value-Added Capital Employed (VACA) affects company's financial performance (ROA).
3) Value-Added Human Capital (VAHU) affects company's financial performance (ROA).
4) Structural Capital Value Added (STVA) affects company's financial performance (ROA).

2 RESEARCH METHOD

This research is causal explanative to test and analyze the effect of causal relationship of intellectual capital on financial performance in the real estate and property subsectors listed on the IDX for the period 2014–2016. The sampling technique in this study uses non-probability sampling, namely purposive sampling with the following criteria:

Table 1. Sample criteria.

No	Sample criteria
1.	Company subsector real estate & property listed on Indonesia Stock Exchange before 2014
2.	Company subsector real estate and property subsector that consistently published financial statements for the period 2014–2016
3.	Company subsector real estate and property that presents financial statements in Rupiah

Based on the techniques and sampling criteria, the samples used were 41 companies. Secondary data collection techniques in this study are literature studies. Data were collected using data sources from the

IDX (www.idx.co.id). The collected data is processed and analyzed using SPSS Statistics.

2.1 Outlier test

The outlier test in this study used the Mahalanobis Distance method. The decision criteria with the Mahalanobis Distance method are if the Mahalanobis distance is $\leq X2$. The value of X2 is obtained by looking at the Chi-Square table at the level of $p = 0.001$ is 13.82. In accordance with the decision-making criteria, there are 4 companies with Mahalanobis Distance values greater than 13.82. The list of 4 companies is Fortune Mate Indonesia Tbk (FMII), Nirvana Development Tbk (NIRO), Greenwood Sejahtera Tbk (GWSA), and Lippo Cikarang Tbk (LPCK). The sample used in this study became 37 companies.

2.2 Normality test

Data normality test in this study uses the Lilliefors test method with the following results:

Table 2. Lilliefors test.

	Kolmogorov–Smirnov[a]		
	Statistic	df	Sig.
ROA	0.070	111	0.200[*]

(Source: Output SPSS 22, 2018)

Table 2 shows the significance value of the Lilliefors test is 0.20 which means that the value is greater than 0.05. In accordance with the testing conditions, it can be concluded that the regression model in this study is normally distributed.

2.3 Multicollinearity test

In this study, multicollinearity tests used Variance Inflation Factor (VIF). A good regression model is free from multicollinearity on the basis of decision-making, i.e., if the tolerance value is 10, 0.10, or the VIF value is ≤ 10. Based on these results, multicollinearity does not occur (Satiti & Asyik 2013). The results of the multicollinearity test are as follows:

Table 3. Multicollinearity test.

	Collinearity Statistics	
Model	Tolerance	VIF
VACA	0.648	1.543
VAHU	0.632	1.582
STVA	0.968	1.033

(Source: Output SPSS 22, 2018)

According to the criteria above, it can be concluded that the independent variables in this study are free from multicollinearity.

2.4 Heteroscedasticity test

The heteroscedasticity test in this study uses the Glejser test on the basis of decision-making. If the significant value between independent variables with absolute residual values is more than 0.05, it can be concluded that there is no problem of heteroscedasticity. The results of the heteroscedasticity test are as follows:

Table 4. Multicollinearity test.

Model	Sig.
(Constant)	0.000
VACA	0.744
VAHU	0.686
STVA	0.409

(Source: Output SPSS 22, 2018)

According to the criteria, then it can be concluded that there is no heteroscedasticity problem.

2.5 Autocorrelation test

The autocorrelation test used in this study is the Durbin–Watson test with the following results:

Table 5. Autocorrelation test.

Model	Std. Error of the Estimate	Durbin–Watson
1	0.02984	2.032

(Source: Output SPSS 22, 2018)

Based on Table 5, the Durbin–Watson value was 2.032 after the previous Cochrane–Orcutt test. Through the Durbin–Watson table, the value of du is found to be 1.7472 and the value of dl is 1.6355, so du < d < 4-du (1.7472 < 2.032 < 2.2528). After the comparison between the results was calculated with du and dl, it can be concluded that there is no autocorrelation in this study.

This test aims to determine whether the independent variables simultaneously affect the dependent variable. The results of simultaneous data testing (F-test) is shown in Table 6:

Table 6. F-test (Anova).

Model	F	Sig.
Regression	60225	.000 [b]

(Source: Output SPSS 22, 2018)

Table 6 shows a significance value of 0.000, which means that the value is less than 0.05. It can be concluded that independent variable consisting of VACA, VAHU, and STVA influence simultaneously on dependent variable that is ROA.

This test aims to determine whether the independent variables individually have an influence on the dependent variable. Partial data test results (*t*-test) is shown in Table 7:

Table 7. *t*-Test.

Model	Sig.
(Constant)	0.584
VACA	0.000
VAHU	0.000
STVA	0.071

(Source: Output SPSS 22, 2018)

Table 7 shows that the VACA variable has a significant value of 0.000. The VAHU has a significance value of 0.000 and the STVA has a significance value of 0.071. VACA and VAHU values significance is smaller than 0.05, while the value of STVA is greater than 0.05. Thus, it can be concluded that the independent variables that have an influence on the dependent variable ROA are the VACA and VAHU variables.

3 RESULTS AND DISCUSSION

The coefficient of determination aims to measure how far the ability of independent variables is effective in explaining the dependent variable. The ability of independent variables simultaneously in describing the dependent variable is shown in Table 8:

Table 8. Coefficient of determination.

Model	R	R Square	Adjusted R Square
1	0.792	0.628	0.618

(Source: Output SPSS 22, 2018)

Table 8 shows that when the value of Adjusted R^2 is 0.618, then a yield of 61.80% (0.618 × 100%) is obtained, which explains that simultaneous independent variables consisting of VACA, VAHU, and STVA can explain the dependent variable ROA with a yield of 61.80%. From the results of hypothesis testing using multiple regression analysis, some conclusions can be drawn as follows:

1) VACA, VAHU, and STVA simultaneously affect the financial performance of ROA of 61.80%.
2) VACA affects the company's financial performance of ROA of 47.75%.
3) VAHU affects the company's financial performance of ROA of 50.41%.
4) STVA does not affect the company's financial performance of ROA.

Based on the testing of the data that has been done, the results of this study indicate that the added value generated from intellectual capital consisting of financial capital, quality human resources, and existing infrastructure in the company can affect the company's financial performance in this study using ROA as a measure of the company's financial performance. This shows that with the development of a science-based economy, management of intangible assets, namely intellectual capital, is important. The results of the study show that intellectual capital can affect the profitability of the company. Companies need to have heterogeneous intellectual capital in order to provide unique characteristics that can create competitive advantages that other companies do not have.

The results of the study show that Human Capital is the most important component of Intellectual Capital. Investment in training in Human Resources is an important investment and has economic value for the company because it can increase productivity. Productive Human Resources with a high level of creativity, expertise, knowledge, and experience can be a potential element for companies to increase their profitability. Human Resources will increase if the company is able to explore and utilize the knowledge of its employees to the fullest. In addition, the company also requires Capital Assets as support to realize the ideas of its employees to create innovative projects. Therefore, Human Capital and Capital Asset are two important components that must be managed and utilized efficiently and effectively so that the company's goals to obtain high profits can be achieved.

REFERENCES

Baroroh, N. 2013. Analysis of Intellectual Capital Influence on Financial Performance of Manufacturing Companies In Indonesia. *Journal of Accounting Dynamics* 5(2): 172-182.
Bontis. 1998. Intellectual Capital: An Explanatory Study That Develops The Steps and Models. *Management Decision* 36(2): 63-76.
Cashmere. 2012. *Financial Statement Analysis*. Jakarta: PT. Raja Grafindo Persada.
Devi, B. E., Khairunnisa, K. & Budiono, E. 2017. The Influence of Intellectual Capital on The Company's Financial Performance. *E-Proceeding of Management*: 491-500.
Fahmi. 2012. *Financial Performance Analysis*. Alfabeta.
Hery. 2016. *Financial Ratio For Business*. Jakarta: PT Grasindo.

Iswati, S. & Anshori, M. 2007. The Influence of Intellectual Capital to Financial Performance at Insurance Companies in Jakarta Stock Exchane JSE. *Proceeding of the 13th Asia Pacific Management Conference, Melbourne, Australia*: 1393-1399.

Mashali, F. 2018. Intellectua Capital Effect On Financial Performance and Corporate Market Values Empirical Study in the Company which contains in the LQ45 Index on the Indonesia Stock Exchange 2013-2016. *UNPAS Repositories and Scientific Journal.*

Oktavianti, H. & Wahidahwati. 2014. Factors affecting intellectual capital disclosure. *Journal of Accounting Science & Research*: 1-18.

Pulic. 1998. *Measuring the performance of intellectual potential in knowledge economy.* Retrieved from www.vaic-on.net.com.

Ramadani, V., Rexhepi, G., Gërguri-Rashiti, S., Ibraimi, S. & Dana, L.P. 2014. Ethnic entrepreneurship in Macedonia: the case of Albanian entrepreneurs. *International Journal of Entrepreneurship and Small Business* 23(3): 313-335.

Ross, S., Westerfield, R. & Jordan, B. 2009. *Introduction to Corporate Finance.* Jakarta: Salemba Empat.

Satiti, A. & Fun, N.F. 2013. The Influence of Intellectual Capital on Financial Performance of Insurance Companies. *Journal of Accounting Science & Research* 2(7): 1-20.

Ulum, I.M. 2008. Intellectual Capital Performance of Banking Sector in Indonesia. *Journal of Accounting and finance* 10: 77-84.

Utomo, T.A. 2014. Influence of Good Corporate Governance Mechanism on Financial Performance Empirical Study on Manufacturing Company Listed In Indonesia Stock Exchange Year 2010-2012. *Diponegoro Journal Of Accounting* 3(3).

Woodcock, J. & Whiting, RH 2009. *Intellectual Capital Disclosures by Australian Companies.*

Yuniasih, N.D. 2010. *Exploration of Company Market Performance: Review by Intellectual Capital.*

Global Competitiveness: Business Transformation in the
Digital Era – Abdullah, Widiaty & Abdullah (eds)
© 2019 Taylor & Francis Group, London, ISBN 978-0-367-19442-0

Financial literacy and financial behavior among college students

V.I. Dewi, I. Balian, I.P. Tanimukti & P.E. Sastrooredjo
Parahyangan Catholic University, Bandung, West Java, Indonesia

ABSTRACT: The purpose of this study is to determine the level of financial literacy among college students, to examine the effect of financial literacy on financial behavior. In this study, dependent variable of financial literacy is projected by general knowledge, interest rate and inflation, time value of money, and risk diversification. The measurement is using multiple choice questions and it was calculated based on the percentage of the correct answers. The dependent variable is measured using questions. This study is an applied research using explanatory method. The samples contain 535 college students. The data were analyzed by calculating the percentage of the correct answers to determine the level of financial literacy, and the multiple linear regression and hypothesis testing using F-statistics and t-statistics were used to analyze the effect of the financial literacy on the financial behavior. The results show that respondents answered about 56.6% of financial literacy questions correctly. It indicates that the level of financial literacy remains low. The result of financial behavior indicates that 80% of students still ignore to plan their financial decision. From multiple regression analysis, there is a significant effect of financial literacy on financial behavior.

1 INTRODUCTION

Recently, financial literacy is one of the important issues in the global economy. Financial literacy also becomes one of the policy focus of Indonesian government and financial institutions in Indonesia. National survey on Indonesian Financial Literacy conducted by Indonesian Financial services Authority (Otoritas Jasa Keuangan/OJK) in 2013 indicates that Indonesian population still experiences a relatively low rate of financial literacy. Only 21.8% of the Indonesian population is categorized as financially literate (Kusumaningrum 2014). In 2015, the World Bank conducted a survey of 150 thousand people in 140 countries and found that the financial literacy level of Indonesia was 32% (2 of 3 people in Indonesia are not financial literate).

Financial literacy influences how people manage their financial affairs. It has implications for their capability to leverage their wealth and lifestyle. Financial literacy also affected people's investment decisions. Financial literacy helps to improve the level of understanding of financial matters, which enables to process financial data and issue, filter out the information, and make decisions about personal finance (Sarigul 2014). Financial literacy is crucial to make decisions, especially related to daily activities such as saving, investment, and borrowing funds. Young adults need to have the basic financial knowledge and skill that could help them to make important personal financial decisions (Chen & Volpe 1998). Results of the survey on Financial Literacy of Young American Adults (Mandell 2008)

found that high school seniors and college students have poor financial knowledge.

OECD/INFE International (Atkinson et al. 2016) surveyed 51,650 adults aged 18–79 within 30 countries using the OECD/INFE toolkit to measure relevant aspect of financial literacy indicated by combining score on financial knowledge, behavior, and attitudes to longer term financial planning. The results show that overall levels of financial literacy are relatively low. The minimum target score is answering 70% of the basic financial knowledge questions correctly, but all countries on average achieved only 56%.

The purpose of this study is to determine the level of financial literacy among college students and how is their financial behavior. Furthermore, this study examined the effect of financial literacy on financial behavior among college students.

2 LITERATURE REVIEW

There are some previous studies on financial literacy that have been conducted by researchers, scholars, academicians, and finance professionals. Danes & Hira (1987) studied on money management knowledge of college students. The result showed that students had high level of knowledge in personal loan and record keeping but had low levels of knowledge in insurance, credit cards, and general management. Chen & Volpe (1998) analyzed the personal finance literacy among college students. The sample in this study is 924 college students. The result shows that respondents answer about 53% of questions correctly. Based on the level of financial literacy categorization from Danes & Hira (1987), the mean percentage of correct scores can be grouped into relatively high level of knowledge (for the mean percentage of more than 80%), medium level of knowledge (60%–79%), and relatively low level of knowledge (below 60%). The mean of college students financial literate is categorized in the low level of knowledge. Less knowledgeable students tend to hold wrong opinions and make incorrect decisions.

Van Rooij et al. (2007) conducted Internet survey on 2000 households in the Dutch population. The study measured the level of basic financial knowledge and advanced financial knowledge. Furthermore, they assessed the direction of causality of financial literacy to the stock market. Results show that while the understanding of basic economic concepts is far from perfect, it outperforms the limited knowledge of stocks and bonds, the idea of risk diversification, and the working of financial markets. A respondent who has low financial literacy is significantly less likely to invest in stocks.

Lusardi & Mitchell (2007) explained that financial literacy comprised not only the combination of individual understanding of financial products and concepts but also capability and confidence to take financial risks and opportunities. If the risk happened, they know where to go for help, using information to make choices and doing effective actions to improve their financial well-being. Cole et al. (2009) assessed the level of financial literacy and its relationship to demand for financial services in Indonesia and India. The results of this study show that financial literacy and financial behavior have strong relationship with each other. They find evidence that financial literacy not only has an important correlation to household financial behavior and household well-being, but also financial literacy training program does not affect financial decision. The other interesting finding is that people who open bank accounts was via providing small incentives not by financial literacy training program.

Lusardi et al. (2010) examined financial literacy among the young adults and showed that financial literacy is low, fewer than one-third of young adults possess basic knowledge of interest rates, inflation, and risk diversification. Financial literacy was strongly related to sociodemographic characteristics and family financial sophistication.

Lusardi & Mitchell (2010), took data using ALP Survey (American Life Panel) and Internet-based survey on respondents aged 18 years and above with the characteristics of socioeconomic vector *(age, sex, material status, education, race/ethnicity, income)*. The survey was using *two category: 1) basic financial literacy concept (compound interest, inflation and time value of money); 2) sophisticated financial knowledge (risk/return, difference between stock and bonds, how the stock market and risk*

diversification work, relationship between bond prices and interest rates).

Acording to Bhushan & Medury (2013), the level of financial literacy among individuals with salary was low and this financial literacy was affected by gender, education, income, nature of employement, and place of work.

Scheresberg (2013) studied on financial literacy and financial behavior of American young adults aged 25–34 years, using telephone and an online survey on 4500 samples from National Financial Capability Study (NFCS). The result showed that the financial literacy was low. The respondents who have a high income and have savings for emergency expenses and plan for their retirement have a high level of financial literacy. Navickas et al. (2014) stated that "basic concepts of personal finance is compound interests, investment risk and its management during short and long term periods".

Lusardi & Mitchell (2014) explained financial literacy is a way that can affect financial behavior. The level of *Financial Literacy* can be measured through testing the basic financial knowledge and advanced financial knowledge. Advanced financial knowledge is an understanding of risk diversification that relates to short- and long-term saving and investment.

Preliminary literature research of this study shows that most of the research studies of financial literacy were done in developed countries such as United States, Australia, and United Kingdom (UK). A few research studies have been done in developing countries such as Indonesia, India, Malaysia, and Vietnam. Most studies measure the level of financial literacy correlated to demographics and socio-economics group, but few research studies examined the effect of financial literacy level toward financial behavior. The purpose of this study is to determine that gap.

The following are the objectives of this study: 1) To determine the level of financial literacy among college students; 2) To find out the effect of financial literacy to financial behavior.

Furthermore, the hypothesis of this study are:

H_1: General financial knowledge affects financial behavior.

H_2: Interest rate and inflation affect financial behavior.

H_3: Time value of money affects financial behavior.

H_4: Risk diversification affects financial behavior.

3 RESEARCH DESIGN

This sudy is an explanatory research. The population of this research are people between 17 and 25 years old. By using convenience sampling, the questionnaires were distributed to 535 students at Parahyangan Catholic University using Internet survey. This study used survey methods. A comprehensive questionnaire was designed to cover four dimensions of financial literacy as the independent variable. It includes financial literacy on general knowledge, interest rate and inflation, time value of money, and risk diversification. The respondents were asked to answer seven questions as demographic data and 34 items multiple-choice questions of financial literacy. The score was calculated based on the percentage of the correct answers. The dependent variable was measured using 13 items that consist of financial behavior questions. The validity of the questionnaire was confirmed through face validity by people who have competencies in finance and using Spearman and Pearson correlation. The reliability was assessed using Cronbach's Alpha.

To determine the financial behavior, respondents were asked to choose four categories using Likert scale: 1–4 (Never, Almost, Rarely, Always/Routine).

Furthermore, the analysis technique used to confirm the effect of financial literacy on financial decision and behavior is a multiple regression analysis. Hypothesis testing using F-statistics was used to test the significance of the effect simultaneously and t-statistics was used to test partially, with a significance level of 5%.

4 RESULTS AND DISCUSSION

Detailed demographics of the sample are presented in Table 1. In terms of demographic background, most of the respondents are from 19 to 20 years old. Female respondents represent about 52% of the sample. Forty-five percent of the respondents are third-year students.

Table 1. Demographic of samples and the distribution of financial literacy.

		Number of respondents	%	Mean percentage of correct scores	Level of financial literacy
Gender	Male	258	48%	56.9%	Low
	Female	277	52%	56.3%	Low
Years of Age	17 to 18	16	3%	56.7%	Low
	19 to 20	325	61%	56.6%	Low
	21 to 22	148	28%	56.5%	Low
	23 and over	46	8%	56.2%	Low
Rank	First Year	14	3%	53.7%	Low
	Second Year	109	20%	53.9%	Low
	Third Year	242	45%	56.6%	Low
	Fourth Year and Up	170	32%	56.5%	Low
Income (IDR)	Under 500.000	69	13%	56.5%	Low
	500,001–1.000.000	126	24%	56.6%	Low
	1,000,001–1.500,000	111	21%	56.6%	Low
	1,500,001–2,000,000	136	25%	56.5%	Low
	More than 2,000,000	93	17%	56.6%	Low
Academic Disciplines	Economic Majors	444	83%	56.6%	Low
	Non-Economic Majors	91	17%	53.6%	Low
Amount of Finance Products	None	28	5%	55.8%	Low
	One Products	361	67%	56.6%	Low
	Two Products	104	19%	56.5%	Low
	Three Product	36	6%	56.6%	Low
	Four Products	6	0.1%	57.7%	Low
	Five and More	0			
Type of Finance Products					
	Savings	383			
	Giro	4			
	Deposit	54			
	Credit Cards	53			
	Stock	49			
	Obligation	2			
	Mutual Fund	6			
	Cooperative	1			
	Savings Account	1			
	Insurance	1			
	Cryptocurrency	1			
	None	28			

Source: Data processing results.

Table 2. Mean and median percentage of correct answers to financial literacy questions.

	Level of financial literacy		
	Low below 60%	Medium 60%–79%	High over 80%
Basic General Knowledge	54.5%		
Mean Correct Responses	58.3%		
Median Correct Responses			
Interest Rate and Inflation			
Mean Correct Responses		60%	
Median Correct Responses		66.7%	
Time Value of Money			
Mean Correct Responses		70.9%	
Median Correct Responses		75%	
Risk Diversification			
Mean Correct Responses	52.9%		
Median Correct Responses	58.3%		
Mean Correct Responses	56.6%		
Median Correct Responses	57.6%		

Source: Data processing results.

The distribution of the financial literacy, both basic financial knowledge and advanced financial knowledge indices across demographic variables, such as gender, age, grade, outcome, academic disciplines, and the amount of utility finance product, is determined. Table 1 shows that students from non-economic majors display lower financial literacy than economic majors. Table 1 also indicates that there are no large differences in the mean percentage of correct scores between gender, age, grade, and outcome. These findings are different from those findings by other literacy surveys such as Lusardi & Mitchell (2007).

The overall results on financial literacy level are presented in Table 2. The overall mean percentage of correct scores is 56.6%, indicating the respondents answered only about below 60% of the survey questions correctly. The median percentage of correct scores is 57.6%. This study finds that the financial literacy of students is less adequate or low.

The second purpose of this study was to determine the effect of financial literacy on personal finance decisions, opinions, and financial behavior among college students. The reliability of the questions of the questionnaire is 0.678 for the variable of financial literacy and 0.617 for the variable of personal finance opinions, decisions, and financial behavior. Cronbach's Alpha analysis indicates that the questionnaire is reliable.

There are several hypotheses to be tested. Multiple regression is tested whether or not the independent variable are significant towards the dependent variable. If the significant level is smaller than 0.05, then the independent variables are significant towards the dependent variables.

Based on SPSS output, the result of multiple regression is presented in the following table:

Table 3. The t-test coefficients and significant level.

Variable	Coefficients (B)	Significant level
(Constant)	1.249	0.000
General Knowledge	0.131	0.000
Interest & Inflation	0.127	0.000
Time Value of Money	0.071	0.000
Risk Diversification	0.209	0.000

The results in Table 3 indicate that financial literacy has a significant effect on financial behavior at 5% level of significance.

The linear regression model is:

$Y = 1.249 + 0.131\ X_1 + 0.127\ X_2 + 0.071\ X_3 + 0.209\ X_4 + \varepsilon$

The R-square of the multiple regression model is 0.345, which means that 34.5% of dependent variables could be explained by independent variables. The significant level of general financial knowledge, interest and inflation, time value of money, and risk diversivication are smaller than 0.05, which means that those variables are significant in influencing financial behavior.

Statistical F–Test – The F-test was employed to establish whether the model is significant simultaneously. The result is given in Table 4, where the significance of p-value is compared with the level of significance. With the p-value < 0.05, it implies that the model is significant.

Table 4. The F-test.

Model		Sum of squares	df	Mean square	F	Sig.
		ANOVA[a]				
1	Regression	30.741	4	7.685	69.736	0.000[b]
	Residual	58.408	530	.110		
	Total	89.148	534			

[a] Dependent Variable: Financial Behavior.
[b] Predictors: (Constant), Risk Diversification, Time Value of Money, Basic Financial Knowledge, Interest & Inflation.

5 CONCLUSION

The findings of this research are: First, in average score, respondents answer about 56.6% of financial literacy questions correctly. It indicates that the level is low. Second, knowledge level of Interest & Inflation and time value of money are in medium level. Third, financial Behavior indicates that 80% of students still ignore to plan their financial decision, which shows that financial behavior of the students is in low level. Fourth, there are significant effects of financial literacy on financial behavior simultaneously and partially. The contribution of financial literacy to the financial behavior is 34%.

REFERENCES

Atkinson, A., Monticone, C. & Mess, F.A., 2016. OECD/ INFE International Survey of Adult Financial Literacy Competencies. *Technical Report*, OECD.
Bhushan, P. & Medury, Y. 2013. Financial Literacy and its Determinants. *International Journal of Engineering, Business and Enterprise Applications (IJEBEA)* 13 (145): 155-160.
Chen, H. & Volpe, R.P. 1998. An analysis of personal financial literacy among college students. *Financial services review* 7(2): 107-128.
Cole, S.A., Sampson, T.A. & Zia, B.H. 2009. Financial literacy, financial decisions, and the demand for financial services: evidence from India and Indonesia (pp. 09-117). Cambridge, MA: Harvard Business School.
Danes, S.M. and Hira, T.K., 1987. Money management knowledge of college students. *Journal of Student Financial Aid* 17(1): 1.

Kusumaningrum, K. 2014. *National Seminar UII: Bagaimanakah Tingkat Literasi Keuangan Penduduk Indonesia?* Fakultas Ekonomi Universitas Islam Indonesia.
Lusardi, A. & Mitchelli, O.S. 2007. Financial literacy and retirement preparedness: Evidence and implications for financial education. *Business economics* 42(1): 35-44.
Lusardi, A., Mitchell, O.S. & Curto, V. 2009. Financial literacy among the young: Evidence and implications for consumer policy (No. w15352). National Bureau of Economic Research.
Lusardi, A. & Mitchell, O.S. 2009. How ordinary consumers make complex economic decisions: Financial literacy and retirement readiness (No. w15350). National Bureau of Economic Research.
Lusardi, A. & Mitchell, O.S., 2014. The economic importance of financial literacy: Theory and evidence. *Journal of economic literature* 52(1): 5-44.
Mandell, L. (Eds.). 2008. *The Financial Literacy of Young American Adults*. Washington, DC: The Jumpstart Coalition For Personal Financial Literacy.
Navickas, M., Gudaitis, T. & Krajnakova, E. 2013. Influence of Financial Literacy on Management of Personal Finances in a Young Household, *Verslas: Teorija ir Praktika Business: Theory and Practice* 15(1): 32-40
Sarigul, H. 2014. A Survey of Financial Literacy Among University Student, *Muhasebe ve Finansman Dergisi*: 207-244.
Scheresberg, C.D.B. 2013. Financial Literacy and Financial Behavior Among Young Adults: Evidence and Implications. *Numeracy Advancing Education in Quantitative Literacy* 6(2): 5.
Van Rooij,M., Lusardi, A., Alessie, A. & Rab, J.M. 2007. Financial Literacy and Stock Market Participation. *CFS Working Paper No2007/27*, Econstor The Open Access Publication Server of the ZBW.

Global Competitiveness: Business Transformation in the Digital Era – Abdullah, Widiaty & Abdullah (eds)
© 2019 Taylor & Francis Group, London, ISBN 978-0-367-19442-0

The role of information source in decision-making for investors: Case study at Maranatha Sinarmas Securities Investment Gallery

S. Setyawan
Maranatha Christian University, Bandung, West Java, Indonesia

ABSTRACT: Professional capital market investors need an appropriate source of information to execute their decision about buying, selling, or keeping their portfolio. In making decision about their transaction, investors are expected to be influenced by the news from professionals (financial advice), informal news from relatives (word of mouth), and also from investment media (specialized media). This descriptive study aims to evaluate the type of source that is frequently used to make the appropriate decision. Among 425 investors in Maranatha Sinarmas Securities Investment Gallery, there are 30 investors who are willing to participate as respondents in this research. It shows that specialized media is the most frequently used information because the investor still believes in formal issues.

1 INTRODUCTION

The growth of capital market in Indonesia is quite outstanding. There are 534 companies listed and 473 kinds of bonds traded in Indonesia Stock Exchange (www.idx.co.id). It is also supported by enormous investors in Indonesia. Indonesia Central Securities Depository (KSEI) reported there are 491,116 individual investors in 2016, and it has been growing 26 percent from previous year (www.ksei.co.id).

Investor trading activity in capital market includes buying, selling, or holding. Each second in trading time can be observed at specific trading software. It describes all trading activity in present time. This trading time is recorded and resumed in particular time. The record can describe the pattern of investor's decision behavior.

An investor as securities consumer has unique behavior when facing capital market trading. The behavior can be conservative, speculative, or opportunistic (Mistry 2015), analyst both technical and fundamental (Maditinos et al. 2007), based on feeling or theoretical (Jaiyeoba & Haron 2016) and other kinds of behavior.

In making their stock transaction decision, investors are expected to be influenced by several inputs such as financial advice, word of mouth (WOM), and specialized media (Tauni et al. 2016). Financial advice is obtained from a paid professional who supervises individuals for their financial matters (Cruciani 2017). WOM can be described as informal information from social environment. It is a powerful communication, especially in electronic communication era. For today's generation, electronic WOM (eWOM) has become one of the most important ways to communicate (Steffers & Burgee

2009). Specialized media is a formal financial media and formally issued by certain companies. The common specialized media are corporate financial report (Al-Ajmi 2009) and mass media (Davis 2006).

Maranatha Sinarmas Securities Investment Gallery (*Galeri Investasi Maranatha Sinarmas Sekuritas*) was founded in 2007. It used to be Maranatha Sinarmas Securities Indonesia Stock Exchange Corner (*Pojok BEI Maranatha Sinarmas Sekuritas*). The investment gallery itself is supported by Indonesia Stock Exchange to educate students, lecturers, staffs, and also parents as investors of the gallery (www.idx.co.id). One of the objectives is to increase the investors' capital market literacy; furthermore, the investors are confident to trade in capital market. The gallery has four computers with online trading information that can help investor to read the trading pattern in particular time.

The main problem of this investment gallery is the passive investor. It has 452 investors with more than 50 percent as passive investors. They are listed as investors in the gallery but they have no transaction. Most of them are beginner investors who are not confident to make the trading decision for they are lack of information source. Misunderstanding about source of information may result in loss for the investor, although understanding information may not be creating profit. Therefore, they want to understand the pattern of advanced investors in making their investment decision.

This research wants to describe the type of source of information that is used by advanced investors; moreover, the decision is also based on their decision behavioral pattern. It is also expected that the result can increase the beginner investors' confident to trade in Indonesia Capital Market.

2 LITERATURE REVIEW

2.1 *Behavior pattern*

Economically, investors expect to gain profit in trading at capital market. To gain the profit, investors have to decide whether they buy, sell, or even keep their investment. Nevertheless, investors should face the risk to gain the profit. This obstacle creates investors' behavior pattern.

Behavior pattern can be identified by decision process. Rani (2014) states that consumer (or investor in this matter) goes through a decision process. There are recognition problem, information search, and evaluation of alternatives, purchase decision, and post-purchase behavior. Based on this decision process, this research adapted Rani's (2014) theory and made it as a decision behavior for investors from identification the needs of stock until the execution about buying or selling the stock. It is called the four steps of investors' decision behavior.

Table 1. Four steps of investors' decision behavior.

Step	Behavior
1	Identify the needs of stocks
2	Search the information of stocks
3	Evaluate the alternative of stocks
4	Execute the decision stock

Source: Adapted from Rani (2014).

In the first step, investors should identify their needs of stock, whether it is important, interesting, or even just follow the trend. Then they should search the information about the issuers (companies), which will be discussed in this research. After having complete information, investors should evaluate which stocks are feasible to be executed. The last step is executing the decision, whether to buy, sell, or even hold the stock.

Tauni et al. (2016) investigate the impact of sources of information on trading behavior by analyzing the influence of investor personality in Chinese futures market. Based on their research, the sources of information consist of three types of sources, i.e. financial advice, word of mouth, and specialized media.

2.2 *Source of information*

Zhang (2014) measures the face-to-face financial advice provided by an authorized financial adviser. Financial adviser could be someone who is advanced in capital market and usually works in capital market. Tauni et al. (2016) define financial advice as advice obtained by an investor from professionals such as bank manager, financial advisor, or broker advice. Zhang (2014) concludes that investor who

gets information from financial advice will have a better return. Investors will behave positively if there is information from financial advice. In this research, financial advisor could be a gallery investment's officer or staff, securities broker, banker, or financial planner.

In this discussion, WOM can be said as an informal chain of financial information between investors whether in offline (viral) or online (buzz) form (Kotler & Keller 2016). This research used friends, family members, lecturers, students, or other investors as the forms of WOM. Special media is a mass media which discuss specifically about finance and investment. The media could be local media (Deshpande & Svetina 2011) or international media. This research used financial statement (Al-Ajmi 2009), financial newspaper, financial magazine, newsletter from securities, television, or website.

3 METHODS

This research tries to describe the situation in Maranatha Sinarmas Securities Investment Gallery. There are 30 out of 452 investors who are willing to share the information. The questionnaire was adopted from Tauni et al. (2016) encompassing three parts of source of information, i.e. financial advice, WOM, and specialized media. The respondents were asked to confirm whether they never or always use the specified source of information. The questions used 6-likert scale to prevent neutral or undecided answer.

4 RESULTS

There are lots of sources of information for the investors to form their decision. According to respondents as advanced investors, they gathered the information from particular sources as depicted in Table 2.

The first part is financial advice. Most of the respondents gathered the information from the person who is appointed at the investment gallery, i.e. the head and staff. It is believed that they usually or almost meet the head and staff in investment gallery to execute their trading. The head and staff get the information from securities industries. Respondents are rarely using financial planner for they have to pay for the services.

The second part is WOM. Most of the respondents believe other investors in investment gallery. Many of them also trust investment and capital market lecturer at campus for their expertise in theory. On the other hand, they do not gather information from their own family members who have no understanding about capital market.

The last part is specialized media. Most of the respondents believe in official news; nevertheless,

Table 2. Respondent's source of information.

Source of information	Average	
Panel A: Financial Advice		
Head and staff in investment gallery	4.03	2.35
Investment gallery's securities industry staff	2.90	
Other securities staff	2.10	
Banking staff	1.63	
Private financial planner	2.07	
Other financial planner	1.37	
Panel B: Word of mouth		
Investors at investment gallery	3.73	2.45
Investors at host securities	2.60	
Other investors	2.40	
Investment and capital market lecturer	3.03	
Other lecturer	2.33	
Students in investment and capital market class	2.40	
Other students	1.90	
Family as investor	2.53	
Family but not as investor	1.13	
Panel C: Specialized media		
Financial report	3.53	2.80
Newsletter from host securities	2.90	
Newsletter from other securities	2.60	
Television	2.70	
Internet	2.93	
Newspaper or magazine	2.13	

corporate financial report is higher than mass media. This result supports previous researches stating that investor's perception is high at specialized media, especially financial report (Al-Ajmi 2009) and mass media as the source of information for the investor (Davis 2006).

Moreover, this result also shows that group of specialized media are the most popular source of information, followed by WOM and financial advice. Unfortunately, the difference test between these groups is rejected, i.e. there are no differences between groups. On top of that, although specialized

Table 3. Specified Specialized Media.

Media	Name	Total
Television	Metro TV	6
	IDX Channel	2
	Others	4
Internet	www.kontan.com	4
	www.idx.co.id	3
	Others	8
Newspaper or magazine	Kontan	5
	Bisnis Indonesia	2
	Kompas	1

media is the most popular, investors also use other source of information to make their investment decision.

Mass media also takes part of investors' decision-making. Therefore, this research also shows the kind of mass media that is used as source of information. Table 3 exposes the sources of specialized media based on type of media, i.e. television, Internet, and newspaper or magazine. It shows that local media is trusted to be the source of information. This result also supports Deshpande & Svetina (2011) saying that local mass media can help investor to decide their investment.

5 CONCLUSION

This descriptive research wants to show what kind of source of information is used by advanced investors to decide on their investment. Using previous research about four steps of investors' decision behavior (Rani 2014) and source of information (Tauni et al. 2016), it is obvious that most of Maranatha Sinarmas Investment Gallery uses specialized media, along with WOM and financial advice. Most of them also use local mass media to make their investment decision.

The formal specialized media, especially financial report and newsletters, are the most reliable sources used by investors, as these provide reliable description for the investor to execute their investment decision. Moreover, investors also believe in informal news from their trusted sources, i.e. other investors at gallery, and investment lecturers.

REFERENCES

Al-Ajmi, J. 2009. Investors' use of corporate reports in Bahrain. *Managerial Auditing Journal* 24(3): 266-289.

Cruciani, C. 2017. Understanding Investor Behaviour. In C. Cruciani, *Investor Decision-Making and the Role of the Financial Advisor: A Behavioural Finance Approach* (pp. 3-26). Cham, Switzerland: Palgrave Macmillan.

Davis, A. 2006. The role of the mass media in investor relations. *Journal of Communication Management* 10 (1): 7-17.

Deshpande, S. & Svetina, M. 2011. Does local news matter to investors? *Managerial Finance* 37(12): 1190-1212.

Jaiyeoba, H. & Haron, R. 2016. A quantitative inquire into the investment decision behavior of the Malaysian Stock Market investor. *Quantitative Research in Financial Markets* 8(3): 246-267.

Kotler, P. & Keller, K. 2016. *Marketing Management* (15 ed.). Essex, England, UK: Pearson Education Limited.

Maditinos, D., Sevic, Z. & Theriou, N. 2007. Investors' behavior in the Athens Stock Exchange (ASE). *Studies in Economics and Finance* 24(1): 32-50.

Mistry, K. 2015. A study of individual investor's behavior in stock market - with special reference to Indian Stock

Market. *International Journal of Management and Commerce Innovations* 3(1): 541-545.

Rani, P. 2014. Factors influencing consumer behavior. *International Journal of Current Research and Academic Review* 2(9).

Steffers, E. & Burgee, L. 2009. Social ties and online word of mouth. *Internet Research* 19(1): 42-59.

Tauni, M., Fang, H. & Iqbal, A. 2016. Information sources and trading behavior: does investor personality matter? *Quantitative Research in Financial Markets* 8(2): 94-117.

www.idx.co.id. (n.d.). Retrieved April 2017, from Indonesia Stock Exchange.

www.ksei.co.id. (n.d.). Retrieved April 2017, from Indonesia Central Securities Depository.

Zhang, A. 2014. Financial advice and asset allocation of individual investors. *Pacific Accounting Review* 26(3): 226-247.

Global Competitiveness: Business Transformation in the
Digital Era – Abdullah, Widiaty & Abdullah (eds)
© *2019 Taylor & Francis Group, London, ISBN 978-0-367-19442-0*

Investment behaviour in manufacturing companies in Indonesia: Study on leverage, company growth, and cash holding

A.C. Nugroho & A. Rizki
APP Polytechnic Ministry of Industry, Jakarta, Indonesia

N.A. Nasution
Master Student in Sustainability and Business, University of Leeds

ABSTRACT: Decision in investment is critical for company's performance, competitiveness, profitability and their survival. This study was aimed to demonstrate empirically how manufacturing company's leverage and growth affect their investment decision in Indonesian context. This study utilized annual financial statements of companies in the manufacturing sector listed on the Indonesia Stock Exchange (BEI) within the period of 2007 to 2016. The results of analysis showed that leverage has a control function on management. Company growth has positive effect on the investment. Meanwhile, free Cash Flow has negative impact on investment that can be proven by their cash holding behaviour. In addition, this study demonstrated that the companies' growth rate does not strengthen nor weaken the effect of leverage on the investment decisions of the manufacturing companies in Indonesia. The fact is assumed to be happened due to the financial constraint issues when the company intended to perform external financing for their investment in Indonesia.

1 INTRODUCTION

Manufacturing company investment behaviour is different from companies in other sectors. Investment behaviour of these manufacturing companies tends to be less affected by regulation, different from finance company, and the nature of the activities that are different from utility companies (Aivazian et al. 2003).

Investment projects can be operational or have a strategic focus. In strategic investments, usually large amounts of investment, involving high levels of risk, produce results that are difficult to measure, and have a significant long-term impact on company performance (Alkaraan & Northcott 2006). Wrong investment decisions can negatively impact the company over the long term, not just in short term.

Various studies on investment decisions in companies within the agency theory framework in manufacturing firms have been conducted, particularly on the topic of leverage influence as a firm's control. But the studies haven't yielded consistent results. This indicates the existence of different corporate condition characteristics or environment.

Indonesia manufacturing companies are experiencing financial constraints that affect their investment behaviour (Ajide 2017, Prasetyantoko 2007). With this financial constraints condition, Indonesian manufacturing companies become an interesting object to be investigated in terms of its leverage relationship with and company growth influence on investment decision.

The investment decisions are important because they will affect future conditions on both macro and micro environmental levels. On the macro environmental level, Kiel et al. (2014) stated that investment in infrastructure of transportation can affect the competitiveness of a region whereas on the micro environmental level. The investment itself is divided into intangible and tangible investments. Investments in intangible assets including investments in training and advertising and these will increase the company market values (Zambrano et al. 2017). Similarly, in investment in tangible assets, investment decisions are important as they will affect the company value (Andreou et al. 2017, Vranakis & Chatzoglou 2012).

Optimizing the company value can be achieved through the implementation of proper financial management. The financial decision taken will affect other financial decisions and have an impact on the company value (Fama & French 1998). Study on investment decisions conducted by Fama & French (1998) and Chen et al. (2014) revealed that the company investment decisions significantly affected the company performance as they responded positively to better investments and profits from investments increased the company profitability.

Having the same sound, Aivazian et al. (2003) and Lang et al. (1996) stated that one of the important aspects in the company is investment decision and the decision made by the company is important for the company competitiveness. Savolainen et al. (2017) pointed out that the choice of financial structure is essential to maximize shareholder value.

According to Firth et al. (2012), in addition to shareholders, there is also a debt-holder who will monitor the company performance and business decisions of the company including investment decisions with the existence of leverage. The agency problem in Aivazian et al. (2003) is "over-investment" because of the conflict between management and shareholder. Managers have a tendency to scale-up their company expansions and pay less attention to their future company value after investments. More-over, they also take unnecessary or poor investment projects that may reduce shareholder wealth. The management ability to implement the policy is limited by the availability of cash flow and this constraint can be further minimized through leverage. By issuing its debt, the company has to pay interest and principals that put pressure on that management so that it will not allocate the company funds for poor investment projects.

Accordingly, in their studies, Anwar & Sun (2014), Aivazian et al. (2003), and Guney et al. (2011) stated that leverage affected investment decisions. Jensen (1986) and Stulz (1990) predicted a negative relationship between leverage and investment but emphasized that this might be beneficial to shareholders in low-growth companies, as managerial flexibility over debt limits exceed free cash flow.

According to Lang et al. (1996), management uses leverage based on private information on the future company growth. The existing capital structure literature suggests that managers in companies with good company growth opportunities should prefer lower leverage because the companies will not be able to take advantage of investment opportunities if they have to raise funds from outside.

In company investment decisions, the growth variable of the company is an indicator that is noticed by manager (agent), debt-holder, and shareholder. Aivazian et al. (2003) and Lang et al. (1996) used Tobin Q as a measure of company growth. The Tobin Q variable has been used much earlier as a control variable in the regression model which sees the company growth effect on company investment and this variable was used by Jiang et al. (2015), Firth et al. (2012), Giroud & Mueller (2011), Chen et al. (2013), Aivazian et al. (2003), and Lang et al. (1996).

According to Aivazian et al. (2003), the ratio of Tobin Q serves as a proxy for easy access to capital markets. The companies with high growth can be easier to refinance and recapitalize in the capital market. In this capital market, investors (debt-holders and shareholders) will pay attention to the company Tobin Q when the company takes investment decisions. Meanwhile, Aivazian et al. (2003) and Lang et al. (1996) had conducted studies showing that the variable of company growth rate will assess the effect of over-investment or under-investment on the company investment.

Given the presence of interest cost and creditor supervision, management will be more cautious in investing (Anwar & Sun 2014, Guney et al. 2011, and Aivazian et al. 2003). Leverage is often used to prevent over-investment and increase control over the company management.

In regards to the presence of leverage, there is a conflict among shareholders, management and debt-holder, and this conflict can be examined through the agency theory. Nonetheless, there are also different results from the research on agency theory in capital structure as conducted by Banga & Gupta (2017) in businesses in India stating that the leverage determination was affected by the implementation of pecking order and trade off theories, however, there is no evidence of agency theory. Furthermore, empirical results of the research by Dawar (2014) in India highlighted that the leverage had a negative effect on the financial performance of Indian companies, contradicting the assumption of agency theory as it is generally accepted in both developed and developing countries.

Although a number of studies have shown that leverage has an effect on investment, there are still in-consistent results. As revealed in the research by Ajide (2017) showing that the leverage does not affect company investment and the study also showed that Tobin Q had a negative effect on the company investment; however, this result was inconsistent with studies conducted by Aivazian et al. (2003) and Lang et al. (1996) in which the Tobin Q had a positive effect on the company investment.

The research results of Aivazian et al. (2003) and Lang et al. (1996) showed that the company diversification based on the company growth rate affected leverage on company investment. Nevertheless, this is different from the current research results that do not indicate any effects of the company growth rate and this is presumably due to the financial constraints.

This is in accordance with Ajide (2017) stating that the presence of financing constraints will affect the company-specific effect on the decision making on the company investment. Meanwhile, Prasetyantoko (2007) stated that in Indonesia, some financial constraint issues come up; therefore, the research became interesting as it was conducted in Indonesia in which there were issues of financial constraint occurring as the companies who intended to invest using leverage. Subsequently, empirical proofs are required for this matter.

2 RESEARCH OBJECTIVES

Despite the importance of company investment decisions, there were inconsistencies from the previous researches on the leverage and company growth effect on investment decisions as well as the presence of financial constraints in Indonesia. Therefore, this research was necessary to be conducted. The objectives of this research were to analyze the effect of leverage and company growth on investment decisions and to further analyze whether the growth rate of the company would have an effect on leverage functioning as the management control.

3 THE RELATIONSHIP BETWEEN LEVERAGE, GROWTH, AND INVESTMENT

Aivazian et al. (2003) examined the impact of financial leverage on company investment decisions by using information obtained from the Canadian industrial companies. The results showed that leverage was negatively related to investment and this negative effect was significantly stronger for companies with low growth opportunities compared to high growth opportunities. Jensen (1986) and Stulz (1990) predicted a negative relationship between leverage and investment; nonetheless, they emphasized that this might be beneficial to shareholders in low-growth companies as the managerial flexibility over debt limits exceeds free cash flow.

According to Firth et al. (2012), in addition to shareholders, there were also debt-holders who monitored the company performance and business decisions including investment decisions due to leverage. Firth et al. (2012) examined the relationship of cash inflows and financing channels for listed companies in China. The results show that negative investments are related to low cash flow rates, yet they were positively related to high cash flow rates. These results are consistent with those reported by Cleary et al. (2007) for companies in the US and by Guariglia & Yang (2015) for those in the UK.

Lang et al. (1996) conducted a study using pooling regressions and putting aside the effect of individual companies. The results found that pooling regression tended to ignore the impact of leverage on investment and most appropriate fixed-effect model specification. The results showed that leverage had a significant negative impact on investment for Canadian companies and had a strong negative impact on companies with low growth opportunities.

Dawar (2014) examined agency theory by examining the effect of capital structure on company performance in the emerging economy country of India using the data panel. The empirical results indicated that leverage had a negative effect on the financial performance of Indian companies, as opposed to the assumption of agency theory as it is generally accepted in developed and developing countries. Consequently, agency theory postulate should be examined through different perspectives in India considering the market basic characteristics and the dominance of state-owned banks on lending for the company sector.

Aivazian et al. (2003) and Lang et al. (1996) utilized Tobin Q as a measure for company growth. According to Aivazian et al. (2003), Tobin Q defines the market value of the company total assets divided by the book value of total assets as a proxy of the company growth opportunities. Lang et al. (1996) used Tobin Q as a control variable for growth measures. Companies with higher Q values have better growth opportunities as argued by Lang et al. (1996). In contrast, the low Tobin Q ratio indicates that the company does not have good investment opportunities for new investors. Therefore, Tobin Q is utilized as a proxy of company growth.

McConnell & Servaes (1990) examined the non-financial corporations in the US in 1976, 1986, and 1988. His research divided the samples into two, the company with a strong growth opportunity and the company with a weak growth opportunity. The results show that the company value is negatively correlated with leverage for the company with a strong growth opportunity (as indicated by high Tobin's Q) and positively correlated with leverage for the company with a weak growth opportunity (as indicated by the low Tobin Q value).

According to Aivazian et al. (2003), companies with high Q scores (those with strong growth prospects) have higher cash flow expectations or net assets and can reduce the moral risks and adverse selection issues inherent in the credit supply to companies in the capital market. Companies with high growth can more easily refinance and recapitalize in the capital market, while in companies with low Q values, leverage will become more stringent constraints and limit the investment; as a result, companies will face difficulties in recapitalizing due to their weak growth prospects.

High Tobin Q value reflects better company performance in the market and reflects the company's prospects in the future so that it is easier to get funding from external parties (Brigham & Gapenski 1996). Thus, high Tobin's Q value tends not to encounter financial constraints.

According to Fazzari et al. (1988), the presence of asymmetric information related to external funding sources will cause external funding costs to be higher than internal funding, resulting in financial constraints in which they lack access to external funding. Due to this limitation, investment decisions of companies tend to be sensitive to cash flow. Myers (1977) showed that with a high level of leverage, a positive net present value project (NPV) could not be funded due to the emergence of debt overhangs from the previous debt financing.

Companies in investment funding can obtain funds through internal and external funds. Leverage is used by corporations as external funding, which is proven by various studies related to the investment decisions, has an impact on management control functions on investment decision. If company use leverage, the management will be more selective on their investment decision and will make sure that their investment decision will have a positive impact on company profit. Based on this result, leverage predicted will have a negative impact on corporate investment. Company that has a high growth will have greater possibilities to get capital funding for company investment. Based on studies on relationship between company growth and investment, it can be concluded that company growth will have a positive effect on corporate investment. However, Indonesian cases with the financial constraint occur in manufacturing company give room for improvement on the present study. This condition is never in consideration in previous studies. With this condition, it is expected that there will be difference result in this analysis. In this case, the impact of leverage, company growth, and interaction both of leverage and company growth on investment decision will be different compared to the previous studies.

4 RESEARCH METHOD

This study used annual financial statements of 50 companies in the manufacturing sector listed on the Indonesia Stock Exchange (BEI) within the period of 2007 to 2016 as data to be investigated. Fifty companies were selected through sorting/selection process with several criteria. The criteria cover: the companies have completeness of financial statement data, they are listed on ISE within the period of 2007 to 2016 and they have a positive profitability. We employed panel data regression to analyze the data in which investment was used as the dependent variable while leverage, cash flow, sales, and Tobin-Q were used as the independent variables. The definitions of these variables are further described in Table 1.

Three types of Tobin Q measured were used in this study. This research used Tobin Q as the proxy of the company growth. A number of Tobin Q were utilized to examine the robustness of the Tobin Q effects on the company investment. Tobin Q was distinguished by its method of calculation. TQ-a is a calculation of Tobin Q based on Jiang et al. (2015), Firth et al. (2012), and Giroud & Mueller (2011). Meanwhile, TQ-b is a calculation of Tobin Q based on Chen et al. (2013), Fazzari et al. (1988), Whited (1992), Baker et al. (2003), and McLean et al. (2012). Lastly, TQ-c is a calculation of Tobin Q based on Aivazian et al. (2003) and Lang et al. (1996).

Table 1. The variable measurements.

Variable	Note
I	Net investment (I)/lag of net fixed assets (K) = {Capital expenditure-Depreciation}/lag of net fixed assets
FCF	Free cash flow are divided by from the book value on the current assets
TQ	a. The ratio of the total stock market value is divided by the book value of the total assets at the beginning of the year. b. The result of the market value in equity minus the book value in equity added by the book value on asset is divided by the book value on asset. c. {The total of liabilities + common stock market value + estimated market value in preferred stock}/book value of total assets (TQ_C)
LEV	Total of liabilities/assets
SALES	Net Sales (Sales)/fixed assets (K)
D_TQ	Dummy variable equal to 1 if Tobin's Q> 1, and 0 for the reverse

5 RESULTS AND DISCUSSION

5.1 Descriptive statistics

The descriptive statistical analysis of this research was obtained from the data from the 50 manufacturing financial report from 2008 until 2016. The following is the result of the statistical descriptive variables presented in Table 2.

Table 2 presents the descriptive statistical information for investment (I) and other variables including cash flow (CF), Tobin Q (TQ_A, TQ_B, TQ_C), leverage (LEV), and Sales (SALES). The results on Table 2 showed that the average investment of manufacturing companies in Indonesia from 2007 to 2016 was 0.1167 with a standard deviation of 0.1977. The large standard deviation value indicates that investment in the manufacturing companies in Indonesia had a high variation or diversity.

Meanwhile, the cash flow had an average value of 0.2196 with a standard deviation of 0.6195. The value of Tobin Q had a fairly good average value of more than 1 indicating that the growth opportunity of the company was relatively good, yet the high standard deviation indicates that Tobin Q value of manufacturing companies in Indonesia had a high variation or diversity. Leverage had an average value of 0.4115 with a standard deviation of 0.1738. The result highlights that the companies preferred to use their own capital (equity) rather than their liabilities as the business capital. The sales value from manufacturing companies in Indonesia from 2007 to 2016 had an average of 4.7764 with a standard deviation of 4.1694.

5.2 Effects of leverage and company growth on investment

This research used the panel data regression analysis approach to observe the effects of leverage and company growth on investment of the manufacturing companies in Indonesia. This research adopted the regression model applied by Aivazian et al. (2003). The following is the basic model of this research:

$$I_{it} = \gamma_0 + \gamma_1 FCF_{it} + \gamma_2 TQ_{it-1} + \gamma_3 Lev_{it-1} + \gamma_4 Sales_{it} + \varepsilon_{it} \quad (1)$$

I_{it} is the investment of company i in the period of t; CF_{it} is the *cashflow* of the company i in the period of t; TQ_{it-1} is the lag of Tobin Q; Lev_{it-1} is the lag of *leverage*; $Sales_{it}$ is the sales of company i in the period of t. γ_0 is intercept; γ_1, γ_2, γ_3, and γ_4 are coefficient, and ε_{it} is an error term.

The above model is fitted using three different methods we consider in this study namely: pooled least square analysis (PLS), fixed equation model (FEM), and random equation model (REM). The results of the analysis are presented in Table 3. Table 3 shows that leverage is associated with all of

Table 2. The variable descriptive statistics.

	I	CF	TQ_A	TQ_B	TQ_C	LEV	SALES
Mean	0,1172	0,2376	1,2123	2,0267	1,6291	0,4141	4,8198
Median	0,0633	0,0954	0,4765	1,2410	0,9272	0,4101	3,7566
Maximum	1.5370	3,5846	17,9473	18,9424	18,6404	0,8940	34,8741
Minimum	-0,2053	-4,7697	0,0021	0,1223	0,2008	0,0711	0,2254
Std. Dev.	0,1986	0,6245	2,2937	2,3419	2,2855	0,1749	4,1953
Std. Error	0,0094	0,0294	0,1081	0,1104	0,1077	0,0082	0,1978

Table 3. Data panel regression analysis of the effect of leverage and company growth on investment.

	TQ_A			TQ_B			TQ_C		
	PLS	FEM	REM	PLS	FEM	REM	PLS	FEM	REM
Intercept	0.164***	–	0.180***	0.151***	–	0.166***	0.164***	–	0.180***
	(6.163)	–	(5.552)	(5.521)	–	(4.988)	(6.140)	–	(5.534)
CF	-0.115***	-0.144***	-0.127***	-0.117***	-0.144***	-0.129***	-0.115***	-0.144***	-0.127***
	(-7.338)	(-7.268)	(-7.582)	(-7.503)	(-7.277)	-(7.683)	(-7.358)	(-7.268)	(-7.592)
TQ	0.012***	0.007	0.011**	0.014***	0.010	0.013***	0.012***	0.007	0.011**
	(2.906)	(0.753)	(2.215)	(3.440)	(1.052)	(2.680)	(2.932)	(0.745)	(2.232)
Lev	-0.171***	-0.321***	-0.209***	-0.171***	-0.320***	-0.207***	-0.183***	-0.328***	-0.220***
	(-3.279)	(-3.196)	(-3.298)	(-3.283)	(-3.194)	(-3.291)	(-3.506)	(-3.269)	(-3.482)
Sales	0.008***	0.010	0.008***	0.008***	0.010***	0.008***	0.008***	0.010***	0.008***
	(3.450)	(2.783)	(3.260)	(3.504)	(2.814)	(3.3055)	(3.459)	(2.782)	(3.263)
Chow test	4.66E-06			1.12E-05			4.87E-06		
Hausman test		2.01E-05			4.00E-05			2,09E-05	
LM test			0.1713			0.2065			0.1763
R-Square	0.122	0.146	0.130	0.128	0.147	0.134	0.122	0.146	0.130

This table presents the regression results of the effect of leverage and company growth (TQ) on the investment decision of manufacturing companies. T-statistics values are presented under the coefficient value. TQ A, TQ B, TQ C were differentiated based on the variable calculations of TQ as discussed in the research method.
*** Significant at the level of 1%, ** Significant at the level of 5%, * Significant at the level of 10%

the three measures of the market value. The sign and magnitude of the estimate indicate that a unit increase in company's leverage will decrease the mean of market value by around 0.18 in the PLS model.

Based on Table 3, leverage had an effect on company investment that is in accordance with the previous research conducted by Aivazian et al. (2003). Leverage coefficient had a negative value indicating that it has a negative impact on the company investment. This finding highlights that there was an agency theory on the capital structure of the company investment. With the presence of leverage, there was a conflict of interest among debt-holders, management, and shareholders.

According to Myers (1977), leverage can have a negative effect on investment due to an agency issue between shareholders and bondholders. If managers work for the benefit of shareholders, they may provide a positive net present value due to the debt overhang. The results of this empirical research are also strengthened by the studies conducted by Lang et al. (1996), Jensen (1986), Stulz (1990), and

Grossman & Hart (1982) showing that leverage has a negative effect on investment opportunities.

Tobin Q representing the company growth had a positive effect on the company investment on each Tobin Q with different methods of calculation. Tobin Q positive coefficient on the investment indicated the notion that the greater the company growth, the greater the company investment. Tobin Q ratio was measured from the market value of the company compared (shared) to its book value. Therefore, Q value became higher if the market value was higher than the book value.

A higher market value indicates that investors see a growth opportunity of the company. Higher company values are better for investors; thus, companies will find it easier to get fresh funding when they conduct a right issue. This causes Tobin Q to be the proxy for company growth affecting company investment decisions. According to Aivazian et al. (2003), differences in empirical results of the companies with high and low Q are due to the fact that Q value serves as a proxy for easy access to capital markets.

The cash flow variable had a negative effect on investment decisions of the manufacturing companies in Indonesia. This is in contrast with the results obtained by Aivazian et al. (2003) who examined Canadian companies, yet it is in line with the results obtained by Prasetyantoko (2007) and Fazzari et al. (1996). The negative cash flow coefficient value indicates that the companies prioritized funding from their operating cash flow and used funding from debts for company investment afterwards.

The negative cash flow coefficient value indicates that go-public companies in Indonesia tend to have financial constraints as argued by Prasetyantoko (2007). According to Fazzari et al. (1996), if cash flow is not sufficient for investment funding, the company will take on debts. In company investment activities, the primary funding should be from the internal funding prior to the use of external funding.

Moreover, the sales variable as the proxy of profitability in the future had a positive effect on corporate investment indicating that the greater the company sales, the greater the profitability that in turn will increase the opportunity for companies to invest. The results of this study are in accordance with Aivazian et al. (2003) research, Lang et al. (1996), and Prasetyantoko (2007) showing that sales had a positive effect on the company investment.

The analysis on the effect of leverage and company growth on investment in manufacturing companies in Indonesia in this research was conducted through data panel regression analysis. In the data panel regression, there were three methods of analysis i.e. PLS model, fixed equation model (FEM), and random equation model (REM). The Chow test was used to determine the PLS or FEM model use. Meanwhile, Hausman test was used to determine the model of FEM or REM use, and LM test was utilized to see the chosen REM or PLS model. In this study, the results of these tests show that the REM model was chosen as the overall preferred model used for analysis.

5.3 Does growth rate have effects on the relationship of leverage and company investment?

According to Aivazian et al. (2003), Zwiebel (1996), and Novaes & Zingales (1995), there is a difference in negative effects between investment and leverage in companies that have high growth and those with low growth. Therefore, interaction variables were used between company growth rate and leverage in this research model.

$$I_{it} = \gamma_0 + \gamma_1 CF_{it} + \gamma_2 TQ_{it-1} + \gamma_3 Lev_{it-1}$$
$$+ \gamma_4 Sales_{it} + \gamma_5 D_{TQ_{it-1}} \quad (2)$$
$$+ \gamma_6 D_{TQ_{it-1}} * Lev_{it-1} + \varepsilon_{it}$$

D_TQ is a dummy variable i.e. 1 if Tobin's Q is > 1, and 0 if Tobin's Q is <1. Tobin Q which is less than one indicates a low growth of the company whereas Tobin Q of more than 1 indicates high growth of the company. However, in this research, the company growth rate (DTQ) had no effects on the company investment. The company insignificant growth rate (DTQ) shows that it did not affect the over-investment or under-investment of the manufacturing companies in Indonesia for the period of 2007-2016. The growth rate in this research showed different results from the findings of Aivazian et al. (2003) and Lang et al. (1996) revealing that companies in Indonesia do not have agency conflicts in the assessment of over-investment or under-investment on net present value of the investment project.

Similarly, the company growth rate does not significantly affect the leverage (DTQ_Lev) on the company investment which highlights that the company growth rate did not strengthen or weaken the leverage effects on the investment of manufacturing companies in Indonesia from 2007-2016 (see Table 4). The results of this study are different from Aivazian et al (2003) revealing that the dummy interaction of Tobin Q and leverage affected the company investment.

The results of this research indicate that the company growth rate does not strengthen or weaken the effect of leverage on investment. This shows that the determination of the use of leverage for company investment funding is not affected by the company growth rate. Companies with high and low growth rates will continue to prioritize funding from cash flow funds or internal company as it is not easy to obtain debts (leverage). This is presumably because companies in Indonesia have faced financial constraints in their investment as seen from their cash flow that had a negative effect on company investment. As shown by the results obtained by Prasetyantoko (2007) who found that there were financial constraints in investing, faced by the companies in Indonesia. In contrast to the research by Aivazian et al. (2003), this result shows that cash flow had a positive effect on investment.

Meanwhile, other variables obtained results which is in accordance with the regression results of the basic model in this study showing that leverage negatively affected the company investment, but Tobin Q had a positive effect on the company investment. Cash flow negatively affected the company investment, meanwhile sales positively affected the company's investment. In addition, the results of the different Tobin Q calculating method also produced the same value. Therefore, the regression results indicate that the results obtained were robust.

Table 4. Data panel regression analysis of the effect of interactions between company growth and leverage variables.

	TQ_A			TQ_B			TQ_C		
	PLS	FEM	REM	PLS	FEM	REM	PLS	FEM	REM
Intercept	0.196***	–	0.209***	0.156***	–	0.179***	0.174***	–	0.189***
	(4.695)	–	(4.579)	(3.845)	–	(3.953)	(4.475)	–	(4.404)
CF	−0.116***	−0.144***	−0.129***	−0.116***	0.144***	−0.129***	−0.116***	−0.144***	−0.127***
	(−7.388)	(−7.225)	(−7.638)	(−7.412)	(−7.253)	(−7.648)	(−7.358)	(−7.251)	(−7.538)
TQ	0.014***	0.009	0.014**	0.013***	0.010	0.013**	0.013***	0.006	0.012**
	(2.943)	(0.918)	(2.404)	(2.887)	(1.070)	(2.431)	(2.835)	(0.606)	(2.076)
Lev	−0.222***	−0.023***	−0.254***	−0.184**	0.345***	−0.234***	−0.198**	−0.336***	−0.237***
	(−2.813)	(−2.791)	(−2.897)	(−2.386)	(−2.964)	(−2.704)	(−2.519)	(−2.790)	(−2.703)
Sales	0.008***	0.010***	0.009***	0.008***	0.010**	0.009	0.008***	0.010***	0.008***
	(3.478)	(2.823)	(3.301)	(3.515)	(2.836)	(3.322)	(3.455)	(2.748)	3.252
DTQ	−0.045	−0.023	−0.044	−0.011	−0.028	−0.023	−0.017	0.003	−0.018
	(−0.897)	(−0.356)	(−0.816)	(−0.221)	(−0.398)	(−0.409)	(−0.369)	(0.044)	(−0.358)
DTQ*Lev	0.061	0.008	0.050	0.043	0.064	0.056	0.021	0.010	0.030
	(0.553)	(0.052)	(0.416)	(0.390)	(0.426)	(0.456)	(0.207)	(0.083)	(0.282)
Chow test (P-value)	4.04E-06			1.27E-05			5.19E-06		
Hausman test (P-value)		2.68E-05			4.59E-05			2.48E-05	
LM test (P-value)			0.4768			0.3807			0.3593
R-Square	0.124	0.147	0.133	0.129	0.148	0.135	0.123	0.146	0.129

This table presents the regression results of interactions between company growth and leverage variables. T-Statistics values are presented under the coefficient values. TQ_A, TQ_B, TQ_C were differentiated based on TQ variable calculations discussed in the research method chapter.
*** Significant at the level of 1%, ** Significant at the level of 5%, * Significant at the level of 10%

6 CONCLUSION

This study has shown empirically the association between leverage and company growth and between interaction of company growth rate and leverage toward investment of manufacturing companies in Indonesia. Tobin Q measurement as a proxy of company growth utilized three approaches to examine the robustness of the obtained results. The regression analysis in this research showed that leverage has a negative impact on company investment indicating that the funding of debt can control the company management to be selective in deciding company projects and can reveal the presence of agency issues between bondholders and shareholders. The negative relationship between FCF and Investment indicated that presence of free cash flow are creating agency problem between shareholders and management and indicates that go-public companies in Indonesia tend to hold their cash that could be a sign of financial constraint.

Furthermore, the company growth was found to have a positive effect on the company investment that also proves that companies with better growth can obtain better funding in the capital market. This study showed that the company growth rate does not influence the effect of leverage on investment decisions of the manufacturing companies in Indonesia due to the financial constraints they face when they intend to make external funding for the company investment. In general, the results of this empirical study support and emphasize the agency theory on the presence of leverage which is able to discipline companies in making their investment.

REFERENCES

Aivazian, V., Ge, Y. & Qiu, J. 2003. The impact of leverage on firm investment: Canadian evidence. *Journal of Corporate Finance* 11(1-2): 277-291.

Ajide, F.M. 2017. Firm-specific, and institutional determinants of corporate investments in Nigeria. *Future Business Journal* 3: 107–118.

Alkaraan F. & Northcott D. 2006. Strategic capital investment decision-making: a role for emergent analysis tools? A study of practice in large UK manufacturing companies. *The British Accounting Review* 38: 149-173.

Andreou, P.C., Karasamani, I., Louca, C. & Enrlich, D. 2017. The impact of managerial ability on crisis-period corporate investment. *Journal of Business Research* 79: 107–122.

Anwar, S. & Sun, S. 2014. Can the presence of foreign investment affect the capital structure of domestic firms?. *Journal of Corporate Finance* 30: 32-43.

Baker, M., Stein, J.C. & Wurgler, J. 2003. When does the market matter? Stock prices and the investment of equity-dependent firms. *Quarterly Journal of Economics* 118: 969-1005.

Banga, C. & Gupta, A. 2017. Effect of firm characteristics on capital structure decisions of Indian SMEs. *International Journal of Applied Business and Economic Research* 15(10): 281-301.

Brigham, E.F. & Gapenski, L.C. 1996. *Intermediate Financial Management*. Fifth Edition, New York: The Dryden press.

Chen, C., Li, L. & Ma, M.L.Z. 2014. Product market competition and the cost of equity capital: evidence from China. *Asia-Pacific Journal of Accounting & Economics* 21 (3): 227–261.

Chen, R., Ghoul, A.E., Omrani, G. & Wang, H. 2013. Do state and foreign ownership affect investment efficiency? *Evidence from Privatizations* 42: 408-421.

Cleary, S., Povel, P. & Raith, M. 2007. The U-shaped investment curve: theory and evidence. *J. Finance. Quant. Anal* 42(1): 1–40.

Dawar, V. 2014. Agency theory, capital structure and firm performance: some Indian evidence. *Managerial Finance* 40(12): 1190-1206.

Fama, E.F. & French, K.R. 1998. Value versus growth: the international evidence. *The Journal of Finance* 53(6): 1975-1999.

Fazzari, S., Hubbard, R.G. & Petersen, B. 1988. Financing constraints and corporate investment. *Brooking Papers on Economic Activity* 1: 141-195.

Fazzari, S.M., Hubbard, R.G. & Petersen, B. 1996. Financing constraints and corporate investment: Response to Kaplan and Zingales. *Brookings Papers on Economic Activity* 19: 141–195.

Firth, M., Malatesta, P.H., Xin, Q. & Xu, L. 2012 Corporate investment, government control, and financing channels: evidence from China's listed companies. *Journal of Corporat Finance* 18: 433–450.

Giroud, X. & Mueller, H.M. 2011. Corporate governance, product market competition, and equity prices. *Journal of Finance* 66: 563–600.

Grossman, S. & Hart, O. 1982. Corporate financial structure and managerial incentives. In McCall, J. (ed.), *The Economics of Information and Uncertainty*: 107–140. Chicago: University of Chicago Press.

Guariglia, A. & Yang J. 2015. A balancing act: Managing financial constraints and agency costs to minimize investment inefficiency in the Chinese market. *Journal of Corporate Finance* 36: 111-130.

Guney, Y., Li, L. & Fairchild, R. 2011. The relationship between product market competition and capital structure in Chinese listed firm. *International Review of Financial Analysis* 20: 41-51.

Jensen, M.C. 1986. Agency cost of free cash flow, corporate finance, and take-overs. *American Economic Review* 76: 323–329.

Jiang, F., Kim, K.A., Nofsinger, J.R. & Zhu, B. 2015. Product market competition and corporate investment: evidence from China. *Journal of Corporate Finance* 35: 19-210.

Kiel J., Smith R. & Ubbels, B. 2014. The impact of transport investments on competitiveness. *Transportation Research Procedia* 1: 77–88.

Lang, L.E., Ofek, E. & Stulz, R. 1996. Leverage, investment and firm growth. *Journal of Financial Economics* 40: 3–29.

McConnell, J.J. & Servaes, H. 1990. Additional evidence on equity ownership and corporate value. *Journal of Financial Economics* 27: 595–612.

McLean, R.D., Zhang, T. & Zhao, M. 2012. Why does the law matter? Investor protection and its effects on investment, finance, and growth. *Journal of Finance* 67: 313-350.

Myers, S. 1977. Determinants of corporate borrowing. *Journal of Financial Economics* 5: 147–175.

Novaes, W. & Zingales, L. 1995. *Capital structure choice when managers are in control: entrenchment vs efficiency*. Cambridge: National Bureau of Economic Research.

Prasetyantoko, A. 2007. *Financing constraint and firm-level investment folowing a financial crisis in Indonesia*. Jakarta: Working paper GATE 2007-14.

Prasetyantoko, A. 2007. *Foreign ownership and firm financing constraint in Indonesia*. Jakarta: Atma Jaya Catholic Univesity.

Savolainen, J., Collan, M. & Luukka, P. 2017. Analyzing operational real options in metal mining investments with a system dynamic model. *The Engineering Economist* 62(1): 54-72.

Stulz, R.M. 1990. Managerial discretion and optimal financing policies. *Journal of Financial Economics* 26: 3–27.

Vranakis, S.K. & Chatzoglou, P. 2012. A conceptual model for machinery & equipment investment decisions. *International Journal of Business and Management* 7(1): 36-56.

Whited, T.M. 1992. Debt, liquidity constraints, and corporate investment: Evidence from panel data. *Journal of Finance* 47: 1425-1460.

Zambrano, L.G., Catellanos, A.R. & Merino, J.D.G. 2017. Impact of investments in training and advertising on the market valuerelevance of a company's intangibles: The effect of the economic crisisin Spain. *European Research on Management and Business Economics* 24: 1-6.

Zwiebel, J. 1996. Dynamic capital structure under managerial management. *American Economic Review* 86: 1197–1215.

Global Competitiveness: Business Transformation in the
Digital Era – Abdullah, Widiaty & Abdullah (eds)
© *2019 Taylor & Francis Group, London, ISBN 978-0-367-19442-0*

Determining the value driver of value-based management using Du Pont extended formula in retail companies in digital marketing era

M. Sibarani
Pascasarjana Universitas Katholik Parahyangan, Bandung, Jawa Barat, Indonesia

K.K. Putra
Sekolah Tinggi Ilmu Ekonomi Harapan Bangsa, Bandung, Jawa Barat, Indonesia

ABSTRACT: Value-based management (VBM) is a managerial process which effectively links strategy, measurement, and operational processes with the result of creating shareholder value. VBM is an approach to management whereby the company's overall aspirations, analytical techniques, and management processes are all aligned to help the company maximize its value. Decision-making is made based on the key drivers of value. Du Pont formula decomposes the value creation drives in terms of margin, turnover, leverage, pullover and, book to value ratio or market to book value ratio. Digital marketing strategies have replaced conventional marketing strategies and caused many retail company outlets or supermarkets closed and some listed retail companies noted declining sales. This paper analyzes two indicators that represent fundamental performance is margin profit and market performance is PER before and after application of digital marketing. This study aims to analyze the application of Du Pont formula in company retail in the present era of digital marketing. Research methods used are descriptive qualitative and Wilcoxon analysis for comparison. The results showed that the ability of retail companies in sales supported by value driver profit margin showed no significant effect of profit margin before application of digital marketing compared with that after application of digital marketing. The company's ability to keep stock prices supported by PER value drivers shows no significant change in PER effect before implementation of digital marketing when compared with that after the application of digital marketing, in today's business world.

1 INTRODUCTION

The creation of value is the primary goal of managers in leading companies. Organizations exist to create value for all constituencies (constituencies include customers, owners, managers, employees, suppliers, investors, and society in general). Organizations determine the degree to which they will prioritize the interests of each stakeholder group and will therefore balance performance goals accordingly.

Value-based management (VBM) is a corporate management that uses a tool and process to focus an organization to the main purpose of creating the shareholder value. Manager with staff's company makes decisions toward strengthening stock prices over the long term (Athanassakos 2007).

VBM provides a dynamic assessment and high-performance organization based on the strength of finance. This research used Du Pont formula as value driver to stakeholders' company. Du Pont formula decomposes the value creation drives as described from margin, turnover, leverage, pullover, and book to value ratio or market to book value ratio.

E-commerce is a growing sales system after the found of the Internet. This marketing or sales system can reach the whole world at the same time without having to set up branch offices in all countries. It can also be done 24 hours without a stop. By simply going through a computer unit connected to the Internet, the company can market its products.

Buyers can conduct transactions anytime anywhere, and with the growth of these online companies, competition became a threat for the existing retail companies.

Table 1. Number of visitors in 10 e-commerce sites in Indonesia.

E-Commerce site	Numbers of visitors
Lazada.co.id	49,000,000
Tokopedia.com	39,666,667
Elevenia.co.id	32,666,667
Blibli.com	27,000,000
Bukalapak.com	25,666,667
Mataharimall.com	18,666,667
Alfacart.com	16,000,000
Blanja.com	4,800,000
JD.id	3,666,667
Bhinneka.com	3,166,667

Source: Gracivia (2017)

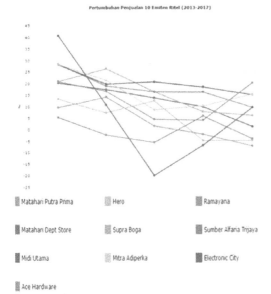

Matahari Putra Prima

Hero

Ramayana

Matahari Dept Store

Supra Boga

Sumber Alfaria Trijaya

Midi Utama

Mitra Adiperka

Electronic City

Ace Hardware

Figure 1. Sales information of 10 retail companies listed in BEI (2013–2017).
Source: Nasution et al. (2018)

Digital marketing strategies have replaced conventional marketing strategies and caused many retail company outlets or supermarkets closed (such as Seven Eleven, Ramayana, Lotus, Debenhams) and some listed retail company noted declining sales. The emergence of the phenomenon about the online shopping since 2014 influenced sales growth of retail companies downward in the past five years (Bright 2017).

Based on Figure 1, three retail companies such as PT Ramayana Lestari Tbk (RALS), PT Hero Supermarket Tbk (HERO), and PT Matahari Putra Prima Tbk (LPPF) suffered decreased sales last year from the previous year. The total sales of 10 retail issuers in 2017 only grew 6.41% from the previous year, whereas in 2013, it recorded a growth of more than 21% from the previous year. This study aims to analyze the application of Du Pont formula in retail companies in the present era of digital marketing.

2 VALUE-BASED MANAGEMENT

"Value based management is an approach that ensures corporations are run consistently on value" (Young & O'Byrne 2001), "Values-based management is an approach to managing in which managers establish, promote, and practice an organization's shared values. An organization's values reflect what it stands for and what it believes in" (Robbins & Coulter 2016). VBM is a managerial process which effectively links strategy, measurement, and operational processes to the end of creating shareholder value (Munteanu et al. 2012).

3 EVENT STUDY

The event study method is a powerful tool that can help researchers assess the financial impact of changes in corporate policy (McWilliams & Siegel 1997). It is a study of market reaction to an event where the information is published as announcement. Event study can be used to test the information content of an announcement and can also be used to test a market that is half strong and commonly used to determine the effect of an event on the price of securities.

Research on this topic has typically focused on theories of event study when digital marketing method had been used in many retail companies. Their approach assumes that the announcement of digital marketing, or buy online usually publicized in the business press, is used as information by market analysts to evaluate the potential profitability of digital marketing method, thereby affecting the firm's competitor (Agrawal & Kamakura 1995).

4 DU PONT EXTENDED ANALYSIS

The Du Pont Company of the US pioneered a system of financial analysis, which has received widespread recognition and acceptance. This system of analysis considers important interrelationships between different elements based on the information found in the financial statements (Melvin 2014).

Du Pont formula is a useful analytical instrument to dissect a company's financial statements and assess the company's financial condition (Gitman & Zutter 2012). Du Pont aims to find the return on common equity as a measure for investors' profits received from each share they plant; higher values will be preferred for investors (Gitman & Zutter 2012) which shows how effective the company uses the capital invested by shareholders (Herciu et al. 2011).

Market ratios are used for the owners of capital so that the capital they plant in assets is in the risk and return expected. There are two ways to calculate market ratios:

- The ratio to profit (price/earnings ratio) is used as a measure of the amount of money that investors are willing to pay for each money-generated company. Subramanyam & Wild (2009) explain that the price-to-profit ratio is inversely related to the cost of capital, if the price-to-profit ratio is high, which means the cost of the share capital is low and vice versa.
- The ratio of market value to book value (market/book ratio) is used as an investor's valuation of the company.

5 RESEARCH METHOD

The population in this research are all retail companies listed on the Indonesia Stock Exchange (IDX) in 2010–2017. Sample in the study is determined by purposive sampling method (selected with a criteria); the criteria are those companies included in the top 6 retail companies listed on the IDX.

The research object is the 6 largest retail companies listed on the stock exchanges Indonesia namely Ace Hardware Indonesia (ACES), Alfaria (AMRT), Ramayana Department Store (RALS), Matahari Department Store (LPPF), Matahari Putra Prima (MPPA), and Hero Department Store (HERO).

This research is a descriptive research that describes a symptom, event, or incident happening at present. Descriptive research focuses on actual problems as they were at the time of the study. Through descriptive research, researchers try to describe the events that became the center of attention without giving special treatment to the event. The variables studied can be single (one variable) or multiple (McMillan & Schumacher 2010, Lind et al. 2012). Research methods used descriptive qualitative with apply a model Du Pont extended to the company so acquired a conclusion.

Measurement of variables consists of 2 variables, namely profit margin and price earning ratio, as follows:

$$Profit\ Margin = \frac{Net\ Income}{Sales} \qquad (1)$$

$$Price\ Earning\ Ratio = \frac{Price\ of\ share}{Earning\ per\ share} \qquad (2)$$

The analytical technique in this research is to test the difference of average profit margin and price earning ratio four years before applying digital marketing and four years after applying digital marketing. Before the hypothesis test, the data to be researched is tested for its normality first, by using Kolmogorov–Smirnov test. When the data is normally distributed, the next test is done by using parametric method for two paired samples with paired sample t-test. Conversely, if the data is not normally distributed, then the next test is done using non-parametric testing methods of two paired samples with Wilcoxon Signed test.

The testing hypothesis for profit margin before the application of digital marketing and after the application of digital marketing is:

$\mu_1 = \mu_2$

$\mu_1 \neq \mu_2$

μ_1 is the average profit margin before the application of digital marketing and μ_2 is the average profit margin after the application of digital marketing. If sign > 0.05, then H_0 is accepted.

The testing hypothesis for price earning ratio before the application of digital marketing and after the application of digital marketing is:

$\mu_{R1} = \mu_{R2}$

$\mu_{R1} \neq \mu_{R2}$

μ_{R1} is the average price earning ratio before the application of digital marketing and μ_{R2} is the average profit margin after the application of digital marketing. If sign > 0.05, then H_0 is accepted.

6 RESULTS AND DISCUSSION

This study wants to see the condition of value drivers before and after digital marketing by using two aspects of Du Pont that represent the company's fundamental performance which is profit margins and the company's market performance which is PER.

Before performing statistical tests, the first step to be done is to test the normality of data using Kolmogorov–Smirnov. The results of normality test data indicate that the two variables to be tested indicated significance value less than 0.05 (see Tables 2 and 3).

The data show that means will be tested using Kolmogorov–Smirnov test, which is a paired two-sample test for abnormal data.

6.1 Hypothesis testing

The results of hypothesis testing 1 listed in Table 4 shows that there is no significant difference in profit margin in the period before application of digital marketing compared with the period after the application of digital marketing, because the value of asymp. Sig. > 0.05. This means the rejection of hypothesis 1 indicates no difference in profit margin contribution as value driver before the implementation and after the implementation of digital marketing that occurs in the

Table 2. Normality test of profit margin data.

Subject	Kolmogorov–Smirnov
	Asymp. Sig.
ProfitM Pre	0.000
ProfitM Post	0.000

Source: Processed secondary data, 2018.

Table 3. Normality test of price earning ratio.

Subject	Kolmogorov–Smirnov
	Asymp. Sig.
PER Pre	0.200
PER Post	0.000

Source: Processed secondary data, 2018.

Table 4. Hypothesis testing of profit margin.

Subject	Z	Asymp Sig	Result
Average before– Average after	−0.449	0.668	H_1 rejected

Source: Processed secondary data, 2018.

business world today. It can also be said that the sale for 6 largest retail companies listed on the BEI is relatively uninterrupted by the emergence of marketing methods of digital marketing in online companies.

The results of hypothesis 2 testing listed in Table 5 show that there is no significant difference for price earning ratio in the period before application with profit margin compared with the period after the application of digital marketing, because of the asymp value. Sig. > 0.05. This means the rejection of hypothesis 2 indicates no difference in the contribution of price earning ratio as a value driver before the implementation and after the application of digital marketing that occurs in the business world today. It can also be said that the share price per share for 6 largest retail companies listed on BEI is relatively uninterrupted by the emergence of marketing methods of digital marketing at online companies.

The emergence of Internet-based social media has made it possible for one person to communicate with hundreds or even thousands of other people about products and the companies that provide them. Thus, the impact of consumer-to-consumer communications has been greatly magnified in the marketplace (Mangold & Faulds 2009).

The development of digital marketing methods in the retail business world when the emergence of online companies did not disrupt the sale and stock prices of the 6 largest retail companies is listed on the IDX in the period 2010–2017.

Digital marketing expert Genc (2018) said that companies must pay attention to business environment conditions such as politics, economics, social, and technology to survive in competition. Political factors relate to policies that are in force. Economic factors relate to market conditions and people's purchasing power. Social factors relate to the pattern of society in seeking information, which is currently through social media, celebrity endorse, and online shopping. The technological factor in marketing today is

Table 5. Hypothesis testing of price earning ratio.

Subject	Z	Asymp Sig	Result
Average before– Average after	−0.857	0.391	H_1 rejected

Source: Processed secondary data, 2018.

non-human interaction and transactions made by handphone or search engine technology. Business strategy adjustments that can be used are:

– Restructuring, means company does not close their business but do renewal.
– Revitalization, means company uses a new model such as digital marketing strategy.
– Restructuration, means company closes unprofitable product.

Reframe, means company makes new target or new vision.

7 CONCLUSION

Hypothesis 1 and Hypothesis 2 were rejected because there is no difference about value driver indicated by profit margin and price earning ratio before implementation and after implementation of digital marketing method in business.

Profitability and market ratio PER as value driver in VBM are not decreased in 6 largest retail companies.

The impact of non-human interaction in marketing strategies or digital marketing has been greatly magnified in the marketplace but the development of digital marketing methods in the retail business did not disrupt the sale and stock prices of the 6 largest retail companies listed on the IDX in the period 2010–2017.

REFERENCES

Agrawal, J. & Kamakura, W.A. 1995. The economic worth of celebrity endorsers: An event study analysis. *The journal of marketing* 59(3): 56-62.

Athanassakos, G. 2007. Value-based management, EVA and stock price performance in Canada. *Management Decision* 45(9): 1397-1411.

Bright, 2017. Digital and Media Marketing. https://www.brightnetwork.co.uk/career-path-guides/marketing-pr/all-about-digital-media-marketing, Accessed on July 11th, 2018

Gitman, L.J. & Zutter, C.J. 2012. *Principles of Managerial Finance*. New Jersey: Prentice Hall.

Gracivia, L. 2017. *Number of Visitors 10 E-Commerce Sites in Indonesia*. [Online]. Available at www.cnnindonesia.com, Accessed on July 11th, 2018.

Genc et.al. 2018. From Bazaars to Digital Environment: A Short History of Marketing in The Turkish Context, in Selcen Ozturkcan, Elif Yolbulan Okan (ed.) Marketing Management in Turkey (Marketing in Emerging).

Herciu, M., Ogrean, C. & Belascu, L. 2011. A Du Pont analysis of the 20 most profitable companies in the world. *Group* 13(1.58): 18-93.

Lind, D.A., Marchal, W.G. & Wathen, S.A. 2012. *Statistical Techniques in Business and Economics*. New York: Mc Graw Hill.

Mangold, W.G. & Faulds, D.J. 2009. Social media: The new hybrid element of the promotion mix. *Business horizons* 52(4): 357-365.

McMillan, J.H. & Schumacher, S. 2010. *Research in Education: Evidence-Based Inquiry.* 7th Edition. Virginia: Pearson Education Inc.

McWilliams, A. & Siegel, D. 1997. Event studies in management research: Theoretical and empirical issues. *Academy of management journal* 40(3): 626-657.

Melvin, John, Boehlje, Michael, Dobbins, Craig, Allan Gray, 2004. "The Dupont profitability analysis model: an application and evaluation of an e-learning tool", Agricultural Finance Review, Vol. 64 Issue: 1, pp.75-89.

Munteanu, V., Danaita, D., Hurbean, L. & Bergler, A. 2012. The Value-Based Management Approach: From the Shareholder Value to the Stakeholder Value. *Proceedings of the International Management Conference* 6(1): 39-44.

Nasution, Damhuri; Prasetyawan, Wahyu; Cahyadi, Gundy. 2017. Katadata Market Sentiment Index, Katadata Insight Center Publish.

Robbins, S.P. & Coulter, M. 2016. *Management.* Boston: Pearson Education Inc.

Subramanyam, K.R. & Wild, J.J. 2009. *Financial Statement Analysis.* New York: Mc Graw Hill.

Young, S. & O'Byrne, S. 2001. *EVA and Value Based Management.* New York: McGraw-Hill.

Human Capital

Global Competitiveness: Business Transformation in the
Digital Era – Abdullah, Widiaty & Abdullah (eds)
© 2019 Taylor & Francis Group, London, ISBN 978-0-367-19442-0

Building organizational commitment of generation Y at workplace: A theoretical perspective

R.G. Munthe, A. Aprillia & R. Setiawan
Maranatha Christian University, Bandung, West Java, Indonesia

ABSTRACT: In the era of digitalization, companies are required to adapt to the rapid changes that occurs. The future success of the organizations is measured by companies learning capacity to adapt. This learning capacity will have impacts on workers as human capital who require updated skills. Unfortunately, many companies nowadays often take shortcuts by stealing others' human capital or often referred as headhunting strategy. This strategy is considered to be effective after considering that Y generation dominates today's workforce. The characteristics of Y generations who do not have the expectation to work in the same position for a long time make them being known as a generation who have high turnover within the workplace. This paper proposes suggestions for Y generation human capital to change their mindset towards their work and their workplace and have high organizational commitment to prevent any hijacking from the competitors.

1 INTRODUCTION

Today's era of digitalization bring new changes that effects human life. The impact has also entered areas such as: politics, economics, socio-culture, defence, security, and information technology. Digital era is born with the emergence of digitalization and Internet network, especially computer information technology. Moreover, the growing sophistication of today's digital technology is making great changes to the world and the birth of a variety of advanced digital technologies.

The development of digital technology facilitates business organization in the way of accessing information in different ways. Moreover, business organizations are also enabled to make use of the digital technology freely yet still under-controlled. Organization is no longer merely run by employees but through the use of machines. The current example starts to happen in banks such as transfer services, cash withdrawals or cash deposits where it already use the machine instead of employees (Kasali, 2017).

Artificial intelligence, super connectivity, sophisticated digital tools, real-time information, virtual environments, and innovations are some of the breakthroughs that become a part of people's daily life. Accordingly, many companies are required to follow such changes very quickly in order to survive. The same scenario are seen in the majority of retail companies (especially in Indonesia), when they show changes in the way they offer discount, open new stores, and shut down many of their store or in the way they shrink the size of the company due to the threat of digitalization era (Sundjaja 2013).

In this millennial age, the capacity of the organization actually lies in the collection of individuals' thoughts within the company. The individuals are not only required to be able to adapt to the changes the era offer, but also to drive the changes as well as to innovate quickly as the organizational change is the transformation of humans within it (Ege et al. 2017). Therefore, the organizational change can not be separated from the learning capacity of the people in it to adapt to the changes. One of the crucial factors for changing the internal environment within the organization is its employees. Employees are an active resource that plays a major role in corporate survival considering the fact that the success of future organizations comes from organizations whose employees have a good learning capacity at the present time (Sudharatna & Li, 2004).

Further, companies and organizations' innovation certainly needs competent human capital in responding to the rapid changes of customer demands. Not only that employees' capability in terms of information technology aspects that is important, encouragement and commitment of all organizational personnel is also indispensable (Robbins & Judge 2013). This means that Human Capital play major role in driving the progress of the company. Without qualified and competent human resources towards their work, the company will not able to make any progress in terms of its innovation. An innovative organization is an organization that is willing and is able to keep learning to adapt to changes in its environment.

Human Capital is lifeblood in achieving organizational success because they are the source of innovation and improvement as human capital is a source of very useful knowledge, skills, and competencies in an organization or company. It reflects the company's collective ability to produce the best solution based on the knowledge possessed by the people in the company (Manuti et al. 2017). However, human capital is also a difficult component to measure.

The current Human Capital is dominated by "Generation Y" or "Nexters" or "Generation Me" or "Millennials" that refers to the youngest generation in the workforce. This generation was born between the year 1980 and 1994. Generation Y in comparison to the other two generations at work, have a very different job values. In addition, Generation Y are also different in terms of personalities and expectations in relation to the job/task they are given (Kuron et al. 2015). For the Y generation, supports from supervisors/superiors by giving independent responsibility as well as chances to be actively involved in completing a job/task (accountability) are ones of the requirements for them to work maximally (Kultalahti & Viitala 2015). Gaining achievements and appreciations in their workplace is a kind of job satisfaction that they themselves need to feel in their workplace (Kuron et al. 2015).

However, Generation Y often have high turnover in the workplace that has been proven that they tend to stay in a job for about 18-36 months only (Wan 2012). When Generation Y did not get the achievement in their workforce, they will not any consideration of staying longer in the company. Towards this issue, headhunting strategy has been widely applied by many competitors to steal others' human capital in the current workforce that is dominated by Y generation with the characteristics that have been mentioned above.

2 RESEARCH METHOD

The type of research used in the study is literature study.

Literature study method refers to a series of activities related to library data collection methods whose main goal is to find the foundation to acquire and build the theoretical base and frame of thinking (Zed 2008). Library study was applied in this research since its primary purpose was to develop both theoretical and practical aspects of benefit. In the present study, the data were collected by reading, recording, and managing research materials under the issues being investigated.

3 RESULTS AND DISCUSSION

One of the attempts to suppress the turnover of talents of Y generation is to understand them, so as to treat, direct and lead them according to their characteristics and needs (Weyland 2011). Recent study found that accountability is a stressor that affects organizational commitment. Accountability can be seen as a barrier or an obstacle which prevents the achievement of a goal or can also be seen as an opportunity to achieve a goal. In order to see this as an opportunity to achieve the goal, there must be an emotionally-bound commitment that comes from person-environment fit (Laird et al. 2015) which in another language from the person that has a calling to do it.

"Calling" is viewed from a neoclassical perspective focusing on the individual's internal and individual choices on the outside and both of them are in the same path (fit) then it is called "calling". This perspective emphasizes the importance of realizing personal value as well as emphasizing the importance of meeting the needs of society. The Neoclassical Perspective believes that the sense of call encompasses both itself and beyond, that is, the function of the work is to realize the individual's self-worth and fulfil the function as part of the environment and social contribution. So, it can be concluded that Neoclassical Perspective has a function of combining "personal interests" and "social interests" (Wang & Dai 2017). In other words, that Calling Orientation will give meaning to the Y Generation and thus they will have Affective Commitment that can impact their intention to stay within the company.

Therefore, in order to make the organization succeed, employees are required to improve their competence in accordance with the demands of changes. Organizations need a stable yet always changing circumstance (Abrahamson 2000). Ironically, the process of change can destabilize the foundations built for future organizational success by undermining the motivational base of employees in the form of 'trust'. This can be a serious threat to the success of the organization because 'trust' is the psychological ties of the organization and its members (Robbins & Judge 2013). The low level of trust between the two is the biggest barrier in creating change in the organization. Trusts perfect the mechanism of an innovation and greater responsibility. It is reciprocal. When a trust is present, employees feel that they are respected and given the power to make decisions. They will be able to work with integrity and demonstrate their abilities optimally. In order to form trust, employees must feel that they have been treated fairly and that their manager is honest and the organization has a goal worth fighting for. Furthermore, employees should be prepared to learn new skills and commit to the organization. Therefore, growth, opportunities for learning and increased experience, is important. If an employee has been motivated to perform better, he or she needs a bigger and more challenging job which provides opportunities for growth. Employees need the opportunity to learn skills in carrying out their work, and to be supervised and developed accordingly (Mondy 2010). They must understand their role in achieving organizational goals and their limits in making new breakthroughs.

Employees need support and guidance in performing their roles rather than being blamed when making mistakes. Most people want to keep learning and growing in order to increase their capacity. This capacity will impact Generation Y employees as human capital since they have renewed their skills. The company's investment in training and development is a key to show not only about the organization's commitment to its employees but also its commitment to grow its human capital. Unfortunately, many companies today often take shortcuts through headhunting strategy in order to gain its competitive advantage within a relatively short time. The uniqueness of the head-hunters are habit of "piracy" of workers in a particular company by offering jobs that are considered to have better chance. The new position in companies that offered by head-hunters should be "tempting" or provide better value to improvement of career or salary increase (Sarjana et al. 2017).

4 CONCLUSION

The Generation Y is marked as a creative employee. Creative employees will show optimal performance and tend to be consistent and even growing. Employee performance can be built through a combination of three main components, namely skills, motivation, and the ability to be creative. An expertise is defined as a set of skills and knowledge of employees in performing various tasks and work. Employees gain expertise derived from their talents or potential and evolve into valuable experiences gained through a range of their actual educational and job programs. If skill is their ability to work, hence motivation is the willingness of employees to work. There are various things that encourage employees to work; ranging from the desire to earn a living, a hobby, looking for a challenge, and to actualize themselves with their work. Motivation relates to the factors within the employees that drive them to continue working. In addition to willingness and creativity, employees must also have a creative soul. In order to grow, the employees must not be in a "compulsion" condition to do something, but they must be in a "willingness" to do something that have an inner impulse (intrinsic motivation) to fulfil his needs such as achievement and recognition. The "willingness" here has a meaning of no burden or in other words how one can "do what you love" (Amabile 1997). Employees

who love their work will devote all their effort toward their spirits; in other words will do everything to progress himself with the work he did and do. In order for a person to "do what you love", an employee must know himself and his personality. By having the will, ability, and creative spirit then the employees will always try to continuously update themselves with the work they do. As a conclusion, the solution to make human capital coming from Y generation have a high intention to remain in their workplace and have high organizational commitment is by giving employees the jobs they want and by offering them the opportunity to develop and advance their careers that in turn will result in a high organizational commitment (Mathieu & Zajac 1990). If organizations do not provide facilities for career development or even limited opportunities to grow, the employees' organizational commitment will decrease. Employees will leave when they are given better opportunities and offers from the competitor companies.

REFERENCES

Abrahamson, E. 2000. Change without pain. *Harvard Business Review* 78(4): 75-79.

Amabile, T.M. 1997. Motivating Creativity In Organizations: On Doing What You Love And Loving What You Do. *California Management Review* (40)1: 39.

Ege, T., Esen, A. & Dizdar, Ö.A. 2017. Organizational Learning and Learning Organizations: An Integrative Framework. *Int. Journal of Management Economics and Business* 13(2): 439-460.

Kasali, R. 2017. *Disruption: Nothing Can Not Be Changed Before Facing, Motivation Only Is Not Enough.* Jakarta: Gramedia Pustaka Utama.

Kultalahti, S. & Viitala, R. 2015. Generation Y – challenging clients for HRM? *Journal of Managerial Psychology* 30(1): 101-114.

Kuron, L.K.J., Lyons, S.T., Schweitzer, L. & Ng, E.S.W. 2015. Millennials' work values: differences across the school to work transition. *Personnel Review* 44(6): 991-1009.

Laird, M.D., Harvey, P. & Lancaster, J. 2015. Accountability, entitlement, tenure, and satisfaction in Generation Y. *Journal of Managerial Psychology* 30(1): 87-100.

Manuti, A., Impedovo, M.A. & Palma, P.D.D. 2017. Managing social and human capital in organizations: Communities of practices as strategic tools for individual and organizational development. *Journal of Workplace Learning* 29(3): 217-234.

Mathieu, J.E. & Zajac, D.M. 1990. A review and meta-analysis of the antecedents, correlates, and consequences of organizational commitment. *Psychological Bulletin* 108: 171-194.

Mondy, R.W. 2010. *Human resource management.* 11th Edition. Upper Saddle River, New Jersey: Pearson Prentice Hall.

Robbins, S.P. & Judge, T.A. 2013. *Organisational behaviour.* 15th Edition. New Jersey: Pearson Education

Sarjana, S., Khayati N., Warini L. & Praswiyati, P. 2017. Strengthening of Intellectual Capital Dimension. *Jurnal Dinamika Manajemen* 8(2): 216-232.

Sudharatna, Y. & Li, L. 2004. Learning Organization Characteristics Contributed to its Readiness-to-Change: A Study of the Thai Mobile Phone Service Industry. *Managing Global Transitions* 2(2): 163-178.

Sundjaja, A.M. 2013. Implementation of Business Intelligence on Banking, Retail, and Educational Industry. *International Journal of Communication & Information Technology (CommIT)* 7(2): 65-70.

Wan, H.L. 2012. Employee Loyalty at the Workplace: The Impact of Japanese Style of Human Resource Management. *International Management Journals* 3 (1): 1-16.

Wang, J. & Dai, L. 2017. Calling: A Literature Review and Prospect. *Journal of Human Resource and Sustainability Studies* 5: 94-100.

Weyland, A. 2011. Engagement and talent management of Gen Y. *Industrial and Commercial Training* 43(7): 439-445.

Zed, M. 2008. *Library Research Method*. Jakarta: Yayasan Obor Indonesia.

Global Competitiveness: Business Transformation in the Digital Era – Abdullah, Widiaty & Abdullah (eds)
© 2019 Taylor & Francis Group, London, ISBN 978-0-367-19442-0

Analysis of relationship between job satisfaction and performance of field employee: A case study in PT. Trisna Naga Asih

R.A.P.N. Suharto, A. Novieningtyas & S. Dwikardana
Faculty of Economy Parahyangan Catholic University, Bandung, Indonesia

ABSTRACT: This study was aimed to examine the relationship of job satisfaction with the performance of field employees of PT. Trisna Naga Asih. The research was conducted to determine the extent of relationship between job satisfaction and the performance of the field employees. This research was set as a quantitative approach and employed survey data collection technique to collect data. The study involved 68 field employees of PT. Trisna Naga Asih as respondents. The results of the analysis found that job satisfaction and job performance of field employees of PT. Trisna Naga Asih have positive relationship with the intensity of a (+) 0.607, which belongs to the category of a strong relationship, indicating that the better the job satisfaction, the better the job performance of the employees. The results of this study propose an SOP that can be used by companies to manage all activities within the company.

1 INTRODUCTION

1.1 Background

A dynamic business environment requires every company to have an advantage so that it will be able to survive in the market competition. In order to win that competition, the company needs financial capital, machinery, technology, and fixed capital. However, it cannot be denied that in a capital company, the most important is intangible capital in the form of human capital. Human capital is human resources that support the company in achieving its goals.

Human resources are very important for the organization because any activity in the organization must be related to humans. Without any human intervention, the company may not be able to achieve the desired goals. In the process of achieving its goals, each company certainly expects all the employees to be willing and able to work diligently, and have a positive attitude towards their work in order to produce optimal performance in terms of quantity and quality being achieved as expected (Khan 2010).

In order to achieve the optimal performance, it needs to be supported by a high willingness to work. Working capabilities are in line with the content of work, a comfortable work environment, income that can meet the minimum living needs, adequate social security, human working conditions, and a harmonious working relationship. Therefore, optimal performance ultimately grows from the way and attitude of work (Suwatno & Tjutju 2013).

One of the scopes of human resource management discusses matters relating to employees' job satisfaction. Employees' job satisfaction is a factor that is considered important as it can affect the overall organization or company. For the employees, job satisfaction is an individual factor and a tool to achieve maximum productivity and performance.

McCormick & Tiffin (2002) stated that job satisfaction is closely related to one's attitude towards their own work. The higher level of satisfaction of a person will be reflected from his/her positive work attitude. Conversely, dissatisfaction with one's work will lead to a negative work attitude. Positive and negative attitudes of a person follow the level of perceived job satisfaction. A person with a high level of job satisfaction shows a positive attitude towards work, while someone who is not satisfied with his/her job tends to show a negative attitude towards work (Robbins & Judge 2015).

PT. Trisna Naga Asih is an organization that has human resources as their main asset. According to Mello (2011), asset is something of value and worth or something that has value and meaning. High values possessed by humans will produce high value for the organization because humans with high value will produce a high contribution to the achievement of organizational goals. Therefore, it is unavoidable for the company to be able to manage assets that are owned properly so that employees can optimally perform the capabilities they have.

One thing that can be done by the company to encourage employees so they can provide maximum performance for the company is by filling employee satisfaction. Job satisfaction is an attitude or one's perspective about their work when they compare between expectations and what they get in the reality. Ideally, the higher the assessment of the work that is perceived to suit the individual's desires, the higher the job satisfaction (Mathis & Jackson 2011).

Therefore, satisfaction is an evaluation that describes a person's feeling whether they are happy or not and whether they are satisfied or dissatisfied with their work. Employees' job satisfaction is also affected by several factors such as salary, benefits and facilities, supervisor and subordinate relationships, relationships between colleagues, opportunity development, work safety, organizational policies, and work performance (Spector 1997).

PT. Trisna Naga Asih is one of the companies in West Java that manages fruit plantations with the main activity of producing dragon fruit. PT. Krisna Naga Asih is also a supplier of various types of dragon fruits such as red, black, and yellow dragon fruit. The main activity of the company is producing dragon fruit. Accordingly, employees are required to be able to meet production targets in each harvest season. Enterprises in the plantation sector are productive work fields that carry out various production activities to achieve results and this sector certainly requires a lot of labor (Pasal 27 ayat 1 UUD 1945).

PT. Trisna Naga Asih always strives to provide the best quality dragon fruit. In addition to its main goal of achieving production targets, PT. Trisna Naga Asih also hopes that its employees can produce good quality dragon fruit. The Director explained that good quality dragon fruit criteria are larger than the size of dragon fruit in general. This large dragon fruit has a high selling value when compared to medium-sized dragon fruit. This larger dragon fruit is sold by the company to the premium market under the brand name "Naga Geulis".

In order to achieve these targets, field employees must carefully tend and control plants in each block as their responsibility. Field employees have a very important role in the company because their work is directly related to the dragon fruit production process. Basically, businesses that are based on food crops and horticulture, other than natural factors, involve the largest workforce in their production activities. Thus, this study involved 68 part-time field employees as objects of research.

According to the results of an unstructured interview with the Director as a preliminary research by the author, it was said that for several times, the company had not been able to meet the company's target. He added that apart from natural factors, the impact of the lack of rigor and patience of field employees in selecting superior seeds and caring for dragon fruit plants caused less optimal yields because the selection and treatment process is one of the important factors that determine the growth of the dragon fruit. It was also explained that field employees were less diligent in caring for dragon fruit plants based on the reports from the head of the block and direct events encountered by the Director as he often saw some field employees doing things that were not their work during working

hours, such as sitting around casually and chatting during working hours when the field workers are not in the block. During working hours, the field employees should have a commitment and responsibility to control and provide care for dragon fruits in each block which is their responsibility. It was also explained that the problem had become a big concern for the company as it is able to disturb company's activities and interrupt the achievement of organizational goals if it is not immediately resolved. On the other hand, in one year, it was reported that some employees request for an increase on their salaries, yet it is still being considered.

Referring to Judge et al. (2001) when we move from the individual level to the organizational level, there is a room for the relationship between satisfaction and work performance. Gibson et al. (1996) explain that job satisfaction increase or decrease employees' performance, indicating that satisfied employees will be more productive than employees who feel dissatisfaction with their work which in turn will decrease their work performance. More specifically, Gibson et al. (1996) reveal that this illustrates the reciprocal relationship between job satisfaction and employee performance.

Based on the description above, the authors are interested in examining whether there is a relationship between the employees' job satisfaction and their job performance by taking the title of research "Analysis of the Relationship between Job Satisfaction and Performance of Field Employees in PT. Trisna Naga Asih".

2 LITERATURE REVIEW

2.1 Job satisfaction

Spector (1997) defines job satisfaction as an "attitude that describes how a person feels about his work as a whole or on various aspects of his work". Wexley & Yukl (1977) added that "Job satisfaction is the way an employee feels about his or her job". Thus, job satisfaction refers to a generalization of the attitude of employees towards their work based on aspects of their work.

A person's attitude towards his work reflects a pleasant or unattractive experience in his work and his hopes for future experiences. Luthans (2006) provides a definition of job satisfaction which includes cognitive, affective, and evaluative reactions or attitudes and states that job satisfaction is "a happy emotional state or positive emotion that comes from an assessment of work or someone's work experience".

Luthans (2006) then concluded that there are two important things in job satisfaction that includes work values and basic needs. Work values are the goals to be achieved that are important and that must be appropriate or helpful to fulfill basic needs.

Therefore, it can be inferred from the explanation above that job satisfaction is an attitude, feeling, and emotion of the employees about their works. Attitudes, feelings, and emotions can be positive and negative and could be related to what the individuals want compared to what is received by them.

2.2 Theory of job satisfaction

Basically job satisfaction is an individual-specific matter. By looking at the psychological side of individual employees, there are 3 well-known job satisfaction theories, namely (Rivai 2011): (1) Equity theory; Robbins & Judge (2015) said that an individual will be satisfied or dissatisfied depending on the presence of justice in the work situation. This theory has some main components that cover input, result, justice, and injustice. *Input* is a valuable factor for employees who are considered being able to support their work, such as education, experience, skills, number of tasks, and equipment used to carry out their work. *Result* is something that is valuable for the employees, such as wages/salaries, side benefits, symbols, status, rewards, and opportunities for success or self-actualization. At the same time, people will always compare someone's progress at the same company or in the other company or it can be himself from the past. Every employee will compare their input ratio with the other employees' input ratio. If the comparison is considered fair, the employee will be satisfied. In contrast, if the comparison is perceived as unfair, it can cause dissatisfaction among employees.

Second is Discrepancy theory. This theory was discovered by Porter and was developed by Locke, and thus it is familiar as Locke's Value Theory. Porter measured someone's job satisfaction by calculating the difference between something that is supposed to be and the perceived reality. However, according to Locke, an individual feels satisfied or dissatisfied is something personal, depending on how he/she perceives the suitability or conflict between his/her desires and the reality (Munandar 2001). So, from discrepancy theory, job satisfaction is related to the difference or conflict between all aspects of work that is owned and all aspects desired, indicating that the greater the difference, the smaller the satisfaction of employees. On the other hand, the smaller the difference, the employee will be more satisfied. Thus, employees will feel satisfied if there is no difference between what they want and perception of reality.

The last theory is Two Factor theory. The theory was first developed by Frederick Herzberg who sees that job satisfaction comes from intrinsic motivators and job dissatisfaction comes from the absence of extrinsic factors (Gibson et al. 1996). According to Herzberg, intrinsic factors are related to job satisfaction. The factors are characterized as motivation factor, such as achievement, recognition, responsibility, advancement, work itself, and possibility of growth (cited in Munandar 2001). Fulfilment of these factors will lead to employees' satisfaction, but not fulfilling these factors doesn't always lead to dissatisfaction.

On the other hand, extrinsic factors that tend to cause dissatisfaction are characterized by Herzberg as hygiene factors, such as salary, job security, working condition, status, company policy and administration, supervision, and interpersonal relations (Munandar, 2001). These factors are needed to fulfill the biological drive and basic needs of the employees. If this factor is not sufficiently fulfilled, employees will not be satisfied. However, if the magnitude of this factor is sufficient to fulfill the needs, employees will not be disappointed even if they are not satisfied.

2.3 Dimensions of job satisfaction

Job satisfaction that is felt by the employees is derived from several dimensions. Luthans (2006) stated 5 dimensions of job satisfaction: the work itself, payment, supervision, co-workers, and opportunity to have promotion.

2.4 Performance

Basically, the definition of performance can be interpreted in many ways. Some experts view performance as the result of work, but the others believed that attitude is important to achieve the desired results. In order to clear the meaning of performance, some understandings of performance are explained below. The following are understandings of performance according to some experts.

Armstrong & Baron (1998) explained more comprehensive opinion such as:

"Performance means both behaviours and results. Behaviours emanate from the performer and transform performance from abstraction to action. Not just the instruments for results, behaviours are also outcomes in their own right – the product of mental and physical effort applied to tasks – and can be judge apart from results."

Besides emphasizing results, the above understanding also sees behavior as part of performance. According to Armstrong & Baron (1998), behavior is important as it will affect the work of an employee.

From the opinion above, performance can be seen from the result of perspective and process or an attitude that leads to achieve the desired goals.

2.5 Factors of performance

Anguinis (2009) said that there are 3 factors that determine performance: (1) Declarative Knowledge, is knowledge or information about work facts, tasks to be carried out, principles in work, and goals to be achieved, (2) Procedural Knowledge that refers to the combination between knowledge and how to do the works. This includes cognitive skill, psycho-motor, physical, and interpersonal skill, and (3) Motivation that is referred to individual behavior in work, such as the desire to work and how the individual attempts to do work. All the factors have multiplicative relations:

Performance = Declarative Knowledge × Procedural Knowledge × Motivation.

If one of the factors has a 0 value, the performance will also have 0 value. Therefore, the three factors above are very important in assessing individual performance.

2.6 Dimensions of performance

Evaluating employees' performance is not only carried out by assessing physical results, but also assessing work performance that covers various fields such as work ability, crafts, discipline, work relationships, and other things according to the level of work and their work fields. Anguinis (2009) explained that performance is multidimensional meaning that it is necessary to consider various types of behavior to understand performance itself. Anguinis identifies performance such as:

- Task Performance, it is the main activity of a job, such as converting raw materials into finished goods. Besides that, task performance is the activity that supports the other main activities such as managing product supply, distributing the product, planning, making coordination, doing supervision and another effective and efficient staff function. Task performance includes some of the work performances: (a) Employees know what to do, (b) Employees do what they have to do, (c) Employees follow all the work steps, and (d) Employees understand the work they have to do.
- Contextual Performance in this case is working by making extra effort and by working happily; do the work that are not part of voluntary work; follow organizational rules and procedures; approve, support, and defend/maintain organizational goals. Contextual performance involved some of work performance such as: (a) Enthusiasm, (b) Effort, (c) Following the rules, working hard, having initiative, and fulfilling the production target.

3 METHOD

The study was set as an explanatory research. In this research, the hypothesis was tested to explain the relationship between job satisfaction and employees' job performance. This research employed quantitative approach that specifically emphasized in measuring variables and proving hypothesis related to the explanation of the relationship. This research used descriptive data analysis to describe the variables about job satisfaction and performance of the employees.

3.1 Population

The population in this research is 68 field employees of PT. Trisna Naga Asih.

3.2 Types and data sources

There are two types of data sources used in this research: (1) Primary data that were obtained from the interview with the Director of PT. Trisna Naga Asih, questionnaires that were distributed directly to the respondents, and also from field observations. (2) Secondary data were collected from books, literature studies, lecture material, scientific journals, the result of similar studies, data provided by the company, and some of the data obtained from the Internet.

3.3 Data collection techniques

The data of the study were collected through some techniques as follows: (1) Literature survey that was carried out by using written sources such as reference, scientific journals, and the results of the similar research to make theoretical basics and also to make the framework. Researchers examined other trusted sources either in writing or in digital format that are relevant and related to the study. The data were then used as study materials and as comparisons to expand the research, (2) Interview, researchers conducted an unstructured interview with the Director of PT. Trisna Naga Asih as well as several field employees to find out more about the company's condition, as the initial stage of research data collection. This process helps find problems of the research, (3) Questionnaire, the study employed closed questionnaire in the form of physical questionnaire through which respondents chose the answer in the questionnaire, (4) Observation, this step was conducted by either by direct observation by visiting the research object and by observing the work environment or activity to find out the employee's behavior. The observation was also employed to find information that actually happened in PT. Trisna Naga Asih.

3.4 Validity

From 34 statements, the sig.r item is less than 0.05 ($\alpha = 0.05$), indicating that each item variable is valid and can be used to measure the research variables.

3.5 Reliability

The decision-making criteria is if the value of alpha reliability coefficient gives a number greater than the passing criteria $\alpha: \geq 0.6$, then the variable is reliable. Alpha coefficient of job satisfaction is 0.874 and performance is 0.854. From the provisions mentioned earlier, all the variables used for this study can be considered reliable.

4 RESULTS AND DISCUSSION

4.1 Descriptive analysis of job satisfaction

In the job satisfaction variable, five indicators were presented, such the work, payment, supervision, co-workers, and opportunity of promotion.

Based on Table 1, it can be seen that most respondents agree with the statements listed in the job satisfaction variable. It can be concluded that most employees have got job satisfaction at PT. Trisna Naga Asih.

4.2 Descriptive analysis of performance

The employees' performance was seen from two indicators, namely task performance and contextual performance.

Table 2 revealed that most respondents agree with the statements offered in the performance variable. Thus, it can be concluded that most of the employees feel that they have performed optimally for the company.

4.3 The relationship between performance and job satisfaction

The statistical calculation of Spearman correlation test resulted significant value (2-tailed) output of above 0.01. This value is smaller than the significance with a value of $\alpha = 5\%$ or 0.05. Based on these results, Ho is rejected; Ho's statement that "There is no relationship between job satisfactions with the performance of employees of PT. Trisna Naga Asih" is rejected in this study. This indicates that there is a relationship between job satisfaction and the performance of employees of PT. Trisna Naga Asih.

5 CONCLUSION

- Generally, the results showed that the perception of field employees towards their job satisfaction at PT. Trisna Naga Asih is quite good. It means, the employee is quite satisfied with the company. However, some of the field employees claimed to be less satisfied with the company, especially in the dimensions of salary and supervision.
- Perception of field employees towards their performance at PT. Trisna Naga Asih is quite good. Field employees feel that they have provided a pretty good performance to the company. However, there are still some field employees who confessed that sometimes they make mistakes during their working hours.
- This research has revealed that job satisfaction has a positive relationship with the field employees' performance of PT. Trisna Naga Asih that can be proven by correlation coefficients +0.607, indicating that there is a strong correlation between job satisfaction and employee performance.

The results of this study confirmed theories and findings from previous research stating that there is a positive relationship between job satisfaction and employees' performance.

Table 1. Answer frequency distribution job satisfaction variable.

Answer Category	Frequency	%
SS	163	10.89%
S	848	56.68%
KS	423	28.27%
TS	61	4.08%
STS	1	0.07%
TOTAL	1.496	100%

Source: Questionnaire Data.

Table 2. Frequency distribution of answer category.

Answer Category	Frequency	%
SS	115	12.08%
S	660	69.32%
KS	169	17.75%
TS	6	0.63%
STS	2	0.21%
TOTAL	952	100%

Source: Questionnaire Data.

REFERENCES

Anguinis, H. 2009. *Performance Management (2nd ed.).* Upper Saddle River NJ: Pearson Prentice Hall.

Armstrong, M. & Baron, A. 1998. *Performance management: The new realities.* London: State Mutual Book & Periodical Service.

Gibson, J.L., Ivanevich, J.M. & Donelly, J.H. 1996. *Organisasi.* Jakarta: Binarupa Aksara.

Judge, T.A., Thoresen, C.J., Bono, J.E. & Patton, G.K. 2001. The job satisfaction–job performance relationship: A qualitative and quantitative review. *Psychological bulletin* 127(3): 376.

Khan, M.R. 2010. The Impact of Organizational Commitment on Employee Job Performance. *European Journal of Social Sciences* 15(3): 292-298.

Luthans, F. 2006. *Organizational Behavior.* New York: McGraw-Hill.

Mathis, R.L. & Jackson, H.H. 2011. *Manajemen Sumber Daya Manusia.* Jakarta: Salemba Empat.

McCormick, E.J. & Tiffin, J. 2002. *Human Resource Management.* Singapore: Prentice-Hall.

Mello, J.A. 2011. *Strategic Human Resource Management.* Stamford: Cengange Learning.

Munandar, A.S. 2001. *Psikologi Industri dan Organisasi*. Jakarta: UI Press.

Rivai, V. 2011. *Manajemen Sumber Daya Manusia Untuk Perusahaan: Dari Teori Ke Praktik Edisi Ketiga*. Jakarta: Rajawali Pers.

Robbins, S.P. & Judge, T.A. 2015. *Perilaku Organisasi, Edisi: 16*. Jakarta: Salemba Empat.

Spector, P. 1997. *Job Satisfaction: Application, Assesement, Causes, Consequence*. United Kingdom: Sage Publication, Inc.

Suwatno, S. & Tjutju, Y. 2013. *Manajemen Sumber Daya Manusia*. Bandung: Alfabeta.

Wexley, K. & Yukl, G. 1977. *Organizational Behavior and Personnel Psychology*. USA: Irwin Home wood Illinois.

Global Competitiveness: Business Transformation in the
Digital Era – Abdullah, Widiaty & Abdullah (eds)
© 2019 Taylor & Francis Group, London, ISBN 978-0-367-19442-0

The benefits and challenges of digitalization for employee performance management in a medium-sized company in Kecamatan Lembang, West Java, Indonesia

I. Nuraida
Parahyangan Catholic University, Bandung, Indonesia

ABSTRACT: One key to successful management of agro-tourism business is performance management which should be related to service quality. Performance management research is generally done on a profit-oriented company, but employee performance management research which is related to digitalization has never been done in the agro-tourism sector, especially for medium-sized enterprises which are not always profit-oriented. This research was set as a case study and was conducted in a middle-sized enterprise of agro-tourism sector at Kecamatan Lembang. The study was aimed to complete the model of employee performance management by finding out what kind of benefits and challenges of digitalization can improve the application of the model. The limitation of this paper is the output model that can be used only to agro-tourism sector in this enterprise. However, this framework will be useful for every researcher who is interested in employee performance management for tourism-service sector.

1 INTRODUCTION

Digitalization is one of the most significant ongoing transformations of contemporary society and is able to encompass many elements of business and everyday life (Hagberg et al. 2016). Digitalization is the process of making all of this information available and accessible in a digital format. Digitalization means making digitalized information work for employee of the company. Digital transformation is the process of devising new business applications that integrate all this digitalized data and digitalized applications. Taking advantage of digitalization could be used to create completely new business concepts.

Digitalization can be used to support human resource management, especially in the service sector. Agro-tourism is one of the service sectors that offers 3 S, something to see, something to buy, and something to do. The outputs of agro-tourism are (1) agricultural/plantation/livestock products, which can be sold or just exhibited/shown to be enjoyed by tourists, and (2) tourism services, and service quality. One of the keys to successful management of agro-tourism sector is in the employee performance management.

Nuraida (2017) has proposed employee performance model for five research objects of small- and medium-sized enterprises at Kecamatan Lembang, Parongpong, and Cisarua. The question is how far the role of technology has been used for employee performance management of those small- and medium-sized enterprises? According to Nuraida

(2017), small- and medium-sized businesses are often associated with limited capital and capabilities, and have fewer employees than larger businesses. Generally, they have simple organizational structure, short organizational level, narrow span of management; they also make the flow of information, communication, and distance, between superiors and subordinates, become fast. Supervision and control can be done directly. Small and medium enterprises have simpler business processes and activities so they generally do not feel the need of office media in the form of letters, forms, and reports (Nuraida 2014). Do they need to apply technology to support their business?

Usually small- and medium-sized enterprises run their business informally, unlike larger and measurable modern businesses in terms of its capacity, institutional, financial, and managerial resources. Informal means 1) allocation of work time, 2) leadership, 3) communication model, 4) unrestricted office space, can be anywhere, 5) do not use financial standard report, even when they borrow money from financial institutions (no visibility study and its reporting), 6) human resources do not rely on certification, and 7) there is no Standard Operating Procedure (Nuraida 2017). Thus, limitations of capital and employee capabilities restrict small- and medium-sized enterprises in utilizing technology in its business operations.

Employee performance management in the agro-tourism sector could be supported by digitalization. In this digital era, with many limitations of small and medium enterprises, it becomes interesting to know how far the role of digitalization can improve this model of employee performance management. Based on previous empirical research, Nuraida (2017) has proposed employee performance management model for small- and medium-sized enterprises at Kecamatan Lembang, Parongpong and Cisarua, which consists of 5 stages that cover: 1) defining performance, 2) performing and monitoring performance, 3) giving performance appraisal, 4) giving performance appraisal feedback, 5) giving performance reinforcement and utilization of performance appraisal. All of these stages are intended to improve employee performance. Furthermore, employee performance management research which is related to digitalization has never been done in the agro-tourism sector, especially for medium-sized enterprises. The purpose of this paper was to find out benefits and challenges of digitalizing for employee performance management, especially in Kopi Luwak Cikole at Kabupaten Lembang, in order to support employee performance management model proposed by Nuraida (2017). The reason for selection of research object is because Kopi Luwak Cikole has been appointed by local government as a pilot model of Luwak coffee production development in Indonesia. Another reason of this selection is because Kopi Luwak Cikole is derived from natural faeces of mongoose, in contrast to other brands in Indonesia, which produce white luwak coffee from chemical processes.

2 RESEARCH METHOD

The case study was carried out in Kopi Luwak Cikole by conducting in-depth interviews with the owners to obtain data about the role of digitalizing, so that it could be added to the performance management model that had been disseminated previously.

"The case study which is an examination of studies done in other similar organization situations, is also a method of solving problems, or for understanding phenomena of interest and generating further knowledge in that area. Case study involves in-depth, contextual analyses of matters relating to similar situations in other organizations" (Sekaran & Bougie 2010).

3 RESULTS AND DISCUSSION

According to Parry & Strohmeier (2014), digital technologies play an increasingly prominent role in both the lives of employees and human resource management (HRM). This seems to be affected in multiple ways. The first major area called "digital employees" figuratively refers to assumed larger changes in the core subject matter of the HR profession: labelled with various terms such as "digital natives" (Prensky 2001), "millennials" (Deal et al. 2010), or "next generation" (Tapscott, 2008), it is

assumed that the early, intimate, and enduring interaction with digital technologies has shaped a new generation of people with distinctively different attitudes, qualifications, behaviors, and expectations. A second major area might be called "digital work", referring to the content as to the organization of work. Relating to work content, the ongoing digitalization implies an increasing automation of manual and routine work and a slow but steady change of remaining tasks towards brain and information work. The third major area called "digital employee management" refers to the planning, implementation, and in particular application of digital technologies to support and network the HR profession, a phenomenon also known as electronic HRM (Bondarouk & Ruël 2009, Strohmeier 2007).

Employee performance management model of Nuraida (2017) is illustrated in Figure 1. Figure 1 is explained in Tables 1–5 and each table is added with narrative explanation found in the case examples of 5 research objects. The models are made from supply side (black colour) and demand side (red colour). Supply side is obtained from owner, manager, and employees, while demand side is obtained from visitor perception on service quality and its influence to satisfaction. The performance management model is derived from quantitative and qualitative methods. Quantitative methods are differentiated with qualitative methods by adding information about loading factors in every stage.

Based on an in-depth interview with the owner of Kopi Luwak Cikole, this model was added with the application of digitalization, which is marked in blue color in each table along with the explanation. The explanation of stage 1 Defining Performance until stage 5 Performance Reinforcement and Utilization of Performance Appraisal is as follows.

Explanation of stage 1: Defining Performance covers the following issues.

1. Confirmation of vision, mission, strategy, objectiveThe visions are to preserve the environment andto educate nature and the. The mission is to provide land and cultivation for agriculture/plantation/livestock, provide an environmental education and agrobusiness (agrotourism), provide natural products of livestock/plantation/

Figure 1. Employee performance management model of small- and medium-sized enterprises at Kecamatan Lembang, Parongpong, and Cisarua.

Source: Nuraida (2017).

132

Table 1. Stage 1 defining performance.

No	Activities	Explanation
1.	Confirmation of strategic plan	Vision, mission, strategy, goals
2.	Identify Key Success Factor (KSF)	Have a certain uniqueness
3.	The process of making plans	Past performance evaluation, competition anticipation, routine and non-routine job identification, top-down and elaborated at operational level, instruction and briefing, assignment of priority task scale
4.	Plans	Job description + valid indicators (loading factor>0.5), job specification + valid indicators (loading factor>0.5), job performance standard, performance management plan, identify routine and fluctuate works, Critical Success Factor (CSF), Key Performance Indicator (KPI) for tangibility, empathy, reliability, assurance, and responsiveness, each has valid indicators (loading factor>0.5) and reliable (probabilities<0.1), responsiveness influence satisfaction the most, valid satisfaction indicators (loading factor>0.5) and *reliable* (probabilities<0.1)
5.	Form of plans	Oral, written (paper and digitalization)
6.	Office media	Letters, forms, paper, or online reports, finger print, CCTV, video, email, Whatsapp, Line, Instagram
7.	Place	Each block
8.	Period	Differentiate between managerial and operational work, permanent employees, casual workers
9.	Actors involved	Owner, supervisors, employees

agriculture, and to increase employee welfare. The strategies were applied to make the visitor have good experience, make them satisfied, and come again. Objective goals: pay all operating expenses, achieving the target of Rupiah and number of visits.

2. Identify Key Success Factor is by providing certain uniqueness that is not found in any place. For example, Begonia flower seeds imported from Germany, Luwak coffee produced from luwak of the local forest which have been cultivated in agro-tourism.

3. The process of making plan: A) Evaluating performance in the past. B) Creating competition through promoting natural-cultural richness-typical local customs of West Java, making innovative and creative programs, conducting foreign

language courses for tour guides, making informal education of employees, providing outbound services and event organizers, franchise opening, and improving facilities and work infrastructure. C) Identification of routine and non-routine jobs (fluctuating orders). D) Broadly the tasks, duties, and responsibilities are tailored to the needs of the job and are given top-down and they are then elaborated, followed up by each unit/employee. E) Direct supervisor provides daily job description and briefing (especially for casual employees with primary education level). F) Direct supervisors provide more structured briefings to improve service quality of employees. G) Tasks are divided into priority scale, i.e., priority 1 is immediately implemented, priority 2 is consideration of time and human resources needs, priority 3 is tailored to the needs/flexible.

4. Plans.
  1. Job description

  - There are closely related ideas of cultivation, maintenance of the environment and its contents (gardens, farms, and livestock), service to visitors, tasks related to human resources, finance, marketing.
  - Make Standard Operating Procedure.
  - A valid job description indicator (loading factor>0.5): agro-tourism leaders invite employees with a minimal background of high school graduates to jointly develop job descriptions to set standards and performance weights.

  2. Job specification

  - Diploma/bachelor degree employee and managerial level are expected to have management skill, communication skill, leadership skill, time management skill, people management skill, analytical thinking, knowledge in Microsoft Office, and problem solving skill.
  - A valid job-specification indicator (loading factor>0.5): the agro-tourism leader asks the employee's opinon about requirements that are appropriate for the task description.

  3. Job performance standard: serving happily, applying motto Concise-Neat-Care-Diligent-Clean, giving more rewards to the employees showing good performance, determining performance standards after 3 months of work.

  4. Daily work plan related to routine tasks (case example: making plant maintenance schedule, planting time and harvest time, animal rearing) and fluctuating duties (case example: group visit, training request).

  5. Performance appraisal plan: giving appraisal depends on supervisor' policy, should be based on monitoring and trust of superiors to subordinates, giving appraisal personally between superiors and subordinates, giving

appraisal can be done every day for freelancers or once a year for permanent employees.

6. Critical Success Factor: changing the atmosphere regularly, seeing is believing, training tour guide role to persuade visitors, facilitating agribusiness education, and providing honest products.

7. Key Performance Indicator: KPI service quality in Kopi Luwak Cikole is made based on feedback from visitors, i.e., smile, greetings, initiative, courtesy.

Based on the results of quantitative data processing of AMOS confirmatory analysis on service quality and its effect on visitor satisfaction in 5 research objects, there is feedback in the form of valid visitor satisfaction indicator (loading factor>0,5) and reliability or significance (probability<0.1), that cover: 1) performing good activities; 2) willingness to come again to the location of agro-tourism; 3) giving recommendation of the agro-tourism to the nearest relatives; 4) giving companion the closest relatives to come together to the location of agro-tourism. To improve the customers' satisfaction, the agro-tourism object should improve its responsiveness. KPI indicators for valid responsiveness (loading factor>0.5) and reliability or significance (probability <0.1) cover: 1) employees taking the initiative to help visitors overcome confusion and problems; 2) employees are alert in giving fast response to visitors' needs and complaints; 3) employees give fast responses in solving customers' problems; 4) employees are always ready when they are needed

Other factors also needed to be considered by agro-tourism object. Each has valid indicators (loading factor>0.5) and reliable or significant (probability <0.1); they are as follows.

1. Empathy refers to several aspects; they are 1) hospitality, courtesy of employees; 2) employees paying attention to the needs/wishes of visitors, and offering personal assistance; 3) employee relationships with visitors; 4) communication of employees with visitors.

2. Tangibility that covers: 1) appearance of employees; 2) body language; 3) agro-tourism facilities (toilet, prayer room, parking lot, restaurant, seating, etc.); 4) agro-tourism should always look good, maintain cleanliness, beauty, and also be secure and orderly.

3. Reliability that covers: 1) accuracy and accountability of information; 2) effectiveness and efficiency of service procedures (timely service); 3) overall product quality; 4) service quality as a whole.

4. Assurance that includes: 1) knowledge; 2) ability; 3) skills; 4) attitude and behavior; 5) security guarantees for visitors.

5. Form of plans in both oral and written. Written form can be made through: A) making daily "to do list" form that is reported to the supervisor every afternoon, B) making time table about the details of the activity schedule, how much, and when to finish the tasks in distributing fluctuating tasks, C) making written notes from the owner using paper, email, Whatsapp, Line, etc., D) Distributing format of paper reports or online daily and weekly stock opname reports. The benefit of these online reports are 1) they are real-time feedback 2) they are easily accessible from other parties at any time, 3) they are flexible to provide detailed customized reports 4) they are easy to be accessed anywhere they are needed, 5) employees can easily upload photos and videos from events without worrying about reducing file size to email, zipping files, 6) Employees can store the report information online so we can easily access reports in the future to compare company's progress from year to year. 7) Reports are kept safe via password-protected websites so that key stakeholders can have access to the critical information.

6. Office media. The office media covers letters, forms, papers, online reports, daily attendance form, finger print, Closed Circuit Television (CCTV), video, email, Whatsapp, Line, Instagram. The benefit of fingerprint identification methods is that employee attendance can be monitored by their supervisor easily. Meanwhile, CCTV is beneficial for recording employees and working activity in a certain spot. It is used not only to prevent crime, but also to create a sense of security for employees in the workplace, including monitoring employee performance during work. In addition, email is beneficial as it is accessible by other parties at any time, can deliver email faster so that all data and information regarding the planning, implementation, progress, and results of employee performance can be immediately known by supervisor to be evaluated or given follow-up actions. Whatsapp and Line media are beneficial as they are able to send faster messages and quick replies. Instagram media is also advantageous since it can promote company profile to represent its business in various facets, such as a salesperson, tour guide, or part of the support team.

7. Place: at the agro-tourism site and each block.

8. Period: A) Managerial level: compiled per month and per year. B) Fixed employees (operational level). For routine work, it is done per week, per month, per year, and for fluctuate work, it is compiled per day, per week, and per month. C) Freelancers (operational staff) who work for routine and fluctuating jobs: compiled per day, per week.

Table 2. Stage 2 performing and monitoring performance.

No	Activities	Explanation
1.	What is monitored	Processes, behaviors, results
2.	Monitoring methods	Increase monitoring to give better service quality to visitors: informally, feedback, coaching, counseling, on-the job training, mentoring, lure of incentives/wages
3.	Actors involved	Employees, direct supervisors, owner, feedback from visitors
4.	Monitoring time	Every day, every week, based on time table/volume of work
5.	Monitoring place	As per work requirement.
6.	Monitoring media	Written, oral, recording, CCTV, finger print, Whatsapp, Line, Instagram
7.	Valid indicators of monitoring (loading factor>0.5)	Guidance, motivation

9. Actors involved: employees, direct supervisor, and the owner.

Explanation of Stage 2: Performing and Monitoring Performance stage is described as follows:

1. What is monitored? Implementation of works in terms of its processes, behavior, results, day to day operation so once a problem comes up, it can be directly corrected.
2. Monitoring methods cover A) Informal: daily monitoring meeting that was done through briefings every morning, face to face, reports, inspections of the stakeholder to the field; weekly monitoring can be done through discussion. B) The role of important and multifunctional leaders: A leader is responsible in providing feedback, coaching, counseling, job training, mentoring, feedback, the lure of providing incentives for employees who have given the best contribution. C) Monitoring method for freelancers (elementary school educational background) was done by a) calculating wages based on work contribution per day, b) reminding freelancers that they are considered as a co-worker, not telling or giving orders but asking for help, c) increasing employees supervision to encourage employees giving better service quality.
3. Parties involved: employees, direct supervisors, owner, and feedback from visitors.
4. Monitoring time: every working day, every week, or by time table, or by volume of work.
5. Monitoring place: sporadic as needed where the work is available, according to the block of each.

6. Monitoring media: office documents (daily workmanship reports, attendance, notes held by immediate supervisors) or based on the memory of superiors, recording, CCTV, Whatsapp, Line, phone call, and Instagram. These digitalization tools are useful to support the monitoring process of performance management, but sometimes employees forget to use it or to report data and information completely.

Table 3. Stage 3 performance appraisal.

No	Activities	Explanation
1.	Input of performance appraisal Purpose of performance appraisal	Implementation and performance results, latest reports, time tables, online applications, recording, CCTV, finger print, video, email, Line, Whatsapp, Instagram. Improve performance, ensure successful work, rewards, promotions.
2.	Administrative procedures Socialization of performance appraisal	According to the needs. According to the needs.
3.	Performance appraisal method	Interviewing, coaching, counseling, discussion, monitoring, inspection, communication way, how to assess good and bad performance.
4.	Media of performance appraisal	Office documents and or non-documents.
5.	Aspects, standards, and weight of performance appraisal	Aspects assessed are results, behaviors, processes. For standard and weight, there are differentiation based on manager level and operational level of primary and secondary education.
6.	Valid performance appraisal indicators (loading factor>0.5)	Objectives, aspects, and measures are clear and complete; ratter is capable and fair; standards communicated; preparing supportive office media.
7.	Period of performance appraisal	Based on the time table of each project, differentiated between freelancers and permanent employees.
8.	Actors involved	Direct supervisor, mutual cross check in weekly discussions.
9.	Output of performance appraisal	As expected or not, what factors are inhibiting or supporting good performance.

7. Based on the results of statistical data processing in 5 research objects, a valid performance monitoring indicator (loading factor>0.5) covers A) Supervisors directly guide employees to correct inadequate assessment component. B) Supervisors directly motivate lazy employees.

Explanation of Stage 3: The Performance Appraisal aspects are explained as follows.

1. Input that is needed for performance appraisal covers: results–process–behaviours which are collected from implementation and work monitoring, weekly report accumulation, online application, time table reports, recording, CCTV, finger print, video, email, Line, Whatsapp, and Instagram. The purpose of performance appraisal is to improve employees' performance, ensure successful work/success, determine rewards, and determine promotion decision.

2. Procedures and socialization of performance appraisal administration are adjusted to the needs: giving dissemination during observation period is not necessarily needed if daily monitoring has been performed, checking whether the work is in accordance with the instructions of the supervisor, checking whether the tasks have been done consistently and consequently, holding morning briefings, and checking attendance. Dissemination of performance regulations is conducted as needed in the field: reduce–reuse–recycle, reduce pesticide use.

3. Performance appraisal method covers: A) Reviewing assessment results followed by interviews, coaching, counseling, and conducting personal or group discussions. B) Conducting daily direct monitoring and unannounced inspections. C) Having communication: informal, personal between supervisor and employee. D) Rating good or bad performance that is conducted based on the results of the supervisor's monitoring results, complaints, or feedback from visitors, conditions of agro-tourism products enjoyed/sold, daily work report, and based on sudden inspection to the field.

4. Media of performance appraisal that covers: A) office documents, e.g. workmanship form, attendance, supervisors note, photo, soft copy, KPI. B) non-office documents, e.g. direct communication between superiors and subordinates.

5. Aspects, standards, and weight of performance appraisal:
   - Rated aspects that cover A) Operational employees who have primary level of education: work (e.g. physical quality and output), working processes (e.g. working performance when if it is not monitored, working conflicts), working behavior (honesty, friendliness of visitors). B) Operational employee who have secondary levels of education: working performance and processes (e.g.

skills in work, attendance, consistent work, and responsibility), attitude behaviors (e.g. friendly, good manners, honesty, loyalty, discipline). C) Supervisors/managers level tertiary education: the working performance and working process (cooperation, consistent work, responsibility, leadership, ideas, working knowledge, decision-making, problem-solving skills), attitude behavior (friendly, courteous, honest, loyalty, discipline).
   - Standard and weighted performance appraisal: A) Operational employees who have secondary levels of education: observed directly by supervisor based on its contribution to the company, KPI. B) For supervisor/manager level tertiary education: KPI. C) Depending on the policy of the immediate supervision.

6. Performance appraisal indicators. The supervisor needs to pay attention to the necessary matters that are acceptable to the employee and are applied fairly as it has a direct impact on employees' satisfaction and motivation to improve their working performance. The results of statistical data processing towards 5 research objects, with a valid performance appraisal indicator (loading factor>0.5), are as follows:
   - Performance appraisal was intended to improve employees' performance and needs to be conducted annually and objectively for permanent employees.
   - Performance appraisal was conducted A) adequately B) to reflect the critical matters of the employees' working performance (no contamination is not relevant); C) as measures to assess aspects of performance appraisal that are made clear and complete (no deficiency/not all assessed); D) as a description of measurable (quantitative) working aspects (productivity) that have been made clear and complete; E) as a description of the aspects that cannot be measured (qualitative); F) as an assessment towards aspects of the working process of employees in agro-tourism; G) as an assessment towards attitude aspect/employee working behavior in agro-tourism made completely.
   - Appraisers of performance: A) Different appraisers provide the same assessment if the measured object does not change. B) Assessment is not much different from the assessment at different times if the measured object does not change. C) Appraisers have an understanding and ability to assess the performance. D) Fair appraisal is needed in assessing employee performance outcomes. E) Performance appraisal standards need to be fulfilled: need to be communicated to the employees, made completely and clearly, and need to be updated.

- Employees' performance appraisal system is understandable and applicable.
- Prepare the office media for adequate monitoring and performance appraisals (e.g. forms, soft copies, etc.).

7. Period of performance appraisal. In the case of examples in 5 research objects, the period of performance appraisal was conducted as follows: A) Freelancers: each day to determine the wages of freelancers for the day, annually for the distribution of the net income/surplus. B) Permanent employee: weekly and annually. C) Based on time table and time line for fluctuating/non-routine jobs.
8. Parties involved: direct supervisors or cross-check each other in weekly routine discussions.
9. Output of performance appraisal: the results of the evaluation of the direct supervisor reveal the effectiveness of the program, factors inhibiting good performance, factors supporting good performance, and complaints from visitors.

Explanation of Stage 4: Performance appraisal feedback was conducted as follows.

1. Performance appraisal feedback was conducted through: A) Discussion and interview, coaching, and counseling. B) Determining how to correct poor performance by reprimanding, giving personal approach through examples, giving warning letters, giving training/workshop/outbound/demotion/by firing, cutting incentives, asking whether performance is as expected as in the initial agreement and then asking them for the solution if it is not. Feedback is given with tolerance, meaning that less performance is still praised but the employee is encouraged to improve their performance. For freelancers who have elementary school education background or lower, supervisors encourage them to find their own answers to mistakes they make and to create a co-worker's atmosphere. C) Determining strategies to maintain/develop good performance: trusted to find other ideas or do more complex tasks, incentives, tips, and study tour.
2. Parties involved: employees, direct supervisors, and owner.
3. Timing of performance appraisal feedback: anytime/every execution of job, every morning briefing, weekly discussion, weekly personalized feedback for freelancers, weekly and annual personal feedback for permanent employees according to time table.
4. Based on AMOS confirmatory analysis of quantitative data, a valid performance feedback indicator (load factor> 0.5) covers: A) The time interval between providing performance feedback and performance appraisal times should be short. B) The supervisor directly informs the component of the assessment to be corrected by the employee. C) Employees understand how to improve performance that is less based on feedback from supervisors.

Table 4. Stage 4 performance appraisal feedback.

No	Activities	Explanation
1.	Performance appraisal feedback method	Discussion, interview, coaching, counseling, determining performance correction of how good and how bad performances are
2.	Actors involved	Employee, direct supervisors, owner
3.	Timing of performance appraisal feedback	Anytime, every day/every briefing, every week, according to the time table, distinguished for freelancers and permanent employees.
4.	Valid indicators of performance feedback (loading factor>0.5)	Quickly, employees understand.

Table 5. Stage 5 performance reinforcement and utilization of performance appraisal.

No	Activities	Explanation
1.	Determine rewards for good performance Determine punishment for poor performance	Distinguished for permanent employees and freelancers. Given fairly, it can be a warning, warning letter, demotion, paycheck, fired, do not pay attention, punish those who do not give good service quality to visitors.
2.	Utilization of performance appraisal to improve functional areas of human resource management	Standard of Operating Procedure for performance appraisal system Recruit new employees Employee promotion Update KPI Foreign language course for tour guide Correct the system of rewards and punishment. Update, improve, and develop digitalization for better performance.
3.	Valid indicators of reinforcing performance and utilization of performance appraisal to improve functional areas of human resource management (loading factors>0.5)	Rewards and punishment are given fairly; there are implications of performance appraisal of employment decisions.

Explanation of Stage 5: Reinforcement Performance and Utilization of Performance Appraisal.

1. Rewards for good performance are as follows.
   - Supervisor buys some food for employees, praised, increase salaries, holidays.
   - Compensation package of permanent employees are: A) Basic salary is paid according to company regulations (per week, per month). B) Benefits: religious holiday allowance, transportation, health, attendance, and lunch. C) Rewards for achievement above standard net income. D) Incentives awarded based on employees' performance output in providing the best contribution or can be evaluated by the number of visitors. E) Overtime pay. F) Premiums for additional work.
   - Compensation for freelancers that cover: A) Daily wage below or equal to regional minimum wage depending on capability. B) Incentives: depending on the performance of employees in providing the best service, it can be in the form of tips/premiums for additional work. C) Benefits like attendance money and lunch. Punishment for poor performance includes: A) Reprimanding, warning letters 1–3, demotions, incentives cutting, fired. B) Freelancers who have primary education level or never gone to school are given punishment in the form of soft warning or cut daily wage, being fired if they are caught stealing or harming outsiders. C) Punishment for employees who do not serve visitors well.

2. Utilization of performance appraisal to improve functional areas of human resource management: A) Adding foreign language courses, especially for tour guides. B) Adding new employees. C) Making promotion for employees with good performance. D) Creating Standard of Operating Procedure for performance appraisal system. E) Improving recruitment and selection process: recruit friendly employees, making banners, requiring applicants to write job application letter. F) Improving rewards system: freelancers should not be paid daily, but need to get paid in accordance with the resulting performance. G) Increasing training to improve service quality to visitors. H) Updating, improving, and developing digitalization for better employee performance.

3. Valid indicators of reinforcing performance and utilization of performance appraisal to improve functional areas of human resource management (loading factor>0.5) are: A) Appreciation for work performance is given fairly. B) Giving rewards to employees who are loyal to agro-tourism. C) Punishment sanction for poor performance and should be applied fairly. C) There are implications of employee performance appraisal of employment decisions.

4 CONCLUSION

As a medium-sized company of agrotourism sector especially at Kecamatan Lembang, Kopi Luwak Cikole employ non-digitalized employees because they have to serve visitors directly and satisfactorily. They are slightly related to digital work because they need to give services to visitors by socializing, communicating, persuading to yield visitor satisfaction. They didn't much apply digitalization into their work and into their digital employee management.

However, use of digitalization has been widely applied by Kopi Luwak Cikole, especially in the field of marketing and has been very helpful in promoting the products and the place (marketing aspect). For the field of human resources, the owner of Kopi Luwak Cikole used the simplest first, ranging from absentee employees who use finger print at the location in Lembang, which is directly accessible at Bandung office and processed by the administration team there. The owners also tried to optimize social media facilities to monitor, assess, train, and develop employee performance such as tour guides who have an important role in educating visitors. Performance is adapted to standard operating procedure in each section. The principle of what is written is done, and what it does is what is written. Related to this matter, Kopi Luwak Cikole has a recording processed by each head of unit and reported every night to the administrative team in Bandung, via email or Whatssapp including daily reporting of stock and sales used to measure production and marketing team work. Another example is recording tour guide to educate visitors about civet mongoose, how to process mongoose to eat coffee snack to produce coffee low of caffeine from faeces, how to process and produce sterilization of civet coffee hygienist to be consumed by visitors. Videos can be used to assess the performance of the tour guides; also videos of the Cikole Kopi Luwak can be displayed on Youtube and websites, as it can promote the uniqueness of coffee product with low caffeine, etc., create brand awareness of Kopi Luwak Cikole, promote the culture of West Java with traditional instrument and custom, which thereby greatly affect the increase in the number of visitors and sales online. In addition, there is CCTV installed in the cashier, café, production section, which is useful as a tool to monitor team performance.

Generally, digitalization cannot be applied optimally in small and medium enterprises of agro-tourism sector, especially at Kopi Luwak Cikole. Kopi Luwak Cikole has its own challenge in applying it for complete digitalization. This is due to the limited quality of human resources that most of them have never studied in college. This becomes the greatest challenge for owners. But digitalization has a prominent role in supporting and helping owner and managers, especially to monitor and appraise employee's performance. For Kopi Luwak Cikole, digitalization is used in the form of video, recording performance, online application, Whatsapp, Line, Instagram, finger print, email. These tools become useful media to help and support defining performance, monitoring performance, conducting performance appraisal, and utilization of performance appraisal to maintain or develop good performance. It's also useful to promote the video through Youtube and website. In addition, recording performance becomes one input for performance appraisal. Manager and employees can discuss the advantages and disadvantages of employee performance by reviewing the performance that has been previously recorded. Stage performance appraisal feedback from managers to employees is more effective using face to face communication to create more harmonic relationship, improve mutual understanding, develop trust, and reinforce the employees' performance.

REFERENCES

Bondarouk, T.V. & Ruel, H.J.M. 2009. Electronic Human Resource Management: challenges in the digital era. *The International Journal of Human Resource Management* 20(3): 505-514.

Deal, J.J., Altman, D.G. & Rogelberg, S.G. 2010. Millennials at work: What we know and what we need to do (if anything). *Journal of Business and Psychology* 25 (2): 191-199.

Hagberg, J., Sundstrom, M. & Egels-Zandén, N. 2016. The digitalization of retailing: an exploratory framework. *International Journal of Retail & Distribution Management* 44(7): 694-712.

Nuraida, I. 2014. *Administrative Office Management*. Revised Edition. Yogyakarta: Kanisius.

Nuraida, I. 2017. Employee Performance Management Framework for Medium-Sized Enterprises of Agrotourism Sector. *Noble International Journal of Business and Management Research* 1(4): 74-93.

Parry, E. & Strohmeier, S. 2014. HRM in the Digital Age – Digital Changes and Challenges of the HR Profession. *Employee Relations* 36(4).

Prensky, M. 2001. Digital natives, digital immigrants part 1. *On the horizon* 9(5): 1-6.

Sekaran, U. & Bougie, R. 2010. *Research Method for Business: A Skill-Building Approach*. Fifth Edition. New Jersey: John Wiley & Sons Ltd.

Strohmeier, S. 2007. Research in E-HRM: Review and Implications. *Human Resource Management Review* 17 (1): 19-37.

Tapscott, D. 2008. *Grown up Digital: How the Net Generation is Changing Your World HC*. New York: McGraw-Hill.

Global Competitiveness: Business Transformation in the
Digital Era – Abdullah, Widiaty & Abdullah (eds)
© 2019 Taylor & Francis Group, London, ISBN 978-0-367-19442-0

Examining the effect of compensation motivation and work period on employee performance

N. Nawiyah, T. Endrawati, M.R. Cili, R.T.H. Parnanto & A. Wahyudin
Polytechnic APP Jakarta, Ministry of Industry, Indonesia

ABSTRACT: The research was aimed to determine the effect of compensation, motivation, and work period on employee performance before and after the performance allowances at the Academy of Corporate Leadership Jakarta. The analysis was based on managerial implications. The research used quantitative with multiple linear regression analysis technique to determine the effect of compensation variable (X_1), motivation variable (X_2), and work period variable (X_3) on employee performance (Y). The population of this research was 60 employees of Academy of Corporate Leadership, and census technical sampling method was used. The data were collected through questionnaires distributed to employees of the Academy of Corporate Leadership that consists of two sources of data namely primary data and secondary data. The result of the research showed that before the performance allowances, compensation had positive and significant effect on the employee performance while motivation and work period had no effect on the employee performance. After the performance allowances, compensation and motivation have positive and significant effect on employee performance, while work period has no effect on employee performance. The implication from this research is motivation and compensation can give encouragement to employee more than hard work.

1 INTRODUCTION

Human resources in the organization make a contribution to the achievement of organizational goals. Such contribution is usually referred to as work or performance. Each job has a specific job criterion or a working dimension that identifies the most important elements of a job. Organizations need to know the various weaknesses and advantages of employees as a foundation to fix weaknesses and strengthen the advantages. This is to increase productivity and employee development so that the performance of employees in the organization can be optimized for the achievement of organizational goals.

The performance appraisal is in accordance with PP. 10 year 1979 namely DP3 assessment system (List of Job Implementation Assessment). In 2011 was issued Government Regulation no. 46 of 2011 on the assessment of the performance of civil servants who are expected to contribute well in terms of assisting government agencies in measuring employee performance. Furthermore, on November 17th, 2012, Presidential Regulation of the Republic of Indonesia Number 101 of 2012 was published, on employee performance benefits within the Ministry of Industry. This Presidential Regulation is issued as a manifestation of the implementation of Bureaucracy Reform within the Ministry of Industry; the Academy of Corporate Leaders follows the applicable regulations. This Presidential Regulation starts to be implemented and the performance appraisal system is also adjusted to this Presidential Regulation.

Moeheriono (2010) states that the factors affecting employee performance cover expectations regarding rewards, encouragement, ability, needs and nature, perceptions of job, external and internal rewards, perceptions of reward levels, and job satisfaction. Compensation and motivation play an important role in implementing employee performance. In addition, the work period can contribute to the performance of an employee; the longer the employee work, the higher the knowledge of the job.

Based on the background described above, this study was intended to obtain empirical evidence on "whether there is effect of compensation, motivation, and work period on employee performance at the Academy of Corporate Leaders Jakarta before and after the existence of performance allowances".

Performance, as stated by Mangkunegara (2005), refers to work performance or achievement that is actually achieved by someone in quality and quantity in performing their duties in accordance with the responsibility given to him/her.

The Regulation of the Minister of Industry of the Republic of Indonesia. No. 112/M-IND/PER/12/2012 definition of performance allowances is followed for the allowance given to employees based on discipline and employee performance appraisal. Assessment of the discipline is the assessment of the working hours of Civil Servants stipulated under the regulation.

Compensation is a Human Resource Management (HRM) function that deals with each type of reward an individual receives in return to the performance of the organization's jobs. Employees exchange their energy to get financial reward and non-financial reward (Kadarisman 2012).

Motivation, on the other hand, is a set of attitudes and values that affect the individual to achieve the specific goal in accordance with the individual goals. Such attitudes and values are an invisible one that provides the power to encourage individuals to achieve their goals (Veitzhal 2004).

Last, the work period is the period of time people have started working until the current working time. The period of work can be interpreted as a long piece of time where a workforce entered into a single area of business until a certain time limit (Suma'mur 2009).

2 METHOD

2.1 Population and sample

The research was conducted at the Academy of Corporate Leadership and it involved 60 lecturers and employees of the Academy of Corporate Leadership. The participants were selected by saturated sampling technique/census where all employees become target of sampling.

2.2 Research variable

Dependent variable in this research is employee performance before and after existence of performance allowance. Employee performance indicators in this study are the quality of work, the quantity of work, the utilization of time, the level of attendance, and cooperation.

There are 3 independent variables in this research, namely compensation (X_1), motivation (X_2), and work period (X_3). The compensation (X_1) indicators in this research are justice, expectation and achievement, prosperity, and spirit. The motivation (X_2) indicator in this the study covers actualization, appreciation, achievement, promotion, creativity, direction, and stimulation. Meanwhile, the work period (X_3) indicator in this research is referred to the working period from the beginning of employee become civil servant until 2012 for the regression model before the performance allowances and 2013 after the performance allowances.

2.3 Analysis

The data were analyzed using multiple regression test with equation (1) to test the regression model before the existence of performance allowances and equation (2) to test the regression model after the existence of performance allowances. Here are the equations of the regression model.

$$Y = a + b1 \text{ compensation} + b2 \text{ Motovation} + b3 \text{ Work Period} + e \quad (1)$$

$$Y = a + b1 \text{ compensation} + b2 \text{ Motovation} + b3 \text{ Work Period} + e \quad (2)$$

Further partial test (t-test) and simultaneous test (F-test) in each regression model with 95% confidence level or significance of 0.05 were carried out.

3 RESULTS AND DISCUSSION

This section presents the results of data processing and analysis to answer the research issues that have been put forward thereafter. The correlation formula of Pearson Product Moment is used for testing the validity of the questionnaire. From the validity test performed, it was found that all r-arithmetic is positive and r-count > r-table at significant value 0.05. It is therefore concluded that all item statements in the instrument/questionnaire are valid. The truth and reliability of the questionnaire were tested by Alpha Cronbach method. The reliability test showed that the value of Alpha Cronbach > 0.70. Thus, it is concluded that all items statement in this research instrument is reliable or consistent and can be used as an instrument in this research.

3.1 Classical assumption test

The first test is normality test using the Kolmogorov–Smirnov test method. From the test results, it was revealed that there is a significance value of 0.624 in the regression model before the performance allowances and 0.190 after performance allowances. These values are significant because both values are above the value of α of 0.05, meaning that the error is normally distributed.

The second test is the Heteroscedasticity test with the scatterplot test method. After analyzing the data, the scatter plot charts show that the points do not form a particular pattern on both regression models. This condition indicates that there isn't any heteroscedasticity in the regression model before and after the performance allowances.

The third test is a Multicollinearity test symbolized by a Variance Inflation Factor (VIF). The analysis revealed that VIF value is less than 10 and Tolerance value is more than 0.10. This condition means that all independent variables in both regression models show no multicollinearity or no linear relationship between independent variables.

The fourth test is an Autocorrelation test by calculating Durbin Watson. From the output of the regression model, the regression model before the performance allowances is 2.123 and the regression model after the performance allowances is 1.892. Whereas from Durbin Watson table with significant 0.05 and samples (n) 60 obtained dL = 1.4794 and dU = 1.6889. Durbin

Watson values in both regression models are in the region between dU and 4-dU, implying that there is no autocorrelation in both regression models.

3.2 *Regression model before performance allowances*

The result of multiple regression test before performance allowances was obtained from the equation as follows:

$$Y = 23.573 + 0.395 \text{ compensation}$$
$$+ 0.136 \text{ Motovation} - 0.067 \text{ Work Period} + \varepsilon$$

Furthermore, the partial test is performed between each independent variable and the dependent variable. With t-table 1.67356, the results of partial test are as follows:

− There is a positive and significant effect of compensation on employee performance before performance allowances because t-count (1.995) > t-table with positive regression coefficient.
− There is no effect of motivation on employee performance before performance allowance because t-count (1.056) < t-table.
− There is no effect of work period on employee performance before performance allowance because −t-count (−0.151) > −t-table.

Then, another test that simultaneously investigated relationship between compensation, motivation, and work period of employee performance before performance allowance was also conducted. With the determined of F-table value of 2.77, the result of simultaneous test showed that F-count is 3.663 > F-table. Thus, it can be concluded that simultaneously, there is an effect of compensation, motivation, and work period on employee performance before performance allowance.

The next test is the determination coefficient test to determine the dependent variable explained independent of any heteroscedasticity variable. The test results showed that the value of Adjusted R Square is 0.164, meaning that 16.4% performance variables before performance allowances are explained by compensation, motivation, and work period, whereas 83.6% is explained by other factors.

3.3 *Regression model after performance allowances*

Meanwhile, another focus of the study to investigate multiple regression tests after performance allowances was carried out by using the equation as follows:

$$Y = 27.428 + 0.545 \text{ compensation}$$
$$+ 0.255 \text{ Motovation} - 0.375 \text{ Work Period}$$

After that, the partial test was carried out between each independent variable and the dependent variable. Using the determined t-table value of 1.67356, the results of partial test are:

− There is a positive and significant effect of compensation on employee performance after performance allowances because t-count (5.101) > t-table with positive regression coefficient.
− There is a positive and significant effect of motivation on employee performance after performance allowances because t-count (3.557) > t-table with positive regression coefficient.
− There is no effect of work period on employee performance after performance allowances because −t-count (−1.411) > −t-table.

Further, the study also tested simultaneously the relation between compensation, motivation, and tenure of employee performance after performance allowances. With the determined value of 2.77 for F-table and the gained result of simultaneous test of F-count (30.177) > F-table, it can be concluded that, simultaneously, there is an effect of compensation, motivation, and work period on employee performance after performance allowances.

The next test is the determination coefficient test to determine the dependent variable explained by the independent variable. From the calculation, it was revealed that the Adjusted R Square test results show the value of 0.618, meaning that 61.8% variable performance after performance allowances was explained by compensation, motivation, and work period. Meanwhile, 31.2% is explained by other factors.

The findings revealed that partially, there is a positive and significant effect of compensation on employee performance before and after the existence of performance allowances. This condition means that with the presence or absence of performance allowances, employees have a professional performance in accordance with their respective duties and responsibilities.

Before the existence of performance allowances, there is no effect of motivation on employee performance, and after existence of performance allowances, there is positive and significant effect of motivation on employee performance. This condition indicates that there is a difference in motivation in the period before and after the performance allowance. With performance benefits, employees are more motivated to work.

Meanwhile, before and after the existence of performance allowances, there is no influence of working period on employee performance. This means that the working period of employees does not affect the results of their work.

4 CONCLUSION

Before the performance allowances, compensation has a positive and significant effect on employee performance, whereas motivation and work period have no effect on employee performance. Meanwhile, after the performance allowance, compensation and motivation have positive and significant influence on employee performance, whereas work period has no effect on employee performance.

REFERENCES

Kadarisman, M. 2012. *Compensation Management*. Jakarta: PT. Raja Grafindo Persada.

Mangkunegaran, A.P. 2005. *Corporate Human Resource Management*. Bandung: Rosada Karya.

Moeherionoo, M. 2010. *Competency Based Performance Measurement*. Second printing. Jakarta: Ghalia Indonesia.

Suma'mur, S. 2009. *Analysis of Factors Affecting Employee Performance in the Regional Personnel Agency of Central Tapanuli Regency*. Jakarta: Open University, Final Project Master Program (TAPM).

Veithzal, R. 2004. *Leadership and Organizational behavior*. Jakarta: PT. Raja Grafindo Persada.

Global Competitiveness: Business Transformation in the
Digital Era – Abdullah, Widiaty & Abdullah (eds)
© 2019 Taylor & Francis Group, London, ISBN 978-0-367-19442-0

Organizational strategy in permanence and newness

F.H. Ismadi

Parahyangan Catholic University, West Java, Indonesia

ABSTRACT: An organization is a group of multiple human beings that interact with each other and have a common purpose. Each member establishes itself in the dialectic of permanence and newness, which is done in the interaction with other beings within the organization. As a whole, the organization is an entity that is independent, intact, and has a certainty. There is also the dialectic in an organization between the past and the future. The past and the future of an organization are together in its present, in the atmosphere of competition. The organization is new, but at the same time, is still old. Both permanence and newness are a part of the present of the organization. In this dialectic between permanence and newness, each organization formulates its strategy whose aims are to maintain its life and to achieve its goals of being in the midst of competition with other organizations. By conducting research in various literatures, this study was aimed to uncover the organizational strategy in the dialectic of permanence and newness.

1   INTRODUCTION

The reality of a human being is in the present. In different ways, the present contains all of a being's past and its future. In its present, a human being is living together with other beings in the dialectic of permanence and newness.

Permanence and newness are concepts in philosophy that speak about the existence of human beings. To deepen the concept of these two themes, literature review was carried out using philosophical writings. These two themes are discussed in Human and Metaphysical Philosophy.

Meanwhile the organization is a concept of management that refers to an entity consisting of beings that are men and women who interact with each other. The human interaction in the organization makes the organization develop itself; there is always newness but there are also permanent elements. To understand this, one must study the writings that discuss the organization and the writings about changes in the organization.

In this dialectic between permanence and newness, each organization formulates its strategy that was aimed to maintain its life and to achieve its goals of being in the midst of competition with other organizations. To understand how to build a strategy, literature review was carried out from the writing of Henry Mintzberg and from two books recently published about disruption and blue ocean shift strategies.

It is supposed that an organization is a group of multiple beings which interact with each other and have a common purpose. Each of them establishes itself in the dialectic of permanence and newness which is done in interaction with other beings within

the organization. As a whole, the organization is an entity that is independent, intact, and has a certainty. Therefore, the organization, in some sense, has the qualities contained in a being, causing the organization to thrive and to move in a similar framework to a being.

There is the dialectic in an organization between the past and the future. In previous literatures, there are some organizations that are satisfied with past performance and achievements, some are satisfied with managing loyal customers who are more profitable than looking for new customers (Kasali 2017). Meanwhile, other organizations try to find a way to get new customers through innovation and technology, using ideas that were not thought of in the past (Kim & Mauborgne 2017).

In its present, the organization is shaped by its past and in the process of becoming its future. The past and the future of an organization are together in its present, in the atmosphere of competition with other organizations. The result of this process is an organization that is always new, but at the same time, is still old. Both permanence and newness are a part of the present of the organization.

This paper discusses how an organization builds a strategy considering the dialectic of permanence and newness in organization.

2   METHOD

A literature review was conducted to uncover the organizational strategy in the dialectic of permanence and newness. To understand how an organization builds a strategy, literature review was carried out to the writing of Henry Mintzberg and to two books about disruption and blue ocean shift strategies. To deepen the concept of permanence and newness, literature review was carried out using philosophical writings. These two themes were discussed in Human and Metaphysical Philosophy.

3 LITERATURE REVIEW

3.1 *The present is a summary of the past and the future*

A being is a substance that is not a superficial fact, but a completely unique independent state. A being expresses what is real in "I" as reality (hey on - Greek). The word "being" is a classic term in various languages: to on (Greek), ens (Latin), das Seiende (German), un être (French). In each of these "being" has an independent state, wholeness, and autonomy (Bakker 1992).

The being is with other beings. In being together with other beings, a being attains consciousness of himself. Therefore, the independent state of a being requires the existence of others (Bakker 1992).

"The present of a being" is the most central. A being has its past, but the past is only real because it is settled in its present/now. A being also has its future, but the future is only real as a project, hope, and desire contained within its present. All the past and the future are present and are summarized in the present. At every moment, a being becomes itself wholly. In its present, a being experiences a real identity (Bakker 1992).

The past is a fact that cannot be changed, making a being with a certain existence. All past facts together efficiently form a being. The relevance of each past value is structured according to a particular order or value scale. There is a continuity between the past and the present (Hadi 1996).

The future is always in touch with the present. The facts of the present contain the foundations to be developed in the future. The future is embedded in contemporary reality as anticipation (Hadi 1996).

Newness is not the same as change. Newness is creation, bringing out something from nothing (Schulz 2001). People think about the future always as a continuation of the past. But the power of divine creation endowed with the gift enables a being, especially human, to have ideas about new possibilities that were not thought of in the past (Hadi 1996, Hurtubise 2003).

3.2 *The dynamics of a being*

A being experiences itself in its present, but the present is not static. In each moment a being moves from one present to the next present. A being comes out of himself, but at the same time it remains itself completely. It is not the other being; it is permanent and at the same time continuous and new (Bakker 1992).

The dynamics of beings are in togetherness. A being experiences and manifests itself in correlation with all other beings (Bakker 1992). The presence of other beings helps to recognize the existence of a being, which is different from the presence of another. Each has its own, unique dynamics, but the personal dynamics are not separated or unrelated to others.

The dynamic unity between all comes in (happens in) the present. In togetherness, each being integrates its own present, so in this togetherness there are similarities and differences (Bakker 1992).

3.3 *Organizational strategy in permanence and newness*

An organization is an entity comprised of multiple people, such as institution or an association that has a collective goal and is linked to an external environment (Chandra 2016). An organization is an aggregate of interacting and purpose-based beings. Each member establishes itself in permanence and newness, which is done in interaction with other members within the organization. As a whole, the organization is a being that is independent, intact, and has a certainty. Therefore, the organization in some sense has the qualities contained in a being, causing the organization to evolve and move in a similar framework to a being (Bakker 1992, Chandra 2016).

Organizations are in tension between the past and the future. In the present, the organization is shaped by its past and in the process of becoming its future (Bakker 1992, Hadi 1996). All of that is in the present of the organization dealing with the reality of the atmosphere of competition with other organizations (Kasali 2017). The organizations in the competitive environment attempt to maximize their performance by improving their position in relation to other organizations. The attempt to maximize performance becomes more and more difficult as the level of competition continues to intensify (Feurer & Chaharbaghi 1995).

In togetherness and competition, the organization seeks to recognize and shape itself and find a unique position. An organization does not evolve to be a duplication of another organization, but remains itself. The organization is both the same and new. It is the same because the present state is the formation of the past. It is new because the creative ideas that manifest in innovation and technology make the organization a new one. Therefore, the past, the present, and the future of an organization as a being are related (Bakker 1992).

A different point of view is found in the research of Koeppen et al. (1995) with the background of health care organizations. According to this research, the vision set for the future of the organization is independent of past experience. The organization's mission is formulated based on the organization's vision of the future. The strategy developed is to realize the mission of the organization. Nevertheless, she argued that the vision of the future cannot be generated from a vacuum and the implementation of an organizational strategy must be based on the current status of the organization in order to expand the future activities of the organization.

In organizations, strategies play a very important role. Strategy is a management process, the relationship between the organization and its environment, consisting of strategic planning, capability planning, and change management. Strategy should have two characters together, which are deliberate but at the same time emergent. Strategy becomes a planned general vision but develops in its implementation. The organizational strategy is simple because it involves the reality of itself in the past, but is responsive because it responds to the challenges of an ever-changing environment (Mintzberg et al. 1998).

Strategies originate in patterns from the past, then become plans for the future, and ultimately become perspectives to guide overall behaviour. The complex and unpredictable nature of the organizational environment hinders a deliberate strategy (Mintzberg et al. 1998). Therefore, strategy making must take the form of the learning process from time to time, in the dialectic between permanence and newness.

In a saturated environment of competition between organizations, two organizational strategy models emerged, namely Disruption Strategy and Non Disruption Strategy called Blue Ocean Shift.

Some organizations that are satisfied with the performance and achievements of the past are satisfied with managing loyal customers who are more profitable than looking for new customers. When an organization talks about its market share, it is an evaluation of the performance it has made over a certain period in the past, not the current market situation (Kasali 2017). Kasali (2017) argued that in a highly saturated competitive environment, organizations must compete for market share that ensures the sustainability of the organization. To achieve this goal, an organization can conduct disruption, a strategy to gain a wider new market by undermining consumers from other organizations. The benefits achieved are the effect of losses suffered by other organizations.

The romanticism of past success is often an excuse for not changing. Organizational reluctance to change in the middle of the technological era becomes an opportunity for competitors to disrupt, seize the consumer and ultimately lead to the destruction of the organization (Kasali 2017). If organizations or individuals within the organization are well-established with the situation, they will think that it is useless to change. Changes will only add work and there is no guarantee that it will benefit them. This group of like-minded organizations or individuals is called the inertia group (Battilana et al. 2009, Tuzlukaya & Kirkbesoglu 2015). Executives of most providers focus their planning on maintaining practices of the past (Koeppen et al. 1995).

Meanwhile, some organizations are trying to make a breakthrough to get new customers. The focus of organizational planning is on how an organization should adapt to meet the changing needs of customers (Koeppen et al. 1995). Organizations that try to leave a market that is already saturated with competition and try to shift to another market are using a blue ocean strategy. This blue ocean is a non-disruption strategy in which organizational benefits do not come from losses to other organizations (Kim & Mauborgne 2017). Innovations that power the shift to blue oceans are value innovation, innovation that ties in value to consumers (Kim & Mauborgne 2017).

In a blue ocean strategy, executives do not create a strategy to build competitive advantage, but to make the competition irrelevant. Organizations are secretly indifferent to what competitors do. They do not feel that they have to do what their competitors are doing. Their concern is focused on strategies to reach larger consumers (Kim & Mauborgne 2017).

Both of these strategy models place the organization in the dynamic between the past and the future that is presented in its present time. In today's organization, reviewing past performance and making leaps in innovation enable organizations to design more promising strategies in the future. In this frame of mind, analysis and evaluation of past performance get their meaning (Feurer & Chaharbaghi 1995). In the dynamics between the past and the future, the organization is in its present design of existence (Bakker 1992).

4 RESULTS AND DISCUSSION

Organizational strategies are made with attention to past performance, using creative ideas to help organizations leap forward to gain new and more promising markets. The dynamics between the past and the future are summarized in the present-day organization.

This leap does not make an organization a different being. It remains as the original because the current state is influenced by the past; however, it is at the same time new because it is also shaped by an unintelligible creative idea in the past.

This dynamic takes place in togetherness. The presence of other organizations, and the competition that is part of the dynamics of organizations, helps the organization recognize and shape itself, finding its unique position in togetherness.

Disruption and Blue Ocean Shift Strategies can be made by an organization dealing with the competitive environment with other organizations. Disruption is taken when the organization intends to get a new market by grabbing another company's consumer or while holding out from its competitors. Blue Ocean Shifts are pursued when organizations try to get out of the saturation of competition, to create new markets, and thus do not benefit from the loss of other organizations. Both of these strategies assume that in the present, the organization reflects on its past to create new markets in the future.

5 CONCLUSION

Strategies of an organization are built with attention to past performance, using creative ideas to help organizations to gain new and more promising markets. The dynamic of the past and the future of the organization and the dynamic of permanence and newness take place in togetherness. The presence of other organizations and the competition that is part of the dynamics of organizations, help the organization recognize and shape itself, finding its unique position in togetherness.

The two strategies, Disruption and Blue Ocean Shift, assume that in the present, the organization reflects on its past to create new markets in the future.

REFERENCES

Bakker, A. 1992. *Ontologi atau Metafisika Umum: Filsafat Pengada dan Dasar-Dasar Kenyataan.* Yogyakarta: Penerbit Kanisius.

Battilana, J., Leca, B. & Boxenbaum, E. 2009. How Actors Change Institutions: Towards a Theory of Institutional Entrepreneurship. *The Academy of Management Annals* 3(1): 65–107.

Chandra, D.R. 2016. *Handbook of Research on Global Indicators of Economic and Political Convergence.* Beaverton, USA: Business Science Reference.

Feurer, R. & Chaharbaghi, K. 1995. Strategy Development : Past, Present, and Future. *Management decision* 33(6): 11-21.

Hadi, P.H. 1996. *Jatidiri Manusia: Berdasar Filsafat Organisme Whitehead.* Yogyakarta: Penerbit Kanisius.

Hurtubise, D. 2003. God and Time in Whitehead 's Metaphysics : Revisiting the Question. *American Journal of Theology* 24(2): 109-128.

Kasali, R. 2017. *Disruption.* Jakarta: PT Gramedia Pustaka Utama.

Kim, W.C. & Mauborgne, R. 2017. *Blue Ocean Shift, Langkah Langkah Teruji untuk Menghadapi Perubahan.* Jakarta: PT Gramedia Pustaka Utama.

Koeppen, L.L., Mess, M.A. & Trott, K.J. 1995. Effective planning for managed care. *Healthcare Financial Management : Journal of the Healthcare Financial Management Association* 49(11): 44–47.

Mintzberg, H., Ahlstrand, B. & Lampel, J. 1998. *Strategy Safari - A Guided Tourthrough the Wilds of Strategic Management.* New York: The Free Press.

Schulz, M. 2001. The uncertain relevance of newness: Organizational learning and knowledge flows. *Academy of management journal* 44(4): 661-681.

Tuzlukaya, S. & Kirkbesoglu, E. 2015. A Theoretical Model for Institutional Change: The Relationship between Institutional Entrepreneurship and Social Capital. *International Journal of Business and Management* 10(3): 91–98.

Global Competitiveness: Business Transformation in the
Digital Era – Abdullah, Widiaty & Abdullah (eds)
© 2019 Taylor & Francis Group, London, ISBN 978-0-367-19442-0

The role of inclusive leadership on job performance through mediators in interior design and construction companies in Vietnam

H.T.N. Le
Van Hien University, Ho Chi Minh City, Vietnam

P.V. Nguyen, T.V.A. Trinh & H.T.S. Do
International University-Vietnam National University, Ho Chi Minh City, Vietnam

ABSTRACT: This study was intended to develop a conceptual model to investigate the indirect effects of inclusive leadership on job performance throughout the mediating factors, including person-job fit, employee well-being and innovative behaviour. The paper conducted a structural equation model approach to test the research hypotheses through questionnaire survey of 387 employees who were working at twelve interior design and construction companies. The results revealed that person-job fit and employee well-being had a significant direct impact on job performance with estimated results supported all hypotheses. Interestingly, employee well-being, person-job fit, innovative behaviour are considerable mediators that statistically support indirect effect of employee well-being on job performance. The findings highlighted a theoretical and empirical contribution to further understanding the impact existence of leader-member exchange policies on job performance. In other words, the results proposed some managerial implications to enhance job performance by strengthening self-worth through innovative behaviour in the workplace and reinforcing inclusive leadership practices.

1 INTRODUCTION

Recently, researchers have focused on employee well-being and innovative behaviour (Mumford et al. 2002, Scott & Bruce 1994) as major predictors of organizational performance (Huhtala & Parzefall 2007).

In general, leadership has significant impacts on employee well-being and innovative behaviour (Arnold et al. 2007, Gong et al. 2009). However, the linkages among these factors in a specific setting have rarely been studied. Several scholars encouraged further studies to examine relational leadership since an increasing emphasis is based on building a relationship between supervisors and subordinators, which calls for leaders' contribution to create an inspiring workplace (Uhl-Bien 2006, Carmeli et al. 2010). Accordingly, deeper investigations have been conducted into one key facet of the relational leadership, inclusive leadership, because of its distinguished features from those of other leadership styles (Hollander 2012) to build up a positive working ambiance (Carmeli et al. 2010).

Although some studies demonstrated a strong relationship between person-job fit and specific

styles of leadership (Mulki et al. 2006), employee well-being (Singh & Greenhaus 2004), and innovative behaviour (Afsar et al. 2015), few studies have identified the mediating effect of person-job fit.

In the Asian context, Vietnam highly represents collectivism and high uncertainty avoidance (Wang & Yi 2011). In such society, employees are more comfortable and intrinsically motivated by sharing an intimate relationship with their colleagues and leaders. Therefore, this study stresses the importance of leadership practices, specifically inclusive leadership, and its effectiveness in shaping a supportive working climate. In a creativity-intensive field like architectural and engineering design sector, employees should acquire particular abilities to match with the job requirements. These factors, which can be fostered under the encouraging working environment, ultimately stimulate high performance. To fully understand job performance and its predictors, we propose the conceptual model to test the relation between inclusive leadership, person-job fit and innovative behaviour, and in turn, the findings enable us to suggest some practical implications to enhance job performance.

2 LITERATURE REVIEW

2.1 Inclusive leadership and employee well-being

The inclusive leadership is identified by three facets consisting of "openness, accessibility, and availability to pay attention to employee ideas" (Carmeli et al. 2010). It enhances the beliefs that members' voices are genuinely appreciated which proposes the positive emotional leader-member ties (Choi et al. 2017). Hence, it has a significant effect on employee well-being. Thus, hypothesis 1 was proposed as follows:

H1: the inclusive leadership has a positive impact on employee well-being.

2.2 Inclusive leadership and personal job-fit

According to Shin (2004), person-job fit has been recognized as the perception of harmonizing between employees' qualities and job demand. Three potential ways illustrate that the inclusive leadership is significantly associated with person-job fit. Firstly, according to (Choi et al. 2015), the inclusive leadership's openness may help reduce followers' uncertainty and ambiguity of their roles. Next, the inclusive leadership creates a supportive work climate that strengthens the belief of person-job fit (Tims et al. 2011). Finally, mastery experience through managers' constant support is able to foster employees' self-evaluation in their capacities through positive feedback about their performance (Tims et al. 2011).

Therefore, the following hypothesis is suggested:

H2: the inclusive leadership has a positive impact on person-job fit.

2.3 Inclusive leadership and innovative behaviour

Innovative behaviour is described as "the intentional introduction within one's work role of new and useful ideas, processes, products, or procedures" by West (1990). Previous studies demonstrated that specific leadership styles motivate employee innovation (Shalley & Gilson 2004) such as transformational leadership (Afsar et al. 2015, Sharifirad 2013) and ethical leadership (Yidong & Xinxin 2013).

The prior studies found the relationship between the inclusive leadership and innovative behaviour in three different ways. Firstly, the leaders with supportive behaviour motivate their employee's engagement in innovative work because they receive emotional and cognitive resources (Vinarski-Peretz & Carmeli 2011). Secondly, employees' novel ideas are stimulated in the supportive working climate. They contribute to the foundation of perception of support for employees' creativity and innovation (Cerne et al. 2013). Lastly, availability and accessibility of the inclusive leader result in clarity of employees' work, thereby implementing innovative ideas (Carmeli et al. 2010). Therefore, we propose hypothesis 3:

H3: the inclusive leadership has a positive impact on employee innovative behaviour.

2.4 Person-job fit and employee well-being and performance

Person-job fit is associated with employee well-being and job performance in several ways. First, employees who well perceive that the requirements of the job are within their capabilities often feel more fulfilled in their work (Quinn 2005). Second, the positive perception of person-job fit results in less pressure and burnout (Singh & Greenhaus 2004) and less worry (Quinn 2005). As a result, it enhances their well-being at work. Finally, combination of employees' capabilities and job demands help them to manage the tasks more effectively (Brkich et al. 2002, Hamid & Yahya 2011). Hence, we suggest two hypotheses (H4) and (H5):

H4: Person-job fit has a positive impact on employee well-being.
H5: Person-job fit has a positive impact on job performance.

2.5 Employee well-being and job performance

Previous studies have found the positive linkage between employee well-being and job performance (Lyubomirsky et al. 2005). Wright (2014) suggests that "Emotion-based employee well-being is attained by an employee when s/he experiences psychological well-being in the form of lack of stress and emotional burnout, and positive affectivity." It was also pointed out that emotion-based employee well-being is more likely to have a positive relation to job performance (Wright & Hobfoll 2004). Additionally, the state of enthusiasm, activeness, and consciousness play a predicting role in several job outcomes (Choi & Lee 2014). Therefore, the following hypothesis (H6) is suggested:

H6: Work well-being has a positive impact on employee job performance.

2.6 Person-job fit and innovative behaviour

When employees self-evaluate themselves for being qualified for the job, they form a sense of contentment, achievement, and confidence (Xie & Johns 1995). These positive emotions encourage them to be strongly committed to the job, foster supportive ideas for innovative development and repress fear for potential mistakes (Cerne et al. 2013). Positive expectations, consequently, triggers motivation for idea generating process (Cerne et al. 2013). Moreover, employees' positive self-evaluation of their qualities to fit job characteristics stimulates flexibility and creativity in thinking, which is one essential feature of innovative behaviour (Avolio et al. 2004). Therefore, we propose the following hypothesis (H7):

H7: Person-job fit has a positive impact on innovative behaviour.

2.7 Innovative behaviour and job performance

The innovative behaviour includes discovering new technologies, introducing new techniques to meet objectives, applying new task methods, and investigating resources for generating new ideas (Janssen 2000). Employees' willingness to learn, explore and initiate ideas results in resolution of pressing problems; consequently, triggering higher job performance (Amabile et al. 2005). Thus, hypothesis 8 is suggested:

H8: Innovative behaviour has a positive impact on job performance.

3 RESEARCH METHODOLOGY

3.1 Measurement

All measurements items were rated on the five-point Likert scale, ranging from 1 (strongly disagree) to 5 (strongly agree). Particularly, Appendix 1 shows the measures of variables with the relative sources.

3.2 Methodology

3.2.1 Questionnaire design
The questionnaire covers two main parts: (1) respondents' profile including age, gender, education level and working position and (2) 36 questions relating to the hypothetical model. It was translated into the Vietnamese language with some adjustments to be more compatible within the Vietnamese context.

3.2.2 Data collection
The data were collected through two phases: a pilot test and official survey, which was conducted in Ho Chi Minh City, Vietnam. Pilot test with the sample size of 37 was carried out to check the measurement scale. After the minor revision, the questionnaires were then distributed to 409 respondents that include employees working in twelve interior design and construction companies. Eventually, 387 valid samples were used to test the hypothetical model.

4 RESULTS

4.1 Demographic characteristics

By gender, the percentage of the male is dominant, at 52.7%, while respondents whose age ranging from 21 - 40 takes the proportion of round 95%. Last demographic information revealed that the number of employees who have the academic level of undergraduate and above was nearly ¾ of the total samples.

Table 1. Reliability analysis.

Var	Items	Mean	SD	Cronbach's Alpha	Factor Loadings
IL	IL5	4.06	.747	.854	.747
	IL4	4.19	.759		.742
	IL6	4.21	.786		.722
	IL3	3.90	.797		.645
	IL2	3.99	.821		.642
	IL1	4.08	.722		.628
PJF	PJF2	3.87	.853	.808	.854
	PJF3	3.72	.778		.749
	PJF1	3.61	.876		.731
EWB	EWB1	3.87	.834	.902	.813
	EWB3	3.72	.788		.803
	EWB2	3.91	.803		.792
	EWB4	3.79	.812		.755
	EWB5	3.79	.767		.731
IB	IB5	3.96	.756	.851	.778
	IB4	3.73	.779		.766
	IB6	4.24	.697		.707
	IB3	4.24	.699		.643
JP	JP3	4.22	.663	.857	.761
	JP4	4.17	.644		.754
	JP6	4.06	.655		.716
	JP2	4.09	.673		.686
	JP5	4.19	.681		.654
	JP1	4.07	.720		.484

4.2 Reliability analysis

To analyze the reliability, a calculation of Cronbach's alpha coefficients was made by implementing exploratory factor analysis (EFA) by using the software SPSS 20.0. According to (Kline 1998), all of the Cronbach's alpha coefficients and factor loadings of all items reach the required standard (above 0.5), excluding that the factor loading of JP1 equals 0.484 which is close to the requirement (See in Table 1).

4.3 Confirmation factor analysis

Based on the Table 2 below, the analysis of fitness of structural model through conducting confirmation

Table 2. Composite reliability and average variance extracted.

Variables	CR	AVE
IL	.854	.494
PJF	.816	.598
EWB	.902	.650
IB	.851	.588
JP	.859	.505

factor analysis (CFA) including Composite Reliability (CR) and Average Variance Extracted (AVE) indicated the statistical significance of proposed hypotheses according to Hair et al. (1998).

4.4 Structural equation modelling & Hypothesis testing

Structural equation modelling (SEM) was conducted with the software AMOS 20.0. It was observed that all values of model fit indices are acceptable (see Table 3).

Figure 1 shows the testing results.

Table 3. Model fit indices in CFA and SEM.

Model fit indices	Thresholds	CFA	SEM
CMIN/df	≤ 2**, ≤ 3*	2.530	2.598
GFI	≥ 0.9**, ≥ 0.8*	0.877	0.873
AGFI	≥ 0.8*	0.847	0.844
CFI	≥ 0.9**	0.925	0.921
TLI	≥ 0.9*	0.914	0.910
RMSEA	≤ 0.05**, ≤ 0.08*	0.063	0.064

** good, * moderate. CMIN/df = Chi-square/df, GFI = Goodness-of-Fit Index, AGFI = adjusted GFI, CFI = Comparative Fit Index, TLI = Tucker Lewis Index, RMSEA = Root Mean Squared Error of Approximation.

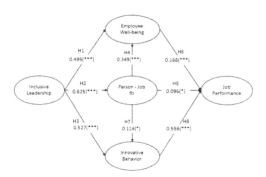

Figure 1. Testing results.

Table 4. Reliability analysis.

Hypothesis	Estimate	S.E.	C.R.	P	Result
IL → EWB	.499	.080	6.209	***	Accepted
IL → PJF	.625	.071	8.854	***	
IL → IB	.527	.067	7.865	***	
PJF → EWB	.349	.071	4.909	***	
PJF → JP	.096	.049	1.962	.050	
EWB → JP	.168	.041	4.089	***	
PJF → IB	.114	.054	2.118	.034	
IB → JP	.556	.060	9.285	***	

5 DISCUSSION

Table 4 illustrates that all hypotheses are statistically significant.

It was proposed that employee well-being and innovative behaviour could be fostered through inspirational leadership style (Sharifirad 2013). The findings demonstrated that the inclusive leadership has a positive influence on employee well-being and innovative behaviour. These results are consistent with prior studies (Arnold et al. 2007, Choi et al. 2017, Gong et al. 2009, Carmeli et al. 2010, Cerne et al. 2013).

Leadership is considered essential to trigger employees' engagement in generating innovative ideas in a knowledge-intensive, complicated and creative environment like the interior design industry in Vietnam (Mumford et al. 2002, Carmeli et al. 2010). Leaders' supportive behaviour may strengthen the relationship with their employees, which in turn results in fuelling employees' motivation and organizational commitment to the innovating process.

Next, the current study investigated the inclusive leadership which is distinctive from general leadership style (Carmeli et al. 2010) by centering and prioritizing employees' needs over collective interests to enhance their well-being (Hollander 2012). It is in line with a previous finding (Shuck & Herd 2012). Specifically, leaders' attentive behaviour to employees' needs can create a motivational workplace.

The results also show that the correlation between the inclusive leadership and innovative behaviour and employee well-being becomes stronger through person-job fit. By studies of Brkich et al. (2002) and Singh & Greenhaus (2004), our result discovers the suitability between employees and job characteristics enhance their well-being. Similarly, person-job fit also has a positive influence on employees' engagement in innovative activities (Afsar et al. 2015).

Other findings of the study also suggested a promising path for future research on the mediating role of person-job fit in the linkages between different styles of leadership and employee well-being and innovative behaviour with distinct characteristics in Vietnam. In addition to prior research that discovers the impact of person-job fit on several job-related outcomes (Cable & DeRue 2002), the correlation between person-job fit and job performance is statistically supported. This study calls for further research on person-job fit as determinant of job performance.

Finally, the innovative behaviour is clarified to be the most significant predictor of job performance. It warrants further investigation into this promising factor on job performance.

5.1 Managerial implications

Results of the study have confirmed the role of employee well-being, person job-fit and innovative behaviour as mediators in relation to the inclusive leadership and job performance. The inclusive leadership takes a decisive role in shaping the working climate, thereby fostering managers to be more attentive to their leadership practices (Vinarski-Peretz & Carmeli 2011). Providing sufficient training, performance evaluation, and rewarding policies are feasible approaches to advance employee well-being, person job-fit, and innovative behaviour (Choi et al. 2015).

First, to maintain a good performance, employees' well-being should be enhanced by making them feel valued. Proper feedbacks and praise would strengthen employees' process of self-development. Adequate resources (tools, budget, information) and immediate training (coaching and mentoring) on improving employee knowledge and skills would be helpful as guidelines for them to well accomplish the assigned tasks (Hamid & Yahya 2011).

Second, as an important mediator, person-job fit should be managed effectively. Managers must carefully identify employees' strengths that are compatible with the required qualities of the job and company's core value, which in turn unleashes their potential to generate better performance. During working processes, "managers' constructive feedbacks and appropriate mentoring" make a substantial contribution to enhancing employees' perspective on person-job fit (Choi et al. 2017).

Last, innovative behaviour's role in heightening job performance must be centralized. Managerial practices would shape a supportive working environment where employees can actualize innovative ideas (Carmeli et al. 2010) such as being receptive to employees' creative approaches and willing to take any risk that is entailed in. This cultivates independence and confidence in employees to commit themselves to high performance.

6 CONCLUSION

The findings have emphasized the influence of the inclusive leadership on job performance through the mediating role of employee well-being, person-job fit, and innovative behaviour. The study added to the literature suggesting that in order to enhance these factors, the inclusive leadership practices plays a crucial role. In addition, the results also highlighted the potential mechanism of these effects on forming a motivating working climate for employees to achieve better performance. Investigating innovative behaviour as a significant driver of job performance opens a promising path for future research of inclusive leadership and job performance.

REFERENCES

Afsar, B., Badir, Y. & Khan, M.M. 2015. Person-job fit, person-organization fit and innovative work behavior: The mediating role of innovation trust. *Journal of High Technology Management Research* 26(2): 105-116.

Amabile, T.M., Barsade, S.G., Mueller, J.S. & Staw, B.M. 2005. Affect and Creativity at Work. *Administrative Science Quarterly* 50(3): 367-403.

Arnold, K.A., Turner, N., Barling, J., Kelloway, E.K. & McKee, M.C. 2007. Transformational Leadership and Psychological Well-Being: The Mediating Role of Meaningful Work. *Journal of Occupational Health Psychology* 12(3): 193.

Avolio, B.J., Gardner, W.L., Walumbwa, F.O., Luthans, F. & May, D.R. 2004. Unlocking the mask: A look at the process by which authentic leaders impact follower attitudes and behaviors. *The Leadership Quarterly* 15(6): 801–823.

Brkich, M., Jeffs, D. & Carless, S.A. 2002. A global self-report measure of person-job fit. *European Journal of Psychological Assessment* 18(1): 43.

Cable, D.M. & DeRue, D.S. 2002. The convergent and discriminant validity of subjective fit perceptions. *Journal of Applied Psychology* 87(5): 875.

Carmeli, A., Reiter-Palmon, R. & Ziv, E. 2010. Inclusive leadership and employee involvement in creative tasks in the workplace: The mediating role of psychological safety. *Creativity Research Journal* 22(3): 250-260.

Cerne, M., Jaklic, M. & Skerlavaj, M. 2013. Authentic leadership, creativity, and innovation: A multilevel perspective. *Leadership* 9(1): 63-85.

Choi, S.B., Tran, T.B.H. & Kang, S.W. 2017. Inclusive Leadership and Employee Well-Being: The Mediating Role of Person-Job Fit. *Journal of Happiness Studies* 18 (6): 1877–1901.

Choi, S.B., Tran, T.B.H. & Park, B.I. 2015. Inclusive leadership and work engagement: Mediating roles of affective organizational commitment and creativity. *Social Behavior and Personality: An International Journal* 43 (6): 931–943.

Choi, Y. & Lee, D. 2014. Psychological capital, big five traits, and employee outcomes. *Journal of Managerial Psychology* 29(2): 122–140.

Gong, Y., Huang, J.C. & Farh, J.L. 2009. Employee learning orientation, transformational leadership, and employee creativity: The mediating role of employee creative self-efficacy. *Academy of Management Journal* 52 (4): 765-778.

Hamid, S.N.A. & Yahya, K.K. 2011. Relationship between person-job fit and person-organization fit on employees' work engagement: A study among engineers in semiconductor companies in Malaysia. In *Annual Conference on Innovations in Business and Management London* (Vol.6, pp. 1–30). Citeseer.

Hair, J.F., Anderson, R.E., Tatham, R.L. & Black, W.C. 1998. *Multivariate data analysis*. New Jersey: Upper Saddle River.

Hollander, E. 2012. *Inclusive leadership: The essential leader-follower relationship*. London: Routledge.

Huhtala, H. & Parzefall, M.R. 2007. A review of employee well-being and innovativeness: An opportunity for a mutual benefit. *Creativity and innovation management* 16(3): 299-306.

Janssen, O. 2000. Job demands, perceptions of effort-reward fairness and innovative work behavior. *Journal of Occupational and Organizational Psychology* 73(3): 287-302.

Kline, R.B. 1998. Software Review: Software Programs for Structural Equation Modeling: Amos, EQS, and LISREL. *Journal of Psychoeducational Assessment* 16 (4): 343-364.

Lyubomirsky, S., King, L. & Diener, E. 2005. The benefits of frequent positive affect: Does happiness lead to success? *Psychological Bulletin* 131(6): 803.

Mulki, J.P., Jaramillo, F. & Locander, W.B. 2006. Emotional exhaustion and organizational deviance: Can the right job and a leader's style make a difference? *Journal of Business Research* 59(12): 1222-1230.

Mumford, M.D., Scott, G.M., Gaddis, B. & Strange, J.M. 2002. Leading creative people: Orchestrating expertise and relationships. *The Leadership Quarterly* 13(6): 705–750.

Quinn, R.W. 2005. Flow in Knowledge Work: High Performance Experience in the Design of National Security Technology. *Administrative Science Quarterly* 50(4): 610-641.

Scott, S. & Bruce, R. 1994. Determinants of innovative behavior: A path model of individual innovation in the workplace. *Academy of Management Journal* 37(3): 580-607.

Shalley, C.E. & Gilson, L.L. 2004. What leaders need to know: A review of social and contextual factors that can foster or hinder creativity. *The Leadership Quarterly* 15 (1): 33–53.

Sharifirad, M.S. 2013. Transformational leadership, innovative work behavior, and employee well-being. *Global Business Perspectives* 1(3): 198-225.

Shin, Y. 2004. A person-environment fit model for virtual organizations. *Journal of Management* 30(5): 725–743.

Shuck, B. & Herd, A.M. 2012. Employee engagement and leadership: Exploring the convergence of two frameworks and implications for leadership development in HRD. *Human Resource Development Review* 11(2): 156–181.

Singh, R. & Greenhaus, J.H. 2004. The relation between career decision-making strategies and person-job fit: A study of job changers. *Journal of Vocational Behavior* 64(1): 198–221.

Tims, M., Bakker, A.B. & Xanthopoulou, D. 2011. Do transformational leaders enhance their followers' daily work engagement? *The Leadership Quarterly* 22(1): 121–131.

Uhl-Bien, M. 2006. Relational Leadership Theory: Exploring the social processes of leadership and organizing. In *Leadership, gender, and organization* (pp. 75-108). Springer, Dordrecht.

Vinarski-Peretz, H. & Carmeli, A. 2011. Linking Care Felt to Engagement in Innovative Behaviors in the Workplace: The Mediating Role of Psychological Conditions. *Psychology of Aesthetics, Creativity, and the Arts* 5(1): 43.

Wang, S. & Yi, X. 2011. It's happiness that counts: Full mediating effect of job satisfaction on the linkage from LMX to turnover intention in Chinese companies. *International Journal of Leadership Studies* 6(3): 337–356.

West, M.A. 1990. The social psychology of innovation in groups. In M.A. West & J.L. Farr (eds.) *Innovation and creativity in work: Psychological and Organizational Strategies* (pp. 309-333). London: Wiley.

Williams, L.J. & Anderson, S.E. 1991. Job Satisfaction and Organizational Commitment as Predictors of Organizational Citizenship and In-Role Behaviors. *Journal of Management* 17(3): 601-617.

Wright, T.A. 2014. Putting your best "face" forward: The role of emotion-based well-being in organizational research. *Journal of Organizational Behavior* 35(8): 1153-1168.

Wright, T.A. & Hobfoll, S.E. 2004. Commitment, psychological well-being, and job performance: An examination of conservation of resources (COR) theory and job burnout. *Journal of Business & Management* 9(4): 389-406.

Xie, J.L. & Johns, G. 1995. Job scope and stress: Can job scope be too high? *Academy of management journal* 38 (5): 1288-1309.

Yidong, T. & Xinxin, L. 2013. How ethical leadership influence employees' innovative work behavior: A perspective of intrinsic motivation. *Journal of Business Ethics* 116(2): 441–455.

APPENDIX 1 MEASURES

Variables (sources)	Code	Measures
Inclusive leadership (Carmeli et al. 2010)	IL1	My manager is attentive to new opportunities to improve work processes (openness)
	IL2	My manager is open to discuss the desired goals and new ways to achieve them (openness)
	IL3	My manager is available for professional questions I would like to consult with him/her (availability)
	IL4	My manager is ready to listen to my requests (availability)
	IL5	My manager encourages me to access him/her on emerging issues (accessibility)
	IL6	My manager is accessible for discussing emerging problems (accessibility)
Person-Job Fit (Mulki et al. 2006)	PJF1	My skills and abilities perfectly match with my job demands
	PJF2	My personal likes and dislikes match perfectly with my job demands
	PJF3	There is a good fit between my job and me
Employee Well-being (Arnold et al. 2007)	EWB1	In the past 6 months, I have felt motivated
	EWB2	In the past 6 months, I have felt energetic
	EWB3	In the past 6 months, I have felt enthusiastic
	EWB4	In the past 6 months, I have felt lively

(Continued)

Variables (sources)	Code	Measures
Innovative Behaviour (Janssen 2000)	EWB5	In the past 6 months, I have felt joyful
	IB1	I search out new working methods, techniques, or instruments
	IB2	I generate original solutions for problems
	IB3	I make important organizational members enthusiastic for innovative ideas
	IB4	I transform innovative ideas into useful applications
	IB5	I introduce innovative ideas into the work environment in a systematic way
	IB6	I evaluate the utility of innovative ideas
Job Performance (Williams & Anderson 1991)	JP1	Perform tasks that are expected of him/her
	JP2	Engages in activities that will directly affect his/her performance evaluation
	JP3	Goes out of way to help new employees
	JP4	Takes time to listen to co-workers' problems and worries
	JP5	Passes along information to co-workers.
	JP6	Attendance at work is above the norm.

Global Competitiveness: Business Transformation in the
Digital Era – Abdullah, Widiaty & Abdullah (eds)
© 2019 Taylor & Francis Group, London, ISBN 978-0-367-19442-0

Influences of social support on job satisfaction and organizational commitment

R. Setiawan, R.G. Munthe & A. Aprillia
Maranatha Christian University, Bandung, West Java, Indonesia

ABSTRACT: Employees' work attitudes determine their performances at company. Situation at the company and social support enable employees to feel happy at work and be loyal to the company. Social support refers to any active attention and care showed by peers and managers to employees in accomplishing the tasks assigned. Job satisfaction is a positive feeling experienced by employees in doing their job while organizational commitment refers to a tendency of employees to do at their best for the success of the company and at the same time keep staying in the company for long. The objectives of this study were to test the influence of social support on job satisfaction as well as its influence on organizational commitment. The respondents of this study were 43 first-line and middle managers working in several private banks in Bandung, Indonesia. Using simple linear regression analysis, the study found that there is a positive influence of social support on both employees' job satisfaction and employees' organizational commitment.

1 INTRODUCTION

Employees are the only active resources that contribute their aspirations and creativities to the performance of their company. The success of a company's performance is determined by the performance quality of its employees. Employees' performance is a function of ability, motivation, and opportunity (Appelbaum et al. 2000). According to Maslow's motivation theory, employees can be motivated by five levels of needs, which one of them is social needs (Onah, 2015). Specifically, social needs refer to needs of affection, belongingness, acceptance, and friendship. Employees' social needs can be fulfilled through social support that is given by people around them at their workplace. Social support has positive psychological impact time after time (Holahan & Moos 1981, George et al. 1989, Lee & Robbins 1998, Kendler et al. 2006, Hill et al. 2011, Hyde et al. 2011). Social support from co-workers and supervisor becomes employees' motivation in showing positive work attitudes in a company. Job satisfaction and organizational commitment are two important work attitudes in most research (Moynihan & Pandey 2007).

Many studies, which have been conducted all over the world across some different industries, have proven that job satisfaction and organizational commitment are the result of social support. The respondents of those studies were workers at information technology companies in the United States (Liu 2004), workers at fashion companies in New Zealand (Bateman 2009), workers at five-star hotels in Bodrum, Turkey (Colakoglu et al. 2010), workers at services sector companies in Catalonia, Spain (Garcia et al. 2011), workers at education and health-care companies in Turki (Emhan 2012), workers at a company engaged in postal services in Indonesia (Pradesa et al. 2013), elementary school teachers in Turkey (Gündüz 2014), workers at non-profit public sector companies in Malaysia (Zumrah & Boyle 2015), workers at manufacturing companies in Taiwan (Chou 2016), workers at higher education institutions in South Africa (Donald et al. 2016), workers at large companies in Nairobi (Miring'u 2016), workers at private libraries in South-West, Nigeria (Olaojo et al. 2016), and security guards in Singapore (Nalla et al. 2017). In order to confirm the results of those previous studies, there is a need to conduct another research on the same topic with specific respondents in different industry, in this case bank managers. Bank is a company that offers services to the consumers. Satisfied and loyal bank customers are resulted from satisfied and loyal frontline bank employees; conversely, those competent staffs derived from satisfied and loyal managers, including first-line manager and middle manager. Those managers play major roles in managing relationship between front liner and top management (Robbins & Coulter 2016). This research was intended to investigate the influence of social support on both job satisfaction and organizational commitment of first-line and middle bank managers at several private banks.

2 LITERATURE REVIEW AND RESEARCH DEVELOPMENT

Job satisfaction is a pleasurable emotional state coming from the appraisal of one's job as achieving or facilitating the achievement of one's job values (Locke 1969). Organizational commitment is the relative strength of an individual's identification with and involvement in a particular organization (Porter et al. 1974). If job satisfaction involves the employees' positive feelings toward their work, then organizational commitment has a broader context; organizational commitment relates to positive feelings of employees to the company where they work that can be demonstrated through employees' loyalty, including acceptance of organizational values, devotion, and loyalty to the company. Social support is an interpersonal transaction containing affection (love, liking, respect, admiration), affirmation (agreement, acknowledgement of appropriateness or rightness of other's behavior), and aid (direct service or giving of material supplies) (Turner 1983). Employees who work in the company have the role of human beings in their daily lives, namely as individual beings and social beings. To become a full employee, employees must demonstrate individual achievements that support the company's progress. In addition, they also need interaction, communication, and information flow from colleagues and their managers in the form of psychological and moral support to feel comfortable in their workplace and feel at home in the company where they work.

Employees who get support from colleagues or supervisors tend to have a high level of satisfaction with their work (Robbins & Judge 2016). The existence of co-workers and supervisors who provide support, both in terms of work and personal or family issues, will make employees feel appreciated and this will encourage the emergence of positive emotions that manifest in the work employees do. Employees who have fun friends will motivate themselves to be always excited and enthusiastic in completing each of their jobs. Employees who meet their social needs will feel comfortable in their work environment. They do not feel alone if they face some problems because both colleagues and supervisors are always willing to help. Employees who are satisfied with their work and social environment in the workplace tend to feel reluctant to leave the company where they work. They are convinced by the familiar atmosphere of the family at work, their work will be well resolved, and can even encourage them to improve their work performance. Employees who get support from colleagues and supervisors tend to have a high level of commitment to the organization (Tansky & Cohen 2001). Employees who feel their social needs are being fulfilled as a sense of respect as a fellow employee of the company in which they work, whether by their co-workers or supervisors, will be motivated to retain their membership within the organization; in particular, they will have willingness to perform more for the organization progress and agree with the values and goals of the organization. The existence of social support

from colleagues and supervisors towards fellow employees will create stronger cohesiveness and ties to jointly commit to the organization. Even if employees do not have a high organizational commitment, but with the support and transmission of organizational commitment through social support from colleagues and supervisors, they tend to think twice in leaving the company where they work because of strong bonds of brotherhood as their biggest consideration. The emergence of a sense of reluctance to leave a friendly and welcoming family and laziness to adapt to the new environment leave employees committed to the company where they work.

Thus, the study tried to investigate the influence of social supports on both employees' job performance and on their organizational commitment by testing two research hypotheses as follows:

H1: Social support positively affects employees' job satisfaction

H2: Social support positively affects employees' organizational commitment

3 RESEARCH METHOD

The study involved 43 employees who work at first-line and middle managerial level in several banks (branch regional offices) in Bandung, Indonesia as respondents. As a matter of privacy, the investigated banks' names are hidden and protected from any kinds of publications. Some of these banks are among the top ten largest banks in Indonesia based on the amount of assets at the time of this study being conducted. The data of the study were collected by survey (questionnaire) and literature study. This is a causal explanatory research that measures linkages among three variables namely social support, job satisfaction, and organizational commitment. Job satisfaction was measured using eighteen items of questions adapted from the questionnaire developed by Brayfiel & Rothe (1951). Organizational commitment was measured using nine item questions developed by Mowday et al. (1979). Meanwhile, social support (from supervisors and co-workers) was measured using twelve item statements developed by Caplan et al. (1975). Because the objectives of the study were to examine influences, hypotheses tests used is simple linear regression. The first simple linear regression analysis was conducted to test the influence of social support on job satisfaction and the second hypothesis is to test influence of social support on organizational commitment. To ensure eligibility of regression analysis tests, this study also conducted validity and reliability as well as normality and heteroskedasticity test. All instrument, data, and hypotheses test were analyzed by using SPSS version 20.

4 RESULTS AND DISCUSSION

The statistical calculation revealed some results. First, the Cronbach's alpha coefficient value of job satisfaction is .885 with item-total correlation values ranging from .266 to .81 and significant value equals to .000. Second, the Cronbach's alpha coefficient value of organizational commitment is .902 with the item-total correlation values ranging from .581 to .880 and significant value equals to .000. Finally, the Cronbach's alpha coefficient value of social support variable is .905 with item-total correlation values ranging from .622 to .796 and significant value equals to .000.

The data collected were proven normal through Kolomogorov–Smirnov's test with significant values, respectively, being .788 and .735. The research data were also free from heteroskedasticity proven by Glejser's test with significant values, respectively, at .892 and .599. The results of hypotheses test in this study are presented in Tables 1 and 2.

JS: Job Satisfaction, SS: Social Support.

Table 1 shows that social support significantly and positively affects job satisfaction, as indicated by significant value of .003 and beta value of .451. This result indicates that more the social support perceived by the employees, the more satisfied they feel towards their job. Social support brings excitement to employees at workplace. Therefore, the first hypothesis was not rejected.

OC: Organizational Commitment, SS: Social Support

Showing the same result, Table 2 reveals that social support have also significant and positive influence on employees' organizational commitment, as indicated by significant value of .006 and beta value of .414. The result implies that the more the social support perceived by the employees, the more the committed employees to their organization. Social support brings engagement for employees to their organization. The second hypothesis was not rejected either.

5 CONCLUSION

This study has shown that both research hypotheses proved that social support has a positive and significant impact both on job satisfaction and organizational commitment. Furthermore, these results confirmed the alignment of the previous researches on the similar topic on social support and its impacts towards employees' job satisfaction and organizational commitment. Employees, who feel that they have support from their co-workers and their direct supervisors tend to have job satisfaction and show organizational commitment at a better level. Companies need to create and develop a more family-friendly culture and policies, to look after the

Table 1. Test on first research hypothesis.

Coefficients^a

Model		Unstandardized Coefficients		Standardized Coefficients		
		B	Std. Error	Beta	t	Sig.
1	(Constant)	37.583	8.352		4.500	.000
	SS	.583	.183	.451	3.192	.003

a. Dependent Variable: JS.

Table 2. Test on second research hypothesis.

Coefficients^a

Model		Unstandardized Coefficients		Standardized Coefficients		
		B	Std. Error	Beta	t	Sig.
1	(Constant)	14.764	6.384		2.313	.026
	OC	.402	.140	.414	2.880	.006

a. Dependent Variable: OC.

conditions of their employees, to understand the conditions and situations they face, to better understand their fellow employees, to help those who are in trouble both physically and psychologically, to look for solutions to personal and collective problems, and to encourage their co-workers and supervisors to be more proactive sympathetically and empathetically towards their social environment in the workplace (Mondy & Martocchio 2016). Any managerial employees should feel that employees' problems will be a problem for them as well, even the company as a whole. Thus, there will be a sense of brotherhood among fellow employees. Social support that is perceived by employees, whether in work or personal matters, will motivate them to be more courageous in facing all these problems because they feel that they are linked each other as united members of the company making them realize that they will be able to strengthen each other even with organizational problems. Social support sourced from a sincere heart and a wise mind will create a cohesive, strong, dynamic, growing, evolving, and positive organizational environment. By sowing well begins with small things, done from now, and begins with personal initiative; then in time, it will inevitably reap great happiness, on an ongoing basis, and affect many people. Positive treatment will be a chain that will be passed from one generation to the next in the company's sustainability.

Research means *re* and *search*, a continuous searching process through better methods and process. Therefore, the study proposes some suggestions for the future research. First, there are many consequences of social support in terms of work behaviors, such as organizational citizenship behavior and pro-social behavior. The study about the aforementioned results of social support will be conducted as the future research. Second, this study only tested managers from banking industry. Studies with the same topic at different industries (non-profit organization, community, public company) can be conducted as the future research. Third, this study only used a simple linear regression. With the complexity of variables and relationships, the future research can be conducted with model test, such as structural equation modeling. Fourth, social support in this context is attention and help that people give at workplace. For the future research, social support can be expanded as interactions and interrelationship among people through social media, thus broadening the scope of social support and comparing the difference between influence from direct and indirect social support.

REFERENCES

Appelbaum, E., Bailey, T., Berg, P. & Kalleberg, A.L. 2000. *Manufacturing advantage: Why high-performance work systems pay off*. London: Economic Policy Institute: Cornell University Press.

Bateman, G. 2009. *Employee perceptions of co-worker support and its effect on job satisfaction, work stress and intention to quit*. Dissertation in Master of Science in Applied Psychology at the Department of Psychology, University of Canterbury

Brayfield, A.H. & Rothe, H.F. 1951. An index of job satisfaction. *Journal of Applied Psychology* 35: 307-311.

Caplan, G., Cobb, S., French, J., Van Harrison, R. & Pinneau, S. 1975. *Job demands and work health: main effects and occupational differences*. Washington, D.C.: U.S. Government Printing Office.

Chou, P. 2016. The effects of social support on employee's behavioural support for organizational change: an empirical study in Taiwan. *International Journal of Economics, Commerce and Management* IV(2): 22-41.

Colakoglu, U., Culha, O. & Atay, H. 2010. The effects of perceived organisational support on employees' affective outcomes: evidence from the hotel industry. *Tourism and Hospitality Management* 16(2): 125-150.

Donald, M.F., Hlanganipai, N. & Richard, S. 2016. The relationship between perceived organizational support and organizational commitment among academics: the mediating effect of job satisfaction. *Investment Management and Financial Innovations* 13(3): 267-273.

Emhan, A.E. 2012. Relationship among managerial support, job satisfaction and organizational commitment: a comparative study of non-profit, for-profit and public sectors in turkey. *International Journal of Business, Humanities and Technology* 2(5): 179-190.

Garcia, J.A.M., Bonavia, T. & Losilla, J.M. 2011. Exploring working conditions as determinants of job satisfaction: an empirical test among Catalonia service workers. *The Service Industries Journal* 31(12): 2051–2066.

George, L.K., Blazer, D.G., Hughes, D.C. & Fowler, N. 1989. Social support and the outcome of major depression. *British Journal of Psychiatry* 154: 478–485

Gündüz, Y. 2014. The effect of organizational support on organizational commitment. *Anthropologist* 18(3): 1041-1057.

Hill, J., Holcombe, C., Clark, L., Boothby, M.R.K., Hincks, A. & Fisher, J. 2011. Predictors of onset of depression and anxiety in the year after diagnosis of breast cancer. *Psychological Medicine* 41: 1429–1436.

Holahan, C.J. & Moos, R.H. 1981. Social support and psychological distress: a longitudinal analysis. *Journal of Abnormal Psychology* 90: 365–370.

Hyde, L.W., Gorka, A., Manuck, S.B. & Hariri, A.R. 2011. Perceived social support moderates the link between threat-related amygdala reactivity and trait anxiety. *Neuropsychological* 49: 651–656.

Kendler, K.S., Gatz, M., Gardner, C.O. & Pedersen, N.L. 2006. A Swedish national twin study of lifetime major depression. *American Journal of Psychiatry* 163: 109–114.

Lee, R.M. & Robbins, S.B. 1998. The relationship between social connectedness and anxiety, self-esteem, and social identity. *Journal of Counselling Psychology* 45: 338–345.

Liu, W. 2004. *Perceived organizational support: linking human resource management practices with important work outcomes*. Dissertation in Doctor of Philosophy at Faculty of the Graduate School of the University of Maryland.

Locke, E.A. 1969. What is job satisfaction? *Organizational Behaviour and Human Performance* 4: 309-336.

Miring'u, W. 2016. *Perceived influence of organisational support on organisational commitment in githunguri dairy co-operative society limited*. A Research Project Submitted in Partial Fulfilment of the Requirement for the Degree of Master of Business Administration (MBA) School Of Business, University Of Nairobi.

Mondy, R.W. & Martocchio, J.J. 2016. *Human Resource Management*. 14th Edition. New Jersey: Pearson Education

Mowday R., Steers R. & Porter L. 1979. The measure of organizational commitment. *Journal of Vocational Behaviour* 14(2): 224-227.

Moynihan, D.P. & Pandey, S.K. 2007. Finding workable levers over work motivation: comparing job satisfaction, job involvement, and organizational commitment. *Administration & Society* 39(7): 803–832.

Nalla, M.K., Paek, S.Y. & Lim, S.S. 2017. The influence of organizational and environmental factors on job satisfaction among security guards in Singapore. *Australian & New Zealand Journal of Criminology* 50(4): 548–565.

Olaojo, P.O., Oyeboade, J.A. & Gbotosho, A.S. 2016. Social support, work motivation and work commitment of library personnel in selected private university libraries in south-west, Nigeria. *Qualitative and Quantitative Methods in Libraries (QQML)* 5: 11-22.

Onah, F.O. 2015. *Human Resource Management*. 4th Edition, Enugu: John Jacob's Classic Publisher, Ltd.

Porter L.W., Steers R.M., Mowday R.T. & Boulian P.V. 1974. Organizational commitment, job satisfaction, and turnover among psychiatric technicians. *Journal of Applied Psychology* 59(5): 603-609.

Pradesa, H.A., Setiawan, M. & Rahayu, D.M. 2013. The relationships of perceived organizational support (pos) with positive work behaviour: mediating role of job satisfaction, affective commitment, and felt obligation. *IOSR Journal of Business and Management (IOSR-JBM)* 13(3): 23-34.

Robbins, S.P. & Coulter, M. 2016. *Management*. 13th Edition. New Jersey: Pearson Education

Robbins, S.P. & Judge, T.A. 2016. *Organisational behaviour*. 17th Edition. New Jersey: Pearson Education

Tansky, J.W. & Cohen, D.J. 2001. The relationship between organizational support, employee development, and organization commitment: an empirical study. *Human Resource Development Quarterly* 12: 285-300.

Turner, R.J. 1983. Direct, indirect, and moderating effects of social support on psychological distress and associated conditions. In H.P. Kaplan (ed.) *Psychosocial Stress, Trends in Theory and Research*. New York: Academic Press

Zumrah, A.R. & Boyle, S. 2015. The effects of perceived organizational support and job satisfaction on transfer of training. *Personnel Review* 44(2): 236-254.

Global Competitiveness: Business Transformation in the
Digital Era – Abdullah, Widiaty & Abdullah (eds)
© 2019 Taylor & Francis Group, London, ISBN 978-0-367-19442-0

Organizational culture as a self-reflective approach to create organizational identity (Case study: A private school in Bandung, Indonesia)

R. Sanjaya

Sekolah Tinggi Ilmu Ekonomi Harapan Bangsa, Bandung, Indonesia

ABSTRACT: High competition among private educational institutions in Bandung triggered schools to pursue achieving competitive advantage. Forming appropriate organizational culture that is reflected in the identity of the organization is an option. This study was aimed to determine the kind of culture that manifested in organizational identity perceived by its employees. This research used OCAI (Organizational Culture Assessment Instrument) and a qualitative survey in the opening relational aspects of organizational culture within an educational institution. The open-ended questions in this survey were constructed in four sections that cover general practice and comparison, history, relational experiences, and leadership practices. In addition, the context for this research was a classical elementary school. The findings of the qualitative survey revealed the relative nature of the school in terms of the collegiality and reciprocity of care between those parties in leadership and between the teachers and the staffs in general. Furthermore, the majority of employees emphasized their identities as a "big family".

1 INTRODUCTION

The education system in developed countries such as Finland, Japan, and New Zealand often becomes a barometer of the designing of education system in developing countries. Those developed countries have both public and private schools who have an organizational culture that tends to be homogeneous as they emphasize equality for their citizens so that the quality between public and private school is relatively the same. Indonesia is a developing country whose quality of public schools is not evenly distributed. Consequently, many private schools have sprung up to answer this need by offering different uniqueness that can become their competitive advantages. Rivalry at private educational institutions area in big cities in Indonesia is so intense including in Bandung. This rivalry can be characterized by several indicators such as admission of new students held earlier as even from previous years, and private schools are competing to attain competitive advantage by providing products, facilities, and services as best as they can which in turn results in more expensive school entrance fee. Schools hunt for a good reputation on the eyes of stakeholders. The organizational reputation can be molded through the contribution of the organizational identity. Therefore, to form an organizational identity, top management must be able to create the desired organizational culture in which values and norms are shared by all employees at all levels of management (Hatch & Schultz 2002). Implementation of cultural values needs to be carried out consistently so that they will be manifested in the identity of the organization elements. The

implementation needs to be done in short time and through continuous efforts to ensure the cultural values displayed become the identity of the organization and can always be realized in the daily life of the organization as reflected by the attitude of the members of the organization (Huang Horowitz & Freberg 2016). Organizational culture also exists in schools. Each school needs a clear identity to be accurately recognized by stakeholders. One of the ways to reveal it is assessing and mapping their culture properly. All too often, educational leaders are busy with data associated with the future directions of an educational enterprise. Educational leaders can make assumptions from their interactions with teachers and staff in the business of leadership and management doing everyday jobs. The open-ended survey has the potential to provide thematic information that relates to specific narratives within an organization through perceptions of what the organization was valuing in practice. A study by Giles & Yates (2012) has found that the success of the experience, findings, and learning on the part of the educational leader has led to the trailing of this organizational tool in the context of an elementary primary school.

One of those schools attempting to shape their identity is Sekolah Klasikal Terang Nusantara (SETARA). Based on in-depth interviews with the headmistress of SETARA, the school was founded based on wishes of some leaders of a local church in Bandung which were eager to serve and be a blessing. They are burdened with an affordable education for those who cannot afford a good education because of limited fund. Good education is identical to the high cost. The headmistress stated: "Good education is expensive. But we believe that we are able to provide education on low budget without sacrificing the quality of education itself and decreasing the proper education standards. That's why SETARA is trying to answer the need for good education at an affordable cost. I am personally called to dedicate myself in education area, especially to facilitate the underprivileged to get a good quality education".

SETARA has vision to prepare the students to build the nation through a Christian perspective that loves and serves others. Its mission is to deliver an educational environment that focuses on Christ, which inspires children to love learning and to equip them with a biblical worldview that they can practice it through thinking wisely and acting with a purpose of advancing their nation, for the glory of God. The motto of the school is "Life-long learning" and its philosophy is a classical Christian school with advantages in active, global, and thorough learning. The core values of SETARA are as follows: excellence, integrity, compassion, whole-heartedness, courage, divine, serve (SETARA 2018). In order to manifest these values in the behavior of their academic community, SETARA equipped them with strong Christianity value, clearly making the principle of focusing on biblical perspective the most important thing within the teachers. On the one hand, the biggest challenge is maintaining harmony among human resources because they are the backbone of the organization. On the other hand, there is a policy to develop the human resources by taking part in ACSI (Association of Christian School International) seminars and providing scholarships for post-secondary schools.

According to data from the Ministry of Education and Culture (Kemdikbud 2018), in 2017, there are 467 primary schools (274 public and 193 private) in Bandung. Particularly in sub-districts where SETARA is located there are 18 kindergartens (1 public and 17 privates) and 10 primary schools (5 publics and 5 privates). Therefore, as a relatively new school, in order to have competitive advantage, SETARA needs to know first where the organization's position is nowadays in the context of its identity in the eyes of its employees. Because of that reason, the importance of mapping organizational culture is very crucial for SETARA. Where SETARA is today and how deep its values are embedded nowadays among employees are very essential questions to be answered. The answers could bring benefits such as giving insights and valuable facts to provide basic foundation for becoming adaptive successfully and realizing a competitive advantage. This study was aimed to explore the cultural values of SETARA that are manifested in its identity which is perceived by the employees.

1.1 Organizational culture and identity

Robbins (2013) see the organizational culture (OC) as a system of shared meaning held by members that distinguishes one organization from other organizations.

OC is believed to last for a long time but it is never static. This enables the organization to periodically evaluate the values, actions, and norms of the organization because of rapidly changing environment so the organization could succeed in becoming adaptive by establishing a new organizational culture that supports operational processes. OC involves all organizational members, initiates and matures at all hierarchical levels, and is founded on a broad-based history that is realized in the artifacts of the organization (e.g. its names, products, buildings, logos and other symbols, including its top managers). Conducive OC has been identified as an indispensable organizational stabilizer and growth driver. OC represents the assumptions, beliefs, and norms of an organization shared by members of the organization. Organizational scholars conceived that OC can be expressed in a number of ways described as manifestations. One of the notifying artifacts is identity (Hatch & Schultz 1997). Understanding OC is fundamental to understand what underpins an organization's operation. OC is also considered as the glue holding individual and organization together. Cultural profile thus provides a comparative benchmark for an organization that directs how people in an organization behave, what assumptions govern their behavior, and what organizational systems impact the change process. Organizational identification can be distinguished from the manifestations of basic organizational assumptions because organizational assumptions underline values and individuals infer their assumptions of the known values. In this connection, OC gives the identity of an organization and the sense of belonging that may result from organizational culture and organizational identification (Cheung et al. 2011).

Cameron & Quinn (2011) declare that the Competing Values Framework is a framework formed based on interactions between two main dimensions that determine the effectiveness of the organization that together form 4 quadrants of Organization Culture Profile (OCP). This cultural dimension is often regarded as a competing value or as a determinant of indicators that affect organizational effectiveness. There are at least two main dimensions whose indicators are grouped into 4 types of cultures:

- The first dimension distinguishes organizational effectiveness indicators that emphasize flexibility, discretion, and dynamic with indicators of effectiveness that emphasize organizational stability, order, and control. The axis of this dimension is Flexibility and Discretion (also called people) and Stability and Control (also called process).
- The second one distinguishes effectiveness indicators that emphasize internal orientation, integration, and unity with indicators of effectiveness that emphasize external orientation, differentiation, and competition. The axis of this dimension is Internal Focus and Integration (also called Operational) and External Focus and Differentiation (also called strategic).

Figure 1. Organization culture profile.

The effectiveness indicators in these 2 dimensions illustrate the values that the company members adopt about organizational performance. The things identified are what they consider to be true in their view. Each quadrant forms a basic assumption, orientation, and values that define the type of organizational culture as listed in Figure 1. Four Organizational Culture Profiles (OCP) are formed from the interaction between the 2 previous dimensions:

- The Hierarchy Culture has the characteristics of a clear line of authority in decision-making, has regulatory standards or procedures within the organization that control all members of the organization, the implementation of control, and accountability as the criterions of success, and there is also a clear working structure. The role of leadership in this culture is vital because as the coordinator and the organizer are within the organization, the leader has to ensure that organization can perform activities smoothly or without experiencing any problems.
- The Market Culture aims to produce strategies for organization facing competitive challenges. This culture is focused on the external environment rather than the internal one. The focus of the problem is on external issues that include suppliers, customers, government, the environment around the organization, and so on. Meanwhile, the main focus is competition and productivity by emphasizing the external position of the organization and control. Market culture assumes that clear goals supported by aggressive strategies will result in productivity and profit. The criterion for success is determined in terms of market share and penetration.
- The Clan Culture emphasizes the shared values and goals in the organization, unity, personality, participatory attitudes, and sense of community. The term "Clan" of this culture is because of the type of organization that adheres very similar to a large family. Teamwork, employee engagement, and employer's commitment to employees characterize clan culture. In a clan culture environment, organization places emphasis on teamwork (not individual), employee development, and considers customers as partners within the organization.
- The Adhocracy Culture. Ad hoc means something that is dynamic. The main purpose of adhocracy

is to develop adaptability, flexibility, and creativity within the organization. An important challenge for adhocracy organization is to always be innovative in delivering products and services, and adapt quickly to opportunities and change.

Generally, a company will not have one type of culture. However, the culture of an organization can be seen from the most dominant side. The identification of the organization's cultural relationships is determined by three factors: strength, harmony, or congruence. OC will support the organization's effectiveness (See in Figure 1). The advantage of competing values framework is the ability to provide an overview of the cultural type of an organization. In addition, this framework can provide the cultural projections expected by the members of the organization because the basic concept of the framework is to map out the cultures embraced in the present and the culture expected in the future. Cameron & Quinn (2011) stated that to identify harmony or suitability of organizational culture adopted must be based on 6 dimensions as follows:

- Dominant Organizational Characteristics determine the most prominent characteristics perceived by members of the organization.
- Organizational Leadership: the role and function of leadership in the organization.
- Management of Employees: the organization's ability to train, develop, and empower employees.
- Organizational Glue: things that unite employees in terms of relations and socialization.
  Strategic Emphasis: long-term planning of the organization for all employees.
- Criteria of Success: determines the success standards of an organization.

Organizational identity (OI) has been defined as the enduring characteristics of an organization that contribute to the distinctiveness and uniqueness of an organization. OI is based on a self-reflective approach and it captures the main enduring and distinctive organizational features (Albert & Whetten 1985). Then OI is also established through two main criteria: unique identity and unique organization (Whetten & Mackey 2002).

Based on Figure 2, intellectual capital models and reports of companies identify and define OI and Corporate Reputation as strategic intangible assets that are capable of generating sustainable competitive advantages (Bueno et al. 2015). From an interpretative perspective, OI is the result of a social process of self-description and it reflects employees' general agreement on "who they are as an organization". OI is developed by the internal stakeholders through interaction and it is the result of a social process of self-description (Gioia 1998). The same processes that form identity at the individual level occur in organizations, though with far greater complexity due to the number and variety of people involved in the identity conversation (see Figure 2). Like individuals, organizations receive feedback from their environment.

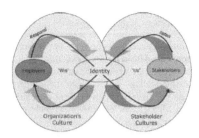

Figure 2. The organizational identity dynamics model.

To preserve a healthy identity, they must learn to balance what they hear about themselves (that which produces the organizational "me" or "us") against what they know themselves to be (the organizational "I" or "we") (Hatch & Schultz 2009).

2 METHODS

SETARA is a school that was established on September 1, 2014 and was built initially to meet the educational needs of some children with single parents, starting from the earliest stage of Kindergarten and Play Group. SETARA continues to grow rapidly in number of students enrolling in the span of 4 years. Since 2014, the number of students has been increased from 11 children to 182 children in 2017 for kindergarten, play group, and primary stages. The number of employees also increased from 2 people (1 teacher and 1 staff) to 36 people (25 teachers and 11 staffs) right now. This research used census sampling method and the survey was given to all 29 SETARA's members, both teachers and staffs. For the first time, the investigation was conducted in the form of combination of an OCAI questionnaire and open questions consisting of 11 questions in 4 categories (Giles & Yates 2012) as shown in Table 1.

The data were analyzed for emergent themes across the participants for each group of questions that straightforwardly related to characteristics or experiences of being in the organization. Emergent themes within each question were first sought. Nevertheless, later analysis focused on participant's

Table 1. Open-ended questions.

General practice and comparison	(1) What do you perceive to be some of the strengths of the relationships within your organization?
	(2) What do you perceive to be some of the challenges of the relationships within your organization?
	(3) How do your relational experiences compare to other organizations you have worked in?
History	(4) What aspects of the organization's history appear to be sustained at present?
	(5) From your experiences and observations, what do you see the organization valuing in practice?
	(6) What keeps you in this organization?
Relational experiences	(7) Can you describe a relational experience from your time in this organization that exceeded your expectations?
	(8) Can you describe a relational experience from your time in the organization that pleasantly surprised you?
	(9) How is leadership practiced within the organization?
Leadership practices	(10) Can you describe an organization initiative that appears to have strengthened individuals' practice?
	(11) How does the leadership at this organization enable your practice?

responses to each group of questions. The emergent themes are trends across the participants.

3 RESULTS

Twenty-nine participants filled the entire OCAI questionnaire, and the results can be seen in Table 2.

Table 2. OCAI survey.

Dimension	Clan	Adhocracy	Market	Hierarchy
Dominant Characteristics	24	0	0	5
Organizational Leadership	23	0	0	6
Management of Employees	22	0	2	5
Organizational Glue	26	1	1	1
Strategic Emphasis	25	1	0	3
Criteria of Success	27	0	2	0

Table 2 shows that 24 respondents describe SETARA as Clan in dominant characteristics dimension and only 5 respondents describe it as Hierarchy. Then, 23 and 22 members, respectively, define SETARA as Clan in organizational leadership and management of employees' dimensions; meanwhile, 6 and 5 members, respectively, define SETARA as Hierarchy. Dominantly, in the other three dimensions, more than 86% of contributors outline SETARA as Clan as well. It is concluded that the most dominant organizational culture at SETARA in 2017 is clan culture. The organization is considered a big family, where every team formed within the school is always emphasized to continue to have good relations, communication, and teamwork. The most notable characteristics are the school's commitment to employees, teamwork, and employee engagement. The findings also have been drawn from participant responses from all teachers and staffs. A summary of direct quotes from the participants for each question is described in Table 3 as follows.

4 DISCUSSION

The recurring themes for general practice and comparison category of questions relate to the communication, relationships, and valuing within the school. The kinship atmosphere is dominant; no one considers a person superior to the others. For instance, staffs said that they "feel welcomed warmly since the first day" and they also welcome others' ideas and views; that rephrased, another respondent stated, "in order to use of any facilities, employees always consider who needs more first". However, clear boundaries must remain in order not to interfere fellow member's personal affairs as a member specified, "There are those who have not been able to distinguish the work affairs with personal issue. Although prioritizing kinship, employees should strive for becoming professionals and do not interfere other's personal affairs". These challenges can impact the "family atmosphere that the school has been famous for", so these issues must be addressed wisely.

The significant repeated theme across the responses to history category of questions was the "compassionate environment" that has been continued within the school over time. One member captured the views of many, writing that, "A compassionate heart towards students and fellow co-workers, as well as humbleness". As another respondent also stated, "As a single parent, I'm impressed of the educational environment in SETARA which is very supportive and focus on helping underprivileged parents financially". Restated by another as well who stated that "Student's character is much appreciated, not just his/her intelligence". Employees described initiatives that

Table 3. Summary of open-ended survey.

(1) What do you perceive to be some of the strengths of the relationships within your organization?
The headmistress's leadership style supports kinship and togetherness, as well as "no favoritism" atmosphere.

(2) What do you perceive to be some of the challenges of the relationships within your organization?
How to understand each other's character in order to strengthen the relationship between co-workers so that miscommunication could be minimized.

(3) How do your relational experiences compare to other organizations you have worked in?
It is easier to solve problem or friction with fellow employees at SETARA than in other organizations.

(4) What aspects of the organization's history appear to be sustained at present?
Greet students before entering and exiting school gate, teach students to keep behaving politely, classical methods, and Christian values.

(5) From your experiences and observations, what do you see the organization valuing in practice?
Life-long learning. SETARA greatly equips teachers and staffs with trainings to develop professionalism and facilitates prayer, devotion, and even counseling for them. Christianity principles are applied directly in all activities.

(6) What keeps you in this organization?
Given the opportunity to develop both hard skills and soft skills. As well as a fact that SETARA is different from others in emphasizing process and goal-oriented very essential, not just merely results.

(7) Can you describe a relational experience from your time in this organization that exceeded your expectations?
Getting something more than just an organization, that is kinship. Relationship with headmistress is like maternal relationship.

(8) Can you describe a relational experience from your time in the organization that pleasantly surprised you?
Experiencing mutual pray, respect each other, and character building.

(9) How is leadership practiced within the organization?
Leadership that explains why I should do and should not do, over and above, does not judge my faults but leads me to do the right thing.

(10) Can you describe an organization initiative that appears to have strengthened individuals' practice?
The existence of internal trainings and external seminars (including ACSI training and scholarships to continue studying) is very helpful for self-development, but more important is SETARA also keep supporting employee's spirituality.

(11) How does the leadership at this organization enable your practice?
The headmistress always underlines that make differences and encourage others to work confidently as teachers and as educators in general are very critical. It motivates us to strive to recognize individual's strengths and needs in practices.

relate to "essence of educating is to build noble character" and "school-wide mentoring support" as evidence of a valuing and recognition of individual's strengths and experiences.

The focus of the employee's experience points to the overwhelming "care". The care surpasses expectation and surprises many. In moments where the generosity of employee is seen, or the pleasure of a collegial spirit is felt, individuals sense "care". It is as if care finds employee in unexpected ways. Students really care their teachers. "The headmistress even noticed about my wedding plan. Some colleagues helped me until overtime". "Initially I just worked for getting money but when I see and know more about SETARA, I feel there is something in my heart that makes me still have to be here". The primary aim of education is to produce people who will engage successfully in caring relations. The educational endeavor then is a caring profession with a concern for relationships (Noddings 2010). The experience of care extends to personal challenges, as one participant said: "I am very touched when the headmistress asked about food I like and invited me to eat it for several times. She always pays attention to employee's health as well". Then the experiences of care extend to the authenticity and sincerity such as "Birthday party" surprise and "hang out together".

Finally, the frequent themes for leadership practices category of questions relate to valuing and recognizing individual's strengths and experiences. Two of the most frequently used expressions for the staff should be "freedom" and "exploring new ideas and innovative ways" which enable them to be encouraged and grow professionally, as one respondent said: "I was asked to make an annual album design for all classes. It was the first experience for me because I usually design it for personal use". The headmistress is said to "lead by example" in a "very supportive way". She leads with good heart who value people, especially who makes the best out of followers.

5 CONCLUSION

All six dimensions of The Competing Values Framework at SETARA are dominated by Clan. Top management within the organization has done exemplary mentoring to employees, facilitating the physical and psychological needs of employees in the workplace, and has given trust to them to be more responsible and committed to organization. Thus, the most dominant organizational culture profile at SETARA today is Clan Culture, a culture that considers organizations very similar to a large family whose characteristics are teamwork, employee engagement, and organization's commitment to employees. SETARA emphasizes teamwork (not individual) and employee development, meaning that the current Competing Values Framework is Flexibility and Discretion as well Internal Focus and Integration. Flexibility and discretion are called people. Consequently, the

identity of SETARA is a Christian Classical School that focuses on developing character of its employees by generating an atmosphere of kinship based on Christian values, and at the end of the day, it's all about people. The open-ended survey gave the idea to be a tool that addresses the pressing concern for educational leaders to stay attuned to the nature of their organizational culture as this represents the organization's storyline (Giles & Yates 2012). In addition to the tool, OCAI survey can be used by schools as confirmation to organizational identity as a "label" which is valuable to leverage its competitive advantage relating to the rivalry by constantly living up this Clan Culture and demonstrating the values of care, humble, and compassion towards its stakeholders, especially teachers, staff, students, and parents.

REFERENCES

Albert, S. & Whetten, D.A. 1985. Organizational Identity. *Research in Organizational Behavior* 7: 263-295.
Bueno, E., Longo-Somoza, M., García-Revilla, R. & Leon, R.D. 2015. Relationships Between Organizational Identity and Corporate Reputation: Management Challenges. In *European Conference on Intellectual Capital* (p. 34). London: Academic Conferences International Limited.
Cameron, K.S. & Quinn, R.E. 2011. *Diagnosing and changing organizational culture: Based on the competing values framework*. New Jersey: John Wiley & Sons.
Cheung, S.O., Pang, H.Y., Tam, S.Y. & Chan, H.Y. 2011. Identity as a manifestation of organisational culture. *International Journal of Disaster Resilience in the Built Environment* 1(1): 748-761.
Giles, D. & Yates, R. 2012. Enabling educational leaders: qualitatively surveying an organization's culture. *International Journal of Organizational Analysis* 22(1): 94-106.
Gioia, D.A. 1998. From Individual to Organizational Identity. In D.A. Whetten & P.C. Godfrey (ed.) *Identity in Organizations: Building Theory Trough Conversations* (pp. 17-31). Thousand Oaks: Sage Publication.
Hatch, M.J. & Schultz, M. 1997. Relations between organizational culture, identity and image. *European Journal Marketing* 31(5/6): 356-365.
Hatch, M.J. & Schultz, M. 2002. The Dynamics of Organizational Identity. *Human Relations* 55(8): 989-1018.
Huang-Horowitz, N.C. & Freberg, K. 2016. Bridging organizational identity and reputation messages online: a conceptual model. *Corporate Communications: An International Journal* 21(2): 195-212.
Kemdikbud. 2018. Data referensi pendidikan. [Online]. Accessed on July 10. Retrieved from http://referensi.data.kemdikbud.go.id/index21.php?level=3&kode=026003&id=1
Noddings, N. 2010. Complexity in caring and empathy. *Abstrata* 6(2): 6-12.
Robbins, S.P. 2013. *Organizational Behavior. 15th Edition.* New Jersey: Prentice-Hall, Inc.
SETARA. 2018). Visi dan misi. [Online]. Accessed on July 1. Retrieved from http://setara.gb3.org/index.php/academics/visi-dan-misi
Whetten, D.A. & Mackey, A. 2002. A Social Actor Conception of Organizational Identity and Its Implications for the Study of Organizational Reputation. *Business and Society* 41(4): 393-414.

Global Competitiveness: Business Transformation in the
Digital Era – Abdullah, Widiaty & Abdullah (eds)
© 2019 Taylor & Francis Group, London, ISBN 978-0-367-19442-0

Safety behaviour of manufacturing companies in Indonesia

I. Djastuti, M.S. Perdhana & S.T. Raharjo
Diponegoro University, Central Java, Indonesia

ABSTRACT: The high rate of accidents in the workplace makes employees safety be a priority in manufacturing companies. This is because work safety is closely related to employees' survival. The paper was aimed to analyze the safety behaviour of employees in manufacturing companies by looking at the influence of three variables namely safety climate, job satisfaction, and safety motivation. This research was carried out in one of the manufacturing companies in Indonesia that produce musical instruments and furniture. The sample was employees in the production section with nonprobability sampling technique. There were 300 respondents who participated in this research, but only 190 questionnaires that were feasible to be processed. This study found that the safety climate and job satisfaction have a positive and significant impact on the safety of employee motivation. Safety motivation also has a positive and significant effect on employee safety behaviour. **However, the safety climate does not have a negative effect and not significant on the safety behaviour.** Then, job satisfaction has a positive effect but not significant on the safety behaviour. Safety climate and job satisfaction have direct effects to the safety motivation, and safety motivation has a direct effect to the safety behaviour. Then, safety motivation is able to mediate safety climate and job satisfaction on the safety behaviour. Based on the lowest indicator index value of each variable, things that need to be considered are safety support from supervisors, wages, safety behaviour willingness, and safety rules. Therefore, a company need to consider taking a policy in implementing a safety climate and increasing employee job satisfaction in order to improve the safety motivation, which is then expected to create good safety behaviour within the company.

1   INTRODUCTION

Accidents that occurred in the industrial companies in Indonesia showed a high rate. Although there has been a decline since 2014, the number of accidents that occur are still quite large at over 100 thousand cases. Based on data from BPJS Ketenagakerjaan, the number of accidents in 2016 still reached 101 367 cases. The high number of accidents surely must be a concern of all parties to find a solution.

Safety is a very important thing to be a major concern of companies, especially manufacturing companies and high-risk enterprise. This is because safety is directly related to the survival of the worker or employee. Quoted from Prihatiningsih & Sugiyanto (2010), Labour Law No. 13/2003 article 86 and 87 explain the importance of workplace safety.

Generally, work accidents occurred due to a weak system of corporate work (O'Toole 2002). Various attempts were made to reduce the number of accidents at the company, such as creating technical solutions, human factors, and regulation. However, those solutions will be meaningless if it is not followed by employee feedback. So it becomes important to analyse the behaviour of the safety among the employees.

To produce employees with good performance, including how to work with a good safety standard would require a stage that is not easy, in addition to motivation, knowledge, and competence,

organizational culture must be built on safety-oriented behaviour in order to avoid safety problems. Employee performance is influenced by two factors, namely factor in job satisfaction and organizational commitment as well as external factors, namely leadership, security, safety, and organizational culture.

Safety motivation mediates the relationship between safety climate and safety behaviour (Neal & Griffin 2006). Huda (2016) found that safety motivation has an effect on adherence to safety procedures until 6 months later.

Based on the Maslow theory of needs, people are motivated to meet and satisfy a number of needs that exist in every human being. Employees will feel satisfied if they received feedback from the company in excess of what they expected (Robbins 2013). Employees will be motivated to do anything, including in terms of the behaviour of the working salvation (Huda 2016).

This research was conducted at a manufacturing company located in the city of Semarang where one company performance target is to make safety a top priority. Management companies should have demonstrated a commitment to fully support all efforts related to anticipation of a safety issue. Even if the company and the management has implemented a safety management system with a good, tight, and disciplines including forming department of Health Safety and Environment (HSE), but there are still cases of accident work as shown in the Figure 1:

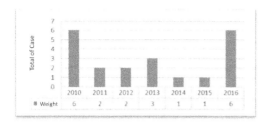

Figure 1. Serious accidents of manufacturing company in Semarang.

From the data above, it can be implied that problems between the targets of the first strategy of Indonesian Manufacturing in 2016 is zero occupational accidents with the data safety performance in 2016 as there is still a severe increase in cases of work accidents.

2 THEORETICAL FRAMEWORK AND HYPOTHESES

2.1 Definition of safety climate

Seo (2004) defines the organizational climate as an overall perception that a person has about the settings in their workplace. Climate often referred to as something temporary and subjective. While the safety climate is a picture of perceptions related to policies, procedures and safety practices (Prihatiningsih & Sugiyanto 2010). Meanwhile, according to Zohar & Luria (2005), safety climate is defined as the perception of the safety of employees who describe their confidence in the safety priorities. That perception reflects the expectation of the results of their work behaviour.

Social perceptions of safety will give description against employees how management commitment to the health and safety of their work. Perception of safety appears with a variety of experiences on the extent to which the management employees to invest in protecting them. A positive safety climate can improve the safety behaviour of employees working in the hazardous working environment and vice versa.

2.2 Definition of job satisfaction

Job satisfaction is not a single concept whereby one can be satisfied with some aspects and feel not satisfied with other aspects (Kreitner & Kinicki 2010). Job satisfaction is an attitude or behaviour which is owned by the individual common to the work that he did (Robbins & Judge 2015). When an individual has a high satisfaction with the job then he is likely to display positive behaviours or attitudes, and vice versa.

Luthans (2011) defines job satisfaction as a person's perception of how good and important the job they have. It can be concluded that job satisfaction is a feeling that arises because of the perception of their work shown in attitude or behaviour towards the work itself.

2.3 Definition of safety motivation

The term safety motivation refers to the individual's willingness to make an effort to enforce safe behaviour and valence associated with these behaviours (Neal & Griffin 2006). Individuals have to be motivated to comply with safe work practices and participate in safety activities if they feel that there is a positive safety climate in the workplace. According to Huda (2016), motivation can be divided into two dimensions, which will boost safety behaviour and willingness to conduct workplace safety.

2.4 Definition of safety behaviour

Hsu (2008) states that conducting employee safety is always abode by the rules and safety procedures. Employees can play it safe or unsafe when they do their job. Therefore, the behaviour of employees in the workplace is very important to minimize safety concerns. In addition, the safety behaviour was found to prevent accidents from happening (Martínez-Córcoles et al. 2011). Previous studies' results implied that the safety behaviour is the right approach in reducing accidents in the workplace. To determine the safety behaviour, there are two dimensions of behaviour that cover safety compliance and safety participation.

According IOHS (Institution of Occupational Safety and Health direction 06.1), safety behaviour is part of the development of the safety management of the approach that is very prescriptive through systems engineering or procedural that are mostly applied in progressive companies that are long established. It should also be applied in the companies as workers are adult human beings with a genuine interest to improve their welfare and who will give their best, but they also need to realize of their own safety in working. To change the behaviour, a transition needs to be done to change the culture of the working group involved so that this approach does not give instant results.

Human behaviour is often categorized as a reflex/automatic which can be considered as a habit. The behavioural approach focuses on custom category but not for blaming or punishing workers, a kind of action that is mostly counterproductive in any case. An effective approach is to identify and measure the secured and non-secured (risky) behaviour that happens in the workplace and manage it well. Measuring behaviour may provide a health and safety system with more proactive management. This is for the stability of the safety.

According to Neal & Griffin (2006), behavioural safety of employees can be divided into two dimensions, namely safety compliance and safety participation. Safety compliance refers to the core activities of the individual to be done to maintain safety in the workplace. This behaviour includes following standard operating procedure and wearing personal protective equipment. Safety participation describes the behaviour that does not directly contribute to an individual's personal safety but helps develop an environment that supports safety. This behaviour includes activities such as participating in a voluntary safety activities, help colleagues with the issues related to safety, and attend safety meetings.

The present study tried to investigate the influence of safety variables by testing five hypotheses as follows:

Hypotheses (See in Figure 2):

H1: Safety Climate has a positive and significant effect on the safety motivation.

H2: Job satisfaction has a positive and significant effect on the safety motivation.

H3: Safety Climate has a positive and significant effect on the safety behaviour.

H4: Job satisfaction has a positive and significant effect on the safety behaviour.

H5: Safety Motivation has a positive and significant effect on the safety behaviour.

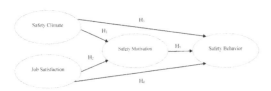

Figure 2. Research framework.

3 RESEARCH METHOD

The population is defined as the entire group of people, events, or things to be investigated by researchers (Sekaran, 2006). Further, population is also referred to a generalization region consisting of the objects/subjects that have certain qualities and characteristics defined by the researchers to be learned and conclusions drawn (Sugiyono 2008). The population involved in this study were employees of a manufacturing company.

The sample is a fraction of the number and characteristics of a population (Sugiyono 2008). Samples are some members of the population. A researcher can analyze samples when the population is too large for the overall study and constrained limitations of time, effort, and funds. The sampling design used in this research is to nonprobability (nonprobability sampling). Nonprobability sampling is a sampling technique that does not give the same opportunity or chance on every member of the population to be used as a sample (Sugiyono 2008).

The study employed purposive sampling as the researchers have understood that the required information can be obtained from a particular group that is able to provide the desired information and they have fulfilled criteria determined (Ferdinand 2014). The tool used to process the data in this study is SEM (Structural Equation Model) which is operated by AMOS (Analysis of Moment Structure).

4 RESULTS AND DISCUSSION

4.1 Overview of respondents

The number of respondents who filled out questionnaires is 300, yet only 190 eligible questionnaires were analysed. Of the total number of 190 respondents, 49 percent (n = 93) were women, and the remaining 51 percent (n = 97) were male. In terms of employment, employees with longer than two years to dominate 53 percent, n = 101), followed by employees with a working time of 6 months - 1 year (27 percent, n = 51), employees with long work for more than 6 months (10 percent, n = 19), and employees with long working 1-2 years (10 percent, n = 19) (See in Table 1).

4.2 Measurement models

Chi-square is the most fundamental measure that indicates the conformity of the overall model. If the value of Chi-Square it will produce a small probability of large, it indicates that the sample covariance matrix of the covariance matrix of the model did not differ significantly (Ghozali 2016), fit structural equation model Chi-Square if the value is small and the probability of > 0.05. The use of Chi-Square is only suitable for use in the study sample totalled 100-200 and if the sample size is outside the range of the sample size, the significance tests become less reliable (Ferdinand 2014). In this study, Chi-Square values obtained at 189.113 with a probability of 0.087, so it can be said that the structural equation model has been developed well.

Level of significance of probability is a statistical measure that is fundamental in determining whether H_0 (null hypothesis) can be rejected. In the analysis, using structural equation modelling approach (SEM) is expected.

H_0 is not rejected, it is different with hypothesis testing in general. Good model should not reject H_0. Thus, the significance of the expected probability is greater than 0.05 or 0.10 in order not to reject H_0. If the results of this research data generating significance probability of 0.087, while the implied value

Table 1. Goodness of fit test results overall feasibility model Structural Equation Model (SEM).

Goodness of Fit Index	Cut-off Value	Results Model	Details
Chi-Square	<147.010 (df = 98)	189.113	Marginal
Probability	≥ 0.05	0.087	Good
GFI	≥ 0.90	0.911	Good
AGFI	≥ 0.90	0.886	Good
CFI	≥ 0.95	0,990	Good
TLI	≥ 0.90	0.989	Good
RMSEA	≤ 0.08	0,028	Good

168

for the level of significance probability is ≥ 0.05, thus it can be concluded that there is sufficient evidence to negate H_0. It means that the alternative hypothesis cannot be accepted. Therefore, it can be concluded that there is no difference between the matrix of variance/covariance matrix samples with variance/covariance population.

Goodness of Fit Index (GFI) is a non-statistical measure which reflects the level of accuracy of the model obtained from the predicted residual quadratic models compared to the actual data, which has a range from 0 to 1 and getting closer to 1 indicates the model is getting better. In this study, the limit values for states GFI fit model is ≥ 0.90 and GFI value between 0.8 up to 0.9 is said to be marginal fit. GFI value in this research is 0.911, so the model can be considered good.

Adjusted Goodness of Fit Index (AGFI) is a development of GFI adjusted to the degree of freedom for the proposed model. A model is said to be fit when the value AGFI ≥ 0.90 and AGFI value between 0.8 - 0.9 is said to be marginal fit. In this study, the value of AGFI amounted to 0.886, so that the structural equation model we tested is said to be marginal fit.

CFI value of 0,990 above the value of 0.95 which is a CFI value required, so it can be stated that the condition of good standard CFI value. Furthermore, the TLI value of 0.989 is more than 0.90, which is the value TLI required, meaning that the value of a good standard TLI. Then, for a value of 0.028 RMSEA below 0.08 which is an RMSEA value required, so that the value of a good standard RMSEA.

4.3 Hypotheses testing

Once the model has been declared fit, then it was followed by hypothesis testing that was carried out by looking at the significance of the estimated value, the critical ratio, and probability (See in Table 2). Table 2 shows that all the significant value of parameter estimation of each relationship has a value of <0.05 unless the value of the estimated

parameter significance workplace safety climate on the behaviour of worker safety and job satisfaction on behavioural safety (0.012 and 0.039). The results of data analysis has shown that the climate effects on motivation Safety have CR = 2.613 and p = 0.007 (<0.05), so it can be said to be significant. This indicates a safety climate can increase the motivation of the perceived safety among the employees. Therefore, safety climate has positive and significant impact on the employees' safety motivation in manufacturing companies in Indonesia. Thus, it can be concluded that H_1 is accepted.

The results of data analysis has shown that the effect of job satisfaction on motivation safety has CR = 3.005 and p = 0.005 (<0.05), so it can be said to be significant. This indicates that job satisfaction can increase the motivation of the perceived safety of employees. Therefore, job satisfaction has significantly and positively affects employees' safety motivation (H_2 is accepted).

Different results were obtained from data analysis showing that climate influences on behavioural Safety have CR = -2.431 and p = 0.012 (> 0.05), so it can be said to be not significant. This indicates a safety climate have not been able to increase the perceived safety behaviour of employees. Therefore, it can be deduced that the H_3 is rejected.

Another result of data analysis revealed that the effect of job satisfaction on safety behaviours have CR = 2.713 and p = 0.039 (> 0.05). This indicates that job satisfaction has a positive effect but not significant on the safety behaviour. Therefore, job satisfaction has a positive effect but not significant on the safety behaviour of employees in manufacturing companies in Indonesia (H_4 is rejected).

The last results of data analysis showing that the effect of occupational safety motivation towards work safety behaviours has CR = 3.201 and p = 0.005 (<0.05), so it can be said to be significant. The result implies that safety motivation can improve the perceived safety behaviour among employees, or in other words, safety motivation has a positive and significant effect on the safety behaviour of employees (H_5 is accepted).

Table 2. Regression weight structural equation modelling.

				Estimate	SE ML	CR	p-value ML	SE Bootstrap	p-value Bootstrap
MKK	<—	IKK	H1	0215	0082	2,613	.009	.081	.007
MKK	<—	KK	H2	0229	0076	3005	.003	.082	.005
PKK	<—	IKK	H3	-0183	0075	-2431	.015	.080	.012
PKK	<—	MKK	H4	0237	0074	3,201	.001	.079	.005
PKK	<—	KK	H5	0152	0070	2173	.030	.075	.039

5 CONCLUSIONS, IMPLICATIONS, SUG-GESTION, AND LIMITATIONS

The main objective of this study was to look at the role of occupational safety climate and job satisfaction to employees' safety behaviour. In addition, this study also attempted to determine the effect of occupational safety motivation in mediating the safety of the working climate on employee safety behaviour. The research conducted at one of the manufacturing companies in Indonesia.

Based on the hypothesis testing, it can be concluded that among the five hypotheses being tested, H_3 which tested the effect of safety climate and H_4 which tested the effect of job satisfaction on work safety behaviour were rejected. This indicates climate safety and job satisfaction have no connection with occupational safety behaviour. Moreover, the causal relationship between safety climate and job satisfaction on employee safety behaviour has a negative impact and insignificant.

However, the findings showed that H_1, H_2, and H_5 testing are consistent with the hypothesis drawn up at the beginning. The results showed that the climate of industrial safety and job satisfaction has positive and significant impact on the motivation of safety (H_1 and H_2). Then, occupational safety motivation also the positively and significantly affects the behaviour of safety (H_5). The findings indicate that the climate of safety and job satisfaction can increase motivation safety of employees. Vice versa, if a safety climate and poor job satisfaction will decrease the motivation of workplace safety. In addition, the findings also indicate if the motivation safety can improve the safety behaviour of employees.

The results of the indicator index analysis of each variable showed which indicators are perceived to be the highest and lowest. From safety climate dimension, competency level is an indicator that has the highest index and the lowest index is safety support from the supervisors. Therefore, it is necessary to increase the intensity of providing support from supervisors to their subordinates. From job satisfaction dimension, working conditions have the highest index and the lowest index is about wages. That indicates that employees are satisfied with their working conditions, but still need attention about wages.

Then, from safety motivation dimension, the highest index is about the importance of helping co-workers when in the danger and the lowest index is about safety behaviour willingness. This indicates that attention is still needed to increase the willingness of employees to their safety while working. From safety behaviour dimension, indicators that have the highest index is about safety participation and the lowest index is about safety rules. This indicates that companies need to improve the safety rules applied to employees. Based on the lowest indicator index value of each variable, things that need to be considered are safety support from supervisors, wages, safety behaviour willingness, and safety rules.

Direct and indirect relationships between variables using path analysis indicate that the variables safety climate and job satisfaction directly influence safety motivation. Then, safety motivation has a direct effect on safety behaviour. Safety climate on the safety behaviour directly has a negative effect, but if through the safety motivation through the safety behaviour, it becomes positive. The results of the Sobel Test showed that safety motivation can mediate safety climate and job satisfaction on the safety behaviour.

The results showed a positive correlation between safety climate, job satisfaction, and motivation safety of the employees' safety behaviour in manufacturing companies in Indonesia. Considering the possibility of potential work accidents whether mild or severe, the company needs to pursue some policies on a regular basis by conducting a survey measuring the behaviour of the employees by a factor measured is the level of compliance of safety (safety compliance) and participation in anticipating danger, considering the frequent turnover for system contract. The survey followed up by a policy in anticipation of declining employee safety behaviour including improving the quality of safety motivation.

The limitation in this study is the reduction of indicators in research in order to get the model Fit in quantitative data processing as there is still fit criteria which do not meet that standard with marginal results Probability. In addition, the sources of respondents are still limited that only 300 respondents and the number of questionnaires that can be analysed only 190.

Some suggestions for future research are also proposed. The first suggestion for further research is to explore the relationship between safety climates on the safety behaviour as studies focusing on this issue very limited literature. Secondly, it is necessary to do research again on the relation of safety climate employees' safety behaviour because there is still a gap between the research results with one another. Third, future research needs to do research on the positive side and negative on the safety of employees' behaviour in addressing the safety climate in an organization. It is able to provide solutions to organizations in taking climate policy in applying safety and increase employees' job satisfaction in order to increase the motivation of safety and to create good safety behaviour within the organization. Then, it is suggested for future research to conduct study in a larger scope since number of respondents in this study is limited in order to meet the test of goodness of chi-square test.

REFERENCES

Ferdinand, A. 2014. *Metode Penelitian Manajemen*, 5th ed. Semarang: Badan Penerbit Universitas Diponegoro.

Ghozali, I. 2016. *Aplikasi Analisis Multivariate Dengan Program IBM SPSS 23*, 8th ed. Semarang: Badan Penerbit Universitas Diponegoro.

Hsu, S.H. 2008. A Cross-Cultural Study of Organizational Factors on Safety: Japanese vs. Taiwanese Oil Refinery Plants. *Accident Analysis and Prevention* 40(1): 24–34.

Huda, U.F. 2016. Model Perilaku Keselamatan Kerja Karyawan Pada Industri Berisiko Tinggi. *Jurnal Manajemen Teknologi* 15(1): 51–66.

Kreitner, R. & Kinicki, A.J. 2010. *Organizational Behavior*. New York: McGraw-Hill.

Luthans, F. 2011. *Organizational Behavior : An Evidence-Based Approach*. New York: McGraw-Hill.

Martínez-Córcoles, M., Gracia, F., Tomás, I. & Peiró, J.M. 2011. Leadership and employees' perceived safety behaviours in a nuclear power plant: A structural equation model. *Safety science* 49(8-9): 1118-1129.

Neal, A. & Griffin, M.A. 2006. A Study of the Lagged Relationships among Safety Climate, Safety Motivation, Safety Behavior, and Accidents at the Individual and Group Levels. *Journal of Applied Psychology* 91(4): 946–953.

O'Toole, M. 2002. The Relationship between Employees' Perceptions of Safety and Organizational Culture. *Journal of Safety Research* 33(2): 231–243.

Prihatiningsih & Sugiyanto. 2010. Pengaruh Iklim Keselamatan Dan Pengalaman Personel Terhadap Kepatuhan Pada Peraturan Keselamatan Pekerja Konstruksi. *Jurnal Psikologi* 37(1): 82–93

Robbins, S. 2013. *Organizational Behavior*. London: Pearson Higher Education.

Robbins, S.P. & Judge, T.A. 2015. *Perilaku Organisasi*. Jakarta: Salemba Empat.

Sekaran, U. 2006. *Metodologi Penelitian Untuk Bisnis*, 4th ed., Jakarta: Salemba Empat.

Seo, D.C. 2004. A Cross-Validation of Safety Climate Scale Using Confirmatory Factor Analytic Approach. *Journal of Safety Research* 35(4): 427–445.

Sugiyono. 2008. *Metode Penelitian Bisnis*. Bandung: Alfabeta.

Zohar, D. & Luria, G. 2005. A multilevel model of safety climate: cross-level relationships between organization and group-level climates. *Journal of applied psychology* 90(4): 616.

Global Competitiveness: Business Transformation in the
Digital Era – Abdullah, Widiaty & Abdullah (eds)
© 2019 Taylor & Francis Group, London, ISBN 978-0-367-19442-0

Developing company viability based on virtue and human potentials (Study on SME in West Java)

B. Gomulia
Faculty of Economy, Parahyangan Catholic University, Bandung, Indonesia

ABSTRACT: The company viability, particularly in relation to virtue and human potentials, has scarcely been discussed in today's field of business and management. However, in line with the more dynamic and complex company milieu, establishing the viability as its adaptive and flexible capacities is urgent. The purpose of this study is to explore and confirm this specific "intrinsic" company performance and its determinant factors. The study is conducted with 47 SME industries located in West Java. The data was collected by survey taken from 905 workers, and from interviews with the owners or managers. Factor analysis method was conducted to verify the validity of the variables and its model proposition as to come to a valid form of research model and hypothesis to analyze. The results of path analysis showed that the company viability is significantly influenced by the management commitment and intrapreneurial spirit; both variables can be explained at R^2 0.93. Meanwhile, the intrapreneurial spirit is explained by the work spirit, innovative learning, and compliance significantly, at R^2 0.94. The study also explained the role of mutual trust. The results of this study is expected to be the basis of a more thorough research on the psychosocial aspects contributing to enhance the intrapreneurial spirit for developing the company viability.

1 INTRODUCTION

1.1 Company viability and workers' roles in West Java

Economy crisis taken place in the 1997–1998, brought a big impact in West Java. Many companies were bankrupt; however, a few survived the crisis. The data of company mortality in West Java during 1996–2000 showed that 2.680 units or about 43.4% of all the companies in 1996 of companies were able to survive (as a first data position), and only 19% of companies could show the ability to progress better, provided the progress is viewed from the rising of total number of workers. Moreover, it is also seen that the large-scale companies and middle-scale companies were able to survive and develop at once (see Table 1).

Table 1. Company viability value in West Java in 1996–2006 (in unit).

The total of companies in 1996 (first position)	6.175
The total of survived companies in 2006 (last position)	2.680 (43.4%)
The total of companies with increasing workers	1.181 (19%)
The total of small companies which experienced development	500
The total of medium companies which experienced development	355
The total of big companies which experienced development	326
The total of new companies during 1996–2006	912

*The data are processed from Manufacture Industry Directory, 1996 and 2006.

Many factors and aspects determine the company's ability to survive and develop. The worker factor is deemed as one of the factors which determine the success of business development. Statistic data in West Java in 2012–2014 show the increasing of workers and their productivity.

Table 2. The development of processing industry productivity in West Java.

Explanation	2012	2013	2014
The total of processing industry:			
UM	1.622	1.709	1.826
UB	929	979	1.090
The total of workers-person:			
UM	454.082	498.372	522.325
UB	2.149.315	2.270.763	2.374.805
Labour productivity-million Rp.:			
UM	182,75	190,05	197,50
UB	174,52	182,48	190,05

* The data are processed from BPS Indonesia and West Java BPS, UM=medium business, UB=large business.

The role and position of workers for the company are not equal to the machine, material, and asset on the production process. Different from the machine and any other resources, workers have reasoning and conscience to assess the appropriateness of the demands. Mele & Canton (2014) said the difference between other creations and human is that human has free will.

"Free will - We are owners of our acts of choice, the desires accepted by our will, and thus we are responsible for them".

The attitude and behavior of the workers are determined by the harmony and the conformity between the norm and value applied in the society. The workers can choose to be the ethical person on working and business. This assumption becomes the reason why this study submitted the concept of company viability that is based on virtue and workers' potentials (Moore & Spence 2006, Solomon 2004, Pirson & Lawrence 2010).

The purpose of the study is to find out the virtue and human potentials that contribute to the development of company viability. In specific, the questions are formulated as follows:

– How is the company viability constructed to face the environmental challenges?
– How the community member's willingness to give the best for the company can contribute to the enhancement of the company viability?
– How the spirit of community member to change for the future challenges can contribute to the enhancement of the company viability?

2 PROPOSITION MODEL

2.1 *Dynamic environment and company viability*

Beer (1985) stated for the first time about a concept of organization viability that "system's ability to maintain its independent existence within a specified environment". Viability is articulated as a system ability (organization) to keep its existence independently and autonomously in a way of developing the flexibility and adaptability. In general, the viability is defined as an ability of a company to survive, advance, and well grow up. A healthy company's life is interpreted as company which is responsible consistently not only economically but also socially towards its member, and the community served.

The company viability is considered as a form of successful business, which is multidimensional and also contingent and contextual. A company cannot survive to face the dynamic environment situation by relying on the system and management structure which tends to be mechanistic, instead of flexibility and high adaptability that are needed (Thompson 2017). The member of the company who has an opportunity and responsibility on facing the challenges can only provide this flexibility.

A well-survived company is a company which can operate, maintain, and update the working system in a short term or long term with the direction of the aspirations to be achieved in the future. A

company which can maintain its viability is marked by the ability to maintain consistency and continuity of operation (Thompson 2003). The external or internal community support in order to maintain the stock and process directly and indirectly gives company the flexibility and adaptability to deal with the changes occurring (De Geus 1997, Freeman et al. 2007). This viability is developed on the basis of trust and good will on developing together between stakeholders and companies (Cameron et al. 2004a, Cameron et al. 2004b, Chun et al. 2011, Freeman 2004).

2.2 *Intrinsic dimensions of the company performance*

In this study, the company viability does not use a hard-dimensional measurement such as the long company life, company growth, maturity stage, and other measurement because these kind of dimensions only show how far the company is able to survive. Meanwhile, the future company deals with the dynamic environment which is different from its previous condition, then the soft dimension is needed to be stated in this study which becomes the basis of the company's ability to build on the internal capability. This capability can maintain the company's long-term viability (Collins 2001, Drucker 2014).

To express the company viability adequately, some dimensions which characterize the intrinsic capability will be identified. First, sensitivity to the market – it reflects the company's ability to fulfill the consumer needs for the products and services which fluctuate quickly. So far, the consumer is consistently loyal to the company. Second, a balance and fairness transaction – a fair treatment for the stakeholders, which brings a win-win situation on working and business run by the company. This business relationship is the best guarantee to maintain business viability in a long term. Third, vision to build people's capabilities – reflection from the company aspiration and desire to develop the future, which supports the positive and innovative member's innovation. These three dimensions are expected to reveal the flexibility, adaptability, innovation, and company standards to run business and create a fair and responsible working environment.

2.3 *Company viability based on the virtue and human potentials*

On the company viability concept, human is placed in the central role and position in the company management; people benefit from various things cannot be seen as a ready resource, but it can be considered and treated as a human resource which has virtue and potential for the actualization (Hartanto 2009, Peterson & Seligman 2004). Hartanto (2009) also viewed human potentials as a strong character, which grow from the confidence, belief, and emotion about positive things in a working life and social life. If this human potential is loaded with a beauty, moral superiority, concern for other people, then those potentials are often called as a virtue.

From the assumptions that company viability can only be manifested through working and management effort, and by company members who will and are able to work synergistically (Hartanto 2009), the proposition is submitted that the company viability is influenced by Management Commitment and Intrapreneurial Spirit to the company. The meaning of the virtue and two potentials explicitly are described as follows:

- Management Commitment – Management commitment is one of the forms of work ethic which reflects management determination to build support from all of the community members to produce performances expected by the company continuously, and the capability to contribute consistently even though the working and business environment is less conducive (Chun et al. 2013, Cullen et al. 2000, Porter et al. 1974, Rhodes & Eisenberger 2002)
- Intrapreneurial Spirit – The entrepreneurship shows the company member's readiness to study, change, adapt, and innovate consistently in accordance with the working demands development in the daily operation, in present and future (Kao 1995, Kuratko et al. 2011)

The intrapreneurial spirit itself seems to be influenced by the company members' spirit and behavior. The spirit and behavior are defined as follows:

- Working Spirit – This spirit is needed to maintain the sustainable working in a full of challenging situation.
- Innovative Learning Spirit – This spirit is needed to bring out renewal and innovation in a constantly changing situation.
- Accountability – This spirit is needed to ensure that working is in a law and ethic corridor, in addition to maintaining decision-making done responsibly.

Human is a social being; therefore, the attitude and other people in the surroundings affect behavior. Likewise, the virtue and worker's potentials can develop corresponding to the society situation and the situation of the company community at the same time (Solomon 2004). There are some working environment aspects which are estimated to influence the behavior and working life. Ethical climate, social climate, and mutual trust are believed to affect the company viability. Complete research proposition model to be tested is presented in Figure 1.

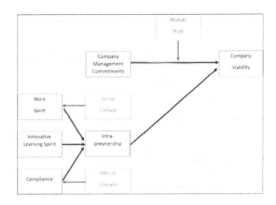

Figure 1. Proposition model.

3 RESEARCH METHOD

Research sample is from 47 medium- and small-scale manufactures that have been running for at least fifteen years in West Java. The total of the sample is sufficiently estimated, because this type of study usually requires at least 30 companies (rule of thumb). Bigger sample is required to ensure the validity of the result.

The variable is measured perceptually through the workers' or management member perception for community or company behavior. The instruments used are general opinion questions on "psychosocial". In this study, workers and management member as the observation units filling the survey is as many as 905 individuals.

The statistical analysis consists of factor analysis and path analysis which used SPSS version 21 (Statistical Package for the Social Sciences).

3.1 Factor analysis

In this study, the test was conducted in two stages; first stage is conducting a validity and reliability variable constructing test with the exploratory factor analysis as well as confirmatory factor analysis. Second stage is conducting a test towards reconstructed research model. The confirmation is is used as the research model and hypothesis from the relationships between research variables; finally, the Research Model is obtained and analyzed further.

4 RESULTS AND DISCUSSION

After conducting a factor analysis to the research variables, which are submitted on the proposition model, a redefinition variable is obtained. This variable is a representation from the psychosocial condition which is perceived in the company environment. The exploratory and confirmatory factor analysis success in identifying dimension and variable that contribute to the improvement model quality of company viability is shown in Figure 2.

4.1 Company performance – viability

The company viability turns out to be a concept, which has to be holistically seen from three dimensions including (1) Attention to Operational, (2) Market Adaptation, (3) Responsibility. All the dimensions consist of company capability to maintain the operational dynamics in order to answer the development of challenges and market chances.

The long-term company viability is not only driven by external stimuli, but also appear implicitly as a consciousness from company members to self-development in order to meet the challenges in the future. This can be seen from the manifestation contents of each company viability dimension, which consist of people development aspects.

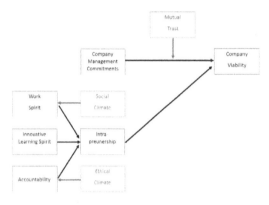

Figure 2. Research model.

4.2 Management commitment and intrapreneurial spirit in rising company viability

Table 3 shows the result of path analysis, from which research model submitted can be confirmed as significant, even though not all hypotheses submitted are accepted. With the explanation level of R^2 0.93, most of the company viability can be explained by Management Commitment and Intrapreneurial Spirit. The company viability has been proven positively and significantly by Management Commitment and Intrapreneurial Spirit. From the results, it can be concluded that company viability can be increased if there is an effort and real concern from the management (and owner) to the workers, as well as the spirit of innovation in the internal company environment. The rising of intrapreneurial spirit, which is found in the company environment, will affect company viability positively and significantly. Thus, it can be seen that the spirit felt in the company environment contributes to the company capabilities to deal with the internal and external challenges.

Table 3. Management commitment (KMP) and intrapreneurial spirit (SKI) towards company viability.

Variable	β	p
KMP	0.221**	0.038
KMPxRSP	0.012**	0.044
SKI	0.684**	0.029
$R^2 = 0.929$		

The mutual trust, which is felt in these company environments, is as expected. This mutual trust has been proven to increase the positive influence of the management commitment towards the company viability. Thus, the companies have actually been proven to have assets yet unable to use them for productive work.

Table 4. Work Spirit (GK), Social Climate (IS), Innovative Learning (SBI), Compliance (PP), and Ethical Climate (IE) toward Intrapreneurial Spirit.

Variable	β	p
SBI	−0.142*	0.067
GK	−0.071*	0.054
GK × IS	−0.037***	0.009
PP	0.045**	0.045
PP × IE	0.174***	0.007
$R^2 = .94$		

Table 4 shows that the intrapreneurial spirit which is discussed in this study is adequate, because the value of R^2 0.94; it means that intrapreneurial existence can be explained by Work Spirit, Innovative Learning, and Compliance. Nevertheless, as per psychosocial research, this research model still needs to be refined and enriched, so that the complete and comprehensive description can be obtained.

The increase of innovative learning spirit available among company members makes a decrease in intrapreneurial spirit. It is suspected due to one or more reasons as follows:

- Innovative learning spirit, which is marked a lot by dialog, discussion, and asking each other, is considered as disrupting daily production activities and the achievements of production target. This phenomenon isin line with the practice, in which the researched company orders workers to focus their attention on the achievement of production target and it needs no renewal because it is considered as management responsibility.
- Innovative company members who learned a lot yet get their opinions ignored or rejected by the

management will increase their diasspointment. Consequently, this situation will decrease the company's performance.

The increase of working spirit has negative effect towards intrapreneurial spirit. It is estimated among 47 researched companies that are still transactional and raised by external stimuli such as performance achievement, which is related to the reward. This situation is strengthened by working condition which tends to be mechanistic with clear and certain working conditions. All of the renewal and innovations which want to be implemented in the working environment tend to be considered inhibit working opportunities to achieve production target and big reward. The working spirit is usually associated with the effort to pursue more rewards which will automatically reduce the willingness to implement new ideas, and this is reflected in the working environments. When the renewal is still considered as a disruption for the production activities, then renewal spirit of the companies will tend to decrease.

The obedience to the rules and work plan turn out to increase the intrapreneurial spirit significantly. Even the impact is getting stronger and significant when the company members experience ethical atmosphere. If the members obey the rules and work ethically, manager can concentrate more to the renewal and innovation, because in the company environments, the supervision can be reduced. This matter can increase the company dynamic and viability.

5 CONCLUSION AND SUGGESTION

To conclude from all of the results and analysis stated before, the observed companies show a dynamic and good viability indeed; however, the viability still relies on the manager capability which is also the owner who is not in the virtue. The company members tend to be treated as a resource and production factor, not as a human being who has virtue and potential that can be invited to think about the company future and directly involved in contributing more to the increasing of company viability. It is estimated that if the member is given an opportunity to engage and contribute in production activities as well as the roles and responsibility, the company viability will be long guaranteed.

In line with the suggestions to the management, commitment should be enriched to be collective, which is supported by the results that company members' mutual trust can be increased from management's commitment towards company viability. Thus, it is suggested that mutual trust between members should be increased constantly through real efforts in the form of member involvement in the production activities and innovation. These efforts need to be implemented consistently by tolerant management, which is reflected through the following attitude and behavior:

- Have a willingness to learn from the honest mistake.
- Have a readiness to listen and consider new ideas of utilization coming from members.
- Respect to the useful members' criticism.

The key to success of this management is determined by the management's willingness to keep the implementation consistently, because the goodwill of the management is usually tested by the members before the management's attitude and behavior accepted as the new habits of the members.

The findings reveal that the work spirit developed in the company environment is still transactional, so that the intrapreneurial spirit need to be paid attention by the management, because in long term, this transactional-based work spirit will impede the company capabilities to develop and adapt with the external environment. Transactional atmosphere will make the company mechanistic increasingly. Management need to develop reward system which reduces members' transactional, like the application of bonus system that gives appreciation to the innovation and renewal ideas, the involvement in social responsibility implementation, and the improvement of teamwork quality.

The management's willingness for the utilization of the renewal ideas sincerely comes from this effort which will determine the usefulness of this suggestion. If it is actualized, the work spirit may develop into more transformational with positive impact on the intrapreneurial spirit. Obedience should be associated all this time as an actualized condition so that workers do not interfere the renewal and innovation spearheaded by the management. The meaning and understanding in the workers cycle become a readiness for the innovative working needs to be developed constantly in the regulation and applicable ethics. Here, it needs to be developed the definition of rules of obedience that does not go against the innovation and renewal.

REFERENCES

Beer, S. 1985. *Diagnosing System for Organisations*. Chichester: Wiley.

Cameron, K.S., Bright, D. & Caza, A. 2004a. Exploring the relationships between organizational virtuousness and performance. *American Behavioural Scientist* 47(6): 766-790.

Cameron, K.S., Barker, B.A. & Caza, A. 2004b. Ethics and Ethos: Buffering and Amplifying Effect of Ethical Behaviour and Virtuousness. *Journal of Business Ethics* 52(2): 169-178.

Chun, J.S., Shin, Y., Choi, J. N. & Kim, M.S. 2013. How does corporate ethics contribute to firm financial performance? The mediating role of collective organizational commitment and organizational citizenship behaviour. *Journal of Management* 39(4): 853-877.

Collins, J. C. 2001. *Good to Great*. Colorado: Harper Collins Publisher.

Cullen, J.B., Johnson, J.L. & Sakano, T. 2000. Success through commitment and trust: The soft side of strategic alliance management. *Journal of World Business* 35(3): 223-240.

De Geus, A. 1997. *The Living Company: Habits for Survival in a Turbulent Business Environment.* Boston Massachusetts: Harvard Business School Press.

Drucker, P. 2014. *Innovation and entrepreneurship.* London: Routledge.

Freeman, R.E., Harrison, J.S. & Wicks, A.C. 2007. *Managing for stakeholders: Survival, reputation, and success.* Yale University Press.

Freeman, R.E., Wicks, A.C. & Parmar, B. 2004. Stakeholder theory and "the corporate objective revisited". *Organization science* 15(3): 364-369.

Hartanto, F.M. 2009. *Paradigma Baru Manajemen Indonesia: Menciptakan Nilai dengan Bertumpu pada Kebajikan dan Potensi Insani.* Bandung: PT. Mizan Media Utama.

Kao, R.W. 1995. *Entrepreneurship: A wealth-creation and value-adding process.* New Jersey: Prentice Hall.

Kuratko, D.F., Morris, M.H. & Covin, J.G. 2011. *Corporate innovation and Entrepreneurship.* Madison, USA: South Western Publishing.

Mele, D. & Canton, C.G. 2014. *Human Foundation of Management: Understanding the Homo Humans.* Spain: IESE-Business School, CUNEF-Universidad Complutense, Palgrave Macmillan.

Moore, G. & Spence, L. 2006. Responsibility and Small Business. *Journal of Business Ethics* 67:219–226.

Peterson, C. & Seligman, M.E.P. 2004. *Character Strengths and Virtues: a Handbook and Classification, an American Psychological Association Publishing.* New York: Oxford University Press.

Porter, L.W., Steers, R.M., Mowday, R.T. & Boulian, P.V. 1974. Organizational commitment, job satisfaction, and turnover among psychiatric technicians. *Journal of applied psychology* 59(5): 603.

Pirson, M.A. & Lawrence, P.R. 2010. Humanism in business–towards a paradigm shift? *Journal of Business Ethics*, 93(4): 553-565.

Rhoades, L., & Eisenberger, R. 2002. Perceived organizational support: a review of the literature. *Journal of applied psychology* 87(4): 698.

Solomon, R.C. 2004. Aristotle, ethics and business organizations. *Organization Studies* 25(6): 1021-1043.

Thompson, A. 2003. *Business feasibility studies: Dimensions of business viability.* Perth: Best Entrepreneur.

Thompson, J.D. 2017. *Organizations in action: Social science bases of administrative theory.* London: Routledge.

177

Information System and Technology

Global Competitiveness: Business Transformation in the
Digital Era – Abdullah, Widiaty & Abdullah (eds)
© 2019 Taylor & Francis Group, London, ISBN 978-0-367-19442-0

Enterprise architecture as a tool to embrace change due to technological development

S. Andhella
Parahyangan Catholic University, Bandung, West Java, Indonesia

ABSTRACT: The recent technological development creates a new challenge for the management team within an organization, as its survival depends on its ability to adapt to the development. Hence, the new approach called enterprise architecture can be used as a tool to meet the challenge. Enterprise architecture aims to create synchronization among operational, information, and communication technology within an organization. This paper aims to illustrate the importance of enterprise architecture as a tool for assisting such change especially for businesses in Indonesia. Moreover, the organization capability to adapt to the change also depends on its personnel.

1 INTRODUCTION

As organizations encounter an increasingly complex, dynamic, and threatening environment, attention must be focused on both handling day-to-day affairs and adapting toward the changing of environmental conditions (Thibodeaux & Favilla 1996). According to Murray & Greenes (2006), the vast changing environmental condition faced by the organizations is mainly due to the technological development. Therefore, organizations should link their strategy, knowledge, and performance in order to gain its competitive advantage and finding the right strategy to deal with technological development (Berman & Marshall 2014). First, this paper will discuss the concept of strategic management, using the new approach of strategic formulation according to Berman & Dalzell-Payne (2018) that could be implemented by organization in order to deal with the recent technological change. This paper believes that enterprise architecture can be used as a tool to deal with the technological changes that are happening in Indonesia.

2 THEORETICAL BACKGROUND

2.1 Strategic formulation – technology

As cited by Smith et al. in Thibodeaux & Favilla (1996), the term strategic management itself is a guidance of a selection of decision and action processes with the core purpose to help organizations increase their performance by the improvement of effectiveness, efficiency, and flexibility. Moreover, the transformative breakthrough of digital computing and other emerging technologies has globally re-shaped the industries. Digital technologies are considered as a tactical advantage as well as the key to transformational strategic opportunities. Technology provides a different economic value propositions, as it can reinvent customer experiences as well as employee capabilities without increasing any cost (Leavy 2005). Therefore, in order to stay ahead, executives need to embrace technology, even though it creates an exceptional challenge for corporate strategists (Carneiro 2005). The new approaches of strategic formulations are:

– Including experienced technologists in the strategic team.
– Applying innovation as the core.
– Implementing an agile strategy.
– Doing decision-making 2.0. (Berman & Dalzell-Payne 2018)

The organization's ability to keep with the technological changes can be achieved through innovation as it captures the imagination power of the individuals (Leavy 2005). One of the factors that would contribute toward a successful change is to have the right mindset and it should not be constrained by passing success or being limited by the company resources. From the perspective of innovation networks, knowledge and technology are considered to be the central object that shapes the relationship; it creates know-how as well as extending the relationship among the actors itself. Furthermore, as innovative networks appeal to be more rational and collaborative, a flexible and adaptive form of organization appears to be a more suitable agent for innovation.

2.2 Enterprise architecture

Enterprise architecture aims to create synchronization among operational, information, and communications technology layers of an organization. It also accommodates the management of organizational change, supporting the foundations of information technology and communications, replacing uncertain systems, planning, promotion or expansion of information and communication systems, as well as creating a common organizational language (Jahani et al. 2010). Enterprise architecture should not only be considered as a project that can be done once, it must be constantly managed within the organization instead. It should also be updated according to the organization's need and aligned with the changes that occur within it. It should be considered as a permanent program that must be adjusted to the organizational process and foundations (Jahani et al. 2010). However, aligning IT investment to business strategy is not enough. Organizations need to be sure that their enterprise architecture is flexible and constantly optimizing their IT delivery efficiency as it also needs to be synchronized with their strategic planning processes (Varghese & Kurien 2004).

3 RESULTS AND DISCUSSION

The above literature review demonstrated that organizations should be able to learn, innovate, and transform in order to overcome the challenges. More importantly, the new approaches in strategic formulation are: including experienced technologist in the strategic team, applying innovation as the core, implementing an agile strategy, and lastly doing the decision-making 2.0. Those strategies can be accomplished through enterprise architecture.

Since enterprise architecture assists employees in managing their knowledge, skills, and expertise, it creates an innovative network that provides a bigger chance for innovation values to take place. As previously mentioned, enterprise architecture can accommodate change as it can also influence the design decision and investment behaviour. Having an effective communication system that would link the strategic formulation with technological tools is highly advantageous. Most importantly, the architecture provides decentralization of the hierarchical structure through local communication channel. This would be highly beneficial especially for organization that employs and understands the significance of its millennial employee. Millennial in general is a technological savvy generation. Therefore, utilizing their insight would be valuable for an organization. Decentralization through local communication channel means that ideas can be distributed in a faster and more efficient way (i.e., replacing memo with email), and since it also gives less personalization feeling into it, it gives employees more confidence in expressing their thought or ideas.

4 CONCLUSION

Despite the significant relationship between IT unit and business unit, some of the personnel within the organization failed to understand its importance. In addition, organization deals with a condition of insufficient skills and expertise from the people in the organization that could result in misinterpretation and mismanagement during the implementation. The lack of knowledge could also have resulted in incorrect technological investment and the inability to effectively use the given technology (Carneiro 2005, Iyamu & Mphahlele 2014). It is crucial for the personnel within the organization to believe that they are capable of performing and sometimes overcoming the implication of the change that occurs. Therefore, future research would be conducted within businesses in Indonesia, especially in the field of human resources management. This paper will contribute toward a better understanding of Indonesian workers on their understanding of technological changes that occur and the effectiveness of enterprise architecture as a tool during such changes. In order to achieve such findings, questionnaires would be distributed toward 150 respondents from a different working environment.

REFERENCES

Berman, S. & Dalzell-Payne, P. 2018. The interaction of strategy and technology in an era of business reinvention. *Strategy and Leadership* 46(1): 10–15.

Berman, S. & Marshall, A. 2014. Reinventing the rules of engagement: Three strategies for winning the information technology race. *Strategy and Leadership* 42(4): 22–32.

Carneiro, A. 2005. How technologies support winning strategies and productivity. *Handbook of Business Strategy* 6(1): 257–263.

Iyamu, T. & Mphahlele, L. 2014. The impact of organisational structure on enterprise architecture deployment. *Journal of Systems and Information Technology* 16(1): 2–19.

Jahani, B., Reza Seyyed Javadein, S. & Abedi Jafari, H. 2010. Measurement of enterprise architecture readiness within organizations. *Business Strategy Series* 11(3): 177–191.

Leavy, B. 2005. Value pioneering - How to discover your own "blue ocean": Interview with W. Chan Kim and Renée Mauborgne. *Strategy and Leadership* 33(6): 13–20.

Murray, A.J. & Greenes, K.A. 2006. In search of the enterprise of the future. *VINE* 36(3): 231-237.

Thibodeaux, M.S. & Favilla, E. 1996. Organizational effectiveness and commitment through strategic management. *Industrial Management and Data Systems* 96 (5): 21–25.

Varghese, J. & Kurien, P. 2004. IT imperatives beyond strategic alignment: enterprise architecture flexibility and IT delivery efficiency. *Handbook of Business Strategy* 5(1): 275–280.

Global Competitiveness: Business Transformation in the Digital Era – Abdullah, Widiaty & Abdullah (eds)
© *2019 Taylor & Francis Group, London, ISBN 978-0-367-19442-0*

Prospects and challenges of virtual reality adoption for destination marketing

N. Muna, A.K. Murti & S. Hidayat
Politeknik APP Jakarta, South Jakarta, Jakarta, Indonesia

K. Soyun
Seoul National University, Seoul, South Korea

A. Yusriana
Universitas Dian Nuswantoro, Semarang, Central Java, Indonesia

ABSTRACT: Virtual Reality (VR) is a cutting-edge technology that has been widely adopted for promotional purposes. In tourism industry, VR is favored due to its interactivity characteristics on delivering experience of tourist destination. The objective of this research is to explore the prospects and challenges of VR adoption for destination marketing. This study is a qualitative research in which the data are collected through observation and in-depth interview with 3 informants, i.e. a virtual reality maker, an advertising agency, and a traveler. The result indicates that VR as destination promotional tools is evolving in number and types of virtual reality formats that have been used, e.g. 3D image, application and 360° video. It offers different visualization and effectiveness in capturing users' attention. However, VR as promotional tools faces several challenges in terms of cost, system development, visualization, and creativity as a package of tourist destination marketing.

1 INTRODUCTION

Virtual Reality (VR) has been extensively discussed and developed for tourism industry over the years (Guttentag 2010, Huang et al. 2013, Martins et al. 2017, Tussyadiah et al. 2018, Williams & Hobson 1995). In Indonesia, VR has gained massive attention since academics and practitioners have recently adopted VR for destination promotional purposes (Hari & Hendrati 2018, Lengkong et al. 2017). The development of information and communication technologies (ICTs) has arrived to the era of interactivity between destination and travelers that possibly substitute tourism experiences (Guttentag 2010, Huang et al. 2013). Moreover, VR has powerful effect on simulating actual situation and tasks that incrementally provide an accurate control of the state experienced by its users (Innocenti 2017). It also provides opportunity for mass virtual visitation to actual tourism destination (Tussyadiah et al. 2018).

There are numerous researches on the adoption of VR for destination marketing focusing their research on visit intention (Aluri 2017, Huang et al. 2013, Tussyadiah et al. 2018) and emotional effects of VR adoption (Debbabi et al. 2013). Although VR proved to have effect on visit intention, there are some discussions on how VR influences virtual affective and conative image during the adoption process (Hyun & O'Keefe 2012).

The idea is dealing with the advanced technology that is able to create imaginary worlds that resemble the real world (Gutiérrez et al. 2008). In addition, VR enables its users to transport to a virtual environment and experience it as if it was real; the evolving features of VR comes with multi-sensory virtual system where several senses such as visual (sight), auditory (hearing), and tactile (haptic) are stimulated at the same time to present "real experience" in virtual environment (Gutiérrez et al. 2008, Martins et al. 2017).

Moreover, VR evolves to some extent that includes olfactory (smelling) and gustatory (tasting). Thus, the users may engage in rich experiences that enhance the level of connectivity and interaction with the users (Barnes et al. 2015). The main goal of VR can be seen from physical and psychological points of view; immersion and presence. VR is a closed computer system consisting of software and hardware that create immersive physical environment which allows interaction between human and computer. Simply, immersion is dealing with the physical configuration that user may interface when using VR application. Meanwhile, presence is related to the psychological aspects of the users' state of consciousness. It can refer to "telepresence" to describe the feeling of being in virtual environment (Gutiérrez et al. 2008, Hyun & O'Keefe 2012, Muhanna 2015).

The advancement of VR has incrementally changed the way destination marketing practices nowadays; people adopt it for several reasons such as assessing real-life brand value (Barnes et al. 2015), enhancing virtual brand image (Hyun & O'Keefe 2012), and proposing experiential marketing strategies (Martins et al. 2017). Meanwhile, the adoption of VR for destination marketing is related to promote place-based marketing that enables travelers to experience the virtual view of the scenery and feelings as they were already at the tourist destination. This paper provides an insight of the future adoption of VR and its gaps for promotional tools of destination marketing in Indonesia. The use of VR for promotional purposes has entered its early stage of Indonesia tourism destination; besides its hypes in providing informative and entertaining new media for promotion tools, VR may lack in several areas such as the affective and conative effect on its adoption.

2 METHODS

The objectives of this research is to explore prospects and challenges of VR for destination marketing. Qualitative approach using in-depth interview and experiment was administered to investigate the current trend and deficiency of VR adoption for destination marketing in Indonesia. In-depth interview involved intensive individual interview with a small number of respondents to explore their perspectives on a certain idea or situation. It was used to obtain detailed information about a person's thought and behaviors regarding new issues in-depth. This technique covered the "how" and "why".

In doing so, several qualified informants were selected according to their expertise and qualification related to the topic. The informants were Virtual Reality maker (Glugu Creative), Visual Design Creative (Digini.co), and a traveler. Glugu Creative was established by communication visual design academicians and practitioners in Semarang, Central Java. They have been making VR application partnering with several private and public stakeholders. Meanwhile, Digini.co provides visual design including VR content specialized in advertising purposes. Meanwhile, the traveler (Yuki) is Paper-Backer founder, and travel blogger based in Semarang. The traveler was selected to gain insight on the users' perspective towards the VR technology adoption. The interview was 45–90 minutes covering some questions related to introduction of VR, characteristics, benefits, VR creation process, the powerful effect of VR, adoption of VR especially in destination marketing, prospect of VR for future development and adoption, current situation of VR adoption in Indonesia, prospect of VR for marketing tools, and challenging things of VR adoption in Indonesia.

Experiment was continued by in-depth interview with informant for the traveler. VR video promotion is shown to the informant and the informant was interviewed for about 40–60 minutes to give the details of feelings and thought after viewing destination promotional VR video. The data will be transcribed and analyzed accordingly relevant to the topics.

3 RESULTS AND DISCUSSION

Based on the observation and in-depth interviews, there are several findings in terms of prospects and challenge of VR adoption for destination marketing in Indonesia. First section discussed about VR adoption in Indonesia for destination marketing, the characteristics of VR for promotional purposes, and challenges in VR adoption for marketing tools.

3.1 Vitual reality adoption in Indonesia

VR is categorized as new and growing multimedia technology in Indonesia. It was first introduced around 2015 which is popularized by gaming application (PokemonGo) and gaming industry like Nintendo. It was widely used in several industries after Oculus Rift got released in the following years. Ministry of Tourism is one of pioneers in Indonesia which adopted VR for destination marketing. Ministry of Tourism exhibited Wonderful Indonesia project in form of VR at World Travel Market (WTM), London.

Based on online observation regarding the adoption of VR in destination marketing, there were several practices of tourism promotion tools using VR in the past 5 years as listed below.

Table 1. Virtual reality for Indonesian destination marketing.

Year	Virtual Reality Technology
2018	Virtual Reality Jogjakarta, Solo, Semarang (Joglosemar) In 360° Video 4K
	Travel Vlogger Documentation (Sentani, Air Terjun Padas Awu, Pantai Watu Leter, Gedung Songo, Museum Keris, Prambanan)
	Travel Agent (Lemukutan)
2017	Minahasa Ethnic Dance Virtual Reality 360° video
	Bali Virtual Tour Guide application
	North Sulawesi introduction Android-based Virtual Reality application
	Sheraton Bali Kuta Experience VR Video
	First Person View (FPV) virtual 3D application for Pantai Lakban Ratatotok
	Wonderful Indonesia Virtual Reality 360° video Riau Island
	Wonderful Indonesia Virtual Reality 360° video Banyuwangi
	Wonderful Indonesia Makassar in 360° video

(Continued)

Table 1. (Cont.)

Year	Virtual Reality Technology
	Virtual 3D Museum BRI
	Virtual Reality Reef Scene Alor
	Travel Vlogger documentation (Bali, Lombok, Anambas, Raja Ampat, Makassar, Dusun Bambu Bandung, Dunia Fantasi, Taman Begonia, Farmhouse, Flores, Malang)
2016	Wonderful Indonesia Virtual Reality Promotion Video at Air Asia Travel 2016, Eastern Plaza, Tawau, Malaysia
	360° video VR Surabaya City
	Wonderful Indonesia – Jakarta in in 360° video
	Wonderful Indonesia – Bali in in 360° video
2015	Wonderful Indonesia Virtual Reality Promotion Video at World Travel Market (WTM), London
	Interactive Virtual Museum
2014	None

VR was first introduced in 1963 by Sutherland through his Ph.D. dissertation and has evolved tremendously nowadays (Muhanna 2015). In Indonesia, VR has been adopted for tourism promotion in the last 5 years in many forms, i.e. 360° video, 3D, game, and Android-based applications. Each type of VR formats offers different effects and technical production hardware and software. 3D (three-dimensional) VR is described as computer-generated 3D environment that uses stereoscopic 3D displays, both 3D graphics and 3D imaging, that offer spatial and immersive interaction (Guttentag 2010, Huang et al. 2013, Marasco et al. 2018).

Meanwhile, 360° video is a photography technique which portrayed a borderless and seamless photo effect from any angle. It doesn't produce 3D effect, hence with the help of head-mounted display (HMD), 360° VR video takes its users to be in reality as it shows in the video. It mixes virtual and reality at the same dimension and times. Moreover, it allows syncretism between photographic technique techniques and VR. Therefore, 3D image and 360° video could be included as VR if they are incorporated with wearable devices as head-mounted display (HMD) to enforce the visual, immersive, and interactive effects (Marasco et al. 2018, Putra et al. 2018).

3.2 Characteristic of virtual reality

VR is computer representations of the real world; based on in-depth interview with VR maker, design visual designer, and traveler, VR is the next big thing in destination marketing field. It offers several characteristics that perfectly fit for destination promotional tools as follows:

3.2.1 Virtual experiential marketing
"in virtual reality, we can be part of the world and control the environment with our eye movement for example to choose certain option, to turn our head left and right and look around us, the point of virtual reality is bringing ourselves to the virtual world we created" (Glugu)

Based on the interview, interactivity is the key point of VR, experiencing the virtual worlds that resemble the reality, and that gives users the ability to interact with and modify the virtual world (Muhanna 2015). The perception of interactivity increases the telepresence as it provides users with an environment to interact and create a feeling of presence (Hyun & O'Keefe 2012, Williams & Hobson 1995).

The essential part of VR as a promotional tool is the experience that takes us to the real destination. VR is one kind of virtual experiential marketing that offers involvement of five dimensions which are sense, interaction, flow, pleasure, and community. The interactivity between user and computer-stimulated sensory experience leads to mental model of "telepresence" (Chen et al. 2008, Li et al. 2001).

3.2.2 Immersive visualization
VR involves users to be part of the computer-generated environment or virtual environment, as the informant said:

"VR is fully computer-generated reality that we model, we create and we would like user to experience nearly the same as the world present it …..I said nearly because we need to re-create…. make a modelling of the reality to be virtual…so, precision is important" (Glugu)

In addition, informant for traveler shows positive feedback after simple experiment using VR devices (VR Box) in viewing Wonderful Indonesia 360° video in Bali. The video duration is 3.09 minutes, mostly showing the life in Bali. He said:

"Woooww,,,, I'm mesmerized!!!! I can see everything around me,,,,, the road, the people, the car, the food,,,,,,, I feel like I am in Bali,,, the girl beside me is so real" - Yuki

VR video exhibits vividness to its users since it offers visualization components such as 3D image, visual acuity (resolution), and a look around capability. The immersion is created through high-quality visualization (Williams & Hobson 1995). Regarding VR formats mentioned above, the greater the quality, the more realistic the experience.

3.2.3 Attention and recall
"………………….we enjoy VR for ourselves, like for example video 360°, VR pull us to the video and take us to certain location in part of the world, the video talk itself, especially advertising video that has been made seriously to persuade people, with VR, the video get fully attention from user and not only that, people are involved in the video"(Digini.co)

VR is the most appropriate display when trying to evoke physiological response. Moreover, VR creates "novelty effect" as the users valuing the uniqueness of the experience more than their own environment (Higuera-Trujillo et al. 2017).

The effectiveness of VR as a promotional tool can be measured from users' attention and recall regarding the video, during 3.09 minutes of experiment, Yuki was very attentive to watch the video from the beginning to the end. At the end of experiment, he could retell the story line of the video and mention the details about the video as he said follows:

"…….I can see the beach, two foreigners boy and girl, a pool, rice field as I was in a car, the dancer, clear sky…although it's slow for me but it's relaxing."

Since VR is enjoyed by putting VR device close to our eyes, users extensively pay full attention to the video. More importantly, VR potentially captures user's attention which leads to promotional effectiveness; users' visual attention can be affected by the viewing task and the amount of time allowed for viewing (Li et al. 2016).

3.3 Prospect of VR for destination marketing

In tourism, experience is the currency for the business. The main reason tourists make times and itinerary if they visit tourist destination is because they want to explore and get the experience. However, Indonesia is rich in culture with hidden gems of tourist destinations where tourists need to explore. Therefore, VR takes its place as a new marketing tool to get into potential customers and offers customer to experience it at anywhere and anytime.

Based on the observation, the technological improvement and ubiquitousness of VR has reached many tourism stakeholders that have already adopted VR as marketing tools, i.e. travel agent, travel blogger, and government. People are more tech savvy and aggressive in promoting tourist destination.

3.4 Challenges of VR for destination marketing

Although VR undeniably offers fascinating characteristics for marketing tools, however, there are several challenges that need to be addressed

3.4.1 Cost
In advertising, to produce high-quality video that is rich in visual cues and compelling story line basically requires high investment. The technology is available to be used; however, the investment to adopt and use that technology is high.

3.4.2 Competent developer
Although the technology is available, competent VR makers are quite few in number, especially VR in terms of 3D modeling, application, etc. It requires special effects and careful re-modeling the real world to the virtual world.

3.4.3 Visualization and creativity
The most important thing in adopting VR as a promotional tool is the ability of the video to create dramatic effects to the audience instead of the interaction effect. Dramatic effect is related to how powerful the

visualization and how compelling the story lines are offered to the audience to capture their attention.

4 CONCLUSION

VR is the next big thing as marketing tools for promoting tourism industry in Indonesia. VR has powerful impact on physical and psychological effects on how users sense the world. In Indonesia, VR has countered several interfaces in presenting tourist destination. However, the cost of VR production is high because it requires powerful visualization and compelling story lines to capture user's attention. Besides, the competent developers who understand the system development and creation are considered low in Indonesia. The need to collaborate between visual designer and program designer is essential.

REFERENCES

Aluri, A. 2017. Mobile augmented reality (MAR) game as a travel guide: insights from Pokémon GO. *Journal of Hospitality and Tourism Technology* 8(1): 55-72.
Barnes, S.J., Mattsson, J. & Hartley, N. 2015. Assessing the value of real-life brands in Virtual Worlds. *Technological Forecasting and Social Change* 92: 12-24.
Chen, J., Ching, R.K.H., Luo, M.M. & Liu, C.-C. 2008. Virtual Experiential Marketing on Online Customer Intentions and Loyalty. *Hawaii International Conference on System Sciences, Proceedings of the 41st Annual* (pp. 271-271). IEEE.
Debbabi, S., Baile, S., des Garets, V. & Roehrich, G. 2013. The impact of telepresence in an online ad on forming attitudes towards the product: The relevance of the traditional experiential approach. *Recherche et Applications en Marketing (English Edition)* 28(2): 3-24.
Gutiérrez, M.A., Vexo, F. & Thlmann, D. 2008. *Stepping into Virtual Reality*. Berlin, Germany: Springer.
Guttentag, D.A. 2010. Virtual reality: Applications and implications for tourism. *Tourism Management* 31(5): 637-651.
Hari, F. & Hendrati, O.D. 2018. Pemanfaatan Augmented Reality untuk Pengenalan Landmark Pariwisata Kota Surakarta. *Jurnal TEKNOINFO* 12(1): 7-10.
Higuera-Trujillo, J. L., Lopez-Tarruella Maldonado, J. & Llinares Millan, C. 2017. Psychological and physiological human responses to simulated and real environments: A comparison between Photographs, 360 degrees Panoramas, and Virtual Reality. *Appl Ergon* 65: 398-409.
Huang, Y.-C., Backman, S.J., Backman, K.F. & Moore, D. 2013. Exploring user acceptance of 3D virtual worlds in travel and tourism marketing. *Tourism Management* 36: 490-501.
Hyun, M.Y. & O'Keefe, R.M. 2012. Virtual destination image: Testing a telepresence model. *Journal of Business Research* 65(1): 29-35.
Innocenti, A. 2017. Virtual reality experiments in economics. *Journal of Behavioral and Experimental Economics* 69: 71-77.
Lengkong, O., Kusen, V. & Dauhan, C. B. 2017. Perancangan Aplikasi Virtual Reality Pengenalan Tempat Wisata di Sulawesi Utara Berbasis Android. *E-Proceedings KNS&I STIKOM Bali* (pp. 575-580), *10 Agustus 2017*. Bali: STIKOM Bali.

Li, H., Daugherty, T. & Biocca, F. 2001. Characteristics of Virtual Experience in Electronic Commerce: A Protocol Analysis. *Journal of Interactive Marketing* 15(3): 13.

Li, Q., Huang, Z.J. & Christianson, K. 2016. Visual attention toward tourism photographs with text: An eye-tracking study. *Tourism Management* 54: 243-258.

Marasco, A., Buonincontri, P., van Niekerk, M., Orlowski, M. & Okumus, F. 2018. Exploring the role of next-generation virtual technologies in destination marketing. *Journal of Destination Marketing & Management* 9: 138-148.

Martins, J., Gonçalves, R., Branco, F., Barbosa, L., Melo, M. & Bessa, M. 2017. A multisensory virtual experience model for thematic tourism: A Port wine tourism application proposal. *Journal of Destination Marketing & Management* 6(2): 103-109.

Muhanna, M.A. 2015. Virtual reality and the CAVE: Taxonomy, interaction challenges and research directions. *Journal of King Saud University - Computer and Information Sciences* 27(3): 344-361.

Putra, E.Y., Wahyudi, A. & Tumilaar, A. 2018. Virtual Reality 360 Interaktif Wisata Digital Kota Tomohon dengan Tampilan Stereoscopic. *Cogito Smart Journal* 4: 104-112.

Tussyadiah, I.P., Wang, D., Jung, T.H. & Tom Dieck, M.C. 2018. Virtual reality, presence, and attitude change: Empirical evidence from tourism. *Tourism Management* 66: 140-154.

Williams, P. & Hobson, J.S.P. 1995. Virtual reality and tourism: fact or fantasy? *Tourism Management* 16(6): 423-427.

Global Competitiveness: Business Transformation in the
Digital Era – Abdullah, Widiaty & Abdullah (eds)
© 2019 Taylor & Francis Group, London, ISBN 978-0-367-19442-0

Role of enterprise resource planning: A review of practices, trends, theory and opportunities in expanding field of research

P. Permatasari & V. Natasha
Parahyangan Catholic University, West Java, Indonesia

ABSTRACT: Since the inception of Enterprise Resource Planning (ERP) concept in 1990, many companies have started to implement ERP. The popularity of ERP software has steadily increased from $ 28 billion in 2006 to about $ 48 billion in 2011. ERP is expected to integrate all parts of the company and facilitate the flow of information both from within and outside the company. Manufacturing companies have some problems that occur in the production cycle. To overcome those problems, they decided to implement ERP. ERP is expected to integrate all parts of the company and facilitate the flow of information both from within and outside the company. This paper provides a review of fifty articles dating from 2001 to 2017 from journals related to ERP. This study aims to identify the roles of ERP in production cycle. We specifically illuminate factors influencing the implementation, adoption, the role, and the success of its adoption. It is found that the role of ERP varied across companies. Besides, cost and benefits of ERP implementation become the main consideration for adoption decision. Further research should investigate more deeply about the role of ERP in each activities in each production cycle and should involve more companies as the sample.

1 INTRODUCTION

The information technology has been developing rapidly in recent decades. The development of technology causes the competition more rigorous. This development causes changes in the company's accounting information system. Information is the output of an information system. Information must be useful and meaningful. The quality of information according to Romney & Steinbart (2015) includes relevant, reliable, complete, timely, understandable, verifiable, and accessible.

The latest accounting information system model continues to be found to overcome the weaknesses that exist in the previous accounting information system. The accounting information system model continues to evolve from the manual process model, flat file model, database model, REA model, to ERP (Hall 2011).

Since the inception of the ERP concept in 1990, many companies have begun to start implementing ERP. According to Hwang & Min (2013), the popularity of ERP continues to increase as evidenced by the increase of ERP software sales from $ 28 billion in 2006 to about $ 48 billion in 2011. More than 50% of ERP users are companies that are in the manufacturing industry.

Manufacturing companies are companies that process raw materials into intermediate goods or finished goods. Therefore, the production cycle become very important cycle for companies in the manufacturing industry. The production cycle is a set of business activities and information-processing operations related to the manufacture of a product. The activities that

exist within the production cycle involve many departments. Activities in the production cycle include product designing, planning and scheduling, product operation and cost accounting. In order for the production cycle to run properly, the information flowing in each activity must be qualified.

The problems that occur within the production cycle cause enormous losses to the company. Problems that occur are often due to the low quality of information relating to production. According to Xu et al. (2002), ERP is implemented to minimize these problems; however, the implementation of ERP is not easy (Booth et al. 2000). Companies need to adapt to ERP software. If ERP is successfully implemented it can integrate all the business functions that exist within the company. ERP facilitates the flow of information both within and outside the company and improves the quality of information required in the production cycle. Therefore, the research questions on this study are:

– What is the figure of production cycle in a – non-ERP manufacturing company?
– What factors affect the successful implementation of ERP?
– What is the role of ERP in company's production cycle?

2 RESEARCH METHOD

This study use descriptive analytic method. This method allows researchers to: understand the characteristics of a group in a situation, thinking systematically about aspects in a situation, providing ideas about future research, and making a decision.

In this study, we used the secondary data. The data were obtained from the literatures related to the topic. The Literatures were studied in form of journals, articles, books, and other sources from Indonesia and other countries published in last sixteen years. As many as fifty journals were used as the sources in this literature study.

The data collection technique in this study is literature study. The data was analysed by using content analysis. Online literature searches were conducted from the database Proquest, Emerald, Wiley, Springer, Ebsco, Sinta with the following criteria: (1) the year of publication of the journal was limited from 2001 to 2017, (2) the keywords used in the journal search were: "enterprise resource planning" "ERP" "production" "manufacturing", (3) abstracts in journals have conformity with the topic to be studied.

3 RESULTS AND DISCUSSION

3.1 *Production cycle in non – ERP companies*

The discussion in this section will be separated by the stages/activities of the manufacturing cycle.

3.1.1 *Product design*
According to Romney & Steinbart (2015), the purpose of product design activities is to produce products that meet customer needs in terms of quality, durability, and function while minimizing production costs. The following section will discuss in detail about the problems happened in this stage.

– Improper Communication between Sales and Production Department: According to Vries & Bonstra (2012), in creating a product design, production department (especially design sections) needs to know and respond to customer's needs in a timely manner in order to design products that meet customer needs at the right time. During this production department has difficulty to know the needs of customers in a timely manner. Sales departments and production departments work independently and generate a silo effect. According to Hsu & Chen (2004), it was found that sales department often did not inform well about customer order taste to production department. Therefore it ultimately led to design mistakes.
– Mistakes in Bill of Material (BOM) Preparation: According to Vries & Boonstra (2012), before a company implements ERP, there is often some mistakes in making BOM. This can be due to poor communication with sales department. The sales department only delivers the specifications as customers want to production department

orally. Because of that, the production department sometimes does not understand the specifications described by the sales department, as a result, the production department misinterprets in determining number and type of components to be used.

3.1.2 *Planning and scheduling*
According to Romney & Steinbart (2015), mistakes in determining the amount of production will cause error in deciding amount of raw materials purchased. Based on some previous studies, there are several causes of mistakes in determination of the amount of production i.e.:

– Error in Sales Forecast: According to Relich et al. (2014), prior to ERP implementation, there was significant difference between actual demand and company's inventory. It is due to wrong estimation in demand forecasting. Too much production and store inventory makes losses because of high cost of storage. Excessive storage costs includes opportunity cost in cost of keeping inventories and other storage-related costs such as warehouse rental fees, insurance fees, and costs incurred due to obsolete inventory. The same finding was also expressed by Hsu and Chen. According to Hsu & Chen (2004), company had difficulties in making accurate sales forecast because the data was too much and spread in several different departments.
– Inaccurate Inventory Data: Kennerley & Neely (2001) found that many companies did not have clear and accurate information relating to their inventories. Inventories spread across several departments within the company. When each department has their owned inventory records they often found some differences in the records because lack of data integration.
– Lack of raw materials: Razi & Tarn (2003) suggested that companies should not have lack of raw materials to keep their operation well. According to Kennerley & Neely (2001), when raw materials in one department run out then the production department staff need to replace their raw materials from other production departments or warehouses. If the raw materials in are not available, then purchasing department need to order them from suppliers and further the suppliers need some more time to deliver the orders. All of these steps could cause late production activities.

3.1.3 *Product operation*
There would be some problems that occur during the production activities, i.e.:

– Production Time Delay: According to Portougal (2005), prior to implementing ERP, production scheduling is only known by production managers. Therefore, it could result in delay in the production process. Otis & Hampson (2017) also found that poor production scheduling will result in the production process runs slowly and costly.

- Improper inventory control: Kennerley & Neely (2001) found that before implementing ERP, companies did not have clear and accurate information about inventory. Therefore, it could result in some potential fraud related to the inventory.

3.1.4 *Cost accounting*

The following section will discuss more about the problems that occur related to cost accounting.

- Low Quality Data: Data is the input of an information system. When the data is not qualified then the resulting information is also not qualified. Xu et al. (2002) identified some data quality problems faced by companies, i.e. the accuracy of data: data is not objective, incomplete data, data that is not timely, too much data, too little data, and the same data are input by several different departments. According to Haug & Pedersen (2009) the same data but inputted by different departments will cause the data in the company duplicated and inappropriate. Some data can be easily manipulated by employees. Kennerley & Neely (2001)'s study found that taking data from different departments requires a lot of time and cost.

- Inaccuracy calculation of production cost: According to Muhtadi (2015), before implementing ERP, each department has its own format to record production cost data. It took a long time to complete the production cost calculation before it could be combined into the same format. Another problem is that personnel in one department often forget to include cost components in the calculation. Employees can easily manipulate those production cost data.

- Incorrect product mix decision: Error in determining product mix can be caused by inaccurate calculation of production cost or inaccurate actual customer demand data.

3.2 *Factors affecting the successful implementation of ERP system*

According to Verville & Hallingten (2003), ERP implementation process in a company is not easy since people must adapt to ERP software. Dezdar & Ainin (2011) found that the success level of ERP implementation depends on the viewer's perspective. In this study, we will analyse eight main factors that affect the successful ERP implementation within a company.

- Top management support: According to Al-Mudimigh et al. (2001), top management support is the desire of top management to provide resources and support to achieve successful ERP implementation. Seng Woo (2007) found that top management is important to develop vision and policy

direction, to help employees find their passion and energy to run the business and implement ERP. Top management engagement becomes essential to generate adequate resources, make decisions quickly and effectively, resolve immediate conflicts, bring all personnel to agree on thought, build collaboration in different groups within the company.

- Project Management: According to Al-Mudimigh et al. (2001), ERP implementation needs to be carefully regulated and monitored. Effective project management is needed to control the implementation process, avoid excessive budget usage, and ensure that the project is completed on time.

- Change Management: Companies should manage the cultural and structural changes that occur as a result of implementing ERP. Company's commitment to dealing with change is needed to face the problems of implementing ERP (Al-Mudimigh et. al, 2001).

- Education and Training: Al Mashari et al. (2003) found that often investing millions of dollars in ERP fails because the company does not apply a good training system. The challenge faced today is to determine the best training method for end users. ERP training should be tailored to the needs of the users.

- Teamwork and composition: According to Seng woo (2007), having the right composition in a team is important but difficult to achieve. Each team member must have good technological skills and understand the company's business thoroughly. Besides, the team should consist of a mix of cross-functional, external consultants and internal staff with the best knowledge and skills in the company (Gargeya & Brady, 2005).

- Communication: Communication is an excellent tool for announcing, explaining, preparing people for change. It is also needed to build knowledge and understanding from users about the new system. Communication should be started as soon as possible (Maditinos et al. 2012). Good communication should at least explain the following: an overview of the whole new system, the reason companies choose to implement the new system, changes that will occur with the new system implementation and its plan and how the new system will help simplify the business processes that take place inside the company.

- Consultant Support: Maditinos (2012) found that consultants play an important role because he has knowledge and skills needed to assist the company during ERP implementation process. Consultants need to have a high ability to solve problems faced by the company in order to make good communication with their clients.

- Clear goal and objective: Upadhyay et al. (2011) found that the companies need clear plans and objectives to be able to control time limit. Besides, having vision, mission, and policy or strategy is also very important to achieve successful ERP implementation. The Vision & mission should be detailed to measurable goals, step, and strategies.

3.3 The role of ERP in the company's production cycle

The following section will describe the role of ERP in each activity in the production cycle.

3.3.1 Product design

- Better communication between sales and production department: Hsu & Chen (2004) found that after implementing ERP, sales/marketing and production department can share information and knowledge. Bharadwaj et al. (2007) also found that after ERP implementation the relationship between marketing and manufacturing departments were better. Marketing/sales team could input customer order data directly into the system and at the same time the design team section could immediately create a product design that matches with the customer's order. Besides, bill of material and the operation list could be inputted into the system. If there is any mistake in product design, the source of errors could be detected to avoid blaming among departments.
- Accuracy of Bill of Material: Lee et al. (2011) found after implementing ERP, company has only one bill of material (BOM) for the same product. The engineering department of the production department must input BOM into ERP software. When production department gets information about product modifications to match with customer desires, the BOM in ERP will be modified to match with the customer order specifications.

3.3.2 Planning and scheduling

According to Romney and Steinbart (2015: 447), there are two types of methods used for production planning. MRP-II is a method of producing products based on customer demand expectations. Lean manufacturing is a method of producing products based on customer demand. The role of ERP in this activity are:

- Better production planning: According to Portougal (2005), after implementing ERP, managers can easily check production plan made by production staff. The plan is also informed to the various departments involved and the production manager will review and approve the plan. Thus, this step can minimize the risk of mistakes in production plan and the risk of error in choosing products to be produced.
- Better sales forecasts: Razi and Tarn (2003) found that ERP facilities enable companies to make accurate sales forecasts by analysing past sales patterns. Portougal (2005) also mention that

ERP assists companies by estimate the number of stocks to be sold based on demand history analysis.

- Better actual sales information: Powell (2013) research found that after implementing ERP, company has better information on customer orders since the orders are directly inputted into the system
- Accurate and transparent information about inventory: According to Bharadwaj et al. (2007), after company implements ERP, they has transparent data on inventory. Kennerley & Neely (2001) also found that company could have better production plan after ERP implementation. Besides, company could have more detail information about inventory (including the age and time of inventory expiration).
- Better raw material supply management: According to Hwang & Min (2013), supply chain is very important in to assure the smooth production process in companies that apply lean manufacturing. The ERP implementation will integrate companies and their suppliers and improve coordination between them.

3.3.3 Product operation

- Efficient use of equipment and labour: Otis & Hampson (2017) found that after implementing ERP, company has better production scheduling. This better production scheduling can improve the efficiency of equipment usage, reduce change over time and further it decrease the amount of labour (Otis & Hampson 2017, Kakouris & Polychronopoulos 2005).
- Faster production time: After implementing ERP in the company, production time will be faster since production department gets up to date, accurate and timely information about problems that occur during production such as about raw materials that will run out (Hsu & Chen 2004).
- Better Inventory Control: According to Kennerley & Neely (2001), the role of ERP in production activities is the presentation of clear and accurate information about inventory including the price and amount of available inventory. Company can control the inventory better. It can minimize the company risk because of inventory loss. This can also minimize the risk of fraud associated with inventory. Besides, after a company implemented ERP, they can find out information about inventory turnover within the company and it will be used b to determine various policies related to inventory (Muscatello et al. 2003).

3.3.4 Cost accounting

- Improve data and information quality: According to Haug & Pedersen (2009), after the company implemented ERP, same data will be inputted only once to the system therefore it could increase the level of data accuracy. After implementing ERP, company also has complete production data. Besides, the retrieval of information from different departments becomes easier and quicker after the company implements ERP (Verville & Hellingten 2003).

- Increase the accuracy of Cost of Goods Manufactured calculation: Muhtadi (2015) found that cost of production calculation process is easier after implementing ERP since each department could input the cost data into the system ERP directly. Besides, the format used in each department is the same. All of these facilitate the production cost data consolidation process.
- Improve the quality of product mix decision: Lea (2007) focus to examine about product mix decision issues related with the ERP implementation. To decide on product mix, companies need data about production cost, production report, and demand forecast data. The data comes from various departments. With the ERP implementation, inter department can communicate easily through one database. Data will be available in a timely manner in an understandable format. Information is updated as soon as changes and fluctuations occur. Company could get up to date information about actual sales data directly from its customers. This information is useful for decision making process and further the decisions will be more qualified because they do not use outdated information.

4 CONCLUSIONS

The conclusions that can be drawn from results of the literature review of the role of ERP are:

- The production cycle consists of four main activities. Prior to implementing ERP, companies implemented a standalone information system. Some of the problems related with the product design are poor communication between sales department and production department and Mistakes in Bill of Material Preparation. In planning and scheduling stage, the problems includes error in sales forecast, inaccurate of inventory data and lack of raw materials. Problems related to product operation are delay in production time and lack of inventory control. Problems related to cost accounting include the low quality of data, inaccurate of production cost information, and wrong product mix decision.
- The success in ERP implementation depends on some factors i.e.: (1) top management support; (2) project management; (3) change management; (4) education and training; (5) teamwork and composition; (6) communication; (7) consultant support; (8) clear goal and objective.

- The roles of ERP can vary among company. Most of companies in this study got considerable benefits from implementing ERP. Benefits related to planning and scheduling are having better production planning, better sales forecasts (for companies that implement MRP), more accurate actual sales and inventory information (for companies implementing lean manufacturing), and easier raw material demand. Benefits related to product operation are efficient use of equipment and labour, faster production time, better inventory control. Benefits related to cost accounting include improving the quality of data and information, increasing the accuracy of cost of production, and increasing quality of product mix decision.

REFERENCES

Al-Mashari, M., Al-Mudimigh, A. & Zairi, M. 2003. Enterprise Resource Planning: A Taxonomy of Critical Factors. *European Journal of Operational Research* 146(2): 352–364.

Al-Mudimigh, A., Zairi, M. & Al-Mashari, M. 2001. ERP Software Implementation: An Integrative Framework. *European Journal of Information Systems* 10(4): 216–226.

Bharadwaj, S., Bharadwaj, A. & Bendoly, E. 2007. The Performance Effects of Complementarities Between Information Systems, Marketing, Manufacturing, and Supply Chain Processes. *Information Systems Research* 18(4): 437–453.

Booth, P., Matolcsy, Z., & Wieder, B. (2000). The impacts of enterprise resource planning systems on accounting practice–the Australian experience. *Australian Accounting Review* 10(22): 4-18.

Dezdar, S. & Ainin, S. 2011. The influence of organizational factors on successful ERP implementation. *Management Decision Journal* 49(6): 911-926.

Gargeya, V.B. & Brady, C. 2005. Success and Failure Factors of Adopting SAP in ERP System Implementation. *Business Process Management Journal* 11(5): 501-516.

Hall, J.A. 2011. *Accounting Information Systems*. United States: South-Western.

Haug, A., & Pedersen, A. 2009. A Classification Model of ERP System Data Quality. *Industrial Management & Data Systems* 109(8): 1053-1068.

Hsu, L.-L. & Chen, M. 2004. Impacts of ERP Systems on the Integrated-Interaction Performance of Manufacturing and Marketing. *Industrial Management & Data Systems* 104(1): 42-55.

Hwang, W. & Min, H. 2013. Assessing the impact of ERP on supplier performance. *Industrial Management & Data Systems* 113(7): 1025-1047.

Kakouris, A. & Polychronopoulos, G. 2005. Enterprise Resource Planning (ERP) System: An Effective Tool for Production Management. *Management Research News* 28(6): 66-78.

Kennerley, M. & Neely, A. 2001. Enterprise Resource Planning: Analysing the Impact. *Integrated Manufacturing Systems* 12(2): 103-113.

Lea, B.-R. 2007. Management accounting in ERP integrated MRP and TOC environments. *Industrial Management & Data Systems* 107(8): 1188-1211.

Lee, C., Hwan, I. & Leem, C. 2011. PDM and ERP Integration Methodology Using Digital Manufacturing to Support Global Manufacturing. *International Journal Advance Manufacturing Technology* 53(1-4): 399–409.

Maditinos, D., Chatzoudes, D. & Tsairidis, C. 2012. Factors Affecting ERP System Implementation Effectiveness. *Journal of Enterprise Information Management* 25(1): 60-78.

Muhtadi, M. 2015. Analisis Penerapan SAP (System Apllication Product) Terhadap Sistem Informasi Biaya Produksi Untuk Meningkatkan Keakuratan Perhitungan Biaya Produksi Perusahaan Manufaktur (Studi Kasus Pada PT SPINDO). *EQUITY* 1(2): 25-32.

Muscatello, J.R., Small, M. & Chen, I. 2003. Implementing Enterprise Resource Planning (ERP) Systems in Small and Midsize Manufacturing Firms. *International Journal of Operations & Production Management* 23(8): 850-871.

Otis, P.T. & Hampson, D. 2017. Improve Production Scheduling to Increase Energy Efficiency. *Chemical Engineering Progress Journal* 103(3): 45.

Portougal, V. 2005. ERP Implementation for Production Planning at EA Cakes Ltd. *Journal of Cases on Information Technology* 7(3): 98-109.

Powell, D. 2013. ERP Systems in Lean Production: New Insights from a Review of Lean and ERP Literature. *International Journal of Operations & Production Managemen* 33(11/12): 1490-1510.

Razi, M.A., & Tarn, J. 2003. An Applied Model for Improving Inventory Management in ERP Systems. *Logistics Information Management* 16(2): 114-124.

Relich, M., Witkowski, K., Saniuk, S. & Sujanova, J. 2014. Material Demand Forecasting: an ERP System Perspective. *Applied Mechanics and Materials Journal* (527): 311-314.

Romney, M.B. & Steinbart, P.J. 2015. *Accounting Information Systems*. England: Pearson Education Limited.

Upadhyay, P., Jahanyan, S. & Dan, P. 2011. Factors Influencing ERP Implementation in Indian Manufacturing Organisations. *Journal of Enterprise Information Management* 24(2): 130-145.

Verville, J. & Halingten, A. 2003. Analysis of the Decision Process for Selecting ERP Software: The Case of Keller Manufacturing. *Integrated Manufacturing Systems* 14 (5): 423-432.

Vries, J.D. & Boonstra, A. 2012. The Influence of ERP implementation on the Division of Power at the Production-Sales Interface. *International Journal of Operations & Production Management* 32(10): 1178-1198.

Seng Woo, H. 2007. Critical success factors for implementing ERP: the case of a Chinese electronics manufacturer. *Journal of manufacturing technology management* 18 (4): 431-442.

Xu, H., Nord, J., Brown, N. & Nord, D. 2002. Data Quality Issues in Implementing an ERP. *Industrial Management & Data Systems* 102(1): 47-58.

193

Global Competitiveness: Business Transformation in the
Digital Era – Abdullah, Widiaty & Abdullah (eds)
© 2019 Taylor & Francis Group, London, ISBN 978-0-367-19442-0

An android supply chain application system for automation order processing

M.T. Siregar & Z.P. Puar
Polytechnic APP Jakarta, Ministry of Industry, Jakarta, Indonesia

P. Leonard
Polytechnic STMI Jakarta, Ministry of Industry, Jakarta, Indonesia

ABSTRACT: The objectives of this research is to add value function to the application (software) which has been previously developed registered with copyright number HKI 2-01-000007457 in 2016. The reason that this became the topic of this research is because nowadays, most industries want to utilize information systems for operating their business activities through easy-to-use application, and if possible connected to the smart phone. This research adopted the System Development Life Cycle (SDLC) method because it is necessary for developing this new application based on previous application which is web-based. The benefit of this application is that the application system has been developed into an android-based system, which is easier, simpler, and can be connected to the android electronic devices such as smart TV and smartphone. Therefore, companies can utilize this application for monitoring their daily business operation; the main functions of this application is for automation order processing. A feasibility survey is conducted with the 40 experienced respondents, in three categories of industries. The method for analysis was AHP (Analytical Hierarchy Process) method. The result of this survey found almost all industries are suitable to use this application, 30.7% in retail, 39.2% in manufacturing, and 30.1% in restaurant.

1 INTRODUCTION

In the present global industrial era, the availability of stock of goods is one of the important factors for the industry to maintain the quality, quantity, and continuity of its production activities. However, the industry tends to need raw materials in fixed quantities, considering the industry has a strategic potential in the development of the nation's industry. Therefore, the industry must be supported by the procurement of raw materials in terms of time, place, form, quantity, and price. Thus, the availability of raw materials greatly determines the implementation of the production process optimally, so that the production plan can be realized.

In the previous research, an integrated system is an interesting challenge in software development because its development must continue to refer to the consistency of the system, so that existing and operational sub-systems are still functioning properly as they integrate the system before and after the integration (Tam et al. 2017). Integrated system is a set of processes to connect multiple computerized systems and applications (software) both physically and functionally. The integrated system will incorporate sub-system components into one system and ensure the functions of the sub-system as a single system. A human–android interaction experiment shows that the integrated system provides relatively human-like interaction (Chikaraishi et al. 2008).

Based on the problems and opportunities existing for developing industrial supply chain applications, this research has objectives to develop current applications (software) to integrate with friendly operating systems, especially simple android operating system.

2 RESEARCH METHOD

This research is conducted through SDLC (System Development Life Cycle) technique with the application of industrial supply chain information system (No. HKI 2-01-000007457) that was previously developed, which will then be connected to the Android operation systems. The details are in Figure 1. Analysis was made by calculating the acceptance of this application using AHP (Analytical Hierarchy Process) method by using 40 respondents who are direct users of the goods/services ordering system. The research stage is shown in Figure 1 (Jogiyanto & Abdillah 2011).

2.1 Scope definition

In this study, the scope consists of the development of monitoring tools are integrated with industrial supply chain in information system of application.

2.2 Problem analysis

This study created problem-solving analysis that occurs in the industry andwhat causes the planning

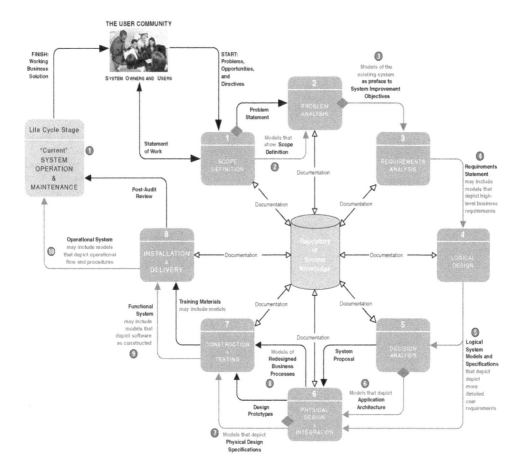

Figure 1. Research stages.

and control of raw materials which are often problematic in overcapacity.

2.3 Requirement analysis

After the problems have been described, then needs analysis was performed in information systems, where the application programming edit is needed to adjust the needs in solving the problem.

2.4 Logical design

The system has been designed and then adjusted to the specification of the equipment that will be connected into the application equipment used in this research which include a smart TV and a smart phone.

2.5 Decision analysis

The result of designing a device specification with an ERP application wasconnected to an integrated system so that data entered into the system will appear in the planned monitoring tool as the output of digital numbers.

2.6 Physical design and integration

The monitoring tools are designed so to connect the application of supply chain information system with display equipment, which are smart TV and smart phone, so that the equipment can work with computer. The display equipment created is a digital system as in Figure 2 (Bin-Abbas & Bakry 2014).

After the programming is appropriate to the system, then it is connected with android studio applications to change the application function into the android smart phone. The android system connected to system circuits resulted in the application of the supply chain information system integrated automatically with the actual conditions on the android smart phone in real time (O'Brien & Marakas 2010).

2.7 Construction testing

Monitoring tools that have been connected with the application are then tested to see the level of accuracy of automation tools to the application. In this test, the result is expected to get 100% accuracy level (see Figure 3).

195

Figure 2. Design application connected to Android system.

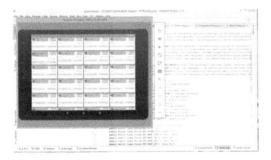

Figure 3. Application testing connected android system.

2.8 *Installation and delivery*

The results of the integrated tools trial will be checked in final phase to avoid errors and damage, and then formed into a more secure package, so that enterprise users can try the tool as a new tool for monitoring raw material needs. The AHP method is used to measure the acceptability of the monitoring tools regarding the suitability of the industry to utilize it. The results of the AHP calculation will then be used to analyze the feasibility of the monitoring system by comparison with conventional methods that have been used in the industry.

3 RESULTS AND DISCUSSION

This application is a repository for business applications that are integrated on Android smartphones to facilitate users when ordering goods from the warehouse. This application also makes it easy for the user, for example front-liner on the tenant-shop to simplify the work with the mobile device so that the front-liner can start placing orders, dynamically updating the goods without having to print new items, or the option to cancel reservations from consumers.

3.1 *Main menu*

Main Menu in this application consists of Dashboard menu, Transactions menu, and Settings menu.

Dashboard menu contains the global information required by the manager such as recapitulation of transaction amount, amount of transaction volume in Rupiah, last order number, and others. The Transaction menu is used in the following sections:

• Waiter that contains the results of the activity of filling the order goods application on the Android app, which starts from:
 a. Determine the number of places tenants to order goods
 b. Ordering food items containing the results of transaction activity of goods order selection

• Cashier containing the order recapitulation result made by Waiter on behalf of a certain tenant before proceeding to Warehousing
• Warehousing contains warehouse layout tables and the following order in each warehouse number including the status of the order is being ordered, is being carried out the delivery process, or has finished the delivery process and continued by Waiter to deliver the order to tenant.

The Setting menu contains the number of tenants as well as the layout of the tenant number sequence and so on, which is possible from various floors. Administrators can set the layout on each floor. See Figure 4.

The Dashboard menu contains the global information required by the manager such as the recapitulation of the transaction amount, the amount of the transaction volume in Rupiah, the last order number, and others if necessary. To display this Dashboard stuff, the system performs the calculation of data based on the order data of goods entered by the waiter and that has been done data recording.

3.2 *Purchase order menu*

Front-liner/Waiter request goods from certain tenants can access this menu. In this process, Transaction menu will do the following steps:

• Waiter shall first record personal data to the extent possible,
• Reservation Code will be set automatically from the system.

Figure 4. Design application connected to Android system.

Figure 5. Purchase order menu.

Figure 6. Order menu.

- The data can still less be filled by the Waiter himself. The filled data are:
  a. Tenant Name
  b. Phone number
  c. E-mail
  d. Reservation Date (auto-set)
  e. Shop layout number code
  f. Maximum length of delivery

- Based on customer's choice, Waiter will click Menu Selection to select the items available (e.g. Food, Fashion, or Accessories). These items can be set up at the beginning of the application. Purchase order menu is given in Figure 5.

3.3 Order menu

After Front-Liner clicks on the Item Options, the details of the item will be accessible by Waiter to serve the request. The following steps shall be taken:

- Each item has been set with the price so that the user can swipe the goods, then the system performs data analysis based on order data items entered by the waiter and record data as well as the number of orders and the amount of Rupiah orders.
- For the process of change, then the old data will be updated with the new data and saved to the existing database on the computer cashier.
- After the verification by clicking the PAY button, then the screen at the cashier will show the payment items along with the details.

Order menu can be seen in Figure 6.

3.4 Cashier menu

The cashier contains the details of the items that have been approved by the customer and have been shipped by the front-liner (Figure 7). In this item, Name of Goods Details, Unit Price per Detail Goods, Order Number (QTY), and Total Price per Goods will be written. It will also display Discount when there is a promo program, VAT tax, and Service Charge, and the total performance to be paid.

Figure 7. Cashier menu.

For payment options, there is Cash and External Credit-Visa. After the payment, the cashier will click Complete Order on the warehousing so that the employee in the warehousing will see the order directly to be done, and can also use the printer as a medium order.

Cashier Menu can also be viewed by recap (list) by clicking the left pop-up menu, so the application program will display the menu as follows (Figure 8):

Figure 8. Recapitulation cashier menu.

3.5 *Warehouse menu*

In this Warehouse Menu, the following steps will be done (Figure 9):

Figure 9. Warehouse menu.

- After receiving the verification from the cashier, the warehousing section will appear with additional order items ordered so that the chef in the warehousing officer will see the order directly to be done.
- The completed order result is inputted into the application system. Then the food items can be immediately transferred to the customer, and if the waiter has delivered the goods to the tenant with a certain number of layouts, then the waiter will click the layout so that the table display on the screen will be DONE (completed).
- Results of transactions that have been done synchronize the process in the online data server that has been provided (Ayat et al. 2011).

4 ANALYZING AND TESTING

For testing the application using the AHP method by conducting a survey on 40 respondents who work as industry players, it is needed to determine the acceptance of applications if the application is applied in the industry (see in Figure 10).

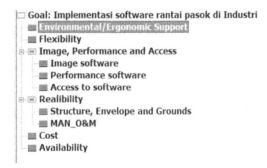

Figure 10. AHP criteria.

Figure 11. Weight attribute industry suitable.

Figure 12. Weight attributes.

Input data is inserted that has a purpose of "Implementation of industrial supply chain software", with 6 attributes; environment, this application can be used without damaging environment; flexibility, this application can be used not only by computer user but multi-users; image performance is the appearance of software; reliability is real time; cost is the price of the application; availability is the easiness to access the application. The attributes are elaborated with three alternative companies: property A (retail industry), property B (manufacturing industry), and property C (restaurant). The result of the test by the AHP method with the survey based on the questionnaire resulted in the following results (Siregar & Puar 2018).

From Figure 11, it is known that various industries are suitable to use this application; 30.7% in the retail industry, 39.2% in the manufacturing industry, and 32.1% in the restaurant. This indicates that the three industries are suitable for using the program applications that have been created with android system integration and display tools (Endrawati & Siregar 2018).

Based on the testing of priority attributes in Figure 12, it is found that the priority things of this application are cost with 25.7% and performance with 24.7%. Therefore, costs and application performance are quite necessary concerns for development of this application in the future (Puar & Siregar 2017).

5 CONCLUSION

The physical form of integrated monitoring tool is an electronic display device with android operating system connected to the smart TV and smart phone. Performance of work system between smart TV and smart phone device can be integrated in real time by using wireless function and FTP (file transfer protocol) function. The results of the survey of acceptance of applications in the industry show that 39.2% of the application is suitable for manufacturing industries. Priority factors required in this program are cost and systems performance. Technology requirement is needed by industries to strengthen their business in the markets. Research studies concerning with technology applied to the industries need to directly solve industry-related problems.

REFERENCES

Ayat, M., Masrom, M. & Sahibuddin, S. 2011. Issues in implementing it governance in small and medium enterprises. *Proceedings of the 2nd International Conference on Intelligent Systems, Modelling and Simulation (ISMS)*, Phnom Penh, Cambodia.

Bin-Abbas, H. & Bakry, S.H. 2014. Assessment of IT governance in organizations: A simple integrated approach. *Computers in Human Behavior* 32: 261-267.

Chikaraishi, T., Minato, T., & Ishiguro, H. 2008. Development of an android system integrated with sensor networks. In *Intelligent Robots and Systems, 2008. IROS 2008. IEEE/RSJ International Conference on* (pp. 326-333). IEEE.

Endrawati, T. & Siregar, M.T. 2018. Analysis of logistic distribution performance of good supply from PT.

Mentari Trans Nusantara distribution centre to branches using Smart PLS 3.0. *In AIP Conference Proceedings* 1941(1): 020007.

Jogiyanto, H.M. & Abdillah, W. 2011. *Sistem Informasi Teknologi Informasi*, Yogyakarta: Andi Publisher.

O'Brien, J.A. & Marakas, G. 2010. *Foundation Concept: Information Systems in Business in Management Information System*. New York: The McGraw-Hill Companies Inc.

Puar, Z.P. & Siregar, M.T. 2017. Rancangan Sistem Elektronik Kanban Untuk Meningkatkan Efektivitas Produksi Just in Time. *Jurnal manajemen industri dan logistic* 1(1): 86-93.

Siregar, M.T. & Puar, Z.M. 2018. Implementasi Lean Distribution Untuk Mengurangi Lead Time Pengiriman Pada Sistem Distribusi Ekspor. *Jurnal Teknologi*, 10(1): 1-8.

Tam, K., Feizollah, A., Anuar, N.B., Salleh, R. & Cavallaro, L. 2017. The evolution of android malware and android analysis techniques. *ACM Computing Surveys (CSUR)* 49(4): 76.

Global Competitiveness: Business Transformation in the
Digital Era – Abdullah, Widiaty & Abdullah (eds)
© 2019 Taylor & Francis Group, London, ISBN 978-0-367-19442-0

Perception analysis on Indonesian university governance disclosure

A. Setiawan, D. Tanumihardja, G. Lusanjaya, M. Sylviana & C. Melinda
Accounting Department, Parahyangan Catholic University, Bandung, Indonesia

ABSTRACT: Corporate accountability depends on information disclosures by the company to its stakeholders. Since each group of stakeholders needs different types of information, it is necessary to identify what type of information each of them needs. In developed countries, university governance is regulated by issuing prevailing standard across the nation. Adequate transparency is needed to actualize stakeholders' involvement and accountability of an organization. The aim of this study is analyzing the perception of stakeholders about Indonesian University Governance Disclosure. In Indonesia, good university governance must cover (1) autonomy of higher education institutions, (2) the management system of higher education institutions, (3) university governance, and (4) public accountability. The data collected through questionnaire was sent to primary stakeholders. The result of this study discovered that: (1) for lecturers in Indonesia, who are required by the regulator to improve their professionalism, HR qualification becomes the main information they want to know; (2) each aspect of information is considered important for the regulator to observe transparency of certain university. Despite considering university's website as the most favorite channel to obtain information about certain university, respondents do not browse further for its operations, financial management, HR qualification, and organizational structures.

KEYWORDS: good university governance, accountability, transparency

1 INTRODUCTION

Indonesia Corruption Watch (ICW) has reported 37 cases of alleged graft in higher education institutions within the last ten years (Yuntho 2016). Alleged graft cases in higher education institutions were not only found in Indonesia, but also in other countries, such as Singapore (Straits Times 2014) and Georgia (Janashia 2004). Even though a university is perceived as the source of knowledge, which produces quality scholars, this institution is not free from the risks of abuse, especially corruption. Both profit organizations and not-for-profit organizations (NFPs) may function properly and be able to achieve their goals if managed correctly. A lot of research on good corporate governance dealing with profit organization have been conducted, whereas only a few dealing with NFPs. This evidence motivates this research to put its focus on NFPs. Besides, NFPs also have significant impacts on the community in general.

This significant impact encourages many governments in developed countries to establish regulations on good governance for NFPs, such as in Canada (Canada Not-for-Profit Corporations Act), Singapore (Code of Governance for Charities), and U.K. (The Good Governance Standards for Public Service). NFPs may take form as organizations in education, health, or other sectors. Meanwhile, in developing countries, there is no regulation on good governance.

This research focuses on education because it is important in educating young generation as the future of the nation. To achieve its goals, a university must ensure to undertake its organizational focus, perform internal operations effectively, manage risks adequately, involve all stakeholders, and demonstrate accountability properly (Office for Public Management, 2004). Therefore, it is necessary to have a good management by implementing university governance.

Principles of Good Governance, including Good University Governance, consists of (1) focusing on the organization's purpose and on outcomes, (2) performing effectively in clearly defined functions and roles, (3) promoting values for the whole organization and demonstrating the values of good governance through behavior, (4) taking informed, transparent decisions and managing risks, (5) developing the capacity and capability of the governing body to be effective, (6) engaging stakeholders and making accountability real (Office for Public Management, 2004; Tamin 2015; Suryani 2015). Based on the sixth principle, adequate transparency is needed to actualize stakeholders' involvement and accountability of an organization.

Stakeholders of a university consist of: (1) lecturers, (2) students, (3) parents, (4) education observers, (5) regulator, and (6) alumni/community. Each group of stakeholders has different interest on university management. The five stakeholders can be categorized as education observers, so education observers are excluded in this research. To meet their expectations, information transparency is important. Transparency of a university is communicated through information disclosures using media acceptable for all parties. In this era of information and communication technology (ICT), a university may use its official website to disclose information.

The benefits of this research are as follows: (1) for the regulator in Indonesia, this research may serve as an input in developing advanced regulation on the management of higher education institutions; (2) for regulators in other countries, this research can be referred in developing regulation based on the case sample in emerging country; (3) for university management, this research may provide some insight to enrich consideration in decision-making regarding information disclosure for public.

2 LITERATURE STUDY AND RESEARCH QUESTIONS

2.1 University governance

In developed countries, university governance is regulated by issuing common standard across the nation. One example is Committee of University Chairs in the U.K., which issues The Higher Education Code of Governance in 2014 to support members of governing bodies identifying the key values and practices of effective governance (Committee of University Chairs, 2014). Meanwhile, in the Netherlands, an evidence-based management approach is developed for creating effective higher educational institutions (Waal & Kerklaan 2015). It is important that all evidence should be disclosed for all the stakeholders. Hence, transparency is required to support the evidence-based management approach. Research in Europe discovered three modes of university governance, namely (1) state-centred model, (2) market-oriented model, and (3) academic self-governance model (Dobbins et al. 2011). Meanwhile, in Japan, university governance emphasizes on the accountability of funding (Yonezawa & Shimmi 2015).

In Latin America, there was a change of external bodies which urged universities to be more concerned about information disclosures undertaken for their stakeholders (Balan 2006), whereas Thailand began to establish national standard dealing with communication and information technology (Subsermsri et al. 2015). However, the similar fact can also be found in developed countries such as Australia (Ali & Green 2007). Meanwhile, in Ghana, a university may choose one of three given models of university governance, i.e. (1) traditional model, (2) business model, and (3) trusteeship model (Tetteh & Ofori 2009).

RQ#1: How does university governance in Indonesia regulated?

2.2 Transparency and disclosure

Disclosure is any form of corporate communication conducted voluntarily, either on website or in other company reports (Bhasin 2010). Corporate accountability depends on information disclosures or publications by the company to its stakeholders. However, there is no general standard on the form, content, and reliability of the disclosures, either established by the regulator or related parties, such as companies who perform the disclosures and stakeholders as the users (Spira & Page 2010). Since each group of stakeholders needs different types of information, it is necessary to identify what type of information each of them needs.

RQ#2: What are types of information needed by each group of stakeholders?

2.3 Relationship between disclosure and satisfaction

Many organizations assume that the users of their disclosures are satisfied, but results show dissatisfaction with this disclosure (Ferchichi & Paturel 2016). To analyze this phenomenon, this research will identify relationship between disclosure and satisfaction. Based on the result of RQ#2, respondents' satisfaction toward media will be measured, connected with information disclosure.

RQ#3: What is the relationship between disclosure and satisfaction?

3 METHODOLOGY

The first data collection was conducted by identifying regulations in other countries and comparing those with regulation in Indonesia. Meanwhile, second data collection was exercised by employing focus group discussion (FGD) to obtain preliminary data used for the questionnaire. Invited stakeholders were to identify preliminary information about information needed by the stakeholders in the FGD. Finally, the third data collection was performed by distributing questionnaires via email. In other words, this research was conducted through several steps as follows: (1) the FGD involving all stakeholders to compose a questionnaire, (2) Preliminary survey by distributing questionnaires in 2 weeks for identifying information needed by lecturers and students as primary stakeholders (while alumni/community are categorized as secondary stakeholders due to their interest of the governance of the university), and (3) Research survey by distributing research questionnaire to all stakeholders.

This research was conducted through three stages: (1) FGD, (2) preliminary survey, and (3) research survey. The first stage is used to answer RQ#2 and confirm RQ#1, whereas the third stage is employed to resolve RQ#3.

4 RESULT AND DISCUSSION

4.1 *Regulation of university governance*

There is no global standard of regulation on good university governance. In developed countries, such as Canada (Jones et al. 2001), a research on the evolution of university governance found out that there are differences in management due to size, as well as socio-culture and political environment of each university. However, they all shared universal principles, namely (1) more transparent governance process, (2) more exceptional faculty and student participation, and (3) more significant role of governing boards and Senates. Meanwhile, in the U.K., there is a shift of focus in university governance and management (Johannesson et al. 2012). Currently, the focus is on quality assurance and accountability. It is related to university funding and government regulation on the mechanism to audit its performance to ensure public accountability.

Thailand, as a developing country, has involved ICT implementation in supporting university governance (Jairak & Praneetpolgrang 2013). Meanwhile, in Indonesia, good university governance must cover (1) autonomy of higher education institutions, (2) the management system of higher education institutions, (3) university governance, and (4) public accountability (Pemerintah Republik Indonesia 2014). Based on the abovementioned explanation, the first research question is resolved. It can be deduced that transparency is a source of information needed by all stakeholders.

4.2 *The need of information of university's stakeholders*

RQ#2 is answered through FGD followed by preliminary survey. FGD aims to obtain preliminary information from variety of stakeholders for their information needs. As a result, a university is expected to disclose transparency on: (1) operations, (2) financial management, (3) HR qualification, and (4) organizational structures. Based on the result of FGD, preliminary survey was conducted on some stakeholders to investigate the extent of information needed, the information channel used, and which stakeholder has the largest interest on information disclosure of a university.

The result of survey from 307 respondents in Indonesia can be observed in Table 1. The profile of the respondents is as follows: 60.5% are female and 39.5% are male; 96.4% are domicile in Java; 53% are students, 6.9% are lecturers, 4.7% are parents, 2.3% are regulators, and 33.9% are alumni/community. In this research, the community and alumni are put in one category because the alumni can become a member of community and has similar interest. To be concluded, HR qualification is the main information needed by lecturers, whereas parents consider financial management is less important than

Table 1a. Information need of stakeholders #1.

Transparency	Lecturers	Students	Parents
Operations	95%	86%	100%
Financial management	90%	85%	87%
HR qualification	100%	85%	100%
Organizational structures	95%	86%	100%

Table 1b. Information need of stakeholders #2.

Transparency	Regulator	Alumni/ Community
Operations	100%	97%
Financial management	100%	97%
HR qualification	100%	97%
Organizational structures	100%	91%

transparency of university operations, HR qualification, and organizational structures. Meanwhile, alumni and community prioritize information transparency on university operations, financial management, and HR qualification rather than information about organizational structures.

Tables 1a and 1b indicate that different experiences and interests of each respondent group resulted in different information needs. For lecturers in Indonesia who are required by regulator to improve their professionalism, HR qualification becomes the primary information they want to know. They concern HR qualification of their university compared to others. Meanwhile, each aspect of information is considered necessary for regulator to observe transparency of certain university. For parents, information about educational operations, which may affect the success of study in the university, must be more important than that of its financial management. As for alumni/community with indirect interaction with university governance, information on organizational structures is less important than transparency of other aspects.

Regarding the channel of information, respondents were asked to choose three primary media as their preferences to obtain information about a university. The result presented in Tables 2a and 2b

Table 2a. Preference of information channels #1.

Channels	Lecturers	Students	Parents
Website	95%	90%	100%
Publication	81%	70%	80%
News	33%	29%	27%
Social Media	24%	33%	20%

Table 2b. Preference of information channels #2.

Channels	Regulator	Alumni/Community
Website	100%	89%
Publication	100%	77%
News	0%	23%
Social Media	100%	30%

demonstrates that website becomes the primary information channel chosen by all stakeholders. Surprisingly, social media as today's favorite of the younger generation is not the first choice. It is assumed that, for formal communication, it is preferred through formal channel, namely website or email. However, the table shows a shift in social media usage for information based on age group. Assumed as the oldest generation among respondent groups, only 20% parents use social media as source of information. The percentage increases to 24% among lecturers and 30% among alumni/community, whereas students as the youngest generation become the largest social media user with 33% among all respondent groups. Therefore, universities should prioritize website in information disclosure practices since it is the first preference of information channel.

4.3 Relationship between disclosure and satisfaction

RQ#3 can be answered by research survey, which only involved 3 respondent groups, namely lecturers, students, and alumni/community as stakeholders of university information disclosure based on preliminary survey conducted before. The questionnaires were distributed to respondents consisting of 49 lecturers from 13 universities in Indonesia, 512 students from 56 universities in Indonesia, and 164 members of alumni/community.

Table 3 displays average scoring of importance level of information. The scoring system ranges from 1 as the minimum score, which means the information is very unimportant, to 5 as the maximum score, which means the information is very important. Compared to other respondent groups,

lecturers gave the highest scores for transparency in operations, financial management, HR qualification, and organizational structures. On the contrary, students gave the lowest scores for those areas of transparency. Based on the result, it can be concluded that respondent group having direct interest on university management will give higher scores than those given by respondent group with indirect interest on the subject. Regarding the respondent group of students, despite having direct interest on the subject, it is assumed that they have little concern on university governance and transparency because of their maturity level. Older respondents have more concern on the information while younger ones have been more indifferent about information disclosed by the university.

In identifying factors correlated with website satisfaction, a correlation analysis was conducted. The correlation analysis is conducted to four areas of information disclosed by the university.

Tables 4a and 4b present correlation analysis between website satisfaction and the four areas of transparency, namely operations, financial management, HR qualification, and organizational structures of a university. The result shows that those four areas of transparency have no significant correlation with website satisfaction. Therefore, it can be concluded that despite considering university's website as the most favorite channel to obtain information about the certain university, respondents do not browse further for its operations, financial management, HR qualification, and organizational structures.

Table 3. Average scoring of importance level.

Transparency	Lecturers	Students	Alumni & Community
Operations	4.47	3.94	4.39
Financial management	4.51	4.12	4.49
HR qualification	4.61	4.14	4.57
Organizational structures	4.71	4.22	4.41

Table 4a. Correlation analysis #1.

	Website Satisfaction	Operations
Website satisfaction	1	
Operations	0.0429	1
Financial management	0.0153	0.6441
HR qualification	0.0355	0.591
Organizational structures	0.0852	0.5493

Table 4b. Correlation analysis #2.

	Financial management	HR qualification
Website satisfaction		
Operations		
Financial management	1	
HR qualification	0.5694	1
Organizational structures	0.487	0.6317

5 CONCLUSION

Stakeholders' need of information reflected prevailing regulation in Indonesia, i.e. need of transparency. Therefore, it is recommended that a university disclose information based on priority as follows: (1) operations, (2) HR qualification, (3) organizational structures, and (4) financial. Regarding channel of information, respondents of this research chose university's website as their first preference, followed by university's publication. Furthermore, website satisfaction had no correlation with information transparency. As a recommendation, advance researches can be conducted to examine (1) the extent of university's website in providing information needed by stakeholders, and (2) the relation between different generations and information and communication technology.

REFERENCES

Ali, S. & Green, P. 2007. IT Governance Mechanisms in Public Sector Organisations: An Australian Context. *Journal of Global Information Management* 15(4): 41-63.

Balan, J. 2006. Reforming Higher Education in Latin America. *Latin American Research Review* 41(2): 228-246.

Bhasin, M.L. 2010. Corporate Governance Disclosure Practices: The Portrait of a Developing Country. *International Journal of Business and Management* 5(4): 150-167.

Committee of University Chairs. 2014. *The Higher Education Code of Governance*. London: Committee of University Chairs.

Dobbins, M., Knill, C. & Vogtle, E.M. 2011. An analytical framework for the cross-country comparison of higher education governance. *High Education* 62(5): 665-683.

Ferchichi, J. & Paturel, R. 2016. Supply and Demand of Intellectual Capital Information in the Annual Reports in an Emerging Country: The Tunisian Case. *Journal of Business Studies Quarterly* 8(1): 77-99.

Jairak, K. & Praneetpolgrang, P. 2013. Applying IT Governance Balanced Socrecard and Importance-performance Analysis for Providing IT Governance Strategy in University. *Information Management & Computer Security* 21(4): 228-249.

Janashia, N. 2004. Fighting Corruption in Georgia's Universities. *Academe* 90(5): 43-46.

Johannesson, J., Palona, I., Salazar Guillen, J.F. & Fock, M. 2012. UK, Russia, Kazakhstan and Cyprus governance compared. *Corporate Governance: The international journal of business in society* 12(2): 226-242.

Jones, G.A., Shanahan, T. & Goyan, P. 2001. University Governance in Canadian Higher Education. *Tertiary Education and Management* 7(2): 135-149.

Office for Public Management. 2004. *The Good Governance Standard for Public Services*. London: The Chartered Institute of Public Finance and Accountancy.

Pemerintah Republik Indonesia. 2014. *Penyelenggaraan Pendidikan Tinggi dan Pengelolaan Perguruan Tinggi*. Jakarta: Pemerintah Republik Indonesia.

Spira, L.F. & Page, M. 2010. Regulation by disclosure: the case of internal control. *Journal of Management Governance* 14(4): 409–433.

Straits Times. 2014. *Singapore Courts & Crime*. Retrieved from Straits Times Singapore: http://www.straitstimes.com/singapore/sex-for-grades-case-takes-a-surprising-turn. Accesed on October 25, 2017.

Subsermsri, P., Jairak, K. & Praneetpolgrang, P. 2015. Information technology governance practices based on sufficiency economy philosophy in the Thai university sector. *Information Technology & People* 28(1): 195-223.

Suryani, I. 2015. Good University Governance. *Jurnal Riset Akuntansi* 7(2): 51-71.

Tamin, R.Z. 2015. *Governance Perguruan Tinggi*. Jakarta: Direktorat Kelembagaan dan Kerjasama Ditjen Pendidikan Tinggi.

Tetteh, E.N. & Ofori, D.F. 2009. An exploratory and comparative assessment of the governance arrangements of universities in Ghana. *Corporate Governance* 10(3): 234-250.

Waal, A.D. & Kerklaan, L. 2015. Developing an Evidence-based Management Approach for Creating High-performance Higher Educational Institution. *Academy of Educational Leadership Journal* 19(3): 85-104.

Yonezawa, A. & Shimmi, Y. 2015. Transformation of University Governance through Internationalization: Challenge for Top Universities and Governmanet Policies in Japan, *High Education* 70(2): 173-186.

Yuntho, E. 2016. *Anti Korupsi*. Retrieved from Perguruan Tinggi Antikorupsi: http://www.antikorupsi.org/id/content/perguruan-tinggi-antikorupsi. Accesed on October 21, 2017.

Global Competitiveness: Business Transformation in the
Digital Era – Abdullah, Widiaty & Abdullah (eds)
© 2019 Taylor & Francis Group, London, ISBN 978-0-367-19442-0

Boosting global competitiveness in Indonesia: Is Industry 4.0 the answer?

K. Gupta
Australian National University, Canberra, Australia

I. Vierke, A. Ibrahim, J. Suwandi & A. Selowidodo
Politeknik APP, Jakarta, Indonesia

ABSTRACT: The Fourth Industrial Revolution, or Industry 4.0, is coming. It allows us to further utilize information technology, such as networking and cloud computing, to manufacturing principle. Indonesia responds the wave with the launching of Making Indonesia 4.0. It discloses how Indonesia can utilize Industry 4.0 to boost manufacturing and expand market to a growth-led export level. It claims to help increase GDP growth by 2% from the baseline and improve manufacturing productivity. The plan seems bold especially since Indonesia's technological readiness is lagged behind and its economy is relatively not open. We argue that the plan is not concise enough in explaining how Indonesia can adopt Industry 4.0 to Indonesian manufacturing. Making Indonesia 4.0 needs to have better indicators and specific action for businesses to make sense of the plan.

1 INTRODUCTION

The Fourth Industrial Revolution, which is a combination of information and technology to manufacturing, is big. Germany was the first nation, specifically in 2011, which dubbed the Fourth Industrial Revolution with the term "Industrie 4.0", which shapes their high-technology vision for 2020 (Hermann et al. 2016). Industrie 4.0 would change the way how we live in the future, and boost economic growth in general (Hermann et al. 2016). This concept then was adopted by World Economic Forum, and generalized the idea with the term "Industry 4.0". It is only natural for many countries to join the race to develop such plan for themselves, including Japan, China, United States, and ASEAN countries, Indonesia included (Kearney 2018).

Indonesia joins the train. In the early second quarter of 2018, Indonesia launched its own Industry 4.0. The natural question to emerge is, Will the plan be successful? We review some literatures on the definition of Industry 4.0, and find out what we need Industry 4.0 to succeed. Furthermore, we review Indonesia's presentation about "Making Indonesia 4.0", Indonesian's Industry 4.0. Benchmark from literatures is used to evaluate this plan's success.

This article starts with the concept of Industry 4.0 (in general), including what it means, the challenges, and the opportunities. Second, we briefly describe "Making Indonesia 4.0". Next, we evaluate whether it will be successful, and we analyze further, how the plan affects business and Indonesia in general.

2 WHAT IS INDUSTRY 4.0?

Since Germany first launched Industrie 4.0, many scholars devote their time and effort to research about this field. However, many stakeholders seem to have diverse understanding on what they mean by Industrie 4.0, especially for non-German-speaking people (Lasi et al. 2014). However, Lasi et al. (2014) and Hermann et al. (2016) are able to neatly summarize the term to a general understanding. Our description of Industry 4.0 mainly focuses on their view. For further discussion, we will use Industry 4.0 to avoid confusion with Germany's Industrie 4.0.

Industry 4.0 is characterized by quicker "time to market", personalized products, flexibility, and higher resource efficiency (Lasi et al. 2014). We are seeing a very fast blueprint-to-product time, where design can quickly be marketed to consumers. It also offers personalized products, in a sense that we might no longer see a classification of textile products amid the ability to match the products exactly as the size of a particular consumer. This will, in turn, increase efficiency greatly.

To be called an Industry 4.0 adapter, a factory needs to have four fundamental concepts (Hermann et al. 2016). First, there must exist interconnections among humans and machines. This is the core of cyber-physical system. Second, the factory has to adapt information transparency. This ensures big and contextualized data for a system to learn and to adapt. Third, decision-making needs to be decentralized to a level where even a machine make decisions. Finally, technical assistance is where high-skilled labor comes, which only needed to fix specific issues.

Globally, countries' readiness in adapting Industry 4.0 varies. Martin et al. (2018) developed a metric called Country Readiness Index (CRI). The index mainly consists of two components, namely structure of production and drivers of production. On a two-dimensional Euclidean space, the two components create four quadrants of country archetypes: Leading, High-potential, Legacy, and Nascent. Using this framework, they assess 100 countries on how ready are they in reaping the benefit of Industry 4.0, and divide those countries into four archetypes. Figure 1 shows the graphical position of the countries in the Euclidean space, taken from Martin et al. (2018).

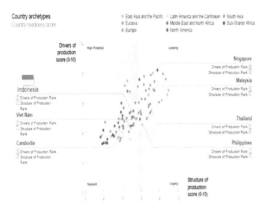

Figure 1. CRI of 100 countries in 4 quadrants.

There are currently only 25 countries, which are ready for Industry 4.0, and are located in the Leader quadrant. Unfortunately, Indonesia is not among them. Indonesia is included in the Nascent archetype, along with Cambodia and Viet Nam (Martin et al. 2018). Indonesia is lagged behind with respect to its neighbors, namely, Philippines and Thailand (Legacy); and Malaysia and Singapore (Leading).

Nascent archetype is the archetype that requires much more catching-up due to many fundamental problems. For Indonesia's case, the problems are its human capital, R&D spending, limited Internet connection, low-quality infrastructure, and its relatively protected economy. The only driver of Indonesia's readiness is its high demand amid high population and positive net-export of manufactured goods.

Table 1. Indonesia's CRI.

Components	Rank	Score
DRIVERS OF PRODUCTION		
Technology & Innovation	61st	4.0
Human Capital	55th	5.0
Global Trade & Investment	61st	5.1
Institutional Framework	69th	4.6
Sustainable Resources	94th	4.1
Demand Environment	15th	6.4
STRUCTURE OF PRODUCTION		
Complexity	73rd	4.3
Scale	6th	7.1

Table 1 summarizes Indonesia's CRI taken from Martin et al. (2018). Industry 4.0 is not without its problem. According to Marr (2016), some problems related to technologies are data security, and reliable communication between cyber and physical. Maintaining the integrity of a system can also be a hard work, especially in a decentralized, near-fully automated system with smaller human supervision. Industry 4.0 would also raise the bar for skill-intensive producer and labor. Progressive countermeasure towards less tech-savvy producers (such as Small and Medium Enterprises) and low skilled labor should not be taken lightly.

3 MAKING INDONESIA 4.0

Indonesia makes sure it is ready for the future and has its own Industry 4.0 plan. On early April 2018, Indonesia held an event called "Indonesia Industrial Summit 2018", which is the first time Indonesian government introduces the concept called Making Indonesia 4.0. The event was opened by the President and keynoted by mostly ministries in his cabinet. The speak revolves mainly on the ideas of how to implement Making Indonesia 4.0 by each stakeholder (i.e., Ministry of Higher Education on how to build a curriculum supporting Making Indonesia 4.0).

According to Ministry of Industry (2018b), 4IR gives Indonesia the opportunity to not only revitalize its industry, but also the way people do things. With no intervention, there is a good chance of Indonesia's manufacturing sector to contribute less and less fraction of GDP, compared to the growing service sector (Ministry of Industry 2018b). 4IR is said to help Indonesia to have top 10 highest GDP in the world by 2030, and to have a 10% of GDP worth of net-export (Ministry of Industry, 2018b). The Minister proposes 5 main sectors to be focused on, namely food and beverage, textile and apparel, automotive, electronics, and chemical (Ministry of Industry 2018b).

The Ministry of Industry (2018a) acknowledges 10 fundamental problems. These 10 problems then become 10 national priorities. Later on, these national priorities distributed to other ministries accordingly under a national committee called National Industrial Committee (KINAS). The 10 national problems are:

1. Relies on import for intermediate input.
2. Unoptimized geographical potential.
3. Markets require higher standards.
4. Lagged Small and Medium Enterprises.
5. Weak digital infrastructure.
6. Limited fund.
7. Quantity over quality of labor.
8. Lack of Innovation centre.
9. Not enough incentive to develop 4IR.
10. Uncoordinated policies.

Kearney (2018) discloses some of other countries' implementation on their own Industry 4.0. In ASEAN region, Singapore, which already started Industry 4.0 since 2015, currently leads. It focuses on robotics and 3D printing. Next, there is Thailand, which has started since 2016. Malaysia is still on its planning phase, but already succeed in inviting Chinese and German firms to invest there in robotics and manufacturing. Indonesia is currently sitting at the same level as Philippines and Viet Nam.

To sum up, Indonesian government tries to utilize Industry 4.0 to improve its manufacturing growth. It then relies on manufacturing to improve net export, hence the export-led growth. The 5 industries of choice reflect Indonesia's current comparative advantage, especially in manufactured goods, which is good if Indonesia opts for export-led growth strategy.

4 WILL MAKING INDONESIA 4.0 WORK?

Industry 4.0 requires hard technological infrastructures. Australian Government (n.d.) stated that their version of Industry 4.0 needs to rise data volumes, computational power, and connectivity that is more reliable. This presents a big challenge for Indonesia, which, technology-wise, sits at rank 61 from 100 countries, mainly amid low Internet coverage (Martin et al. 2018). Currently, only half of Indonesia is covered with LTE, Long Term Evolution, connection (Kementerian Komunikasi dan Informatika 2018). Any radical plan to change this fact is currently non-existent.

Indonesia also suffers from a soft infrastructure problem, which halts innovations, including low patent application and scientific and technical publication (Martin et al. 2018). The answer to this soft infrastructure is also not included in Making Indonesia 4.0. The plan does target to achieve 2% GDP of R&D, even though we cannot find the exact way to reach this number.

Making Indonesia 4.0 knows which sector it needs to focus. The basis of picking these sectors is mostly economic indicators such as their share to manufacturing GDP, share to export, and share to total manufacturing employment. However, in utilizing Industry 4.0, we need to know their technological level. The plan does not disclose what specific infrastructure or technology these sectors are currently sit at, and needed, to reach the four principles of Industry 4.0. For example, it does not seem that the plan says anything about how many firms utilize 3D printing technology, or how smart their factories are.

Making Indonesia 4.0 does not mention anything on opening the economy more and improving business climate. The plan is clear in that Indonesia needs a huge fund from abroad in a way that it stays in Indonesia. Export-led growth strategy also requires us to restrict our trade barrier to a minimum to comply with equal treatment principle. Global trade and investment is also one reason Indonesia is sitting in the Nascent archetype, and we do not see any strategy to tackle this situation.

With that being said, Indonesia is actually seeing a good trend on Information and Communication Technology (ICT) service development. The sector is currently liberalized and subsidized in some places where private sector involvement is not feasible (Setiawan et al. 2017). This trend should be something we all cheer on. Internet development is definitely something that Industry 4.0 requires at the very basic.

However, to ensure the personalization part, the connection has to be even across region. Sujarwoto and Tampubolon (2016) find that this is not the case. Internet coverage in Indonesia is highly unequal, and it will only get worse. Allocated limited funds have to choose between concentrating to increase the quality and increase the quantity to other region of Indonesia. Technology allows for faster Internet, and as the richer part of Indonesia adopts such technology, the less rich part will have even harder time to catch up.

While Industry 4.0 potentially increases regional economic inequality, it can also cause problem in distributing wealth between capital owner, skilled labor, and unskilled labor. Principally, Industry 4.0 requires machine to take over many humanized tasks. In countries with aging population, this strategy makes sense, but can be problematic in Indonesia, which is facing demographic bonus in the near future, complemented with a low-quality human capital. The best short-term way to change low human capital is to allow a higher degree of mobility people, but without proper distributional policy, the problem of inequality will persist, or even gets worse.

Capital-wise, the plan also states the need to have a massive flow of Foreign Direct Investment (FDI) to Indonesia. This makes sense amid Indonesia's Nascent archetype. Unfortunately, Indonesia's FDI hardly grows since 2013 (Ministry of Industry 2018a). This will be problematic especially if we are lagged behind not only in terms of capital formation, but also on innovation. The plan indeed acknowledges the lack of fund as one of its fundamental problems, which is a good sign in its own right.

However, this problem can be proved hard to address. Indonesia-Investment (2018) estimates loss of around 24 billion US dollar in the form of canceled investments due to bad investment climate. There are many reasons why it is so hard to invest in Indonesia, even though the government keeps on selling the investment story. Among these reasons are regulation uncertainties, bad coordination among governments especially between central and local government, and the lack of basic infrastructure (Indonesia-Investment 2018).

5 WHAT WE SHOULD EXPECT?

Keep in mind that the plan disclosed in this paper is by no means technical. It is very general, and there is a very good chance that the more specialized plans exist in lower hierarchy. Until the more specific regulations happen, it is hard to tell whether the plan will work or not.

We expect to see a more decentralized plan. For Making Indonesia 4.0 to work, we need to see ministry levels of regulation come up from each stakeholder. For example, we should see what kind of regulations Ministry of Research and Higher Education imposes amid Making Indonesia 4.0.

Other than the regulations, we can use 10 fundamental problems as our benchmark. In response to tackle the 10 fundamental problems, Making Indonesia 4.0 discloses 10 National Priorities. There is no particular target regarding tackling the 10 fundamental problems, but we can somewhat guess any good proxies for them. Not all of them are straightforward, but there are at least six targets that we can measure.

For the first problem, the government aims to reduce the reliance Indonesia's manufacturing sectors to intermediate imports. There is nothing in the plan, which says how to do this, but we should expect lower imports of intermediate inputs. If you own a company which produces intermediate inputs, this might be your chance to shine.

Second, Indonesian government would like to help 3.7 million of SMEs through technologies such as e-commerce and funding. Indonesia is widely known for its high growth in e-commerce, even when the government do nothing. This makes the growth of e-commerce a certainty but makes evaluating the government in this area somewhat harder. Nevertheless, the growth of e-commerce is something we need to expect, and embrace.

Third, expecting a faster growth of digital infrastructure, the government aims to get 5G and pushes fiber-optics connection to get 1 Gbps. It is uncertain how the government aims to get this, but certainly, this is a room for private firms to chime in.

Fourth, increasing the FDI flow. Indonesia's FDI has been stagnant so far, so a small growth of FDI should be easily spotted. Many international firms would like to expand to Indonesia. It is only a matter of whether Indonesia really wants it or not.

Fifth, human capital wise, it is not clear how the government will fix Indonesia's low-quality human capital. Changes in education will take a long time to evaluate. Short-term solution is to open the labor market. If this is the case, then we should expect a less-restricted labor market in Indonesia. This will show up in the form of a relaxed expatriate policy by Ministry of Labour and increased number of expatriates in Indonesia.

The last problem is the number of Research and Development. More incentive related to R&D activities is expected. We can see this through exempted R&D from tax calculation, for example. R&D budget to GDP should also increase. This is an obtainable indicator. This, with the addition to human capital incentive, is the answer to innovation center.

Other indicators are much harder to observe, at least in the short run. The best way to evaluate geographical potential is through GDP in province level. It will take a significant amount of infrastructure and time, something we cannot quickly observe. We do know that Indonesia is currently focusing on regional infrastructure, so at least we are heading to right direction.

Higher standard of markets requires very detailed indicators. It is hard to imagine how Indonesian government assists this. One thing that government can do is to make regulation about standards, such as Indonesian National Standard (SNI) and Good Manufacturing Practices requirement.

Observing incentive to build 4IR technology should be in line with incentive to have R&D. The only catch to this indicator is, Indonesia has yet to develop the definition of 4IR in a more detailed level. Without this definition, the government has no instrument to target firms, which want to grab the incentive. So far, the definition of 4IR in this paper is gained from literatures, which by no means legal to Indonesian government.

Uncoordinated regulation is also something that is very hard to identify. How to measure "coordinated regulation"? Something we can think of is the reduction of the number of regulations. However, a lower number of regulation does not really tell us much about coordination. We need to read each regulation in order to know if it is a "coordinated regulation". How regulations affect business is much more important. That is why expecting to see "coordinated regulation" is not practical.

To be bold, there are at least six indicators that we can observe to see if the implementation of "Making Indonesia 4.0" happens as it promises. We will see less import of intermediate inputs, higher penetration of e-commerce, faster Internet, higher FDI, fiscal incentives for R&D activities, and more expatriates coming to work in Indonesia.

There are opportunities for private firms to expand their business to intermediate inputs such as spare parts, and embrace e-commerce to increase sales. Prepare any form of R&D activities, so when the regulations on R&D activities provide incentives, you are ready to claim the incentives. Be prepared to join in the hunt for highly skilled expatriates and investment, as attracting overseas resources will be the only viable short-term solution for investment and human resources.

6 CONCLUSION

Industry 4.0 is coming, and it is coming fast. It allows for more efficient and personalized production of things. Indonesia does not want to be lagged behind, hence the plan Making Indonesia 4.0. It shows grand ambition to push Indonesia's economy to top 10 in the world.

However, reaching Industry 4.0 is not a trivial task. Indonesia lacks of basic requirement such as digital infrastructure and low-quality human capital. These facts result in nascent position of Indonesia in the CRI. The plan does not really capture how it will change the game.

It is argued that the government will continue producing more specific policies to get to its goals. This paper offers some indicators to evaluate how far the government commits to the plan. Some of them are investment that is more open and labor policies, increases in digital infrastructure, and higher R&D activities.

The plan is a good start, in the sense that Indonesian government is aware of Industry 4.0 potential. However, making Indonesia 4.0 does not answer yet how to utilize Industry 4.0. It needs more concrete programs, targets, and indicators, as well as commitment to budget, both public and private.

REFERENCES

Australian Government. n.d. *What everyone must know about industry 4.0.* [Online]. Retrieved from https://bit. ly/2tvoKFO. Accessed on 2018-06-25.

Hermann, M., Pentek, T. & Otto, B. 2016. Design principles for industry 4.0 scenarios. In *System Sciences (HICSS), 2016 49th Hawaii International Conference on* (pp. 3928-3937). IEEE.

Indonesia-Investments. 2018. *Indonesia misses billions because of troubled investment climate.* Jakarta: Indonesia-investments. [Online]. Retrieved from https://bit. ly/2DqUi3K. Accessed on 25 May 2018.

Kearney, A.T. 2018. *Benchmarking implementasi industri 4.0.* Jakarta: Indonesia Industrial Summit 2018. [Online]. Retrieved from https://bit.ly/2yHUexF. Accessed on 2018-06-25.

Kementerian Komunikasi dan Informatika. 2018. *Strategi penguatan infrastruktur & regulasi digitalisasi ekonomi untuk penerapan industri 4.0.* Jakarta: Indonesia Industrial Summit 2018.

Lasi, H., Fettke, P., Kemper, H.-g., Feld, T. & Hoffmann, M. 2014. Industry 4.0. *Business & Information Systems Engineering* 6(4): 239-242.

Marr, B. 2016. *What everyone must know about industry 4.0.* [Online]. Retrieved from https://bit.ly/2yHYHAj. Accessed on 2018- 06-25.

Martin, C., Samans, R., Leurent, H., Botti, F., Drzeniek-Hanouz, M., Geiger, T. & Blaylock, A. 2018. *The Readiness for the Future of Production Report 2018* (Tech. Rep.). Swiss: World Economic Forum.

Ministry of Industry. 2018a. *Inisiatif strategis untuk membangun industri manufaktur berdaya saing di era industri 4.* Jakarta: Indonesia Industrial Summit 2018.

Ministry of Industry. 2018b. *Making Indonesia 4.0.* Jakarta: Indonesia Industrial Summit 2018.

Setiawan, A.B., Rafizan, O. & Sastrosubroto, A.S. 2017. Development of the information and communication technology service industry in Indonesia. *Australian Journal of Telecommunications and the Digital Economy* 5(3): 50.

Sujarwoto, S. & Tampubolon, G. 2016. Spatial inequality and the Internet divide in Indonesia 2010–2012. *Telecommunications Policy* 40(7): 602-616.

International Issues

Global Competitiveness: Business Transformation in the
Digital Era – Abdullah, Widiaty & Abdullah (eds)
© 2019 Taylor & Francis Group, London, ISBN 978-0-367-19442-0

Product competitiveness and international trade inequality on ASEAN countries

N. Nawiyah, H. Hasnin, B.P. Sutjiatmo & R. Wikansari
Polytechnic APP, Ministry of Industry, Jakarta, Indonesia

D. Susanti
Policy Science, Ritsumeikan University, Osaka Ibaraki, Japan

ABSTRACT: Nowadays, trade imbalances or inequality has become an important issue on international trade. Different competitive advantages among countries tend to widen trade inequality in region such as ASEAN. This study tries to analyze and identify Indonesia's competitive products relative to its peers in ASEAN and its correlation with regional trade inequality in ASEAN. It employs Revealed Competitive Advantage (RCA) method in order to identify product competitiveness and Williamson Index for calculating regional trade inequality. The results show that product competitiveness has an impact on regional trade inequality in ASEAN. However, implementation of local currency settlement framework among Indonesia, Malaysia, and Thailand on trade seems to be positive for export and import growths and therefore might reduce trade inequality. As an implication, the framework could be extended to other countries in ASEAN.

1 INTRODUCTION

The economic development of ASEAN countries will theoretically transform into a big economic block comprising Southeast Asian countries. Currently, ASEAN has entered the era of ASEAN Economic Community (AEC), which will economically merge into a single economic power in Southeast Asia. At this stage, the ASEAN economy is like a European Union that is economically integrated in production, consumption, and trade. The absence of trade barriers among ASEAN countries has increased internal trade among these countries.

The unification of the ASEAN economy into a single market has affected economic decisions of the business actors between countries in terms of production, investment, consumption, and trade. In addition to providing opportunities, AEC also generates considerable challenges for its member countries, including Indonesia. The movement of resources, especially human resources, will also be more flexible so to increase the competition between countries of human resources, especially in areas of work that have been approved free mobility in ASEAN countries.

In the field of trade, competitive advantage is the main issue compared to comparative advantage. Comparative advantage cannot guarantee the increase of national exports, while competitive advantage will guarantee an increase in exports and international trade of a country. Trade among countries in ASEAN is a separate issue, given the proportion of internal trade ASEAN is smaller than the external ASEAN, although both grow positive (ASEAN Secretary 2017).

This internal ASEAN trade growth will remain the focus for ASEAN's future, especially for increasing export of Indonesian products on ASEAN market. Therefore, an analysis of product competitiveness of Indonesian products to other ASEAN countries' trade products is necessary. Such an analysis would also be useful for the development of trade products and policies for the development of Indonesia's industry and trade for the near future.

The second issue is related to the trade inequality among countries in ASEAN. Countries such as Indonesia in fact has lower share of exports compared to Malaysia, Thailand, and Singapore in ASEAN. Therefore, in sense of trade per capita, exports per capita in Indonesia is much lower compared to those other countries since Indonesian population is much larger than its counterpart's countries.

Krugman (1991) mentioned that trade deficit was not the real issue but the effects of international competition on the mix product that a country produced. Based on this statement, the variation of competitive products on economy becomes the important issue, especially for developing countries, including Indonesia. The high variation on competitive products produced by countries tends to increase international trade balance, and therefore would increase international trade inequality in the region, such as ASEAN.

The third issue related to increasing trade among ASEAN countries is the establishment of bilateral local currency settlement framework among central banks of Indonesia, Malaysia, and Thailand. The purpose of this agreement is to use Indonesian Rupiah and Malaysian Ringgit for international trade transactions between countries rather than using US Dollar. The framework is also for using Rupiah-Thailand Bath and Ringgit-Bath. This framework has been implemented effectively since January 2018.

Based on the above background, the research objectives to be obtained from this research are: (1) to analyze and identify Indonesia's product competitiveness relative to other countries in ASEAN, (2) to analyze regional inequality of international trade in ASEAN. The last purpose of this research is to analyze the effect of bilateral local currency settlement on international trade intra-ASEAN, especially among Indonesia, Malaysia, and Thailand.

2 METHODOLOGY

In order to analyze product competitiveness among countries in ASEAN, we use Revealed Competitive Advantage (RCA). RCA can be formulated as follows (Balassa 1965, Dalum et al. 1998, Laursen 1998):

$$RCA_j^i = \frac{X_j^i / X_n^i}{X_j^r / X_n^r} \qquad (1)$$

where x_{ij} is the total export from country i in the product (based on the SITC product code) j. The value of r reflects the export value of all countries except country i, and the value of n reflects the value of all products except products (based on SITC product code).

The value of the RCA index ranges from $0 < RCA < \infty$. If the value of $RCA_{ij} > 1$, then the country i has a comparative advantage in the product j. Conversely, if $RCA_{ij} < 1$, then country i does not have a comparative advantage in the product j.

For regional trade inequality, we employ Williamson Index. The Williamson Index is a measure of income inequality to analyze how big is the gap between regions/regions. The basis of calculation is by using real GDP per capita in relation to population per area, to measure inequality of regional development. However, to deliver the objective of this study, we use export per capita and/or import per capita for calculating the Williamson Index:

$$V_w = \frac{\sqrt{\sum_{i=1}^n (y_i - y)^2 \left(\frac{f_i}{n}\right)}}{y} \qquad (2)$$

Where V_w denotes Williamson index, y_i represents per capita export from country i, y is the mean of per capita export for all countries in the region, f_i represents population of country i, and n denotes total population in the region. Williamson Index ranges from zero to one. If the index is close to 0, the inequality in export or import distribution among countries in ASEAN is low. Therefore, if the index approaches to 1, the trade distribution in the region is high inequality.

3 EMPIRICAL EVIDENCES

In Indonesia, based on RCA calculation, in fact the number of competitive products is relatively fluctuating. The higher number had been reached in 68 product groups. However, the number of competitive products had declined in 2010 then increased again in 2015 as much as 61 products. The contrary trend can be seen for Malaysia. Its competitive products had been increased up to 61 products in 2015. In Thailand case, the pattern is quite same with Indonesia but its competitive products are higher than Indonesia and Malaysia. It had 78 competitive products in 2015. The details are in Table 1.

Based on: RCA > 1, STIC Rev 3 with 3 digits.

Competitive advantage becomes one of the many reasons why there is international trade imbalance or inequality in ASEAN. Countries with many competitive products tend have larger value in export compared to countries with few competitive products. Therefore, an increase of inequality on the number of competitive products among countries in ASEAN will increase the international trade inequality.

Meanwhile, based on Figure 1, the regional inequality on international trade trend is fluctuating also. From 1998–2002, there is a decreasing trend of

Table 1. Number of competitive products of selected ASEAN countries 1990–2015.

Year/ Countries	Number of Competitive Products		
	Indonesia	Malaysia	Thailand
1990	44	37	56
1995	47	38	58
2000	68	34	89
2005	57	40	77
2010	55	48	75
2015	61	61	78

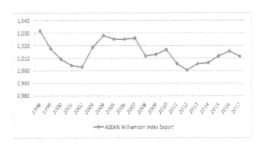

Figure 1. ASEAN regional inequality index of exports, 1998–2017.

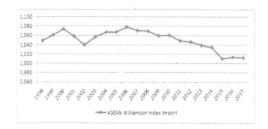

Figure 2. ASEAN regional inequality index of exports, 1998–2017.

Table 2. Correlation on variation of competitive products and regional inequality on trade.

	Sdv. #Competitive products	WI-Export	WI-Import
Sdv. #Competitive products	1.0000		
WI-Export	-0.1792	1.0000	
WI-Import	0.7880	0.3051	1.0000

inequality, but last five years of the analysed data seems to be increased on inequality.

However, the regional inequality on imports is relatively different compared to exports. The trend of regional inequality on imports seems to be decreased since 2006 (Figure 2).

In Table 2, we correlate the variation of the number of competitive products of Indonesia, Malaysia, and Thailand to export and import Williamson indices. We find that the variation of the number of competitive products among those three countries has positive correlation on regional inequality of import in ASEAN. However, we also find a negative correlation of the number of competitive products among those countries to regional inequality index on export.

As we have mentioned earlier, central banks of Indonesia, Malaysia, and Thailand have established an agreement on local currency settlement in order to promote international trade among those countries. It has been implemented since January 2018. It seems that after the implementation of this agreement, Indonesian export growths to Malaysia and Thailand in total are positive compared to January–April 2017 (Table 3). The import growths from them are also relatively positive (Table 4).

Based on increasing trends of trades, both exports and imports among countries (Malaysia, Indonesia, and Thailand), it seems that local currency settlement framework has a promising impact on international trade among these countries. However, it still need time to find a solid evidence that this framework reduces the trade imbalance or trade inequality on the region.

Table 3. Indonesia's exports after and before agreement for local currency settlement framework Indonesia, Malaysia, and Thailand (US $ Million).

Year Month/country	2018 (after agreement) Malaysia	Thailand	Total	2017 (before agreement) Malaysia	Thailand	Total	Growth (%) Malaysia	Thailand	Total
January	729	577	1306	739	483	1223	−1.4	16.3	6.4
February	737	569	1306	666	483	1149	9.6	15.1	12.0
March	841	596	1437	740	613	1353	12.0	−3.0	5.8
April	782	529	1310	663	450	1112	15.2	14.9	15.1

Table 4. Indonesia's imports after and before agreement for local currency settlement framework Indonesia, Malaysia, and Thailand (US $ Million).

Year Month/country	2018 (after agreement) Malaysia	Thailand	Total	2017 (before agreement) Malaysia	Thailand	Total	Growth (%) Malaysia	Thailand	Total
January	768	740	1507	690	656	1346	10.1	11.3	10.7
February	643	895	1539	821	727	1548	−27.5	18.7	−0.6
March	773	943	1715	782	778	1560	−1.2	17.4	9.0
April	786	890	1676	719	741	1460	8.5	16.7	12.9

4 CONCLUSION

The results show that the variation of the number of product competitiveness might have an impact on regional trade inequality in ASEAN, especially for imports. Moreover, the implementation of local currency settlement framework among Indonesia, Malaysia, and Thailand seems to be positive for Indonesian export and import growth. These findings imply that local currency settlement could be expanded not only for those three countries but also for all countries in ASEAN.

REFERENCES

ASEAN Secretary. 2017. *Trade Statistics*. Jakarta: ASEAN Secretary.
Balassa, B. 1965. Trade liberalization and revealed comparative advantage. *The Manchester School* 33(2): 99-123.
Dalum, B., Laursen, K. & Villumsen, G. 1998. Structural change in OECD export specialization patterns: despecialization and stickiness. *International Review of Applied Economics* 12(3): 447-467.
Krugman, P.A. 1991. Myths and realities of U.S. competitiveness. *Science* 254(5033): 811-815.
Laursen, K. 1998. Revealed comparative advantage and the alternatives as measures of international specialization. *Eurasian Business Review* 5(1): 99-115.

Global Competitiveness: Business Transformation in the
Digital Era – Abdullah, Widiaty & Abdullah (eds)
© 2019 Taylor & Francis Group, London, ISBN 978-0-367-19442-0

How Trump's steel and aluminium tariff shapes future world trade

K. Gupta
Australian National University, Canberra, Australia

B.P. Sutjiatmo & M.S. Kurniawan
Politeknik APP, Jakarta, Indonesia

ABSTRACT: In this information era where globalization and advancement of technology helps reduce trade cost, Trump just proposed his idea of having a tariff to help The United States' steel and aluminium industry. Many pro-free trade economists still argue that the policy will hurt world trade. The cost can be so high; Australia, Japan, and European Union are trying to get exemption from the tariff. We show there is terms of trade gain for implementing import tax for a big player such as the United States of America (USA). This turns into a tit-for-tat game, which the best response for the rest of the world is to retaliate. In turn, WTO's role turns questionable and international trade gets harder to predict. Furthermore, we provide theoretical explanation why this will hurt the world as a whole.

1 INTRODUCTION

International trade has been seeing increased trends since the last 15 years at the level where history has never seen before (World Trade Organization 2018). Economic openness has helped boosting developing countries' standard of living and has helped many people escape poverty. There is very little legitimate reason as to why a country wants to close your economy in the sense of growing your country's pie size (Obstfeld 2006).

There is, however, a problem in distributing the share of the pie. International Trade creates winner and loser. International trade can be seen also as zero sum game. Sector or agent, which enjoys protection from rigid movement of goods, will face fiercer competition. This was demonstrated well by Ricardo-Viner where a factor of production cannot move (Obstfeld 2006).

In fact, this is the main reason why the USA was creating World Trade Organization (WTO) in the first place. Trade is, in a sense, similar to prisoner's dilemma where cheating is in the interest of the traders. The United States of America (USA) proposed the creation of WTO to keep the playing field even, and has been working well so far (Stiglitz 2018). The irony is, now the USA is threatening the very existence of WTO.

Donald Trump was elected, and promised to bring inclusive growth to the US soil. He suggested a major change to US international economic policy, and Trump's wish persist in moving the USA toward a further protectionist side (Stiglitz 2018). Trump has just delivered his promise by imposing tariff to steel and aluminium import, which are 25% and 10%, respectively (Denton 2018).

With a country as influential as the USA, the whole world will surely be affected. In this piece, we discuss how Trump's logic actually has some sense. First, we debunk Trump's trade balance argument. Second, we use standard trade model proposed by Obstfeld (2006) to see how protection can benefit steel and aluminium processing sector. More importantly, we analyze how Indonesian government and private sector should react to this policy. Finally, we conclude.

2 THE LOGIC BEHIND TRUMP TARIFF

2.1 *Trade balance argument*

Trump has repeatedly proposed that trade balance is bad. He states that having a negative net export means the USA "lost" to its trading partner. To what extent is that story true?

According to Goerge (2018), it is important to describe between two things that are often discussed in the same sentence: the trade deficit and the US Government's budget deficit. These things interact, but they are very different. The trade deficit is simply the amount of money from the annual value of imports exceeding the annual value of exports.

When the USA runs a trade deficit, say with China, it implies that after Chinese consumers have purchased all the American goods and services they want in a given year, they still have some US dollars left over. Whenever the Chinese investors switched from the dollars to their own currency (Yuan), this would increase the value of the Yuan relative to the dollar. This would imply that the prices for Chinese exports would be higher in the USA, which the

Chinese manufacturing industries for sure do not want. Rather, the Chinese purchase US treasury securities – bonds – that are essentially loans from the US government. Then, the trade surplus supplies the US government with a setup source by low-interest loans, which aid to finance its annual budget deficits (Goerge 2018).

We also have to remind the President how powerful US dollar is. Many countries hold US dollar as their reserve, including Indonesia. The US dollar is eligible currency in Ecuador, El Salvador, and East Timor, but it circulates on the side with many others (Goerge 2018). It is approximated that at least two-thirds of the US currency now in circulation is used outside the country (Goerge 2018). The fact that this money helps create the negative trade balance should imply how far the USA is leading this world instead of losing.

2.2   Winner and the terms of trade

The "standard" trade model is very powerful in showing that free trade is pare to optimal, with a very little exceptional cases where trade protectionism can do better (Obstfeld 2006). Free trade has its own problem, however. One of them is creating losers.

When a country opens to trade, it will import goods that it produces poorly, and export goods that it is comparatively better at producing. Price then adjusts: the goods exported get increased price, and the goods imported get the price reduced. Moreover, under free movement of factors among sectors, Factor Price Equalization (FPE) should hold (Obstfeld 2006).

However, free movement of factors can be a too heroic of an assumption. This means labor and capital of a sector can move freely to other sector. The import sector will be contracted due to import competition, then capital and labor move to export sector, which need more capital and labor due to expansion to meet foreign demand. Problem happens when factors cannot move. Cheap steel from China means lower wage and capital rent in steel industry. Under free movement of factors, this labor can easily get another job, which has better salary. However, this might not be the case.

It gets more dramatic when we observe Chinese side. From the viewpoint of the exporting country, Chinese steel workers should get increased wage, chasing US steel workers' wage. This is indeed the case, as observed by Xing (2018). This essentially removed the US workers' salary to their Chinese counterpart, which suggest that US' steel labors are among the losers. This should also hold true for capital owner's rental rate. This creates incentive for factor owners in US' steel industry to lobby for protection.

Usually, this problem is sector-specific. If the government's interest is in the whole country, then accepting the lobby may be less efficient. The reduction of steel sector should be less big than the increase of export sector such as agriculture should. Moreover, export sectors, which use cheap steel from China, such as health equipment and automotive industries, should benefit even more. Trade should then be good for overall welfare of the country. However, this might not be true for big countries like the USA.

Tariff, most of the times, creates dead weight loss for the economy, making it less efficient (Obstfeld 2006). For big countries, however, this is not the case. Import tariff reduces demand, and for big country, it causes world price to drop. Under this advantage of terms of trade, the impact of the tariff to demand is reduced (amid lower world price), and the government can potentially reap big enough tariff revenue to cover dead weight loss.

The logic is easier explained with a graph. Consider Figure 1, in which the USA is the importing nation. Under autarky, the US' steel price is in Pm, while China trades at Px. Under free trade and the condition Px < Pm, the USA becomes the importer with China as the exporter, with the market price down to Pw. Suppose both countries are price taker, any trade restriction will lead to a deadweight loss for both of them. This is not true with a big country assumption.

Consider the tariff by Trump, which leads the price in the USA to increase to Pw+t, with t being an ad-valorem tariff. The increased domestic price reduces the demand in the USA, which will not affect the world price if USA is small. But suppose the USA is a big country, big enough such that its reduced demand alone leads to lower world price, to Pw'. Like any tariff, there will be deadweight loss. However, the decreased world price leads the tariff gained by the government, which may cover the deadweight loss. Small country can only collect a tariff as big as (Quantity import × (Pw+t-Pw)), but big country gets (Quantity import × (Pw+t-Pw')). For the USA, it is rational as long as the shade ((Pw-Pw') × Quantity import) is bigger than the deadweight loss.

This gain, however, comes at the expense of the other country, which is China. Not only that its revenue reduced by not producing for the USA, but also for the decreased world price. In fact, the world as a whole will be hurt by the tariff. This is what happens

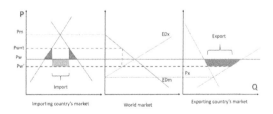

Figure 1. Trade wars illustration.

if China chooses to sit idly doing nothing. However, doing nothing is not the best response to the tariff. The best response is to retaliate.

By comparative advantage, the USA also has sectors, which they rely on Chinese market. They will use the same trick to the USA on this market and get the surplus enough to cover the loss in the steel and aluminium market. This is the best way China can do, sadly at the expense of the whole world.

3 HOW THE WORLD REACT?

The previous section argues the logic behind Trump's background to tariff, which is mostly debunked. However, the policy has been done, and the world reacts to it. When main problem arises with having a (big) country impose tariff on foreign good, the best way for its trading partner to react is retaliation.

China will take counter-measures of the same proportion and scale if the USA imposes further tariffs on Chinese goods (The Guardian n.d.). China announced tariffs on imports of US food and other goods in response to US tariffs on imports of aluminium and steel. China tariff on US soybeans could cost Iowa farmers up to $624 billion. Soybeans are among hundreds of US products China has singled out for tariffs. The USA has an equally long list that includes taxing X-ray machines and other Chinese goods. US soybean prices have fallen about 12% since March 2018, when the US–China trade dispute began. China already has smacked farmers with an additional 25 percent tariff on pork, and Mexico plans a 20% tariff on ham and pork shoulders.

Those moves could cost the US pork producers $360 million over the year; Mexico is weighing tariffs on $4 billion of US corn and soybeans, while the European Union and Canada are considering tariffs on a range of US products. In addition, US farm competitors will take in to capture as much of the Chinese soybean market as possible. It will be South America – Brazil and Argentina – and parts of Western Europe – Russia and the Ukraine – that will replace US farmers to fill China market (Eller 2018).

Not just China, Trump declared the USA would change tariffs on imports of steel and aluminium also from Canada, Mexico, and the European Union in an effort to cut down trade unbalances with the three important allies. Trump also established an investigation that may result in similar limitations on imported automotive trade between the USA, Canada, and Mexico. Besides the tariffs, Trump's strong line in the renegotiation of the North American Free Trade Agreement, or NAFTA, has left the future of that negotiation in uncertainty. Trump said all of the processes are planned to cut down the trade deficit between the USA and other countries (Brian 2018).

Reported by Bank of America Merrill Lynch, the portion of the total US trade deficit attributable to

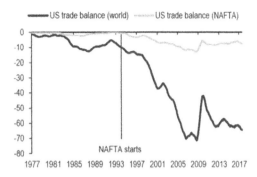

Figure 2. US Trade Balance (Brian 2018).

Canada and Mexico is under 10%. In fact, since NAFTA's implementation in 1994, the trade deficit with America's neighbors has only increased reasonably, although the global deficit ballooned (Brian 2018). The details are in Figure 2.

Should the situation escalate, the consequences could be terrible. Should the USA and EU ramp up various tariffs, including on cars, the impact could knock 0.4% from US growth and 0.3% from the EU (The Guardian, n.d.). The USA has a trade in goods deficit with the EU of about $38 billion, with about $78 billion exported to Europe from the USA, and $116 billion goes the other way. If the tariffs were raised by 10% above the proposed levels, global trade potentially drops by about 6% (The Guardian, n.d.). The EU has said it will retaliate by slapping tariffs on a range of high-profile American goods and will start a case against the USA at the WTO.

4 WHAT THIS MEANS FOR INDONESIA?

Trade wards this big (and potentially gets bigger), surely will affect Indonesia in several ways. One thing for sure, in this section, we are further predicting what the world is going to do, and how we should fit in.

First, we should be prepared to see a change in trade pattern. Indonesia's steel export to the USA consists only 2.58% of its global steel export (World Integrated Trade Solution n.d.). Indonesian steel exporter should prepare to shift the market to some other place. However, due to predicted lower steel price, this should not be a big issue. In fact, Indonesia as the world's top 10 importer of steel should benefit. China and other net steel exporter will need to find alternative market. This will help industries that use steel as intermediate input (such as automotive) to get cheaper inputs.

Second, in terms of other goods, we can actually benefit from the trade war. Steel and aluminium exporting countries will retaliate against US' agricultural products. Meaning, their farmers will need to shift market. Indonesia, which enjoys US' agricultural products (such as soybean), will get reduced price.

Third, whoever gain and lose in trade wars, global trade will surely decrease. We need to bear in mind two things. One thing is logistics activity. Less trade means less movement of goods across the oceans and the sky. Logistics player should prepare to halt its expansion, facing fiercer competition. The other thing is the flow of capital. Expect greater movement of capital due to increased trade cost. Harley-Davidson in fact has already moved some of its production to European Union territory due to retaliation tariff against US' automotive products (Lynch & Long 2018).

Finally, regardless of the plans in the hands of the USA, as long as the rest of world are looking to get more progressive trade deals, we can simply ignore the USA and move on. While Trump announced that the USA declined the Trans Pacific Partnership (TPP), other members are continuing the TPP (Reynolds & Tweed 2018). This should hold true to other Trade Agreements also. This scenario isolates the USA, while at the same time opens opportunity to our manufacturers to find other markets. How deep the USA is isolated, we may still see two great powers on trade: WTO and the isolated USA (along with whoever decides to befriend with them).

5 CONCLUSION

The escalation of trade wars only gets fiercer and faster. The USA just imposed tariff for its steel and aluminium import. However, flawed the logic behind the policy, the best its trading partners can do is to retaliate. This leads to huge disruption to the global trade, especially if the escalation gets even fiercer.

The trade wars can potentially place two poles of trade power: the USA and the world. We need to understand where to stand. We argue that trade wars can benefit Indonesia in the sense that everything that we import could get cheaper as our main trade partners need to switch market. What we sell to America is not yet protected, so we can at least breathe easy for now.

Whoever gains from the trade wars, however, the world's GDP is going to contract. Expect slower movement of goods especially for logistics firm. Overall consumption will further shrink and export-led growth strategy will be less powerful.

Need to keep in mind that Trumpism might only last as long as Trump is the president. We need to take a closer look at US' presidential election, more so than ever.

REFERENCES

Brian, B. 2018. *One chart shows why trump's trade fight with Canada and Mexico is misguided.* [Online]. Retrieved from https://bit.ly/2tCxGcJ. Accessed on 2018-06-25.

Denton, J. 2018. *Trump's tariffs explained: What are they, how has the world reacted and what are the implications for Britain and global trade?* [Online]. Retrieved from https://bit.ly/2lIjWbZ. Accessed on 2018-06-25.

Eller, D. 2018. *China tariffs on US soybeans could cost Iowa farmers up to $624 million.* [Online]. Retrieved from https://dmreg.co/2LZmxJU. Accessed on 2018-06-25,

Goerge, H. 2018. *Protection or free trade.* [Online]. Retrieved from http://www.truefreetrade.org/amap.htm. Accessed on 2018-06-25.

Lynch, D.J. & Long, H. 2018. *Trump says he's 'surprised' har-ley-davidson is moving work overseas after tariffs take effect.* [Online]. Retrieved from https://wapo.st/2yZfzTq. Accessed on 2018-06-25.

Reynolds, I. & Tweed, D. 2018. *Tpp is a big deal, with or with-out the US.* [Online]. Retrieved from https://bloom.bg/2EHSpyA. Accessed on 2018-06-25.

Stiglitz, J.E. 2018. Rethinking Globalization in the Trump Era: US-China Relations. *Frontiers of Economics in China* 13(2): 133-146.

The Guardian. n.d. *Us on brink of trade war with eu, canada and mexico as tit-for-tat tariffs begin.* [Online]. Retrieved from https://bit.ly/2Jkdwgv. Accessed on 2018-06-26.

World Integrated Trade Solution. n.d. *Indonesia metal export by country 2016.* [Online]. Retrieved from https://bit.ly/2tHJqL3. Accessed on 2018-06-25.

World Trade Organization. 2018. *World trade statistical review 2017.* [Online]. Retrieved from https://bit.ly/2izQnbF. Accessed on 2018-06-25.

Xing, Y. 2018. Rising wages, yuan's appreciation and China is processing exports. *China Economic Review* 48: 118-122.

*Global Competitiveness: Business Transformation in the
Digital Era – Abdullah, Widiaty & Abdullah (eds)*
© *2019 Taylor & Francis Group, London, ISBN 978-0-367-19442-0*

Can cryptocurrency help business to be more competitive?

D.S. Ratana
Politeknik APP Jakarta, Jakarta, Indonesia

K. Gupta
Australian National University, Canberra, Australia

ABSTRACT: Recently, cryptocurrency has been a huge debate among leaders in business and finance, especially in the way it can revolutionize finance and transaction. Chicago Mercantile Exchange trades Bitcoin futures, and there are merchants who accept cryptocurrencies as payment. As the development of cryptocurrency will only get faster, we review literature and Indonesian government stance and law. We argue that business should be conservative in adapting to cryptocurrency amid its limited uses, volatility, and relatively small market cap.

1 INTRODUCTION

Money has three functions: medium of exchange, unit of account, and store of value (Mankiw 2014). To be a medium of exchange, money had to be widely accepted, and so the first money was made of gold, silver, etc. Then, in 1800s, the gold standard was adopted so that people don't have to bring their heavy gold to transact anymore and use paper money. This model was accepted because government would redeem the paper money for its value in gold. We no longer use the gold standard, but the money we have still have value because of trust in the government that issued it. Money includes currency, that is, the paper bills and coins issued by the government and the deposits in the banks. Even though these deposits can be transferred to any other account as a medium of exchange, supposedly the cost to transfer are too high, particularly to another country.

In short, our current system of payment still relies on two things. First, it relies on how well the government keep our trust to the money. Without any backup, Government can easily play around with this money, leaving us with second-guessing the value in a presence of a bubble (Shriver 2018). Nowadays, we try to deal with this first problem by hedging the value of money with something else, such as futures or foreign currencies. Second, it relies on a middle man (or men) to bridge the transaction, which incurs additional cost.

This is where cryptocurrency comes in. Technology has been a prominent driver for growth. It helps business in various ways. Gap of information is getting closer and closer with faster transportation and communication.

Businesses nowadays are able to manage risk using developed instruments such as insurance and futures. Transaction wise, we invent something today we call money. Cryptocurrency is a kind of money which can be "mined" by everyone and is a technological breakthrough. It has limited amount, just like precious metal (Shriver 2018) which means, regulating the value of cryptocurrency will be less trivial than printing money or switching interest rate. Moreover, cryptocurrency can be traded without any middle man, thanks to unique key which is impossible to impersonate (Simonite 2011). The question, then rises: should business utilize cryptocurrency?

We assign the paper in to three parts. First, we discuss about what is cryptocurrency and its features. Second, we identify how these features helpful for business. Finally, we conclude.

2 UNDERSTANDING CRYPTOCURRENCY

Cryptocurrency has been widely talked about, yet people struggle to clearly define it. The definition of cryptocurrency according to Merriam Webster is "any form of currency that only exists digitally, that usually has no central issuing or regulating authority but instead uses a decentralized system to record transactions and manage the issuance of new units, and that relies on cryptography to prevent counterfeiting and fraudulent transactions". Note the key words here: currency, digitally, decentralized system, and cryptography. We will address all of this in the following section.

The first known cryptocurrency is Bitcoin, which was proposed in 2009 by a mysterious character being called Satoshi Nakamoto (Simonite 2011). However, it was in 2013 when Bitcoin started its first hype (Collins 2018). In 2015, Bitcoin is getting more seriously taken when United States gave them

Table 1. Cryptocurrencies with highest market caps, taken 28 June 2018.

No.	Name	Symbol	Market Cap (mil-USD)	Price (USD) lion
1	Bitcoin	BTC	104,135.7	6,083.26
2	Ethereum	ETH	42,809.1	426.65
3	Ripple	XRP	18,050.0	0.46
4	Bitcoin cash	BCH	11,983.0	696.43
5	EOS	EOS	6,759.4	7.54

Source: coinmarketcap.com

status "commodity" (Collins 2018). Up to 2017, Bitcoin received 18× growth of value (Collins 2018).

Since Bitcoin enjoys a hike in market capitalization, other currencies start to emerge. Among the top gainers of market caps are Ethereum, Ripple, and EOS. Table 1 summarizes the top 5 market caps of currently traded cryptocurrency (CoinMarketCap 2018). Almost all of these currencies just change the parameters of the block chain from the Bitcoin platform and try to find markets of their own. Ethereum, for instance, provides ether as digital currency and a platform for those who want to sell and buy decentralized application. Essentially, it is a market place without a centralized server. This should make Ethereum a more valued platform because for anyone who wants a product developed, they can post a contract and wait for someone who would provide the service. Such service would utilize the Ethereum platform, with miners already in place. But this proves otherwise, the platform still produces other altcoins – yet another Cryptocurrency. An exception to this might be Ripple, where it is currently still somewhat controlled by its creator (Orcutt 2018).

Bitcoin is built with no central bank to which control of double spending and spending of non-existent money is difficult. Bitcoin tackles this issue using every nodes/miners as ledgers keepers which doubles as coin distribution mechanism (Tschorsch & Scheuermann 2016). For any transaction, the system made a sophisticated puzzle which requires quite a computational power. The first miner to solve the puzzle gets an incentive in the form of the currency itself. After the puzzle gets solved, it was then written in a block which will be carried over to the next transaction. This system is called a block chain. This in itself provides anonymity, independence from central authority, and double spending attack protection. No other group of currencies, beside cryptocurrencies, has combination of these features (Lansky 2018). They further classified the approach of countries into 5 levels in both directions, negative and positive, with level 0 ignoring cryptocurrency and level 5 completely integrating or banning the currency. The level goes as follows (Lansky 2018):

Level 0 – ignoring: the state authority does nothing with the existence of cryptocurrencies. **Level 1 – monitoring**: the state authority issued a statement that it is aware of the existence of cryptocurrencies but no recommendation was issued. **Level 2 – recommendation**: the state authority issued a statement that it is aware of the existence of cryptocurrencies and is issuing recommendation that most view crypto negatively.

Level 3 – guidance: the state authority has issued guidance to govern the method of using cryptocurrencies and usually accompanied by a warning against cryptocurrency risks.

Level 4 – regulation: provision of cryptocurrency-related services requires an explicit authorization from the relevant state authority.

Level 5 – ban or integration: the state authority has issued the refusal or the full adoption of the cryptocurrency concept.

As you will see, this will prove very interesting for Indonesia, because the stances of the authority are not only on a different level, but also at different polarity.

On February 6, 2014, Bank Indonesia states Bitcoin and other virtual currency are not a valid currency payment instrument in Indonesia. Such statement is only an affirmation to the public since it is already stated in the Government Law no. 7 2011. This was reaffirmed multiple times through Bank Indonesia Regulation no 17/3/PBI/2015 and public statement with an added warning clause (Das 2017). This essentially removes cryptocurrency as a legal currency, at least in Indonesia. Anyone who accepts or uses any cryptocurrency will get penalized by the Central Bank, particularly financial institution. Implementing the law on anonymous transaction is obviously hard, and merchants are still using US dollar in business transactions, particularly in imported consumer goods. Cryptocurrency made that even easier, so if a product was imported with cryptocurrency, it will also exchange with cryptocurrency.

Despite this, Indonesian cryptocurrency exchanges are still operational and thriving. In fact, on June 5th, BAPPEBTI said that they had legalized Bitcoin and other cryptocurrency as commodities and can be traded as futures (Bosnia 2018). The move was made by BAPPEBTI to lure foreign investors as there are a few countries that allow the trade. It is confusing to have governmental institutions of the same country yet with two different stances, but both institutions are adamant with their stand and said the other institution did not collaborate with them.

3 HOW USEFUL IS CRYPTOCURRENCY TO BUSINESS?

Anonymity and double spending attack protection are inherent in fiat currency so there is no added benefit from these characteristics. Independence from central authority, however, can lead to much smaller fee and faster transaction. Smaller fee can happen because more than one entity recording the transaction provides competition, and competition always benefit customers by pushing prices down. The down side is that it's possible that no one wants to record it if the fee or incentive to process the transaction is too low. Although with centralization, it can get pricey, all transaction will always be completed even if there is no incentive for some transactions.

Transferring from one central authority to another can take a lot of time, but within a central authority scope, one can transfer fund instantaneously everywhere, even abroad. In contrast, in cryptocurrencies, this depends on the system they adopt. While Bitcoin can take as fast as 10 minutes, other cryptocurrency may do faster on the expense of less security. Note that this 10 minutes' confirmation time on Bitcoin is the fastest and is not very secure. One does not care about security when he/she only buys a cup of coffee, but 10 minutes' waiting time is obviously too long. This can be hastened by giving an optional transaction fee for the successful miner (Barber et al. 2012), and again such fee can only feasible if the transaction value is big enough to justify the fee.

The main arguments against cryptocurrency are its legal status and its high volatility value (Ivashchenko 2016). Legality might not be a huge issue since there is only small number of countries that openly ban cryptocurrency, with Indonesia being not among those countries. Moreover, executing the ban is a non-trivial task amid its decentralized nature (Lansky 2018). We then left with the volatility problem.

Volatility, then, is a huge problem. Stable price is one of the main requirements for transaction medium. Moore & Stephen (2016) find that Bitcoin can only be a safe hedge for a country's reserve if it consists only 0.01% of total reserve. There are, however, potential solution to this problem.

First, we can now trade Bitcoin futures as well. Some people are skeptical about Bitcoin futures, but people were also skeptical when the first futures were sold (Collins 2018). Second, some fiat currencies of some countries are also volatile. Bitcoin is a much safer bet if we want to trade with Venezuelan or Zimbabwean (Lansky 2018). Finally, due to its decentralized nature, cryptocurrencies' value is dictated by the market (Collins 2018). This leads to a possibility of predicting cryptocurrencies' value using market sentiment such as forums (Kim et al. 2016).

But there are many other issues with using cryptocurrency. According to European Banking Authority (2014), one example is its low market cap in general. This is one source of its volatility. Bitcoin is already highly volatile, but other cryptocurrencies are performing even worse in terms of stability of value (Lansky 2018). Cryptocurrencies are still growing in a sense that we are seeing the emergence of more and more new Initial Coin Offering (ICO), but it is hard to imagine a new one would take over the safest, highest market cap Bitcoin.

The main feature of cryptocurrency for business is its fast, decentralized transaction. However, its volatility presents more risk than return. The relatively small market cap of cryptocurrency might also means adopting to it will only present with marginal benefit. Moreover, cryptocurrency and the technology behind it is still developing. Some method of delivering cryptocurrency is also varying, from completely decentralized like Bitcoin to somewhat controlled like Ripple. It is probably best for business to wait until a clearer pattern emerges from this technology.

4 CONCLUSION

Technology powers the emergence of a new decentralized digital currency called cryptocurrency. Unlike conventional currencies, cryptocurrency is fast and free from any central bank's control. While adopting cryptocurrency will be certainly beneficial in the sense of reducing the cost of transaction and dropping the reliability to the government, existing cryptocurrencies are highly volatile and still have a relatively small market cap in contrast to conventional instrument. We believe that it is better to wait to adopt cryptocurrency for investment uses until we understand this relatively new technology.

REFERENCES

Bank Indonesia. 2014. *Pernyataan bank indonesia terkait bitcoin dan virtual currency lainnya*. [Online]. Retrieved from https://bit.ly/2KfBc78. Accessed on 2018- 06-25.
Barber, S., Boyen, X., Shi, E. & Uzun, E. 2012. Bitter to better—how to make bitcoin a better currency. In *International Conference on Financial Cryptography and Data Security (pp. 399-414)*. Berlin, Heidelberg: Springer.
Bosnia, T. 2018. *Bappebti: Bitcoin cs masuk kategori komoditas bursa berjangka*. [Online]. Retrieved from https://bit.ly/2yWVRaG. Accessed on 2018-06-25.
CoinMarketCap. 2018. *Crypto-currency market capitalizations*. [Online]. Retrieved from https://coinmarketcap.com/all/views/all/. Accessed on 2018-06-25.
Collins, D.P. 2018. *The problem with cryptocurrencies. Modern Trader, 61*. Canberra: The Australian National University.
Das, S. 2017. *Bitcoin banned as a payment method, adopters will be 'dealt with': Indonesian central bank*. [Online]. Retrieved from https://bit.ly/2KqTQF5. Accessed on 2018- 06-25.
European Banking Authority. (2014). Eba opinion on virtual currency. [Online]. Retrieved from https://eba.europa.eu/documents/10180/657547/EBA-Op-2014-08+Opinion+on+Virtual+Currencies.pdf. Accessed on 2018- 06-28.
Ivashchenko, A.I. 2016. Using cryptocurrency in the activities of ukrainian small and medium enterprises in order

to improve their investment attractiveness. *Problemy Ekonomiky*. 3, 267-273.

Kim, Y.B., Kim, J.G., Kim, W., Im, J.H., Kim, T.H., Kang, S.J. & Kim, C.H. 2016. Predicting fluctuations in cryptocurrency transactions based on user comments and replies. *PloS one* 11(8).

Lansky, J. 2018. Possible state approaches to cryptocurrencies. *Journal of Systems Integration* 9(1): 19-31.

Mankiw, N.G. 2014. Principles of macroeconomics. *Cengage Learning*.

Moore, W. & Stephen, J. 2016. Should cryptocurrencies be included in the portfolio of international reserves held by central banks?. *Cogent Economics & Finance* 4(1): 1147119.

Orcutt, M. 2018. *No, ripple isn't the next bitcoin*. [Online]. Retrieved from https://bit.ly/2DnYIbl. Accessed on 2018-06-25.

Shriver, L. 2018. *Why cryptocurrency is the answer*. [Online]. Retrieved from https://bit.ly/2E55oKH. Accessed on 2018-06-28.

Simonite, T. 2011. What bitcoin is, and why it matters. *Technology Review*, May, 25, 10A1.

Tschorsch, F. & Scheuermann, B. 2016. Bitcoin and beyond: A technical survey on decentralized digital currencies. *IEEE Communications Surveys and Tutorials* 18(3): 2084-2123.

Operation and Supply Chain

Global Competitiveness: Business Transformation in the
Digital Era – Abdullah, Widiaty & Abdullah (eds)
© *2019 Taylor & Francis Group, London, ISBN 978-0-367-19442-0*

Supplier development: Practices and measurement

M. Sulungbudi
Universitas Katolik Parahyangan, Bandung, Indonesia

V. Yanamandram & S. Akter
University of Wollongong, Wollongong, Australia

L. Tam
University of Technology, Sydney, Australia

ABSTRACT: When competition is no longer among firms yet among supply chains, firms are encouraged to establish beneficial collaborations in the supply chain. Supplier development is one of the popular practices believed to be able to create values in supply chain. Studies have discussed that supplier development is defined as developing measurements and exploring its implementation in organizations. However, although customer support in inter-supplier collaboration is believed as one of the supplier development practices, it is never being included in supplier development measurements. This current study makes a significant contribution by developing a measurement model of supplier development with the inclusion of customer support in inter-supplier collaboration, together with direct involvement, supplier evaluation and future business incentives. Moreover, the study supported the view that supplier development is a second-order construct consisting of four first-order constructs, namely direct involvement, supplier evaluation, future business incentives, and customer support in inter-supplier collaboration.

1 INTRODUCTION

Resource scarcity, technological change acceleration, market shifts, global competition, political turbulence and government intervention in supplier markets have led firms to pay attention to the purchasing function as a strategic function, and to the need to manage supplier relationships in addition to customer relationships (Hahn et al. 1990). Traditional supplier relationships, where firms relied on suppliers in product and technology R&D, are no longer considered sufficient, with a closer and more collaborative approach being suggested by scholars (Blenkhorn & Banting 1991). Suppliers may not be able to produce and deliver products that meet customer specifications, so customer firm purchasing staff may have to participate heavily in identifying the best purchasing solution for their needs (Biemans & Brand 1995).

Supplier development is defined as any effort taken by a buying firm with its supplier to increase performance and/or the capabilities of the supplier to meet the buying firm's supply needs (Krause and Ellram 1997). A customer/buyer may assist a supplier to improve its capabilities and performance through various combinations of supplier development activities (Hines 1994, Sucky & Durst 2013). On the other hand, a supplier may access important knowledge, and develop, coordinate, and integrate a new set of capabilities with its customer through supplier development that could lead to performance improvement (Danneels 2002).

Indonesian firms, with their collectivist culture (Hofstede et al. 2010), may value supplier development as more important considering it to be relationship investment which would be less the case in countries with individualist cultures (Barry & Doney 2011). One indication of the collectivist culture is the common practice of associations and collaboration culture that is called *gotong-royong* (YDBA 2014). The *gotong-royong* culture is the reason why Indonesians are accustomed to collaborating in groups to attain a shared goal and to prioritize common interests over private interests (Nasroen 1967, Taylor et al. 1991). Therefore, the Indonesian automotive industry might provide one of the best examples of inter-supplier collaboration, when considered in addition to Japanese manufacturers as the initiator of inter-supplier collaboration.

The purpose of this study is to develop a measure of supplier development with the inclusion of customer support in inter-supplier collaboration. Sections to follow discuss the types of supplier development practices, item generation for each dimensions of supplier development measurement, and findings from Indonesia automotive industry.

2 SUPPLIER DEVELOPMENT PRACTICES AND TYPOLOGIES

Various ways can be employed to support a supplier's performance. From the current study's thorough literature review, eight different activities were identified and are summarized as: (1) training and education; (2) providing on-site consultation; (3) conducting employee exchanges; (4) evaluating, assessing and informing the supplier about their performance; (5) motivating suppliers to improve their performance by offering future business incentives; (6) motivating suppliers to collaborate with each other; (7) stimulating competition between suppliers; and (8) providing capital investment and/or financial support.

2.1 Training and education

For a long time, training and education have been known as supplier development efforts used by large multinational companies (MNCs) to share common knowledge and best practices. Toyota has been providing various training programs for its supplier associations (*kyohokai*) since 1943 (Dyer & Nobeoka 2000). Boeing started to train its suppliers in statistical quality control in the 1980s (Leitner 2005). However, supplier training and education were not really popular and tended to be avoided in the US in the late 1990s, due to the need for long-term commitment by customers (Krause 1997).

2.2 On-site consultation

Suppliers, by themselves, often do not have sufficient knowledge on how to improve their performance and tend to appreciate customer support or help in the form of on-site consultations (Krause et al. 2000). Customers can perform consultations or provide advice to suppliers in one or more specific areas, such as quality management, manufacturing processes, and technology and product development. Customers may also guide their suppliers to adopt best practices, for example, Toyota with its Toyota Production System (TPS) (Dyer & Nobeoka 2000).

2.3 Employee exchange

The practice of employee exchange is well known not only among Japanese firms, but also in other Asian firms. The literature documents that Toyota practices employee exchanges with suppliers, called *shukko* (Dyer & Nobeoka 2000). A large Korean electronics company was reported to have created supplier development teams from the mid-1980s to help suppliers in improving quality, processes and administration (Choi 1999). Honda of America, General Motors and Ford are reported to send supplier development specialist teams to supplier plants to help the suppliers improve in specific areas (Choi 1999).

Employee exchange between a customer and a supplier can be done in two ways: co-locating the customer's engineers to the supplier's facilities or transferring the supplier's engineers to the customer's facility. Employee exchange facilitates intensive communication between engineers from the two firms that enables tacit knowledge exchange between the two parties (Nonaka 1994).

2.4 Supplier evaluation

Evaluating supplier's performance, comparing supplier's performance with expected performance and planning supplier improvement are considered as the fundamental activities of supplier development (Wagner 2006). Customers may evaluate suppliers based on capabilities, performance, processes in management and/or technical areas (Purdy et al. 1994). By providing feedback and improvement targets to the supplier, customers influence suppliers to change their behavior to achieve targets.

Supplier evaluation can be regularly or occasionally, quantitative or qualitative, formal or informal. Giunipero (1990) found that 46% of his survey respondents used quantitative evaluation to motivate their suppliers to improve their product quality, while 10% of the respondents used a qualitative supplier's performance review. Watts & Hahn (1993) reported that 75% of their respondents from the US evaluated suppliers regularly, but only 47% used formal evaluation.

2.5 Future business incentives

Once supplier evaluation is complete, incentives can be used to motivate suppliers to change their behavior to achieve improvement (Frazier & Summers 1984). Some business incentive practices were documented in supplier development publications, such as promises of higher volume orders of present items and consideration of future business upon improving their performance, sharing the cost savings achieved due to performance improvement, and recognizing supplier improvements through awards (Giunipero 1990, Krause 1997, Krause et al. 2000, Modi & Mabert 2007). Suppliers are often reluctant to commit to a relationship if no incentives are available and incentive promises may increase a supplier's willingness to act according to the customer's demands (Trent & Monczka 1999).

2.6 Customers' support in inter-supplier collaboration

With a tendency to have small supply bases, firms tend to influence their suppliers to collaborate with other suppliers, meanwhile maintaining the distance between suppliers to balance collaborative synergy and competition. Many firms advise that the relationship between themselves and their suppliers is critical (Asanuma 1989) and demand that suppliers collaborate on various projects (Wasti & Liker 1999). This inter-supplier relationship is called "co-opetition" (Choi et al. 2002, Wu et al. 2010). Suppliers are expected to be aware that not only do they have to compete for survival, but they also need to collaborate in learning processes. Suppliers are encouraged to communicate with each other directly and sometimes to exchange materials for efficiency; meanwhile, they are also reminded that they compete to supply similar, or the same, products.

In 1939 in Japan, Toyota established a supplier association, *kyoryoku kai*, and then, in 1943, renamed it as *kyohokai* (Nishiguchi 1994). *Kyohokai* was successful in facilitating information exchange and mutual development between members (Dyer & Nobeoka 2000). In 1989, Toyota replicated *kyohokai* in the US as the Bluegrass Automotive Manufacturers Association (BAMA). In 1977, Toyota also facilitated knowledge sharing in "voluntary study groups" (known in Japanese as *jishukenkyu-kai, kojo jishuken* or *jishuken*) where suppliers assist each other to achieve a specific common goal, such as improvement in quality and products (Dyer & Nobeoka 2000). In 1994, Toyota imitated the *jishuken* in the US by establishing plant development activity (PDA) core groups. Unfortunately, in the first two years, the PDA core groups were not as successful as *jishuken*. In the early 1990s, Allen-Bradley initiated a high-performance manufacturing (HPM) supplier consortium to improve its supplier's performance (Stuart et al. 1998). The consortium succeeded in improving the supplier's performance in the early years but then failed to continue the improvement after 1996, so the learning consortium was terminated in 2002 (Stuart & Deckert 2009).

2.7 *Competitive pressure*

When customers use multiple suppliers to obtain a resource, competition builds between suppliers (Hahn et al. 1986). Inter-supplier competition is traditionally used to force suppliers to improve their capability and performance (Giunipero 1990), especially when the customer uses a low purchase price purchasing strategy (Hahn et al. 1986). Although competitive pressure is considered to be part of supplier development, the supplier development literature suggests that competitive pressure has many drawbacks: resulting in high transaction costs, deteriorate customer-supplier relationship, poor product quality and poor communication between the supplier and the customer (Liker & Choi 2004, Hahn et al. 1986, Krause 1997).

2.8 *Capital investment and financial support*

Small suppliers sometimes find that they cannot afford to provide the equipment and tools needed to improve their performance, or that they do not have access to the capital needed (Choi 1999). Blenkhorn & Banting (1991) and also Biemans & Brand (1995)

suggested that customers could provide financial support to a new developing supplier that was expected to fulfil the customer firm's needs.

Ford was among the first organizations reported to have supported its suppliers with capital assets (Seltzer 1928). A successful Korean electronics company supports its suppliers financially. As a result, this support helped one of the suppliers to increase its annual sales tenfold which then benefited the customer with millions of dollars of savings (Choi 1999).

Various typologies, as discussed below, have been used in the literature on supplier development activities, the most common typology being based on the level of the customer's involvement in activities or resource investment (Krause et al. 2007, Sucky & Durst 2013). Krause (1997) proposed three factors of supplier development, namely direct firm involvement, incentives, and enforced competition. He defined direct firm involvement as active involvement and resource investment in the supplier's efforts to improve performance. He also stated that the three factors of supplier development might be used in any combination as the activities are independent and complement each other. Krause et al. (2000) and Krause & Scannell (2002) categorized supplier development as direct involvement, supplier assessment, supplier incentives and competitive pressure.

Modi & Mabert (2007) partially replicated Krause et al.'s work and proposed "operational knowledge transfer activities" to replace their dimension of "direct involvement supplier development activities". Scannell and Calantone's work also used competitive pressure, evaluation, certification and future business incentives as other dimensions of supplier development.

Humphreys, Li, Chan and colleagues (Humphreys et al. 2011, Humphreys et al. 2004) proposed that transaction-specific supplier development and infrastructure factors of supplier development influence customer–supplier's performance improvement. Humphreys et al. (2004) defined transaction-specific supplier development as a core practice of supplier development that represents the direct involvement of the buying company in developing suppliers. Humphreys and colleagues added capital support and recognition of supplier progress in the form of awards as parts of transaction-specific supplier development.

The current study adopts Wagner's direct supplier development definition of a customer's commitment or investment to transfer its knowledge as relationship-specific resources to its supplier in order to improve the supplier's capability and performance (Wagner 2010). In addition, supplier evaluation, future business incentives and inter-supplier collaboration were suggested as the customer's communication approach used to force or encourage its supplier to improve its own performance and/or capabilities (Wagner 2010).

3 GENERATION OF SCALE ITEMS

Wagner's scale of direct involvement supplier development was adapted to reflect this conceptualization (Wagner & Krause 2009, Wagner 2011, Wagner 2010), as it thoroughly identified key activities of supplier development and based on systematic scientific discussions on supplier development (Sucky & Durst 2013). The direct involvement supplier development scale consists of seven items, with each of these items representing activities that show customer's commitment to transfer knowledge.

In addition to direct involvement, the current study adopted four items measuring supplier evaluation from the scale developed by Wagner (Wagner & Krause 2009, Wagner 2010); four items on the scale measuring future business incentives from Modi & Mabert (2007); and six items on the scale measuring the customer's support in inter-supplier collaboration from Wu et al.'s scale of buyer influence (2010). Wu et al.'s scale of buyer influence was adopted to measure the customer's support in inter-supplier collaboration since each item of the scale represent activities that show customer's support in inter-supplier collaboration. The current study did not measure competitive pressure due to its tendency to have a negative impact on performance and on the customer–supplier relationship, leading to its avoidance in the customer–supplier cooperative relationship (Shahzad et al. 2016, Wagner 2010).

A six-point Likert scale measuring the degree of agreement with the items ranging from 'strongly disagree' to 'strongly agree' was applied to measure the multi-item variables used in the current study. Scales were reworded to make it possible for the items to be interpreted from the point of view of the supplier as respondents of the study. All items in the questionnaires were pre-tested in Indonesian, and changes were made to the English version and Indonesian versions iteratively. The final Indonesian versions were later translated back to English by a professional translator for a validity check.

4 DATA COLLECTION

A list of original equipment manufacturers (OEMs) in the automotive industry that were representative of the desired target population was obtained from a report of the Association of Indonesian Automotive Industries (GAIKINDO, 2014). The report listed 14 OEMs; however, information was inadequate as to whether all these OEMs were providing supplier development for their suppliers. The current study focused on the automotive industry due to its size and relevance in the economies of Indonesia and South East Asia. Emails were sent to each of the 14 OEMs listed in the association, asked if they would be able to assist in the recruitment of respondents. Four OEMs, who had more than 60% production share of the industry, indicated their willingness to provide supplier lists. They came from the first and second of the four biggest conglomerate corporations that are engaged in the Indonesian automotive industry. The four firms were identified as Firm A, B, C, and D in the current study.

In total, 376 suppliers were on these supplier lists. However, some suppliers' names were duplicated indicating that some suppliers had received supplier development from more than one customer. In all, 310 distinct suppliers were on the final consolidated supplier list.

The data collection techniques of the current study were a combination of closed web questionnaires, emails with attachment questionnaires, and group distribution of paper questionnaires. The appearance of the questionnaires attached to the emails was similar to the paper questionnaires. The target respondents were given a choice of the most convenient survey instrument for them to respond to in the study. Of the 310 questionnaires distributed, 31 pairs of questionnaires were completed via web questionnaires, five pairs were completed via web and paper questionnaires, and 127 pairs were completed via paper questionnaires. Of 158 complete responses, 151 responses from 100 suppliers were usable. The questionnaires that were discarded (seven cases) failed to meet screening criteria, had severe amounts of missing data or were found to be multivariate outliers. The sample characteristics can be found in Table 1.

Table 1. Sample characteristics.

Supplier firm size (N=100)		Percentage
Number of Employee	Micro	0.0%
	Small	8.0%
	Medium	25.0%
	Large	66.0%
	Unknown	1.0%
Customer identity (N=151)		
Firm A		33.8%
Firm B		12.6%
Firm C		10.6%
Firm D		7.9%
Other customer		13.2%
Unknown		21.9%
Product category (N=151)*		
Main parts and components for 4-wheelers		47.7%
Supporting parts and components for 4-wheelers		47.0%
Main parts and components for 2-wheelers		11.9%
Supporting parts and components for 2-wheelers		13.2%
Jigs and fixtures		15.9%
Moulds and dies		16.6%
Others		7.3%

* Suppliers may support the customer with more than one product category.

5 ANALYSIS

Confirmatory factor analysis (CFA) was conducted to examine and refine the measurement model of supplier development. Appendix 1 presented 21 items to measure the four dimensions of Supplier Development construct.

Some of the standardised regression weights for the supplier development initial measurement model had moderate loadings and their item reliability coefficients or squared multiple correlations were less than 0.50. Therefore, the initial model had to be revised to meet the CFA requirement. The initial measurement model of supplier development was revised two times, by removing one indicator at a time, with all the indicators of Direct Involvement and Supplier Evaluation retained. One indicator of Future Benefit (SuD_FB_03) and one indicator of Inter-Supplier Collaboration (SuD_IC_06) were eliminated for their low loadings and squared multiple correlation values. The resulting fit indicators were χ^2 = 242.698, df = 146, p = 0.00; Bollen–Stine bootstrap p = 0.367; χ^2/df = 1.662; TLI = 0.939; CFI = 0.948; RMSEA = 0.066 (0.051; 0.081); SRMR = 0.057. The standardized regression weights, critical ratios and squared multiple correlation are presented in Table 2. As indicates, the standardized regression

weight of SuD_Di_03 was 0.694 that was very close to the acceptable value of 0.70. The critical values of all observed variables were indicating statistical significance of parameter estimates, as the critical values were greater than 1.96 (Byrne 2010), with the lowest critical value was 9.427. All the standardized residual values did not exceed the cut-off point of |2.58| (Jöreskog & Sörbom 1993, Byrne 2010). Although some of MIs were somewhat larger than 7.882, their par changes were not greater than 0.40. This indicates that there is no modification that would improve the par change high enough, thus no need to remove or modify any indicator (Jöreskog & Sörbom 1993). Therefore, the four-factor model represents an adequate and reliable description of supplier participation in supplier development (Cunningham 2008, Byrne 2010).

All the first-order construct factor correlation moderately to highly correlate with each other, with the lowest correlation being 0.647 and the highest correlation being 0.752, suggesting that the second-order model for supplier development could be further analyzed (Cunningham 2008).

Figure 1 shows the second-order measurement model for supplier development construct. Four first-order constructs, namely, direct involvement, supplier evaluation, future business incentives and inter-supplier collaboration performed as indicators of the second-order supplier development construct. The resulting fit indicators for the second-order model for

Table 2. CFA results for first-order models.

Factor and Item	Standardised Regression Weight (Factor Loading)	Critical Value (t-value)*	Squared Multiple Correlation (Item Reliability Coefficient)
Direct Involvement			
SuD_Di_01	0.717	9.863	0.515
SuD_Di_02	0.790	11.322	0.625
SuD_Di_03	0.694	9.427	0.481
SuD_Di_04	0.794	11.397	0.630
SuD_Di_05	0.824	12.069	0.680
SuD_Di_06	0.759	10.674	0.576
SuD_Di_07	0.745	10.387	0.554
Supplier Evaluation			
SuD_Ev_01	0.837	12.275	0.700
SuD_Ev_02	0.802	11.518	0.644
SuD_Ev_03	0.877	13.210	0.769
SuD_Ev_04	0.727	9.990	0.528
Future Business Incentives			
SuD_FB_01	0.855	12.537	0.731
SuD_FB_02	0.877	13.032	0.770
SuD_FB_04	0.727	9.924	0.528
Inter-supplier Collaboration			
SuD_IC_01	0.734	10.125	0.539
SuD_IC_02	0.787	11.190	0.620
SuD_IC_03	0.840	12.326	0.705
SuD_IC_04	0.746	10.343	0.556
SuD_IC_05	0.812	11.713	0.659

* statistically significant, p < 0.001, n=151

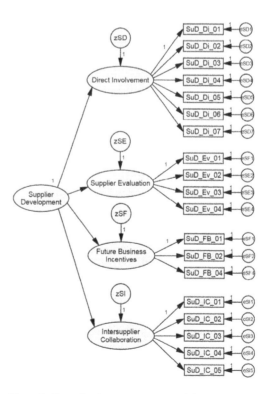

Figure 1. Second-order measurement model.

supplier development were χ^2= 244.922, df= 148, p= 0.00; Bollen–Stine bootstrap p= 0.384; χ^2/df= 1.655; TLI = 0.940; CFI= 0.948; RMSEA= 0.066 (0.051; 0.081); SRMR= 0.058. All the fit indicators for the second-order model were comparable to the first-order construct model indicates that the models were equivalent and the second-order model was acceptable for further analysis (Cunningham 2008, Byrne 2010).

The standardized regression weights, critical ratios and squared mltiple correlation for the second-order model are presented in Table 3. As indicated, most of standardized regression weights for model were greater than 0.70, with the lowest value being 0.695 (SuD_Di_03) that was considered as 0.70 after rounding to two decimal places. Furthermore, the regression between the supplier development construct and its four first-order constructs showed significantly high factor loadings, with the lowest factor loading value being 0.796. Most of the obtained item reliability coefficients were greater than 0.50, with the lowest value

Table 3. CFA result for second-order model.

Factor and Item	Standardised Regression Weight (Factor Loading)	Critical Value (t-value)*	Squared Multiple Correlation (Item Reliability Coefficient)
Supplier Development (Second-Order)			
Direct_SD	0.796	8.009	0.634
SuD_Ev	0.849	9.808	0.722
SuD_FB	0.862	10.073	0.742
SuD_IC	0.828	8.391	0.685
Direct Involvement (First-Order)			
SuD_Di_01	0.717		0.515
SuD_Di_02	0.788	9.296	0.620
SuD_Di_03	0.695	8.201	0.483
SuD_Di_04	0.794	9.370	0.630
SuD_Di_05	0.823	9.716	0.678
SuD_Di_06	0.762	8.995	0.581
SuD_Di_07	0.744	8.786	0.554
Supplier Evaluation (First-Order)			
SuD_Ev_01	0.839		0.703
SuD_Ev_02	0.800	11.430	0.640
SuD_Ev_03	0.878	13.035	0.770
SuD_Ev_04	0.725	9.942	0.525
Future Business Incentives (First-Order)			
SuD_FB_01	0.857		0.734
SuD_FB_02	0.875	12.800	0.765
SuD_FB_04	0.728	10.017	0.529
Inter-supplier Collaboration (First-Order)			
SuD_IC_01	0.734		0.538
SuD_IC_02	0.786	9.432	0.618
SuD_IC_03	0.840	10.091	0.706
SuD_IC_04	0.746	8.927	0.556
SuD_IC_05	0.812	9.755	0.660

* statistically significant, p < 0.001, n=151

being 0.483 (SuD_Di_03) that also acceptable for analysis (Cunningham 2008).

The critical ratios of all observed variables are above 1.96, with the lowest value being 8.201, indicating statistical significance of parameter estimates (Jöreskog & Sörbom 1993, Byrne 2010). None of the standardized residual values exceed the cut-off point of |2.58| (Jöreskog & Sörbom 1993). Although some of MIs were somewhat larger than 7.882, their par change were not greater than 0.40, this indicates there is no modification that would improve the par change high enough, suggests it is no need to remove or modify any indicator (Jöreskog & Sörbom 1993). The results were consistent with the first-order construct model. Therefore, supplier development could be analyzed as a second-order construct in the structural model (Cunningham 2008).

The correlations between the second-order construct with its four first-order constructs and with all 19 indicators were significant ($p < 0.001$), supported the nomological validity of the supplier development scale and confirmed that supplier development was validated as a second-order construct model (Spiro & Weitz 1990).

6 CONCLUSION

CFA supports the view that supplier development is a higher-order construct. To the best of the researcher's knowledge, there is no previous empirical study that proposed and tested direct involvement, supplier evaluation, future business incentives, and customer support in inter-supplier collaboration as first-order constructs of the higher-order supplier development. Therefore, although customer support in inter-supplier collaboration has never been included as a factor of supplier development in supplier development empirical studies, the current study confirmed that inter-supplier collaboration is a part of supplier development. This finding is based on the concept of "co-opetition" that balances collaborative synergy and competition among suppliers suggested by Choi et al (2002), Hines's (1994) prescription to facilitate supplier association and supplier development literature that reported supplier development best practices (Nishiguchi & Beaudet 1998, Dyer & Nobeoka 2000, Stuart & Deckert 2009, Stuart et al. 1998). The inter-supplier collaboration is important and has big opportunity to develop in Indonesia, since Indonesia is a country with a collectivist culture, the *gotong-royong* culture causes Indonesians to collaborate to attain a shared goal (Nasroen 1967, Taylor et al. 1991) and the automotive industry in Indonesia is dominated by Japanese multinational companies, which, reported utilizing supplier associations (Hines 1994, Nishiguchi 1994, Dyer & Nobeoka 2000).

REFERENCES

Asanuma, B. 1989. Manufacturer-supplier relationships in Japan and the concept of relation-specific skill. *Journal of the Japanese and international economies* 3(1): 1-30.

Barry, J.M. & Doney, P.M. 2011. Cross-Cultural Examination of Relationship Quality. *Journal of Global Marketing* 24(4): 305-323.

Biemans, W.G. & Brand, M.J. 1995. Reverse Marketing: A Synergy of Purchasing and Relationship Marketing. *International Journal of Purchasing and Materials Management* 31(2): 28-37.

Blenkhorn, D.L. & Banting, P.M. 1991. How Reverse Marketing Changes Buyer – Seller Roles. *Industrial Marketing Management* 20(3): 185-191.

Byrne, B.M. 2010. *Structural equation modeling with AMOS: basic concepts, applications, and programming.* New York: Routledge.

Choi, T. 1999. Reverse Marketing in Asia: A Korean Experience. *Business Horizons* 42(5): 34-34.

Choi, T.Y., Zhaohui, W., Ellram, L. & Koka, B.R. 2002. Supplier-supplier relationships and their implications for buyer-supplier relationships. *IEEE transactions on engineering management* 49(2): 119-130.

Cunningham, E. 2008. *Structural equation modeling using AMOS.* Melbourne: Statsline.

Danneels, E. 2002. The dynamics of product innovation and firm competences. *Strategic Management Journal* 23(12): 1095-1121.

Dyer, J.H. & Nobeoka, K. 2000. Creating and Managing a High-Performance Knowledge-Sharing Network: The Toyota Case. *Strategic Management Journal* 21(3): 345-367.

Frazier, G.L. & Summers, J.O. 1984. Interfirm Influence Strategies and Their Applications within Distribution Channels. *Journal of Marketing*, 48, 43-55.

GAIKINDO 2014. Indonesia Automotive Industry: Report on 2013 Auto Market. *In: 20th Automotive Dialogue Beijing.* Beijing, China: Asia-Pacific Economic Corporation (APEC).

Giunipero, L.C. 1990. Motivating and Monitoring JIT Supplier Performance. *Journal of Purchasing and Materials Management* 26(3): 19-25.

Hahn, C.K., Kim, K.H. & Kim, J.S. 1986. Costs of Competition: Implications for Purchasing Strategy. *Journal of Purchasing and Materials Management* 22(3): 2-7.

Hahn, C.K., Watts, C.A. & Kim, K.Y. 1990. The Supplier Development Program: A Conceptual Model. *Journal of Purchasing and Materials Management* 26(2): 2-7.

Hines, P. 1994. Internationalization and Localization of the Kyoryoku Kai: The Spread of Best Practice Supplier Development. *The International Journal of Logistics Management* 5(1): 67-72.

Hofstede, G., Hofstede, G.J. & Minkov, M. 2010. *Cultures and organizations: software of the mind: intercultural cooperation and its importance for survival.* New York: McGraw-Hill.

Humphreys, P., Cadden, T., Li, W.-L. & Mchugh, M. 2011. An investigation into supplier development activities and their influence on performance in the Chinese electronics industry. *Production Planning and Control* 22(2): 137-156.

Humphreys, P.K., Li, W.L. & Chan, L.Y. 2004. The impact of supplier development on buyer–supplier performance. *Omega* 32(2): 131-143.

Jöreskog, K. & Sörbom, D. 1993. *LISREL 8: Structural equation modeling with the SIMPLIS command language,* Lincolnwood: Scientific Software International, Inc.

Krause, D.R. 1997. Supplier development: Current practices and outcomes. *International Journal of Purchasing and Materials Management* 33(1): 12-19.

Krause, D.R. & Ellram, L.M. 1997. Critical elements of supplier development The buying-firm perspective. *European Journal of Purchasing and Supply Management* 3(1),21-31.

Krause, D.R., Handfield, R.B. & Tyler, B.B. 2007. The relationships between supplier development, commitment, social capital accumulation and performance improvement. *Journal of Operations Management* 25(2): 528-545.

Krause, D.R. & Scannell, T.V. 2002. Supplier Development Practices: Product- and Service-Based Industry Comparisons. *Journal of Supply Chain Management* 38(1): 13-21.

Krause, D.R., Scannell, T.V. & Calantone, R.J. 2000. A structural analysis of the effectiveness of buying firms' strategies to improve supplier performance. *Decision Sciences* 31(1): 33-55.

Leitner, P.A. 2005. The Lean Joerney at the Boeing Company. *ASQ World Conference on Quality and Improvement Proceedings* 59: 263-271.

Liker, J.K. & Choi, T.Y. 2004. Building Deep Supplier Relationships. *Harvard Business Review* 82(12): 104-113.

Modi, S.B. & Mabert, V.A. 2007. Supplier development: Improving supplier performance through knowledge transfer. *Journal of Operations Management* 25(1): 42-64.

Nasroen, M. 1967. *Falsafah Indonesia.* Jakarta: Penerbit Bulan Bintang.

Nishiguchi, T. 1994. *Strategic Industrial Sourcing: The Japanese Advantage.* New York: Oxford University Press.

Nishiguchi, T. & Beaudet, A. 1998. The Toyota Group and the Aisin Fire. *Sloan Management Review* 40(1): 49

Nonaka, I. 1994. A dynamic theory of organizational knowledge creation. *Organization science* 5(1): 14-37.

Purdy, L., Astad, U. & Safayeni, F. 1994. Perceived Effectiveness of the Automotive Supplier Evaluation Process. *International Journal of Operations and Production Management* 14(6): 91-103.

Seltzer, L.H. 1928. *A financial history of the American automobile industry: a study of the ways in which the leading American producers of automobiles have met their capital requirements,* Boston and New York, USA: Houghton Mifflin Company.

Shahzad, K., Sillanpaa, I., Sillanpaa, E. & Imeri, S. 2016. Benchmarking supplier development: An empirical case study of validating a framework to improve buyer-supplier relationship. *Management and Production Engineering Review* 7(1): 56-70.

Spiro, R.L. & Weitz, B.A. 1990. Adaptive Selling: Conceptualization, Measurement, and Nomological Validity. *Journal of Marketing Research (JMR)* 27: 61-69.

Stuart, I. & Deckert, P. 2009. The value of learning consortia for achieving performance excellence in manufacturing. *Ivey Business Journal* 73.

Stuart, I., Deckert, P., Mccutcheon, D. & Kunst, R. 1998. A Leveraged Learning Network. *Sloan Management Review* 39(4): 81-94.

Sucky, E. & Durst, S.M. 2013. Supplier development: current status of empirical research. *International Journal of Procurement Management* 6(1): 92-127.

Taylor, P.M., Aragon, L.V. & Rice, A.L. 1991. *Beyond the Java Sea: Art of Indonesia's Outer Islands*, New York: National Museum of Natural History/Abrams.

Trent, R.J. & Monczka, R.M. 1999. Achieving world-class supplier quality. *Total Quality Management* 10(6): 927-938.

Wagner, S.M. 2006. Supplier development practices: an exploratory study. *European Journal of Marketing* 40(5/6) 554-571.

Wagner, S.M. 2010. Indirect and direct supplier development: performance implications of individual and combined effects. *IEEE Transactions on Engineering Management* 57(4): 536-546.

Wagner, S.M. 2011. Supplier development and the relationship life-cycle. *International Journal of Production Economics* 129(2): 277-283.

Wagner, S.M. & Krause, D.R. 2009. Supplier development: communication approaches, activities and goals. *International Journal of Production Research* 47(12): 3161-3177.

Wasti, S.N. & Liker, J.K. 1999. Collaborating with suppliers in product development: a US and Japan comparative study. *IEEE Transactions on Engineering Management* 46(4): 444-460.

Watts, C.A. & Hahn, C.K. 1993. Supplier development programs: An empirical analysis. *International Journal of Purchasing and Materials Management* 29(1): 10-17.

Wu, Z., Choi, T.Y. & Rungtusanatham, M.J. 2010. Supplier–supplier relationships in buyer–supplier–supplier triads: Implications for supplier performance. *Journal of Operations Management* 28(2): 115-123.

YDBA 2014. *Directory of YDBA's Partner Manufacturing SMEs*. Jakarta: Yayasan Dharma Bhakti Astra.

APPENDIX 1

Direct Involvement:

SuD_Di_01: Customer X undertook supplier development with our firm through giving manufacturing-related advice (e.g. processes, machining process, machine set-up)

SuD_Di_02: Customer X undertook supplier development with our firm through training of our employees.

SuD_Di_03: Customer X undertook supplier development with our firm through transferring their employees to our facilities.

SuD_Di_04: Customer X undertook supplier development with our firm through giving product development-related advice (e.g. processes, project management).

SuD_Di_05: Customer X undertook supplier development with our firm through giving technological advice (e.g. materials, software)

SuD_Di_06: Firm X undertook supplier development with our firm through giving quality-related advice (e.g. use of inspection equipment, quality assurance procedures)

SuD_Di_07: Customer X undertook supplier development with our firm through transferring our employees to their firm.

Supplier Evaluation

SuD_Ev_01: Customer X undertook supplier development with our firm through setting improvement targets

SuD_Ev_02: Customer X undertook supplier development with our firm through auditing our firm

SuD_Ev_03: Customer X undertook supplier development with our firm through providing feedback about our performance

SuD_Ev_04: Customer X undertook supplier development with our firm through strong formal supplier evaluation

Future Benefit

SuD_FB_01: Customer X promised increased volume order of items supplied by our firm for improving current performance

SuD_FB_02: Customer X promised consideration for improved business in the future for delivered improvements in our performance

SuD_FB_03: Customer X shared the cost savings achieved due to our performance improvements

SuD_FB_04: Customer X recognised our improvements through awards

Inter-supplier Collaboration

SuD_IC_01: Customer X provided occasions (e.g. social settings, meetings, forums and conferences, etc.) where suppliers can meet and talk.

SuD_IC_02: Customer X encouraged suppliers to work together on operations issues (i.e. quality, delivery, forecast, process engineering, etc.).

SuD_IC_03: Suppliers' ability to work as a team was an important supplier evaluation/selection criterion for Customer X.

SuD_IC_04: Customer X's contractual agreements promoted collaboration between suppliers.

SuD_IC_05: Customer X encouraged suppliers to help each other out if we encounter production problems.

SuD_IC_06: Customer X encouraged suppliers to coordinate our activities without their direct involvement.

*Global Competitiveness: Business Transformation in the
Digital Era – Abdullah, Widiaty & Abdullah (eds)*
© 2019 Taylor & Francis Group, London, ISBN 978-0-367-19442-0

Structuring Indonesia maritime logistics system through shipping industry, port service provider, and government perspective

Y. Sunitiyoso, S. Nuraeni, T. Inayati, F. Hadiansyah, I.F. Nurdayat & N.F. Pambudi
Institut Teknologi Bandung, Bandung, Indonesia

ABSTRACT: In 2012, as a political will to improve price of goods equality, Indonesian government initiated a program named as Motorways of the Sea Program (*Tol Laut*). Ramification of the program is that large number of stakeholders in Indonesia maritime logistics should be accounted in the design and implementation processes. In order to empower multi perspective in development, stakeholders' involvements shall be considered based on their interests, barriers, and expectations. This study aims to identify those interests, barriers, and expectations from stakeholders in developing and implementing Motorways of the Sea program. Those identification processes will be used as considerations to obtain support from important stakeholders especially government, shipping industry, and ports. Critical system heuristic is used to describe distinctive interests between stakeholders in maritime logistic system. Interviews are conducted with several stakeholders such as shipping companies, government, port infrastructure providers and port operators. Interview results have been triangulated using field observations in several Indonesia main ports. This study is producing a systemic map of each stakeholder's interest, barriers, and expectations that will eventually enable policy makers to have holistic view of the situation, which is important to design policy that generate shared value in the Motorways of the Sea implementation.

1 INTRODUCTION

Indonesia has an estimate of 17,500 islands located within its borders. Therefore, inter-island trade has been an important factor for Indonesia economic development. Indonesia's trading relies heavily on sea transportation because of its capability to transport large volume of goods in relatively lower cost compared to other transportation modes (Siahaan et al. 2013). Furthermore, to keep the cost low, chain of distribution is often divided into more focused divisions such as port service, shipping, stevedoring, and trucking. On the other hand, coordinating and managing these stakeholders is a challenging task. Each stakeholder often has conflicting interest and strategy, presumably because each side wants to maximize their own gain and benefit. Output of this research aimed to develop holistic view of Indonesia maritime system in Indonesia. This holistic view could consider as policy evaluation and give further description gap between perceived and ideal situation in Indonesia maritime logistics.

In some conditions, only sea transportation can send trade goods. On the other hand, although maritime logistics cost is relatively cheap, it is not adequately low to create equal price across the country. Indonesia's production activity is mainly concentrated in several main islands such as Java and Sumatra (Ralahalu & Jinca 2013). This condition has created unfavorable position for regions that are located relatively far from the production centers.

Based on World Bank's report in 2016, Indonesia was ranked as the 63rd country based on its logistic performance index, which was still below in comparison with neighboring countries' ranks. Indonesia was also considered as one of the countries with most expensive logistic cost where it still consumes 26% of its GDP. Major discrepancies in terms of development between regions or islands still exist. One of the most apparent phenomena to be observed as a sign of unequal development is the vast difference of basic commodities prices in different region in Indonesia. It is commonly known that the price of commodities such as gasoline in eastern part of Indonesia could reach 400% higher than the gasoline price in western part of Indonesia. The situation exists because of the high logistic cost to transport the commodities to the eastern part Indonesia. Hence, the government sees maritime logistic as one of the priority issues to be solved to reach its development goals.

Indonesian government sees that maritime logistics issue as an important factor for their success on realizing an equal development throughout the country's broad region. In 2012, as a political will to improve price of goods equality, the Government initiated a program to tackle this issue named as *Pendulum Nusantara*, and in 2014 it was named as the Motorway of the Sea (*Tol Laut*) program. The main idea of the program is to decrease logistics cost by optimizing the utilization of sea transportation and the mobility of inter-island decentralized commodities production center. Ramification of the program is that large number of stakeholders in Indonesia maritime logistics should be accounted in the design and implementation processes. Democratic, decentralized, and pluralistic nature of Indonesia's government, culture, and bureaucracy has put challenge on the implementation of the *Tol Laut* Program. In order to make the program successful, stakeholders' involvements shall be considered based on their interests, barriers, and expectations (Direktorat Transportasi 2015).

BAPPENAS policy paper is to disseminate detailed government plan for *Tol Laut* implementation. Tol Laut strategy mainly focuses on development of 24 strategic ports. This port was chosen to build hub and spoke transportation system. Hub and spoke system aimed to boost shipping efficiency. Other policy is to non-commercial port that is not able to be self-sustained from operation activities (Direktorat Transportasi 2015). All of them will be under government control through Ministry of Transportation. Government also encourages shipping company to operate in certain routes. Government incentives were applied to attract shipping company. All this complex activity is run and monitored by Indonesia central government.

On the other hand, Indonesia's maritime logistics system consists of many different stakeholders, which made the implementation of the government's maritime logistics policy become more intricate. Hence, it is essential to see how the stakeholders view and react to the policy employed by the central government. Therefore, this study aims to explore stakeholders' perspective towards current Indonesia maritime logistics system; especially shipping industry, port service provider, and government.

2 LITERATURE REVIEW

Maritime logistics problem in previous studies mainly focus on efficiency issue. Inefficient operation of route and ship is the main cause of inflated logistics cost, especially in Indonesia (Ralahalu & Jinca 2013, Fahmiasari & Parikesit 2017, Tu et al. 2017). A study about implementation of Tol Laut and Pendulum Nusantara could increase efficiency 10 times compared to previous network. To meet that condition, eastern hub ports, such as in Bitung and Sorong, need to be developed (Fahmiasari & Parikesit 2017). Furthermore, a unique strategy to formulate maritime logistics in Indonesia's growing market is required (Tu et al. 2017). This view leads government to set and prepare prerequisite condition and calculate optimum parameter for each controlled element, such as number of ports, which ports should become a hub, and which route should be the most efficient in particular ship size.

Maritime logistics problem in previous studies mainly focus on efficiency issue. Inefficient operation of route, and ship is the main cause of inflated logistics cost, especially in Indonesia (Ralahalu & Jinca 2013, Fahmiasari & Parikesit 2017, Tu et al. 2017). A study about implementation of Tol Laut and Pendulum Nusantara could increase efficiency 10 times compared to previous network. In order to meet that condition, eastern hub ports, such as in Bitung and Sorong, need to be developed (Fahmiasari & Parikesit 2017). Furthermore, there is required unique strategy to formulate maritime logistics in Indonesia's growing market (Tu et al. 2017). This view lead government to set and prepare prerequisite condition and calculate optimum parameter for each controlled element, such as number of ports, which ports should become a hub, and which route should be the most efficient in particular ship size.

Research of maritime transport from 2000 – 2014 in main maritime transport journal has shown growing portion of quantitative approach (Shi & Li 2017). The focus of these researches is mainly on shipping and port topics. This phenomenon indicates that maritime logistics is viewed as sectoral optimization (Mangan et al. 2008). On the other hand, maritime logistics include many parties that created multi perspectives and interests in the system. Thus, research to investigate who the stakeholder is and what their interest and aspiration toward maritime logistics are, especially in Indonesia, is needed to define Indonesia maritime logistics system (Wicaksana 2017).

Largely maritime logistics referred to as an integral process of planning, implementing, and managing the flow of goods and information where ocean carriage acts as the medium (Nam & Song 2011). Song & Panayides (2015) stated that maritime logistics perspective applies to maritime transport issues where logistics and supply chain theoretical context were employed. This indicates that maritime logistics relates to a vast network of actors/components. Moreover, there are three key players in maritime logistics which Nam & Song (2011) identified: shipping companies, port operators, and freight forwarders. Linked to the previous description of maritime logistics, this further showed the complexity involved in the study of maritime logistics, especially maritime logistics as a system.

When analysing environmental conflict issues, where stakeholders are basically the indispensable part of it, it is crucial to analyse and identify the worldview; this includes the interest and position, of the stakeholders involved in the said issues. Policy development is highly related to environmental conflict where its implementation will fundamentally decide the consequences, which relevant stakeholders will receive. It can be concluded that stakeholders view is needed when developing policy for a system.

Based on the study of Vitsounis & Pallis (2012), all members of relevant ports and community influence and contribute to the framing of port system. Furthermore, they conclude that pooled and reciprocal interdependencies that existed in ports are the ones which help promotes the emergence of value co-creation scheme. This indicates that, related to maritime logistics where the port system is one of its components, the understanding of relevant stakeholders' views is needed to analyse maritime logistics system thoroughly.

3 METHODOLOGY

Critical System Heuristics (CSH) was a qualitative analysis method developed by Ulrich (1996), that is, a reference for system or a system of concern. It defines and structures the situation of an issue into a map of situation or design for changing. In practical, CSH can be used to assess an intervention or used for intervention (Reynolds & Holwell 2010). CSH uses boundary judgments as constraint to frame situation. The boundary *method* is used to make up a feature situation through mapping a phenomenon into two frames, namely descriptive frame and normative frame (Reynolds & Holwell 2010). Descriptive frame is that existing condition or known as "what is" condition. Normative frame is that ideal condition or known as "what should" condition.

In the first stage of Critical System Heuristics (CSH), identifying stakeholders carried out from secondary data. In this stage, the reference system is the SISLOGNAS, that being identified by the research and using the boundary questions to identify which stakeholders that have certain social roles. In the second stage of CSH, on constructing the descriptive frame, certain semi-structured interview was conducted to justify the identified stakeholders as well as their social roles and key problems.

This paper is utilising qualitative data to generate analysis. Data are collected through interviews with 3 representatives from different stakeholders. First respondent is a representative from one of the largest port service provider companies that is government owned and is authorised in managing government-owned sea ports concentrated in 10 provinces in Indonesia. Second respondent is a representative from a private-owned shipping company in Indonesia established since 1964. Last respondent is a representative from The Committee for Acceleration of Priority Infrastructure Delivery (KPPIP). All interviews were conducted from April 2018 until June 2018. These interviews were conducted using semi-structured interview where all interviewed were recorded upon the agreement of the respondents through interviewees' consent. Interview guides were constructed using previous research, report, and critical system heuristics question guidelines (Ulrich, 2005).

4 RESULTS AND DISCUSSION

There will be two kinds of analyses: 'ought to' analysis and 'is' analysis. The "ought to" analysis will be conducted based on the boundary categories and questions of CSH adapted from Ulrich (1996). The analyses will perform ideal mapping of Indonesia maritime logistic system as the reference system based on its source of motivation, control, knowledge, and legitimacy from participating stakeholders. The analysis will define which part is the involved and which part is the affected from the implementation of maritime logistic system. The "ought to" analyses for maritime logistic system can be seen in Table 1.

Table 1. shows the 'ought to' analysis for maritime logistics. The 'is' analysis reflects the claims about current conditions by stakeholders. Government and state-owned enterprise are the intended beneficiary of the maritime logistic system. There is still less opportunity for domestic private-owned enterprises especially shipping industries to become one part that benefits from maritime logistic system. The involvement of domestic private sectors, especially in shipping industry, is considered important. However, Indonesian government chooses to have relationships with foreign private sectors. This condition forces domestic private sectors to diversify their products and services. Therefore, companies build non-shipping divisions or subsidiary companies. For instance, they build container, trucking, ports, warehousing, and distribution centre. Maritime logistic is less beneficial for domestic private-owned enterprise and its influence make less contribution for them to develop the system.

Whether government, shipping companies, and port service provider have the same goal in maritime logistic system, the main goal is minimizing total logistic cost. The improvement to achieve the goal in port service provider mainly focused to speed, reliability, transparency, and technology. The improvement is also affecting the logistic cost applies to shipping industries as customer in port service. Minimizing logistic cost also develop fair price of products in Indonesian area although it cannot be guaranteed that the effect will occurs directly. If cost of goods is still expensive but the logistics cost in shipping has decreased, then trading system in land has to be analysed. Traders may have increased their margin price. One way to cope with this problem is by establishing trading house managed by the Government.

Fair price and economic development is controlled by government to measure the improvement in order to seek the real impact of minimizing total logistic cost from shipping industries and port service provider. The rule of shipping should be that the vessel follows trade, but what happens currently is the other way around. Building ports need to be conducted where there are economic opportunities in that area. This causes the inefficiency of shipping logistics hence increased costs. However, the condition is the other way around. Government had spent major amount of money to pioneer harbour instead of commercial harbour, which is counter intuitive action according to commercial perspective.

Development of motorways of the sea in maritime logistic system, by providing several routes in Indonesian archipelago, should be supported by clear potential commodities in each destined location that

Table 1. Ought to analysis for maritime logistics system.

Boundary Judgments Informing Maritime Logistics (S)			
Source of Influence	*Social roles (Stakeholders)*	*Specific concerns (Stakes)*	*Key Problems (Stake holding issues)*
Source of motivation	*1. Beneficiary* Shipping companies, port service provider, industries, communities	*2. Purpose* Minimizing the total logistic cost that should be paid by customer such as shipping companies, port service provider, industries, and communities.	*3. Measure of Improvement* Fair price and stable demand in the destined location for transporting the product to the communities. Economic development in the communities in destined location to produce significant commodities.	**The involved**
Source of Control	*4. Decision Maker* Government by its regulations and policies.	*5. Resources* The dwelling time in the port and the balance demand and supply in a route that implemented in maritime logistic system.	*6. Decision Environment* The dwelling time definition should be clear and standardized to bring transparent and fair performance measurement and not intend to avoid the problem of it in the port activities. The market environment should bring balance supply and demand to get an efficient maritime logistic, therefore economic development in destined location should be prioritized.	
Source of Knowledge	*7. Expert* Local government, industries, practitioners and academicians.	*8. Expertise* Technical knowledge and expertise of maritime transportation logistic, including management and technology related subject.	*9. Guarantor* Experts that promote holistic view and mutual understanding of the system	
Source of legitimacy	*10. Witness* The people and goods producers in Indonesia, both in the present and also in the future.	*11. Emancipation* Related ministries or entities open to criticism or questions from affected parties	*12. Worldview* Ecosystem that promote coordination between communities, local industries, local government, central government, shipping industries, and port service provider.	**The Affected**

will bring efficient loading on shipping process of logistic. Economic development should be guaranteed by local government and communities' activities that will be helped by the availability of product from shipping routes. There is a problem from local government who often gives additional demands to the infrastructure specification such as exit gate for toll road in their area. Decentralized government should be coordinated with the creation of shared values and goals between local government and central government to minimize intervention and sabotage during infrastructures delivery.

In other perspective, to support the economic development on the destined location may involve marketing aspect. The communities' ability to produce as well as consume different commodities could be pointed out through the marketing channel. Therefore, the coordination of several participating industries should be implemented. The said participating industries are retail companies, warehousing, and trucking companies. The goal is to bring the economic development in the communities to produce leading commodities. Then, the commodities can be transported to another area that can support efficiency of the shipping route in maritime logistic system.

Still in the context to maintain economic development, acceleration of infrastructure delivery is also important. Factors that subjected to the development of maritime logistic infrastructure are policy, sabotage, and market factor. Policy factor discusses the urgency of action that can support the acceleration of infrastructure delivery. Sabotage factor will be focused on the uncertainty during infrastructure delivery should be minimized especially in social and political issues. Market factor will determine whether the targeted area where the infrastructure will be built is economically well developed and has the needed potential or not.

Government as a decision maker has prioritized which infrastructure are critical to be built with the hope to manage its limited financial capability. The demand of infrastructure is often higher than the capability of government to build them. Infrastructure development should be done in good coordination between central governments, local governments, and private industries. Such manner is needed to give opportunities to private companies take part in supporting government's financial capability and develop a potential business from its infrastructure. However, the government only manages major ports that have high potential of profit. Smaller ports are offered to private-owned companies. These ports are considered to be less profitable compared to ports owned by government-owned companies. Government-owned companies are supposed to conduct public services for the citizens; instead, they are aiming for profit. Small ports should be managed by government-owned companies rather than handing them to private-owned companies. Other phenomena showed that the planning of ports development in Indonesia was considered being too hasty in its process, whilst the development should be carefully planned yet being sustainable. This can occur with cooperation with local government. However, local government's budget for infrastructure allocation is small. One possible solution is to bring this matter to ministry level. In addition, public private partnership may also be incorporated to generate more funding.

Operational aspect, dwelling time and productivity in port are also becoming important measurements in developing maritime logistic system. However, the definition of dwelling time in the port should be standardized and adjusted to the condition of the port itself. The regulation must be supportive to the system in port to maintain the clean and clear statement of the arriving logistic. The problem should not be avoided by using the regulation, but the regulation must bring the deliberating of authorization to deal the administrative demand in port. There must be appointed personnel or system to replace longer bureaucracy process. Government is the main decision maker with its regulations and policies. On the other hand, integrated system/platform including custom and administrative process of the logistics involving 18 authorized ministry and department in Indonesia need to be developed. Thus, it may consider the deliberating authorization of respected personnel in the department or ministry. The approval process should be able to be done in the port area to minimize the waiting time of transporter in port and total logistic cost for customer. The system is also become transparent via the implementation of cashless and one gate bureaucracy system. The system will minimize human interaction and the payment can be done in the system directly anytime and anywhere the customer wishes to pay.

The productivity in the port itself is significant to be increased to reduce delays and dwelling time in the said port. Therefore, port management needs to be considered as essential booster of productivity.

Changing the capacity of the ships may generate the decrease of occupancy almost to half of previous occupancy. Hence, with the decrease of pier usage rate, the delays of dwelling time on ports will also decrease. Efficiency of the logistics system does not depend solely on gears or machines, but also human resources. Sufficient trainings are needed for workers in every level in order to ensure the efficiency of time and productivity. The strategy will be delivered firstly by doing a re-layout of the port, continued with the solving of human resources and operational activities' problem. Lastly, implementing related and relevant technologies can do the improvement in equipment and system.

The actual condition may still lack of coordination especially between government, state-owned enterprise, and domestic private companies. The priority of infrastructure development still has inadequate potential market to generate profit. Thus, private companies are reluctant to participate. This condition also exacerbates with less guarantee from government for developing infrastructure in maritime logistics. Yet, government relies more on their collaboration with state-owned enterprises and foreign private companies to get more funding in developing port infrastructure for its maritime logistic system. However, there is mutual interest from government, state-owned enterprises, and private companies in maritime logistic system to promote productivity and efficiency in port for minimizing the total logistic cost. Different stakeholders claim several practical solutions based on each experience for minimizing the total logistic cost.

5 CONCLUSION

As the largest archipelagic country in the world, Indonesia's maritime logistics system is very fundamental and significant whose problems should be taken by initiatives as quickly as possible. When discussing about a system, stakeholders are having major roles in creating and implementing it; however, stakeholders must have different perspectives and interests at hand. Therefore, this paper's purpose is to identify interests, barriers, and expectations from stakeholders who have important roles in this system by utilizing a methodology identified as Critical Systems Heuristics. Our findings after gathering data through interviews with several stakeholders show that there are discrepancies of how the system ideally should be and how it really is in terms of operations, supply chain, human resources, financing, even the policies and implementation by the Government. Building integrative system that can benefit all stakeholders, although difficult, is yet still doable. Further recommendation is to gather important stakeholders to coordinately create not only beneficial maritime logistics systems but also sustainable.

REFERENCES

Direktorat Transportasi. 2015. *Implementasi Konsep Tol Laut 2015-2019*. Jakarta: BAPPENAS.

Fahmiasari, H. & Parikesit, D. 2017. Container shipping network efficiency comparison in Indonesia: Nusantara Pendulum and Sea Tollway. *The Asian Journal of Shipping and Logistics* 33(2): 79-84.

Mangan, J., Lalwani, C. & Fynes, B. 2008. Port-centric logistics. *The International Journal of Logistics Management*. 19(1): 29-41.

Nam, H.S. & Song, D.W. 2011. Defining maritime logistics hub and its implication for container port. *Maritime Policy & Management*. 38(3): 269-292.

Ralahalu, K.A. & Jinca, M.Y. 2013. The Development of Indonesia Archipelago Transportation. *International Refered Journal of Engineering and Science (IRJES)*. 2(9): 12-18.

Reynolds, M. & Holwell, S. 2010. *Systems approaches to managing change: a practical guide*. Berlin: Springer Science & Business Media.

Siahaan, D.L., Jinca, M.Y., Wunas, S. & Pallu, M.S. 2013. Container Sea Transportation Demand in Eastern Indonesia. *International Refereed Journal of Engineering and*.

Shi, W. & Li, K.X. 2017. Themes and tools of maritime transport research during 2000-2014. *Maritime Policy & Management*. 44(2): 151-169.

Song, D.W. & Panayides, P. 2015. *Maritime logistics: A guide to contemporary shipping and port management*. London: Kogan Page Publishers.

Tu, N., Adiputranto, D., Fu, X. & Li, Z.C. 2018. Shipping network design in a growth market: The case of Indonesia. *Transportation Research Part E: Logistics and Transportation Review* 117: 108-125.

Ulrich, W. 1996. *A Primer to Critical Systems Heuristics for Action Researchers*. Hull, UK: University of Hull, Centre for Systems Studies.

Ulrich, W. 2005. A brief introduction to critical systems heuristics (CSH). *Web site of the ECOSENSUS project, Open University, Milton Keynes, UK*.

Vitsounis, T.K. & Pallis, A.A. 2012. Port value chains and the role of interdependencies. In *Maritime Logistics: Contemporary Issues (pp. 155-174)*. Bingley: Emerald Group Publishing Limited.

Wicaksana, I.G.W. 2017. Indonesia's maritime connectivity development: domestic and international challenges. *Asian Journal of Political Science* 25(2): 212-233.

Global Competitiveness: Business Transformation in the
Digital Era – Abdullah, Widiaty & Abdullah (eds)
© 2019 Taylor & Francis Group, London, ISBN 978-0-367-19442-0

Design of decision support system "reverse supply chain management" based on Android

I. Dharmayanti & W. Kartika
APP Polytechnic, Jakarta, Indonesia

E.H. Yossy
Bina Nusantara University, Jakarta, Indonesia

ABSTRACT: Reverse supply chain is the backward movement of product in supply chain. This paper proposes a reverse logistics decision support system which can ease product information tracking for customers, company (decision-maker), and service center regarding products returned. The model in this paper is inspired by various papers published in the literature and real-life examples of repairing smartphones at the authorized service center. The proposed model considers important elements of reverse supply chain which are initial screening process of reverse (gatekeeping), collection, sorting, and recovery (treatment). Activity diagram of each element reverse supply chain is described. Implementation of a decision support system based on android is also presented. The proposed model will help the parties involved in reverse activities and also help academics in developing better decision reverse supply chain model, especially for electronic products that have shorter life cycle.

1 INTRODUCTION

Reverse supply chains (RSC) include collection and reprocessing activities of used manufactured products in order to recover their remaining market value (Filip & Duta 2015). Due to environmental concerns, RSC now is becoming an important strategy to increase customer satisfaction and also how the material is recovered, and who will execute and manage the various reverse operations are important issues (Liao 2018). Many companies do not manage the flow of goods and materials well, as some assume that reverse is a burden to the company, which cannot be predicted with certainty unless with additional data and related information. However, reversing this SCM (Supply Chain Manager) can provide benefits to the company economically, socially, and environmentally. RSC management needs to be done in order to increase the company's competitive advantage in providing services to its customers (Blumberg 2005).

In every RS system, it is essential to make decisions concerning the returns management, efficient communication between the different parties involved, product identification, handling, and treatment (Turki & Mounir 2014). Based on related literature, the researches seem to focus on the whole process of reverse flow and there is few who have mentioned the Decision Support Systems (DSS). Lambert et al. (2011) proposed decision conceptual framework RSC process in general. There is no single reference model to make their RSC more efficient; each company must find the best solution to specific situation. Turki &

Mounir (2014) who proposed a DSS for reverse logistics uses a web-based application by adding three more elements to complete the reverse flow management. These elements are (1) the coordinating system, (2) the gatekeeping, (3) the collection, (4) the sorting, (5) the information system, (6) the disposal system. This paper proposes a DSS concept on RSC process of smartphone product based on android operation system. The use of android-based information technology will make the application more attractive and easier to use, and can be used by the company that includes some for partnership such as parts production, warehouse, sender, and other stakeholders such as distributors, service centers, and consumers as the user, without fixating on the availability of computer hardware, because this application is designed with android operating system that can be accessed by using a smartphone. It is expected that by the creation of this application, both companies and the public can obtain the ease and benefits of reverse process materials or products from consumers to electronics manufacturing companies, and thereby achieve the effectiveness and efficiency of reverse services.

2 LITERATURE REVIEW

2.1 *Closed-loop supply chain management*

Closed-loop supply chain (CLSCM) can be defined as a system of design, control, and operation to maximize creation of the value throughout the product life cycle by recovering the value of the product dynamically, because the type and volume of the returned product are not the same at different time (Guide et al. 2003). This activity is a combination of forward and RSC activities.

According to Blumberg (2005), CLSCM activity is a sustainable approach to the engineering activity design in product development or system operation.

2.1.1 Forward logistics and direct supply chain management

Management of activities and overall forward logistics control from material, part, and finished product streams to the main warehouse, distributed, and up to the end user.

2.1.2 Reverse logistics

Coordination activity and control of taking materials, parts, and products that have been used from consumers, sent to the recycling process, and then back to the consumer if it can be reused.

2.1.3 Depot repair, processing, diagnostic, and disposal

The activity of receiving returned product through reverse logistics process, inspection, recondition, and redistribution process through main line, secondary market, and disposed as waste. In general, RSC activities may include reuse, repair, remanufacturing, recycling, and disposal. Reverse logistics is the most important part of the CLSC, because without a reverse flow, there is no loop in the supply chain.

Furthermore, for high-technology products such as smartphones, Blumberg (2005) spelled out a reverse model, from the four CLSC models he presented. The models are shown in Figure 1.

In high-tech products, original equipment manufacturer (OEM) sells its products to consumers and is directly responsible for the RL (Reverse Logistics) process. Such products as sub-assembly, part, and returned component will be recovered by the OEM through a designated dealer as an OEM representative

or an OEM service center itself. In this model, direct supply chain and RL are controlled by OEM. However, the reverse process also can be done directly independently without going through an OEM.

2.2 Reverse supply chain

According to Guide et al. (2003), reverse supply chain is a series of activities to take back products that are not used by consumers and those that can be reused or become waste later. There are five main RSC processes: product acquisition; reverse logistics (the activity of transferring/shipping of the acquired product to the handling); inspection and disposition (disassembly), inspection, testing, sorting of returned products to identify quality, choosing appropriate treatment and appropriate recovery strategies); reconditioning (repair, re-furbished, or remanufactured); redistribution and sales (sales of products that have been reconditioned and re-usable).

The first step to designing an RSC is to choose the proper take-back path process from the return product, to return to manufacturing. The process of taking its products is made directly to the consumer; through the intermediary retailers; as well as through third-party services. For the latter, there are two collection models namely Centralized and Decentralized RSC.

2.3 Utilization of information technology in reverse supply chain management

The information technology development provides various positive impacts to increasing productivity of many sectors, including logistics and supply chain management. Bhandari (2016) argues that the latest technologies being used in logistics and supply chain management are segregated into:

- Automatic Identification Technology: Bar coding, Radio Frequency Identification (RFID), Radio Frequency Tags (RFTs)
- Communication Technology: Electronic Data Interchange (EDI), Very Small Aperture Terminal (VSAT), Geographical Positioning System (GPS), Geographical Information System (GIS), Web-Based Tracking, Automated Guided Vehicle System (AGVS) and
- Information Technology (IT): The IT tools used in logistic and SCM are Enterprise Resource Planning (ERP), Distribution Requirement Planning (DRP), and Automated Inventory Tracking System (AITS).

The more complex a business gets, the more complicated the decision-making is. Some factors such as the need to respond quickly to the markets; a rapidly changing environment and the uncertainty of its impact; need for quick and real-time monitoring and information; as well as the need to coordinating the decision-makers who are not in the same location, made manual decision-making more difficult. It makes

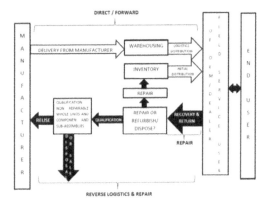

Figure 1. Closed-Loop Supply Chain for high-tech products (Blumberg, 2005).

computer-based information system necessary in analyzing and exploring various alternative decisions.

The instrument in this decision-making is said to be DSS. Turban (2007) suggests that the DSS component consists of Data Management, Model Management, and User Interfaces.

Filip & Duta (2015), who studied the DSC on Reverse SCM in several European countries, exposed the important issues and the attributes of DSS that can be used on Reverse SCM. However, this paper is a literature review and case studies are not explained.

RSC research has previously focused on reverse processes as a whole, but few have combined with DSS. There is research on Reverse Logistic DSS, but it still focuses merely on one phase, like recovery process or delivery.

Turki & Mounir (2014) drafted the DSS model in the RL process by taking issues related to product recovery activities, vehicle routing, and end-of-life product handling issues. The proposed DSS integration on RL activities is used to facilitate tracking product information, shipping, storing, referencing, and reporting for managers as decision-makers. The Turki and Mounir research adds four main activities: gatekeeping, collection, sorting, and disposal, with three additional activities of coordination, treatment, and information systems, as shown in Figure 2. Research conducted by Turki & Mounir (2014) creates customer value by providing accurate information to customer and provider through web portal.

The current study will propose a DSS concept on RSC process of smartphone product based on android operation system. The steps of the research include: (1) identifying the SCM flow, (2) identifying possible reverse activities as indicator of each activity, (3) designing RSC model, (4) conceptualizing model validation, (5) designing logic models of the DSS features, (6) validating logic model, (7) designing the simulation model (interface), (8) modeling validation and verification, (9) having trials, and (10) implementing the results.

In this paper, the discussion is limited to DSS conceptual on RSC element and design the simulation model (interface).

3 PROPOSED MODEL

The proposed model is based on literature review and interviews with smartphone service centers. From the literature, Lambert et al. (2011) stated that RL system considers four steps: gatekeeping, collection, sorting, and treatment or recovery. The disposal is not mentioned because of the nature of a product. The goal of this model is to propose an android-based RL system DSS for smartphones. Activity diagram for each step is presented in the subsections below.

3.1 *Step 1: Gatekeeping*

Gatekeeping is a filtering process in which returned products are allowed to enter RL system (Giuntini & Andel 1995). For smartphones, activity diagram of gatekeeping is adopted from Lambert et al. (2011). A preliminary gatekeeping leads to communication between customer and company whether return authorization should be required. If a return authorization is necessary, and verification should be done, customers will then receive a return authorization number to service if verification is accepted by the company. After the company receives the product, the company decides whether recovery is possible or not. Activity diagram DSS for gatekeeping is shown in Figure 3. A customer who is refused through the gatekeeping process may send their product back to the company in accordance with the terms and conditions apply. A decision needs to be made on whether the product should be retuned; if a return authorization is necessary, verification should be done.

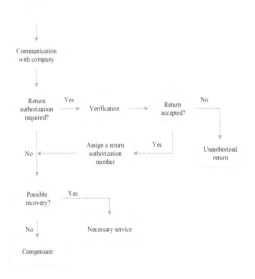

Figure 3. Activity diagram of DSS: Gatekeeping (Lambert et al. 2011).

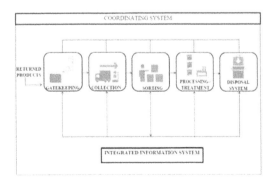

Figure 2. Seven RL activities (Turki & Mounir 2014).

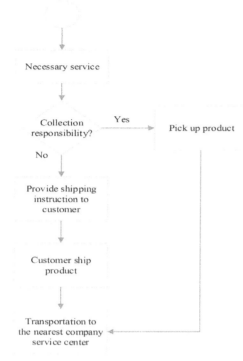

Figure 4. Activity diagram of DSS: Collection.

3.2 Step 2: Collection

Collection is a process of receiving returned products from customers, as illustrated in Figure 4. If the company is required to take responsibility for the collection process, product pick-up should be done; otherwise, customers send the product to the nearest company representative service center based on shipping instruction.

In the electronics industry, the technician visits the customer to repair onsite, if possible. If the company is not responsible for returning the product, the company must give clear instructions on packaging, returning address, etc. Thus, a decision needs to be made and may include whether responsibility for collection should take place which will also determine the nearest company service center.

3.3 Step 3: Sorting

A preliminary sorting takes place after receiving the returned products and authorization process is given to the gatekeeper, as illustrated in Figure 5. The company decides which products are acceptable or not. In this step, company must determine the criteria for accepting to avoid differences in decision-making. These criteria will be inputted into the database in the DSS. According to Rogers & Tibben-Lembke (1999), returned products have different reasons. A decision needs to be made and may include return reason and further handling.

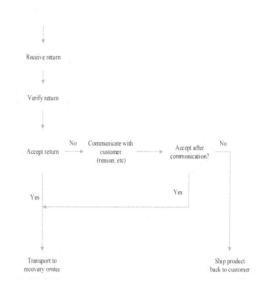

Figure 5. Activity diagram of DSS: Sorting.

3.4 Step 4: Recovery

This step involves activities with recovery options such as repair, upgrade, and cannibalization. They are considered for smartphones because they are proposed RL system until they arrive at a service center. This activity diagram is shown in Figure 6. Determining the initial state of the returned products influences recovery options. According to De Brito et al. (2002), several types of recovery can be distinguished. They are separated by product recovery,

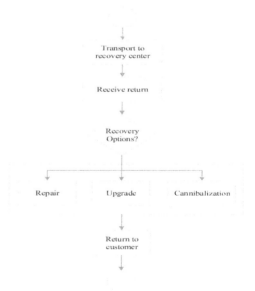

Figure 6. Activity Diagram of DSS: Recovery.

component recovery, material recovery, and energy recovery. In this model, recovery decision is separated by product recovery and component recovery. Product recovery contains repair and upgrade; then component recovery is cannibalization (components are taken off and used to repair another unit of the same product).

3.5 Android-based DSS of RL system

After presenting a conceptual RL system for smartphones, this section presents some screenshots from the proposed DSS model based on android. It shows interface register (Figure 7), return authorization (Figure 8), types of complaint or product return (Figure 9), and recovery suggestion (Figure 10).

Interface register shown in Figure 7 presents initial process in RSC (gatekeeping). Customers should register before they return their product. Information required are username, email, and phone number. Based on customer data, the company decides whether the return is accepted or not.

If customer data are verified, the company will send return authorization number to the customers via email. Then, the customers complete user return

Figure 9. Type of complaint from screenshot.

Figure 10. Recovery suggestion from screenshot.

authorization as shown in Figure 8. It is required to know information about product return.

Types of complaint shown in Figure 9 present reasons of return. Reasons of return for smartphones are LCD, power, audio, camera, battery, etc. According to De Brito et al. (2002), a product is returned because the product is not working properly.

Recovery suggestion presents decision from the company after the returned product is examined directly. Customer receives that information through the application which is shown in Figure 10. Based on previous explanation, recovery options are repair, upgrade, and cannibalization.

4 DISCUSSION

In the proposed DSS model, the parties involved are customers, companies (decision makers), and authorization service centers (recovery centers). The main objectives proposed a reverse logistics decision support system which can ease product information tracking to products returned, especially smartphone customer using an android-based application. According to Turki & Mounir (2014), to create a

Figure 7. Register from screenshot.

Figure 8. User return authorization from screenshot.

customer value through the return process, we make sure that necessary and the correct information are provided. All customers fill in and send a return request form to the company. A return request form should be available on the application. Only customers who are registered while purchasing the product in the first place can send a return request. By this purchase, data of both the customer and the product are saved into database. Customers who use this application do not have to come to service center.

However, in this model, sorting is the most crucial issue because the company must determine the criteria for accepting a return. Each type is concerned with specific criteria, which are different from the others (Lambert et al. 2011).

5 CONCLUSION

The conclusion of this paper is that an android-based DSS model can be developed to improve the efficiency and effectiveness of RSC management.

This model is designed to ease product returned information tracking to customers in the reverse process. As consumers can know the possibility of damage experienced, they also know where they should send the product, provide an alternative way to collecting process by looking for delivery without having to come to the service center, and get estimated treatment time, and the estimated cost if they must pay. Thus, the consumers can decide whether to proceed to immediate recovery or not.

This model does not include the disposal stage. Also, the DSS model in smartphone Reverse SCM designed has not yet reached the manufacturing level. The model is designed to determine the type of recovery/treatment type in service center.

Considering those facts, further research is expected to develop a DSS model that covers all reverse SCM activities on smartphone products.

REFERENCES

Bhandari, R. 2014. Impact of technology on logistics and supply chain management. *IOSR Journal of Business and Management* p.19-24

Blumberg, D.F. 2005. *Introduction to management of reverse logistics and closed loop supply chain processes.* Boca Raton, FL, USA: CRC Press.

Rogers, D.S. & Tibben-Lembke, R.S. 1999. *Going backwards: reverse logistics trends and practices (Vol. 2).* Pittsburgh, PA: Reverse Logistics Executive Council.

Brito, M.D., Flapper, S.D. & Dekker, R. 2002. *Reverse logistics.* Rotterdam: Econometric Institute Research Papers.

Filip, F.G. & Duta, L. 2015. Decision support systems in reverse supply chain management. *Procedia Economics and Finance* 22, 154-159.

Giuntini, R. & Andel, T. 1995. Master the six R's of reverse logistics - Part 2. *Transportation and Distribution* 36(2): 73-77.

Guide, V.D.R. & Wassenhove, L.N. 2003. *Business aspects of closed-loop supply chains (Vol. 12, pp. 86-93).* Pittsburgh, PA: Carnegie Mellon University Press.

Lambert, S., Riopel, D., Kader, W.A. 2011. A reverse logistics decision conceptual framework. *Computers & Industrial Engineering* 61(3): 561-581.

Liao, T.Y. 2018. Reverse logistics network design for product recovery and remanufacturing. *Applied Mathematical Modelling* 60: 145-163.

Turban, E. 2007. *Information technology for management: Transforming organizations in the digital economy.* Hoboken, New Jersey: John Wiley & Sons, Inc.

Turki, W. & Mounir, B. 2014. A proposition of a decision support system for reverse logistics. *In Advanced Logistics and Transport (ICALT), 2014 International Conference on (pp. 120-125). IEEE.*

Global Competitiveness: Business Transformation in the
Digital Era – Abdullah, Widiaty & Abdullah (eds)
© *2019 Taylor & Francis Group, London, ISBN 978-0-367-19442-0*

Developing green manufacturing framework through reverse logistics using system dynamics simulation

E. Fatma & D. Jayawati
Politeknik APP Jakarta, Jakarta, Indonesia

C.P. Wulandari
National Taiwan University of Science and Technology, Taipei, Taiwan

ABSTRACT: This paper proposes to create a system simulation model to simulate e-waste management to support the development of green manufacturing framework by considering economic and environmental concerns. This paper uses system dynamics simulation based on literature studies and related previous research. The initial stage of this research was carried out by identifying the barrier of e-waste management and factors that influence e-waste management. Then, a conceptual model of e-waste process management through a reverse logistics system was developed. The conceptual model was developed into a simulation which consists of several related sub-models including manufacturer, distributor, government, recycle provider and environment sub-model. From the proposed causal and stock and flow model, it is found that government regulation and incentives play an important role in developing green manufacturing framework.

1   INTRODUCTION

The rapid technological developments and market changes have triggered electronics manufacturers to compete in producing new products frequently. However, this development led to a shorter life cycle of electronics products. Shortened electronic life cycles may cause the product to be no longer used or depleted faster which will lead to the increase of electronic waste (e-waste). Balde et al. (2014) reported that e-waste produced globally between 2010 and 2015 has reached 48 million tons. E-waste management becomes important since various components consisted in e-waste are classified as toxic and can be harmful to the health and the environment. Meanwhile, e-waste recycling processing business is profitable (Krishnadas & Radhakrishna 2014). Unfortunately, e-waste treatments are scattered and hard to control; and only a small percentage of total e-waste has been appropriately managed.

Fernando & Rupasinghe (2016) reveal that there is an increasing awareness about e-waste and its impact on environmental sustainability. Increasing environmental concern has led manufacturers to manage their e-waste and develop green manufacturing (Lu et al. 2015). On the other hand, e-waste management is a complicated process due to the contents of the hazardous material composition which will affect environments (Robinson 2009). E-waste operational factors which need to be considered include cost-benefit analysis, transportation, warehousing, recycling, etc. (Rahman & Subramanian 2012).

Consequently, e-waste management requires a multi-stakeholder including consumers, manufacturers, government, and environmentalists. Some references suggest that reverse logistics is one of e-waste management solutions. In e-waste management, reverse logistics is defined as a system for returning defective, time-consuming, or outdated electronic products to producers or suppliers for further processing (Janse et al. 2010). Activities in e-waste reverse logistics may include remanufacturing, refurbishment or final disposal. This paper attempts to develop e-waste reverse logistics system simulation to develop sustainable manufacturing. System simulation will be built by considering manufacturing, regulatory, consumption, distribution and environmental aspect in developing e-waste management.

2   LITERATURE REVIEW

Reverse logistics is a process of planning, executing and controlling the flow of materials, and information from the point of consumption back to its beginning points for reprocessing or appropriate disposal (Rogers & Tibben-Lembke, 2001). Reverse logistics in electronics industry aims to return the value of reusable electronic components back to its producer or supplier, as the form of corporate environmental responsibility to the product that has been produced (Tonanont et al. 2008).

Some EU countries have implemented Waste of Electronic and Electricity Equipment (WEEE) policy since 2012. This policy requires each

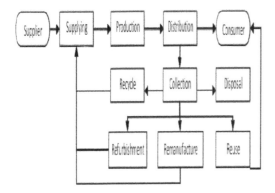

Figure 1. Closed loop supply chain in the electronics industry.

producer to reprocess waste generated from their used products using environmentally friendly methods. This policy strives to increase the involvement of environmental performance of all parties involved in the life cycle of electronics products (Ongondo et al. 2011). The process should be managed efficiently to minimize the cost of the required process (Hanafi et al. 2008). The complexity of e-waste management can be considered as a dynamic process (Georgiadis & Besiou 2008).

Dynamic simulation system approach has been used to analyze the mechanisms, patterns, and trends of e-waste management, as the sequence of future events depends on the current policy (Stock 1998). System Dynamics is used to observe the structure of underlying complex situations and identify the patterns with the behavioral patterns generated by the system over time (Forrester 1994).

Figure 1 represents the general closed-loop supply chain system, at the beginning materials flow from supplier to consumer; which is known as forward logistics. When the product is no longer used, it expectantly flows backward to the suppliers or manufacturers. Reverse logistics facilitates the flow of returns products which include following activities: collecting, recycling, processing, or disposing the material into the landfills. Various research studies have been conducted in the field of e-waste reverse logistics which covers various topics including the design of logistics networks, location-allocation problem, optimal allocation problem, optimal transportation route, manufacturing design and other related topics. Previous research on e-waste reverse logistics is summarized in Table 1.

3 RESEARCH FRAMEWORK

This research uses system dynamics simulation to create a framework for developing green manufacturing policy through reverse logistics. This research identifies the barrier and trigger of e-waste reverse logistics management. In the first stage, the

Table 1. Previous research related to e-waste management.

Authors (Year)	Factors observed	Method
Georgiadis & Besiou (2008)	raw materials, serviceable inventory, distributor's inventory, recyclable products	System dynamics simulation
Janse et al. (2010)	awareness, partnerships, performance visibility, strategic focus in avoiding returns, reclaiming value from returns	TOPSIS and Fuzzy analytic network process
Chiou et al. (2012)	economic, environmental, and social needs, recycled volumes, recycling costs, sales volume	Fuzzy analytic hierarchy process
Banar et al. (2014)	the site of the recycling of electrical and electronic equipment wastes plants location	Multi-Criteria Decision Making (MCDM)
Agrawal et al. (2015)	reverse logistics, reverse logistics network, disposition forecasting product returns, outsourcing	Review and literature analysis
Fiksel J. (2003)	challenges encountered in sustainable and resilient system design in manufacturing	Comparative assessment and simultaneous simulation

formulation of the whole system will be discussed. The next step is to analyze the factors that influence the re-verse logistics as e-waste problem solutions. Based on literature review and system analysis, a conceptual model of e-waste management through reverse logistics was developed. The conceptual model was developed into a simulation model which consist of several related sub-models. Reverse logistics causal model framework can be simulated to predict system response in e-waste management. This paper proposes to create a system simulation model to simulate e-waste management development to support the establishment of the green manufacturing.

3.1 System definition

The development of a closed loop supply chain in e-waste management requires involvement and cooperation from various parties to ensure its effectiveness. The observed system is a combination of various activities, for instance, material procurement, production, distribution, utilization, e-waste collection, which include sorting, recycling and final disposal. In this model, the system was grouped into several sub-models to facilitate system behavior analysis and to see linkages between activities. This system involves several parties, such as suppliers, manufacturers, distributors, retailers, consumers, recyclers and governments.

In supply chains, suppliers act as raw materials source to producers. In e-waste management, suppliers are forced to take the role of using parts of recycled or reused component, extracted from e-waste. Since some parts of electronics devices are extracted from non-renewable natural resources, these recycling and reusing efforts will possibly help to preserve natural resources and the environment. Manufacturers are also having responsibilities for their e-waste processing. Some developed countries have implemented Extended Producer Responsibility regulation that forces manufacturers to have a great responsibility to organize and operate their own e-waste management (Gottberg et al. 2006), so it will not be harm the environment.

Distributors and retailers have a role in delivering finished products from producers to end-consumers. As a point that is directly connected to consumers, retailers can act as an e-waste collection center by offering a promotion to some products that may appeal to end-consumers. It will make some amount of e-waste are entering back the e-waste management system (Tonanont et al. 2008).

The end-consumer is also considered as a central point of e-waste management. Consumer behavior can be measured subjectively through the consumer awareness regarding preserving the environment. Consumers with high awareness will consciously recycle or reduce their e-waste (Chen & Chai 2010).

The government, as a regulator, has a role in the making of e-waste management policy and regulation. In some countries, governments play a substantial role, not only in the formulation of legislation but also engaging in the implementation; meanwhile, in other countries, governments only play a small role, and further encourage the voluntary mechanism of the company (Balde et al. 2014). The government can give an incentive to industry to promote and encourage e-waste management or have a firm regulation about pollution.

E-waste recycling actors can be grouped into informal and formal recyclers. Kumar et al. (2011)

reveals that most e-waste collections are through informal channels. E-waste is then dismantled and reused in the market, while its non-functional components are disposed of. High-value components are then sold to the processing industries to recover or recycle those materials to supply industrial needs. Recyclers engage in the collection, pre-processing/ recycling of any raw materials. A small proportion of this informal sector may contribute to negative impacts on human health and into the environment due to its unhealthy processing techniques. Problem arise from informal sector is that the volume of processed e-waste is not properly documented any may use unsafe e-waste processing methodology.

Community service or non-governmental organizations play a significant role in raising public awareness of problems caused by e-waste. Organizations may have a good collaboration with others parties. This initiative should come from various stakeholders, especially from governments, suppliers, producers, recyclers, as well as the consumers, to provide a broader e-waste management system. Based on the movement of e-waste and the involvement of each actor within, the closed supply chain of electronic products can be drawn into a causal loop system as illustrated in Figure 2.

3.2 Model development

The causal-loop in Figure 2, was then developed into system dynamics stock-flow diagram. The system dynamics structure contains both level and auxiliary variables. The level is defined as the accumulation of values occurring in the system, while the variable represents the movement of flow in the system (Forrester 1994). The flow is generated from the decision-making process and other conditions that may influence or be influenced by decisions made (Fatma 2015). Figure 3 shows the system dynamics of e-waste activity framework. The arrows in Figure 3 illustrate the relationship between variables and the arrows show the direction of its influence. The (+) or (-) sign at the top of the arrows indicates the effect of each activity. The (+) sign shows that the Variables will change to the same value; if the sign is (−), variable changes to the opposite value. Figure 3

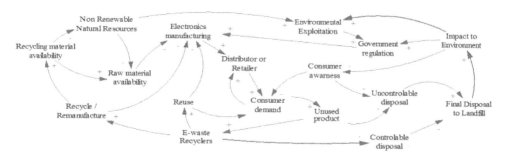

Figure 2. Causality diagram of the green manufacturing development framework.

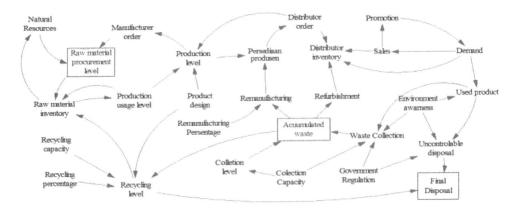

Figure 3. Reverse logistics for electronics industry framework.

shows the relationship between variables in the development of sustainable electronics industry through reverse logistics system of e-waste. Based on the proposed model, it can analyze what factors can be done to develop green manufacturing through reverse logistics of e-waste.

3.3 Manufacturing sub-model

Market demand determines the number of raw materials needed for production. If demand increases, the number of raw materials needed will increase as well. Consequently, the existing source of raw materials for electronics will be exploited, and its availability in nature will decrease. It encourages the manufacturer to utilize recycled raw materials, which come from e-waste. Increased recycling may increase the availability of recycled raw materials. On the other hand, the recovery process requires a processing cost that may impose a manufacturer (Andel 1997). However, if a company can manage their reverse logistics correctly, the company will get economic and environmental profits by performing it (Stock 1998).

3.4 Government sub-model

The Government regulations might encourage producers and suppliers to procure recycled materials as their raw materials. They allow manufacturers to take advantage of e-waste for recycling before re-entering the manufacturing process (King et al. 2006). This sub-model affects the environment sub-model which triggers manufacturers to utilize recycled raw materials. In the causality model, it was assumed that there is a flow of information that describes the effect of regulation on the actions of the manufacturer, consumers, and distributors. Consistency and firmness in the implementation of the government regulations will enhance the companies, consumers or others compliance of in e-waste treatment. This compliance must be offset by the collection and treatment capacity of the related parties (Kang 2013).

3.5 Distribution and consumption sub-models

Consumers play an essential role in a closed supply chain system of e-waste. It is revealed that consumers tend to dispose of electronics products even though the product is still feasible to use. Consumption has a positive relationship between the consumption of electronics and an increase in the amount of e-waste. This behavior is also driven by the manufacturers that keep on increasing electronics product sales.

Manufacturers can also raise consumer environmental awareness of their users concerning on the dangers of e-waste. Increasing awareness of the users will reduce e-waste in the environment; on the other hand, it will increase the volume of e-waste processed by the processing facility, which needs to be considered and prepared by both producer or government.

3.6 Recycle provider sub-model

E-waste collected form the end-consumer is transported to recycle provider for further processing. After the recovery process, e-waste is transported to its original producers or other producers which use recycled materials (Georgiadis & Vlochos 2004). In e-waste reverse logistics, recycle provider may act as a storage site operator where e-waste is sorted or classified based on its conditions, they will classify e-waste either to recycle or process it into a final treatment and landfill for final disposal (Wang & Yang 2007). Recycling process involves cost and revenue that may encourage recyclers to process e-waste (Das & Dutta, 2013). E-waste processed by recycle provider is constrained by its processing capacity.

3.7 Environmental sub-model

Awareness of environment and sustainability is one of the success drivers of e-waste reverse logistics. Reverse logistics brings a competitive advantage to manufacturers that combine business goals and environmental sustainability. In addition, "green manufacturer" image is an important marketing element which might drive the increase in their sales (Chen et al. 2012). Reverse logistics is performed to ensure that environmental protection from e-waste has been done. Manufacturers will no longer rely on new raw materials, instead, they may use recycled materials. Increasing e-waste volume leads to a positive loop on the use of raw materials and reduces the exploitation of natural resources to acquire new materials which simultaneously leads to a negative loop for the environment (Amankwaa 2013).

4 CONCLUSION

This study has identified some perspectives involved in developing green manufacturing in electronics industries. A conceptual model to develop green manufacturing development through reverse logistics has been constructed. The causal-loop and-flow diagrams were constructed using previous studies and qualitative method of system dynamics. The proposed model represents flows of e-waste and its reverse logistics network to develop green manufacturing policy which involves multiple parties. Reverse logistics process provides reuse, repair, recycling and refurbishes option in controllable e-waste management.

Based on the developed model, it is shown that Government regulation and consumer awareness play an important role to encourage the development of e-waste reverse logistics. In addition, particular emphasis should be performed to the relations among the chain members themselves and commitment from all manufacturers, retailers to work collectively, in terms of e-reverse logistics processing and costs sharing. Further model development is needed by using statistical data to capture real system in e-waste management.

REFERENCES

Agrawal, S., Singh, R.K. & Murtaza, Q. 2015. A literature review and perspectives in reverse logistics. *Resources, Conservation and Recycling* 97: 76-92.

Amankwaa, E.F. 2013. Livelihoods in risk: Exploring the health and environmental implications of e-waste recycling as a livelihood strategy in Ghana. *The Journal of Modern African Studies* 51(4): 551-575.

Andel, T. 1997. Reverse logistics: a second chance to profit. *Transportation & Distribution* 38(7): 61-66.

Balde, C.P., Wang, F., Kuehr, R. & Huisman, J. 2014. The global e-waste monitor. *United Nations University, IAS-SCYCLE, Bonn.*

Banar, M., Tulger, G. & Özkan, A. 2014. Plant Site Selection for Recycling Plants of Waste Electrical and Electronic Equipment in Turkey by Using Multi-Criteria Decision Making Methods. *Environmental Engineering & Management Journal (EEMJ)* 13(1).

Chen, T.B. & Chai, L.T. 2010. Attitude towards the environment and green products: consumers' perspective. *Management science and engineering* 4(2): 27.

Chen, C.C., Shih, H.S., Shyur, H.J. & Wu, K.S. 2012. A business strategy selection of green supply chain management via an analytic network process. *Computers & Mathematics with Applications* 64(8): 2544-2557.

Chiou, C.Y., Chen, H.C., Yu, C.T. & Yeh, C.Y. 2012. Consideration factors of reverse logistics implementation-A case study of Taiwan's electronics industry. *Procedia-Social and Behavioral Sciences* 40: 375-381.

Das, D. & Dutta, P. 2013. A system dynamics framework for integrated reverse supply chain with three-way recovery and product exchange policy. *Computers & Industrial Engineering* 66(4): 720-733.

Fatma, E. 2015. Development of sustainable tuna processing industry using system dynamics simulation. *Procedia Manufacturing* 4: 107-114.

Fernando, K.J.S. & Rupasinghe, T.D. 2016. A Conceptual Framework for E-waste Management through Reverse Logistics: A Case Study from Australia. *Management* 5 (4): 190-211.

Fiksel, J. 2003. Designing resilient, sustainable systems. *Environmental science & technology* 37(23): 5330-5339.

Forrester, J.W. 1994. System dynamics, systems thinking, and soft OR. *System dynamics review* 10(2-3): 245-256.

Georgiadis, P. & Besiou, M. 2008. Sustainability in electrical and electronic equipment closed-loop supply chains: a system dynamics approach. *Journal of Cleaner Production* 16(15): 1665-1678.

Georgiadis, P. & Vlachos, D. 2004. Decision making in reverse logistics using system dynamics. *Yugoslav Journal of Operations Research* 14(2): 259-272.

Gottberg, A., Morris, J., Pollard, S., Mark-Herbert, C. & Cook, M. 2006. Producer responsibility, waste minimization and the WEEE Directive: Case studies in eco-design from the European lighting sector. *Science of the total environment* 359(1): 38-56.

Hanafi, J., Kara, S. & Kaebernick, H. 2008. Reverse logistics strategies for end-of-life products. *The International Journal of Logistics Management* 19(3): 367-388.

Janse, B., Schuur, P. & de Brito, M.P. 2010. A reverse logistics diagnostic tool: the case of the consumer electronics industry. *The International Journal of Advanced Manufacturing Technology* 47(5): 495-513.

Kang, D.H.P., Chen, M. & Ogunseitan, O.A. 2013. Potential environmental and human health impacts of rechargeable lithium batteries in electronic waste. *Environmental science & technology* 47(10).

King, A.M., Burgess, S.C., Ijomah, W. & McMahon, C.A. 2006. Reducing waste: repair, recondition, remanufacture or recycle?. *Sustainable Development* 14(4): 257-267.

Kumar, V., Garg, R., Rahman, Z. & Kazmi, A.A. 2011. Sustainability and E-waste management scenario in India. In *the first International Conference on Interdisciplinary Research and Development* (Vol. 31).

Lu, C., Zhang, L., Zhong, Y., Ren, W., Tobias, M., Mu, Z. & Xue, B. 2015. An overview of e-waste management in China. *Journal of Material Cycles and Waste Management* 17(1): 1-12.

Krishnadas, N. & Radhakrishna, R.P. 2014. Green information technology: Literature review and research domains. *Journal of Management Systems* 24(1): 57-79.

Ongondo, F.O., Williams, I.D. & Cherrett, T.J. 2011. How are WEEE doing? A global review of the management of electrical and electronic wastes. *Waste management* 31(4): 714-730.

Rahman, S. & Subramanian, N. 2012. Factors for implementing end-of-life computer recycling operations in reverse supply chains. *International Journal of Production Economics* 140(1): 239-248.

Robinson, B.H. 2009. E-waste: an assessment of global production and environmental impacts. *Science of the total environment* 408(2): 183-191.

Rogers, D.S. & Tibben-Lembke, R. 2001. An examination of reverse logistics practices. *Journal of business logistics* 22(2): 129-148.

Stock, J.R. 1998. Development and implementation of reverse logistics programs. In *Annual Conference Proceedings, Council of Logistics Management*.

Tonanont, A., Yimsiri, S., Jitpitaklert, W. & Rogers, K.J. (2008, January). Performance evaluation in reverse logistics with data envelopment analysis. In *IIIE Annual Conference. Proceedings* (p. 764). Institute of Industrial and Systems Engineers (IISE).

Wang, I.L. & Yang, W.C. 2007. Fast heuristics for designing integrated e-waste reverse logistics networks. *IEEE Transactions on Electronics Packaging Manufacturing* 30(2): 147-154.

Other Related Issues

*Global Competitiveness: Business Transformation in the
Digital Era – Abdullah, Widiaty & Abdullah (eds)*
© 2019 Taylor & Francis Group, London, ISBN 978-0-367-19442-0

A new strategy of SME governance in new Indonesia era: Better or worse?

R. Deti, A.V.S. Hubeis, I. Sailah & L.M. Baga
Institut Pertanian Bogor, Bogor, Indonesia

ABSTRACT: This paper explains the new transformation of Small and Medium Enterprises (SMEs) governance in Indonesia by discussing the development of related regulations. As a developing country, Indonesia faces many challenges such as human development issues in SMEs governance. Data identify that SMEs governance needs some concrete actions besides regular regulations to support SMEs. There is a need of human development action to advance SMEs' performance. Special connection between human development and labor productivity also cannot be denied. The analysis is based on Labor Market Assessment of SMEs in West Java Province, Indonesia, as the most densely populated province in Indonesia. To address this gap, this study suggests a new strategy for building individual skills by developing Financial Life Skill Training.

1 INTRODUCTION

Small and Medium Enterprises (SMEs) development is one of the popular topics to discuss in global economic development. Previous research discussing the development of Chinese SME revealed the importance of government and enterprises relations for creating conducive situation (Chen 2006). Topics of regulation and government role do not only occur in China but have emerged as significant issues in the United Kingdom (Bacon & Hoque 2005). In Poland, for instance, the discussion about SMEs comes up with the failure of government SMEs program. Development of SMEs needs structured supporting program from government (Klonowski 2010).

Experiences from many countries show that the transformation for SMEs governance needs government role. In this case, it will emphasize on historical regulations of SMEs in Indonesia. Furthermore, a research study in Cameroon argued that SMEs development is more complex because it requires the supportive business environment. It needs some efforts to create good environment such as enhancement of human resource (St-Pierre et al. 2015). Hence, this research not only discusses the power of regulation to improve SMEs governance but also needs of developing human resource.

From 1997 to 2013, the number of SMEs in Indonesia has increased from 39,765,110 to 57,895,721 (Badan Pusat Statistik Indonesia 2016). Growth number of SMEs drives to the complexity of SMEs governance. It comes to be more challenging because of internal and external factors (Bank Indonesia 2015). This article discusses human development as an internal factor and regulation as an external factor. It needs inline connection between internal and external factors. To this day, Indonesia has so many regulations to support SMEs development. However, it needs more active actions to accelerate the development, especially for human development issues.

2 INDONESIAN GOVERNMENT STRATEGIES FOR SMEs DEVELOPMENT

Government in developing countries tend to direct policies to achieve by focusing on creating occupations, short-term business development, poverty alleviation, and long-term economic growth (Azis & Rusland 2009). SMEs development is one of the government actions as transformation of economic development to help achieving the goals above. According to Indonesia's Act 20/2008, SMEs aim to increase and expand the enterprises to develop Indonesia's economic based on fair economic democracy in Indonesia.

Indonesian government has been concerned about development of SMEs since 1990s by regulating these matters as one of the actions to maintain stability of economic condition in Indonesia. This is also a continuation phase of financial crisis impact in 1998. Based on *Badan Pusat Statistik* report, SMEs did not have any disruption. It could survive from financial crisis in 1997 and provide workforce for unemployed people in Indonesia up to 107 million until 2012 (Bank Indonesia 2015).

Indonesia has been concerned about maintaining SMEs since the last period of New Order Era. The empowerment and development of small enterprises regulated by Act 9/1995 and Government Regulation 32/1998 aims to expanded workforce and increased income distribution. These regulations continued by Presidential Instruction 10/1999 about empowerment of medium enterprises aimed to increase expansion by using technology in order to improve product quality, and other marketing methods.

In Post-New Order Era, SMEs increased and survived to even become more stable in financial and helped in controlling numbers of unemployment in Indonesia. Hence, SMEs have been recognized in domestic economic activities as sources of livelihood for many households, employment regeneration, and poverty alleviation (Tambunan 2007, Padachi & Lukea Bhiwajee 2016, Agyei 2018), but it is still not good enough to help increasing Indonesia GDP growth until several years after Post-New Order Era. SMEs have helped in decreasing numbers of unemployment but still weak in terms of GDP contribution which needs more than financial stability, such as capital, human resource, technology, and market access (Tambunan 2007).

Table 1. SMEs Contribution to Indonesian GDP.

Indicator	2011	2012	2013
SMEs Contribution to GDP (Billion Rupiah)	1,369,326.00	1,451,460.20	1,536,918.80
Percentage of SMEs Contribution to GDP Growth (%)	6.76	6.00	5.89

Source: Badan Pusat Statistik Indonesia (2016).

Furthermore, government regulated SMEs into Act 20/2008 supported by Government Regulation 17/2013, contained further development for micro, small, and medium enterprises. This action can be considered as improvement regulation to enhance SMEs strategies, because regulation and policy must be dynamic and adjusted to new situation. As a result, SMEs have been shown a good pace in order to maintain economic activities and have a big hand to Indonesia GDP growth.

From the data above, we can see SMEs contribution to GDP was increasing with increased percentage of more than 5% every year. This is one of the results of government concerns toward empowerment and development of SMEs. According to Ministry of Industry Website, SMEs contribution to the number of GDP has been improved up to 60% within 5 years (KOMPAS, 2016). One of the key indicators in GDP is human resources. In order to develop quality and standard for SMEs workforce, government regulated Guidelines for Education and Training for Human Resources of Cooperatives, Micro, Small, and Medium Enterprises. This act aims to improve knowledge, skills, attitude, and behavior of SMEs workforce to increase productivity and business competitiveness.

Since 2015, Indonesia has been concerned about the growth of ASEAN Economy Community (AEC),

which are providing market access for enterprises and human resources to compete freely based on capability and skills. ASEAN countries also have been doing collaboration to reinforce competitiveness and sustainability of SMEs, strengthened by ASEAN Strategic Action Plan for Small Medium Enterprises Development (SAP SMED) 2012–2015 and the latest are for 2016–2025. This document offered strategic goals, explanation about opportunities, and access for SMEs in ASEAN to expand their business and network, supported by policies and regulations applied in each country.

These strategies are still unfamiliar for SMEs people in Indonesia, whereas they just need to utilize the opportunities to expand their business to another step. Indonesia government also has been encouraging SMEs people to expand their business through several strengthening strategies such as convenience financial facility, empowering human resources through vocational training center, and other activities based on government programs and regulations.

In reality, there are still SMEs people who are ignorant and resistant to regulation (Bacon & Hoque 2005), which impacted on SMEs performance. For these kinds of issues, improvement related to internal factors in SMEs is needed such as human resource development because through good policies, regulations, and programs, the SMEs governance just need more concrete actions to advance SMEs performance.

3 IMPROVING HUMAN DEVELOPMENT IN SMES

As we mentioned before, SMEs have been showing a good impact in several aspects on employment and financial stability but are still weak in terms of Indonesia GDP contributions. It needs improvement in several aspects such as in human resources. Human development has an important and distinct impact on economic growth and performance, whereas GDP also has influence on Human Development Index (HDI) (Ulas & Keskin, 2017, Khodabakhshi 2011). Human Development Index is a summary measure of long-term progress for human development, consisting of three basic dimensions: a long and healthy life, access to knowledge, and a decent standard of living. Knowledge level is also measured by access to learning.

Several studies stated that human capital attributes such as education, experience, and skill of employees and managers are important to determine SMEs outcomes (Huselid 1995, Pennings et al. 1998, Georgiadis & Pitelis 2012). Education and training are important to enhancing opportunities and quality in a job. These actions are also considered investment in human capital which can increase productivity, raise employment participation, and direct sources of innovation and competitiveness (Holzer et al. 1993, Barron et al. 1999, Conti 2004, Hunt et al. 2007). SMEs have external benefits on efficiency, innovation, and also increase productivity growth

(Tambunan 2007). To advance SMEs growths, SMEs people, both employees and managers, have to improve their competitiveness to survive because there are great market opportunities and access available, but usually SMEs are weak on human capital development. To achieve this goal, SMEs must enhance human skills of SMEs people and thereby productivity growth (Opeyemi & Victor 2017).

Productivity growth is also related to how human resources can improve and develop their individual skills to give great impacts on business. However, SMEs people do not really have access to develop their skills because training in SMEs is considered as informal approach to enhance skills with little provision and systematic approach because SMEs do not really have luxury to train employees (Kotey & Slade 2005, Beaver & Hutchings 2005).

Literatures argue that human resources aspects in SMEs are in need of training and development to create a better organizational culture (Beaver & Hutchings 2005, Padachi & Lukea Bhiwajee 2016). In a changing environment where global competition becomes more intense, human development is one of the aspects required to support SMEs (ASEAN 2015). ASEAN Strategic Plan has several desired outcomes such as enhancing productivity and human capital development (ASEAN 2015). These outcomes can be effectively done with skill development. Improving skills is one of the strategies used to create a better SMEs performance, because coherent and dedicated strategies for employees can provide useful goals to work with their best efforts (Georgiadis & Pitelis 2012).

Besides requirement for hard skills, soft skills also have significant role in enhancing employees' performance in SMEs. Soft skill development is important in order to survive in the industry and increase productivity of SMEs. In order to enhance individual performance, three factors should be improved: motivation, ability, and opportunity to participate (Armstrong 2009).

Nowadays, HRD has shifted its direction from training in general to being provided individuals to develop capability for the future of their own benefit and for the benefit of their organizations (Beaver & Hutchings 2005). Knowledge from training can be applied to overcome challenges that emerge in the market and give great influences to business, because results of education and training of the workforce in SMEs will tend to be positively related to the profitability of SMEs (Georgiadis & Pitelis 2012).

4 NEW STRATEGY: FINANCIAL LIFE SKILL TRAINING

Many strategies regulated by Indonesia government tend to improve SMEs performance. However, in Indonesian case, improving SMEs performance is beyond the role of regulations. In fact, it also requires skilled labors. Hence, for better transformation of SMEs governance, it needs a new strategy to improve their skills.

A literature review also showed that fragile financial life skill of labor will affect the productivity. For getting known about what kind of labor might be needed by SMEs, we had done Labor Market Assessment (LMA) in West Java Province.

As we mentioned before, West Java had been chosen because of its high population number. The number of micro enterprises (MIEs) in West Java Province is around 24,669 (Dinas Koperasi dan Usaha Kecil Provinsi Jawa Barat, 2017). Specific areas selected for doing LMA are Bandung, Indramayu, Tasikmalaya, and Sukabumi. This research conducted quantitative survey and qualitative in-depth interview. It involved 169 entrepreneurs from SMEs for quantitative survey. For Focus Group Discussion (FGD), it involved 16 government institutions and 146 entrepreneurs.

LMA result showed that there is a gap in labor soft skills so that SMEs might need upgrading labor soft skills such as technical knowledge, managing personal financial, accounting, computerizing, and communication. Figure 1 emphasizes 7 biggest gap soft skill assessments in West Java Province.

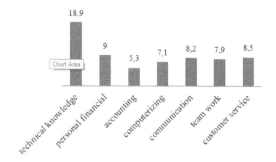

Figure 1. LMA for Gap in Soft Skill.

Furthermore, those data showed that we have to make some strategies to improve labors' soft skills. Technical knowledge might need some training from each SME because it would be different for each. It depends on the type of SME industries. However, in general, all of SMEs labor needs personal financial soft skill. As we discussed before, personal financial problems might decrease labor productivity so that it

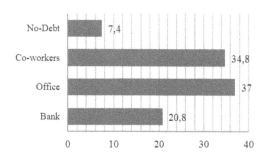

Figure 2. Labor debt.

is necessary to be more concerned about personal financial labor.

LMA showed that only 7.4% of SMEs labors are stable with personal financial state. Around 92.6% labors have credits in different sources. The highest number is labors with debt in office. As SMEs are nothing but small and medium enterprises, this also in one way means that the financial situation will also be in small or medium level. If many labors borrow money from office, it would drive to unstable financial condition for SMEs. Hence, we have to put more concerns to the personal financial labor issues.

This research aims to promote a new strategy for SMEs development in terms of personal financial life skill. SMEs need employees who could manage personal finance so that they would be productive employees in terms of enhancing SMEs performance. Indonesian government needs action to improve the performance because at some points, SMEs have been assumed as risky institution (Nunoo & Andoh 2012). Therefore, it needs some improvements to encourage trust for SMEs. One of the strategies that might be effective is financial life skill training for labors.

In this case, we also tried to do a survey on SMEs entrepreneurs about considering the need to implement financial life skill training. We want to make sure that whether it is needed for labors only or also for employers. The result of survey showed that 93.9% for SMEs entrepreneurs expect about having this kind of training for themselves. They consider joining it because they realize that it is an important training for their businesses to develop. In this survey, most of the SMEs entrepreneurs are managing company's finance by their own.

Furthermore, 73.9% of them are having some credits from difference sources. It shows that financial literacy is one of popular discussions in the case of SMEs. This research has also found that 53.3% of SMEs entrepreneurs had been joining soft skill training; this shows that they seem interested for having this kind of training. Hence, they argue that SMEs entrepreneurs are supposed to have financial life skill training not only for labors but also for the entrepreneurs and employers.

From some surveys, we assume that Indonesia might need an action to improve SMEs performance. We need governance transformation of SMEs, which is supposed to be more concerned with financial life skill. Regulations are important, but we could not deny that human resource development is also a crucial issue in SMEs. As we already discussed, SMEs give a significant impact for economy development in Indonesia.

5 CONCLUSIONS

Indonesia has various strategies for improving SMEs governance, one of which is making regulation. Furthermore, it is getting better year by year. By regulating some public policies, it has been proven that Indonesia starts to be concerned with SMEs development. However, in this case, we could not ignore the importance of human resources. For improving SMEs performance, skilled labors or employees are required. Hence, personal training would be needed to get them. This research suggests a new strategy, which puts some attention of upgrading financial life skills of labors. By collecting some data from observation, interview, and survey, we have found that personal financial skill is one of the human development issues in terms of improving SMEs performance.

REFERENCES

Agyei, S.K. 2018. Culture, Financial Literacy, and SME Performance in Ghana. *Cogent Economics & Finance* 6 (1): 1463813.

Armstrong, M. 2009. *Armstrong's Handbook of Human Resource Management Practice 11th Edition*. London and Philadelphia: Kogan Page.

ASEAN. 2015. *ASEAN Strategic Plan for SME Development 2016-2025*. Jakarta: ASEAN Secretariat.

Azis, A. & Rusland, A.H. 2009. Peranan Bank Indonesia di dalam Mendukung Pengembangan Usaha Mikro, Kecil, dan Menengah. *Dalam Seri Kebanksentralan* 21.

Bacon, N. & Hoque, K. 2005. HRM in the SME Sector: Valuable Employees and Coercive Networks. *The International Journal of Human Resource Management* 16 (11): 1976-1999.

Badan Pusat Statistik Indonesia. 2016. *Ekonomi dan Perdagangan: Badan Pusat Statistik Indonesia*. [Online]. Retrieved from https://www.bps.go.id Accessed on 2018- 01-05.

Bank Indonesia. 2015. *Profil bisnis usaha mikro, kecil dan menengah (UMKM)*. Jakarta (ID): Lembaga Pengembangan Perbankan Indonesia.

Barron, J., Berger, M. & Black, D. 1999. Do Workers Pay for On-The-Job Training. *The Journal of Human Resources* 34(21): 236-252.

Beaver, G. & Hutchings, K. 2005. Training and Developing An Age Diverse Workforce in SMEs: The Need for A Strategic Approach. *Education + Training* 47(8/9): 592-604.

Chen, J. 2006. Development of Chinese small and medium-sized enterprises. *Journal of Small Business and Enterprise Development* 13(2): 140-147.

Conti, G. 2004. Training Productivity and Wages. *The Sixteenth Annual European Association of Labour Economists (EALE)*. Lisbon.

Dinas Koperasi dan Usaha Kecil Provinsi Jawa Barat. 2017. *Profil Koperasi Provinsi Jawa Barat*. Bandung: Pemerintah Provinsi Jawa Barat.

Georgiadis, A. & Pitelis, C.N. 2012. Human Resources and SME Performance in Services: Empirical Evidence from the UK. *The International Journal of Human Resource Management* 23(4): 808-825.

Holzer, H., Block, M. & Knott, J. 1993. Are Training Subsidies for Firms Effective? The Michigan Experience. *Industrial and Labor Relations Review* 46(4): 625-636.

Hunt, I., Hennessy, M., O'Brien, E. & Sherry, R. 2007. The Graduate and the SME. *Education, Knowledge & Economy* 1(2): 199-210.

Huselid, M. 1995. The Impact of Human Resource Management Practices on Turnover, Productivity, and

Corporate Financial Performance. *Academy of Management Journal.* 38(3): 419-443.

Khodabakhshi, A. 2011. Relationship between GDP and Human Development Indices in India. *International Journal of Trade, Economics and FInance* 2(3): 251-253.

Klonowski, D. 2010. The effectiveness of government-sponsored programmes in supporting the SME sector in Poland. *Post-Communist Economies* 22(2): 229-245.

KOMPAS. 2016. *Berita Industri.* [Online]. Retrieved from http://www.kemenperin.go.id/artikel/14200/Kontribusi-UMKM-Naik Accessed on 2018- 01-10.

Kotey, B. & Slade, P. 2005. Formal Human Resource Management Practices in Small Growing Firms. *Journal of Small Business Management* 43(1): 16-41

Nunoo, J., & Andoh, F. K. (2012). Sustaining small and medium enterprises through financial service utilization: Does financial literacy matter. In *(Unpublished Paper) presented at the Agricultural & Applied Economics Association's 2012 AAEA Annual Meeting, Seattle, Washington.*

Opeyemi, A. O. & Victor, A.A. 2017. An Analysis of Human Capital Development and Productivity Growth-Case Study, Nigeria. *Review of Innovation and Competitiveness* 3(3): 61-84.

Padachi, K. & Lukea Bhiwajee, S. 2016. Barriers to employee training in small and medium sized enterprises: Insights and evidences from Mauritius. *European Journal of Training and Development* 40(4): 232-247.

Pennings, J. M., Lee, K. & Van Witteloostuijn, A. 1998. Human Capital, Social Capital and Firm Dissolution. *Academy of Management Journal* 41: 425-440.

St-Pierre, J., Foleu, L., Abdulnour, G., Nomo, S. & Fouda, M. 2015. SME development challenges in cameroon: an entrepreneurial ecosystem perspective. *Transnational Corporations Review* 7(4): 441-462.

Tambunan, T. 2007. Development of SME and Women Entrepreneurs in a Developing Country: The Indonesian Story. *Small Enterprise Research* 15(2): 31-51.

Ulas, E. & Keskin, B. 2017. Is There a Relation Between HDI and Economic Performance? *17th Annual Conference on Finance and Accounting* (pp. 61-70). Switzerland: Springer.

259

*Global Competitiveness: Business Transformation in the
Digital Era – Abdullah, Widiaty & Abdullah (eds)
© 2019 Taylor & Francis Group, London, ISBN 978-0-367-19442-0*

Data analytics in the era of industry 4.0

A. Gusnanto
University of Leeds, Leeds, UK

ABSTRACT: In the era of globalization, the presence and information and communication technolgy is inevitable. Its rapid growth demands industrial aspects to employ effective data analytics. This paper highlights the importance, impacts, and challenges of data analytics in the fourth industrial era. In this paper, the journey and estabslishtment of industrial revolution has been discussed in the Introduction part preceding the discussion of the importance of data analytics, particularly in the fourth industrial revolution. The focus of data analytics is this paper is big data which will benefit both business and academic sectors. It has been proven that big industries impacted by big data are mostly related to telecommunication and manufacturing. However, there are also challenges of data analytics. Some of the challenges include weak ability to identify problems, absoption of genetal statistical principles, information technology infrastructure, and data governance and legal aspects of data.

1 INTRODUCTION

The Government of Germany has adopted the *Industrie 4.0* initiative (Bundesministerium für Bildung und Forschung 2019) that elaborates the goverment's strategy in dealing with the fourth industrial revolution. Similar initiatives are also adopted by major industrial and developing economies, such as *Industrial Internet (of Things)* (Jeschke et al. 2017) and *Internet+* (Keane 2016). The fourth industrial revolution is considered a continuation of the first to the third industrial revolutions. The first one started around the 18th-19th century, which was characterised by energy revolution where the manufacturing processes were transformed with the advent of steam engines. This was followed by the second industrial revolution around the turn of the 19th to 20th century that was indicated by more efficient manufacturing process, and the use of electricity and internal combustion engines. The third industrial revolution was characterised by digital revolution, the invention of personal computer and automation process around 1970-1980s. The fourth revolution is indicated by cyber physical system (Lee et al. 2015), where automation process is characterised by data exchanges in the internet of things (Zhong et al. 2017).

In this fourth revolution, data is at the heart of everything. For example, the concept of 'smart manufacturing' is a system in which data exchanges are pivotal in the communication between sensors (as data generation tools) and the controllers, so that they can give feedback to the system to adjust the manufacturing process to be optimal (Davis et al. 2012). The feedback itself is interpreted as data by the control system. In a general context, Industry 4.0 has to embrace the arrival of big data (Kusiak 2017), which

is characterised by 4 V's: Volume, Velocity, Variety, and Veracity (Hashem et al. 2015, Yin & Kaynak 2015). The volume of data that are generated everyday grow exponentially and it is no longer uncommon to find businesses that generate gigabytes of data everyday (Lee et al. 2014). The term velocity refers to the type of data that are considered as streaming data. A famous example would be data that are generated by hundreds of millions of users in social media. The data are generated continuously and massively, across a wide network (Wollschlaeger et al. 2017). However, it is also possible to have this type of data in general when, for example, business operations involved are also 'continuous' such as airline travel, traffic or logistic network, broadcasting, hotels or services, and other online internet networks (Wang & Wang 2016). In terms of variety, the types of data that are generated in Industry 4.0 vary quite considerably. Some of them are in text format, while some others are, for example, in picture, voice and video format (Hashem et al. 2015). Each of these types of data needs analytical tools that are specific for them. Lastly, the term veracity refers to the situation where either, first, the information in the data are 'thinly' spread in the whole data and they are only meaningful when we combine that information or, secondly, the relevant information are located in a small unknown part of the whole data (Gandomi & Haider 2015). The latter means that other parts of data may be relevant for our context, but they are not necessarily relevant for the problem at hand.

2 IMPORTANCE OF DATA ANALYTICS

With such characteristics, data analytics becomes crucial in the era of Industry 4.0. In this paper, we shall highlight some of the benefit of data analysis, particularly with big data. The first and foremost benefit is accurate prediction (Lee et al. 2014). In the current business climate and other factors that often change, many businesses and organisations depend on accurate prediction to adapt with current changes. Long time ago, these changes happened within years or months. Accurate prediction with data analytics was not urgent because all parties have time to digest what was going on and had enough time to adapt. However, at the moment, the changes can happen in hours and minutes. Data analytics becomes crucial to create prediction because with many information in the data, our mind may not be fast enough to focus on the most relevant bits of the information. Even if we can focus on them, it still takes time to digest the bits of information before any action can be considered (Vercellis 2011).

Accurate prediction can advantage businesses in many different ways. The main one is to increase and improve business operation, especially in managing resources and inventories, and to increase business efficiency (Gregori et al. 2001, Wen et al. 2003). A famous example of this is the pricing method for airline tickets that have to take into accounts many factors to make accurate prediction on how much ticket should be sold to maximise profit and occupancy, in real time. Another advantage of accurate prediction is to optimise marketing campaign by tailoring the campaign to potentially suit individual customers, mainly in the context of online transaction (Chen et al. 2012). The prediction is done based on the customersâ historical data, to identify what the customers need. Businesses then can tailor promotions or discounts on products or services that they need (Linoff & Berry 2011). On the other side of this prediction, the same principle can also be used to detect fraud and abuse of service. This is because, based on past historical data, businesses can predict "reasonable" behaviour of their customers and will flag a behaviour that out of the ordinary, probably in quite a big way (Chen et al. 2012). Banks and card service providers have implemented this principle in their system that would detect account fraud, for example (Cardenas et al. 2013).

Another benefit of data analytics is that, using statistical principles, it can turn data into knowledge and knowledge into insight (LaValle et al. 2011). Why is this important? Because decision maker can then turn the insight into action. Data analytics is critical to understand the underlying, possibly unobserved, patterns of the data. To get into insight, statistical principles need to be considered even from the start when any idea was still conceived. An example of this is utilisation of customer survey by businesses. Many believe that survey is a method to get customer feedback. However, if statistical principles are adhered, survey is not only a reflection of how a business gives service to its customer, but also how they operate.

As an implication of the above, data analytics enables decision making to be taken quickly where relevant (Provost & Fawcett 2013). With fierce competition and so much data around us, it is no longer adequate to rely on intuition only when making business decision. Data analytics is able to give guidance to make decision quickly, which is a major advantage. Business competitiveness is about staying ahead in the competition, and this business trait will give that advantage to stay ahead.

3 INDUSTRY IMPACTED BY DATA ANALYTICS

Which industry will be impacted by (big) data analytics? Virtually all industries will be impacted by data analytics, especially those industries that involve big data such as telecommunication and manufacturing (Gandomi & Haider 2015, Sagiroglu & Sinanc 2013). Optimising service quality, development of new products, efficiency, and waste reduction are some examples of "target" of data analytics that will give great impact to industries. Retail industry is an example where data analytics gives a major impact, where online transaction, customer segmentation, marketing, pricing, and optimisation of logistics and distributions have benefited from data analytics (Linoff & Berry 2011). Other industries, from finance to transportation, from healthcare to agribusiness are expected to get much greater impact in the future (Chawla & Davis 2013, Groves et al. 2013, Lv 2015, Waller & Fawcett 2013, Wolfert et al. 2013).

Big industries are not only the ones that will be impacted by data analytics. Small and medium enterprises have begun to benefit from data analytics. A small ice cream shop in Leeds (UK) managed to understand their ice cream sales (Brennan & Mark 1994). They recorded their sales in detail including the types of ice cream they sell, and they also record the weather and their posts in social media. The data was then analysed, and the results indicate that the increase in sales happened when the shop posted pictures of ice cream in social media. This is just a simple example where data analytics can benefit small businesses. Other examples exist in the context of restaurants, suppliers to big supermarket chain, and other services Bi 2014, Coleman 2016, Watson 2014).

4 CHALLENGES AHEAD

Looking forward, data analytics in the era Industry 4.0 face four main challenges, especially in the developing countries. The first and main one is a weak ability to identify problem. Data analytics serves as a solution to a problem, since the it is shaped by the formulation or definition of the problem. Now, many believe that the absence of 'bottleneckâĂŹ in their business process is a sign that there is no problem. Others believe that a reasonable growth or profit is a sign that there is no problem. These cannot be further from the truth. Almost all of the disruptions in Industry 4.0 target those businesses that tend to be 'complacent' or easily satisfied. These businesses consider that processes that have been going on are those that should have been going on, when this is not necessarily true. Therefore, to identify problems, businesses have to be critical of themselves and always test their business processes. After all, changes that take place from within is always better than those that are forced from outside.

The second challenge is the absorption of general statistical principles. Statistical principles are needed in data analytics since they are able to guide us in understanding the problem, getting the right information, understanding the results, and taking conclusions. This does not mean that everybody has to take a course in statistics or become a statistician. However, there are some general principles in statistics that are useful to deal with the above challenges.

The third challenge is the information technology infrastructure that are in urgent need to be further developed, especially in the developing world. In the era of big data, technology is critical for data analytics and all other activities that support data analytics, including cloud technology, network, storage, etc. They make sure that data, as information, can flow seamlessly and data analytics can be performed while their results, in themselves are 'new' data, can be communicated to relevant parties.

The last challenge in data analytics is the data governance and legal aspects of data. Some countries have different levels of privacy setting to protect their citizens. It is therefore still a challenge to provide adequate level of privacy protection in some of them (Sadeghi & Wachsmann 2015). European countries have set an excellent example in this aspect where they recently implemented the general data protection regulation (GDPR), in which the data governance is outlined in detail (EU Commission 2016). With this regulation, every party recognise their share of responsibility in ensuring that data privacy is protected while at the same time allow data analytics to be conducted.

REFERENCES

Bi, Z. & Cochran, D. 2014. Big data analytics with applications. *Journal of Management Analytics* 1(4): 249-265.

Bundesministerium für Bildung und Forschung. 2019. *Digitale Wirtschaft und Gesellschaft: Industrie 4.0.* [Online]. Retrieved from: https://www.bmbf.de/de/zukunftsprojekt-industrie-4-0-848.html. Accessed on 6 January 2019

Cardenas, A.A., Manadhata, P.K. & Rajan, S.P. 2013. Big data analytics for security. *IEEE Security & Privacy* 11 (6): 74-76.

Chawla, N.V. & Davis, D.A. 2013. Bringing big data to personalized healthcare: A patient-centered framework. *Journal of Genera Internal Medicine* 28(3): 660.

Chen, H., Chiang, R. & Storey, V. 2012. Business intelligence and analytics: From big data to big impact. *MIS Quarterly* 36(4): 1165-1188.

Coleman, S., Göb, R., Manco, G., Pievatolo, A., Tort-Martorell, X. & Reis, M.S. 2016. How can smes benefit from big data? Challenges and a path forward. *Quality and Reliability Engineering International* 32: 2151-2164.

Davis, J., Edgar, T., Porter, J., Bernaden, J. & Sarli, M. 2012. Smart manufacturing, manufacturing intelligence and demand-dynamic performance. *Computers & Chemical Engineering* 145-156.

EU Commission. 2016. *Regulation (EU) 2016/679 of the European Parliament and of the Council of 27 April 2016 on the protection of natural persons with regard to the processing of personal data and on the free movement of such data, and repealing Directive 95/46/EC (General Data Protection Regulation).* [Online]. Retrieved from: https://eur-lex.europa.eu/legal-content/EN/TXT/?qid=1528874672298&uri=CELEX%3A32016R0679. Accessed on 6 January 2019.

Gandomi, A. & Haider, M. 2015. Beyond the hype: Big data concepts methods, and analytics. *International Journal of Information Management* 35(2): 137-144.

Brennan, P.M. & Mark, R.M. 1994. *Personal communication service with mobility manager.* Washington, DC: U.S. Patent and Trademark Office.

Gregori, D., Casati, F., Dayal, U. & Shan, M.C. 2001. Improving business process quality through exception understanding, prediction, and prevention. *Proceedings of the 27th VLDB Conference*, Roma, Italy.

Groves, P., Kayyali, B., Knott, D. & Van Kuiken, S. 2013. The 'big data' revolution in health- care: Accelerating value and innovation. *McKinsey Quarterly*

Hashem, I.A.T., Yaqoob, I., Anuar, N.B., Mokhtar, S., Gani, A. & Khan, S.U. 2015. The rise of "big data" on cloud computing: Review and open research issues. *Information Systems*, 47: 98-115.

Jeschke, S., Brecher, C., Meisen, T., Özdemir, D. & Eschert T. 2017. Industrial Internet of Things and Cyber Manufacturing Systems. In: Jeschke, S., Brecher C., Song H. & Rawat D. (ed.), *Industrial Internet of Things. Springer Series in Wireless Technology. Springer, Cham.*

Keane, M. 2016. Internet+ China: Unleashing the innovative nation strategy. *International Journal of Cultural and Creative Industries* 3(2): 68-74.

Kusiak, A. 2017. Smart manufacturing must embrace big data. *Nature* 544: 23-25.

LaValle, S., Lesser, E., Shockley, R., Hopkins, M.S. & Kruschwitz, N. 2011. Big data, analytics and the path from insights to value. *MITSloan Management Review* 52(2): 21-31.

Lee, J., Bagheri, B. & Kao, H.A. 2015. A cyber-physical systems architecture for Industry 4.0 based manufacturing systems. *Manufacturing Letters* 3: 18-23.

Lee, J., Kao, H.A. & Yang, S. 2014. Service innovation and smart analytic for industry 4.0 and big data environment. *Procedia CIRP* 16: 3-8.

Linoff, G.S. & Berry, M.J.A. 2011. *Data mining techniques: For marketing, sales and customer relationship management.* New Jersey: John Wiley & Sons.

Lv, Y., Duan, Y., Kang, W., Li, Z. & Wang, F.Y. 2015. Traffic flow prediction with big data: a deep learning approach. *IEEE Transactions on Intelligent Transportation Systems* 16(2): 865-873.

Provost, F. & Fawcett, T. 2013. Data science and its relationship to big data and data driven decision making. *Big Data* 1(1): 1.

Sadeghi, A., Wachsmann, C. & Waidner, M. 2015. Security and privacy challenges in industrial Internet of Things. *52nd ACM/EDAC/IEEE Design Automation Conference (DAC)*. San Francisco, CA, pp. 1-6.

Sagiroglu, S., & Sinanc, D. 2013. Big data: A review, *International Conference on Collaboration Technologies and Systems (CTS)*. San Diego, CA, pp. 42-47.

Vercellis, C. 2011. *Business intelligence: Data mining and optimization for decision making*. New Jersey: John Wiley & Sons.

Waller, M.A. & Fawcett, S.E. 2013. Data science, predictive analytics, and big data: A revolution that will transform supply chain design and management. *Journal of Business Logistics* 34: 77-84.

Wang, L. & Wang, G. 2016. Big data in cyber-physical systems, digital manufacturing and industry 4.0. *International Journal of Engineering and Manufacturing* 4: 1-8.

Watson, H.J. 2014. Tutorial: Big data analytics: Concepts, technologies, and applications. *Communications of the Association for Information Systems* 34: 65.

Wen, H.J., Lim, B. & Huang, H.L. 2003. Measuring e-commerce efficiency: A data envelopment analysis (DEA) approach. *Industrial Management & Data Systems* 103 (9): 703-710.

Wolfert, S., Ge, L., Verdouw, C. & Bogaardt, M.J. 2013. Big data in smart farming – a review. *Agricultural systems* 153: 69-80.

Wollschlaeger, M., Sauter, T. & Jasperneite, J. 2017. The future of industrial communication: Automation networks in the era of the Internet of Things and Industry 4.0. *IEEE Industrial Electronics Magazine* 11(1): 17-27.

Yin, S. & Kaynak, O. 2015. Big data for modern industry: Challenges and trends [Point of View]. *Proceedings of the IEEE* 103(2): 143-146.

Zhong, R.Y., Xu, X., Klotz, E., Newman, S.T. 2017. Intelligent manufacturing in the context of industry 4.0: A review. *Engineering* 3(5): 616-630.

Global Competitiveness: Business Transformation in the Digital Era – Abdullah, Widiaty & Abdullah (eds)
© *2019 Taylor & Francis Group, London, ISBN 978-0-367-19442-0*

Examining the perceived career growth, organisational justice and intention to stay among traffic wardens in the City Traffic Police, Lahore

S.A. Mehmood, D. Nadarajah & M.S. Akhtar
University Putra Malaysia, Selangor, Malaysia

ABSTRACT: This study aimed to investigate intention to stay among officers in the City Traffic Police Lahore in relation to their perceptions of organisational justice and career growth. 224 traffic wardens working in Lahore participated in survey. Apart from procedural justice and professional ability development, all dimensions of organisational justice and perceived career growth were found to significantly influence traffic officers' intention to stay. Moreover, promotional speed emerged as the strongest predictor of the intent to stay. The findings of this study may guide police authorities in dealing with issues on turnover by initiating policies which can strengthen employee retention intention. This paper enhances understanding of turnover issues by investigating retention intention of traffic police officers in an Eastern culture. Specifically, this research contributes to literature by examining the predictive role of organisational inducement factors (organisational justice and career growth) on attitude (intention to stay). Additionally, both the exogenous constructs of interest are used at the dimensional levels.

1 INTRODUCTION

Employee retention in the police force has grown into a critical challenge (Howes & Goodman-Delahunty 2014). The turnover of 1145 out of 3000 officers from the City Traffic Police Lahore (CTPL) within 10 years (Bajwa, 2015) captivated our attention and necessitated the need for this research.

A range of factors rationalises why understanding the issue of employee turnover is essential for researchers and organisations. Among these factors include the recruitment and training of new staff, which entail some financial costs (Blumberg et al. 2015). That is, to become an accredited police officer, one is required to go through several specialised training programs; thus, recruiting well-trained sworn officers straight from the general public may be infeasible (Lynch & Tuckey 2008). Moreover, police recruits are compensated during training and certification period, though they are not yet providing service to the public (Blumberg et al. 2015). Other consequences of turnover are the productivity and performance losses (Howes & Goodman-Delahunty 2014). In 2006, over 3300 young graduates were instated as traffic wardens in Lahore to transform the police culture into public-friendly policing. Initially, they performed up to expectations, but due to high workload, they eventually exhibited various counter-productive behaviors indicative of their waning performance (Mehmood et al. 2018). Another factor that may be associated with turnover is employee demoralization (Chew 2005). Apart from these, loss of job-specific and organizational knowledge has also been identified as a contributing factor for employee turnover (Reina et al. 2017).

Career shifting is becoming increasingly common unlike in the past (Weng & McElroy 2012). High employee turnover particularly in police organisations is becoming a crucial issue (Hur 2013). As, policing is considered as one of the most taxing occupations in the world (Van Craen & Skogan 2016). Therefore, to help police officers cope with their stressful roles, it is important to consider the factors that may increase their intention to stay (Reukauf 2018).

Intention to stay refers to employees' conscious and deliberate willingness to stay with the organization (Tett & Meyer 2006). The focus of researchers and management professionals is shifting away from employee turnover, and has already made progress in discovering useful retention methods (Ghosh & Gurunathan 2015). However, the number of studies on intention to stay is rather limited compared to investigations on intention to leave (Kim 2015). Most researchers concerned with the retention of professionals and other workers tend to concentrate on aspects of the job or organization that make them decide to leave; whereas, surprisingly less focus seems to have been accorded to organizational and job components that make employees stay (Akhtar et al. 2018). Intention to stay has been measured amongst many occupational groups such as physician assistants, IT personnel, service sector employees in Turkey, engineers in Malaysia, and personal support workers

(Mehmood et al. 2018). As such, this study will greatly enhance our knowledge on intention to stay among police officers.

Despite significant implications and the opportunity to prevent voluntary turnover, there has been limited research on the nature of turnover in police organizations (Yun et al. 2015). In particular, very few published works on policing have been found in the Pakistani context. Pakistan, regarding its cultural values is the very high level of uncertainty avoidance and power distance. It is known that employees in cultures with high uncertainty avoidance are sensitive to little changes. That is, they are driven by strict rules, values and procedures, and they react more quickly on justice perception (Shao et al. 2011). In addition, the vast majority of research on turnover have focused on intention to quit. Accordingly, contemporary investigations argue that the determinants of intention to quit may differ from those of intention to stay (Akhtar et al. 2018, Lee et al. 2017). Therefore, knowing about the determinants of staying intention may help practitioners realize how to transform reluctant stayers into enthusiastic stayers (Lee et al. 2017). In addition, there is a call for future research to empirically investigate the organisational justice and career growth as determinants of staying intention (Mehmood et al. 2018).

2 THEORETICAL FOUNDATION AND HYPOTHESIS DEVELOPMENT

2.1 Social exchange theory

The social exchange theory (SET) provides an explanation on the relationship of intention to stay with organisational justice and perceived career growth. In this theory, Blau (1964) defined social exchanges as 'voluntary actions' in response to an organisation's treatment of its employees, expecting that such treatment will be repaid in the long run. The social exchange theory has been widely applied to explain the nature of employee-employer relationship (Cropanzano et al. 2016). Social exchange relationships develop when an organisation shows concern for its employees. The concept of social exchange proposes that workers are more devoted to their organisational task when they perceive a well-balanced and reasonable system of exchange (Blau, 1964). If an employee perceives that the organisation has benefited from him but failed to reciprocate within the expected period of time, some unfavourable effects on the growth of their mutual relationship may ensue (Cropanzano et al. 2016, Liu & Liu 2016). Such situation may lead to trust deficit wherein an employee's loyalty would be compromised.

2.2 OJ and ITS

Organisations hardly survive without the key employees. However, the well-being, perceptions and feelings of employees within an organisation will considerably determine their intentions to stay or leave (Owolabi 2012). To build trust in employees, organisation has to take a fair approach in all aspects connected to daily work. It has been revealed that employees' perceptions of justice are important in their decisions to leave or stay with an organisation (Nadiri & Tanova 2010). Moorman (1991) explained that organizational justice (OJ) is concerned with the ways in which employees determine if they have been treated fairly in their jobs and how they affect other work-related variables. OJ is composed of three dimensions: distributive, procedural and interactional justice. Distributive justice (DJ) refers to "employees' perceptions of the rewards they receive such as pay and promotions" (Moorman 1991). The concept was initially derived from (Adams et al. 1976), who used equity theory to evaluate fairness. While, procedural justice(PJ) is defined as "the fairness of the manner in which the decision-making process is conducted" (Folger & Konovsky 1989). The notion of PJ was first introduced by (Walker & Thibaut 1975) in third-party dispute proceedings such as arbitration and mediation. Muzumdar (2012), a sociologist, defined interactional justice (IJ) as the level of dignity and respect received by individuals. In particular, it deals with the interpersonal treatment that people experience when procedures are carried out. IJ in the workplace is rooted in the social exchange theory and concern about the feelings and well-being of employees, and quality of treatment when procedures are enforced (Muzumdar 2012). According to Greenberg (1988), the two dimensions of interactional justice are interpersonal justice and informational justice. Interpersonal justice pertains to personal treatment such as politeness, respect and dignity. On the other hand, informational justice is about actions taken by the management, including how information is disseminated to the employees (e.g., listening to the employees' concerns, providing adequate explanations for decision-making, and demonstrating care towards their well-being). Primarily, it explains how information is conveyed and presented to the people.

From the social exchange perspective, employees expect to receive fair and respectful treatment from their organisation or its representatives (Bakri & Ali 2015). When they receive fair treatment, they will have greater satisfaction with their job (Ahmadi et al. 2012) and better work outcome (Sahni & Sinha 2018). Researchers suggest that justice perceptions directly relate to organisational outcomes such as turnover intentions and other withdrawal behaviours (Rhoades & Eisenberger 2002). The relationship of OJ and turnover intention had widely been studied in literature. For instance, (Rusbadrol 2018) conducted a systematic literature review of 46 studies and discovered that all dimensions of OJ negatively correlate with turnover intention. Consistent with previous findings, we propose following hypothesis:

H1 : OJ is significantly related to ITS.
H1(a) : DJ is significantly related to ITS.
H1(b) : PJ is significantly related to ITS.
H1(c) : IJ is significantly related to ITS.

2.3 *PCG and ITS*

While 'career' is understood as a succession of lifetime work experiences of an individual (Arthur et al. 2008), 'career growth' is defined as "one's perceptions of the chances of development and advancement within an organisation" (Jans 1989). According to (Weng & McElroy 2012), perceived career growth consists of four factors, namely, career goal progress (CGP), professional ability development (PAD), promotion speed (PS), and remuneration growth (RG). Career goal progress is the degree to which one's current organisation creates an environment that allows the person to meet his career goals. Professional ability development is about acquiring new knowledge, skills and abilities. Promotion speed is the degree to which the organisation reinforces accomplishments through promotions. Compensation describes the degree to which one's remuneration may increase. Career goal progress and professional ability development account for intrinsic career growth, whereas promotion speed and compensation contribute to extrinsic career growth (Spagnoli 2017).

Weng & McElroy (2012) studied career growth and its influence on turnover intentions. Perceived career growth has also been linked to work outcomes, such as job satisfaction (Spagnoli 2017), employee voice, organizational commitment (Weng et al. 2010), turnover intention (Chen et al. 2016), and performance (Spagnoli 2017). Inferring from the social exchange theory, a conceptual support of intention to stay and its relationships with perceived career growth is proposed by this study. Thus, the following seven hypotheses were postulated in this empirical investigation

H2 : PCG is significantly related to ITS.
H2(a) : CGP is significantly related to ITS.
H2(b) : PAD is significantly related to ITS.
H2(c) : PS is significantly related to ITS.
H2(d) : RG is significantly related to ITS.

As shown in Figure 1, the model includes both OJ and PCG as potential predictors of ITS.

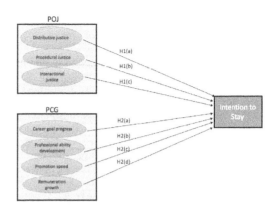

Figure 1. Conceptual framework.

3 METHOD

Chief traffic officer was formally requested to grant permissions for their staff to participate in the research survey. A total of 650 potential respondents were approached using stratified random sampling. The sample consisted of 224 traffic wardens working in 30 sectors in City Traffic Police Lahore was gathered. In order to avoid potential biases and problems which may stem from the hectic nature of a traffic officer's job, data gathering was carried out during the morning briefing time, when employees were more mentally and physically fresh. Furthermore, social desirability bias was minimized by ensuring the confidentiality of the responses of respondents. Moreover, he length of questionnaire was minimised and phrased so as to retain logical flow of questions as well as the interest of the respondents.

4 MEASURES

Intention to stay, as opposed to turnover intention, is defined in this study as a conscious and deliberate wilfulness to leave the organisation (Bayazit & Mannix 2003). Consistent with this definition, intention to stay was measured using a three-item scale with a Cronbach's alpha coefficient of 0.83, and was developed by (Stassen & Ursel 2011). A sample item is: "If I were completely free to choose, I would prefer to continue working in this organisation."

Distributive justice refers to "the fairness associated with decision outcomes and distribution of resources" (Loi et al. 2006). In accordance to this, distributive justice was measured using a six-item scale developed by Price and Mueller (1986), that has a reported Cronbach's alpha coefficient of 0.94. A sample item is: "I am rewarded fairly, considering the responsibility assigned to me."

Procedural justice refers to "the fairness of the processes that lead to outcomes" (Loi et al. 2006).

Accordingly, procedural justice was measured using a six-item scale developed by Moorman (1991), which has a reported Cronbach's alpha coefficient of 0.94. One of the items is: "My organisation's procedures provide for collecting accurate information for making decisions."

To measure interactional justice, Moorman's (1991) six-item scale that has a Cronbach's alpha coefficient of 0.93 was employed. One of the items in the scale is: "My immediate supervisor treats me with kindness and consideration."

Career progress practices indicate an employer's commitment and concern for their employees' future in the organisation. To assess career goal progress, a scale developed by (Weng et al. 2010) consisting of three items and a Cronbach's alpha coefficient of 0.086 was utilized. A sample item is: "My present job sets the foundation for the realization of my career goals."

Professional ability development is defined as "the development of the knowledge, skills and abilities that employees require to perform their tasks competently" (Nouri & Parker 2013). To measure professional ability development, a three-item scale developed by Weng et al. (2010) that has a Cronbach's alpha coefficient of 0.090 was used. One of the items in the scale is: "My present job encourages me to continuously gain new and job-related skills."

Promotion speed was measured using Weng et al.'s (2010) scale, which consists of three items and a Cronbach's alpha coefficient of 0.087. A sample item is: "My promotion speed in the present organisation is fast." Remuneration encompasses fringe benefits, salary and yearly bonus. In this study, remuneration growth was evaluated using a three-item scale developed by Weng et al. (2010), that has a Cronbach's alpha coefficient of 0.083. A sample item is: "My salary is growing quickly in my present organisation."

All instruments used in this study were answered on a five-point rating scale, with response options ranging from 1 "strongly disagree" to 5 "strongly agree".

5 RESULTS

5.1 Descriptive analyses

Table 1 presents the means, standard deviations, and correlation coefficients between the study variables. The possible range of scores for all variables was 1 to 5, where higher scores indicate greater levels of intention to stay, distributive justice, procedural justice, interactional justice, career goal progress, professional ability development, promotion speed and remuneration growth. Specifically, the range for each variable of interest is: 1.0 – 4.33 for intention to stay, 1.17 – 4.50 for distributive justice, 1.0 – 4.50 for procedural justice, 1.0 – 4.33 for interactional justice, 1.0 – 4.67 for career goal progress, 1.0 – 4.33 for professional ability development, 1.0 – 4.68 for promotion speed and 1.0 – 4.57 for remuneration growth.

5.2 Hypothesis testing

Multiple regression was employed to predict intention to stay (ITS) from distributive justice (DJ), procedural justice (PJ), interactional justice (IJ), career goal progress (CGP), professional ability development (PAD), promotion speed (PS) and remuneration growth (RG). Results from partial regression plots and a plot of studentized residuals against the predicted values showed linearity. The analysis also revealed independence of residuals as measured by a Durbin-Watson statistic of 2.21. Homoscedasticity was likewise established using a visual inspection of a plot of studentized residuals versus unstandardized predicted values. Despite high correlations among the independent variables, there was no evidence of multicollinearity, as evidenced by tolerance values greater than 0.1.

Overall, the multiple regression model significantly predicted intention to stay (F (7,216) = 26.37, $p < 0.05$, adjusted $R^2 = 0.443$). Specifically, 44.3 percent of the variance in intention to stay can be explained by different dimensions of organisational

Table 1. Means, standard deviations and correlation coefficients.

		1	2	3	4	5	6	7	8	Mean	SD
1	ITS	-	0.614	0.541	0.586	0.453	0.505	0.627	0.597	1.899	0.560
2	DJ		-	0.748	0.764	0.716	0.701	0.827	0.753	1.707	0.427
3	PJ			-	0.750	0.711	0.664	0.737	0.722	1.825	0.484
4	IJ				-	0.772	0.704	0.797	0.733	1.672	0.448
5	CGP					-	0.662	0.759	0.674	1.670	0.543
6	PAD						-	0.689	0.717	1.693	0.529
7	PS							-	0.777	1.740	0.570
8	RG								-	1.783	0.568

Note: N=224
Note: Dependent Variable: Intention to stay, *p<0.05

Table 2. Regression analysis.

Variable	B	SEB	β	t	p	Tolerance
	0.480	0.126		3.813		
Distributive Justice	0.279	0.131	0.212*	2.124	0.035	0.250
Procesural Justice	0.059	0.101	0.051	0.582	0.561	0.326
Interactional Justice	0.248	0.123	o.198*	2.007	0.046	0.256
Career Goal Progress	−0.240	0.090	−0.233	−2.662	0.008	0.326
Professional Ability Development	0.003	0.085	0.003	0.041	0.967	0.388
Promotion Speed	0.278	0.106	0.283*	2.629	0.009	0.215
Remuneration Growth	0.187	0.090	0.189*	2.084	0.038	0.303

Note: Dependent variable, Intention to Stay; B= unstandardized coefficient; SEB= Standard error of the coefficient; β= standardized coefficient; *p<0.05

justice and career growth. Further, as shown in Table 2, coefficient estimates demonstrate that five out of seven variables were statistically significant ($p < 0.05$) in predicting intention to stay among traffic wardens. Accordingly, DJ (B = 0.279, t = 2.124, p = 0.035), IJ (B = 0.248, t = 2.007, p = 0.046), CGP (B = -0.240, t = -2.662, p = 0.008), PS (B = 0.278, t = 2.629, p = 0.009) and RG (B = 0.187, t = 2.084, p = 0.038) were significant predictors of intention to stay. On the other hand, PJ (B = 0.059, t = 0.582, p = 0.561) and PAD (B = 0.003, t =0.041, p = 0.967) were not statistically significant in predicting intention to stay. In view of these findings, the regression equation can be written as:

ITS = 0.480 + 0.279(DJ) + 0.248(IJ) - 0.240 (CGP) + 0.278(PS) + 0.187(RG)

6 DISCUSSIONS

The present study set out to investigate the predictive roles of organisational justice and career growth on traffic wardens' intention to stay. Consistent with findings by (Poon 2012), this study showed that there is a significant relationship between distributive justice and intention to stay among traffic wardens of the CTPL. It implies that when officers realize that there is impartial distributive justice in their organisation, they will have a stronger desire to stay. The positive relationship between distributive justice and intention to stay justifies officers' perceptions that they are being treated unfairly in terms of the rewards they receive for the responsibilities assigned to them. Such perceptions may arise when they compare themselves with their colleagues. Being government employees, they are mainly getting the same amount of salary despite the differences in the level of difficulty demanded by the nature of their job. By the same token, traffic wardens, who are strictly required to undergo extensive trainings, may not be appropriately rewarded according to their level of educational attainment

since they are designated to the same ranks as those who completed only a bachelor's degree.

Interestingly, results of this study revealed that procedural justice is not a significant predictor of intention to stay. In support of this finding, a study by (Wittmer et al. 2010) indicated that procedural justice was not directly related to turnover. Results may imply that the CTPL is doing well in maintaining its procedures, as evidenced by the traffic wardens' satisfaction with perceived justice in the organisation. Moreover, it denotes that there is an imbalance between perceived distributive justice and procedural justice which may motivate officers to have the intention to quit.

Furthermore, the significant relationship between interactional justice and intention to stay demonstrates that officers have negative perceptions about supervisory behaviour. In the police force, such phenomenon is not new. Interactional justice has been found to be negatively related to turnover intention (Muzumdar 2012).

Career goal progress was likewise found to have a significant impact on intention to stay. Achieving career goal progress is a typical example of a higher-order need satisfaction (Weng et al. 2010). Results suggest that police officers do not consider their job as a way of fulfilling their career goals. Moreover, they have very few employment opportunities which are in line with their perceived career goals. There is also no stable service structure that can guarantee the realization of their long-term goals. In Pakistan, the negative image of the police may be another reason why officers may not want to have a long-term career in the organisation.

Interestingly, professional ability development was not significant in predicting intention to stay among traffic wardens. This may suggest that a high turnover among wardens is not due to their level of professional development. On the contrary, they may be getting ample opportunities to learn job-related skills. Public dealing, communication skills, traffic management and road knowledge are some of the basic skills that are enhanced through experience. The results from this study revealed that officers were satisfied with their acquisition of job-related knowledge and capabilities. (Hackman & Oldham 1975) argued that experiencing a meaningful work is connected to positive satisfaction as well as decreased staff turnover.

Promotion speed emerged as a very strong predictor of turnover intention. Accordingly, officers seem to be disappointed at the rate at which promotion is granted. The press reports suggest that the slow awarding of promotions most frequently contributes to high turnover. Due to the politicization of the police, it remains as an underdeveloped service structure even after ten years. A study by Weng et al. (2010) revealed that regardless of an employee's ongoing contributions to the organisation, slow promotion speed could diminish his level commitment. Such scenario inevitably triggers turnover intention.

This study also found that remuneration significantly impacts the perception of turnover among wardens. Since CTPL is a state department, salary is paid by the government on an equal basis. The results imply that the salary received by the traffic wardens is not sufficient enough to compensate for the amount and nature of work that they perform. The dissatisfaction resulting from inadequate salary may cause low intention to stay.

7 LIMITATIONS AND FUTURE DIRECTIONS

The present study has offered a framework for understanding the significant predictors of intention to stay among traffic wardens. However, some limitations need to be considered. The regression analysis demonstrated that the model accounted for 44.3% of the variance in intention to say. Despite this promising result, there is still an abundant room for progress in identifying other factors that may directly or indirectly affect employee turnover. In future investigations of intention to stay in the CTPL or similar organisations, other potential predictors may be included in the model, such as level of commitment, job satisfaction, compensation, perception about the job and public perception of police work. Apart from psychological factors, environmental and physical conditions that include adequate equipment, the condition of police vehicles, office space, and the overall state of the police facility may also provide insights on employee turnover; hence, researchers may consider incorporating them in future studies. Along these lines, although the present study collected data on marital status, specific questions pertaining to its association with decisions to leave or remain in the organisation were not asked. In view of this, future studies that explore the effects of family background on turnover intentions could be beneficial.

Moreover, the sample of this research was limited only to current traffic officers. This study did not examine officers who have actually left the law enforcement profession and do not have the intention to return. Further work is needed to gather information from these officers in order to arrive at a better understanding of the factors that prompted them to leave the police profession and seek a new career. Nonetheless, locating former police officers is an arduous challenge as it requires cooperation from the human resource departments of numerous law enforcement agencies. As such, collecting empirical information from them may be difficult to attain due to its complexity and possible legal roadblocks.

Lastly, the present study only investigated intention to stay and was not specifically designed to evaluate factors related to intention to quit. In view of this, further research can be carried out to investigate intention to quit and its relationship with intention to stay. Such an undertaking could enlighten us if intention to stay and intention to quit are closely associated with each other or are two completely different phenomena.

8 CONCLUSION

The present study was designed to determine the relative effects of all the dimensions of organisational justice and career growth on intention to stay among the officers of CTPL. Multiple regression analysis revealed that officer's intention to stay is influenced strongly by their perception of distributive justice and promotion speed. On the other hand, procedural justice and professional ability development are insignificant determinant of officer's intention to stay.

REFERENCES

Adams, J.S., Berkowitz, L. & Walster, E. 1976. *Advances in experimental social psychology. Vol. 9, Equity theory: toward a general theory of social interaction.* Cambridge: Academic press

Akhtar, M.S., Salleh, L.M., Ghafar, N.H., Ahmed Khurro, M., & Mehmood, S. A. (2018). Conceptualizing the impact of perceived organizational support and psychological contract fulfillment of employees pasradoxical intentions of stay and leave. *International Journal of Engineering & Technology* 7(2.5): 9–14.

Ahmadi, S.A.A., Daraei, M.R., Rabiei, H., Salamzadeh, Y. & Takallo, H. (2012). The Study on Relationship Between Organizational Justice, Organizational Citizenship Behavior, Job Satisfaction and Turnover Intentions a Comparison between Public Sector and Private Sector. *International Business Management* 6(1): 22–31.

Arthur, M.B., DeFILLIPPI, R.J. & Lindsay, V.J. 2008. On being a knowledge worker. *Organizational Dynamics* 4 (37): 365-377.

Bakri, N. & Ali, N. 2015. The Impact of Organizational Justice on Turnover Intention of Bankers of KPK, Pakistan: The Mediator Role of Organizational Commitment. *Asian Social Science* 11(21): 143–147.

Bayazit, M. & Mannix, E.A. 2003. Should I Stay or Should I Go? Predicting Team Members' Intent to Remain in the Team. *Small Group Research* 34(3): 290–321.

Blau, P.M. 1964. Justice in Social Exchange. *Sociological Inquiry.* 34(2): 193–206.

Blumberg, D.M., Giromini, L. & Jacobson, L.B. 2015. Impact of Police Academy Training on Recruits' Integrity. *Police Quarterly* 19(1): 63–86.

Chew, Y.T. 2005. Achieving organisational prosperity through employee motivation and retention: A comparative study of strategic HRM practices in Malaysian institutions. *Research and Practice in Human Resource Management* 13(2): 87-104.

Cropanzano, R., Anthony, E.L., Daniels, S.R. & Hall, A.V. 2017. Social exchange theory: A critical review with theoretical remedies. *Academy of Management Annals* 11(1): 479-516.

Folger, R., & Konovsky, M. A. (1989). Effects of Procedural and Distributive Justice on Reactions to Pay Raise Decisions. *Academy of Management Journal* 32(1): 115–130.

Ghosh, D. & Gurunathan, L., 2015. Job Embeddedness: A Ten-year Literature Review and Proposed Guidelines. *Global Business Review* 16(5): 856–866.

Greenberg, J. 1988. Cultivating an Image of Justice: Looking Fair on the Job. *Academy of Management Executive* 2(2): 155–158.

Hackman, J.R. & Oldham G.R. 1975. Development of the job diagnostic survey. *Journal of Applied psychology* 60 (2): 159.

Howes, L.M. & Goodman-Delahunty, J. 2014. Career decisions by Australian police officers: a cross-section of perspectives on entering, staying in and leaving policing careers. *Police Practice and Research* 16(6): 453–468.

Hur, Y. 2013. Turnover, Voluntary Turnover, and Organizational Performance: Evidence from Municipal Police Departments. *Public Administration Quarterly.* 4-45.

Jans, N.A. (1989). Organizational commitment, career factors and career/life stage. *Journal of Organizational Behavior*, 10(3): 247–266.

Kim, J. 2015. What Increases Public Employees' Turnover Intention? *Public Personnel Management*, 44(4): 496–519.

Lee, T.W., Hom, P., Eberly, M. & Li, J.J. 2017. Managing employee retention and turnover with 21st century ideas. *Organizational Dynamics.*

Liu, J. & Liu, Y.H. 2016. Perceived organizational support and intention to remain: The mediating roles of career success and self-esteem. *International Journal of Nursing Practice*, 22(2): 205–214.

Loi, R., Hang Yue, N. & Foley, S. 2006. Linking employees' justice perceptions to organizational commitment and intention to leave: The mediating role of perceived organizational support. *Journal of Occupational and Organizational Psychology* 79(1): 101–120.

Lynch, J.E. & Tuckey, M. 2008. The police turnover problem: fact or fiction? *Policing: An International Journal of Police Strategies & Management* 31(1): 6–18.

Mehmood, S.A., Nadarajah, D., Akhtar, M.S., Brohi, N.A. & Khuhro M.A. 2018. A Conceptual Framework Explaining the Impact of Perceived Career Growth and Organisational Justice on Intention to Stay Among City Traffic Police Lahore. *International Journal of Engineering Technology* 7(2): 22–28.

Moorman, R.H. 1991. Relationship between organizational justice and organizational citizenship behaviors: Do fairness perceptions influence employee citizenship? *Journal of Applied Psychology* 76(6): 845–855.

Muzumdar, P. 2012. Influence of Interactional Justice on the Turnover Behavioral Decision in an Organization.

Nadiri, H. & Tanova, C. 2010. An investigation of the role of justice in turnover intentions, job satisfaction, and organizational citizenship behavior in hospitality industry. *International Journal of Hospitality Management* 29 (1): 33–41.

Nouri, H. & Parker, R.J. 2013. Career growth opportunities and employee turnover intentions in public accounting firms. *The British Accounting Review* 45(2): 138–148.

Owolabi, A.B. 2012. Effect of Organizational Justice and Organizational Environment on Turn-Over Intention of Health Workers in Ekiti State, Nigeria. *Research in World Economy*, 3(1): 28

Poon, J.M.L. 2012. Distributive Justice, Procedural Justice, Affective Commitment, and Turnover Intention: A Mediation-Moderation Framework1. *Journal of Applied Social Psychology*, 42(6): 1505–1532.

Price, J.L. & Mueller, C.W. 1986. *Absenteeism and turnover of hospital employees.*

Reina, C.S., Rogers, K.M., Peterson, S.J., Byron, K., & Hom, P.W. (2017). Quitting the Boss? The Role of Manager Influence Tactics and Employee Emotional Engagement in Voluntary Turnover. *Journal of Leadership & Organizational Studies*, 25(1): 5–18.

Reukauf, J.A. 2018. *The Correlation Between Job Satisfaction and Turnover Intention in Small Business.* (D. S. Burrus, Ed.).

Rhoades, L. & Eisenberger, R. 2002. Perceived organizational support: A review of the literature. *The Journal of Applied Psychology* 87(4): 698–714.

Rusbadrol, N. 2018. *A Systematic Review On the Relationship Between Organizational Justice and Turnover Intention (pp. 58–71).* Presented at the AIMC 2017 - Asia International Multidisciplinary Conference, Cognitive-Crcs.

Sahni, S. & Sinha, C. 2018. Effect of Fairness on Employee Outcome: An LMX Perspective on Indian Banks: *Global Business Review* 32(4): 097215091877927.

Bajwa, A. 2015. *Service structure: Regulations sought for wardens' promotions.* [Online]. Retrieved from https://tribune.com.pk/story/907581/service-structure-regulations-sought-for-wardens-promotions/. Accessed on 2018- 10-14.

Shao, R., Rupp, D.E., Skarlicki, D.P. & Jones, K.S. 2011. Employee Justice Across Cultures. *Journal of Management*, 39(1): 263–301.

Spagnoli, P. 2017. Organizational Socialization Learning, Organizational Career Growth, and Work Outcomes. *Journal of Career Development* 6: 089484531770072.

Stassen, M.A., & Ursel, N.D. 2011. Perceived organizational support, career satisfaction, and the retention of older workers. *Journal of Occupational and Organizational Psychology* 82(1): 201–220.

Tett, R.P. & Meyer, J.P. 2006. Job Satisfaction, Organizational Commitment, Turnover Intention, And Turnover: Path Analyses Based On Meta-Analytic Findings. *Personnel Psychology* 46(2): 259–293.

Van Craen, M. & Skogan, W.G. (2016). Achieving Fairness in Policing. *Police Quarterly* 20(1): 3–23.

Thibaut, J.W., & Walker, L. 1975. *Procedural justice: A psychological analysis*. L. Erlbaum Associates.

Weng, Q. & McElroy, J.C. 2012. Organizational career growth, affective occupational commitment and turnover intentions, 80(2): 256–265.

Weng, Q., McElroy, J.C., Morrow, P.C. & Liu, R. 2010. The relationship between career growth and organizational commitment 77(3): 391–400.

Wittmer, J.L.S., Martin, J.E. & Tekleab, A.G. 2010. Procedural Justice and Work Outcomes in a Unionized Setting: The Mediating Role of Leader-Member Exchange. *American Journal of Business* 25(2): 55–70.

Yun, I., Hwang, E. & Lynch, J. 2015. Police Stressors, Job Satisfaction, Burnout, and Turnover Intention Among South Korean Police Officers. *Asian Journal of Criminology* 10(1): 23–41.

Global Competitiveness: Business Transformation in the
Digital Era – Abdullah, Widiaty & Abdullah (eds)
© *2019 Taylor & Francis Group, London, ISBN 978-0-367-19442-0*

Consumer engagement captured in online endorsement (A case study in hijab endorsement)

F. Fatmasari, N. Muna, A.C. Nugroho & Y. Yudani
Polytechnic APP Jakarta, Jakarta, Indonesia

ABSTRACT: As technology changes rapidly, marketing area has a challenge to have sufficient changes as well as to meet the demands from consumers. Online endorsement is becoming more familiar for being a strategy in digital marketing. This marketing way is often used to introduce a new product or to post a sale of a product. Online endorsements can use celebrities or non-celebrities as endorsees. Both of these can represent attachment to the consumer differently. The engagement could be seen from action people did right after seeing online endorsement. The research aimed to provide an insight on how online endorsees and consumers engaged to each other. A comparison between celebrity endorsees' and non-celebrity endorsees' engagement was also made. It used behavioral metrics implied from the online endorsement. It also used interpretative phenomenological analysis to analyze data. It would take a look at different capture of online endorsement.

1 INTRODUCTION

1.1 *Background*

Millennial lifestyle changes where the Internet of things has triggered a change of promotion policy online. A product is no longer promoted through leaflets, bazaars, and banners, but has touched the consumer's preference through endorsement. Endorsement is a promotion by using a figure, both public figure and non-public figure. This is very boisterously done through social media, such as Instagram, an application that allows members to post visual and audiovisual contents along with texts.

Selection of figures becomes important considering the "figure" is spearhead to increase turnover. The chosen figure usually has hundreds of thousands of followers who can be persuaded to buy after the character is seen using a product that is endorsed. Herein lays consumer engagement (consumer engagement) to the attention. Marzocchi et al. (2013), stated that consumer engagement might be strong predictor of brand trust and affect.

One type of endorsement is known as endorsement using customer-driven approaches. This type of engagement activities is of direct benefit to the customers and does not require much support from a firm or seller; alternatively, customers prefer not to involve the firm in the engagement activities. As suggested by Van Doorn et al. (2010), customer behavioral manifestations related to WOM, customer blogging, helping other customers, and writing online reviews are examples in which it is the customer driving the engagement.

Engagement in online endorsement had different view from usual offline endorsement. Some of the usual ways to know the attachment of the consumer is to observe the behavioral site metric. Although it is not always able to capture consumers, it is one of the things most believed by business owner in terms of such things as the number of followers, likes, and comments on the posting of the products. It is also believed that an internship of social media manager at a moslem clothing line prefers the selection of endorsement artists based on the number of followers and statistical data of social media follower increase owned by his moslem clothing line. Usually, the more followers one account has, the higher the cost they charge; however, it commonly comes with better impact on the product sales as well.

It is now an increasing phenomenon that more common people are being known as "rising star" in some social media. They are now in competition in attracting more people to follow their social media. As they get more followers, endorsement will be starting to come.

Considering the aforementioned facts, it begins to be a benchmark for sellers to make an endorsement for their products. Brand managers usually take a look at web metrics or statistical performance of celebrity endorsement; such as the number of followers, the acceleration of the number of followers, likes and unlikes, and also review. It is also common for endorsement agents to provide statistical data to brand managers routinely. However, there have been a few number of research studies showing the ratio of engagement between consumers to celebrity and non-celebrity endorsees. Thus, the research captured different engagement between celebrity endorsees and non-celebrity endorsees. It comprised followers, likes, views, and comments.

2 LITERATURE REVIEW

2.1 *Consumer engagement*

The concept of consumer engagement has been emerging since Brodie et al. (2011) provided logic that consumer engagement is a psychological state that occurs by virtue of interactive customer experiences with a focal agent/object such as a firm or brand. It is manifested into behavior which can strengthen or weaken the brand or firm (van Doorn et al. 2010, Jaakkola et al. 2014).

More related concept is mentioned about customer voluntary performance (Bettencourt 1997) and customer citizenship behaviors (Rosenbaum & Massiah 2007). They focus on customer contributions to the service quality of a firm through benevolent behaviors that are consistent with the role assigned to the customers by the provider. Thus, the stance of that will be helping the firm according to the plans of the firm. Moreover, Groeger (2016) was capturing value from non-paying customer engagement.

Some previous research provide two types of implications of engagement. First, by giving feedback, review, or information about the product (Kumar et al. 2010), or involving in designing product design or assembly (Hoyer et al. 2010, Kristensson et al. 2004), then affirming new customer or influencing others (Kumar et al. 2010). An opinion against those perspectives leads to new types of consumer engagement (CE) proposed by Jaakkola et al. (2014). They are augmenting, co-developing, influencing, and mobilizing behavior.

An engaged customer will be able to post contents in social media or invent alternative products. They will then be very pleased to participate in test use of a new product. Furthermore, an engaged customer can persuade or recommend a brand. Obviously, a really engaged customer can even ask others to boycott their competitor's brands. In social media platform, engagement between customers and its owner(s) can be reflected through customer feedback and collaboration intention (Carlson, 2018).

2.2 *Endorsement*

Endorsement through digital media is applied to both celebrity and non-celebrity social media users. Recent research has demonstrated that celebrity endorsement leads to a favorable attitude toward the endorsed brand (Till et al. 2008). Celebrity endorsement is considered an effective promotional tool by marketers worldwide. One-in-four advertisements use celebrity endorsement. Celebrity endorsement influences advertising effectiveness, brand recognition, brand recall, purchase intentions, and even purchase behavior (Spry et al. 2011). They can attractively invite new consumer to introduce new products to society. Capturing more consumer engagement in its dimensionalities is being observed by some researchers, for example, Noraini & Napi

(2015). They reveal the effectiveness in celebrity and non-celebrity advertisement, especially in the area of physical attractiveness, trustworthiness, expertise, and brand–consumer congruency (Noraini & Napi 2015).

Endorsement can be applied through many media, either offline or online. In online endorsement, it is usually applied in some platforms, e.g., Instagram or YouTube, etc. Each platform admits each specialty. Instagram, as a favorite platform for millennials, brings out high engagement between its members through visual photography, caption, and its short videos shown in InstaStory or sometimes in their feeds. Similar to it, there is also Facebook. However, YouTube provides much longer audio-video visual to its subscribers. Those three platforms are now the three highest endorsement platforms having high members.

3 METHOD

This research was attained qualitatively by using interpretative phenomenology analysis. It attempted to give an explanation on how participants are making sense of their personal life and social worlds which may reveal personal experiences (Smith & Osborn 2003). This research was also a kind of comparative study between celebrity and non-celebrity endorsement's engagement.

Sample brand endorsement observed is a brand in a Muslim fashion line. It was advertised through Instagram. It is observed for about a month after the product was posted. It would be observed in terms of the number of followers, the acceleration of the number of followers, impact to the brand, and comments. In this context, endorsees were persons, celebrity and non-celebrity, paid to promote a product.

4 RESULTS AND DISCUSSION

As shown in the research, many endorsees, especially in hijab, were millennials. The average age of endorsees was 30 years and below. This encouraged their fanbase who are predominantly teenagers to really follow them. However, the endorsees have a good image to get endorsed. In this study, the endorsees observed were Zaskia Sungkar and Laudya Chintya Bella celebrity endorsees, while Hamidah and Mega Iskanti were non-celebrity endorsees observed in this research. They were endorsing for the same brand in that era.

4.1 *Preference criteria of endorsees*

Choosing an endorser might become a really difficult work for brand managers. Many aspects would be observed through endorsees' portfolio which is delivered soon after an endorsement inquiry is coming. Preference criteria to endorse might be prioritized into the following aspects: (1) image of endorser; (2) the increase in the number of followers in the social media; and (3) endorsement fee.

The image of the endorser often leads to consumers' trust. Image of good moslem women with inner natural beauty and attitude would be highly preferred by brand managers. However, one product to another may have different criteria. In addition, reputation is also a major factor for brand managers to pick an endorsee.

Acceleration of the number of followers is the next important aspect of choosing the right endorsee(s). One motive of brand managers to make endorsement was to catch high engagement with new customers. When there is an increasing number of followers of the brand in its social media, one goal is considered achieved since it indicates that there are more viewers on the product post. This phenomenon often leads to better selling.

Since satisfaction also brings a role in endorser preference, endorsement fee is not a big problem for brand managers. Generally, the higher the engagement, the more money is made. The differences between celebrity and non-celebrity engagement and fees are shown in Table 1.

4.2 Consumer engagement capture in online endorsement

Activities of followers are inevitable for benchmarking how successful the endorsement is. People can see, re-post, and re-mention, or even give their footprints by giving like/unlike and feedback in the comment section.

As a post is free to share to public, anybody can visit and leave without an order. Once it is locked, only some people can leave their footprints, while checking a post, for instance a post by CEr2. In some latest post, there are only less than 10 comments. But when the lock was released, it can reach up to more than 400 comments.

Table 1. An overview for celebrity and non-celebrity endorsement.

Celebrity Endorsee (CEe)		Non-Celebrity Endorse (NCEe)	
1	2	1	2
22m followers	13,5m followers	657k followers	554k followers
2980 posts	3411 posts	1998 posts	1445 posts
Up to 137k likes in a post	Up to 77k likes in a post	Up to 30,2k likes in a post	Up to 28,6k likes in a post
Got 359 comments	Get 441 comments	Get 118 comments	Got 202 comments
Starting from IDR 8m		Starting from IDR 3m	

*Taken per July13, 2018

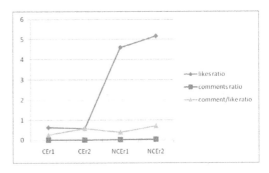

Figure 1. Ratio in consumer engagement.

As celebrity and non-celebrity endorsees reach some awesome number of followers, it will not be neglected that the ratio of footprints will be more challenging. Somehow, the increase in the number of followers should be also followed by the increase in likes or comments. In fact, having more followers does not always mean having more footprint ratio. However, it has been proven that the number of viewers of the post has climbed up significantly.

As seen in Figure 1, it is indicated that NCEr2 has the highest ratio in the number of likes. It could be conceived since the number of previous followers is still uprising.

The interaction between customers and endorsees usually take place in comments. When endorsees provide more feedback in comments, it can improve attractiveness and bring more followers to the account.

Taking a look at the capture, it was reasonable that brand managers would choose an NCEe to endorse the brand with the following reasons: (1) efficient in cost; (2) brought more followers because beginner NCEe are still in an effort of convincing public to trust the brand that he/she endorsed. Yet, CEe could be a good endorser since more followers can bring more viewers on to the brand, so that the awareness to the brand can be climbed up.

5 DISCUSSION AND CONSLUSION

Grasping consumers to get engagement with endorsee was one important key to improving sales. This study has proven that the number of endorsees' followers impact the the number of the brand's account followers. Consequently, this leads to the percentage of the acceleration of followers of the account. In addition, the availability to chat with the endorsees in the comment section also triggers the acceleration of the number of the followers which usually leads to better selling.

This research jumped to the conclusion that preferences of CEe or NCEe would imply on each situation of the brand. More followers will come with more costs. This means that if we try to endorse a brand to a Cee, we have to be ready to prepare more money.

There is a similar research implying that product attitudes were predicted by inferences about the endorser's liking for the product and by attitudes toward the endorser (Silvera 2004). In support of this practice, research indicates that celebrity endorsements can result in more favorable advertisement ratings and product evaluations (Dean & Biswas 2001).

For further studies, it is recommended that the ressearch go in a more in-depth investigation particulalry on the elaboration of the comment section. The analysis can be about the classification of the followers (whether they have real or fake accounts), their loyalty to the products or to the endorsees, and so on.

REFERENCES

Bettencourt, L.A. 1997. Customer Voluntary Performance Customers as Partners in Service Delivery. *Journal of Retailing* 73: 383-406.

Silvera, D.H. & Austad, B. 2004. Factors predicting the effectiveness of celebrity endorsement advertisements. *European Journal of marketing* 38(11/12): 1509-1526.

Dean, D.H. & Biswas, A. 2001. Third-party organization endorsement of products: an advertising cue affecting consumer prepurchase evaluation of goods and services. *Journal of Advertising* 30(4): 41-57.

Hoyer, W.D., Chandy, R., Dorotic, M., Krafft, M. & Singh, S.S. 2010. Consumer Cocreation in New Product Development. *Journal of Service Research* 13(3): 283-296.

Jaakkola, E. & Alexander, M. 2014. The role of customer engagement behavior in value co-creation a service system perspective. *Journal of Service Research* 17: 247–261

Carlson, J., Rahman, M., Voola, R. & De Vries, N. 2018. Customer engagement behaviours in social media: capturing innovation opportunities. *Journal of Services Marketing* 32(1): 83-94.

Kristensson, P., Gustafsson, A. & Archer, T. 2004. Harnessing the creative potential among users. *Journal of product innovation management* 21(1): 4-14.

Kumar, V., Aksoy, L., Donkers, B., Venkatesan, R., Wiesel, T. & Tillmanns, S. 2010. Undervalued or overvalued customers: Capturing total customer engagement value. *Journal of Service Research* 13: 297–310.

Groeger, L., Moroko, L. & Hollebeek, L.D. 2016. Capturing value from non-paying consumers' engagement behaviours: field evidence and development of a theoretical model. *Journal of Strategic Marketing* 24(3-4): 190-209.

Marzocchi, G., Morandin, G. & Bergami, M. 2013. Brand communities: loyal to the community or the brand? *European Journal of Marketing* 47(1/2): 93-114.

Noraini, W. & Napi, W. 2015. *Celebrity and non-celebrity endorsement effectiveness on consumers' attitude towards advertisement.* Kedah: Universiti Utara Malaysia.

Brodie, R.J., Hollebeek, L.D., Jurić, B. & Ilić, A. 2011. Customer engagement: conceptual domain, fundamental propositions, and implications for research. *Journal of service research* 14(3): 252-271.

Rosenbaum, M.S. & Massiah, C.A. 2007. When Customers Receive Support from Other Customers: Exploring the Influence of Customer Social Support on Customer Voluntary Performance. *Journal of Service Research* 9: 257-270.

Smith, J.A. & Osborn, M. 2003. Interpretative phenomenological analysis. In Smith, J.A. (Ed.), *Qualitative psychology: A practical guide to methods (pp. 53-80).* California: Sage.

Spry, A., Pappu, R. & Bettina, C.T. 2011. Celebrity endorsement, brand credibility and brand equity. *European Journal of Marketing* 45(6): 882-909.

Till, B.D., Stanley, S.M. & Priluck, R. 2008. Classical conditioning and celebrity endorsers: An examination of belongingness and resistance to extinction. *Psychology & Marketing* 25(2): 179-196.

van Doorn, J., Lemon, K.N., Mittal, V., Nass, S., Pick, D., Pirner, P. & Verhoef, P.C. 2010. Customer engagement behavior: Theoretical foundations and research directions. *Journal of Service Research* 13: 253–266.

Global Competitiveness: Business Transformation in the
Digital Era – Abdullah, Widiaty & Abdullah (eds)
© 2019 Taylor & Francis Group, London, ISBN 978-0-367-19442-0

The level of organizational communication satisfaction and job satisfaction of global customer fulfilment workers

I. Sualman, F.H.A. Razak & M.I.S. Hamzah
Universiti Teknologi MARA Shah Alam, Selangor, Malaysia

Y. Darwis
Universitas Andalas, Padang, Indonesia

ABSTRACT: Organizational communication satisfaction and job satisfaction are important to people and to organization as to improve workers and company performance. Failing to communicate may affect the company day process. The purpose of this study was to examine the relationship between organizational communication satisfaction and job satisfaction among International Business Machine (IBM) Malaysian Workers. The methods used were Communication Satisfaction Questionnaire by Downs and Adrian, and Minnesota. 80 respondents participated in this study. The selection of the samples was drawn based on the convenient sampling technique. The results found that, level of organisational satisfactions of the respondents showed moderate satisfaction of all dimensions. Moderate satisfaction level was also found on job satisfaction of the respondents. From the eight communication satisfaction dimensions (personal feedback, supervisor communication, subordinate communication, horizontal communication, organizational integration, corporate information, communication climate and media quality), 'communication climate' was found to be the highest correlation with job satisfactions. There was significant correlation between organizational communication satisfaction and job satisfaction among IBM workers. Hence, the company should maintain the organizational communication process applied within the company as to improve performance.

1 INTRODUCTION

In an organisation, employees, managers, or clients communicate with each other using either verbal or non-verbal (gesture or facial expression) communication. The combination of both verbal and non-verbal also happen and often came with emotion. Eze (1998) defined communication as an interaction between humans that involves the process of sharing ideas, thought, experience, or information from one person to another person. This includes written communication which uses tools such as memos, letters, email, slideshow, and so on. According to Crosling & Ward (2002), workplace oral communication reflects the pervasive and powerful role of language and communication in human society.

Richason (2012) stated that the key of effective communication in an organisation is based on interpersonal relationship, which means how good and attractive the process of communication and also how good the listeners are in the organisation. A good listener will react on certain issues or information accordingly. In order to communicate effectively, a good communication process needs to be developed. This is to ensure the information is transmitted fluently and can be understood and accessible to the employees. Pettit Jr (1997) stated that job satisfaction can be influenced by lots of things such as

salaries, promotion, relationship between subordinate and upper level management, working environment and so on.

The outcomes that a person or in this case an employee gets from the transaction process between their self-demand and expectation of employees that matches the company's objectives are called job satisfaction. In completing a company task or business, the management team and also employees need to work as a unit. Thus, managers should be alert with their employees' need and try to meet their demands. The same thing goes with the employees as they need to prove to the company with a good performance so that the company may achieve its objectives and of course increase the revenues. According to Okpara (2004), job satisfaction in work place is a condition whereby positive emotion or positive feelings that occurs result from good or comfortable occupational experience. It is believed that employees' happiness often leads to the company's success.

According to Chiang et al. (2008), communication between employers and workers have to be accurate, complete, clear and consistent to be effective. Communication breakdown will occur when all the principles are not met. Examples of this are poor listening skills, poor communication medium or when communication gets mixed up with sender or receiver's emotional feeling and so on.

In communication, receivers and senders must understand what the information is all about and everyone must focus on the ideas of the messages. Failing to do so may lead to miscommunication which will affect the company's day to day process. This situation makes sense why communication must be a two-way process, receivers can always ask for clear information if they are not clear with the messages that the senders sent to them.

There are few barriers in communication such as language, different personalities, cultural differences and physical factors. When communication difficulty exists, workers communication satisfactions have a tendency to drop off, resulting in decrease of job satisfaction, commitment and also employee performance. Thus, leaders in the certain organisation must always look up and try to provide a good communication medium or communication method in information delivery to their workers.

The key of effective communication in the organisation is based on interpersonal factor, which means how good and attractive the process of communication and also how good the listeners are in the organisation. The absence or lack of communication in the organisation may decrease workers communication satisfaction and lead to decrease of leadership, productivity of the organisation and the most important is workers job satisfaction.

These issues are harmful to the organisations and will impact the quality and services given to their customers. It is critically important for an organisation or employer to be aware of the barriers of communication within the organisation or workplace and how satisfied the workers with the communication process occurred in their organisation. Therefore, this research is undertaken to study the relationship between organisational communication satisfaction and job satisfaction in Global Customer Fulfillment department in IBM Malaysia. More specifically, this study is to assess the level of organisational communication satisfaction and job satisfaction and its relationship as well. Effective organisational communication is very crucial in any organisation in this world. Therefore, it is the responsibility of all categories of workers to build an imperative communication with other subordinates and also clients. The results from this research may help the workers to know their level of communication and job satisfaction. This study investigates the relationship between organisational communication satisfaction and job satisfaction of workers. The results from this study can be beneficial to the organisation to help them to improve their communication and to increase workers' job satisfaction. Moreover, the results from this study may be beneficial as a reference for future research on communication satisfaction and job satisfaction. The purpose of this study is to examine the relationship between organisational communication satisfaction and job satisfaction among IBM Malaysian workers. The specific objectives are:

– To identify the workers' level of communication satisfaction in the organisation.
– To identify the workers' level of job satisfaction in the organisation.
– To analyse the relationship between organisational communication satisfaction and job satisfaction.

The hypothesis of this study were developed as follow:

– H1: There is a significant relationship between good organisational communication and job satisfaction among IBM workers.
– H2: There is a relationship organisational integration and job satisfaction.
– H3: There is a relationship between communicate climate and job satisfaction.

2 RESEARCH METHOD

The research of organisational communication satisfaction and job satisfaction in IBM Malaysia, was conducted in quantitative approaches. In the quantitative research, the aim was to determine the relationship between another (outcome variable) and one thing (an independent variable) in a population. For a precise estimation of the relationship between variables, a descriptive study usually needs a sample of hundreds or even thousands of subjects. Therefore, the research method used was survey research.

The method of data collection that was used in this study was survey and a simple random sampling was used to select the sample. It is a non-representative subset of some larger population. This type of sampling is more convenient and economical compared to other sampling technique. The number of workers (population) who work in IGF department, IBM Malaysia Private Limited was 100 so the sample size was 80. The questionnaire was adapted from Communication Satisfaction Questionnaire (CSQ) of Downs and Hazen (2004) and Minnesota Satisfaction Questionnaire (MSQ) (Weiss & Cropanzano (1996). Downs and Hazen identified three main contexts that should be measured by a communication satisfaction questionnaire which are interpersonal communication, communication in group context, and communication in the organisational context. The Minnesota Satisfaction Questionnaire (MSQ) was designed to measure an employee's satisfaction towards their job. Rather than analysing general measures of job satisfaction, the MSQ provided more specific information on the aspects of a job that an individual find rewarding. The MSQ is also useful in exploring client vocational needs, in counseling follow-up studies, and in generating information about reinforces in jobs. The Likert scale range 1- very satisfied, 2- Dissatisfied, 3 Neutral, 4- Satisfied and 5 Very Satisfied were used to measure the level of satisfaction.

3 RESULTS

3.1 Level of communication satisfaction

Table 1 shows communication satisfaction scores of IBM workers. The highest score dimensions were corporate information (M=4.25) followed by organisational integration (M=4.14) and subordinate communication (M=4.09). The second lowest score dimension was communication climate (M=3.80) and the lowest were personal feedback (M=3.49). Based on the Table 1, the level of organisational communication satisfaction of IBM workers is satisfied.

3.2 Level of job satisfaction

Table 2 represents job satisfaction scores of IBM workers. The highest score dimensions were responsibility (M=4.30) followed by extrinsic reward dimensions (M=3.93) and leadership dimensions (M=3.83). The lowest score was working condition (M=3.59). The Likert scale for job satisfaction range 1- very satisfied, 2- Dissatisfied, 3 Neutral, 4- Satisfied and 5 Very Satisfied. Based on the table, the level of job satisfaction of IBM workers is satisfied.

3.3 Relationship between organisational communication and job satisfaction

Table 3 indicated moderate positive linear correlation between organisational communication and job satisfaction. This moderate positive linear correlation coefficient between organisational communication and job satisfaction (r=.50, p<.05) implied that as perceptions of the organisational communication increased, the job satisfaction of workers also increased. Due to positive linear relationship between organisational communication and job satisfaction, hypothesis 1 was accepted.

3.4 Relationship between organisational integration and job satisfaction

Table 4 indicated moderate positive linear correlation organisational integration and job satisfaction. This moderate positive linear correlation coefficient between organisational integration and job satisfaction (r=.27, p<.05) implied that as perceptions of the organisational integration increased, the job satisfaction of workers also increased. Due to positive linear relationship between organisational integration and job satisfaction, hypothesis 2 was accepted.

3.5 Relationship between communication climate and job satisfaction

Table 5 indicated moderate positive linear correlation communication climate and job satisfaction.

Table 1. Communication satisfaction.

Dimensions	Mean	SD*
Personal feedback	3.49	.771
Supervisor communication	3.91	.522
Subordinate communication	4.09	.717
Horizontal communication	3.86	.490
Organisational integration	4.14	.532
Corporate information	4.25	.479
Communication climate	3.80	.582
Media quality	4.04	.516

*Standard Deviation

Table 2. Job Satisfaction scores.

Dimensions	Mean	SD*
Working condition	3.59	.677
Leadership	3.83	.684
Responsibility	4.30	.538
Extrinsic reward	3.93	.366

*Standard Deviation

Table 3. Correlation between organisational communication and job satisfaction.

Correlations		
		Job satisfaction
Organisational communication	Pearson Correlation	.63**
	Sig. (1-tailed)	.00
	N	80

**. Correlation is significant at the 0.05 level (2-tailed).

Table 4. Correlation between organisational integration and job satisfaction.

Correlations		
		Job satisfaction
Organisational Integration	Pearson Correlation	.27**
	Sig. (1-tailed)	.00
	N	80

**. Correlation is significant at the 0.05 level (2-tailed).

Table 5. Correlation between communication climate and job satisfaction.

Correlations		
		Job satisfaction
Communication Climate	Pearson Correlation	.67**
	Sig. (1-tailed)	.00
	N	80

**. Correlation is significant at the 0.05 level (2-tailed).

This moderate positive linear correlation coefficient between communication climate and job satisfaction (r=.62, p<.05) implied that as perceptions of the communication climate increased, the job satisfaction of workers also increased. Due to positive linear relationship between communication climate and job satisfaction, hypothesis 3 was accepted.

The results of this study indicated that the workers were satisfied in terms of communication in their organisations which means positive feedback regarding the communication practices gathered from the workers regarding their company. However, the findings from Gray & Laidlaw (2004) are in contrast with this study. They found that the employees from the organisations were dissatisfied with all the dimensions of communications. Communication Climate and personal feedback were found least dissatisfying dimensions in Gray and Laidlaw's study. The high satisfaction comes from supervisory and subordinate communication, horizontal communication and media quality, and low satisfaction from, personal feedback, organisational integration, organisational integration and communication climate.

However, in this study, there were no low satisfaction levels found among respondents in every communication satisfaction dimension. The workers and employees showed highest level of satisfaction in media quality, organisational integration and horizontal communication, and lowest satisfaction in personal feedback and communication climate.

Secondly, results of this study found that the sample mean for job satisfaction was higher than 3.5, representing that the respondents were mostly somewhat have high level of job satisfaction areas. The mean scores for job satisfaction across different nations and across academic departments for different aspects of job satisfaction found that majority of its workers were either somewhat satisfied, satisfied, or very satisfied with their current job. Specifically, moderate positive linear correlation was found between organisational communication and job satisfaction in this study. This indicated that as perceptions of the organisational communication increased, the job satisfaction of workers also increased. This study also found positive correlation between organisational communication and job satisfaction, indicating that when workers feel satisfied with their communication in the organisations, it usually leads to job satisfaction. Positive relation between communication and job satisfaction dimension is also found in this study.

4 CONCLUSION

Communication is one of the potential keys which give a positive impact on the employees and we can say that the degree to which a communicator's goals are achieved through effective and appropriate interaction, can affect the employees satisfaction towards their job.

Job satisfaction is the employees' positive feeling about their job as it meets their desires.

When an organization gets more complex in the way they work and structure, it is necessary to reassess the way organisational communication takes place to ensure it works effectively. We need to communicate with others in the organization. Whether exchanging information about tasks or contact information, proper communication helps to improve function, fulfill the goals, and maintain relationships within the organization. In conjunction with organisational communication satisfaction, workers job satisfaction also needed to be reassessed as it plays a big role to workers quality performances especially in the large company in the private sector.

In summary, the study has achieved the entire objectives laid out at the beginning of the paper. Our findings showed that most of the workers communicate every day in order to accomplish their day to day task so a good organisational communication is important in order to avoid miscommunication, and to ensure the flow of completing certain tasks runs smoothly. Thus, we can conclude that there is a positive correlation between organisational communication and job satisfaction of IBM GCF workers and the management should take action towards this result as job satisfaction affects the company business.

REFERENCES

Chiang, C., Jang, S., Canter, D. & Prince, B. 2008. An expectancy theory model for hotel employee motivation: Examining the moderating role of communication satisfaction. *International Journal of Hospitality & Tourism Administration* 9(4): 327-351.

Crosling, G. & Ward, I. 2002. Oral communication: The workplace needs and uses of business graduate employees. *English for Specific Purposes* 21(1): 41-57.

Downs, C.W. & Adrian, A.D. 2004. *Assessing organizational communication: Strategic communication audits.* New York, NY: Guilford.

Eze, I.O. 1998. Speech communication as a tool of modern marking and public relations management. *Journal of communication Art* 1(1): 61-69.

Pettit Jr, J.D., Goris, J.R. & Vaught, B.C. 1997. An examination of organizational communication as a moderator of the relationship between job performance and job satisfaction. *The Journal of Business Communication (1973)* 34(1): 81-98.

Gray, J. & Laidlaw, H. 2004. Improving the measurement of communication satisfaction. *Management Communication Quarterly* 17(3): 425-448.

Okpara, J. 2004. The Impact of Salary on Job Satisfaction. *The Journal of Business Developing Nation* 8.

Richason, O.E. 2012. *What is effective workplace communication?* [Online]. Retrieved from http://smallbusiness. chron.com/effective-workplace-communication-822. html. Accessed on 2018- 06-25.

Weiss, H.M. & Cropanzano, R. 1996. Affective Events Theory: A Theoretical Discussion of the Structure, Causes and Consequences of Affective Experiences at Work. In Staw, B.M., & Sutton, R.I. (ed.), *Research in organizational behavior (Vol. 22).* New York: Elsevier.

Global Competitiveness: Business Transformation in the
Digital Era – Abdullah, Widiaty & Abdullah (eds)
© *2019 Taylor & Francis Group, London, ISBN 978-0-367-19442-0*

Online luxury and in-store luxury shoppers' analysis towards luxury goods

A. Aprillia, R. Setiawan & R.G. Munthe
Maranatha Christian University, Bandung, Indonesia

ABSTRACT: The development of the digital world makes a better marketing application and opens opportunities for sellers to market their products through online stores, including for the sellers of luxury goods. The difference between luxury shoppers and regular shoppers is luxury shoppers willing to pay premium for prestigious products to show their social status. The purpose of this research is to analyze whether there is a difference in shopping behavior between online luxury shoppers and in-store luxury shoppers. The number of samples in this research were 124 respondents. This research uses independent sample t-test. The result shows there is no difference between online luxury and in-store luxury shoppers towards luxury goods.

1 INTRODUCTION

The traditional in-store, which is the out of date marketing application is a direct and tangible interaction between the seller and the buyer. The up to date marketing has begun to shift from traditional in-store to online store. The invention of the internet could become as important as the invention of the automobile in shaping people's daily activities (Farag 2006). The use of Information and Communication Technologies (ICT) has been increasing in recent decades (Mokhtarian 2004). Information technology has played an important role in influencing the scale and nature of retail. In the past few decades we have seen smartphones and other electronic devices used for business transactions. Searching product information and buying goods online are becoming increasingly popular activities (Farag 2006). Online shopping is emerging as one of the most important vehicles for transactions between buyers and sellers (Su 2008).

Based on Google Indonesia survey results in 2016, the trend of online shopping in Indonesia is the highest in Asia with an estimated 71 percent of Indonesians using smartphones for online transactions is 136 minutes per day and uses about 52 minutes of desktop per day. The best-selling products in Indonesia's online shopping are travel products (airfare and hotel), fashion (clothes and accessories), gadgets (smartphones and tablets), electronic products, and e-books (The Daily Oktagon 2017). The products are included in the category of non-luxury goods products. Do shoppers in Indonesia dare or not to buy luxury goods through online channels? As we know luxury goods are expensive goods and considered risky when buying through online channels. Shopping online is not easy to do for all types of product such as luxury goods.

The business of luxury goods has become one of the fastest growing business segments in today's world, this is not confined to any country or segment but is spreading to all groups and countries, especially emerging economies (Sun 2011). The market for luxury goods and services has been enlarging, steadily, and strongly, since the early 1990s (Truong et al. 2008, Truong 2010, Roux et al. 2016), economic recovery in most of the western countries and unshackled economic growth in Southeast Asian countries triggered the purchase of luxury goods (Vigneron & Johnson 1999). The luxury market grew by 5% to an estimated €1.2 trillion globally in 2017 (D'Arpizio et al. 2017).

In the world of luxury brands, it may appear intuitive to think that some brands are more conspicuous than others because they hold more materialistic values, or are more fashionable (Truong et al. 2008). Luxury goods enable consumers to satisfy psychological and functional needs. The consumption of luxury goods involves buying a product that represents values to both the individual and significant others (Wiedmann et al. 2009). Grossman and Shapiro (1986) stated that owning and using luxury goods can convey the owners' perceived social status and prestige.

The difference between luxury shoppers and regular shoppers is luxury shoppers willing to pay premium for prestigious products to show their social status (Veblen 2017). Factors that influence online luxury shoppers and in-store luxury shoppers according to Liu et al. (2013) are price consciousness, product availability, trust, risk aversion, employee attitude, and shopping interaction.

According to Liu et al. (2013), online luxury shoppers are more price consciousness than in-store luxury shoppers. The Internet makes it easy for online luxury shoppers to compare prices from some online stores first and find the cheapest prices. In addition, online luxury shoppers can easily view and compare items from several online stores of a kind, high variety they are looking for and they expect product availability. For in-store luxury shoppers, it is difficult to compare prices and see the availability of products because in-store luxury stores are very few in each region, so their tendency is not too price consciousness and variety seeking. Thus, we present the following hypotheses:

H_1: There is a difference of price consciousness between online luxury shoppers and in-store luxury shoppers.

H_2: There is a difference of value product availability between online luxury shoppers and in-store luxury shoppers.

According to Liu et al. (2013), in-store luxury shoppers feel that shopping in the in-store is safer because they can ensure that the goods do exist and are genuine goods. While they make payments by credit card too, they feel safe because the money spent on luxury goods quite a lot. When online luxury shoppers want to buy luxury goods, they will find a seller with good reviews and ratings to avoid unwanted incident. Thus, we present the following hypotheses:

H_3: There is a difference of level of trust between online luxury shoppers and in-store luxury shoppers.

H_4: There is a difference of level of risk aversion between online luxury shoppers and in-store luxury shoppers.

According to Liu et al. (2013), in-store luxury shoppers prefer to able to see and touch the products. Good customer service and courteous store employees are important to the in-store luxury shoppers while online luxury shoppers enjoy shopping online because of the lack pressure from the salesperson. The in-store luxury shoppers feel that they are not only high valued, but also financially successful through the interaction between in-store luxury shoppers and store employees help in-store shoppers. Thus, we present the following hypotheses:

H_5: There is a difference value of personal store service (employee attitude) between online luxury shoppers and in-store luxury shoppers.

H_6: There is a difference of value shopping interactions between online luxury shoppers and in-store luxury shoppers.

2 RESEARCH METHOD

The current research method replicates and adopts the Liu et al. (2013) research. We used qualitative and quantitative methods. This research used 24 measurement items. 5 items to measure conspicuous consumption motive (CCM), 3 items to measure price consciousness (PC), 3 items to measure product availability (PA), 4 items to measure trust (TR), 3 items to measure risk aversion (RA), 3 items to measure employee attitude (EA), and 3 items to measure shopping interaction (SI).

We referred adult respondents who were at least twenty one years old and live in Bandung and its surroundings. Non-probability sampling used in this research. The numbers of samples were 124 respondents. The age of respondents ranged from 21 to 45 above, there were 60 males and 64 females.

We used a qualitative method to identify which respondents belonged to the category of luxury shoppers. There are two questions asked. First: 'In the last three years, have you bought any luxury brand products?' The second question is about luxury consumption tendency, five scale items were included to measure the construct of conspicuous consumption motive (CCM). Those respondents whose average scores were higher than three were deemed to display a high luxury consumption tendency. Only those respondents who answered "yes" to the first question about their experience in luxury shopping and also scored higher than three on the CCM scale were categorized as luxury consumers. The final sample consisted of 56 respondents, there were 31 males and 25 females.

Next, we divided the 56 luxury shoppers into online and in-store groups. In our surveys, we asked the respondents how frequently they purchased luxury goods online. The respondents needed to select one of six options: "never", "once in two or three years", "once a year", "twice a year", "three times a year", and "over three times a year". The respondents who selected "never" or "once in two or three years" were assigned to the in-store group. The rest of the shoppers were put in the online group. After applying this grouping method, we identified 33 online luxury shoppers and 23 in-store ones.

A quantitative method is used to examine the hypotheses. Hypotheses was tested with independent sample t-test, it compares the means are significantly different.

3 RESULTS

3.1 Validity and reliability

The results of the validity test show the KMO results of 0.717 with a significance level of 0.000, meaning the number of samples in this research is adequate. A common rule of thumb for validity test suggests that a KMO score above 0.5 is adequate and a high Bartlett score with a significance level of 0.5 is significant (Hair et al. 1998). Table 1 presents the results of factor loadings. Based on these results, all items are valid.

Based on Table 2, all items are reliable because the cronbach's alpha value is greater than 0.600.

Table 1. Validity test results.

Rotated component matrix[a]

Component

	1	2	3	4	5	6	7
CCM1	.805						
CCM2	.841						
CCM3	.766						
CCM4	.772						
CCM5	.838						
PC1				.646			
PC2				.858			
PC3				.836			
PA1					.794		
PA2					.683		
PA3					.653		
TR1		.848					
TR2		.879					
TR3		.839					
TR4		.850					
RA1						.817	
RA2						.520	
RA3						.661	
EA1			.744				
EA2			.768				
EA3			.747				
SI1							.596
SI2							.795
SI3							.531

Extraction Method: Principal Component Analysis.
Rotation Method: Varimax with Kaiser Normalization.

a. Rotation converged in 7 iterations.

Source: Results of SPSS processed data (2018)

Table 2. Reliability test results.

Variable/indicator	Cronbach's alpha	Status
CCM	0.870	Reliabel
PC	0.746	Reliabel
PA	0.660	Reliabel
TR	0.896	Reliabel
RA	0.619	Reliabel
EA	0.743	Reliabel
SI	0.612	Reliabel

Source: Results of SPSS processed data (2018)

Rule of thumb for reliability test suggests that the value of cronbach's alpha should be greater than 0.700 (Hair et al. 1998), but other authors say that a value of 0.600 is still acceptable (Sekaran & Bougie 2013).

Table 3. In-store luxury shoppers versus online luxury shoppers.

Hypothesis number	In-store luxury shoppers average	Online luxury shoppers average	Sig. (p value)
H_1: Price consciousness	4.3913	4.1515	0.214
H_2: Product availability	4.0290	3.8081	0.194
H_3: Trust	4.0978	3.9015	0.325
H_4: Risk aversion	4.3478	4.4949	0.283
H_5: Employee attitude	4.1159	4.0404	0.662
H_6: Shopping interaction	3.8406	3.8889	0.727

Source: Results of SPSS processed data (2018)

3.2 Independent sample t-test

Results are shown in Table 3. All hypotheses are not supported because the value of p value is greater than 0.05. First, we did not find support for H_1, online and in-store luxury shoppers showed no significant difference in their behavior towards price consciousness. This results reveals that online and in-store luxury shoppers demonstrate the same behavior towards price consciousness. Second, we did not find support for H_2, online and in-store luxury shoppers showed no significant difference in their behavior towards product availability. This results reveals that online and in-store luxury shoppers demonstrate the same behavior towards product availability.

Third, we did not find support for H_3, online and in-store luxury shoppers showed no significant difference in their behavior towards level of trust. This results reveals that online and in-store luxury shoppers demonstrate the same behavior towards level of trust. Fourth, we did not find support for H_4, online and in-store luxury shoppers showed no significant difference in their behavior towards level of risk aversion. This results reveals that online and in-store luxury shoppers demonstrate the same behavior towards level of risk aversion.

Fifth, we did not find support for H_5, online and in-store luxury shoppers showed no significant difference in their behavior towards value of personal store service (employee attitude). This results reveals that online and in-store luxury shoppers demonstrate the same behavior towards value of personal store service (employee attitude). Sixth, we did not find support for H_6, online and in-store luxury shoppers showed no significant difference in their behavior towards value shopping interactions. This results reveals that online and in-store luxury shoppers demonstrate the same behavior towards value shopping interactions.

This means there is no difference behavior between in-store luxury shoppers with online luxury shoppers towards price consciousness, product availability, trust, risk aversion, employee attitude, and shopping interaction.

4 DISCUSSION AND CONCLUSION

The results of this research differ from previous research results from Liu et al. (2013). In this research there is no different behavior between in-store luxury shoppers with online luxury shoppers towards price consciousness, product availability, trust, risk aversion, employee attitude, and shopping interaction. This occurs due to cultural differences between samples in previous studies (Western) and this research (Asian). Some researchers claim that there are differences in behavior between Western and Asian related to luxury goods (Dubois & Laurent 1994, Wong & Ahuvia 1998, Wong & Zaichkowsky 1999, Zhang & Schavitt 2003, Veblen 2017, Hofstede et al. 2010, Sun 2011, Hofstede 2011, Hennigs et al. 2012).

Asian shoppers buy luxury goods to elevate their social status, more famous and expensive the brand, more recognition they will get and emphasize to others that they have the ability to afford expensive products. Wearing or using luxury brands, an individual can bring glory and respect to the family and to the wider community as a clear sign of his or her/his success. In addition, Asian shoppers are strongly influenced by the collectiveness and social pressure to conform, they tend to hide their personal opinions, conform to the group and obey manners that are believed to be socially acceptable. Purchase luxury branded products to look the same as their peers.

Thus, Asian shoppers do not really care whether they buy the luxury goods through in-store or online store; therefore, the result of this research did not find the difference of behavior between in-store luxury shoppers with online luxury shoppers towards price consciousness, product availability, trust, risk aversion, employee attitude, and shopping interaction.

Considering the aforementioned facts, we cannot generalize the results of this research because there are only a few samples used and the research area is only in Bandung and its surroundings, not all of Indonesia and even Asia. These are limitations in our research. For further research, it is better to expand the research area and increase the number of samples.

REFERENCES

D'Arpizio, C., Levato, F., Kamel, M.A. & Montgolfier, J. D. 2017. *Luxury Goods Worldwide Market Study, Fall-Winter 2017: The New Luxury Consumer: Why Responding to the Millennial Mindset Will Be Key*. Boston: Bain & Company.

Dubois, B. & Laurent, G. (1994). Attitudes towards the concept of luxury: An exploratory analysis. *Asia Pacific Advances in Consumer Research* 1: 273-278.

Farag, S. 2006. *E-shopping and its interactions with in-store shopping*. Utrecht: Utrecht University.

Grossman, G.M. & Shapiro, C. 1988. Foreign counterfeiting of status goods. *The Quarterly Journal of Economics* 103(1): 79-100.

Hair, J.R., Anderson, R.E., Tatham, R.L. & Black, W.C. 1998. *Multivariate Data Analysis. 5th Edition*, Upper Saddle River. NJ: Prentice-Hall, Inc.

Hennigs, N., Wiedmann, K.P., Klarmann, C., Strehlau, S., Godey, B., Pederzoli, D. & Taro, K. 2012. What is the value of luxury? A cross-cultural consumer perspective. *Psychology & Marketing* 29(12): 1018-1034.

Hofstede, G. 2011. Dimensionalising cultures: The Hofstede model in context. *Online readings in psychology and culture* 2(1): 1-26.

Hofstede, G., Hofstede, G.J. & Minkov, M. 2010. *Cultures and organizations: Software of the mind: Intercultural cooperation and its importance (pp. 6527)*.

Liu, X., Burns, A.C. & Hou, Y. 2013. Comparing online and in-store shopping behavior towards luxury goods. *International Journal of Retail & Distribution Management* 41(11/12): 885-900.

Mokhtarian, P.L. 2004. A conceptual analysis of the transportation impacts of B2C e-commerce. *Transportation* 31(3): 257-284.

Roux, E., Tafani, E. & Vigneron, F. 2017. Values associated with luxury brand consumption and the role of gender. *Journal of Business Research* 71: 102-113.

Sekaran, U. & Bougie, R. 2013. *Research methods for business: A skill-building approach. 6th Edition*. New York: John Wiley & Sons, Ltd.

Su, B.C. 2008. Characteristics of consumer search on-line: How much do we search?. *International Journal of Electronic Commerce* 13(1): 109-129.

Sun, M.W. 2011. *Consumption of luxury fashion brands: The motives of generation y consumers in China*. Auckland: Auckland University of Technology.

The Daily Oktagon. 2017. Perilaku hedonism pada pengguna smartphone, apakah anda salah satunya?. [Online]. Retrieved from https://daily.oktagon.co.id/perilaku-hedonisme-pada-pengguna-smartphone-apakah-anda-salah-satunya/ Accessed on 2018- 06-29.

Truong, Y. 2010. Personal aspirations and the consumption of luxury goods. *International Journal of Market Research* 52(5): 655-673.

Truong, Y., Simmons, G., McColl, M. & Kitchen, P.J. 2008. Status and conspicuousness – are they related? Strategic marketing implications for luxury brands. *Journal of Strategic Marketing* 16(3): 189–203.

Veblen, T. 2017. *The theory of the leisure class*. London: Routledge.

Vigneron, F. & Johnson, L.W. 1999. A review and a conceptual framework of prestige-seeking consumer behavior. *Academy of Marketing Science Review* 1(1): 1-15.

Wiedmann, K.P., Hennigs, N. & Siebels, A. 2009. Value-based segmentation of luxury consumption behavior. *Psychology & Marketing* 26(7): 625–651.

Wong, N.Y. & Ahuvia, A.C. 1998. Personal taste and family face: Luxury consumption in confucian and western societies. *Psychology & Marketing* 15(5): 423-441.

Wong, A.C.Y & Zaichkowsky, J.L. 1999. Understanding luxury brands in Hong Kong. *European Advances in Consumer Research* 4: 310-316.

Zhang, J. & Shavitt, S. 2003. Cultural values in advertisements to the Chinese x-generation: Promoting modernity and individualism. *Journal of Advertising* 32(1): 21-31.

Global Competitiveness: Business Transformation in the
Digital Era – Abdullah, Widiaty & Abdullah (eds)
© 2019 Taylor & Francis Group, London, ISBN 978-0-367-19442-0

The effects of shadow banking on banks' credit consumers

R. Fitriaini & R. Veronica
Parahyangan Catholic University, Bandung, Indonesia

ABSTRACT: Gross regional domestic product (GRDP) of West Java, Indonesia, still relies on household consumption. One of the factors which encourages the development of household consumption is credit. During the period of 2007-2015, the credit consumer position of commercial banks in West Java increased by approximately 44%. Aside from commercial banks, there is another form of financial institution that took part in lending activities, named shadow banks. This raises the question on whether or not shadow banks disrupt the demand for credit consumer of commercial banks in West Java. This research used multi-variate regression method with ordinary least squares (OLS) technique. The results showed that the level of unemployment and interest rates of banks have a significant negative influence, whereas the interest rate of shadow banks and GRDP of West Java was not significant in affecting the number of the commercial banks' credit consumption in West Java.

1 INTRODUCTION

After the global financial crisis of 2008, despite a downturn, Indonesia's Gross Domestic Product (GDP) aggregate continued to show an upward trend. From the sectoral side, the Central Statistics Agency showed that Indonesia's GDP is still dominated by several provinces, one of them is West Java with a composition of 13% of total GDP. In comparison to the other components, household consumption is the main contributor, representing approximately 60% of West Java's Gross Regional Domestic Product (GRDP) from 2007-2015. This was followed by exports of goods and services by 25% and gross domestic fixed capital formation by 20%. Furthermore, one of the factors driving the development of consumption is credit for consumption purposes. According to Suyatno (2007) credit is a loan made by parties who need funds to financial institutions which serve as a provider of financial services. The loans are made under predetermined conditions and within a certain period of time. In economic activities, credit is considered to have several functions, namely to improve the use of money and goods, improve the circulation of money, maintain economic stability, as well as a tool of international economic relations (Muchdarsyah 2000). Generally, financial institutions that provide credit services are banks. According to Mishkin in Aviliani et al. (2015) bank is an important institution in financing economic activity in the real sector. However, if financial crisis happens, moments after that usually banks will become more cautious in choosing the economic units to be financed because of the risks and strict regulations to avoid future crisis conditions (Hofmann 2017). In addition to being more cautious, the

banks created a more stringent standard in determining whether an economic unit is eligible to receive credit, making it more of an exclusive product, because it can only be enjoyed by a group of people (Solarz 2013). This poses a problem for the economic unit that cannot access the credit provided by the bank, hampering the economic activities in the real sector.

However, over time, the problem began to be overcome by the presence of shadow banks. Financial Stability Board (2012) states that shadow banks are non-bank institutions that participate in credit intermediation where activities involve several entities and are conducted outside the regular banking system in whole or in part. In the case of Indonesia, entities involved in shadow banking practices include finance companies, insurance companies, mutual funds, securities firms, private equity, hedge funds and savings and loan cooperatives (Kementerian Keuangan 2013). Even so, the practice of shadow banking in Indonesia is not as complicated as that in developed countries. The practice of shadow banking is still limited to the activities of finance companies that disburse loans to customers by using several sources of funds (Kementerian Keuangan 2013). In its implementation, the finance company has 4 types of business activities, namely leasing, credit card, consumer financing and factoring. Data from Bank Indonesia show that the performance of finance companies in Indonesia is only dominated by two business activities, which are consumer financing and leasing by 60.6% and 36.9% of the total value of business activities of the financing industry, respectively. Consumer financing is a financing activity that is devoted to the procurement of goods based on consumer needs with installment payments. Consumer needs include vehicle financing, home appliance financing, electronic financing, and housing finance. On the other hand, lease is a financing activity in the form of the provision of capital goods, whether under lease with finance lease or an operating lease for use by the lease for a specified period based on periodic payments.

Although the activities of these institutions are still limited in Indonesia, shadow banks can be considered capable of contributing and benefiting the economy. One of which can be seen from the previous explanation that explained how the problem about the difficulty of accessing credit for community groups that are inadequate to meet the creditworthiness standard are compensated by the existence of these shadow banks. According to Ghosh et al. (2012), this is because shadow banks have a function that enables these institutions to efficiently channel funds to those in need. This statement is supported by the results of research Gao (2015) which states that shadow banks can be considered as a source of alternative financing for those who cannot access credit to the banking sector. This is due to how shadow banks offer easier requirements, more flexible loan amounts, and shorter loan approval times than the banking sector. Thus, the debtor will have a higher willingness to pay for the interest rates on loans than the rates set by commercial banks. In addition, when viewed from the consumer side, this can also happen, namely because shadow banks are considered "attractive" for consumers who are not credit worthy by the bank (Solarz 2013).

Mester et al. (2017) also revealed if shadow banks have three functions in the financial sector, (1) alternative funding source, (2) investment opportunities in addition to traditional banking, and (3) risk-sharing from banking sector instruments. In addition, Barth et al. (2015) found that shadow banks in China are proven to be able to diversify China's financial sector to provide greater investment and savings opportunities to consumers and businesses across the country. This positively affects economic growth in China. In addition, he also found that there are significant linkages between shadow banks and commercial banks. At the same time, however, shadow bank financial activities can also be a source of systemic risk. Based on the Financial Stability Board (2012), it is due to the largest source of shadow banking financing comes from the banking sector, where such an interaction between the banking sector and financing institutions could amplify the systemic risk. In addition, some risks that may come up from shadow banking activities include: the potential for excess leverage, procyclicality amplification, funding instability and potential bank run, systemic risk transmission, and arbitration regulation (Ghosh et al. 2012).

Based on the explanation above, it can be inferred that finance companies actually have an influence on the economy and indeed have its own "portion" in

lending activities to the public. Moreover, in the case of West Java, based on the data from the Financial Services Authority, it can be seen that the total loan portfolio by the finance companies in West Java from 2007 – 2015 is considered to have a fairly high rate, especially in the case of consumption credit. However, to find out whether this situation can affect commercial banks' business activities or not still remains a question. Thus, this study aims to determine whether there is an influence caused by finance companies to business activities of commercial banks, especially in the case of consumer credit. This is important, because until now, studies on the effect of shadow banks toward commercial banks in Indonesia are relatively scarce, notably in West Java. In addition, if it is proven that the finance company has a negative impact on the business activities of commercial banks, the financial authorities are expected to create policies that specifically regulate the activities of the finance companies in order not to interfere with business activities of commercial banks and thus can help create economic stability.

2 RESEARCH METHOD

The data used in this study are secondary data from statistical reports on Bank Indonesia, Financial Services Authority, and Central Bureau of Statistics quarterly time-series from 2007-2015. The unit of analysis of this research is commercial banks and finance companies in West Java. The reason the data beyond 2015 is not incorporated is because there is a change in the rules of the companies's business activities as well as in the system of consumer lending after 2015. The following is the details of the data sources used in this study (Table. 1):

Table 1. Data tables.

	Data	Period	Sources
1	Amount of consumer credit of commercial banks in West Java	January 2007-December 2015 (quarterly)	Bank Indonesia and Financial Services Authority (OJK)
2	Gross regional domestic bruto (GRDP)		Central Bureau of Statistics (BPS)
3	Consumer credit interest rate in West Java		Central Bureau of Statistics (BPS)
4	Financial companies's interest rate in West Java		Financial Services Authority (OJK)
5	Unemployment rate in West Java		Central Bureau of Statistics (BPS)

Furthermore, in determining the presence of influence of finance companies on the amount of bank's consumer credit, this research will use Ordinary Least Square (OLS) analysis technique. It is important to be known that before performing the OLS test, the model used must first be free from violation of classical assumptions. The classical assumption test is used to determine the relation between variables, including stationary test, autocorrelation test, multicollinearity test, and heteroscedasticity test. In its operation, this technique distinguishes between dependent and independent variables. The dependent variable used is the amount of consumer credit distributed by commercial banks whereas, the independent variables used are the bank's consumer credit interest rate, finance companies's interest rate, unemployment rate, and gross regional domestic product (GRDP) in West Java. The following is a research model used in this study.

$$KKP_t = \beta_0 + \beta_1 PDRB_t + \beta_2 TSP_t \\ + \beta_3 TSPP_t + \beta_4 TP_t + \varepsilon_t \quad (1)$$

Information:
KKP_t : The amount of consumer credit disbursed by commercial banks (trillion rupiah)
$PDRB_t$: Total gross regional domestic product (GRDP) (billion rupiah)
TSP_t : Consumer credit interest rate (percent)
$TSPP_t$: Financial companies's interest rate (percent)
TP_t : Unemployment rate (percent)
ε_t : Error term

3 RESULTS AND DISCUSSION

Table 2. shows the estimated time series model of commercial banks's consumption credit in West Java in 2007 to 2015.

Based on Table. 2 there is some information that can be known. First, the variable of unemployment rate (TP) and the interest rate of consumption credit of commercial banks (D (TSP)) at alpha level 20 percent showed indications that they have a significant influence on the amount of consumer credit commercial banks, as shown in p-value of 0.001 and 0.174, respectively. In addition, it can also be seen that the coefficients of TP and D (TSP) have a negative sign

Table 2. Estimation results.

Independent variables	Coefficient	Prob.
D(GDRB)	0.000	0.447
TP	-721.004	0.000
D(TSP)	-1199.493	0.174
TSPP	52.668	0.786
C	9479.465	0.001
R-squared = 0,509		

on each coefficient which means that if TP is increased by 1 percent, then the amount of consumption credit of commercial banks will decrease by 721.004. Then, if D (TSP) are increased by 1 percent, the amount of consumption credit of commercial banks, the option on it will decrease 1,199.493 billion rupiahs. This might happen when the involuntary unemployed to total unemployed has a larger portion than voluntary unemployed (Hadad et al. 2004). Furthermore, bank lending rates have a negative effect on the amount of credit of commercial banks. According to Solarz (2013), credit is an exclusive product, so it can only be enjoyed by a group of people. Thus, the possibilities that banks increase their lending rates will make the possibility for deficit units to get loans from commercial banks more limited.

On the other side, although the interest rate of financing company (TSPP) and GRDP of West Java (D (PDRB)) variables have a positive sign, the p-value for the two variables shows an insignificant number. In other words, the TSPP and (D(PDRB)) are proven to positively affect the consumer credit of commercial banks, but not statistically significant. It is possible that from the consumer side, they consider the financial products produced by banks and financing institutions as a complementary item, so that the increase in interest rates of financial institutions does not significantly affect the amount of bank credit consumption. Meanwhile, PDRB does not give a significant effect because the period 2007-2015 is before and after the global crisis, so that economic conditions in West Java were affected. GRDP has a significant positive influence on the amount of credit of commercial banks. The changes of GRDP show the level of prosperity through the increase or reduction of society's income that can represent the pattern of public consumption. This means that the increase of GRDP in a province will be followed with an increase in the amount of credit disbursed by commercial banks in order to fulfill the needs of the people in the related province.

In general, the presence of financing institutions should not be threatening for the banking sector since their finance function is limited to providing financing for customers. Provisions for prospective borrowers that are determined by financing institutions is considered more lenient than banking requirements, even though it is balanced with higher interest rates. Financing economic activities in Indonesia are still limited to consumer financing, credit cards, leases, and factoring. Thus, the financing institution has the opportunity to become another source for the prospective creditors. Funds disbursed by financing institutions are obtained from equity, exchange, and capital loans from banks. This makes the relationship between financial institutions and commercial banks complementary to one another.

4 CONCLUSION

This study aims to determine whether there is an influence caused by finance companies to business activities of commercial banks and how the nature of these influences, especially in terms of consumer credit is. To achieve that, this study used quarterly time-series data from January 2007 to December 2015 which were then processed using Ordinary Least Squares (OLS) analysis technique. The dependent variable used in this study is the amount of consumer credits that are distributed by commercial banks, whereas the independent variables used are the interest rate of consumer financing credit, the interest rate of consumer credit commercial bank, the unemployment rate, and the GRDP. The results seemed to indicate that the presence of shadow banks in West Java do not threaten the existence of the commercial banks. This is due to how the activities of shadow banks in Indonesia are still limited to providing loans to debtors. In addition, the largest source of funds disbursed by shadow banks comes from commercial banks. That being said, when the number of shadow bank customers increases, the funds disbursed will also increase, where based on that, the funds lent by commercial banks to financial institutions should also increase. Therefore, the existence of shadow banks leans more towards being complementary rather than threatening the business activities of commercial banks in West Java.

REFERENCES

Aviliani, S.H., Maulana, T.N. & Hasanah, H. 2015. The Impact of Macroeconomic Condition on The Bank's Performance in Indonesia. *Buletin Ekonomi Moneter dan Perbankan* 17(4): 379-402.

Barth, W., Hulek, K., Peters, C. & Van de Ven, A. 2015. *Compact complex surfaces (Vol. 4)*. Berlin: Springer.

Financial Stability Board. 2012. *Strengthening Oversight and Regulation of Shadow Banking: An Integrated Overview of Policy Recommendations*. [Online]. Retrieved from http://www.fsb.org/2012/11/r_121118/ Accessed on 2018- 06-27.

Gao, S. 2015. Seeing Gray in a Black-and-White Legal World: Financial Repression, Adaptive Efficiency, and Shadow Banking in China. *Texas International Law Journal* 50(1): 95-143.

Ghosh, S., Mazo, I.G. & Robe, I. 2012. Chasing the Shadows: How Significant Is Shadow Banking in Emerging Markets? *Economic Premise* 88: 1-7.

Hadad, E., Rav-Acha, M., Heled, Y., Epstein, Y. & Moran, D.S. 2004. Heat stroke. *Sports Medicine* 34(8): 501-511.

Hofmann C. 2017. Shadow Banking in Singapore. *Singapore Journal of Legal Studies* 18-52.

Kementerian Keuangan. 2013. *Peran Penyaluran Kredit Non Perbankan dan Pertumbuhan Ekonomi: Perspektif dari Negara Emerging G20*. Jakarta: Badan Kebijakan Fiskal Kemenkeu

Mester, É. Tóth, R. & Kozma, T. 2017. Banking Competitiveness. *Management, Enterprise and Benchmarking in the 21st Century*. IV, 258-276.

Muchdarsyah, S. 2000. *Manajemen Dana Bank*. Jakarta: Bumi Aksara.

Solarz, M. 2013. The Importance of Shadow Banking Sector Entities for Population Affected by Credit Exclusion. *Copernican Journal of Finance & Accounting* 2 (2): 189-201.

Suyatno, S. 2007. *Kelembagaan Perbankan*. Jakarta: Gramedia Pustaka Utama.

Global Competitiveness: Business Transformation in the
Digital Era – Abdullah, Widiaty & Abdullah (eds)
© 2019 Taylor & Francis Group, London, ISBN 978-0-367-19442-0

Perception and self-concept analysis as the basis of making family planning ads for male

C.W. Utami, M. Teguh, H.Y. Wono & C. Hongdiyanto
Universitas Ciputra, Surabaya, Indonesia

ABSTRACT: One of the things that is still in the spotlight for the Surabaya City, Indonesia, government is the population density. It makes city officials take strategic steps to increase public participation in family planning program. One of the programs being promoted is male family planning with vasectomy method. In order for this program to be widely known, public service ads will be made. The ads take consideration of perceptions and self-concept of the target. The method used in this research is descriptive qualitative, with in-depth interviews as data collection instruments. This research informant consisted of five people who were the target of the male family planning program using vasectomy methods, namely men, Surabaya residents, aged 25-49 years old, married and already had a child of at least one person. The results show that the target has no negative perception towards the program and willing to participate when they feel it is necessary. They also want to be seen as responsible and useful people for their family and surroundings. Thus the ads to be made are advisable to lift it as the main message.

1 INTRODUCTION

The Surabaya City Government faces one serious problem, namely controlling the population. Until the end of 2015, the East Java Central Statistics Agency (BPS) recorded 2,848,583 residents of the city of Surabaya. The population that is not small is still developing with a population growth rate of 0.63 (Pemerintah Kota Surabaya 2015). This growth has become a problem because the population density in Surabaya has exceeded the limit since 2010. The ideal population of Surabaya city should be 75 people per hectare, according to the Surabaya Population and Civil Registration Service (Dispendukcapil). However, the latest data from the population census in 2010, there were 87 residents per hectare. Various negative impacts of population growth that exceeded the limits were identified. Residents who live in areas that are too dense must compete to meet basic needs such as clothing, food, shelter, education, and jobs to survive. The more people are unable to fulfil their needs, the greater the crime will occur (Khaqim & Andawaningtyas 2013).

With regard to these problems, the Surabaya City Government through the Surabaya City Population Control, Women's Empowerment and Child Protection (DP5A) Office has promoted the Family Planning (KB) program again. One of their programs is the vasectomy method. This male family planning program is expected to grow. So far, women dominate the use of family planning. Women are susceptible to various diseases if they take part in family planning programs such as diabetes, high blood pressure, lung disease, heart disease, systemic or pelvic infections, vaginal bleeding, and allergies. Since 2013, DP5A (formerly the Community Empowerment and Family Planning Agency/ Bapemas KB) has conducted a male family planning group formation program and aims to increase vasectomy user participation. Until 2017 there were around 7 male family planning groups. This family planning group with the longest formation of data was found in Pakal Subdistrict with the name "Siwalan Mesra" group with 150 members. The group with the highest number of participants was named "Karangpilang Bahagia" and had 250 participants.

Regardless of the efforts made, the development of male contraceptives tends to stagnate. 2013 data from Bapemas KB showed a target of around 0.27% of 518,000 fertile age couples in the city of Surabaya. In 2014, the target had reached around 0.38%, and in 2015 the target achievement decreased to 0.32% (Wono & Teguh 2016). Departing from this problem, the Surabaya city government took the initiative to find a solution. According to information from various sources in the field, the cause of the low male KB participation is that people have low knowledge and there are even many myths that are mistaken about male contraception. So far the main action to overcome this is by relying on doctors and physician assistants to follow up on male KB. Unfortunately, the number of health workers is very limited: DP5A only has 6 doctors from the Health Service and 5 doctor assistants from BKKBN who handle all KB participants every year. Because the numbers are very limited, health workers focus more on providing explanations to people who are interested in participating in male family planning rather than socializing to targets who do not understand male KB issues. Therefore, it is necessary to have an alternative to effective and efficient socialization to encourage the participation of male KB users in Surabaya.

The alternative solution chosen by DP5A is to create public service advertisements which are disseminated through the media such as posters, leaflets, booklets, and videos. In order for the public service advertisement to be right and effective to the target, the ad must be able to attract the attention of the audience. Attractive advertising is an ad that can answer the needs of the target audience and they can interpret the content of the ad positively. Conditions that affect a person's interpretation include their perception and self-concept (Khan 2006). This study describes the perceptions and self-concept of target targets related to male family planning programs.

2 LITERATURE REVIEW

Advertising is a promotional message that is generally paid and distributed by a source identified through a communication medium. Advertising often sells a product. However, in its development the contents of the advertisement expanded to include various things such as ideology, public appeal, health and safety issues, social activities and other non-profit matters (Hackley & Hackley 2018). In general, advertisements that aim to convey non-profit messages are called public service advertisements. Public service advertising is a very important approach to promoting health issues. Various changes in people's behavior after being exposed to health service advertisements have been observed. These advertisements are like prevention of melanoma, prevention of uterine cancer, the urge to do more physical activity and the call to stop smoking. These observations show positive results: public service advertisements can increase awareness and change people's behavior effectively (Hu et al. 2017).

In order for the content of the ad message to be well received, the content of the message must have an appeal and pay attention to the attitudes and behavior of the target audience (in this case it can also be said as a consumer of advertising). In terms of attractiveness, there are three attractions that can be developed for advertising messages (Harjanto 2009):

- Factual appeal. This attraction emphasizes the benefits of the product in accordance with the interests and desires of consumers. Messages must highlight rational or factual benefits for consumers such as product basic ingredients, product performance, quality, formula, low prices, and others.
- Emotional attractiveness. This attraction focuses on the emotions of the target audience. Emotions here relate to one's self-concept about feelings of love, pride, feelings of pleasure, fear, hate, shame, guilt, and so on. The trick is to motivate them to act. The messages conveyed usually touch feelings, attract attention, and create feelings that need, want, or like what is advertised.
- Moral attractiveness. This attraction is closely related to the conscience of the target audience, and relates to perceptions of the right things, virtues, or things that should be done. This type of attraction is often used to arouse awareness and conduct activities that benefit the social environment and others.

Self-concept can be described as a situation where a person sees himself and his behavior in everyday life. Self-concept is about how a person sees himself and how they think about him. There are six human self-concepts that can be described as follows (Khan 2006):

- Actual self: how a person sees his true self
- Ideal self: how someone wants to see themselves
- Social self: how someone thinks about what others see about him
- Ideal social self: how someone wants to be seen by others
- Expected self: a self-image that is in the midst of actual self and ideal self
- Situational self: A personal picture of a person when in a specific situation

Ad adjustment to the self-concept of the target group is one way to attract attention. If the ad is too deviated from the target's self-concept, the target group will lose interest in the ad. According to them the advertisement was not intended for them.

Perception is the most important psychological factor in influencing human behavior. Perception of stimuli and situations plays a large role in human behavior. Perception is an important activity that can make individuals feel connected with a group, situation, and various messages and invitations. A study conducted in Ngudilor Hamlet, Bandung Village, Gedeg Sub-district, Mojokerto District showed a relationship between perception and interest in doing a vasectomy. The results of this study stated that the negative perception of the target group caused their low interest in doing a vasectomy. This study took a sample of 62 respondents: 40

respondents had a negative perception of vasectomy, 39 people (97.5%) were not interested in participating in the male family planning program. 22 people have a positive perception, 18 people (81.8%) are interested in participating in the Male Family Planning program (Saudah & Rachmawati 2016). It is important to know the perception of the target group of male family planning users in Surabaya so that an advertising message can be made correctly and then the ad encourages their interest in participating in the family planning program for male.

In advertising, an advertisement can be said to be successful if the advertisement succeeds through the stages in perception as follows (Khan 2006):

- Exposure: the target is exposed by advertising, meaning that the advertisement reaches the target easily
- Attention: does not stop at advertisement delivery to the target group. The target group must be interested in the ad. This means that advertising messages have meaning for them to think and touch their hearts.
- Interpretation: after the target group has been attracted to the ad, then the ad can be interpreted correctly by the target. The correct interpretation is the interpretation that matches the purpose of making the advertisement.
- Memory: after the ad has been interpreted, the ad must be remembered by the target group. It is expected that the target group will be ready to participate because they are able to remember the information or message of the advertisement.

3 RESEARCH METHOD

This research used descriptive qualitative method. This method was used to understand phenomena in a natural and profound way: researchers explored seed and probed all information to obtain specific data (Daymon & Holloway 2008). Data collection methods were carried out through in-depth interview techniques for informants. The criteria of the informants were the people who were the target of the male family planning program using vasectomy methods, namely men, Surabaya residents, aged 25-49 years old, married and already had a child of at least one person. In particular, informants were taken from the area of residence in Semampir, Kenjeran, Tambaksari, Sawahan and Wonokromo sub-districts. These regions were chosen because the region is the region with the lowest male KB penetration in Surabaya. Data from this study were taken from five informants aged 28 years, 33 years, 35 years, 40 years and 48 years. They live in Tambaksari, Kenjeran,

Semampir, Sawahan, and Wonokromo. They work as small traders, online transportation drivers, administrative staff, and security. They have as many children at 1-3. The informant was chosen because it was in accordance with the criteria needed in this study. Transcript results from in-depth interviews were analysed by reducing, presented and drawn conclusions (Miles et al. 2014).

4 DISCUSSION

From the results of the interviews it was found that they generally gathered and socialized around their living area or working area. Therefore their perception is strongly influenced by the household environment and their work environment. The topics of conversation in their daily lives are work, daily living and household needs, hobbies, issues that are currently crowded and events in their environment. They use topics in conversation because the topic is interesting and can be an input to support the work, add new information, and increase familiarity. Apart from the social environment, the informants also got a lot of information from various main media social media and sites on the internet and from television. One of the information they pay attention to is audio visual advertising. Often ads appear when they are browsing on the internet or watching television. The things that make them pay attention to advertising are because they are interested in the content of the ad. If the content of the advertisement is interesting and according to their needs, they will continue to see the ad. If the ad is considered not useful, they will just skip the ad. They also claimed to still get additional information from various types of print media such as brochures, posters or leaflets. Generally they will only read news content if the design in the print media is interesting to them and information is relevant to their needs. If not, even if they get the print media, they are reluctant to read it.

Specifically for health information they generally get information through several channels such as conversations with friends, sharing experiences about health, talking with health center staff or doctors while they are on treatment, browsing internet sites, and posters installed in the surrounding environment. Health information that attracts their attention is information about prevention of disease, the level of risk of various diseases, and the benefits of various health tips. For male family planning or vasectomy, the informants claimed that they had already known about the method. However, they have not explored deeper information because they do not feel the need. The informants actually did not have a negative view of male family planning. They have only a few concerns: they do not understand the vasectomy procedure; they feel afraid of vasectomy procedures, they do not get support from their wives; their wives have joined the family planning program; they are worried about the side effects of vasectomy for the body. If their worries prove to be incorrect, they are willing to use male KB.

While in terms of self-concept, they generally see themselves as people who are good and can be accepted by the social environment. Their ideal self-image is someone who is responsible, independent, does not trouble others, and is able to make the family happy. They feel they are seen by others as a low profile, not much, simple, and consequent person. They want to be seen by others as contributive people, able to share what they have even if they are simple, able to raise children well, and able to maintain harmony in their own homes.

From the informants' perception it can be seen that there is no significant rejection of the vasectomy. But there are things that need to be a concern that their conditions of lack of information. These informations must be included in the ads that will be created. Therefore, information must be included in the advertisement regarding the benefits of vasectomy, vasectomy procedures, the level of safety of the vasectomy for male health and stamina, the safety of the vasectomy for the marital relationship, and the side effects of the vasectomy. Consideration should be given also to include information about who needs a vasectomy and why it needed to be able to encourage interest in the target using vasectomy.

Besides needing to pay attention to the information contained in the advertisement, the theme of the message that will be carried is also important. The theme of the message can pay attention to the self-concept of the informants. They want to be seen as someone who is good and can mingle with the environment as much as possible. In particular, they also want to be seen as a responsible person, not troubling others, and able to contribute to the family and people around them. Therefore, the right picture to be raised in the advertisement is the figure of a father, who is able to work well to make the family happy and contribute to society. Why is the father figure more appropriate than the husband's figure, because the target of the vasectomy program is a father. Therefore, the father figure is much more appropriate to be used in the advertisement that will be made. The father's figure must be described as an active father and able to work diligently. This is needed because the self-image of the informants shows that the ability to work and contribute becomes an important part of their lives. This also simultaneously removes the misperception that the vasectomy will make the user weak and unable to work

properly. Besides that, the father figure must also be described as someone who works for the welfare of the family and the people around him. Why is this important, because the impression of a workaholic father but is not responsible for the family or loner and is not accepted by the environment should also be avoided. This is in addition to answering the ideal picture for a father, as well as providing an impetus those vasectomy users can improve their families' welfare. Because with the ability to plan the number of family members, fathers will also be more responsible for the family's future. Besides that, a father who is not burdened with too many children can also contribute to his social environment.

5 CONCLUSIONS AND RECOMMENDATIONS

From this study it can be concluded that the perception of the target of male family planning programs with vasectomy methods does not tend to be negative: there is no rejection from the target group frontally. However, it is important to pay attention to various concerns that stem from misperceptions about vasectomy procedures. For self-concept, they want to be seen as someone who is responsible and able to contribute positively especially to the family and the surrounding environment. It is recommended that advertising messages can correct the perception that is still wrong about vasectomy. Information that must be entered includes the benefits of vasectomy, vasectomy procedures, the level of safety of the vasectomy for male health and stamina, the safety of the vasectomy for the marital relationship, and the side effects of the vasectomy. Meanwhile, advertising theme and design should refer to the self-concept of program target where the theme and design raised should refer to the figure of a father, who is able to work well to make the family happy and contribute to society.

REFERENCES

Daymon, C. & Holloway, I. 2008. *Metode-Metode Riset Kualitatif dalam Public Relations dan Marketing Communication*. Yogyakarta: Penerbit Bentang.

Hackley, C. & Hackley, R.A. 2018. *Advertising & Promotion 4th Edition*. London: SAGE Publications Ltd.

Harjanto, R. 2009. *Prinsip-Prinsip Periklanan*. Jakarta: Dewan Perguruan Periklanan Indonesia.

Hu, P., Wu, T.T., Wu, C.B., Huang, H., Fu, Z., Du, L. & Zhao, Y. 2017. Evaluation of "being healthy, being away from chronic diseases" public service advertisement in Chongqing, China: A cross-sectional study. *PeerJ Preprints* 5: 1-15.

Khan, M. 2006. *Consumer Behaviour and Advertising Management*. New Delhi: New Age International (P) Ltd., Publishers.

Khaqim, L. & Andawaningtyas, K. 2013. Proyeksi Penduduk Provinsi DKI Jakarta dan Kota Surabaya dengan

Model Pertumbuhan Logistik. *Jurnal Mahasiswa Matematika* 1(3): 232.

Miles, M.B., Huberman, A.M. & Saldana, J. 2014. *Qualitatitve Data Analysis, A Method Sourcebook*. California: SAGE Publication Inc.

Pemerintah Kota Surabaya. 2015. *Informasi Data Pokok Surabaya Tahun 2015*. Surabaya: Dinas Komunikasi dan Informatika Kota Surabaya.

Saudah, N. & Rachmawati, N.L. 2016. Hbungan Persepsi Suami Tentang Kb Vasektomi Dengan Minat Memakai Kb Vasektomi Di Desa Bandung Kecamatan Gedeg Kabupaten Mojokerto. *Jurnal Keperawatan Sehat* 2 (14): 31-43.

Wono, H.Y. & Teguh, M. 2016. Perilaku Konsumsi Media Pada Pria Di Surabaya (Studi Pada Upaya Peningkatan Partisipasi KB Pria). *Jurnal SCRIPTURA* 6(2): 76-81.

Global Competitiveness: Business Transformation in the
Digital Era – Abdullah, Widiaty & Abdullah (eds)
© *2019 Taylor & Francis Group, London, ISBN 978-0-367-19442-0*

Crisis-based transition and family-business organization's growth in 5 Indonesian middle-large family-business organizations

S. Dwikardana & A. Teressia

Parahyangan Catholic University, Bandung, Indonesia

ABSTRACT: The existence of the family-business in today's business competition is an interesting phenomenon to study particularly their ability to survive in the global economic downturn and making large contributions to the economic recovery in many emerging market countries including Indonesia. They have been impressively growing by making smart and effective business decisions during the crisis so that they are able to compete in business. Greiner's thesis states an organization will go through six stages of growth based on age, size and evolution coupled with specific crisis in each phase, organizations will survive if they can overcome the crisis and evolve to the next stage. The family-businesses examined in this study facing crisis which, in contrast to Greiner's assumptions, is not in accordance with the age and scale of the business. The second growth phase, which is growth through direction with specific autonomy crisis, is the longest phase in the family-businesses under studied. This study expected to provide new insights about the management of family businesses so that further study can develop new theories that are more adequate for Indonesian context.

1 INTRODUCTION

The growth and development of organizations has been an area of interest for organizational theorists for decades (Lester 2008). Many organizational scholars have proposed models to classify the lifecycle of organizations (Adizes 1979, Churchill & Lewis 1983, Quinn & Cameron 1983) and most of them agree on the fundamental assumption that organization in general are born, grow, and develop, and possibly die or restore themselves (Mintzberg 1984, Kimberly & Miles 1980), while Greiner (1972) propose a five-stage model, to which he later added a sixth phase, whereby ability to overcome embedded problem in each stage as a basis for subsequent changes in the organization.

On the contrary, there are still limited studies on the growth and development of family-businesses. Family-business organization have specific characteristics, that can be distinguished from non-family business, in which these peculiarities are valuable for their survival and sustainability. Sindhuja (2009) defines family business as company managed by members from a single dominant family group, the management consists of the main family members, and the executives of the company are held by family members.

The survival of the family-business in today's business competition and the global economic downturn is an interesting phenomenon to observe. Survey of PwC Survey (2014) showed at the end of 2013, the family-businesses in Indonesia grew well,

even higher than the world average and is predicted to continue to strengthen until the next 10 years. This means there are unique characteristics of family-business that make it able to survive in the current economic situation. In-depth interviews conducted by SWA Magazine to 10 top management from family-businesses can identify the strengths and weaknesses of family-businesses (Singapurwoko 2013), namely:

Table 1 shows that the growth of the family-business in terms of age and development of the business

Table 1. Strength and weaknesses of family-business.

STRENGTH	%	WEAKNESSES	%
Strong (long term) vision	80	Potential conflict	66.7
There are family values to guide and unite	80	Lack of planning	44.4
The strong feeling of belonging among the family members	70	Lack of management system	44.4
Easy to communicate and can be done informally	70	Only rely on the family figures	11.1
Easy to control	60	Hesitation in the family	11.1
Easily in early detection of family members' capability	50	Personal emotions involved in job decision	11.1
Lean and agile bureaucracy	30	Hard to control family members	11.1
Understand every family member's interest	10	Centralist tendency	11.1

scale is not always followed by maturity of management practices, whereas organizations go through some phases as born, growing, maturity and death like every living organism. Greiner six-stage model employed the need to solve a particular problem inherent during each stage as a basis for subsequent changes in the organization. Greiner's assumption says that companies will evolve in accordance with the growth of age, the development of the scale, level of maturity of management practices, and the crisis that will be faced in each phase (Mulder 2013).

Only a few reviews on different aspects of family businesses' distinctiveness have been carried out in the last decade. However, these studies mostly focused on specific topics including financial performance, corporate governance or internationalization, but did not identify whether the theory of Greiner Model is relevant to the practice of family-businesses in Indonesia (Harms 2014).

2 RESEARCH METHOD

This study uses a qualitative case study method, aimed at understanding the phenomenon of family business in Indonesia. This study specifically explores and understands the objects which are 5 companies with their 500 respondents from managerial level. A case study research aims to reveal the unique characteristics contained in the case under study. The case itself is the cause of the research and become the object of research, therefore everything related to the case, including the case, activities, functions, history, physical condition of the case, and various other matters relating and influencing the case must be examined, so that the purpose of explaining and understanding the case can be achieved comprehensively.

The data analysis technique used in this study is interactive analysis, namely: data collection is done at the company's location by conducting interviews, focus group discussions, observation and documentation; whereas data reduction is done by determining cases in 5 family-businesses; then triangulation of data is obtained from various sources to draw conclusions.

This study has limitation of not being able to generalize the findings since it is done qualitatively and pay attention to the 5 family- businesses with their 500 managers as respondents and only analyze their dynamics of growth, development, and crisis which might not be the most determinant factors influencing the success as well as failure of the family-business in Indonesia.

3 RESULTS

This section will discuss how the strengths and weaknesses of family business in Indonesia are mapped in the Greiner's model; whether the assumptions about the phase and crisis in Greiner's

model are in line with the development of the family business; whether the results of previous studies stating that there is no relationship between the age of the company and maturity management practices are also evident in the family business in Indonesia.

Characteristics in all the companies studied and the uniqueness of family-businesses are the strong (long term) vision of the founder, family values as a guidance, and centralist tendency, while other characteristics of the table above are not always found in family-business management practices.

The strengths and weaknesses of the family-business from the results of the SWA Magazine survey show most family-business in Indonesia are in phases 2 or 3, and they face a crisis of leadership and autonomy according to Greiner Theory. The same phase of growth and development was obtained from this study, namely phases 2 and 3, but the crisis faced was different, namely the control crisis. The discussion of the growth and development of family businesses in Indonesia in this study can be described as follows:

3.1 Phase 1. Growth through creativity

In this phase, the owner has a full role in managing the company, with a primary focus on creating products, markets, and communicating (both with employees and with customers) informally. The greater business complexity makes it difficult for owners to manage their own businesses and cannot make decisions quickly so that the crisis that occurs in this phase is leadership. The theory of this phase is in accordance with the practice in family-business at the early age and small scale so it is not found in this study.

3.2 Phase 2. Growth through direction

In this phase, professional managers begin to be employed to help manage the company. Functional organizational structure, work standardization, and accounting management are carried out to facilitate the owner in controlling. Communication starts formally following the hierarchy in the organizational structure, but important decisions are still made by the owner so that professional managers feel they do not have sufficient autonomy and the crisis faced is autonomy. From the findings of this study, the second phase is the longest phase of a family-business, where professional managers are only given authority on routine aspects of daily management. Decisions that are considered important are still carried out by top management (here the owner) so that turnover and dissatisfaction rates from professional managers are high, in this research is a distribution company 30 years old but the owner still makes operational decisions, for example in the recruitment process and selection for staff level.

Table 2. Firms vs. character strengths and weaknesses of family-business.

	1	2	3	4	5
Organization's age	55 yrs.	44 yrs.	30 yrs.	50 yrs.	30 yrs.
Greiner's phase	4	3	3	3	2
Crisis	Red-tape	Leadership	Control	Control	Autonomy
Sales and office coverage	National				
STRENGTHS					
1 Strong (long term) vision	Y	Y	Y	Y	Y
2 There are family values as a guidance and to unite	Y	Y	Y	Y	Y
3 The strong feeling of belonging among the family members	N	Y	Y	N	Y
4 Easy to communicate and can be done informally	N	Y	Y	Y	Y
5 Easy to control	N	Y	N	N	Y
6 Easily in early detection of family members capability	Y	Y	Y	Y	Y
7 Lean and agile bureaucracy	N	Y	Y	Y	Y
8 Understand every family members' interest	N	Y	Y	N	Y
WEAKNESSES					
9 Potential conflict	N	Y	Y	Y	Y
10 Lack of planning	N	N	N	N	N
11 Lack of management system	N	Y	N	Y	Y
12 Only rely on the family figures	N	Y	Y	Y	Y
13 Hesitation in the family	N	Y	Y	Y	Y
14 Personal emotions involved in job decision	N	Y	Y	Y	Y
15 Hard to control family members	N	N	Y	N	N
16 Centralist tendency	Y	Y	Y	Y	Y

(Y: yes; N: no)

3.3 Phase 3. Growth through delegation

To overcome the crisis in the second phase, the owner is committed to making numerous changes in the third phase, especially to delegate tasks and communicate according to the hierarchy in the organizational structure. Managers have the responsibility and authority to make decisions at the department level so that each manager focuses on achieving his department's targets. This condition encouraged the emergence of a crisis of control because the owners only evaluated the department's performance from the available reports. From the research conducted, this third phase is a phase that determines management maturity in family-businesses. If the owner feels there are managers who can be trusted then the system, standardization of work, and hierarchy made can be run properly. Examples are distribution company and education services company that have department managers who are considered loyal and have good engagement with the company. Conversely, when the owner does not believe in the existing professional managers, the decision making at the department level remains intervened by the owner so that a family-business is found in the third phase but still faces a crisis of autonomy even though the system and standardization of work are available.

3.4 Phase 4. Growth through coordination

From the research conducted, the readiness of the next generation is an important factor for family-business to achieve this phase, where the next generation has the ambition to develop the company to become more professional, awareness of the importance of compliance with rules, development of human resources, and the importance of getting ISO as a recognition of the company. This phase will also be achieved by family-businesses that are affiliated with external parties (for example foreign investors) who are mature in their management, in this study it is found in a distribution company affiliated with Japanese companies that are required to have a mature management system. The business process of the company is translated into Standard Operating Procedures to regulate coordination between departments so that the existing departments do not go in different directions. Formal planning is the basis for the implementation of the company's operational activities, the activities of each department are communicated at a meeting so that all parties are informed and documented to be accountable. Many rules are made to ensure coordination, efficiency and work effectiveness and costs. Compliance with government regulations and awareness of the importance of developing human resources is increasing because the complexity of companies requires more competent employees. Regulations and SOPs are the basis for carrying out work so that these changes are perceived as a bureaucracy in the company and slow down the decision making process. 4 out 5 family-businesses in this study stated they were not ready to be in this phase because there were no future generations who could carry out modern management practices, also because they wanted to reduce internal risks. Commitment to compliance with rules and employee development is considered one of the inhibiting factors in responding to changes quickly and accurately.

3.5 *Phase 5. Growth through collaboration*

Organizations that are in this phase are no longer using a rigid system. The matrix organizational structure that emphasizes cross functional task teams is the strength of the organization already in this phase. Simple monitoring mechanisms and real time information systems are needed to respond to changes or complaints quickly. The large-scale family-businesses examined in this study have not arrived at this stage.

3.6 *Phase 6. Growth through alliances*

Generally, organizations that are in this phase find it difficult to experience significant internal growth so that alliances with other companies are needed, through mergers, networks or collaboration so the challenge that must be faced is an identity crisis.

From the above discussion, flexibility in internal management is considered the main factor that can be controlled to be competitive in the market for family companies. For example, when the selling price of a product is no longer competitive with an increase in raw materials that cannot be controlled by the owner, the expenditure of human resources will be adjusted so that prices in the market can be re-competitive. Whereas when internal management practices are standardized it will be difficult to make policy changes quickly so that most family-businesses are in the second and third phases.

4 CONCLUSION

This study shows not all the strengths owned by family companies can be utilized to encourage growth and development. More professional management

practices are started when there are several reasons, e.g. company need to develop information technology, the next generations have an open-minded, companies are required to have ISO, investment in large quantities that need to be controlled properly, there are investors who demand more professional management practices. To answer the research question, it is evident that family-business that tend to prioritize informal management have made themselves able to compete in the business and make decisions more quickly and precisely. This fact simultaneously denies Greiner's assumption that all companies will evolve in their management practices in accordance with the growth of age and scale of the company.

REFERENCES

Adizes, I. 1979. Organizational passages: diagnosing and treating life cycle problems in organizations. *Organizational Dynamics* 8(1): 3-24.

Churchill, N. & Lewis, V. 1983. The five stages of small business growth. *Harvard Business Review* 61(3): 30-50.

Greiner, L. 1972. Evolution and revolution as organizations grow. *Harvard Business Review* 50(4): 37-46.

Harms, H. 2014. Review of Family Business Definitions: Cluster Approach and Implications of Heterogeneous Application for Family Business Research. *International Journal of Financial Studies* 2: 280–314.

Kimberly, J. & Miles, R. 1980. *The Organizational Life Cycle*. San Francisco: Jossey-Bass Publishers.

Lester, D.L., Parnell, J.A., Crandall, W.R., & Meneffe, M. L. 2008. Organizational Life Cycle and Performance among SMEs. *International Journal of Commerce and Management* 18(4): 313-330.

Mintzberg, H. 1984. Power and organization life cycles. *Academy of Management Review* 9: 207-224.

Mulder, P. 2013. *Greiner Growth Model*. [Online]. Retrieved from https://www.toolshero.com/strategy/greiner-growth-model/ Accessed on 2018- 09-14.

Singapurwoko, A. 2003. Indonesian Family Business vs. Non-Family Business Enterprises: Which has Better Performance?. *International Journal of Business and Commerce* 2(5): 35-43.

PwC Survey. 2014. *Family Business Survey Findings for Indonesia*. [Online]. Retrieved from https://www.pwc.com/id/en/publications/assets/Family-Business-Survey-2014-Country-Report-Indonesia.pdf Accessed on 2018- 09-14.

Quinn, R. & Cameron, K. 1983. Organizational life cycles and shifting criteria of effectiveness: some preliminary evidence. *Management Science* 29(1): 33-41.

Sindhuja, P.N. 2009. Performance and Value Creation: Family Managed Business Versus Non-Family Managed Business. *Journal of Business Strategy*. VI(3): 66-80.

Global Competitiveness: Business Transformation in the
Digital Era – Abdullah, Widiaty & Abdullah (eds)
© 2019 Taylor & Francis Group, London, ISBN 978-0-367-19442-0

The misinterpretation of organizational creativity: Errors in problem definition

A. Raharso
ISEAD, Singapore

ABSTRACT: Prevailing views of organizational creativity are that organizations need to intervene to enhance individual creativity by adopting structures and practices that facilitate innovation. The core assumption of these views is that employees need training to think creatively and that organizations are fertile grounds which are conducive and supportive for achieving this. We argue that this notion of creativity in businesses has been incorrectly framed. Our proposition is that employees are inherently creative but their creative efforts are thwarted by organizations which in actuality provide hostile grounds for creativity.

1 INTRODUCTION

For the better half of the last century, management theorists have researched on the topic of facilitating creativity in organizations (Drazin et al. 1999, Ford 1996, Mumford & Gustafson 1988, Sternberg 1999, Summers & White 1976, Unsworth 2001, Woodman et al. 1993). Researchers have tried to find answers to why certain individuals, teams or organizations are more likely than others to formulate novel and useful ideas, processes and products (Amabile 1996). It is a matter of concern that despite the plethora of research in this field, researchers are still looking for solutions to address the management's call for the lack of employee creativity. Our main argument is that the discussion on creativity models, mediators and enhancers of organizational creativity, although well-intentioned, has been incorrectly framed. Instead, we propose that employee creativity is present and given in organizations; it is the organizations which are structurally and organically designed to not tap into the employee's creative potential or enhance creativity. Studies of creativity appear to take the perspective or bias of organizations trying to facilitate creativity in which it is presumed creativity channels in employees are defunct and need management intervention in the form of creativity training for innovation in the organization.

Our starting point is that much of this 'creativity imperative' has developed within a largely uncritical vacuum, in which the notion of 'creativity' and 'creative employees' itself has been assumed to be distinct and insufficiently found in organization. Creativity has often appeared only with reference to the business creativity which is defined by creativity for the sake of achievement of organizational goals within a very narrow focus. As organizations are grappling to gain a foothold in their respective industries, they have come to blame the non- achievement

of targets and the innovation gap on a lack of creativity among their employees to come up with unique and targeted solutions. Many research papers claim that management can take steps to promote a creativity stimulating climate (Gaspersz 2005). As a result of this research, organizations create structures and models to enhance creativity; creativity training programmes are set up with the intention to fast-track the process of getting creative ideas. This paper explores the utility of these concepts of creativity enhancement in the form of trainings etc. and aims to assert why creativity in its original sense of understanding is inconsistent with organizations whose primary purpose is making money, and whose primary mode is working through rules and institutionalised practice (Gahan et al. 2007).

Our central argument is that the meaning and expectation of creativity has been restricted by the demands on business creativity by the organizations. We argue that creative employees exist in abundance in organizations but the pressure within organizations to align personal creativity with organization's goal is creating an organizational bias in the understanding of creativity and what leads to innovation.

2 THE CONCEPT OF ORGANIZATIONAL CREATIVITY

2.1 *Definition and models of creativity*

Creativity in the workplace is defined as the production of new ideas about products, services, processes, and procedures that are useful to organizations (Amabile et al. 1996, Oldham & Cummings 1996, Shalley 1991, Zhou & George 2001). In an organizational context, the idea of creativity is viewed both as an 'output' and as something that has value or is appropriate for the enterprise to respond to the changing environment in which it needs to remain competitive (Amabile et al. 1996, Levitt 2002).

The componential model is premised on the idea that intrinsic motivation is the most important facilitator of creativity, especially at the early stages of discovering or defining a problem for which creative ideas or solutions need to be produced and of actually coming up with creative ideas or solutions (Amabile 1983, 1988). The componential model of organizational creativity proposes that individual creativity increases due to concurrent increases in intrinsic motivation, domain-relevant skills and knowledge, and creativity relevant skills and processes (Amabile 1988, 1996). The work environment serves to enhance employee creativity through incremental increases in these three major components. Intrinsic motivation arises from a "positive reaction to qualities of the task itself" (Amabile 1996). Thus, an intrinsically-motivated employee would be interested in and enjoy his/her work due to the qualities inherent in the work he/she performs. Domain-relevant skills refer to one's expertise and knowledge in a specific field. At work, one's domain-relevant knowledge may be reflected though such variables as self-efficacy for one's job tasks and the clear understanding of one's goals and processes at work. Domain-relevant skills at work would be influenced by the availability of training, resources, and information (Amabile 1988, Sawyer 1992). Creativity-relevant skills and processes refer to one's abilities (both innate and developed) to generate creative ideas and to recognize, explore, and solve problems creatively. Examples of creativity relevant processes include involvement in prior creative experiences (including creativity training), personality characteristics related to creativity (e.g., openness to experience; Costa & McCrae 1992), and a cognitive style involving creative thought processes.

To date most research addressing the componential model has focused on intrinsic motivation as a precursor to employee creativity. This research has approached creativity from the perspective of cognitive evaluation theory, which suggests that environments contain both informational and controlling aspects (Deco & Ryan 1985). Informational characteristics promote and controlling aspects inhibit motivation, and subsequently creativity. Researchers exploring the tenets of the componential model have examined several contextual aspects of the work environment that have been proposed to influence employee motivation and creativity. These contextual influences include organizational and supervisory encouragement, work group support of creativity, job autonomy, sufficiency of resources, and workload demands (Amabile et al. 1996).

Woodman et al. (1993) *interactionist* perspective of creativity is grounded in the theory of interactionist psychology (Schneider 1983, Terborg 1981), and premised on the idea that creativity is an individual-level phenomenon that can be affected by both dispositional and situational variables. The perspective further posits that it is the interaction of an individual's disposition or personality and contextual factors that fully predict that individual's creative performance. According to Woodman et al. (1993), creativity in organizations is a function of a host of individual, group, and organizational characteristics that interact to enhance or constrain individual creativity. The individual characteristics include cognitive abilities or styles, personality, intrinsic motivation, and knowledge. The group characteristics include norms, cohesiveness, size, diversity, roles, tasks, and problem solving approaches. The organizational characteristics include culture, resources, rewards, strategies, structures, and technologies. The interactionist model proposes that creative persons, groups, and organizations are inputs that are transformed in the process of creativity or in a creative situation, and in turn facilitate or constrain individual creativity.

2.2 *Creativity in the 21st century*

Because of the rapidly changing economy and continuing globalization of business, employee creativity— referring to the development of novel and useful ideas about products, practices, services or procedures—has become increasingly crucial for the survival and competitiveness of organizations today (Shalley et al. 2009). Successful firms both large and small require a constant stream of new ways of working; this ranges from the shop floor to the boardroom, from products, to processes, to services to concepts. The Boston Consulting Group has been running an annual strategy survey for the last eight years in which creativity and innovation have been the top ranked strategic imperatives for seven out of eight years.

Many academic researchers have begun to converge on the opinion that: "Employee creativity can make a substantial contribution to an organization's growth and competitiveness" (Baer & Oldham 2006). It is hardly surprising that innovation and creativity enable the development of new ways of working that ensure profitability.

Frymire (2006) states in The Economist that "the biggest challenge facing organizations is identifying and developing individuals with brainpower (both natural and trained) and especially the ability to think creatively". These findings have led to companies adopting measures to improve creativity in organizations as illustrated in the succeeding paragraphs.

At the heart of the most admired and successful companies' (such as Google, Apple, and Red Bull widely known for their creative talent) success lies a willingness to develop and encourage creativity across all levels of the firm. The Ernst & Young (2010) Connecting Innovation to Profit study concluded that *"the ability to manage, organise, cultivate and nurture creative thinking is directly linked to growth and achievement"*. Considering this, we can understand that the opportunity lies in companies to take creativity seriously although not at the cost of strategy, leadership, communication and delivery. Thus, creativity is the need of the hour and the focus on developing creative talent and creating innovative organizations has never been more intense.

2.3 Steps taken by management to simulate creativity

In some organizations, actions are taken to simulate creativity and innovation. The steps may have been taken, such as involving personnel in decision making, recruiting and appointing personnel with creative characteristics, setting standards for work performance and giving regular feedback, but creativity and innovation are hampered in other ways (Martins & Terblanche 2003). Gaspersz (2005) suggests some more steps that can be taken by management - promoting open communication, including everybody in the innovation process to suggest new ideas, sharing knowledge, bringing people from different disciplines together, creating a climate with tolerance for failure, setting challenging targets, creating time for creativity, and allowing in-house entrepreneurship. Others have added giving rewards (Weiss 2001), setting clear visions and goals (Shalley 1995, Weiss 2001), providing information and helpful feedback (Zhou 2003), giving encouragement (Deci & Ryan 1987), stimulating a risk taking environment (Woodman et al. 1993, Mumford & Gustafson 1988), evaluating progress in terms of work and not in terms of outcomes (Mumford 2000, Shalley 1995), restricting constraints (Nohria & Gulati 1997, Drazin et al. 1999), structural measuring of creativity and making it part of process reviews, regular planning of brainstorming sessions, and making sure that team members have an equal status (Weiss 2001) in Klijn & Tomic (2010). Organizations also employ using creativity training for their employees. Over the course of the last half century, numerous training programs intended to develop creativity capacities have been proposed. These training sessions in formal techniques include brainstorming, lateral thinking and mind-mapping worthwhile. These programmes focused on development of cognitive skills and the heuristics involved in skill application, using realistic exercises appropriate to the domain at hand (Scott et al. 2004). We will analyze the utility of these trainings programs further into our paper. Despite these measures to enhance creativity, organizations fall flat on their route to innovation. According to the 2007 McKinsey Global Survey, 84% of executives believe innovation is extremely important for their company's growth strategy. However, the successful implementation of innovative products, services, and experiences is a road paved with strain and failure. While building the business, managers often let short-term growth override the long-term vision. Recently Fast Company published its 2009 list of the 50 Most Innovative Companies. An interesting finding was

that 33 of the previous year's 50 did not make to the list. Despite the amount of focus on innovation these days, when it comes right down to innovating, most organizations fail to consciously foster creativity, or at least are ineffective to real, ongoing innovation. In the following sections, we will attempt to explain why despite the measures, creativity is still a hard goal to achieve in organizations by first exploring the definition of creativity followed by examining the organizational environment in which most creativity is to take place.

2.4 Interpreting the barriers to achievement of creativity

There are many barriers to creativity at work using these steps. Organisations do not understand how to identify, nurture, manage and develop creative thinking skills, thus even though these steps are well-intentioned, they are poorly directed. Research conducted by McCombs accounting Professors Kachelmeier & Williamson (2008) shows that rather than encouraging more creative ideas, paying workers for better ideas actually stifles their creativity. It turns out that employees paid to be creative may feel pressured, limiting their output creative and non-creative both.

The core belief of these research studies on enhancing creativity thus far is that management is in a position to affect creativity in the organizations. According to Gahan et al. (2007), despite the fact that companies view creativity to be of immense intrinsic value to their business, they make no attempt to define it in such a way that it means something greater than merely being efficient or competent in the job. In this sense, creativity is actually a new euphemism for old ideas about the basic skills needed in any ordinary workplace. Following this interpretation, the word 'creativity' provides organisational theorists with a tantalising metaphor to conjure with. Ultimately, creativity comes to signify a set of exercises, maxims and handy tips to help even the most creatively challenged in the organization to come up with those breakthrough ideas (Gahan et al. 2007). Thus, creativity has become a symbol of change and progress and not a quality. Organizations have come to treat creativity as a commodity, where it is claimed there is not enough of it (Chaharbaghi & Cripps 2007). In this way, creativity has become the "new problem". This presents a major part of our argument that the definition of creativity has been misconstrued in the organizational context. In the following section, we provide evidence as to how employees in actuality are creative.

3 THE IMPLICIT CREATIVITY OF EMPLOYEES

The 2009 NESTA Everyday Innovation survey proposed that creativity was an integral part of modern work for all of working professionals and not just

Chief Executives or arch-strategists. The findings of the survey were that all employees can find original and useful ways of solving the problems they encounter in their normal course of work. The only caveat being that in some industries and sectors, it may not be so much that 'we can', but rather that 'we must' approach of the employees. The findings went on to suggest that there is no such an employee who does not (at least sometimes) face problems and opportunities at all. When they do, this is when they need to call upon their capacities to develop ideas.

3.1 Redefining creativity

3.1.1 New ways of thinking

Our first point in this paper is to show that employees are creative individuals. The people who come to be hired by companies possess certain creative characteristics for use in the position they have been recruited for. Gurteen (1998) in his research paper on Knowledge, Creativity and Innovation states that individuals are naturally creative and the need to create is a fundamental driving force in human beings. As per Sir William Bragg, well-known British Physicist, "the important thing in science is not so much to obtain new facts as to discover new ways of thinking about them". The same rule is applicable to all aspects of creativity. Creativity does not require lots of new information– what it requires is a need to think about information and knowledge that is already present in abundance in new ways (Gurteen 1998). DreamWorks, the world famous animation studio is a prime example of a company which believes that every employee is creative. They value creative input from every employee, even its accountants and lawyers and actively solicits ideas and receives hundreds of creative thoughts from all workers, according to its Head of Human Resources and Satterthwaite. DreamWorks recognizes that creativity can come from anywhere because people are a product of their experiences and each experience is different as each one has a new way of thinking. According to Epstein (1996) "Behaviour is generative; like the surface of a fast flowing river, it is inherently and continuously novel… behaviour flows and it never stops changing. Novel behaviour is generated continuously, but it is labelled creative only when it has some special value to the community… Generativity is the basic process that drives all the behaviour we come to label creative." Generative research shows that everyone has creative abilities.

Japanese auto manufacturers realize that all employees are ultimately "knowledge workers (Drucker 1973)" a term coined by Peter Drucker to refer to employees whose work was associated with knowledge management. These companies realized that the role of the firm is to both encourage and support problem-solving by all employees. They recognized that front line assembly workers on the factory floor - the antithesis of a conventional view of knowledge workers were in fact essential to performance improvement for the broader firm. In encouraging and supporting problem-solving by these employees, the Japanese auto makers were able to give their work new meaning and unleashed much more passion on the factory floor (Hagel et al. 2010). Thus by deduction, all employees are capable of creativity because the nature of jobs poses problems at all levels and dealing with problems requires creativity.

3.1.2 Right brain and left brain theory

In 2009, Consultants at Bain & Company in their paper Innovation in Turbulent Times mention that in order to be innovative, managers had to make use of both right and left brain or form a partnership with the more left brained person and vice versa. The right and left brain dominance theory was created by Sperry (1981) when he discovered the right brain and left brain structures. Roger Sperry earned the Nobel Prize for Medicine in 1981 for his work with epileptic patients whose corpora callosa – the bundles of nerves connecting their left and right hemispheres – had been severed. When the two hemispheres could no longer communicate with each other, their differences became more obvious. He postulated that the left side of the brain is considered to be adept at tasks that involve logic, language and analytical thinking whereas the right side of the brain is best at creative and imaginative tasks. According to the Left Brain — Right Brain Theory, there is a big difference between the kind of information we process with the different parts of our brain. Also the way we think and approach decisions is therefore quite different. As we are all born with both sides of the brain, one half of the brain is dedicated to creative and imaginative insights. And it is this that makes employees creative by nature. It is however important to note that the left-brain or right-brain capabilities do not always reside purely in the eponymous regions of the cerebral cortex. Almost nothing in people's heads is processed solely by one hemisphere; both contribute to nearly everything. But they do so in different ways, and people's cognitive preferences exhibit significant differences. But most people have strongly preferred approaches for drawing on their brains to solve problems, and few are extraordinarily skilled at drawing on all regions of the brain. There are training programmes which suggest they can increase creativity by tapping on exercising the abilities of the right brain structures (Gorovitz 1982a, b, Herrmann 1981), however these programmes are have been found to be falsely premised as the two brains work together and there is no way to apply theories to just one part of the brain (Hines 1987).

3.1.3 Errors in measuring employee creative self-efficacy

Ford (1996) noted that employees require efficacy to feel motivated to create. Creative employees put in effort that is commensurate to the results of their effort and the ultimate outcome. Because self-efficacy magnitude affects task-related attraction, initiation, and sustenance (Bandura 1997), efficacy levels are likely to influence the extent to which employees enjoy creativity-relevant activities, initiate creative action, and maintain actual creative levels in their work. In the following paragraphs, we will discuss how studies measuring creative self-efficacy have downplayed the role of creativity understanding in organizations. This analysis of these research papers tells us that even studies of creativity tend to incorrectly frame and measure employee creativity.

Tierney & Farmer (2002) examined how self-efficacy predicts creativity. Understanding creativity as the creation of the useful and the novel in a domain, Tierney & Farmer (2002) proposed that creativity in a domain should be predicted both by self-efficacy for that domain and self-efficacy for creativity. The authors proposed that job tenure, education level, job self-efficacy, supervisor support, job complexity, and job tenure would all positively predict creative self-efficacy. Choi (2004) proposed that a number of psychological mediators of creativity, including creative self-efficacy, creative intention, and creative personality, and to test this surveyed 430 students at a business school. Choi's confirmatory analysis showed that creative self-efficacy explained 34% of the variance in creative performance, while creative intention explained 24%, and creative personality did not explain any additional variation, once other variables such as cautious personality were added to a longitudinal structural model. Jaussi et al. (2007) conducted a treatment on 219 professional senior managers. Creative self-efficacy was measured using the Tierney & Farmer (2002) scale, and creativity was measured through co-worker appraisal.

Unfortunately, these studies suffer from methodological flaws which limit their generalizability. Consider how the studies treat creativity: Choi's (2004) definition as "creativity as the generation of novel or original ideas that are useful or relevant" (p. 188), Tierney & Farmer's (2002) definition as "the generation of domain-specific... novel, and useful outcomes" (p. 138), and Jaussi et al. (2007) definition as "the production novel and useful ideas" are all close to each other, and to definitions of creativity used in other articles. However, all of these paper use reports by instructors (Choi 2004), a work supervisor (Tierney & Farmer 2002), or co-workers (Jaussi et al. 2007). Thus, creativity is operationalized as the positive impression one makes on co-workers, rather than paying attention to a field, "all the individuals who act as gatekeepers to a domain," that are the arbitrators of creativity (Abuhamdeh & Csikszentmihalyi 2002). Methodological flaws also weaken the research on creative self-efficacy. Creative self-efficacy is an individual's belief in his ability to perform a task in order to achieve a goal (Bandura 1997, 2006). Efficacy varies in terms of

the magnitude, generality, and strength of the expectation (Bandura 2006). Self-efficacy can come from an individual's own accomplishments, observing a model, persuasion, or emotional arousal. Abuhamdeh & Csikszentmihalyi (2002) present a guide for measuring creativity when they describe it as an individual who operates in a domain to gain recognition by the field. Thus, in the future creativity can be measured by the recognition of the field.

These studies often view creativity from the perspective of supervisors and relied a lot on report of others. And management has a bias to only view only top level executives as possessing creative talent. Some researchers believe people in firms can be grouped into two classes: those who have knowledge and talent and, by implication, those who do not (Hagel et al. 2010). This segmentation is misleading and damaging to firms in the long run. This reporting of creativity levels by others presents a tainted image of creativity. When talking about talent, many executives focus on what Richard Florida calls the "creative class": engineers, scientists, architects, educators, researchers, coders, artists and, more broadly, knowledge workers (Florida 2002). But this focus on the creative class unintentionally diminishes the potential contributions from other parts of the workforce. Thus the creativity variables are many. Management often tend to focus on the top level executives when it comes to driving creativity in their organizations. When executives focus on "knowledge workers", they lose sight of the fact that even highly routinized jobs require improvisation and the use of judgment in ambiguous situations, especially if the goal is to drive performance to new levels. This way, the way we look at creativity, we are miscalculating the creativity of employees and coming up with results that do not reflect the clear picture.

Employees are creative but they may avoid engaging in creative tasks as they might not believe their effort can result in any tangible outcomes because their status in the management hierarchy might not be of a "knowledge worker". Creativity is often a time and effort intensive activity with a high potential for failure so it is paramount that employees have sources of perseverance allowing them to sustain creative action in the face of such conditions (Amabile 1988, Bandura 1997).

According to Peter Mulford, Executive Vice President at BTS, a strategy alignment company, *"the challenge is not lack of resources or creativity but of management capability "*. This leads us to Levitt (2002) and West (2002) argument that the production of creative ideas is far more prevalent than their conversion into actual innovations, which proves to us that creative ideas abound in organizations. However, the opposition that creative ideas likely encounter may have less to do with their worth than with the organizational and personal consequences they imply (Wolfe 1995). Thus, these ideas fizzle out due to the absence of work on them.

In his book 'Where have all the intellectuals gone', Furedi (1994) and Gahan et al. (2007) argues that the notion of creativity has become another feel-good term, indiscriminately applied, and intended to transform the mundane actuality of work into something lofty and significant.

4 HOSTILE MECHANISMS IN ORGANIZATIONS FOR CREATIVITY

So far, we have dealt with issues in the definition of creativity in organizations and have argued in favour of individual creativity of employees. In the following paragraphs, we will examine whether organizations support or does not support creative employees. Our concern is that much of the research about creativity in organizations has a relatively narrow training focus. Thus, we feel there is a need to broaden the outlook to understand the conditions that inhibit creative behaviour of individuals and groups in the work setting. In our propositions, organizations act as effective killing machine of new ideas and thoughts leading to situations where an individual employee gets blamed for the lack of creative ideas. Some of the processes through which this is done are as follows.

4.1 Socialisation of new employees

When new employees are hired in a company, they undergo training to understand the ins and outs of the jobs to be performed. Training, job description and sharing policy expectations are all important parts of welcoming a new employee on board but there are other issues to tend to in order to make a new employee feel like a full, official member of the work team. New employees initially lack identification with their jobs and the activities going on around them, and are less likely to understand the contingencies in their environments for their careers (Kim et al. 2009). Through socialisation processes in organizations, individuals learn what behaviour is acceptable and how activities should function. Norms develop and are accepted and shared by individuals. In accordance with shared norms, individuals make assumptions about whether creative and innovative behaviour forms part of the way in which the organization operates (Tesluk et al. 1997). The basic values, assumptions and beliefs become enacted in established forms of behaviours and activities and are reflected as structures, policy, management practices and procedures. These impact directly on creativity in the workplace, for example, by providing resource support to pursue the development of new ideas or the lack of it (Tesluk et al. 1997). In this way individuals in organizations come to perceive what is considered valuable and how they should act in the workplace. Thus, they unlearn some of the methods of creativity that they had learnt before. The assumptions of personnel in the

organization on how to act and behave within the sub-systems context, as explained above will have an impact on the degree of creativity and innovation in the organization (Martins 2000).

4.2 Abusive supervision and leadership

Team leader's abusive supervision may undermine team member creativity because it reduces team member intrinsic motivation, which refers to the degree to which an individual undertakes an activity for the sake of his/her enjoyment of and interest in the activity itself, rather than as a result of external pressures and rewards (Deci 1972). As per the componential model of organizational creativity, lower the intrinsic motivation, lesser the creative urge. Liu et al. (2012) found in their study that team leader abusive supervision was negatively related to team member creativity. Tepper et al. (2006) estimated that U.S. companies incur a tremendous annual cost of $23.8 billion as a result of abusive supervision's negative influence on employees. They found that abuse in the form of public criticism, loud and angry tantrums, rudeness etc belittled and humiliated employees at work, undermines their intrinsic motivation (Keashly & Harvey 2005) and made them unsatisfied with their jobs and intending to quit (Tepper 2000). Abusive supervision also leads subordinates to doubt whether organizations respect their contributions and whether their jobs are meaningful to their own and organizations' development (Rafferty & Restubog 2011). Accordingly, abusive supervision should reduce employees' enjoyment of their jobs, thereby causing diminished intrinsic motivation towards their jobs. In addition, abusive supervision is viewed as a significant source of psychological distress (Restubog et al. 2011). Abused employees often suffer from depression, anxiety, and emotional exhaustion, and they tend to alienate themselves from their jobs (Aryee et al. 2007, Hoobler & Brass 2006, Tepper et al. 2004). In such a distressed psychological state, abused employees may have little chance of developing interest in their work, so their intrinsic motivation should decline substantially (Deci & Ryan 2008). Team leader's abusive supervision can account for the negative influence of abusive leaders at each level on his or her team member creativity. This is because of Social Learning Theory (Bandura 1986) where managers learn this behaviour from their managers and it trickles downward. This trend of abusive supervision following the interactionist model affects individual creativity in the organization.

4.3 Utility of creativity training programmes

People who think and act beyond reason (a common creativity characteristic) often find themselves feared, resisted, and rejected: feared because such acts cannot be accounted for within accepted reason, thus they increase uncertainty; resisted because creative acts bring about change when it is sometimes unwanted; and rejected because creativity can be seen as contradicting reason – directly challenging the status quo (Chaharbaghi & Cripps 2007). According to Alan Weiss, the President of the Summit Consulting Group in East Greenwich, "creative people do scare the hell out of everyone else. A lot of companies say they want creativity, but what they really want is for employees to find a way to do the job cheaper than they haven't thought of yet" (Filipczak 1997).

Thus, at the organisational level of application, being creative is actually personally dangerous should the idea fail. Yet all creative acts are fundamentally risky. Given the risk factor involved in being creative within an organisational setting, individuals have to make a choice about the level of risk they are prepared to undertake in the conditions that exist at the time (Chaharbaghi & Cripps 2007). Management often has to resort to criticizing and discouraging the reactive behaviour which comes from individual's personal risk evaluation as they are so eager to celebrate successful creativity. Acknowledging reactive behaviour as a rational and sensible response to a particular condition would imply changing the underpinning logic of organising for imaginative outcomes. Thus, in order to protect the underpinning logic of individualism, organizations target the blame on lack of individual creativity rather than group or organizational hostile view towards creative personnel (Chaharbaghi & Cripps 2007). Thus, it can be argued that rationally managed organisations have the potential to demonise the very people that have the potential to break free from the mould and think differently (Argyris 1985).

Ignoring the importance of community permits individual employees to be artificially portrayed as the cause of poor imagination within organisations (Dunn 1991), legitimising the preponderance of training programmes that miss the connections through which creativity emerges (Chaharbaghi & Cripps 2007).

Chaharbaghi & Cripps (2007) have argued that "those who attempt to create conditions to facilitate creativity in organisations are working from a false premise: that the individual is not as important as the collective in the process of creativity". The source of creativity is therefore an individual's capacity, which can be excited by the organization. However, reversing this process will not necessarily boost an individual's creativity because of the conditions in the organizations. In this context, creativity often reflects a process of breaking free from organisational or societal allegiances. Whilst training emphasises the idea of a closed approach, where outcomes are precise in terms of how to do a specific task well or how to achieve clear cut solutions to well defined problems. Education, on the other hand, must be an open approach where the emphasis is on understanding, questioning, and seeing things from a range of alternative perspectives by being critical

(Chaharbaghi & Newman 1998). The paradox of creative training is that whereas training stresses homogeneity and a convergent way of seeing, inherent in education is the notion of heterogeneity, tolerance of difference and shifting understanding. From this perspective, when training obscures education, the potential for creativity can be "trained out" of individuals because the repetitious and convergent approach is adopted to creativity, promoting conformity, thereby contradicting the need for thinking differently and encouraging deviance.

4.4 *Hierarchy in organizations*

In order to be efficient, organizations need an efficient chain of command. Organizations require the supervision of trained managers running their departments and reporting upward to more senior decision makers. However, hierarchies turn out to be remarkably inefficient when organizations are trying to leverage creative ideas and increase their innovation (Burkus 2012).

The chain of command works well for issuing orders and making decisions. In the process creative ideas stand little chance of being utilized unless they are being shared from the top downward. Creative ideas that come from the middle or lower levels of a hierarchy have to work their way up through a series of managers, each with the power to veto but each lacking the power to implement. Innovative ideas are often rejected by supervisors because the people who developed them understand the novelty and applicability of the ideas better than them. The possibility of rejection increases as and when an idea progresses through the different levels as the managers tend to get further away from the domain the idea is applicable to and understanding the true value of the idea in that domain is incomprehensible for them. This led Vanderbilt Professor Dave Owens to conclude that the standard organizational structure contains natural constraints that kill innovative ideas.

4.5 *Mismanagement of freedom*

According to Amabile (2006), managers tend to change goals frequently or fail to define them clearly. Employees may have freedom around process, but when they do not know where they are headed, such freedom is pointless. In fact, some managers grant autonomy only in name. They believe they are 'empowering' the employees to explore the maze as they search for solutions but in fact, the process is proscribed which leads to employees divulging at their own risk. Organizations often create fake deadlines or impossibly tight ones which create distrust and also cause burnout. Keeping resources tight pushes people to channel their creativity into finding additional resources, not in actually developing new products or services.

5 IMPLICATIONS

Our research brings significant implications for both theory and practice. We have shown that the definition of organizational creativity itself is limited in scope which leads to wrong interpretation of actual problem. This phenomenon is widely found among current organizations and needs to be understood thoroughly by management theorists for correct understanding of the issue of innovation. We propose that current creativity researchers recognize how the incorrect framing of creativity can lead to wrongful interpretation of the creative capacity of employees.

Management often undermines the potential for performance improvement with labels that draw artificial boundaries through the workforce. It is time for top executives to relook the purposes that creativity enhancing steps serve for their organization and the employees and how it may actually be hampering innovation. Creativity training may actually be missing the connections through which creativity emerges. Methods and tips to improve creativity have more of a homogenizing effect than exploring the creativity that arises out of differences. There is little hope that individual's creativity can be facilitated by being taught. The potential for creativity can be "trained out" if management follow training methods which are repetitious and convergent. We suggest that it may be time for higher management executives to go back to school and educate themselves in what actually constitutes creativity and create an environment which supports this new thinking.

The IBM Global CEO Survey 2010 that interviewed more than 1500 CEO's from 60 countries and 33 industries concluded that creativity is the most important leadership trait for the future. They suggested that "more than rigor, management discipline, integrity or even vision – successfully navigating an increasingly complex world will require creativity." In light of this, it is important to understand how abusive supervision may actually be hindering creativity. Abusive supervision by top management renders middle-level managers more likely to display abusive behaviours and harm employee creativity across levels. This result ought to serve as a warning to organizations that abusive supervision should be avoided. Management needs to be aware how they may inadvertently be supporting a hierarchical structure which works to dissuade creative ideas. On the other hand, employees should be conscious of the organizational culture and what aspects of it they should or shouldn't adopt as some cultures may adversely affect their creativity thinking through socialisation.

Because the odds of implementing creative ideas can be rather small, organizations and managers need to be aware that some of their potentially most productive ideas may never be realized and that social-political dynamics, rather than issues related to the ideas themselves, may be responsible (Levitt 2002, Mintzberg 1983, Baer 2012). Given the potential for more highly creative ideas to cause conflict and create disruptions, the findings suggest that the implementation of creative ideas is a fragile endeavour that requires systematic attention to a number of conditions if it is to be successfully executed (Baer 2012). Managers cannot be expected to ignore business imperatives but in working toward these imperatives, they may be inadvertently designing organizations that systematically crush creativity. Providing autonomy around the creative process fosters creativity because giving employees freedom in how they approach their work heightens their intrinsic motivation and sense of ownership (Amabile 1988).

The Ernst & Young Connecting Innovation to Profit report (2010) found that fast-moving, agile companies recognise the importance of creative thinking skills, concluding that "the ability to manage, organise, cultivate and nurture creative thinking is directly linked to growth and achievement." Given these findings, it is crucial that managers take steps to understand the problem concerning organizational creativity and take appropriate steps to create an environment which supports creativity and innovation.

6 DIRECTIONS FOR FUTURE RESEARCH

In this paper, we explored many issues concerning creativity in organizations and discussed creativity studies of the past half-century. We believe that more research and analysis needs to be undertaken to understand this issue in entirety. An interesting avenue for further research would be to explore the effectiveness of creativity training programmes in light of our finding about how creativity training may actually have a homogenizing effect on employees, thereby not serving the purpose of generating 'novel' ideas in the organization.

Another valuable extension of our research would be to explore the thinking of management in understanding why they take steps that might actually be detrimental for their organizations. As we explored how sometimes, management focuses only on the top tier of employees to train them in creativity thinking and leadership, they may be ignoring the employees at the bottom of the pyramid who are closest to the work process. We understand the focus on climate and culture for creating innovative organizations but do these imperatives pre-empt the need for creativity training? Creativity training in the 21st century has come to refer to a set of exercises and maxims, although we understand that creativity is a matter of human behaviour and behaviour can be trained. In light of this, we implore researchers to re-interpret creativity training in organizations. Perhaps, creativity thinking can begin training top level executives about the right way of thinking about the human potential in general. Another avenue for further research can be to understand how hierarchical structures may benefit creative thinking. Since most organizations have hierarchies and hierarchies are useful for transfer of information at most times, how can management better use hierarchies for fostering innovation instead of impeding it.

7 CONCLUSION

Research on organizational creativity has been and will go on for as long as organizations exist. This is because no one set theory works for all types of organizations. Despite that, the main contribution of this paper has been the identification of the shortfall with the problem definition of creativity in organizations which leads to incorrect steps to measure creativity and cultivate it. We conclude that the change needs to take place in rational managers' minds before collective organizational creativity can be derived. Management that needs to recognize that creativity is inherent and a part of all employee's job scope. If institutions and, indeed, nations are going to mobilize their entire workforce, then they need to abandon this artificial distinction between who's creative and who's not and look to redefine even jobs that appear highly routine to embrace and extend their creative aspects (Hagel et al. 2010). Performance improvement by everyone counts, not just performance improvement for "knowledge workers." Executives need to redefine all jobs, especially those performed at the front line or the most routine and often ignored jobs in ways that facilitate problem solving, experimentation, and tinkering. This will foster more widespread performance improvement. Everyone, even the most unskilled worker, should be viewed as a critical problem-solver and knowledge-worker contributing to performance improvement and innovation. Perhaps creativity is a process of unlearning, rather than learning as Mobley of IBM had originally suggested. We believe it is difficult to learn to be creative, but easier to become creative people.

REFERENCES

Abuhamdeh, S. & Csikszentmihalyi, M. 2002. The artistic personality: a systems perspective, in R.J. Sternberg, E.L. Grigorenco, & J.L. Singer (eds) *Creativity: from potential to realization*. Washington DC: American Psychological Association.

Amabile, T.M. 1983. *The social psychology of creativity*. New York: Springer.

Amabile, T.M. 1988. A Model of Creativity and Innovation in Organizations. In B. M. Staw & L. L. Cummings (Eds.), *Research in organizational behaviour 10: 123-167*. Greenwich, CT: JAI Press.

Amabile T.M. 1996. *Creativity in Context*. Newyork: Westview Press.

Amabile, T.M., Conti, R., Coon, H., Lazenhy, J. & Herron, M. 1996. Assessing the work environment for creativity. *Academy of Management Journal* 39: 1154-1184.

Argyris, C. 1985. Strategy, Change and Defensive Routines, Pitman, Boston, MA In Chaharbaghu, K. and Cripps, S. *Collective Creativity: Wisdom or Oxymoron, Journal of European Industrial Training*, 31 (8):626-638.

Aryee, S., Chen, Z.X., Sun, L.Y. & Dehrah, Y.A. 2007. Antecedents and outcomes of abusive supervision: Test of a trickle-down model. *Journal of Applied Psychology* 92: 191-201.

Baer, M. 2012. Putting Creativity to Work: The implementation of creative ideas in organizations. *Academy of Management Journal* 55(5): 1102-1119.

Baer, M. & Oldham, G.R. 2006. The curvilinear relation between experienced creative time pressure and creativity: Moderating effects of openness to experience and support for creativity. *Journal of Applied Psychology* 91: 963-970.

Bandura, A. 1997. Self-efficacy: The exercise of control. New York: Freeman and Company In Tierney, P. and Farmer, S.M., *The Pygmalion Process and Employee Creativity, Journal of Management* 30: 413.

Bandura, A. 2006. Guide for constructing self-efficacy scales. In F. Pajares & T. Urdan (Eds.). *Self-efficacy beliefs of adolescents, 5: 307-337*. Greenwich, CT: Information Age Publishing.

Bandura, A. 1986, Social foundations of thought and action: A social cognitive theory. Englewood Cliffs, NJ: Prentice-Hall In Liu, D., Liao, H., Loi, R. *The Dark Side of Leadership: A three-level investigation of the cascading Effect of abusive supervision on employee Creativity Academy of Management Journal*, 55 (5):1187-1212.

Burkus, D. 2012. When migrating stars fail to shine: Individual performance depends largely on the organization as a whole. *Human Resource Management International Digest* 20(4): 24-26.

Chaharbaghi, K. & Cripps, S. 2007. Collective Creativity: Wisdom or Oxymoron. *Journal of European Industrial Training* 31(8): 626-638.

Chaharbaghi, K. & Newman, V. 1998. When Production Management Takes over Education: The Rise and Fall of Organized Education. *Management Decision*. 36(8): 509-516.

Choi, J.N. 2004. Individual and contextual predictors of creative performance: The mediating role of psychological processes. *Creativity Research Journal*. 16 (2&3): 187-199.

Costa, P.T. & McCrae, R.R. 1992. *Revised NEO Personality Inventory (NEO PIR) and NEO Five-Factor Inventory (NEO-FFI) Professional Manual*. Odessa, FL: Psychological Assessment Resources.

Deci, E. 1972. Intrinsic Motivation, Extrinsic Reinforcement, and nequity. *Journal of Personality and Social Psychology* 22: 113-120.

Deci, E.L. & Ryan, R.M. 1987. The Support of Autonomy and Control of Behaviour *Journal of Personality and Social Psychology* 53(6): 1024-1037.

Deci, E.L. & Ryan, R.M. 1985. *Intrinsic motivation and self-determination in human behavior*. New York: Plenum.

Deci, E.L. & Ryan, R.M. 2008. Facilitating optimal motivation and psychological well- being across life's domains. *Canadian Psychology* 49: 14-23.

Drazin R., Glynn M.A. & Kazanjian R.K. 1999. Multilevel Theorising About Creativity in Organizations: A Sensemaking Perspective. *Academy of Management Review* 24(2): 286-307.

Drucker, P.F. 1973. *Management: Tasks, Responsibilities, Practices*. New York: Harper & Row. 839 p.

Dunn, S. 1991. Root Metaphor in the old and new industrial relations. *British Journal of Industrial Relations* 28 (1): 1-31

Epstein, R. 1996. *Cognition, creativity, and behavior: Selected essays*. Westport: Praeger Publishers/Greenwood Publishing Group.

Filipczak, B. 1997. It takes all kinds: Creativity in the work force. *Training* 34(5): 32-40.

Ford C.M. 1996. A Theory of Individual Creative Action in Multiple Social Domains. *Academy of Management Review* 21(4): 1112-1142.

Florida, R. 2002. *The Rise of the Creative Class: And how it's transforming work, leisure, community and everyday life*. New York: Perseus Book Group.

Frymire, B. 2006. The Search for Talent; Business and Society. *The Economist* 8498, 11.

Furedi, F. 1994. Where Have All the Intellectuals Gone? Continuum Press, London In Gahan P., Minahan S. and Glow H. *A Creative Twist: Management theory, Creativity and the Arts, Journal of Management and Organization 13 (1):*41-50.

Gaspersz, J.B.R. 2005. "Compete with creativity", Essay presented at the innovation lecture "Compete with creativity" of the Dutch Ministry of Economic Affairs. The Hague.

Gahan P., Minahan S. & Glow H. 2007. A Creative Twist: Management theory, Creativity and the Arts. *Journal of Management and Organization* 13(1): 41-50.

Gorovitz, E. 1982a. Brain strategies: Applications for change and innovation. *Training and Development Journal* 36(8): 62-68.

Gorovitz, E. 1982b. The creative brain E: A revisit with Ned Herrmann. *Training and Development Journal* 36 (12):74-88.

Gurteen, D. 1998. Knowledge, Creativity and Innovation. *Journal of Knowledge Management* 2(1):5-13.

Hagel, J., Brown, J. S. & Davison, L. 2010. The best way to measure company performance. *Harvard Business Review* 4.

Herrmann, N. 1981. The creative brain. *Training and Development Journal* 35(10): 10-16.

Hines, T. 1987. Left Brain/Right Brain Mythology and Implications for Management and Training. *Academy of Management Review* 12(4): 600-606.

Hoobler, J.M. & Brass, D.I. 2006. Abusive supervision and family undermining as displaced aggression. *Journal of Applied Psychology* 91: 1125-1133.

Jaussi, K.S., Randel, A.E. & Dionne, S.D. 2007. I am, I think I can, I do: The role of personal identity, self-efficacy, and cross-application of experiences in creativity at work. *Creativity Research Journal* 19(2 & 3): 247-258.

Kachelmeier, S.J. & Williamson, M.G. 2010. Attracting creativity: The initial and aggregate effects of contract selection on creativity-weighted productivity. *The Accounting Review* 85(5): 1669-1691.

Keashly, L. & Harvey, S. 2005. Emotional abuse in the workplace In S. Fox & P. Spector (Eds.) *Counterproductive work behaviors: 201-236*. Washington, DG: American Psychological Association.

Kim, T.Y., Hon, A.H.Y. & Crant, J.M. 2009. Proactive Personality, Employee Creativity, and Newcomer Outcomes: A Longitudinal Study. *Journal of Business Psychology* 24: 93-193.

Klijn, M. & Tomic, W. 2010. A review of creativity within organizations from a psychological perspective. *Journal of Management Development* 29(4): 322-343.

Levitt, T. 2002. Creativity is Not Enough. *Harvard Business Review* 80(8): 137-144.

Liu, D., Liao, H., Loi, R. 2012. The Dark Side of Leadership: A three-level investigation of the cascading Effect of abusive supervision on employee Creativity. *Academy of Management Journal* 55(5): 1187-1212.

Martins, E.C. 2000. *The influence of organizational culture on creativity and innovation in a university library*. Pretoria: University of South Africa.

Martins, E.C. & Terblanche, F. 2003. Building organisational culture that stimulates creativity and innovation. *European Journal of Innovation Management* 6(1): 64-74

Mintzberg, H. 1983. Power in and around organizations. Englewood Cliffs, NJ: Prentice- Hall In Baer, M. *Putting Creativity to Work: The implementation of creative ideas in organizations, Academy of Management Journal 55 (5):*1102-1119.

Mumford, M.D. 2000. Managing Creative People: Strategies and Tactics for Innovation. *Human Resource Management Review* 10(3): 313-351.

Mumford M.D. & Gustafson S.B. 1988. Creativity Syndrome: Integration, Application and Innovation. *Psychological Bulletin* 103: 27-43.

Nohria, N. & Gulati, R. 1997. What is the optimum amount of organizational slack? A study of the relationship between slack and innovation in multinational firms. *European Management Journal* 15(6): 603-611.

Oldham, G.R. & Cummings, A. 1996. Employee creativity: Personal and contextual factors at work. *Academy of Management Journal* 39: 607-634.

Rafferty, A.E. & Restuhog, S.L.D. 2011. The influence of abusive supervisors on followers' organizational citizenship behaviours: The hidden costs of abusive supervision. *British Journal of Management* 22: 270-285.

Restubog, S.L.D., Scott, K.D. & Zagenczyk, T.J. 2011. When distress hits home: The role of contextual factors and psychological distress in predicting employees' responses to abusive supervision. *Journal of Applied Psychology* 96: 713-729.

Sawyer, J.E. 1992. Goal and process clarity: Specification of multiple constructs of role ambiguity and a structural equation model of their antecedents and consequences. *Journal of Applied Psychology* (77): 130-142.

Schneider, B. 1983. Interactional psychology and organizational behavior. In L. L. Cummings & B. M. Staw (Eds.), *Research in organizational behavior, 5, 1-31*. Greenwich, CT: JAI Press.

Scott, G., Leritz, L.E. & Mumford, M.D. 2004. The effectiveness of creativity training. *Creativity Research Journal* 16(4): 361–388.

Shalley, C.E. 1991. Effects of Productivity Goals, Creativity Goals, and Personal Discretion on Individual Creativity. *Journal of Applied Psychology* 76: 179-185.

Shalley, C.E. 1995. Effects of Coaction, Expected Evaluation, and Goal Setting on Creativity and Productivity. *Academy of Management Journal* 38: 483-503.

Shalley, G.E., Gilson, L.L. & Blum, T.G. 2009. Interactive effects of growth need strength, work context, and job complexity on self-reported creative performance. *Academy of Management Journal* 52: 489-505.

Sperry, R.W. 1981. *Some effects of disconnecting the cerebral hemispheres. Nobel Lecture. Les Prix Nobel*. Stockholm: Almqvist & Wiksell.

Sternberg, R.J. 1999. A Propulsion Model of Types of Creative Contributions. *Review of General Psychology* 3: 83-100.

Summers & White 1976. Creativity Techniques: Towards and Improvement of the Decision Process. *Academy of Management Review* 1(2): 99-107.

Tepper, B.J. 2000. Consequences of abusive supervision. *Academy of Management Journal* 43: 178-190.

Tepper, B.J., Duffy, M.K., Henle, C.A. & Lambert, L.S. 2006. Procedural injustice, victim precipitation, and abusive supervision. *Personnel Psychology* 59: 101-123.

Tepper, B.J., Duffy, M.K., Hoohler, J. M. & Ensley, M.D. 2004. Moderators of the relationships between coworkers' organizational citizenship behaviour and fellow employees' attitudes. *Journal of Applied Psychology* 89: 455-465.

Terborg, J.R. 1981. Interactional Psychology and Research on Human Behaviour in Organizations. *Academy of Management Review* 6: 569-576.

Tesluk, P.E., Laar, J.L. & Klein, S.R. 1997. Influences of organizational culture and climate on individual creativity. *The Journal of Creative Behaviour* 31(1): 21-41.

Tierney, P. & Farmer, S.M. 2002. Creative self-efficacy: Its potential antecedents and relationship to creative performance. *Academy of Management journal* 45(6): 1137-1148.

Unsworth, K. 2001. Unpacking Creativity. *Academy of Management Review* 26(2): 289-297.

Weiss, R.P. 2001. How to foster creativity at work? *Training & Development* 55(2): 61-65.

West, M.A. 2002. Sparkling fountains or stagnant ponds: An integrative model of creativity and innovation in work groups. *Applied Psychology: An International Review* 51: 355-424.

Wolfe, R.A. 1995. Human resource management innovations: Determinants of their adoption and implementation. *Human Resources Management* 34: 313-327.

Woodman, R.W., Sawyer, J.E. & Griffin, R.W. 1993. Toward a Theory of Organizational Creativity. *Academy of Management Review* 24(2): 293-321.

Zhou, J. 2003. When the Presence of Creative Co-workers is related to Creativity: Role of Supervisor Close Monitoring, Developmental Feedback, and Creative Personality. *Journal of Applied Psychology* 88(3): 413-422.

Zhou, J. & George, J.M. 2001. When job dissatisfaction leads to creativity: Encouraging the expression of voice. *Academy of Management Journal* 44: 682-696.

Author Index